Narration in the Fiction Film

David Bordwell

First published in Great Britain in 1985 by
Methuen & Co. Ltd
First published as a University Paperback in 1986
Reprinted 1988, 1990, 1993, 1995, 1997 by Routledge
11 New Fetter Lane, London EC4P 4EE

Published in the United States of America by
The University of Wisconsin Press

British Library Cataloguing in Publication Data
Bordwell, David
Narration in the fiction film.
1. Moving-pictures—History
I. Title
791.43′09′0923   PN1993.5

ISBN 0-415-01877-3

Narration in the Fiction Film

For Jacques Ledoux

Man of the Cinema

Contents

Preface

This book owes a great deal to many agencies, archives, and persons. A fellowship from the American Council of Learned Societies under a program funded by the National Endowment for the Humanities enabled me to write several early chapters. The generous support of the University of Wisconsin-Madison Graduate School has allowed me to conduct several film analyses and to work over two summers. The British Film Institute, the Library of Congress Motion Picture Division, the Museum of Modern Art, the Wisconsin Center for Film and Theater Research, the UCLA Film Archive, and the Cinémathèque Royale de Belgique provided me with access to films and documents.

A great many people assisted my work by offering criticism, hospitality, suggestions for revision, help with translations, hints of films to see or leads to trace, and aid in finding material: Jeanne Allen, Dudley Andrew, Roy Armes, Jacques Aumont, Jonathan Buchsbaum, Charles Barr, Eileen Bowser, Ben Brewster, James E. Brown, Peter Bukalski, Elaine Burroughs, Ed Buscombe, Joe Cappella, Gabrielle Claes, Keith Cohen, Elizabeth Cowie, Larry Crawford, Rosalind Delmar, Thomas Elsaesser, Maxine Fleckner, André Gaudreault, Gillian Hartnoll, Denise Hartsough, Stephen Heath, Rob and Kit Hume, Kathy Kellermann, Vance Kepley, Don Kirihara, Barbara Klinger, Annette Kuhn, Jacques Ledoux, Jay Leyda, Timothy Lyons, Judith Milhaus, Richard Neupert, Danielle Nicholas, Geoffrey Nowell-Smith, Jim Peterson, David Rodowick, Philip Rosen, Robert Rosen, Emily Sieger, Charles Silver, and Janet Staiger. Portions of the manuscript were typed by Linda Henzl, Ronee Messina, and Betsy Schuette.

I owe particular gratitude to Noël Carroll, who commented upon several portions of the manuscript; to Jerry Carlson and Don Fredericksen, who read the entire text and offered many vigorous criticisms; to Susan Tarcov, whose copy editing improved the manuscript considerably; and to Edward Branigan, who patiently convinced me that filmic narration had to be studied in its own right. As usual, special thanks must go to Kristin Thompson, who helps me even more than she, perhaps, knows.

Note

The following films were distributed in Great Britain under alternative titles.

Pigpen—Pigsty
Monika—Summer with Monika
Kaspar Hauser—The Enigma of Kaspar Hauser
Kagi—Odd Obsession
Love Affair—The Switchboard Operator
The Fiances—I Fidanzati
Not to Speak about all These Women—All These Women
Closely Watched Trains—Closely Observed Trains

Introduction

An Englishman and an American man found themselves both crossing a desert. The Britisher carried a pail of water; the American carried a car door. They trudged alongside one another for many miles, with the Englishman glancing puzzledly at his companion. Finally, the Englishman stopped and demanded: "Excuse me, but why are you carrying that door?"

"I'll tell you," answered the American, "if you'll tell me why you're carrying that pail."

"Very simple," said the Englishman. "When I get hot, I scoop up some water and cool my face."

"Oh," the American replied, "when *I* get hot, I just roll down the window."

A joke is usually a narrative, and we can use this one to illustrate three different ways we can study storytelling. We can treat narrative as a *representation*, considering the story's world, its portrayal of some reality, or its broader meanings. In our joke, we would study a world of deserts, heat, automobiles, and conventional notions of what Englishmen and Americans are like. We would interpret the joke's point as a depiction of the American attachment to cars and comfort, even in an utterly irrelevant context. Most studies of realism or character in fiction exemplify an interest in narrative as representation. Alternatively, we can treat narrative as a *structure*, a particular way of combining parts to make a whole. This approach is exemplified by Vladimir Propp's analysis of the magical fairy tale and by Tzvetan Todorov's studies of narrative "grammar."[1] Under analysis, our joke would reveal a simple binary structure: two men, two nationalities, two treks, two ways of keeping cool, regular alternation of lines of dialogue, and—in order to make the story happen—an exchange (here, of information) that breaks the symmetry.

There is yet another way to study narrative. We could ask how our joke set up a question—why carry a door across the desert?—which in turn relies upon assumptions about normal behavior. We could observe that we share the "point of view" of the Englishman: he knows as little as we, and he is as curious. We could note the way the telling retards the revelation by letting the hapless men march along for several miles. We could focus on how the style deems certain sorts of information unnecessary (no descriptions, no clues as to the car's make), emphasizes certain parallel aspects of the situation (the phrasing and punctuation of the second sentence, the alternating replies), chooses to render conversation in dialogue rather than in summary, and signals the punch line by appeal to the convention of a broken-up quotation ("Oh," the American replied . . .), this last itself motivated by immediately prior phrasing. We can, in short, study narrative as a *process*, the activity of selecting, arranging, and rendering story material in order to achieve specific time-bound effects on a perceiver. I shall call this process *narration*, and it is the central concern of this book.

In practice, the three approaches often crisscross. Claude Lévi-Strauss, for instance, analyzes the structure of myth in order to reveal representational functions.[2] By contrast, John Holloway considers representation and narration only insofar as they affect structure.[3] In setting forth a theory of narration in film, this book will sometimes touch upon matters of representation and structure. But at least the emphasis, the direction of movement, should be clear: I seek an account of the narrative *activity* in fictional cinema.

This book indulges in film theory, which in recent years has become quite staggering stuff. Still, what follows is not quite theory as usual, if only because I do not accept any hard-and-fast distinctions among theory, criticism, and history. Such a split is sometimes handy for mapping out intellectual work, but the theorist, the critic, and the historian remain ideal types only. The scholar asks a question, and the answers may have no regard for disciplinary boundaries.

The historian must be something of a critic or theorist; the critic usually inherits theoretical and historical presuppositions. Indeed, one could argue that the most interesting and powerful questions explicitly cut across the academic division of labor. I am posing a theoretical question: How does narration operate in the fictional cinema? But I hope that the "theory" label will satisfy librarians only, for the task here is to set out reasonably detailed historical and critical arguments as well.

Given the book's topic, it is not implausible to draw upon the work of the Russian Formalist critics of the 1920s—Viktor Shklovsky, Yuri Tynianov, Boris Eichenbaum, and the like. If we except Henry James, these were the most significant theorists of narrative since Aristotle. Concepts like syuzhet and fabula, motivation, retardation, and parallelism have become all but indispensable to contemporary narrative theory. Not incidentally, the Formalists also wrote sensitively about cinema; the 1927 collection *Poetika Kino* ("Poetics of the Cinema") offers many insights into film narrative and stylistics. The Formalists frankly grounded their study of literature in a broader theory of art, as Eichenbaum pointed out:

> The Formalists advocated principles which violated solidly entrenched traditional notions, notions which had appeared to be "axiomatic" not only in the study of literature but in the study of art generally. Because they adhered to their principles so strictly, they narrowed the distance between particular problems of literary theory and general problems of aesthetics. The ideas and principles of the Formalists, for all their concreteness, were pointedly directed towards a general theory of aesthetics.[4]

Fortunately for my project, the Formalists' work does still more: its aesthetic theory encourages the breaking of arbitrary boundaries among theory, history, and criticism.

It is common to think of the Formalists as advocating a rarefied division of scholarly labor. Did they not strive to isolate literary studies from commerce with social, philosophical, and psychological approaches? Was not the search for "literariness" an attempt to specify an intrinsically poetic function which is uncontaminated by extrapoetic demands? While it is true that the Formalists stressed the specificity of the aesthetic function, they were quick to assert the central importance of social convention in defining what any culture counted as a work of art. The difference between "literary" form and practical language varied historically and was thus purely relational and functional, not substantive and essential. More important, the Formalists' attempt to delimit the boundaries of literary study did not, in the manner of Anglo-American New Criticism, sever "practical" criticism from theory or from literary history. Able and perceptive critics, the Formalists recognized the need to base the analysis and interpretation of individual works upon explicit theoretical principles and rigorous historical investigation. A good theory would have to include, at least, categories and propositions pertaining to the artwork's structure, the perceiver's relation to the work, and the broader functions of the work. Historical research would recognize the norms and conventions within which the work takes on saliency. Such research would also suggest how the art medium's social matrix—the "literary working conditions"—shaped the form and function of the work. Far from being entranced by the artwork as a closed, self-sufficient text (in the manner of New Criticism or some brands of continental structuralism), the Formalists introduced a vigorous, if variegated and incomplete, approach to studying the work in multiple contexts.

The value of this approach for film studies would be a little clearer if there were a wider range of work on narrative theory in the field. Unfortunately, the literature on the problem remains thin. There are virtually no theoretical studies of the representational dimension of film narrative, although some work in the theory of genre has been useful.[5] Research into the structural aspects of narrative has been somewhat richer, especially in the wake of French structuralism. Christian Metz's *grande syntagmatique* of the narrative film probably remains the outstanding achievement in this area.[6]

More recently, film theorists have begun to analyze narrative as an activity, and important contributions have been made by Stephen Heath, Raymond Bellour, Thierry Kuntzel, and others.[7] Nonetheless, to some degree *Narration in the Fiction Film* arose out of my dissatisfaction with contemporary theories. Much recent film theory relies upon assumptions about narration that have crucial deficiencies: too many theories rely on weak analogies with pictorial or verbal representation, emphasize certain film techniques, concentrate on isolated narrational devices at the expense of the whole film, and impute a fundamental passivity to the spectator. A good theory, I believe, should possess internal coherence, empirical breadth, discriminating power, and some recognition of historical change. On the basis of these criteria, Chapters 1 and 2 review and criticize the two main trends in the theory of filmic narration.

It is exhilarating but not very enlightening to criticize a position without proposing one of your own. My aim, stated broadly, is to set forth a poetics of narration.[8] Part 2 of this book is an exercise in *theoretical* poetics, constructing a systematic account according to a series of abstract questions. How does cinematic narration work? What does the spectator do in comprehending a narrative film? What features and structures solicit narrative comprehension? What roles can properties of the film medium play in the narrational process? Chapter 3 outlines a theory of the spectator's narrative activity, treating film viewing as a dynamic, perceptual-cognitive process. In Chapter 4 I argue that filmic narration involves two principal formal systems, syuzhet and style, which cue the spectator to frame hypotheses and draw inferences. Chapters 3 and 4 are thus the conceptual center of the book. Chapter 5 seeks to show how this theory of narration can explain narrational operations across entire films. The final chapters in this part examine two stylistic aspects of the film medium, time and space, in their narrational aspects. Throughout, the theory elaborates concepts present in Russian Formalist work and the writings in that tradition by Jan Mukařovský, Tzvetan Todorov, Gérard Genette, Meir Sternberg, and Seymour Chatman.

Although the second part of this book takes "normal cinema" as intuitively given, the third section situates filmic narration in a series of historical contexts. This part of the book exemplifies *descriptive* poetics, the inductive and empirical "fieldwork" that reveals historical manifestations of theoretical categories. Here I am concerned with such questions as these: What narrational procedures exist as unified, long-standing bodies of conventions in various filmmaking traditions? How does each set of conventions weight specific formal and stylistic options? What historical circumstances have constrained or encouraged the development of particular bodies of narrational norms? To answer such questions, I argue that such bodies of norms, which I shall call *modes* are known to both filmmakers and audiences. Chapter 8 sets forth a theory of norms, and the following chapters use the theoretical concepts of Part 2 to describe four major modes: classical narration, art-cinema narration, historical-materialist narration, and parametric narration. Each chapter analyzes the mode's formal presuppositions and sketches its historical development. Chapter 13 tackles the problem of norms from another angle: it takes a single filmmaker, Jean-Luc Godard, and shows how the theory and history of modes can help explain the curious narrational discordances in his films.

Running through Parts 2 and 3 is a concern with film criticism as well. How, we can ask, do theoretical and historical poetics enable us to analyze particular works? And how does the particular work test our categories and periodizations? I offer critical discussions of several films: *Rear Window, Murder My Sweet, The Big Sleep, In This Our Life, The Spider's Stratagem, The Confrontation, La guerre est finie, The New Babylon,* and *Pickpocket.* These analyses do not claim to be exhaustive; they simply illustrate concepts discussed in the book. The critic should not, I think, have the final word, as if criticism were the practice that is the real proof of theory. Nevertheless, critical analysis is indispensable to the inductive study of narration in film history. More broadly, the last section of this book aims to contribute something to a "metacriticism" of film, a study of how critics employ tacit frames of reference that shape what they see *in films*. The narrational norms which I isolate in Chapters 9 through 12 are employed not only by filmmakers and viewers but also by critics, as the grounds and bounds of their discourse.

A few caveats in closing. This book is not a comparison of film and literature, even if this issue turns up throughout. I have not considered documentary film, for while it is often structured on narrative lines, its "nonfictional" status calls for a different theoretical account of narration. I have limited my examples to films from the United States, Western and Eastern Europe, and the USSR, with a few mentions of Japan. The films analyzed vary from well-known titles to works that deserve wider circulation and closer scrutiny.

PART ONE

Some Theories of Narration

*In the sitting–room of Peacehaven, meanwhile,
separated from the sitting–room of The Nook
by only a thin partition, events had been
taking place which demand the historian's
attention. It is to Lord Biskerton and his
affairs that the chronicler must now turn
his all–embracing eye.*

P. G. Wodehouse, *Big Money*

1. Mimetic Theories of Narration

In the *Poetics*, Aristotle distinguishes among the means of imitation (the medium, such as painting or language), the object of imitation (some aspect of human action), and the mode of imitation (how something is imitated). He goes on to isolate three possible modes: "The poet may imitate by narration—in which he can either take another personality as Homer does or speak in his own person unchanged—or he may present all his characters as living and moving before us."[1] The basic difference is between telling and showing. The secondary difference lies within the category of telling: does the poet speak in his own voice or through a character's? These formulations are troubling in many ways, and the dust has not yet settled on all the controversies around them. I shall employ Aristotle's distinction simply in order to demarcate two influential conceptions of narration. *Diegetic* theories conceive of narration as consisting either literally or analogically of verbal activity: a telling. This telling may be either oral or written. I will consider prominent diegetic theories of filmic narration in Chapter 2. *Mimetic* theories conceive of narration as the presentation of a spectacle: a showing. Note, incidentally, that since the difference applies only to "mode" of imitation, either theory may be applied to any medium. You can hold a mimetic theory of the novel if you believe the narrational methods of fiction to resemble those of drama, and you can hold a diegetic theory of painting if you posit visual spectacle to be analogous to linguistic transmission. The Aristotelian distinction enables us to compare the two principal traditions of narrative representation and to examine how film theory has drawn upon each one.

Aristotle's conception of *mimesis* applies primarily to theatrical performance. According to Gerald Else, the earliest meaning of the word was something like "the imitation of animate beings, animal and human, by the body and the voice (not necessarily the singing voice), rather than by artefacts such as statues or pictures."[2] By Plato's time, however, the term had been stretched to include imitations in painting and sculpture. Later, mimetic powers were claimed for language in itself; in the *Cratylus*, Plato himself seems to have held this belief. Gérard Genette has minutely traced the history of those theories of language based on the assumption that oral or written language imitates visual or acoustic properties of the referent. We shall see how the concept of mimesis was extended to prose fiction and, eventually, to cinema. For now, we can briefly consider how mimetic theories were applied in their most proximate domains: theater and painting.

Perspective as Narration

Mimetic theories take as their model the act of vision: an object of perception is presented to the eye of the beholder. This model underlies the changes in representational practice introduced by Greek theater and painting and, later, several Renaissance arts. "Perspective" in its various senses then emerges as the central concept for explaining narration.

What survives of the *Poetics* treats theatrical performance as the principal instance of mimesis, and it is in fifth-century Athenian theater that we can find the key assumptions of the mimetic tradition of narration. The very word *theatron* means "seeing place," and the early Greek theater took as much account of sight lines as of acoustics: seats arranged in a semicircle, an orchestra in the center, and a stage behind the players. The Greek theater differs significantly from the circular staging of primitive cultures and from more processional or ambulatory forms (e.g., parade, carnival), in that a specific space is marked off as fictional and the audience occupies a limited arc of vantage points onto that space. Around 425 B.C., the addition of a wooden proscenium further demarcated the stage space, framing it for viewing. Moreover, the decoration of the stage brought into play principles derived from optics. According to Proclus Diadochus, a commentator on Euclid, optical science includes scenography, "which shows how objects at various distances and of various heights may be so represented in drawings that they will not appear out of proportion and distorted in shape."[3] It is probable that by the fifth century the stage was painted to represent both natural landscapes and architectural settings. Four centuries later, in an ambiguous and contentious passage, the architect Vitruvius speaks of the Athenians' having employed a scenographic construction using lines which "correspond by natural law to the sight of the eyes."[4] From this passage and from fragmentary evidence in surviving Greek painting, Erwin Panofsky and John White have concluded that the Athenian artist possessed a coherent conception of what we would call central linear perspective. At least it seems very likely that Aristotle's Greece had in both its theater and its painting a tacit awareness of how to calculate visual spectacle in relation to the spectator's sight. This awareness inaugurates a mimetic theory of narration in the visual arts.

The Greek theater raised and confronted the central problems that haunt the mimetic tradition: How is the space of the story to be presented, and where is the spectator in relation to it? In theater or painting, story space may be represented as three-dimensional by various means (occlusion or overlap, familiar size, size diminution, lighting effects, etc.). Many nonperspectival painting systems signal depth through these cues. Egyptian painting makes considerable use of overlap to pick out planes, while medieval miniatures add information through size cues. In all representational painting or theater, these factors continue to play a large part. Nonetheless, all these monocular cues are localized in their effect: they do not determine the depth of the depicted world in any homogeneous and systematic way. Nor is the spectator's relation to the total space defined precisely. These became the tasks of various systems of perspective.

In the history of art, the concept of perspective has been most closely bound up with painting, so I will initially confine my exposition to that medium. Only after we have surveyed perspective in the graphic arts can we understand how it has shaped theater as well. Perspective (from the Italian, *prospettiva*) means, we are reminded often enough, "seeing through"—a handy way to recognize that both the object (the depicted world) and the subject (the viewer) are bound together through the picture plane. There are several different perspective systems, distinguished on the basis of how each renders parallel straight edges in the depth of the represented space. (Chapter 7 discusses them in more detail.) Many of these are "nonscientific" in that they rest on no theory of sight; as systems for organizing pictorial space, they remain powerful but intuitive. The "scientific" perspective systems formulated during the Renaissance were of two principal types: linear and synthetic. In linear perspective, orthogonal lines converge to one, two, or three vanishing points. (The most-discussed variant is "central" or Albertian perspective, in which orthogonals converge to a single central vanishing point.) Synthetic perspective, proposed by Leonardo da Vinci, renders some parallel edges as curves on the picture plane. Both "scientific" systems presuppose a rule-governed, measurable scenic space organized around the optical vantage point of an implied spectator.

Except for the disputed passage in Vitruvius, little consistent practice or explicit theory of scientific perspective existed prior to the Renaissance. Before the fourteenth century, there seem to have been few attempts to depict the geometrically correct orientation of the facets of cubical and rectangular solids—rooms, pavements, facades, tabletops, and other familiar features of Western life. Giotto and some Sienese painters began to treat architectural volumes in more depth, usually by employing a vanishing axis construction. In the early fifteenth century many Italian painters started to represent enclosed interiors and finite open spaces through central perspective. The theory, as explained by Alberti, posited that light rays traveled in a straight line (hence the "linearity" of perspective) and gathered in a bundle at the eye, forming a visual pyramid. A picture plane was then a cross section of that pyramid. By use of Euclidean geometry, the artist could make a point-for-point replica of the rays on the picture plane. The scene's space was now

visibly, mathematically measurable—continuous, consistent, and finite. The artist could apply rules of geometrical proportion to make parallel lines meet and to assure that figures diminished as they distributed themselves in depth. Leonardo revised Alberti's account by suggesting that the picture plane show foreshortening not only in depth but also horizontally and vertically and thus make straight lines project as curved. This was an attempt to copy the image's spherical curvature on the retina. With scientific perspective, the painting represented the spectator as a single eye, literally a point of view.[5]

What scientific perspective creates, then, is not only an imaginary scene but a fixed, imaginary witness. No longer are objects the only thing that painting can measure; now the artist can measure empty space—and not just the spaces between objects but the distance between the scene and the beholder. We witness the birth of a theatrical scenography of painting. Space is autonomous, a grid or checkerboard or stage preexisting any arrangement of objects upon it. In 1467, the Paduan painter Squarcione contracted to teach a pupil "the system of the floor, well-drawn in my manner; and to put figures on the said floor here and there at different points, and to put objects on it—chairs, benches, and houses . . ."[6] At the same time, the boundaries of the painting became identified with the edges of a window, and the picture plane becomes as transparent as glass: Alberti asks the painter to imagine "an open window through which I see what I want to paint."[7] Much later, the Soviet Constructivist painter Tarabukin contended that Oriental inverse perspective placed the spectator at the center of a scene that surrounded him.[8] By contrast, in Albertian perspective, the scene exists as a three-dimensional event staged for a spectator whose eye is the picture's point of intelligibility but whose place is closed off from the event witnessed.

In fact, the theory of scientific perspective did not coincide with artists' practice. Northern European painters took up central projection and geometrically correct foreshortening late, and in the wake of Dürer's writings and graphic work the north tended to employ more oblique and "wide-angle" views. In Italy as well there was much mixing of systems. Two- and three-point perspective, to become important in baroque art, introduced complications into the Albertian system. Moreover, the strength of mathematical perspective, its ability to render plane surfaces and regular architectural solids and hollows, did not apply to other subjects, such as landscapes or animate bodies. Not until Leonardo did painters discover that to represent such subjects straight lines afforded less useful schemata than arcs. As a result, the scientific perspective picture often reveals a conflict between an accurate rendition of architectural space and a distorted construction of the human figure. We should also remember that Italian artists violated rules to achieve particular purposes. One problem of central perspective was that the strongest visual spot for the important element was also the most distant point in the picture space; to center something was also to make it small. Painters had to compromise between compositional and scenographic demands. John White has listed ways in which the painter could keep the eye from getting carried off into depth: by breaking orthogonals into short lengths, by putting the vanishing point "within" a foreground object, by using cool colors in the foreground, and so on.[9] Perspective was not an ironclad formula; proportions, orthogonals, and other depth effects could be modified to suit the overall design and the story that the painting had to tell.

Whether or not Vitruvius was describing a system of central perspective in his remarks on Athenian stagecraft, for many centuries theater design and staging made only limited use of perspective principles. In the Hellenistic theater a house at each edge of the stage provided some cues for depth, and in the Roman era, with the stage and proscenium having become the playing space and the site of the story action, the theater architect could calculate sight lines more exactly. During the Middle Ages, staging became even less dependent upon perspective. Scenes might be presented on pageant wagons lumbering past the audience; the stage scene might simply be a neutral, open area; or a "mansion," a curtained cube representing a room or house, would adjoin an unlocalized acting area. In all cases, the dramatic action could be viewed from three or all four sides. Medieval staging practices continued well into the 1500s, long after scientific perspective painting had become the norm. Only with the revival of interest in classical theater and the reprinting of Vitruvius's treatise in 1486 did Renaissance theaters begin to apply Albertian principles to stage space. The Italian theater would contain a modified Roman stage, a platform backed by a continuous facade, but now linear perspective painting would form the basis of scenic design.

Perspective principles shaped the organization of Renaissance stage space, the conception of the spectator, and the architecture of the theater. The characteristic scenic locale became a street vista, which supplied many architectural features and a conventional central vanishing point. At first, scene painters applied perspective to a flat backdrop and two projecting wings; later, angle wings, staggered at regular intervals, yielded a sense of many planes receding into depth. The stage floor could be sloped accordingly. The Renaissance theater also used the proscenium to frame the stage picture. George Kernodle finds many precedents for the proscenium in medieval art and theater, and he shows that in the Renaissance the proscenium (like the curtain) came to demarcate a picture plane for the action.[10] The proscenium also blocked backstage areas from view, thus masking the mechanisms that produced the stage illusion. Like Alberti's windowpane, the proscenium frontispiece finally closed off the spectator from the world of the narrative action.

If the Italian theater thus became truly a "seeing place," around whose vantage point was the spectacle to be calculated? It is significant that the theaters of the populace and the academies never utilized perspective effects to the degree employed in aristocratic theaters. Perspective scenography developed in the context of court festivities, with their large stage mansions and extensive machinery. As a result, the perspective eyepoint was determined by the position of the ruler's box in the auditorium. Indeed, entire theaters came to be built around the vantage point of the duke's or cardinal's seat; the sight lines of other seats were correspondingly distorted.

Subsequent staging elaborated upon Renaissance practice. In the late seventeenth century, the proscenium became a more neutral (though still decorative) border, and scenographers like the Bibiena family exploited oblique perspective to yield two vanishing points. Such effects had already been achieved in baroque paintings, such as Tintoretto's *Discovery of the Body of St. Mark*. Eventually, the Italians' insistence upon a distinct stage space spread to other countries, though England and France were tardy in banishing spectators from the stage. The baroque theater broadened and deepened stage space, no longer planning perspective from the patron's box but still calculating sight lines with respect to the segregation of seats by social class. During the late eighteenth century, the box set began to be employed to represent interiors, on the grounds that it enhanced realism and blocked any view of offstage areas; box sets also employed perspective foreshortening on floors and ceilings. And the limited evidence we have suggests that the placement of actors in the post-Renaissance court theaters conformed to perspective principles, with actors arranged symmetrically around a central axis and grouped into recessive diagonals.[11] In sum, the perspective stage, with its picture, frame, and calculated audience viewpoint, dominated Western theater from about 1645 until the early twentieth century.

Perspective, in its various guises, is the central and most fully elaborated concept within the mimetic tradition of narration. Perspective conventions grew up as storytelling devices. E. H. Gombrich has suggested that Greek art took as its purpose the rendition of characters in action at specific moments in a story.[12] Similarly, the Greek theater sought to represent historical events, and stage painting was to assist this effort. When the Renaissance church demanded that biblical tales and ecclesiastical history be taught through art, perspective painting attempted to represent a story as if seen through the church wall framing it. Alberti laid great stress on *istoria*, the painting's faithful representation of a narrative. The eventual elimination of written language from Western painting can be traced to the greater mimetic role assigned to figurative representation. And the post-Renaissance theater reveals the continuous employment of perspective as the key to the construction of an ideal viewer's orientation toward an enacted story.

In the mimetic tradition, narration equals showing and reception equals perceiving, but the convolutions of scientific perspective in practice reveal that both showing and perceiving need not respect geometrical verisimilitude. Narrative significance is conveyed through an idealized spectacle and an idealized perception. Most painters' compromises with "pure" perspective theory issue from specific demands of storytelling; that is, the best possible way to understand the story action may not correspond to a geometrically consistent construction. And just as the perspective stage is still intelligible when not seen from the patron's box, so the perspective picture coheres even when its implied vantage point contradicts the picture's placement in the church architecture. The narrative pressures of mimesis make perspective, in all its avatars, more a mental system than an optical one.

Perspective and Point of View in Literature

During the sixteenth and seventeenth centuries, writers began to subsume various arts under a single category and started to draw parallels among them. A misunderstanding of one of Horace's remarks led to a doctrine of *ut pictura poesis* ("Poetry should be like a speaking picture"). With the rise of the novel, not only poetry but prose fiction came to be thought of in mimetic terms. "A novel," wrote Smollett, "is a large diffused picture."[13] George Eliot described narration as exemplifying "the superior mastery of images and pictures in grasping the attention."[14] Flaubert criticized his *Sentimental Education* for lacking "the illusion of perspective."[15] For Trollope, creating character was a matter of crowding "the canvas" with "real portraits."[16] Dickens drew the analogy to theater: "Every writer of fiction . . . writes, in effect, for the stage."[17] Indeed, the comparison of novel with play was common in English criticism by the 1840s.[18] It remained for Henry James to suggest a thoroughgoing mimetic theory of literary narration and for Percy Lubbock to popularize the conception of the novel as spectacle.

Like his predecessors, James presupposes the novel to be a pictorial art. "The novelist can only fall back on that—on his recognition that man's constant demand for what he has to offer is simply man's general appetite for a *picture*. The novel is of all pictures the most comprehensive and the most elastic."[19] James develops this commonplace notion by analogies drawn from vision. The writer's technical devices include "reflectors," strategies of "framing and encircling," places of focus, and of course the concept of "point of view." James explicitly develops point of view as a post-Renaissance perspectival metaphor. Dwelling in the "house of fiction," looking through windows that give onto "the human scene" with his eyes or "at least with a field-glass," the writer scans the world.[20]

"Dramatize, dramatize!" With this famous injunction James signals another scenographic assumption in his theory. The novel is not one picture; it is a series of scenes, as on the stage. James boasted of seeing "dramas within dramas" which still created "an object adorably pictorial."[21] His description of point of view in *The Wings of the Dove* evokes an Italianate perspective stage: "So, if we talk of princesses, do the balconies opposite the palace gates, do the coignes of vantage and respect enjoyed for a fee, rake from afar the mystic figure in the gilded coach as it comes forth into the great *place*."[22]

James's principal disseminator, Percy Lubbock, developed the pictorial and theatrical analogies into a set of critical categories. "A novel is a picture, a portrait," he asserts, and refers to fiction's windowed vistas, foreshortening, and point of view.[23] But Lubbock grasps the shortcoming of the pictorial analogy; the "viewless art of literature" unfolds only in time, offering no measurable object like a painting.[24] Therefore Lubbock seeks to strengthen the analogy with drama. The novel can "place the scene before us, so that we may take it in like a picture gradually unrolled or a drama enacted."[25] Lubbock goes on to distinguish two narrational methods: the pictorial, which represents the action in the mirror of a character's consciousness; and the dramatic, which neutrally presents "the visible and audible facts of the case."[26] The novel, in Lubbock's theory, synthesizes the two arts of vision, the perspective painting with its stability and the stage play with its temporal unfolding.

Both James and Lubbock ignore the fact that novels are made of words. To conceive of literary art as a form of spectacle is to treat the novel as having no speaker. James and Lubbock collapse the question "Who speaks?" into the question "Who sees and knows?" In his novels, James strives to find a "center of consciousness" whose restricted point of view motivates the fine sensory and psychological texture of the book's verbal fabric. Lubbock calls this center of consciousness "the mind that really commands the subject."[27] By confining the text to the limited viewpoint of the implied subject of the perspectival picture, the novelist makes language a vehicle for vision. Lubbock contrasts this "scenic" method with one in which the author intervenes "with his superior knowledge."[28] Yet even this intervention is not conceived of as a linguistic act: Lubbock calls this the panoramic method, a way of revealing a wider range of vision than that commanded by a character. Lubbock's very term, borrowed from the visual arts, has its own history, stretching back to Giovanni Servandoni's "mute spectacles" and Daguerre's deceptive panoramas. While Lubbock proposes the scenic and panoramic categories as logically equivalent options, in fact "the scene holds the place of honor."[29] The scenic method plays down language more effectively: instead of stating his attitudes directly, the author can dramatize them. Lubbock criticizes *War and Peace* for its uncontrolled panoramic portions, while praising the farmyard auction in *Madame Bovary* for its lack of authorial intervention. He writes of Maupassant: "The machinery of his telling, by which they [events] reach us, is unnoticed; the story appears to tell itself."[30] For Lubbock, the novel fulfills itself when it imitates an action and when the novelist's language functions as a tactful proscenium frame.

It is not necessary to trace the subsequent developments of the perspectival theory of narration: suffice it to say that in the work of D. W. Harding, Norman Friedman, Wayne Booth, and Wolfgang Iser, the pictorial and theatrical analogies get extended. The new wrinkle is the addition of another art available for comparison—cinema. For Elizabeth Bowen, the novel possesses a "camera eye"; the novelist resembles not a painter but a filmmaker.[31] And Roger Fowler says that the narrator of Hemingway's "The Killers" occupies "a definite viewing position, like a fixed camera."[32] In the mimetic tradition of narration, then, it has become common to compare literary narration to that of a film. All of which assumes cinema to be yet another perspectival art.

The Invisible Observer

Insofar as film theory before 1960 possesses a theory of narration, it is drawn from the mimetic tradition. In film, writes Frances Marion, the story is "not told but *dramatized.*"[33] Hugo Münsterberg and Rudolf Arnheim begin theorizing from the assumption that a film is a string of images, and however much they strive to distinguish cinema from theater, neither writer seeks to define cinema outside the domain of spectacle. Lev Kuleshov advocates plotting actors' movements as if they occurred in a web of rays that ran from the scene to gather at the camera lens—a complete replica of Albertian perspective principles. André Bazin also acknowledges the centrality of visual spectacle: a normal narrative film, he asserts, is like a photographed play, with the changes in camera position selecting and stressing certain details. But traditional film theory goes beyond this general adherence to the mimetic tradition; it creates a perspectival eye for cinema, one we can call the invisible observer.

On this account, a narrative film represents story events through the vision of an invisible or imaginary witness. The idea can be found circulating within American filmmaking fairly early, and some aspects are present in Münsterberg's reflections on cinema. But the most explicit formulation occurs in V. I. Pudovkin's 1926 monograph *Film Technique.* According to Pudovkin, the camera lens should represent the eyes of an implicit observer taking in the action. By framing the shot a certain way, and by concentrating on the most significant details of the action, the director compels the audience "to see as the attentive observer saw." The change of shot will then correspond to "the natural transference of attention of an imaginary observer."[34] Pudovkin works out an elaborate example wherein cutting conveys the impression of a spectator watching a street encounter and casting his glance from one participant to another. Pudovkin even suggests that quickening the tempo of editing can replicate in the viewer the mounting excitement of the invisible witness. In later writings, he extended the theory to sound as well, with the microphone taking the place of the observer's ears. The result of the theory was a conception of film as presenting us with "an observer ideally mobile in space and time."[35]

Pudovkin's formulation came to be widely accepted and served a variety of tactical ends. For one thing, the invisible-observer model presupposed orthodox spatial construction. Continuity editing was implicit in Pudovkin's example of a witness who turns his attention from one detail to another; rooted to the spot, the witness remains on the same side of the axis of action or "180° line." Apologists for mainstream narrative filmmaking seized on this model to explain practices of continuity editing. By cutting from long shot to closer view, write Karel Reisz and Gavin Millar, the director supplies a "psychologically accurate" depiction of the normal process of seeing a detail.[36] At the same time, the invisible observer, incarnated in the camera, could be identified with the narrator. Pudovkin had also claimed that the camera lens was the director's eye and that cutting expressed the filmmaker's emotional attitude. Later writers came to see the camera itself as the film's storyteller, the narrator's "point of view" on the action. Thus the invisible-witness model became classical film theory's all-purpose answer to problems involving space, authorship, point of view, and narration.

The incompatibilities in the invisible-observer account were not so much resolved as patched together. Pudovkin claimed that by utilizing the invisible observer's perceptions, film style could mimic ordinary experience. The shot would correspond to a brute perceptual datum. The cut would then mimic a psychological process, that of the shift of attention. Thus we grasp not only what the invisible observer sees but the manner in which he interprets the surroundings. In practice, however, camera work and cutting often tax the capacities of an invisible witness. A high or low camera angle might violate plausible viewer positions, while cuts from one locale to another could hardly be justified as faithful renditions of perception. Consequently, theorists seized upon Pudovkin's hint that the spectator was *ideally* mobile. According to Ivor Montagu, for instance, cinema makes the viewer an "ideal observer" who can see "aspects which would normally be unavailable to an observer in real life."[37] One Hollywood practitioner writes that the camera is an observer "who can see an object or an occurrence from all and every side, angle, and distance."[38] The invisible witness thus became an omnipresent one as well, endowed with a ghostly ubiquity. Yet this formulation posed new problems. If the imaginary witness represented not only the spectator but, first of all, the artistic consciousness of the filmmaker, any flaunting of the filmmaker's omnipresence could break the basic analogy between film style and phenomenal experience (shots as views, cuts as shifts of attention). Hence some thinkers imposed a sanction: the camera could go anywhere, but it shouldn't. "The ideal spectator," notes Ivor Montagu, "must be an ideally placed *possible* spectator."[39] In effect, many classical theorists were suggesting that a narrative film employs an omniscient narrator, but they insisted that the film should limit our awareness of that omniscience. The invisible observer became the cinematic equivalent of the idealized implied viewer of the perspective picture or the effaced narrating consciousness of Lubbock's "scenic" novel.

As these claims suggest, the theory was initially used to valorize a cinema of cutting, of either the Hollywood or the Soviet variety. Pudovkin and his followers set the invisible-observer approach against a method of filming that was distanced, inert, theatrical, and opposed to our immersion in the flux of everyday life. Eventually, though, the theory's premises were stretched to accommodate other film techniques. Camera movement could be compared to bodily mobility: a pan or tilt represented a turning of the head, a tracking shot corresponded to striding forward or traveling back. In the agile hands of Bazin, even the unmoving long take—the prototype of Pudovkin's "theatrical" cinema— could be likened to the total phenomenal field available to a witness on the scene. Bazin grants that classical editing

mimics human acts of attention; he simply adds that those acts normally operate in an a priori field of choice. Since an event exists within a continuum, a director who cuts denies us the perceptual options that a real observer on the scene would possess. The long take and staging in depth give the spectator the ability to create a mental decoupage as if he were actually on the scene.[40] Whatever technique came to be privileged by any theorist or critic, the anthropomorphic premise of the invisible-observer account went unchallenged.

It is not hard to find empirical fault with the invisible-observer account. It must ignore many stylized techniques which cannot correspond to optical processes (split screen, wipes, negative filming, "impossible" camera positions and movements). It presupposes continuity cutting to be the closest representation of actual perception. It forgets that even in ordinary films, the camera's position changes in ways that cannot be attributed to a shift in a spectator's attention. The model works wholly at a localized, "atomic" level: it seeks to explain only this cut or that image, not whole sequences or films. And the account can ludicrously distort the workings of film style.

Consider one striking example. It is a critical commonplace that the low camera height favored in the films of Yasujiro Ozu corresponds to the viewpoint of an invisible Japanese witness, with the camera lens becoming the eyes of a seated guest. The model here teeters into absurdity, since Ozu uses this height indoors or out, in theaters and factories as well as homes, down the aisles of streetcars, and so forth. Why should an observer be squatting on the street or in an office corridor? Furthermore, a theory of narration that assumes an invisible observer distorts the very data it seeks to explain. Ozu's camera is not at a constant height. In general, his lens axis will cross the filmed object at the middle or at some lower point. If the object is six feet tall, the camera may be three feet off the ground. But if the object is a table or a skyscraper, the camera's height may vary from a few inches to many yards. Looking for an invisible observer has caused critics to miss this simple compositional strategy: the height of a seated person is only one position which

1.1. Lady Windermere's Fan
1.2. Lady Windermere's Fan

Ozu's camera may occupy. The invisible-witness model tempts critics to accept the comfort of banal familiarity and to overlook the specific qualities of particular films.

The model faces more deep-seated theoretical difficulties. Even if we put aside the contradictions in the notion of "an ideally placed possible spectator," we must recognize that analogies to phenomenal perception tend to "naturalize" the operations of film style. Camera and microphone become anthropomorphic, stationed like a person before a real phenomenon. The imaginary observer becomes a subject before the objective world of the story action. Yet staging an event to be filmed is no less part of fictional moviemaking than is camera placement or editing. The imaginary witness account forgets that in cinema, fictional narrative begins not with the framing of a preexistent action but with the construction of that action to start with. As Käte Hamburger has put it, "While a concrete reality exists because it exists, a fictional reality exists only by virtue of the fact that it is narrated."[41]

Figure 1.1 is a fairly ordinary shot. It is not just the camera placement that makes the shot a maximally communicative view of the group. The characters' positions are arranged for the sake of cogent viewing. Few groups of people would spontaneously arrange themselves into such a perfect wedge of visibility—frontal and three-quarters views, careful spacing, unimpaired access to glances and expressions. (The composition in fact employs many of the conventions of perspective painting and theater—heads along horizon lines, recessive placement of figures, modified frontality.) Moreover, as the shot develops, other women gather around the central one, but their final station points all continue to provide a view of her (fig. 1.2). The invisible-observer model, being wholly concerned with space, cannot explain how action develops to prolong maximum visibility. In fact, when another woman comes into the frame and blocks our view of the central figure (fig. 1.3), the shot ends; the temporal development of the shot had its own teleology. In the fiction film, not only the camera position but the mise-en-scène, as it unfolds in time and space, is addressed to the spectator. It is not that the camera chooses the best spot from which to

1.3. Lady Windermere's Fan

capture an independently existing event; figures, lighting, setting, and costume are constructed so as to make sense only from certain vantage points. From this we can draw a conclusion to which we will often return. All film techniques, even those involving the "profilmic event," function narrationally, constructing the story world for specific effects.

Now a classical theorist may reply that we nonetheless ignore artifices of mise-en-scène and believe that the camera and the editing are simply trailing a solid, independently existing world. To which one can agree; with the proviso that this impression of an invisible observer facing an autonomous world is an effect of the film's construction. The invisible observer is not the *basis* of film style but only one *figure* of style. The observer's ubiquity, the verisimilitude of perception, and the very sense that this filmed world could be known independently—all are formal effects. Like the novelist's commanding consciousness or the implied viewer of a picture, the invisible observer is created to be ideal, solely for the purposes of narration.

Historically, the invisible-observer model has fulfilled

some worthwhile functions. It provided classical film theory with a rudimentary conception of narrative representation, one consonant with post-Renaissance assumptions about the properties of perspectival vision. And the model did, however unwittingly, point to one salient stylistic figure of classical narrative filmmaking: the camera as ideal witness. But the model has also led to inexact and insipid analyses of films, and it has blocked our grasping the range of styles at work in cinema. It has leaned excessively upon the eye-camera analogy and minimized the narrational role of other film techniques. In sum, the invisible-observer model lacks coherence, breadth, and discrimination.

Eisenstein: Narration as Scenography

In 1934, Sergei Eisenstein and Lev Kuleshov began to draw up plans for a rehearsal hall in which to train film actors.[42] This building is a paradox, a theater that tries to overcome the heritage of the theater. There is a main stage with two others flanking it. The main stage rotates. The spectators sit on a central disc which also rotates, turning them toward the acting area at the proper moment. Walls may be opened to reveal the landscape outside. A bridge runs from the main stage into the auditorium, so that actors may come forward to play in "close-up." There is also a conveyor belt on which an actor can run in place or "pan" past the spectator. A "cinefied" rehearsal hall, in short, with all the perspectival assumptions of the traditional stage revised in the light of contemporary film practice. Examples of this sort also emerged from Eisenstein's directing classes at the State Cinema Institute, when he would start to plan the staging of a play in an orthodox theater and then introduce complicated stage machinery to simulate what could be simply accomplished in cinema.[43]

In such ways we see Eisenstein's debt to the mimetic tradition. Despite his occasional use of linguistic analogies (film-syntax), he remained committed to the view that the cinema is a spectacle calculated for a spectator. But his vastly elaborate scenography suggests that he pushed the mimetic position to an extreme. A man of the theater, he was formed in a period during which directors began to see the stage in a fresh way. His teachers, Meyerhold most notably, were rethinking the proscenium frame, the representation of depth, the spatial unity of the production, and the place of the audience. Like Meyerhold and Brecht, Eisenstein sought to make the stage a vehicle for an omniscient, ever-present narration. He thereby challenged Aristotle's assumption that theater invariably minimized the author's shaping hand.

Eisenstein's theory is "expressionist" in that it regards narration as the process of making manifest some essential emotional quality of the story. Throughout his career he insisted that representation involved not a simple and flat depiction but a heightening of the import and emotion of what was depicted.

At the earliest stage of his work, Eisenstein cast aside literary aspects of drama and grounded theatrical perform-ance in expressive movement. Influenced by Meyerhold, by "eccentrism" in Soviet experimental theater, by reflex-centered theories of movement, and by the "expressive gym-nastics" of Rudolf Bode, he trained actors to translate emo-tional states into sheerly physical reactions. In an early essay, written with Sergei Tretyakov, he asserted that even speech was a sort of "gesture" of the body.[44] "Realistic" acting was only a flattening and muting of expressive movement; Eisenstein argued for a maximal expressivity, even if this seemed stylized:

> You say, "But there are two," on the last word showing two extended fingers. And how much the persuasive-ness of the phrase itself would be strengthened, the ex-pressiveness of the intonation, if on the first words, you made a recoil movement with the body while raising the elbow, and then with an energetic movement you threw the torso and the hand with the extended fingers forward. Furthermore, the braking of the wrist would be so strongly directed that the wrist would vibrate (like a metronome). In the first instance you are deal-ing with partial thrust, in the second with organically

[word omitted] movement of maximal exertion. Thus the expressiveness of movement, and with it, intonation as well, are not created by representational exactness, but by the energetic intensity of the gesture, which helps to develop the general thrust.[45]

Hence, when discussing cinema in 1922, Eisenstein praised American comedies, *policiers*, and adventure films and such expressive stars as Hart, Pickford, Fairbanks, Arbuckle, and above all Chaplin.[46] That such ideas remained crucial for him is shown by a 1939 photograph of a May Day float in which Eisenstein sits among three huge opened books, symboliz-ing his work in progress, *Direction*: the central volume is opened to the page entitled "Expressive Movement."

The purpose of this expressivity is the "persuasiveness" Eisenstein and Tretyakov mention. The agitprop theater of Eisenstein's time left its mark: throughout his career, he considered representation instrumentally, as a means of affecting the perceiver in specifiable ways. Expressive movement on stage would make the spectator imitate the movement in his or her own body, with a predetermined psychic effect. The viewer "reflexively repeats in weakened form the entire system of actor's movements: as a result of the produced movements, the spectator's incipient muscu-lar tensions are released in the desired emotion."[47] Thus acting becomes real work, the processing of a material—the spectator.

Very soon, expressivity became the basis of the concept of the "attraction," that common denominator of theater which galvanizes the audience's perception. The attraction is a unit of spectatorial impact, gauged by its ability to administer perceptual and emotional shocks.[48] These attractions—not only the actor's movements but also setting, lighting, sound effects, and so on—formed an effective whole through "montage," the judicious assemblage of shocks that would lead the spectator to the proper ideological conclusion. In some respects, Eisenstein's "montage of attractions" was a more abstract reworking of ideas that had already appeared in a 1922 Feks (Factory of the Eccentric Actor) manifesto, but Eisenstein's version became the basis of a full-fledged theory of film. For, as Eisenstein often remarked, cinema is a contemporary extension of theater.[49] Film has attractions too, and these function as stimuli for spectatorial response. These can be associated with one another through montage, which in cinema occurs through the joining of one piece of film with another. Properly controlled, the montage of film attractions would work directly on the spectator's nervous system, associating unconditioned reflexes with specific story events and creating new conditioned reflexes in relation to the theme the film seeks to inculcate. As in theater, the desired effect is at once perceptual, affective, and cognitive.

Eisenstein's 1920s writings on the cinema are chiefly of interest for the light they shed on style. Apparently under the influence of Soviet debates in psychology and philosophy, he sought in 1929 to create a "dialectical" approach to shooting and editing, claiming that graphic composition and other visual factors could create a conflict that would "explode" into the conflict between shots. In the same year he proposed that the filmmaker should seek to manipulate all the stimuli within each editing piece, not simply its "dominant" one; control of the basic "tone" and its "overtones" could yield a richer perceptual effect. By 1932, he was at work on *An American Tragedy*, which would try to render the protagonist's stream of consciousness. In all these years, certain narrational concerns remain central. The goal in *An American Tragedy* is "the expression of those subtleties of the inner struggle in all its nuances."[50] Eisenstein's theory of the dialectics of style is, he says, "fully analogous to human, psychological expression."[51] The methods of montage act on the spectator's "psycho-physiological complex" so as to create a predetermined effect in the manner of attractions.[52] Although Eisenstein's conception of mental activity seems to change significantly around 1930, human expressivity and spectatorial impact remain central.

Partly because of his emphasis on style, Eisenstein has little explicitly to say about plot construction. Indeed, at times he seems impatient that traditional notions of story limit his agitational purpose. It is clear, though, that for him narration in film would be an expressive representation of the story action. In particular writings, Eisenstein skirts many difficulties of the invisible-observer position. Because all that finally counts is response, Eisenstein can refuse Pudovkin's view of the profilmic event as an untransformed reality to be recorded by the camera and adjusted in editing. Instead, the profilmic event, as expressive movement or attraction, is *already* an expressively heightened representation of the thesis. Staging, on Eisenstein's account, is an initial processing of the ideological point to be communicated. Similarly, the camera is not a delegate for the spectator. It is an instrument for transforming the profilmic event so as to maximize effect. Nor does editing mimic the attention of an invisible observer. Editing, as the most palpable stage of montage construction, will often violate verisimilitude for the sake of impact. Perhaps most productive is the assumption that the story action is not in the film but in the spectator's mind; it becomes a construction which the viewer puts upon a configuration of stimuli. Eisenstein cites stereotyped association—e.g., murder inferred from opening eyes, a knife, drops of blood—and suggests that one could use other associations to construct completely new types of "stories" (Marx's *Capital*, Joyce's *Ulysses*).

It is in Eisenstein's notes, essays, and lectures between 1932 and 1947 that his version of a mimetic theory becomes most explicit. Now spectator effect is less bound to an ideological thesis, more allied with absorption in the narrative process itself. He demonstrates how the unfolding of an emotional donnée can become the basis of an entire work, from staging through editing. He posits various techniques to articulate the revelation of the emotional essence of the work. Mise-en-scène projects the emotional essence into the overall patterns of actor movement and stage space. Breaks with verisimilitude in setting or performance are permitted so long as they heighten the basic emotional point. Within mise-en-scène, the human figure is central, and Eisenstein speaks of *mise en jeu* (the actor's overall character portrayal) and *mise en geste* (the marked physical action of performance; individual expressive movements). Both aspects of acting can further intensify the donnée. Editing transforms theatrical mise-en-scène into shots, enjoying perfect freedom to emphasize or "falsify" the profilmic event for the sake of expressive impact. Finally, what he calls *mise en cadre* shapes each action for its composition within the frame.[53]

In Eisenstein's account there is the sense that the text before us, the play or the film, is the performance of a "prior" story. Eisenstein's work, both early and late, presupposes overt narration—not the speaking voice of language or literature, but an invisible master of ceremonies who has staged this action, chosen these camera positions, and edited the images in just this way. The expressionist emphasis of Eisenstein's theory of direction assures a continual awareness of the director's shaping hand. If he had to show a figure fallen from a great height, Eisenstein explained, he would do everything necessary to make the event forceful: incline the surface which the figure falls upon, use diagonal architecture "to nail the attention of the viewer to the figure," have a woman drop crosswise upon the figure, and employ starkly opposed costume colors to emphasize the elements of the design.[54] He did not add that such a maniacally explicit representation points silently but unambiguously to a maker. The very terms he uses stress the creator's intervention—not only "montage" as creative assembly but the recurring prefix *mise* as an acknowledgment that acting and setting and framing are *put in place* by some overriding intelligence. By seeking the maximally expressive unfolding of an emotional essence, Eisenstein makes the entire representation into a narrator's interpretation of the emotional donnée, just as we speak of a stage director's "interpretation" of a play. At one point, Eisenstein even considered representing the narrator on the screen. He recalled that in his scenario for *MMM* (1932–1933), the intrigue becomes so tangled that the camera backs off, the tiled floor of the setting turns out to be a giant chessboard, and while the characters stand waiting, the screenwriter and the director sit tearing their hair trying to solve the plot problem.[55]

Eisenstein's work, even in its late phase, does not constitute a theory of narration. Scrappy, ad hoc, and idiosyncratic, the ideas are geared primarily to his filmmaking practice. Their limitations are often those of the mimetic position generally—an emphasis on vision and a neglect of thinking, a tendency to atomism in the explanation of effects. But in Eisenstein we see a brilliant filmmaker, working in an era that did not pose the problem of narration as we would, straining against the invisible-observer account. His insistence that the profilmic event is already narrational, his attempt to treat all film techniques as potentially equivalent instruments, and his assumption that the spectator constructs the story out of stimuli—all these are indispensable to an adequate theory of narration, and we shall have occasion to return to them throughout this book.

2. Diegetic Theories of Narration

If Aristotle may be credited with founding the mimetic tradition of narrative representation, Plato is the principal ancient spokesman for the conception that narration is fundamentally a linguistic activity. In book 3 of the *Republic*, Plato distinguishes two principal sorts of storytelling. There is simple or pure narrative (*haplē diēgēsis*), in which "the poet himself is the speaker and does not even attempt to suggest to us that anyone but himself is speaking."[1] A lyric poem would be an example. In contrast stands imitative narrative (*mimēsis*), of which drama is the chief instance. Here the poet speaks through his characters, "as if he were someone else."[2] In 1953, the term *diegesis* was revived by Etienne Souriau to describe the "recounted story" of a film, and it has since achieved wide usage in literary theory.[3] "Diegesis" has come to be the accepted term for the fictional world of the story. Calling one tradition of narrative theory "diegetic" brings out the linguistic conception underlying Plato's formulation. For Plato, both pure narrative and theatrical imitation presuppose the priority of the poet's voice; in drama, the poet simply makes his own speech like that of another.

Diegetic conceptions of narration could be traced through the Renaissance, but it is in our own century that diegetic theories have been most prominent. During the years that Anglo-American critics like Lubbock were promoting mimetic theories of literary narration, the Russian Formalist critics were suggesting that literature was above all an affair of language. Vivid effects could be attributed to the writer's manipulation of verbal norms. In the late 1920s and early 1930s, Mikhail Bakhtin claimed that the literary text formed a historically variable mix of discourses. The novel, according to Bakhtin, is not a spectacle organized around Jamesian sight lines; it is a polyphony, even a cacophony, of different registers of speech and written language: a montage of voices. At the same time, Jan Mukařovský attributed "syntactic" and "semantic" features to literature, drama, architecture, and cinema. Finally, it is possible to see Brecht's "literarization" of the theater—the use of episodic structure, voice-over commentary, and inserted captions—as a tactic for bringing out the diegetic aspect which Aristotelian conceptions of theater had effaced.

The most visible developments in diegetic theories of narration have been tied to the vicissitudes of continental structuralism. We can distinguish two periods. First, around 1960, Roland Barthes picked up Saussure's hint that linguistics might form the basis of a more general science of signs—semiology. Barthes sought to apply Saussure's theory of signification to nonlinguistic systems, such as fashions and advertisements. There followed, and still follow, semiotic studies of all manner of cultural phenomena. Media which had seemed analyzable only through mimetic assumptions came to be treated as analogous to verbal language. Semiologists wrote of painting and theater as language systems. For some theorists, language became the master system upon which all others were modeled. "It is far from certain," wrote Barthes on the first page of *Elements of Semiology*, "that in the social life of today there are to be found any extensive systems of signs outside human language."[4] Similarly, Barthes's most comprehensive analysis of narration at this period, "The Structural Analysis of Narratives," declares that every narration depends upon linguistic codes.[5]

The same essay, published in 1966, also indicates a transition to what may be considered the "second semiology." After a very Saussurean analysis of narrative structure, Barthes moves to consider narrative as a transmission from sender to receiver. The essay is symptomatic of structuralism's shift from the study of signification (concentrating on problems of denotation and connotation) to the study of enunciation (concentrating on problems of subjectivity in language). The static, tabular nature of classic structuralist analysis was replaced by a greater emphasis on the process, even the play, of linguistic activity. Semiotic analysis of enunciation did not clearly focus on what Anglo-American linguists call pragmatics, although it did touch on issues of *deixis*, those grammatical categories which encode the person, place, time, or social context of utterance. Nor did many semioticians draw upon the major innovation in Anglo-American linguistics, Chomsky's transformational grammar. Instead, some theoretical essays by the linguist Emile Benveniste, and psychoanalytic theories drawn from Freud and Jacques Lacan, supplied the bases for conceptions of the speaking subject in linguistic and nonlinguistic media. Barthes's 1966 essay, for instance, cites both Benveniste and Lacan to back up an analysis of the "personal" marks of James Bond's speech in a passage from *Goldfinger*.[6]

How has this tradition affected film theory? The Russian Formalists were the first to exploit the analogies between language and film in a detailed way. They isolated a "poetic" use of film parallel to the "literary" use of language they posited for verbal texts. Yuri Tynianov likened the shot to a line of verse and sought the cinematic equivalents of epithets, similes, metaphors, and other poetic devices.[7] For Boris Eichenbaum, film was to photography as poetic language was to practical language. He saw the cinema as having a linguistic basis in several ways, chiefly with respect to "internal speech." Stylistics of the cinema would then be based upon filmic syntax, the way in which the shots were linked into "phrases" and "sentences."[8] These analogies were taken up, in partial fashion, in the writings of Eisenstein, Vertov, Kuleshov, and Pudovkin.

Yet the Formalists did not rigorously compare language as a system to cinema. This was partly because their literary criticism, despite its call for a return to the study of language as a material, did not produce much strictly linguistic analysis of narrative. Formalists studied prosody, some syntactic devices (e.g., parallelism), and certain semantic effects (e.g., metaphor), but they did not construct a comprehensive model using pertinent linguistic categories. Not until

French structuralism and semiology emerge do we find critics systematically employing linguistic theory to analyze film. In this chapter, Colin MacCabe's theory of the "classical realist text" will serve as the most influential instance of a structuralist approach to filmic narration. After a brief examination of MacCabe's theory, I will consider at greater length how the semiotics of enunciation has been applied to cinema.

Film Narration as Metalanguage

Colin MacCabe treats dominant narrative cinema as significantly analogous to the nineteenth-century realist novel. Both, he contends, frame "object languages" by a "metalanguage." "A meta-language 'talks about' an object-language and transforms it into content by naming the object-language (accomplished through the use of inverted commas) and thus being able to identify both the object-language and its area of application. . . . [In the novel] the narrative prose is the meta-language that can state all the truths in the object-language(s) (the marks held in inverted commas) and can also explain the relation of the object-language to the world."[9] The novelistic metalanguage has three attributes. First, by enclosing the object languages, it creates a hierarchy of discourses. Second, the metalanguage "tells the truth"—truth here being conceived of as empirical adequacy to the real. Finally, the metalanguage is "transparent," in that it seems to be issuing from no identifiable speaker. MacCabe takes as an illustration a passage from Eliot's *Middlemarch*, in which the sentences outside quotation marks give a privileged overview of two characters' misconceptions.

According to MacCabe, the same hierarchy of discourses rules narration in classical films. Characters speak, but their discourses are always framed by an equivalent of the novelist's metalanguage: the camera. "The camera shows us what happens—it tells us the truth against which we can measure the discourses."[10] MacCabe's example is the end of *Klute*, where Bree's uncertainty about her relation to John Klute is overriden by the camera: "The reality of the image ensures us that this is the way it will really be."[11] Narration in mainstream film, then, depends upon an opposition "between spoken discourses which may be mistaken and a visual discourse which guarantees truth—which reveals all."[12]

Despite appearances, it is not the term "metalanguage" that signals MacCabe's debt to structuralism. While Barthes uses the term to describe the semiotic process whereby signs of one system become signifieds of another, MacCabe's usage is closer to that of the logician Alfred Tarski.[13] Rather, MacCabe's project is structuralist by virtue of several assumptions. He insists upon levels of coding in a text, he claims the linguistic sign to be constituted by differential operations, and he defines discourse in a Lévi-Straussian way as "a set of significant oppositions."[14] More generally, the idea of a stable, self-sealed text, locking its discourses into compartments and tagging each one unambiguously, is an analytical postulate straight out of that "euphoric dream of scientificity" which Barthes once called early structuralism.[15]

MacCabe's account, a general and loose one, has fundamental drawbacks. For one thing, it is not describing a phenomenon peculiar to literature, let alone the novel. MacCabe's basic assumption—that the classical text takes reality as given, on one side, with language irrevocably on the other—applies to a great many written texts. Scientific treatises, newspaper reports, chronicles and annals, and bureaucratic memoranda all traditionally efface the material traces of speech and rank discourses according to their implicit correspondence to an empirically defined reality. Furthermore, MacCabe's category of the "nineteenth-century novel" does not distinguish among subgenres (e.g., the novel of manners, the Gothic romance) or among varieties of point of view (e.g., omniscient, restricted). This objection is not historical pedantry, for one can argue that MacCabe fails to take account of how formal and generic conventions may make empirical realism a secondary factor. *Little Dorrit*, for instance, creates a formal norm within the text that stipulates that some events, although described as a dream by the third-person narrator, can be understood as *not* being a dream. One can also argue that the descriptions in the Gothic novel and the linguistic play in comic novels do not qualify as instances of language trying to pass itself off as "transparent" or "unwritten."[16] It is even doubtful that Mac-Cabe's descriptions hold good for his singular and prototypical example, *Middlemarch*.[17] But the greatest difficulties spring from the theory's basic conceptions of metalanguage and discourse.

MacCabe identifies the object language with direct discourse, "those words held in inverted commas."[18] Correspondingly, the metalanguage is any chunk of text not enclosed within quotation marks. But this distinction is too crude. Many novels frame characters' speeches not within a "transparent" metalanguage but within the writing or speech of a narrator, either that of a character in the fiction (*David Copperfield, The Moonstone, Huckleberry Finn*) or a more or less personified speaker or writer (*Tom Jones, Pickwick Papers, The Brothers Karamazov*). Two generations of literary critics have shown that such narrators, whether first or third person, need offer no unhampered passage to truth; that the author can use them to create error, distraction, irony, inadequate grasp of an action's significance, and other effects. In fact, no narrator need be present at all: MacCabe must say that an epistolary novel has no metalanguage, since it consists of nothing but (written) character discourse. The "with or without quotation marks" split fails at the stylistic level as well, since it will not distinguish between the different degrees of narrational presence manifested in such techniques as indirect discourse (*She thought that it was wonderful to be alone*) and free indirect discourse (*How wonderful to be alone!*).[19]

The theory's inability to account for such complex effects is traceable to its notable lack of a semantic dimension. MacCabe might reply that his conception of discourse as a set of significant oppositions supplies such a semantics. But a set of semantic oppositions will not of necessity coincide with the surface-level split between character speech and narrative metalanguage. If there is a set of significant oppositions between character "discourse" and narrator "discourse," that too MacCabe must call a discourse.[20] Either

MacCabe holds incompatible conceptions of language or he defines discourse in a loose enough sense to cover both oppositions of signifieds and traits of signifiers (his quotation-marks cue, what Dickens called "the necessity of turned commas"). Thus MacCabe assumes that one can identify the process of narration by locating particular textual marks. But narration includes the structural relations between the text and the story that it represents, and this relation can emerge in a wide variety of ways, even in nineteenth-century texts. MacCabe ignores the semantic and syntactic dimensions of fictional prose and sets aside formal manipulation of time, space, and point of view. Narration comes down to typography.[21]

The degree to which MacCabe has hypostatized the novel and its language may be seen by contrasting his account with the theory set forth by Mikhail Bakhtin, who also sees the novel as a set of discourses. Whereas MacCabe thinks of the nineteenth-century novel as monologic, pinned under one dominant discourse, Bakhtin proposes that the principal novelistic tradition is that of dialogue or heteroglossia: "The novel is the expression of a Galilean perception of language, one that denies the absolutism of a single and unitary language."[22] Far from attempting to provide an unmediated literary representation of reality, the novel tends to criticize discourses which reduce reality in univocal ways. After a close investigation of the history of the novel, Bakhtin shows that the realist tendency which MacCabe takes as pervasive, unitary, and of long duration actually emerged from a particular literary polemic about reality and was by the beginning of the nineteenth century widely criticized and parodied. For Bakhtin, the narrator's interventions in the work of Tolstoy or Eliot constitute heterogeneous attacks upon various predefined conceptions of reality: in these novels, visions of the world struggle in open battle.

The battle is fought by means of various discourses. But Bakhtin denies that there can be any static or stable metalanguage. He shows how the comic novel pioneered a method whereby discourses mingled not only in dialogue exchanges but also within the enveloping narration. A passage from *Little Dorrit* exemplifies the process. "But Mr. Tite Barnacle

was a buttoned-up man, and consequently a weighty one."
Not being in quotation marks, the "consequently" belongs to
what MacCabe must call metalanguage; yet its function is
not simply to claim transparent access to truth. As character
discourse, the word renders the society's judgment of Mr.
Barnacle; as narration, the word mocks logic ("consequently" parodies the inferential "thus") and ironically criticizes a society that equates concealment with importance.
The "consequently" belongs both to Mr. Barnacle's admirers
and to the critical narrator. Even a single word can thus be a
hybrid locution, mixing two or more semantic fields without
signaling any boundary. (Bakhtin points out that putting the
word in quotation marks would not do justice to the word's
double discursive function.) Bakhtin shows that even in the
most "realistic" novels, the narrator's language will interact
dynamically with several discourses, not all of them attributable to direct character speech. Bakhtin's conclusion is
worth quoting at length because it suggests the richness of
novelistic language in a way that MacCabe's scheme cannot
grasp.

> Even when we exclude character speech and inserted
> genres, authorial language itself still remains a stylistic
> system of languages; large portions of this speech will
> take their style (directly, parodically, or ironically) from
> the languages of others, and this stylistic system is
> sprinkled with others' words, words not enclosed in
> quotation marks, *formally* belonging to authorial
> speech but clearly distanced from the mouth of the au-
> thor by ironic, parodic, polemical or some other pre-
> existing "qualified" intonation. To relegate all these
> orchestrating and distancing discourses to the unitary
> vocabulary of a given author, to relegate the semantic
> and syntactic peculiarities of these orchestrating words
> and forms to the specific semantics and syntax of an
> author, that is, to perceive and describe everything as
> linguistic features belonging to some unitary authorial
> language, is just as absurd as blaming the language of
> the author for the grammatical mistakes he has em-
> ployed to flesh out one of his characters.[23]

The basic theoretical difficulty becomes clear: MacCabe has
derived his conception of metalanguage from scattered surface properties of the text, physical marks which do not
necessarily signal the stylistic systems of which Bakhtin
writes, those semantic fields which are mobilized within the
language of narration.

If MacCabe's version of the "classic realist text" drastically
oversimplifies the history of the novel, how much more does
it reduce the range of filmic narration. By equating metalanguage with the camera, MacCabe returns to one habit of the
invisible-observer model: the privileging of camera work
(and at a pinch, editing) over other film techniques. As I
have already claimed, all materials of cinema function narrationally—not only the camera but speech, gesture, written
language, music, color, optical processes, lighting, costume,
even offscreen space and offscreen sound.[24]

But perhaps MacCabe doesn't literally mean to identify
"the camera" with any one technique. Possibly he is simply
claiming that what we *see* in a normal fiction film has stronger narrational force than what we hear. That this is inaccurate is shown by his own example, *Klute*. The film ends with
Klute and Bree soberly preparing to move her out of her
apartment, while her voice-over commentary claims that she
doesn't know if the change will work. There is no reason to
decide, as MacCabe does, that "what she really wants is to
settle in the mid-West with John Klute."[25] The narration is as
conventional as MacCabe suggests, but the convention employed is not that of definite closure but that of ambiguity:
Klute is "open-ended" in a way characteristic of those American genre films influenced by the European art cinema of
the 1960s and 1970s. The only way that this ambiguity can
be achieved is to give image and sound equal interpretive
weight. As Bakhtin points out with respect to literary narration, filmic narration can often be better characterized by the
interplay of potentially equivalent narrational factors than by
the flattening of all elements under a monolithic "metalanguage."

Film Narration as Enunciation

The structuralist aspects of MacCabe's account make it typical of one impulse in the diegetic approach to narration, but more widespread has been the application to film of linguistic categories of enunciation derived from Emile Benveniste.

It would be comforting to be able to outline Benveniste's categories precisely, but they occupy a small portion of his writings and of the work of his peers. The distinction between *histoire* and *discours* has not become part of mainstream linguistic theory, while the *énoncé/énonciation* pairing gets used in ambiguous ways. Moreover, Benveniste has elaborated these concepts relatively little, and his use of terms is less consistent than many film theorists would lead one to believe. Nevertheless, in one guise or another the concepts have slipped into film theory and we must do what we can to sort them out.

The primary distinction is that between the *énoncé* (the "enounced," or the utterance) and the *énonciation* (the enunciation). The utterance is a stretch of text, a string of words, phrases, or sentences linked by principles of coherence and perceived as constituting a whole.[26] The enunciation, on the other hand, is the general process that creates the utterance. According to Benveniste, the enunciation consists, first, of the act itself. This includes the speaker, who puts linguistic codes to work; the listener, partner in a dialogue; and some reference to a shared world. The enunciation also includes the situation, or context, of the utterance. Finally, we find in the enunciation specific linguistic forms, which Benveniste calls "means": pronouns, the person and tense of verbs, syntactic patterns like the interrogative and the imperative, and so forth.[27] Every spoken or written employment of language involves both utterance and enunciation.

Benveniste orginally conceived of enunciation as embracing the entire communicative process—act, context, and linguistic forms. But Catherine Kerbrat-Orecchioni points out that linguists who employed Benveniste's terms began to restrict the concept to the speaker's relation to the product of the act, the traces in the *énoncé* of the subject of enunciation. As she puts it, the study of enunciation has become "the study of linguistic devices (shifters, modalizers, evaluative terms, etc.) by which the speaker leaves his mark upon the *énoncé*, inscribes himself into the message (implicitly or explicitly), and situates himself with respect to it."[28]

Evidently some utterances bear more traces of enunciation than others. "Eliza, fetch me my slippers" explicitly signals the presence of a speaker, listener, and speech context through its use of proper name, first person possessive pronoun, imperative mood, personal pronoun, and present tense. Benveniste calls this mode of enunciation *discours*: "every enunciation assuming a speaker and a hearer, and in the speaker the intention of influencing the hearer in some way."[29] The mode which omits strong enunciative marks is identified as *histoire*: "the presentation of facts observed at a certain point in time, without any intervention of the speaker in the recounting."[30] In French, *histoire* means both "story" and "history," and prose fiction and historical writing furnish Benveniste's principal examples of *histoire*. Here language frees itself from a concrete communicative situation. "There is in fact no longer even a narrator. The events are set forth as they occurred in the story. No one speaks here; the events seem to recount themselves."[31]

I have suggested earlier that the "second semiology" turned to Benveniste's theory as a way out of too static and enclosed a notion of signification.[32] Benveniste's conception of enunciative means offered a method for detecting traces of subjectivity in a text. Barthes, for instance, deployed categories of tense, person, and voice to locate the "writing subject" in even relatively *histoire*-oriented passages.[33] Yet to do this he had to go beyond Benveniste and posit a homology between sentence structure and text structure. Gérard Genette proposed *discours* as the general and "natural" mode of language and took *histoire*—what he called *récit* ("story")—as a particular subset marked by exclusions. This constitutes a distinct deviation from Benveniste's logically exclusive and parallel categories. Like Barthes, Genette recommended that literary critics turn their attention to analyzing the delicate relations between "the requirements of *récit* and the necessities of *discours*."[34] Given such difficulties, it is not surprising that one linguist simply declared all written fiction to be *histoire*.[35]

Film theorists who wanted to use Benveniste's work were even more taxed, since they had to apply linguistic categories by analogy. Assume the film, or some passage of it, to be the utterance. How do we find the enunciation? Who "speaks" a film? To whom is it addressed? In what circumstances is it spoken? What is the film's equivalent for person, tense, mode, and other means of enunciation?

Some answers are supplied by Christian Metz. In "Histoire/discours," he proposes that cinema as an institution has an enunciative dimension by virtue of "the filmmaker's intentions, the influences he wields over the general public, etc."[36] But the traditional film presents itself as *histoire* in that it effaces all marks of enunciation.[37] Like the nineteenth–century novel, the film presents the action in the past tense and an impersonal mode ("I watch it, but it doesn't watch me watching it").[38] Nonetheless, Metz claims, this impression of *histoire* is an illusion; the film is discursive, but covertly so: it "masquerades" as *histoire*. In a traditional film, the camera is an invisible agency of discourse in that it "*puts forward* the story and shows it to us."[39] In fact, Metz asserts, we identify with this all-powerful seeing and even get the feeling of being the enunciating subject ourselves. This film which seems to have no teller seems to be told by us.

Metz's brief essay outlines a core of common premises for critics seeking to build a linguistically based account of filmic narration. The analyst must ferret out the discursive elements that the utterance disguises as *histoire* and find the "speaker" behind what seems unspoken. Three brief examples will show how these assumptions have been employed.

Some critics seek in cinema specific correlatives to the Benveniste-Metz categories. Mark Nash has argued that *Vampyr* displays cinematic equivalents of those marks of person one can find in personal and possessive pronouns. He suggests that an optical point-of-view shot constitutes first-person *histoire* and an ordinary descriptive shot constitutes third-person *histoire*. When subjective and descriptive shots contain personal marks of the author, we are in the realm of *discours*. Nash uses these categories to argue that *Vampyr*'s unexpected shifts from *histoire* to *discours* are analogous to the hesitations in enunciation which Todorov has shown to be at work in the literary genre of the fantastic.[40]

Less stringent has been the application of the Benveniste-Metz conception by two other critics. Raymond Bellour's analysis of *Marnie* assumes *histoire* to be present simply when the plot moves along and the filmic narration follows it through a controlled repetition and variation. We also know that Hitchcock characteristically presents the film as *histoire* by transmitting information through characters' optical viewpoints. But if we dissect the film as a whole, Bellour contends, we find "a central point from which all these different visions emanate: the place, at once productive and empty, of the subject-director."[41] Bellour goes on to isolate moments when this subject reveals his control through specific marks of *énonciation*: a strongly noticeable camera position, the heroine's fleeting glance toward the camera, and in particular a moment when Hitchcock himself, posing as a passerby, stares at Marnie and then looks at the camera. In these images, Bellour claims, Hitchcock no longer presents the camera's look as the character's point of view; he makes his own seeing/speaking presence manifest.

Bellour concentrates upon classical narrative films, works which approximate Metz's notion of the traditional work that hides its discursive operations. Marie-Claire Ropars-Wuilleumier tends to analyze films which flaunt their *discours*. In her discussion of one sequence from *Muriel*, she indicates that the delay of an establishing shot, the discontinuous editing, the disjunction between sound and image, the sudden close-ups, and the manipulation of time make the scene virtually impossible to describe as straight *histoire*. The autonomy of the camera with respect to the action creates enunciative patterns that force us to understand the sequence as a narrator's mediated rendition.[42] Ropars shares with Bellour and Nash the assumptions that a film is an *énoncé* which contains traces of *énonciation* and that the critic must expose when and how *histoire* gives way, even if fleetingly, to *discours*.

Using Benveniste's theory in film study raises three related difficulties. First, critics have not acknowledged the degree to which they have recast his concepts. Metz's "Histoire/discours" essay is the principal instance. Metz claims that the institution of cinema enunciates, but Benveniste does not grant that speaking can be done by any entities except individuals. When Metz asserts that a film is enunciative in that it aims to affect the audience, he transposes one *necessary* condition of Benveniste's definition into a *sufficient* condition for its application to cinema. Moreover, Metz's claim that cinema is discursive by virtue of intent and effects would also apply to the writing of fiction and history, activities which Benveniste labels unequivocal instances of *histoire*. Benveniste furthermore does not propose that *discours* may masquerade as *histoire*; if a text "effaces all marks of enunciation," Benveniste calls it *histoire* pure and simple. Here Metz has confused *discours* (the overt marking in the *énoncé* of the speaker-listener relation) with enunciation itself (which always includes speaker and listener). That traditional cinema is "enunciative" would not automatically make it "discursive" in Benveniste's sense. In a still more farfetched revision, Metz translates verbal activity (Benveniste's research object) into an optical activity: if the film "looks at me," it is discursive; if it does not, it remains *histoire*. And Benveniste makes no provision for the possibility of the hearer's being somehow duped into becoming the enunciator. He does not say that the reader of *histoire* thinks he or she created it. In sum, Metz does not so much borrow from Benveniste as rewrite him, and not for the better.

This would not be an insurmountable problem if the adaptation of the original theory were argued out in detail. What is perhaps most striking about enunciation theories of film narration is the absence of justification for applying linguistic categories. This is the second difficulty of the approach. Why, we can ask, choose Benveniste's theory of language over others, some of which are far more elabo-

rated? The appropriation of Benveniste's categories seems particularly dubious in that they were constructed to solve specific linguistic problems (e.g., verb and person in French); they have been interpreted in a variety of ways; and they have not yet gained general acceptance within linguistic circles. Why, moreover, is the employment of linguistic concepts a necessary condition of analyzing filmic narration? Is linguistics presumed to offer a way of subsuming film under a general theory of signification? Or does linguistics offer methods of inquiry which we can adopt? Or is linguistics simply a storehouse of localized and suggestive analogies to cinematic processes? Such questions must be answered before we can consider a character's glance as equivalent to a speech act or treat the camera as having a "look."

A third set of problems crops up when the theorist does indeed explore the analogy in detail. The closer an enunciation account sticks to the linguistic model, the more troublesome the application to film becomes. Nash's discussion of *Vampyr* is revealing here. Seeking to find marks of *discours* in the film, Nash must reject nearly all of Benveniste's "means of enunciation" (e.g., verb tense, signs of time) as inapplicable. Only the category of person, Nash hypothesizes, has a cinematic equivalent. Yet the comparison breaks down when he fails to find filmic equivalents for the second-person function. He asserts that in cinema the "you" function "bears the marks of the author's address to the implicit reader."[43] His only examples are two expository titles in the film which present questions addressed (perhaps) to the viewer. But what would a second-person *image* look like? Nash can find no instances because we have no idea of what could be pertinent marks. Is a close-up overtly addressed to the reader? Is a carefully framed long shot? In effect, every shot or cut bears some trace of the author's address. The second-person pronoun is a necessary component of Benveniste's conception of *discours*: it brings out the presence of the hearer. But if in analyzing a film we cannot distinguish first-person *discours* (i.e., shots bearing personal marks of the author) from second-person *discours* (i.e., shots bearing personal marks of the viewer) then the category of person has no equivalent in the cinema.

When critics try to avoid the search for stringent parallels to linguistic categories, uses of the utterance/enunciation and *histoire/discours* pairings become variable to the point of pandemonium. Some critics, such as François Jost, speak of heterogeneous enunciative functions, not distinct enunciative signs; others hold with Nick Browne that each camera setup constitutes "a marker of the enunciation."[44] For Jacqueline Suter, discourse is "an ideological position from which a subject 'speaks' (acts/interacts) within the social order"; this formulation makes any social behavior analogous to speech and renders discourse prior to any speech act—surely a vacuous use of terms.[45] Some theorists treat *histoire* as at least intermittently present on the screen, even though it is interrupted by bursts of *discours*. Others, however, hold that throughout the film only *discours* is before us; when it is unnoticeable, we take it for *histoire*. We should not be surprised, then, that there is little discussion of what constitutes a cinematic *énoncé*, the analytical unit upon which the whole edifice rests. Alain Bergala takes the *énoncé* to be the profilmic event, the filmed action; here *énonciation* is firmly identified with camera work and editing.[46] For Ropars, however, the shot is "the smallest *énoncé* possible in cinema."[47] But the shot is a material division, not necessarily a signifying one; in language, the *énoncé* is not defined by its material limits, since it can consist of one word or many sentences. Is one of Miklós Jancsó's ten-minute takes a "smaller" analytical unit than a line of dialogue in the same film? It is perhaps to duck this problem that most analysts of cinematic *discours* have concentrated on films where editing clearly marks narrative units—Bellour on *Marnie* and *The Birds*, Ropars on *Muriel* and *October*. And Nash's analysis of *Vampyr* takes "the duration of an interplay of the codes" as the minimal utterance, a solution that eludes narrowness by fleeing into vagueness.[48]

Because the foundations for a linguistic theory of cinematic representation have not been firmly laid, critics have slipped into habits that recall tendencies of the mimetic tradition. The lack of a clear theory of enunciation leads to an intuitive, ad hoc spotting of *discours*. Camera work and editing, the two techniques privileged by the invisible-observer model, become the principal bases of enunciation, with the proviso that certain applications of them show strong marks. With discontinuous montage, Ropars writes, *discours* is brought to our attention. Bellour suggests, however, that continuity cutting can also betray signs of enunciation, at least when it is organized in strict "rhyming" alternations. Metz takes this still further: editing of any sort creates a more deliberate intervention of the "filming subject" than does a lengthy take.[49] In addition, for Bellour and others, the camera—or rather "the variation in distance between camera and object"[50]—can give access to enunciation. Camera movement, according to Browne, has a strong "enunciative force."[51] We are back to a conception of narration which not only ignores certain film techniques (e.g., music, mise-en-scène) but also treats the diegetic world as a prior unity inflected from the outside by another intelligence: the one that frames the action and puts one image after another. In fact, the slippage from *discours* as speech (Benveniste) to *discours* as "the look" (Metz) has strengthened the pride of place held by the camera. Metz unabashedly anthropomorphizes the camera in describing how the traditional film conceals *discours*. On this account, the characters look, and the camera "looks" at them looking.

"Who" looks through the camera? Bellour answers: the subject producing the *discours*. Ropars: the narrator. Nash: the author. Sometimes this figure is described in linguistic terms—the "enunciator" (Bellour), a "voice" (Ropars). But just as often the entity is described mimetically: Ropars speaks of a camera movement as "the narrator's look," Bellour of Hitchcock as "the kino-eye."[52] Just as this critical paradigm has not yet offered a systematic account of how narration mobilizes all film techniques, so there has as yet been no attempt to define the general properties or qualities of filmic narration or the filmic narrator. Indeed, critics have blurred important distinctions: Ropars equates the narrator with the "implied author," while Bellour talks as if the enunciator in Hitchcock's films is not a critical construct but a certain corpulent Englishman ("the director, the man with the movie camera").[53]

In part, the format of analyzing one film in depth has served to block more abstract theorizing. Nash is concerned with *Vampyr*'s adherence to codes of a literary genre, Ropars concentrates on the modernity of certain directors, and Bellour's analysis of enunciation in the classical cinema has been confined to a few works taken singly. The failure of Nash's analysis suggests that the more stringently one applies concepts like enunciation and *discours*, the less one is able to generate exhaustive and consistent explanations of narration. Film's lack of deictics (person, tense, mode, etc.) makes it difficult to account systematically for the speaker, situation, and means of enunciation.

Stephen Heath has made the most philosophically ambitious attempt to assimilate narrative structure and cinematic technique to an enunciation theory. He has avoided local analogies and sought to work at a far more abstract level. Heath's contribution seems to me valuable, but his appeal to the concept of "subject position" returns to mimetic assumptions in crucial ways. In his essay "Narrative Space," Heath declares that all representation is "a matter of discourse," but he then defines discourse as "the organization of the images, the definition of the 'views,' their construction."[54] Heath then appeals to the concept of position, using it in four different senses: (1) the implied physical vantage point created by an image in linear perspective; (2) a totalized sense of space across several images, a sort of mind's-eye view; (3) a coherent narrative "point of view"; and (4) "subject position," which refers to the stability and unity of the construction of the self. Heath holds that language offers the paradigm for the enunciation of subject positions. If he can show a logical relation among space (senses 1 and 2), narrative (3), and subject position (4), he will have assimilated film style and narrative to linguistic processes.

I believe that Heath's argument establishes only a terminological connection among the four senses of "position." For the concepts are very different. For instance, perspectival positioning (1) involves sensory activities which objectify concrete locales, while narrative "positioning" (3) is simply a metaphor for the intelligibility and coherence achieved in the processing of narrative information. Indeed, senses 2 through 4 are all metaphorical. And even if the relation among these concepts is more than metaphorical, the entire construct does not escape mimetic assumptions. Senses 1 and 2 of "position" presuppose that shots create invisible observers and that editing creates ideal ones. Heath in fact needs these mimetic assumptions to hook up the various senses of "position." To be sure, Heath sometimes criticizes mimetic claims, but this waiver is hard to accept. He often appears to make claims about the actual effects of dominant cinema, in which case nothing that he says counts against the mimetic theory. Perhaps, however, Heath is in fact describing not the effects but the *aims* or the *rationale* of conventional filmmaking. If this is his goal, he is nonetheless led to accept the premises offered by that cinema's "mimetic" apologists.

These difficulties emerge from Heath's discussion of particular cases. Most of his examples (*Wavelength, Print Generation, La région centrale, Poetic Justice*) imply that a unified subject position can be avoided only by avoiding narrative itself. But this says nothing about how a filmmaker could ever avoid "positioning" at the level of the shot or the sequence of shots. Heath's most detailed analysis of an example involves a scene from *Death by Hanging*. He asserts a priori that Oshima's films present a contradictory subject position in sense 4: "Split in the narrativization, the films are thus out of true with—out of 'the truth' of—any single address: the subject divided in complexes of representation and their contradictory relations."[55] What does this claim imply about "positioning" in the other senses of the term? Heath grants that each of the shots furnishes no disruptions of perspectival position. His case rests upon asserting a disruption of that ideal viewing position afforded by normal editing, and this is accomplished by one cut that presents overt incompatibilities in figure position and setting. Yet the stylistic evidence he offers does not differ from that present in many "art films," which can create such spatial incompatibilities from shot to shot—ambiguously comprehensible, as in this case, as either character subjectivity or authorial commentary. (Chapter 10 supplies a detailed discussion.) The fact that Heath finds the sequence obeying optical perspective (sense 1) and, except for that one cut, creating an ideal view (sense 2) again suggests that subject-position theory has not improved on the mimetic explanation of film technique.

Enunciation theory has provided a major impetus for the dissection of film style, and it has set cinephiles thinking about narration in more sophisticated ways. Yet because a film lacks equivalents for the most basic aspects of verbal activity, I suggest that we abandon the enunciation account. We need a theory of narration that is not bound to vague or atomistic analogies among representational systems, that does not privilege certain techniques, and that is broad enough to cover many cases but supple enough to discriminate among types, levels, and historical manifestations of narration. Arguing for such a theory is the business of the rest of this book.

PART TWO

Narration and Film Form

By the way, it's not all jam writing a story in the first person. The reader can know nothing except what Bertie tells him, and Bertie can know only a limited amount himself.

P. G. Wodehouse, *Performing Flea*

3. The Viewer's Activity

The theories of filmic narration discussed in the last two chapters have little to say about the spectator, except that he or she is relatively passive. Perspectival accounts tend to treat the viewer pointillistically, as the sum total of ideal vantage points shifting from shot to shot. But this observer is merely the "all-embracing eye" of the Wodehouse passage cited at the start of Part 1: mimetic theories assign few *mental* properties to the spectator. Of mimetic theorists, only Eisenstein allows the spectator an interesting mental life, including features such as expectation and some powers of inference. Diegetic theories, for all their apparent concern with narrational effects, also tend to downplay the viewer's role. In keeping with the revision of Benveniste whereby *énonciation* gets reduced to marks of the speaker, enunciation theorists have notably ignored the spectator. When the perceiver is discussed, it is usually as the victim or dupe of narrational illusion-making. MacCabe's "metalanguage" and Metz's *discours*-disguised-as-*histoire* fool the viewer into taking the narration for an unmediated and "natural" representation. The passivity of the spectator in diegetic theories generally is suggested not only by the extensive borrowing of mimetic concepts of narration but also by the use of terms like the "position" or the "place" of the subject. Such metaphors lead us to conceive of the perceiver as backed into a corner by conventions of perspective, editing, narrative point of view, and psychic unity. A film, I shall suggest, does not "position" anybody. A film cues the spectator to execute a definable variety of *operations*.

I have no trust that starting a theory of narration with an account of the spectator's work will explain all narrational phenomena. But since the spectator's comprehension of the story is the principal aim of narration, we can usefully begin there. And by not giving the film an immediate pride of place, we can seek to avoid passive notions of viewing. But first a few disclaimers.

I shall try to explain the formal conditions under which we comprehend a film. This means that here the "spectator" is not a particular person, not even me. Nor is the spectator an "ideal reader," which in recent reader-response criticism tends to be the most fully equipped perceiver the text could imagine, the one most adequate to all the aspects of meaning presented. I adopt the term "viewer" or "spectator" to name a hypothetical entity executing the operations relevant to constructing a story out of the film's representation. My spectator, then, acts according to the protocols of story comprehension which this and following chapters will spell out. Insofar as an empirical viewer makes sense of the story, his or her activities coincide with the process I will be describing. For the comprehension of any one narrative film, of course, the "hollow" forms I will be describing must be supplemented by many sorts of particular knowledge. Moreover, my spectator is "real" in at least the sense that she or he possesses certain psychological limitations that real spectators also possess. My spectator, for instance, undergoes the *phi* phenomenon (see p. 32) and thus necessarily perceives apparent motion in films. Finally, my spectator is active; his or her experience is cued by the text, according to intersubjective protocols that may vary (as we shall see in Part 3).

The theory I advance attends to the perceptual and cognitive aspects of film viewing. While I do not deny the usefulness of psychoanalytic approaches to the spectator, I see no reason to claim for the unconscious any activities which can be explained on other grounds. In general, current film theory has underestimated the importance of the spectator's conscious and preconscious work. Study of narrative cognition may in fact be a prelude to psychoanalytic inquiry for the same reason that Freud was at pains to show that psychoanalytic theory finds its best application when cognitive explanations fall short.

As a perceptual-cognitive account, this theory does not address affective features of film viewing. This is not because I think that emotion is irrelevant to our experience of cinematic storytelling—far from it—but because I am concerned with the aspects of viewing that lead to constructing the story and its world. I am assuming that a spectator's comprehension of the films' narrative is theoretically separable from his or her emotional responses. (I suspect that psychoanalytic models may be well suited for explaining emotional aspects of film viewing.) Near the end of this chapter I will suggest how some affective features might be explicable in relation to cognitive processes.

It will come as no surprise that I do not treat the spectator's operations as necessarily modeled upon linguistic activities. I shall not speak of the spectator's "enunciating" the story as the film runs along, nor shall I assume that narrative sense is made according to the principles of metaphor and metonymy. It is by no means clearly established that human perception and cognition are fundamentally determined by the processes of natural language; indeed, much psycholinguistic evidence runs the other way, toward the view that language is an instrument of and guide for mental activity.[1] For such reasons, I do not call the spectator's comprehension "reading" a film. It is, moreover, needlessly equivocal to speak of the spectator's activity as a "reading" when the same word is applied to the abstract propositional arguments characteristic of critical analysis and interpretation. Viewing is synoptic, tied to the time of the text's presentation, and literal; it does not require translation into verbal terms. Interpreting (reading) is dissective, free of the text's temporality, and symbolic; it relies upon propositional language. This chapter and this book try to explain viewing.

A Sketch for a Psychology of Filmic Perception and Cognition

Any theory of the spectator's activity must rest upon a general theory of perception and cognition. I assume here what is called a Constructivist theory of psychological activity; descended from Helmholtz, it has been the dominant view in perceptual and cognitive psychology since the 1960s. According to Constructivist theory, perceiving and thinking are active, goal-oriented processes. (Karl Popper calls this the "searchlight" theory of mind.)[2] Sensory stimuli alone cannot determine a percept, since they are incomplete and ambiguous. The organism *constructs* a perceptual judgment on the basis of nonconscious *inferences*.

Inference making is a central notion in Constructivist psychology. In some cases, the inference proceeds principally "from the bottom up," in which conclusions are drawn on the basis of the perceptual input. Color perception is a good example. Other processes, such as the recognition of a familiar face, operate "from the top down." Here the organization of sensory data is primarily determined by expectation, background knowledge, problem-solving processes, and other cognitive operations. Both bottom-up and top-down processing are inferential in that perceptual "conclusions" about the stimulus are drawn, often inductively, on the basis of "premises" furnished by the data, by internalized rules, or by prior knowledge.[3]

A Constructivist theory permits no easy separation between perception and cognition. Speaking roughly, the typical act of perception is the identification of a three-dimensional world on the basis of cues. Perception becomes a process of active hypothesis-testing. The organism is tuned to pick up data from the environment. Perception tends to be anticipatory, framing more or less likely expectations about what is out there. As E. H. Gombrich puts it, "Groping comes before grasping, or seeking before seeing."[4] The organism interrogates the environment for information which is then checked against the perceptual hypothesis. The hypothesis is thus either confirmed or disconfirmed; in the latter case, a fresh hypothesis tends to appear.[5] Bottom-up perceptual processes, such as seeing a moving object, operate in a fast, involuntary way, but they remain similar to other inferential processes.[6] Top-down processes are more overtly based on assumptions, expectations, and hypotheses. When we scan a crowd to look for a friend, the likelihoods furnished by context and past experience count for a good deal. Cognitive processes help frame and fix perceptual hypotheses by reckoning in probabilities weighted to the situation and to prior knowledge. Typical cognitive activities, like sorting or remembering things, depend on inferential processes.

In all these activities, whether we call them perceptual or cognitive, organized clusters of knowledge guide our hypothesis making. These are called *schemata*. The mental image of a bird is a schema for visual recognition, and the concept of a well-formed sentence functions as a schema in speech perception.[7] Schemata may be of various kinds—prototypes (the bird image, for instance), or templates (like filing systems), or procedural patterns (a skilled behavior, such as knowing how to ride a bicycle).[8] We shall see shortly that schemata play an important part in story comprehension.

The dynamic nature of the Constructivist account makes it highly attractive. The perceiver in effect bets on what he or she takes to be the most likely perceptual hypothesis. Like all inferences, perceptual experience tends to be a little risky, capable of being challenged by fresh environmental situations and new schemata. After some interval, a perceptual hypothesis is confirmed or disconfirmed; if necessary, the organism shifts hypotheses or schemata. This cycle of perceptual-cognitive activity explains the ongoing, revisionist nature of perception. The theory also explains why perception is often a skilled, learned activity; as one constructs a wider repertoire of schemata, tests them against varying situations, and has them challenged by incoming data, one's perceptual and conceptual abilities become more supple and nuanced.

Visual perception has furnished the classic illustrations of Constructivist psychological theory. Taken as a purely sensory experience, seeing is a bewildering flutter of impressions. The eye fixates many times per minute, using short and fast movements (called *saccades*); the eye rotates to compensate for head and body movement; the eye trembles involuntarily; and most of the visual information we receive is peripheral anyhow. Yet we do not experience a flicker or smear of percepts. We see a stable world, smooth movements, constant patterns of light and dark. To the extent that seeing is a bottom-up process, the visual system is organized to make its inferences in an involuntary, virtually instantaneous manner. You "immediately" see a visual array as consisting of objects distributed in three-dimensional space, and you cannot help seeing this. This automatic construction is also affected by schemata-driven processes that check hypotheses against incoming visual data. Julian Hochberg suggests that since only the fovea of the eye sees detail, the saccades purposefully explore the environment, guided by schemata that propose the most fruitful places to look. We assemble our visual world from successive glances which we constantly check against our reigning "cognitive maps." These maps tell us to ignore the eye's physiological tremor and to bring the most significant areas into foveal vision. The schemata also generate hypotheses about what we will see next.[9] Seeing is thus not a passive absorption of stimuli. It is a constructive activity, involving very fast computations, stored concepts, and various purposes, expectations, and hypotheses.[10] A comparable account can be provided for auditory perception.

No one has yet delineated a Constructivist theory of aesthetic activity, but its outlines look clear enough. The artwork is necessarily incomplete, needing to be unified and fleshed out by the active participation of the perceiver. To some extent, artworks exploit the automatic nature of bottom-up processing; in such cases, the work can create illusions. But art is also a domain of top-down procedures. The spectator brings to the artwork expectations and hypotheses born of schemata, those in turn being derived from everyday experience, other artworks, and so forth. The artwork sets limits on what the spectator does. Salient perceptual features and the overall form of the artwork function as both triggers and constraints. The artwork is made so as to encourage the application of certain schemata, even if those must eventually be discarded in the course of the perceiver's activity.

What, then, distinguishes aesthetic perception and cognition from the nonaesthetic variety? In our culture, aesthetic activity deploys such skills for nonpractical ends. In experiencing art, instead of focusing on the pragmatic results of perception, we turn our attention to the very process itself. What is nonconscious in everyday mental life becomes consciously attended to. Our schemata get shaped, stretched, and transgressed; a delay in hypothesis-confirmation can be prolonged for its own sake. And like all psychological activities, aesthetic activity has long-range effects. Art may reinforce, or modify, or even assault our normal perceptual-cognitive repertoire.

A Constructivist account would thus consider film viewing as a dynamic psychological process, manipulating a variety of factors:

1. *Perceptual capacities.* Cinema is a medium that depends upon two physiological deficiencies in our visual system. First, the retina is unable to follow rapidly changing light intensities. At critical "fusion" frequency, more than fifty flashes per second will create the impression of steady light. Second, the phenomenon known as apparent motion occurs when the eye sees a string of displays as a single moving one.[11] This effect depends on the fact that the eye will infer movement from an intermittent input if the jumps are not too large. Flicker fusion and apparent motion illustrate how automatic and mandatory bottom-up processing is: although we know that a film is only a stroboscopic display of fixed frames, we *cannot fail* to construct continuous light and movement. As a medium of illusion, cinema counts on our making "wrong" inferences.[12] Moreover, the theater situation helps control our miscalibration of the stimuli. Darkness reduces distracting visual information and isolates the film for our concentration. And when the perceiver is acclimated to lower light levels, fusion and apparent movement effects operate more strongly.[13]

Other bottom-up processes shape our perceptual experience, such as when we perceive color on the screen. Some tasks, such as constructing the fictional space on the basis of depth cues, involve both bottom-up and top-down processing. (See Chapter 7.)

2. *Prior knowledge and experience.* In watching a representational film, we draw on schemata derived from our transactions with the everyday world, with other artworks, and with other films. On the basis of these schemata, we make assumptions, erect expectations, and confirm or disconfirm hypotheses. Everything from recognizing objects and understanding dialogue to comprehending the film's

overall story utilizes previous knowledge. The rest of this book will consider various schemata specific to narrative comprehension.

3. *The material and structure of the film itself.* In narrative cinema, as we shall see in the next chapter, the film offers structures of information—a narrative system and a stylistic system. The narrative film is so made as to encourage the spectator to execute story-constructing activities. The film presents cues, patterns, and gaps that shape the viewer's application of schemata and the testing of hypotheses.

I have isolated these factors for convenience, but plainly they interact in any single case. Consider the role of time in film viewing. While watching a narrative film, the spectator takes as one goal the arranging of events in temporal sequence. Our prior commerce with narrative and the everyday world allows us to expect that events will occur in some determinate order, and in most films specific cues encourage us to treat each distinct action as following previously presented ones. If the narrative presents events out of chronological order, we must fall back on our ability to rearrange them according to schemata. But such films run the risk of confusing us. Moreover, cinema's viewing conditions add a constraint: under normal conditions, it is not possible to review stretches of a film as one can reread passages of prose. The relentless forward march of stimuli in a film puts an extra strain on the spectator's memory and inferential processes. A filmmaker who presents story events out of chronological order thus risks forcing the spectator to choose between reconstructing story order and losing track of current action. This is probably why most films avoid temporal reshufflings. But we have seen in recent decades that films with complex time patterns can supply audiences with new schemata or encourage them to see the film more than once. The history of film form can thus alter the perceiver's prior experiences.[14] (This history is investigated in Part 3 of this book.)

In opposition to all passive notions of spectatorship, then, we should consider film viewing a complicated, even skilled, activity. Watching a movie may seem as effortless as riding a bicycle, but both draw on a range of practiced acts. Here, perhaps, is the most significant relation between the spectator and the reader. We are accustomed to think of reading printed matter as automatic, but even after the language has been learned, reading is an immensely intricate achievement, requiring the selection of salient cues, the processing of large units, decisions about how to sample the text, anticipations, and the projection of an ongoing semantic whole.[15] Comprehending a painting seems no less formidable. E. H. Gombrich has shown that the beholder needs a knowledge of the medium's constraints and conventions, a sense of the painting's purpose, the ability to fill in what is missing, and a proclivity to compare the painting with pertinent experiences of the world.[16] It would be surprising if a film, with its mixtures of visual, auditory, and verbal stimuli, did not demand active and complex construction.

Narrative Comprehension

The point of the previous section is that the spectator *thinks.* To make sense of a narrative film, however, the viewer must do more than perceive movement, construe images and sounds as presenting a three-dimensional world, and understand oral or written language. The viewer must take as a central cognitive goal the construction of a more or less intelligible story. But what makes something a story? And what makes a story intelligible?

Since the early 1970s, several psychologists and linguists have sought to understand how people comprehend and recall stories.[17] The research is still limited by its reductive assumptions, since the stories are simple, short, written in prose, and shorn of most aesthetic interest. Yet what data the researchers have discovered offer some pointers for theorizing. First, these studies have revealed that even five-year-old children in our culture recognize certain activities as characteristic of storytelling and story-following. Second, the patterns of comprehending and recalling a story are remarkably uniform for all age groups. People tacitly assume that a story is composed of discriminable events performed by certain agents and linked by particular principles. People also share a sense of what is secondary to the story's point and what is essential to it. Third, and most significant from a Constructivist standpoint, people perform operations on a story. When information is missing, perceivers infer it or make guesses about it. When events are arranged out of temporal order, perceivers try to put those events in sequence. And people seek causal connections among events, both in anticipation and in retrospect.

Story research has posed but not yet solved two problems: cross-cultural comprehension, and the relation of learning to innate abilities. It seems likely that, in non-Western cultures, following a story does not take the exact forms it does in ours.[18] And it seems very likely that skill in story comprehension, however much it may operate with innate mental capacities (e.g., perception of time or causality), is acquired. One study found older children more proficient than younger ones in understanding stories with events put out of temporal order. This would support culture-based theories of perception and cognition, as well as late structuralist conceptions of narrative codes' dependence upon "already read" texts. Nonetheless, neither problem is of central importance for us here. For schooled perceivers in contemporary Western culture, narrative comprehension and recall are centrally guided by the goal of creating a meaningful story out of the material presented.

Generally, the spectator comes to the film already tuned, prepared to focus energies toward story construction and to apply sets of schemata derived from context and prior experience. This effort toward meaning involves an effort toward unity. Comprehending a narrative requires assigning it some coherence. At a local level, the viewer must grasp character relations, lines of dialogue, relations between shots, and so on. More broadly, the viewer must test the narrative information for consistency: does it hang together in a way we can identify? For instance, does a series of gestures, words, and manipulations of objects add up to the action sequence we know as "buying a loaf of bread"? The viewer also finds unity by looking for relevance, testing each event for its pertinence to the action which the film (or

scene, or character action) seems to be basically setting forth. Such general criteria direct perceptual activity through anticipations and hypotheses, and they are in turn modified by the data supplied by the film.

We can specify these schemata more exactly. In comprehending a narrative film, the spectator seeks to grasp the filmic continuum as a set of events occurring in defined settings and unified by principles of temporality and causation. To understand a film's story is to grasp what happens and where, when, and why it happens. Thus any schemata for events, locations, time, and cause/effect may become pertinent to making sense of a narrative film. More rigorously, we can follow Reid Hastie in distinguishing among various types of schemata; each has a role to play in narrative comprehension.[19]

"Central-tendency" or *prototype* schemata, Hastie suggests, involve identifying individual members of a class according to some posited norm. In narrative comprehension, prototype schemata seem most relevant for identifying individual agents, actions, goals, and locales. Understanding *Bonnie and Clyde* involves applying prototypes of "lovers," "bank robbery," "small Southern town," and "Depression era." We cannot inventory all the possible prototype schemata that might be pertinent to narrative comprehension; each film will call on a particular configuration of them.

More useful for our purposes is the tendency for such prototypes to operate in a larger structure. Hastie calls such structures *template* schemata, or filing systems. Template schemata can add information when it is absent and test for proper classification of data. The early results of story-comprehension research suggest that in our culture perceivers do tend to presuppose a particular master schema, an abstraction of narrative structure which embodies typical expectations about how to classify events and relate parts to the whole. Perceivers tend to use this master schema as a framework for understanding, recalling, and summarizing a particular narrative. The perceiver expects each event to be discriminable and to occur in an identifiable locale. The string of events should reveal chronological order and linear causality. (For perceivers of all ages, texts with reordered story events or ambiguous causal connections tend to reduce understanding.) Causal connections are especially important; in remembering stories, people tend to invert the order of events more frequently when the link is only sequential ("and then . . .") and not also consequential ("as a result . . .").

Several experiments yield evidence for the schematic function of a "template" of narrative structure in contemporary Western cultures. The perceiver tends to recall a deviant story as being more normal than it was. If the text as presented omits causal connections, perceivers tend to supply them when retelling the tale. This is also strong evidence for the active qualities of narrative understanding: spectators are filling in material, extrapolating and adjusting what they remember. Perceivers also agree about what can be deleted in summarizing a story.[20] And adults have developed strategies to deal with deviations from the master schema, the chief one of which seems to be a toleration of ambiguity. In such ways, basic structural principles continue to serve as reference points for the identification of "less intelligible" narratives. The narrative schema is like those circles, squares, and triangles which artists revise and adorn to permit the portrayal of any object; the perceiver constantly refines the basic schema to fit the narrative at hand.

Nearly all story-comprehension researchers agree that the most common template structure can be articulated as a "canonical" story format, something like this: introduction of setting and characters—explanation of a state of affairs—complicating action—ensuing events—outcome—ending. Distortions in comprehension and recall tend to occur at points when the narrative violates or ambiguates this ideal scenario. There is further evidence that goal orientation is a salient aspect of the schema of causality. One researcher found that comprehension and memory are best when the story conformed to the drive-to-a-goal pattern. When the goal was stated at the end of the tale, comprehension and recall were significantly poorer, but still not so poor as when the goal of the action was never stated. In other words, early statement of the protagonist's goal permitted the perceiver to fill in causal and temporal connections more exactly. And in recalling and summarizing stories which stated the goal tardily, perceivers inserted goal statements earlier in the sequence. Thus the format can be recast as: setting plus characters—goal—attempts—outcome—resolution.[21]

Now, the canonic story formats have a familiar ring; they resemble the formulas for plot construction dear to Freytag, Brunetière, and a hundred lesser theorists of narrative construction. We are thus inclined to suspect a strong cultural bias at work in the experiments' descriptions of story formats. Would an African perceiver necessarily grasp a tale in terms of exposition/complication/outcome? I do not wish to dismiss the possibility of a cross-cultural canonic story, since perhaps at some level of description these formats hold good. But since the matter needs much more study, I suggest only that the formats have heuristic value for analyzing narratives produced and consumed in our culture. The contemporary Western perceiver does typically expect expository material at the outset, a state of affairs disturbed by a complication, and some character ready to function as a goal-oriented protagonist.

As a template for organizing causality and time, the canonic story accords well with a Constructivist theory of narrative cognition. The perceiver gauges how well the narrative at hand can be slotted into the schema. In most cases the perceiver does not patiently isolate each datum (in a film, each movement or shot or sound) and slowly assemble a narrative event such as "buying a loaf of bread." Instead, the spectator selects salient cues, then draws on prototype schemata (e.g., knowledge of bakeries and hunger) and template schemata specific to narrative structure (e.g., what is likely to be causally prominent). Guided by something like the canonic story, the perceiver "chunks" the film into more or less structurally significant episodes. Only some such process can explain how the perceiver understands that very different forms of surface information convey similar meanings. In a film, buying a loaf of bread might consume an instant, a scene, or several scenes. As Roland Barthes remarks, "To read a narrative continuum is in fact to arrange it—at the quick pace set by the reading material—in a variety of structures, to strive for concepts or labels which more or less sum up the profuse sequence of observations."[22] Furthermore, the top-down grasping of an event can run ahead of the data. If a hungry man enters a bakery, "buying a loaf of bread" becomes a likely hypothesis before he places his order. The categorical whole can precede the perceived part.

Prototype schemata and template schemata are employed by what Hastie calls *procedural* schemata, those operational protocols which dynamically acquire and organize information. This is perhaps most clearly seen when a template schema is inadequate for the task at hand. If the film does not correspond to the canonic story, the spectator must adjust his or her expectations and posit, however tentatively, new explanations for what is presented. Even in a more predictable narrative, the search for information and the framing of inferences follow characteristic rules. Some of these procedures were identified long ago by the Russian Formalists under the name of "motivation."[23] By what procedures does the spectator justify a given textual element? How does the element get assigned to a prototype or classified within a pertinent grid?

The spectator may justify material in terms of its relevance to story necessity. We can call this *compositional* motivation. But the spectator may apply other warrants, such as a notion of plausibility derived from some conception of the way things work in the world. "He is the sort of man who would do that": such a rationale exemplifies *realistic* motivation. Or the spectator may justify an expectation or inference on *transtextual* grounds. The clearest case is that of genre: in a Western, we expect to see gunfights, barroom brawls, and thundering hooves even if they are neither realistically introduced nor causally necessary. Finally, and most rarely, the perceiver can decide that something is present simply for its own sake—as an appealing or shocking or neutral element. The Formalists called this *artistic* motivation and thought very highly of it, since it directly focused attention on the forms and materials of the artwork.

In practice, the first three of these procedural rationales often cooperate with one another. If Marlene Dietrich sings a cabaret song, we could justify it compositionally (it's here that the hero meets her), realistically (she plays a cabaret singer), and transtextually (Marlene sings such songs in many of her films; it's one aspect of her star persona). Sometimes too there may be disparity among these rationales, as when we consider a stray "realistic" detail as having no bearing on the unfolding action, or when in the musical genre the causal chain halts to make way for a song and dance. Most films ask the spectator to employ compositional and transtextual motivation. Realistic motivation is usually a supplementary factor, reinforcing expectations already arrived at on other grounds. Artistic motivation is a residual category and remains distinct from the others; the spectator has recourse to it only when the other sorts do not apply. Thus, the concept of motivation brings to light several procedural schemata which the spectator must actively employ.

To what extent, we might now ask, does the viewer possess *stylistic* schemata? Most narratives use their medium (language, film, graphic art, whatever) as a vehicle for narrative information. Perceivers' schemata thus tend to favor narrative patterning and to find purely stylistic patterns difficult to notice or recall. Teun van Dijk writes of the literary text: "Our memory and processing resources are able only in a very restricted way to store and retrieve these kinds of surface structural information, even if the communicative conventions require specific attention to such structures."[24] The same often holds true for visual phenomena: after one checks a clock, one can recall the time but not the shape of the numerals, even though those must have been registered at some stage of perception.[25] This suggests that when spectators are confronted with a film that emphasizes its stylistic features, they will still seek cues for constructing a story.

Film style may usually go unnoticed, but that does not entail that the spectator has no stylistic schemata. On a Constructivist account, the perceiver need be no more aware of applying an aesthetic convention than of any other cognitive operation. We have already seen that many perceptual processes are nonconscious. Perhaps owing to the stylistic uniformity of mainstream cinema, applying stylistic schemata is a top-down process that has become so practiced as to operate automatically. It is clear that on the basis of prior experience, the spectator assumes that certain stylistic schemata will be adhered to, as when we identify a long shot or a nondiegetic commentary on the basis of prototypes. We also employ stylistic templates. In mainstream narrative cinema, a long shot is likely to be followed by a closer view, and a musical bridge is more apt to fade out than to be cut off. Some stylistic alternatives are unlikely and some are completely ruled out. We also know that spectators accustomed to one stylistic tradition can use procedural schemata to comprehend other stylistic options (e.g., "motivate this cut by story necessity"). A Constructivist theory would emphasize that to a great degree spectators can learn to notice and recall stylistic features of any film. At later points in this book we will have occasion to consider how film style can operate as a vehicle for narration and a system in its own right.

What does the viewer do with the schemata? Plainly, many cognitive activities are performed in making sense out of narrative. The viewer posits a more or less stable set of *assumptions*. The spectator assumes, for example, that objects and human beings persist in space even when they are not on screen; that a character possesses the same individual identity on successive appearances; that a film in English will not suddenly lapse into Urdu. We notice such basic assumptions only when a film violates them, as when the same character is played by two quite different performers (as in Buñuel's *Obscure Object of Desire*). The viewer also makes many *inferences*. If our hero bursts into tears, we conclude that he is sad. Like other inductive inferences, such conclusions are open-ended, probabilistic, and subject to correction. Maybe our hero is delighted. *Memory* of course plays a role as well. Again, memory must be seen not as a simple reproduction of a prior perception, but as an act of construction, guided by schemata (as was proposed by Frederic Bartlett over fifty years ago).[26] There is also the cognitive task of *hypothesizing*: the spectator frames and tests expectations about upcoming story information. Since hypotheses exemplify the anticipatory quality of schema-driven perception, I shall try to clarify their operation at a little more length.

Meir Sternberg is one of the few theorists of narrative to give due weight to the process of framing and testing hypotheses. In Sternberg's theory, the pattern of story information withheld in the work prompts the perceiver to make hypotheses of various sorts. A hypothesis may pertain to past action that the text refrains from specifying; Sternberg calls this a *curiosity* hypothesis. By contrast, a *suspense* hypothesis is one that sets up anticipations about forthcoming events. Hypotheses may also be more or less *probable*, ranging from the highly likely to the flatly improbable, and more or less *exclusive*, ranging from either/or choices to mixed sets. And since hypotheses arise in the course of time, they may be held simultaneously or successively, as when one hypothesis simply replaces another.[27] All of these categories will prove of use when we seek to analyze how particular films both cue and constrain the spectator's activity.

There are levels of hypothesis testing. Typically, assumptions and inferences take care of the "microscopic," moment-by-moment processing of the action, but at critical junctures we are tuned to expect particular events. Across scenes, hypotheses emerge with some clarity: will the character do x or y? A more indefinite but highly significant arc of "macroexpectation" may extend across a whole film. The narrative itself can inflect these levels, such as by playing down small-scale portions (transitions, or the secondary actions Barthes calls "catalyses") in order to stress longer-range hypotheses about significant action sequences (Barthes's "kernels" or "hinges").[28] Other narratives may deny us large-scale expectations; in such a case we call the text episodic. Hypotheses also vary in precison according to their placement in the text: they tend to be more "open" at the start of a text; some remain tacitly in force throughout because they are never countermanded.

The primary focus of hypothesis forming remains what Sternberg calls suspense—anticipating and weighing the probabilities of future narrative events. Consider the alternatives. When an action backs up an already confirmed hypothesis, it is redundant and cannot trigger the full anticipatory range of hypothesis casting. "Our whole sensory apparatus," writes Gombrich, "is basically tuned to the monitoring of unexpected change. Continuity fails to register after a time, and this is true both on the physiological and the psychological level."[29] But when the action presented does not confirm a hypothesis, the perceiver is unlikely to turn back to a previous page or halt the teller's tale or stop the film to sort it all out. Instead, the perceiver presses on to see if the unfolding action will explain or modify the challenge to the hypothesis. We can call this the "wait-and-see" strategy.[30] Even in the detective story, which of all genres places most emphasis upon curiosity about prior events, the perceiver seldom pauses if there are snags in answering questions about why the action occurs or what the action shows about the agent. Instead, the perceiver rushes eagerly on. The detective tale offers the story of an investigation, and what the perceiver wants to know is not only "who did it" but how the detective's future actions will bring the solution to light.

The perceiver's tendency to make salient those hypotheses pertaining to upcoming information accords well with the Constructivist assumption that schemata coax us to anticipate and extrapolate. Disconfirming instances make us readjust our expectations. At the same time, the schemata need a firm foothold somewhere. The sequential nature of narrative makes the initial portions of a text crucial for the establishment of hypotheses. Sternberg borrows a term from cognitive psychology, the "primacy effect," to describe how initial information establishes "a frame of reference to which subsequent information [is] subordinated as far as possible."[31] A character initially described as virtuous will tend to be considered so even in the face of some contrary evidence; the initial hypothesis will be qualified but not demolished unless very strong evidence is brought forward.

Between the framing of the hypothesis and the confirming or disconfirming instance in the text there intervenes some time. At a local level, the hypothesis may be validated or invalidated very soon, which is the normal case for our moment-by-moment following of the narrative. Our heroine crosses a room and opens the door; cut to a shot from outside as she walks out into the hall. But when more idiosyncratic and macrostructurally significant narrative action is at stake, the information is typically withheld for some interval. If our heroine is to encounter someone in the hall, perhaps that person's motive or purpose will be withheld from us and

revealed only later. Since the pioneering explorations of the Russian Formalists, we have recognized *retardation* as essential to narrative structure. Because the narrative unwinds in time, the fulfillment of our expectations may be considerably delayed. The narrative begins, but its forward progress must be interrupted by exposition that supplies pertinent background information. The narrative will end, but its conclusion is held back by complications, subplots, or digressions. Viktor Shklovsky called retardation "stairstep construction": a narrative text is less like an elevator than a spiral staircase which, littered with toys, dog leashes, and open umbrellas, impedes our progress.[32] Sternberg goes so far as to describe the narrative text as "a dynamic system of competing and mutually blocking retardatory patterns."[33] Of course, delaying story information will not keep the spectator interested forever; our blocked expectations must be balanced by more immediate ones—usually, suspense hypotheses. In any event, delay in satisfying hypotheses can be exploited to trigger new expectations or to play off different retardatory structures against one another. If, after our heroine goes out her door, we cut to a shot of the hero across town, menaced by the killer whom the heroine seeks, we start to elaborate a hypothesis that she will come to rescue him. And if the landlord holds her palavering at her door, the retardation of each line of action by the other will intensify our interest in finding out whether our hypothesis holds good.

So ongoing and insistent is the perceiver's drive to anticipate narrative information that a confirmed hypothesis easily becomes a tacit assumption, the ground for further hypotheses. But it is still convenient to speak of the perceiver's hypotheses as being clearly validated, invalidated, or left dangling. Most are validated: no narrative surprises us at every turn. Less often, the presentation of story information leads us to disqualify some hypotheses. The character does something we thought unlikely; the chief murder suspect turns out to be the next victim; the narrative swerves off the track. Narratives are composed in order to reward, modify, frustrate, or defeat the perceiver's search for coherence.

To sum up: In our culture, the perceiver of a narrative film comes armed and active to the task. She or he takes as a central goal the carving out of an intelligible story. To do this, the perceiver applies narrative schemata which define narrative events and unify them by principles of causality, time, and space. Prototypical story components and the structural schema of the "canonical story" assist in this effort to organize the material presented. In the course of constructing the story the perceiver uses schemata and incoming cues to make assumptions, draw inferences about current story events, and frame and test hypotheses about prior and upcoming events. Often some inferences must be revised and some hypotheses will have to be suspended while the narrative delays payoff. While hypotheses undergo constant modification, we can isolate critical moments when some are clearly confirmed, disconfirmed, or left open. In any empirical case, this whole process takes place within the terms set by the narrative itself, the spectator's perceptual-cognitive equipment, the circumstances of reception, and prior experience.

Narratives in the aesthetic realm submit all these processes to particular pressures. In ordinary perception, Ulric Neisser points out, perceptual hypotheses tend to be vague and open-ended, and they are seldom vigorously disconfirmed.[34] In art, however, alternative hypotheses tend to be much more explicitly defined, their set tends to be closed, and they get challenged fairly often. Aesthetic perception and cognition encounter situations which are constructed so as to upset the most common assumptions, the most valid inferences, the most probable hypotheses, and the most appropriate schemata. Narratives may arouse perceivers' anticipations and lock in mental sets before presenting information that undermines those very activities. More often than we are usually aware, narratives invoke expectations only to defeat them, plan and time our encounters with information that will upset our assumptions, encourage us to extrapolate and then chide us for going too far, parade a host of positive instances before trotting out the single and crucial exception, hold back basic data while "prattling" (Barthes's term) about irrelevancies—all the while forcing us to keep to a predetermined temporal sequence and (in film and other "time arts") yoking us to a fixed rate of comprehension that makes us err simply by pressure of the clock. Narrative art ruthlessly exploits the tentative, probabilistic nature of mental activity.

Although I am delineating a hypothetical spectator endowed with aspects of human perceptual and cognitive capacities, I might mention the extent to which empirical spectators can err in comprehending a film. These errors can be explained within the theory I have outlined. As I mentioned earlier, a narrative film both triggers and constrains the formation of hypotheses and inferences; it does not uniquely specify or determine them. Physiological factors such as fatigue may thwart or delay perceptual processing, making attention or memory flag. Other misunderstandings of the film may result from applying schemata which later prove to be inappropriate—such as mistaking the hero's goal or not expecting temporal reordering in a flashback. Errors of schemata selection and hypothesis forming may also spring from inadequate knowledge of the narrational norms to which the film appeals; a spectator who lacks the schemata for the 1960s "art film" will miss cues and lose patterning in a film like 8½. Of course, a spectator may also deliberately misconstrue the story, as some French Surrealists did in their "irrational enlargements" of Hollywood B-pictures. Finally, as I have suggested, a film may contain cues and structures that encourage the viewer to make errors of comprehension; in such cases, the film "wants" a short- or long-term "misunderstanding."

To the extent that this theory showcases perception and cognition, it does not have much to say about affect. The theories of affect most compatible with the Constructivist account are those in which emotion is bound up with expectation and its interrupted or delayed fulfillment.[35] It should be evident that emotion is not at all alien to the process of filmic comprehension. When we bet on a hypothesis, especially under the pressure of time, confirmation can carry an emotional kick; the organism enjoys creating unity. When the narrative delays satisfying an expectation, the withholding of knowledge can arouse keener interest. When a hypothesis is disconfirmed, the setback can spur the viewer to new bursts of activity. The mixture of anticipation, fulfillment, and blocked or retarded or twisted consequences can exercise great emotional power. The formal processes of perception and cognition—as Eisenstein well knew—can trigger affect.

Believing and Seeing

Rear Window (1954) has long been used as a small-scale model of the spectator's activity. The chairbound photographer watching without being seen; the windows across the way like movie screens; the apparent freedom from consequences yielded by the viewer's distant vantage point—these have made the film an irresistible analogy for the viewing experience. Such atomistic comparisons are valid; no film I know fits more snugly into a perspectival theory of narration. Yet *Rear Window* can also be used to exhibit the full complexity of the viewing activity. Not just the piquant situation but the very process of the unfolding action lays bare the way we typically construct the story in a fiction film. *Rear Window* is at once typical in the job it hands the spectator and extraordinary in the explicitness with which tasks are spelled out.

The story is well known. Laid up with a broken leg, L. B. Jeffries takes to watching his neighbors across the courtyard. He idly looks in on a married couple and their dog, a composer, a pair of newlyweds, a lonely middle-aged woman, a young female dancer, a sculptress, and the Thorwalds, another married couple. At the moment, Jeff's love affair with the model Lisa Fremont is deteriorating because he sees her as too unlike him: she leads a sophisticated Manhattan life while he tramps around the world pursuing adventure. In his days of rear-window spying, Jeff begins to suspect that Lars Thorwald has murdered his wife. Jeff wins Lisa to his way of thinking, but his friend Detective Lieutenant Doyle remains skeptical. After Lisa breaks into Thorwald's apartment for evidence, Thorwald realizes that Jeff has been watching him and comes to assault him. Jeff is saved in time (although he breaks his other leg), and the film ends with Jeff and Lisa apparently reconciled.

There are thus two interdependent lines of action: the mystery (What has happened to Mrs. Thorwald? Will Jeff prove that she was killed? Can Lisa find evidence?) and the romance (Will Jeff and Lisa break up?). What makes the film useful to us here is its blending of explicit and implicit appeals to spectatorial activity. The mystery plot line tends to state assumptions, hypotheses, evidence, and inferences very baldly. Characters talk about how they build up expectations, select information, and draw conclusions. The spectator shares in the characters' battle for a solution to the mystery. At certain moments in the mystery action, however, the viewer is tossed information which the characters do not possess. Thus we must sometimes qualify or challenge the characters' problem-solving processes. And in the romance plot line, the spectator must construct the story without benefit of such overt cues. For example, the spectator must discover that the absolute opposition which Jeff creates—Lisa and urban boredom versus himself and high adventure—is a false one; one can find adventure in the most mundane urban milieu.

The overall structure of the film confirms expectations grounded in the canonic story format. There is exposition which establishes time, setting, and character relations and which identifies the two primary states of affairs: life in the courtyard and the impasse in Jeff and Lisa's romance. There follows Jeff's decision to achieve a goal—to prove Mrs. Thorwald was murdered—which makes progress but which also encounters several obstacles (counterevidence, absence of tangible proof). Finally Jeff achieves the goal (resolution), and he and Lisa are seen at relative peace at the end.

The film's time scheme also encourages us to unify the action. The story begins on Wednesday and reaches its climax on Saturday, with each day carefully demarcated and a clear rhythm of alternation established between day and night. The temporal unity is strengthened by a set of deadlines: Thorwald may leave before Jeff can prove the murder took place, Thorwald may harm Lisa before the police arrive, Thorwald may kill Jeff before the police rescue him. The viewer thus constructs the story using information not only about causality but about the duration and deadlines that govern the action. Furthermore, the prologue and epilogue are symmetrical, not only spatially (similar camera movements around the courtyard and Jeff's apartment) but in their invitation to compare present with past (e.g., the newlyweds are bickering at the end, Miss Lonelyhearts now knows the composer). The viewer can also quickly grasp the spatial premise: we will be confined to this room (with some exceptions), we will see what Jeff sees (with significant exceptions). Thus we will also have to call on stylistic schemata, such as our knowledge of eyeline-match and point-of-view editing.

From the outset, *Rear Window* emphasizes the probabilistic quality of seeing and knowing. The tour of the courtyard, with the camera panning slowly left to right from within Jeff's window, provides information that is principally visual (supplemented by music and street noises). We see the neighbors composing music, practicing dance, and so on, and we infer that these are habitual and typical activities. When the camera moves into and around Jeff's apartment, our inferences must come thick and fast. Track left to reveal his leg in a cast. (How did the leg get injured?) Then to a shattered press camera. (He's a photographer. Did he break his leg on the job?) Then to photographs of an auto race, a fire, a battered woman, an atomic bomb. (He probably did; he takes hazardous assignments.) Then down a line of cameras and flashbulbs. (Almost certainly a professional photographer.) Finally to a framed negative of a model and to a stack of magazines with the photo on the cover. (He can also do fashion photography.) Yet these inferences remain only probable until the next scene. Now most of the inferences we had made get corroborated by Jeff's phone conversation with his editor. The pattern is set: this film will encourage us to construct a story on the basis of visual information (objects, behavior) and then confirm or disconfirm that construction through verbal comment. After the solitary woman across the way toasts her phantom dinner companion and then breaks down weeping, Jeff's remark, "Miss Lonelyhearts," caps our comprehension of her situation. After Thorwald dials three digits and pauses, Jeff will mutter: "Long distance." As we watch Miss Torso's party, Jeff and Lisa spin yarns about her choice of male companions. Encouraging us to draw conclusions about

story events and then making us wait for verbal corroboration highlights the more or less likely nature of our inferential procedures. Moreover, by having the characters sum up the actions we see by a clichéd label ("nagging wife," "Park Avenue model," "the eat-drink-and-be-merry girl"), the film makes sure that we construct the proper schematic prototypes.

Rear Window asks us to generate several distinct sorts of hypotheses. We frame curiosity hypotheses about the past (Thorwald did murder his wife), and suspense hypotheses about the future (the investigation will reveal more clues). In the first four scenes, the film confines itself chiefly to the romance plot and generates vague suspense hypotheses (Jeff and Lisa will likely remain at loggerheads). After Jeff hears the scream and crash at the close of scene 4, curiosity plays a stronger part; we and Jeff watch Thorwald's mysterious comings and goings until we are prepared to label the action as "domestic murder" and ask more specific questions. And the hypotheses alter with respect to probability. As of scene 4, Jeff and Lisa's romance looks unlikely, but as the murder draws them together, their eventual alliance becomes more probable. That Thorwald has committed murder seems unlikely in scene 4, more likely after Jeff pleads his case, less likely after Doyle's deflating evidence, more likely after the neighbors' dog is murdered, and virtually certain after Jeff discovers that something was buried in the garden.

The process whereby Jeff pursues the mystery displays quite beautifully the activity of the film spectator. He begins, like you and me, in a state of tuned anticipation: "If you don't pull me out of this swamp of boredom, I'm gonna do something drastic. . . . Right now I'd welcome trouble." Jeff is prepared to perceive, but he is so eager for activity that he risks extrapolating too much. In scene 4, after Lisa leaves, he turns to the window and scans the darkened apartment block across the way. Two sensory cues pop out—a scream and a crash. He looks quickly to and fro, but no visual cues are forthcoming. Now he can apply a very loose procedural schema: he will test for lapses in normal activity. As the night goes on, he watches Thorwald leave and return to his apartment. The next morning, he possesses only the roughest hypothesis: "I just can't figure it. . . . I think he was taking something out of the apartment." His nurse Stella quickly suggests the hypothesis that Thorwald is running out on his wife. But then Jeff picks up new information. Thorwald looks across the way in a peculiar fashion. "That's the kind of look a man gives when he's afraid someone might be watching him." In response, Jeff uses his telephoto lens to magnify his view. Thorwald opens a suitcase and wraps a knife and saw in newspaper. By the time Lisa arrives that night, Jeff is convinced that Mrs. Thorwald has been killed.

Note that Jeff's inferential process does not completely mirror our own. In an earlier scene, at six in the morning, we have seen Thorwald leave his apartment, accompanied by a woman dressed in black. But Jeff is asleep. We thus gain information that he does not have, and it creates a hypothesis that competes with the murder hypothesis. Everything that Jeff sees and will later see could also be explained by the hypothesis that the wife took a trip. But this is not to say that we reject Jeff's hypothesis completely. The murder hypothesis, however unlikely in real life, is highly likely in a Hitchcock film (transtextual motivation), and the fact that the film would equivocate about the woman's identity makes the viewer adopt a wait-and-see attitude. Perhaps this new information can be fitted into a more global explanation. (Lisa will show us how later.) For Hitchcock the division of knowledge between characters and audience is fundamental to suspense, which he describes as "providing the audience with information that the characters do not have."[36] This is only a half-truth, though. In most of his films, such data are never pure; they always come filtered through a narration that withholds crucial facts. Though we are more knowledgeable than the protagonists, we remain less knowledgeable than the narration, and the film rubs our noses in the partial and ambiguous quality of our information.

At this point Jeff sums up (Thorwald left late at night, wrapped up his knife and saw) and adds new data: he did not go to work, and he avoided his wife's bedroom. It falls to Lisa to resist Jeff's inference. She suggests that Mrs. Thorwald died; but there is no sign of a doctor or undertaker. Perhaps she's sleeping or sedated; but Jeff points out that she needs constant care. Yet would Thorwald murder his wife with the shades up? Jeff counters that he's being nonchalant to give the impression of normality. And Lisa returns to Stella's point—Thorwald is leaving his wife—adding that indeed very few husbands commit murder. Lisa's rebuke is important in reemphasizing the tentative nature of Jeff's construction of the chain of events; her question "What is it you're looking for?" implies that Jeff has run far beyond the data. But Lisa's competing schemata are defeated when Thorwald finally raises the blinds to reveal the bed stripped, the wife gone, and a steamer trunk being packed. Lisa stands staring. "Let's start from the beginning again, Jeff. Tell me everything you saw—and what you think it means." Her remark concisely reiterates the film's strategy of supplying sensory information ("everything you saw") and then forcing Jeff (and us) to interpret it ("and what you think it means").

The next morning, the nurse Stella is already convinced of Jeff's account and freely pours forth specific hypotheses. ("Now just where do you suppose he cut her up? Of course— the bathtub.") But Jeff's friend Lieutenant Doyle is skeptical, reminding him that there are many alternatives, of which murder is the least plausible. Hypothesizing that the wife took a trip, Doyle sets out to gather evidence. He reports to Jeff that witnesses saw the Thorwalds leave for the railroad station at 6 A.M. the previous morning; this corroborates our view of the couple leaving. Doyle also claims that he found a postcard from Mrs. Thorwald in her husband's mail. Jeff nonetheless resists this evidence and demands proof that she got on the train and that the trunk contains only clothes. Doyle grudgingly agrees to check further. Jeff's tenacity reveals the force of the primacy effect. The first full-blown inference, although less probable than Doyle's, takes pride of place, and subsequent hypotheses are flung against this one.

That evening there is a pitched battle of mutually exclusive hypotheses. Lisa rehabilitates Jeff's original opinion. First, she modifies his initial hypothesis in order to accommodate new evidence. Jeff has seen Thorwald take his wife's handbag from a drawer and go through her jewelry. Lisa (using the highly ideological "realistic" rationale, "What women typically do") asserts that no woman would leave home without her favorite handbag and jewelry. More important, she offers an alternative account of what we saw: "We'll agree they saw a woman, but she was not Mrs. Thorwald. At least, not yet." This removes the last obstacle to our sharing Jeff's inference. (It implies, however, that the film's narration cunningly concealed how and when the second woman got *into* Thorwald's apartment.) Yet Doyle destroys their revised hypothesis. He dismisses Lisa's schema as "woman's intuition" and trots out hard evidence that the Thorwalds have separated. He has the clichéd prototype: "That's what's called a family problem." The trunk contained clothes and was picked up by Mrs. Thorwald in Merrittsville. Doyle turns Jeff's suspicions back on him (Has *he* owned a knife and saw? "Do you tell your landlord everything?") Most compellingly, Doyle points out that no hypothesis is airtight:

JEFF: You mean to say that you can explain everything that's gone on over there and is still going on?

DOYLE: No, and neither can you. That's a secret, private world you're looking into out there. People do a lot of things in private that they couldn't possibly explain in public.

After Doyle leaves, Jeff and Lisa watch Miss Lonelyhearts in an ugly and humiliating quarrel with a man she invites in. Jeff winces and grants that Doyle might be right about private behavior; Lisa agrees that they've become ghouls. Miss Lonelyhearts's episode confirms Doyle's hypothesis, and they accept defeat.

A defeat, however, which is only momentary. In the next scene, Jeff and Lisa are brought frantically to the window by (again) a scream. The neighbors' dog has been killed, and the wife shrieks out to the courtyard at large, denouncing the callousness of her neighbors. Crowds gather at windows and balconies to look down, but Thorwald does not emerge, remaining inside his darkened apartment, quietly smoking. Jeff switches back to his earlier explanation, assuming now that Thorwald killed the dog. But, Lisa asks, why? "Because it knew too much?" The next morning, Jeff uses slides he took of the courtyard to prove that something was buried in the garden. This fits with earlier data—the dog sniffing about the flower bed and Thorwald shooing it away. At this

point, the murder inference is virtually inescapable: it explains more than any other candidate. Later scenes will reconfirm it—Thorwald will respond to a blackmail threat, Lisa will find Mrs. Thorwald's wedding ring—but now the curiosity portion of the viewer's activity is largely finished. (The only question remaining pertains to the disposal of the wife's body.) The new problem is: how to get enough evidence to convince the authorities before Thorwald flees? By the time Jeff makes the blackmail call, he can read his prey's mind as he watches: "Go on and pick it up, Thorwald. You're curious. You're wondering if it's your girlfriend calling you up—the one you killed for." This is the culmination of that story construction we saw in a more rudimentary form earlier: visual cues anchored by verbal interpretation.

If the mystery line of action follows fairly closely the characters' explicit formulations (with the crucial qualifications provided by our privileged view), the romance plot solicits the same sort of viewing activities more tacitly. In early scenes, Jeff reiterates the impossibility of any alliance between himself and Lisa: he mocks marriage, resists Stella's advice, and insists that neither he nor Lisa can change. He employs detailed contrasts to show that with respect to food, clothes, locale, taste, and safety his and Lisa's worlds are mutually exclusive. His rude remarks travesty Lisa's catered dinner and bring her to the edge of breaking off their romance. But he holds back: "Couldn't we just keep things status quo?" "Without any future?" she asks. But in the end, she agrees to see him again tomorrow night. This portion of the film corresponds to the "state of affairs" phase of our canonical story, and what it portrays is a stalemate. It is at this point that Jeff hears the scream that initiates the murder plot.

Jeff tends to utilize schemata that are strictly homogeneous: Thorwald killed/did not kill his wife; Lisa and Jeff are exactly alike/diametrically opposite. One of Doyle's telling points about the putative murder is that not everything can be neatly filed: "People do lots of things in private that they couldn't possibly explain in public." He proposes a more heterogeneous schema. In the romance plot, it is the viewer's duty to be alert for such heterogeneous categories. Jeff's sharp distinctions get blurred when Lisa develops a taste for danger. She eagerly reports the name and address of the mysterious couple; she mulls over the case while at work; she delivers the threatening note to Thorwald and eventually breaks into his apartment. At each step, Jeff warms to her. After she supplies an identity for Thorwald's woman companion, he kisses her. When she returns breathless from her foray across the court, he grins proudly at her enthusiasm. Calling Doyle on the phone, Jeff boasts of her resourcefulness in saving herself from Thorwald. Lisa demonstrates that she can handle the adventurous life that Jeff had believed was foreign to her. From a structural standpoint, the murder plot resolves the romance plot by breaking down Jeff's rigid dichotomy and revealing Lisa's wit and courage.

Whatever the cues in this film, our expectations are funded by knowledge of other films in the tradition. We motivate transtextually. Just as our experience of thrillers leads us to expect that Jeff is right about the murder, our knowledge of narrative conventions lets us expect that the romantic problems will be resolved before the end. They are, but somewhat equivocally. The camera surveys the courtyard in a movement parallel to that of the first scene, revealing the composer and Miss Lonelyhearts together, painters cleaning Thorwald's apartment, the older couple with a new dog, Miss Torso's boyfriend/husband returning from the army, and the newlyweds bickering. The camera then moves inside to reveal Jeff asleep in his chair, now with two broken legs. Pan right to Lisa on his daybed, curled up in a blouse and blue jeans reading *Beyond the High Himalayas*. The joke depends partly on the echo with the glamorous woman on the magazine cover in the first scene; Lisa the model has become Lisa the mountaineer. But then she picks up *Harper's Bazaar* and begins thumbing through it. The spectator can draw either of two conclusions: Lisa has bridged the gap between the two worlds, or she has reinstated the old opposition by revealing that her concession to the rugged life is superficial and provisional. It is not a question here of interpreting the film one way or the other. The throwaway nature of this last shot reiterates the game of visual information and alternative hypotheses that has in-

formed the whole film. After all the demands on the spectator to draw conclusions about murder and romance, the film ends with information that calls up exclusive and equally probable hypotheses about the stability of the couple without firmly backing either one.

Arrival at this ending depends upon careful retardation, or what Hitchcock preferred to call frustration. Jeff's ultimata and the stalemate in the fourth scene leave the romance plot hanging; its resolution is delayed by the murder plot. And the murder plot in turn must be seen as having its own retardatory structure. Jeff's murder hypothesis needs proving, so he searches for clues. The first is the possibility that Mrs. Thorwald's body is in the trunk which later turns out to contain nothing but clothes. The second clue is the patch of zinnias from which Thorwald shoos away the dog; after the dog's death, Jeff infers that there's something buried there, but when Stella and Lisa dig up the flower bed, they find nothing. The crucial evidence is a third clue, the wedding ring which Jeff sees Thorwald handling and which is the target of Lisa's break-and-entry. The wedding ring is the strongest evidence—it convinces Doyle to take a second look—but from a constructional standpoint the ring could have been the first clue Jeff spotted. The trunk and the zinnia patch are red herrings, pure retardatory devices. The same goes, in a more general way, for all the neighbors living their lives adjacent to Jeff and Thorwald. Apart from their considerable value as thematic parallels to the two primary couples, the neighbors often delay the unfolding of the mystery plot by distracting Jeff's (and our) attention from the main issue. Even at a very localized level, the film uses retardation to prolong our expectations. When Jeff writes Thorwald the threatening letter, the camera adopts a distant, high-angle framing so that we cannot see what he is writing; then the camera slowly cranes in, stretching out the gradual revelation of the simple question: "What have you done with her?" *Rear Window* perfectly illustrates Sternberg's point that a narrative can be considered "a dynamic system of competing and mutually blocking retardatory patterns."

This camera movement, like others, exemplifies how the viewer may also make inferences about the stylistic patterns that emerge. The outstanding example in *Rear Window* is the handling of the death of the neighbors' dog. Jeff and Lisa have accepted Doyle's explanation for Mrs. Thorwald's absence. A scream from outside fetches them to the window. Up to this point, all shots have been confined to Jeff's apartment or to what one could see from it. Now, as Jeff and Lisa look, we get a shot from outside their window, looking in at them. People from other apartments peer out into the courtyard, and the freedom of spatial vantage points increases. The camera frames various neighbors in medium shots and from low angles, and it is clear that neither Jeff nor Lisa sees these people. After the neighbor cries out, "Which of you did it?" and denounces life on the courtyard, she and her husband haul the dead dog up to their window. Then we return to a framing of Jeff and Lisa, the camera tracks in on them, and they notice that only Thorwald, smoking in his darkened apartment, did not go to the window. They conclude that he killed the dog.

The scene violates one tacit stylistic assumption we have formed since the start—that we will be confined to what can be seen from Jeff's window. This violation is quite unpredictable (we might speak of stylistic as well as narrative "surprise" here), but it fulfills the narrative function of giving us a slight edge on Jeff and Lisa. The shocked reactions of the neighbors would not be visible from the window, and by showing them to us the narration tells us immediately that they did not kill the dog. Thorwald is thus guilty by elimination. It is left for Jeff and Lisa to draw the positive inference from his indifference to the tumult outside. In a sense, this scene is comparable to that in which the narration let us see the woman leave Thorwald's apartment while Jeff slept. Here, too, we are freed from our restriction to what Jeff knows. In that scene, though, space helped the narration mislead us: confined to Jeff's room, we got an equivocal view of the action. Here, the narration's closer framings do not try to bamboozle us. After this scene, the camera will not leave Jeff's apartment until the final struggle with Thorwald, and again the violation of the film's spatial norm will be justified by giving us information that Jeff doesn't have (the police are arriving). In such scenes, film style not only guides our inductive processes, but becomes, in however general a way, one object of them.

Every film trains its spectator. By the last scenes of *Rear Window* we have honed our story-construction schemata to expect a climax. We are prepared to slot actions into a narrow "outcome" format. We have been explicitly encouraged to construct certain hypotheses, accepting some and resisting others. We have been trained to take purely visual cues as signs of a narrative situation. The telltale glimpse of Thorwald escorting the woman in black, and the romance plot as a whole, have accustomed us to diverging from characters' knowledge, playing their schemata and hypotheses against more heterogeneous and nuanced ones. We are prepared to justify events and motifs compositionally, realistically, and especially transtextually. We know that retardation will be employed to delay satisfaction of our expectations. Now, in a scene of continuous tension, the film makes maximal use of all the lessons it has taught.

As Stella and Jeff watch, Lisa delivers the threatening note to Thorwald's apartment; she is nearly seen by him. Stella then turns her attention to Miss Lonelyhearts in the apartment below Thorwald's; she notices that the woman has poured out a huge quantity of sleeping pills. Our schema pops into place and dictates a (clichéd) hypothesis: Miss Lonelyhearts will try to kill herself. The first phase of this long scene will thus shift between two lines of action, Thorwald and Miss Lonelyhearts, and hence two hypotheses: he will go out in obedience to the note, she will attempt suicide. The narration cleverly lets us attend more carefully to Miss Lonelyhearts than the characters do. Lisa rushes in, and the two women decide to dig among the zinnias; Jeff will call Thorwald out of the apartment for awhile. As they pore over the phone book, cut away to Miss Lonelyhearts lowering the blind; they do not see her. And the Miss Lonelyhearts situation is left dangling while Jeff calls Thorwald. The women leave, and while they dig, Jeff calls Doyle's home and leaves a message. Jeff's attention drifts to Miss Lonelyhearts, who is at a desk writing; he mutters: "Stella was wrong about Miss

Lonelyhearts." But for the viewer, who has seen the fistful of sleeping pills and the despairing lowering of the blinds, her new action "realistically" confirms the suicide hypothesis; we label the gesture "writing a suicide note." By this crucial point we have become so well trained that we can contradict the inference of the character who has been our principal tutor.

Stella and Lisa find nothing in the garden and, setting out on her own, Lisa shinnies up the fire escape to Thorwald's apartment. Jeff watches her through his telephoto lens as she discovers Mrs. Thorwald's handbag, but not the wedding ring. When Stella returns, she notices Miss Lonelyhearts about to swallow her pills. Now the characters catch up with us and recognize that two lines of action have been running simultaneously. (What is surprise for them has been suspense for us.) Jeff can call the police to tell them of Miss Lonelyhearts, or he can call Thorwald's apartment to warn Lisa. A long shot of the apartment block brilliantly stages the problem, as Thorwald returns down the corridor, Lisa hesitates in Thorwald's living room, and Miss Lonelyhearts languishes in the apartment below. As it turns out, Miss Lonelyhearts was only (again) a delaying device, for the sound of the composer's song halts her suicide attempt; but by then Thorwald has discovered Lisa. Jeff calls the police—anticipating the action we are about to see: "A man is assaulting a woman . . ."—but he can then only watch helplessly from his wheelchair as Thorwald grabs her. Like Jeff and Stella, the viewer must wait for the outcome. After the police arrive and arrest Lisa, she signals Jeff that she has the ring. Thorwald looks across the way straight into Jeff's lens.

Thorwald's returning of Jeff's gaze makes Jeff the prey. As Jeff sends Stella out and phones Doyle, we alone see Thorwald leave his apartment. The phone rings and Jeff, wrong expectation in place, answers it unthinkingly: "Tom, I think Thorwald's left. I don't see . . ." Silence and a click. Now Jeff, not Thorwald, has given himself away. Jeff prepares for Thorwald's arrival by switching out the light and waiting with a clutch of flashbulbs (motivated realistically as the weapon to which a photographer would "naturally" turn). In

a neat reversal, we now infer Thorwald's approach by sonic cues instead of visual ones—the slam of a door and heavy footsteps in the hall. The viewer is in that situation of classic suspense astutely described by Noël Carroll: it seems more probable that Thorwald will kill Jeff, but we hope for the less likely alternative.[37] In realistic terms Jeff is likely to lose, but in compositional and transtextual terms we bet that he will not. He does not, although he winds up tumbling from his rear window to the courtyard into which he had stared so avidly.

Hitchcock has claimed that the tempo of the film's cutting steadily increases across the film.[38] The description is not accurate in detail, but certainly the early scenes insist upon longer takes (around thirty-six seconds) and leisurely camera movements, while the climactic sequences (starting with the discovery of the dead dog) are cut much faster, with the average shot length hovering between four and ten seconds. This is not idle bookkeeping, for such rapid cutting can control the pace of our viewing activity. By the end of a film, the tempo of narrative events and cutting can move faster. From the vague, multiple, heterogeneous hypotheses of the opening we have moved to a narrow set of alternatives: Lisa will or will not get caught, Miss Lonelyhearts will or will not kill herself, Jeff will or will not avoid Thorwald's onslaught. We can follow rapid editing because at this point each shot need convey only one of three sorts of information: "this reinforces alternative X," "this reinforces alternative not-X," or "still waiting." When we "lose ourselves" in a film's climactic moments, it is to a large extent because of the power of a perceptual-cognitive activity that, informed by the logic of the film up to that point, sorts information on the basis of a stringently reduced series of possible outcomes and then bets, in rapid interaction with the flow of story cues, upon certain results.

"Tell me everything you saw," Lisa urges Jeff after she finds Mrs. Thorwald gone, "and what you think it means." *Rear Window* shows how powerful can be the effect of a film that overtly grounds its formal method in basic processes of perception and cognition. Every fiction film does what *Rear Window* does: it asks us to tune our sensory capacities to certain informational wavelengths and then translate given data into a story. Lisa's request is made, more implicitly, by every film that solicits narrative comprehension. Of course, not every film reinforces such conventional ideological categories (nagging wife, society model, adventurous photographer, lusty newlyweds, old maid) and places such trust in the connection between seeing and understanding. Some films—and we shall consider several of them later—undermine our conviction in our acquired schemata, open us up to improbable hypotheses, and cheat us of satisfying inferences. But no matter how much a film arouses our expectations only to frustrate them, or creates implausible alternatives that turn out to be valid, it still assumes that the spectator will initially act upon those assumptions which we use to construct a coherent everyday world.

4. Principles of Narration

My account of *Rear Window* does not constitute a critical interpretation. I have not labeled Jeff a voyeur, judged his peeping nice or naughty, or sought to establish him as a "castrated" adventurer fantasizing the dismembering of a woman's body. Indeed, my sketch is not even an analysis of the film, since specifying the spectator's activity cannot itself provide that. For the viewer, constructing the story takes precedence; the effects of the text are registered, but its causes go unremarked. This is not to say that these activities are, strictly speaking, unconscious; most work of narrative comprehension seems to occur in what Freud called the *pre*conscious, the realm of elements "capable of entering consciousness."[1] The spectator simply has no concepts or terms for the textual elements and systems that shape responses. It is the job of theory to construct them, the job of analysis to show them at work. A full theory of narration must be able to specify the objective devices and forms that elicit the spectator's activity. That is the task of this and the next three chapters. Theory must also go beyond the perceiver's relation to the text by situating the text within contexts of which the perceiver is seldom explicitly aware. These contexts are historical ones, and I shall consider those most pertinent to narration in Part 3. What an account of the spectator's work has taught us is that theory and analysis must explain not only localized effects but whole films, treating them as eliciting the spectator's ongoing construction of the story. Eisenstein's advice to his students holds good for the study of narration as textual form: "Think in stages of a process."[2]

From this chapter forward, my focus is on how film form and style function in relation to narrational strategies and ends. As an alternative, we could undertake empirical investigations of how actual spectators construe particular films. While worthwhile, this enterprise would not necessarily lead to insights into how films encourage, sustain, block, or undercut specific viewing operations. As I have said throughout, formal systems both *cue* and *constrain* the viewer's construction of a story. The theory I propose cannot predict any actual response; it can only construct distinctions and historical contexts which suggest the most logically coherent range of conventionally permissible responses.

We have seen theories of narration founder upon superficial analogies between film and other media—literature or theater (the mimetic approach); literature, speech, or writing (the diegetic approach). The theory I propose sees narration as a formal activity, a notion comparable to Eisenstein's rhetoric of form. In keeping with a perceptual-cognitive approach to the spectator's work, this theory treats narration as a process which is not in its basic aims specific to any medium. As a dynamic process, narration deploys the materials and procedures of each medium for its ends. Thinking of narration in this way yields considerable scope for investigation while still allowing us to build in the specific possibilities of the film medium. In addition, a form-centered approach sets itself the task of explaining how narration functions in the totality of the film. Narrational patterning is a major part of the process by which we grasp films as more or less coherent wholes.

Fabula, Syuzhet, and Style

In previous chapters I have assumed a difference between the story that is represented and the actual representation of it, the form in which the perceiver actually encounters it. This crucial distinction may go back to Aristotle,[3] but it was most fully theorized by the Russian Formalists, and it is indispensable to a theory of narration.

Presented with two narrative events, we look for causal or spatial or temporal links. The imaginary construct we create, progressively and retroactively, was termed by Formalists the *fabula* (sometimes translated as "story"). More specifically, the fabula embodies the action as a chronological, cause-and-effect chain of events occurring within a given duration and a spatial field. In *Rear Window,* as in most detective tales, there is an overt process of fabula construction, since the investigation of the crime involves establishing certain connections among events. Putting the fabula together requires us to construct the story of the ongoing inquiry while at the same time framing and testing hypotheses about past events. That is, the story of the investigation is a search for the concealed story of a crime. By the end of the typical detective tale, all story events can be fitted into a single pattern of time, space, and causality.

The fabula is thus a pattern which perceivers of narratives create through assumptions and inferences. It is the developing result of picking up narrative cues, applying schemata, framing and testing hypotheses. Ideally, the fabula can be embodied in a verbal synopsis, as general or as detailed as circumstances require. Yet the fabula, however imaginary, is not a whimsical or arbitrary construct. The viewer builds the fabula on the basis of prototype schemata (identifiable types of persons, actions, locales, etc.), template schemata (principally the "canonic" story), and procedural schemata (a search for appropriate motivations and relations of causality, time, and space). To the extent that these processes are intersubjective, so is the fabula that is created. In principle, viewers of a film will agree about either what the story is or what factors obscure or render ambiguous the adequate construction of the story.

It would be an error to take the fabula, or story, as the profilmic event. A film's fabula is never materially present on the screen or soundtrack. When we see a shot of Jeff looking out his window, his action is a representation which signals us to infer a story event (Jeff looks out his window). The same piece of information might have been conveyed many other ways, many of them requiring no sight or sound of Jeff at all. The staging of the action, as Eisenstein showed, is itself a representational act. This theoretical move lets us

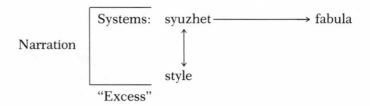

Fig. 4.1 Film as Phenomenal Process

avoid that a priori favoring of certain film techniques charac-teristic of mimetic theories.

The fabula, writes Tynianov, "can only be guessed at, but it is not a given."[4] What is given? What sorts of phenome-nally present materials and forms do we encounter? We can analyze the film as consisting of two systems and a remain-ing body of material, diagramed in figure 4.1. The *syuzhet* (usually translated as "plot") is the actual arrangement and presentation of the fabula in the film. It is not the text in toto.[5] It is a more abstract construct, the patterning of the story as a blow-by-blow recounting of the film could render it. The syuzhet is a system because it arranges components—the story events and states of affairs—according to specific prin-ciples. As Boris Tomashevsky puts it: "The fabula is opposed to the syuzhet, which is built out of the same events, but the syuzhet respects their order in the work and the series of information processes which designate them."[6] "Syuzhet" names the architectonics of the film's presentation of the fabula; hence the rightward arrow in the diagram.[7] Logi-cally, syuzhet patterning is independent of the medium; the same syuzhet patterns could be embodied in a novel, a play, or a film.

Style also constitutes a system in that it too mobilizes components—particular instantiations of film techniques—according to principles of organization. There are other uses of the term "style" (e.g., to designate recurrent features of structure or texture in a body of films, such as "neorealist style"), but in this context, "style" simply names the film's systematic use of cinematic devices. Style is thus wholly ingredient to the medium. Style interacts with syuzhet in various ways; hence the two-way arrow in the diagram.

An example may illustrate how syuzhet and style differ. In *Rear Window*, the syuzhet consists of the particular pattern of events (actions, scenes, turning points, plot twists) depict-ing the tale of Mrs. Thorwald's murder and its investigation and the tale of Lisa and Jeff's romance. When in the preced-ing chapter I described formal patterns of withheld knowl-edge or abrupt revelation, I was referring principally to the construction of the syuzhet. The same film, however, can be described as a steady flow of applications of cinematic

techniques—mise-en-scène, cinematography, editing, and sound. In one scene, Jeff and Stella are spotted by Thorwald. They step quickly back into Jeff's room (figure movement, setting); they whisper (sound) and douse the lamp (light-ing); the camera tracks quickly back to a long shot (cinema-tography); and all of this occurs after the crucial shot of Thorwald turning to look out his window (editing).

Note that in a narrative film these two systems coexist. They can do this because syuzhet and style each treat dif-ferent aspects of the phenomenal process. The syuzhet em-bodies the film as a "dramaturgical" process; style embodies it as a "technical" one. While it would often be arbitrary to separate the two systems in the process of perception, the distinction has precedent in much narrative theory.[8] Indeed, we shall discover one mode of narration that requires us to keep syuzhet and style conceptually separate. Assuming that the distinction is warranted, I want now to spell out the relations between syuzhet and fabula, and syuzhet and style.

In discussing the spectator's activity, I stressed the role of narrative schemata.[9] The theoretical concept of the syuzhet offers a way of analyzing the aspects of a film that the spectator organizes into an ongoing story. It should be clear, though, that the syuzhet is not identical with what Chapter 3 called the canonic story format. The latter, we can now see, comprises schematic assumptions about both the fabula and the syuzhet. The viewer's tendency to assume that charac-ters have goals pertains to causality in the fabula; it does not imply anything about syuzhet organization. But the assump-tion that the spectator will encounter an exposition or an ending pertains to the organization of the syuzhet. The "canonic story" nonetheless offers an example of how assumptions about syuzhet and fabula factors play a considerable role in narrative comprehension.

As a distinction, the fabula/syuzhet pair cuts across media. At a gross level, the same fabula could be inferred from a novel, a film, a painting, or a play. Thus one difficulty of enunciative theories—the forced analogy between linguistic categories and nonverbal phenomena—vanishes. As Meir Sternberg puts it, any narrative medium utilizes "a largely extraverbal logic" that includes "the twofold development of the action, as it objectively and straightforwardly progresses in the fictive world from beginning to end (within the fabula) and as it is deformed and patterned into progressing in our mind during the reading-process (within the syuzhet)."[10] The conception of syuzhet avoids surface-phenomena distinctions (such as person, tense, metalanguage) and relies upon more supple principles basic to all narrative representation. Consequently, and contrary to what some writers believe, the fabula/syuzhet distinction does not replicate the *histoire/discours* distinction held by enunciation theories.[11] The fabula is not an unmarked enunciative act; it is not a speech act at all but a set of inferences.

I asserted that the syuzhet composes story situations and events according to specifiable principles. Chapter 3 showed that when we perceive and comprehend a narrative text, we tend to construct certain patterns among events. We can now see how the film's syuzhet provides a basis for this activity. Three sorts of principles relate the syuzhet to the fabula.

1. *Narrative "logic."* In constructing a fabula, the perceiver defines some phenomena as events while constructing relations among them. These relations are primarily causal ones. An event will be assumed to be a consequence of another event, of a character trait, or of some general law. The syuzhet can facilitate this process by systematically encouraging us to make linear causal inferences. But the syuzhet can also arrange events so as to block or complicate the construction of causal relations. This happens with the false clues in *Rear Window*. Narrative logic also includes a more abstract principle of similarity and difference which I call *parallelism*. Thorwald's murder of his wife has no sig-

nificant effect on most of his neighbors; one function of the courtyard vignettes is to parallel the romantic relations of Jeff and Lisa with other male/female relations. What counts as an event, a cause, an effect, a similarity, or a difference—all will be determined within the context of the individual film.

2. *Time.* Narrative time has several aspects, well analyzed by Gérard Genette. The syuzhet can cue us to construct fabula events in any sequence (a matter of *order*). The syuzhet can suggest fabula events as occurring in virtually any time span (*duration*). And the syuzhet can signal fabula events as taking place any number of times (*frequency*). These aspects can all assist or block the viewer's construction of fabula time. Again, temporal representation will vary with historical convention and the context of the individual film.

3. *Space.* Fabula events must be represented as occurring in a spatial frame of reference, however vague or abstract. The syuzhet can facilitate construction of fabula space by informing us of the relevant surroundings and the positions and paths assumed by the story's agents. The confinement to Jeff's courtyard in *Rear Window* is an instance of the use of syuzhet devices to advance our construction of fabula space. But the film could also impede our comprehension by suspending, muddling, or undercutting our construction of space.

Depending on how the syuzhet presents the fabula, there will be particular spectatorial effects. Armed with the notion of different narrative principles and the concept of the syuzhet's distortion of fabula information, we can begin to account for the concrete narrational work of any film. It is obvious, for instance, that *Rear Window* depends upon withholding certain fabula information; we can now see that our schematizing and hypothesizing activities are guided by the syuzhet's cues about causality, time, and space. The basic-training aspect of the film's early portions—its tendency to give visual cues, let us draw inferences, and then confirm or disconfirm them by verbal statement—arises from manipulation of causal information. To take a specific scene: while Jeff is asleep, we see a woman leave with Thorwald and wonder if she is his wife; the syuzhet has generated this suspicion that Mrs. Thorwald is still alive by not showing us this woman (who is not Mrs. Thorwald) entering the apartment. The syuzhet of *Rear Window* also blocks our knowledge by limiting space; we can use only narrowly restricted views of the courtyard to construct the fabula. And *Rear Window* is not exceptional in its limitations, concealments, and revelations. For theoretical purposes it may sometimes be convenient to take as an ideal baseline an instance in which the syuzhet is constructed so as to permit maximum access to the fabula. But every syuzhet uses retardation to postpone complete construction of the fabula. At the very least, the end of the story, or the means whereby we arrive there, will be withheld. Thus the syuzhet aims not to let us construct the fabula in some logically pristine state but rather to guide us to construct the fabula in a specific way, by arousing in us particular expectations at this or that point, eliciting our curiosity or suspense, and pulling surprises along the way.

In some cases, the syuzhet will include masses of material that block our construction of the fabula. Such material may encourage us to treat the syuzhet as interpreting or commenting on the fabula. In *October,* both Kerensky and General Kornilov appeal to the slogan "For God and Country." Suddenly we cut to a series of statues of gods from many cultures. These shots do not help us to construct the spatial, temporal, or logical connections among story events; in fabula terms they are a digression. Nonetheless, the sequence constitutes syuzhet manipulation. As a little dissertation on the very idea of God, the passage emphasizes the cultural variability of religion and suggests that an appeal to the holy often veils political opportunism. The inserted material insists in its patterned development that we motivate it transtextually, as a species of rhetorical argument. A novelist's commentary, however digressive, forms an integral part of the syuzhet, and so do Eisenstein's essayistic interpolations.

The syuzhet, then, is the dramaturgy of the fiction film, the organized set of cues prompting us to infer and assemble story information. As the diagram on p. 50 suggests, the film's style can interact with the syuzhet in various ways. Film technique is customarily used to perform syuzhet tasks—providing information, cueing hypotheses, and so forth. In the "normal" film, that is, the syuzhet system controls the stylistic system—in Formalist terms, the syuzhet is the "dominant." For example, patterns in the syuzhet's presentation of story information will be matched by stylistic patterns, as when at the close of *Rear Window* a camera movement homologous to that in the opening underlines the changes in the lives of the courtyard's inhabitants.

Still, this is not to say that the systematic employment of film techniques—that is, the film's style—is wholly a vehicle for the syuzhet. When alternative techniques exist for a given syuzhet purpose, it may make a difference which technique is chosen. For instance, the syuzhet may require that two story events be cued as occurring simultaneously. The simultaneity may be denoted by crosscutting from one event to the other, by staging the two actions in depth, by use of split-screen techniques, or by the inclusion of particular objects in the setting (such as a television set broadcasting a "live" event). Whatever stylistic choice is made may have different effects on the spectator's perceptual and cognitive activity. Style is thus a notable factor in its own right, even when it is "only" supporting the syuzhet.

Film style can also take shapes not justified by the syuzhet's manipulation of story information. If in *Rear Window* Hitchcock systematically cut from Jeff's gaze to closeups of misleading or irrelevant objects which he could not see, then the stylistic procedure itself could vie for prominence with the syuzhet's task of presenting the story. True, we might take this stylistic flourish as a syuzhet maneuver to baffle us about causality or space; but if the device were repeated systematically across the film with no clear link to the developing syuzhet and fabula, then the more economical explanation would be that style has come forward to claim our attention independent of syuzhet/fabula relations. Chapter 12 will show how this happens in a variety of films. For analytical purposes, then, we must grant a potential disparity between the stylistic system and the syuzhet system, even if such a tendency is rare.

It is evident that both syuzhet and style invite the spectator to apply the motivational rationales discussed in Chapter 3. At the syuzhet level, when Jeff and Stella recoil from Thorwald's look, the audience justifies this event as psychologically plausible and compositionally necessary for what follows. At the stylistic level, when Jeff scans the apartment block and the next shot is of Thorwald's windows, we assume the shot to be compositionally relevant, grant it a certain realism (Jeff's point of view), and acquiesce to a generic convention (this could be a suspenseful buildup). In the hypothetical example of patterned cutaways to irrelevant objects, we would try to motivate them compositionally, realistically, or transtextually; but if all were unequal to the task set by the style, we would have a case of "artistic motivation," whereby the materials and forms of the medium constitute the chief object of interest.

It is time for a formal definition. In the fiction film, narration is *the process whereby the film's syuzhet and style interact in the course of cueing and channeling the spectator's construction of the fabula.* Thus it is not only when the syuzhet arranges fabula information that the film narrates. Narration also includes stylistic processes. It would of course be possible to treat narration solely as a matter of syuzhet/fabula relations, but this would leave out the ways in which the filmic texture affects the spectator's activity. We have already seen that the spectator possesses stylistic schemata as well as others, and these invariably affect the overall process of narrative representation. Moreover, by including style within narration, we can analyze stylistic departures from the syuzhet's project. In an earlier example, a cut from Jeff's gaze to irrelevant objects would be a narrational act as much as would a cut to relevant ones. Narration is the dynamic interaction between the syuzhet's transmission of story information and what Tynianov called "the movement, the rise and fall of the stylistic masses."[12]

Is there anything in a narrative film that is not narrational? Any image or sound can contribute to narration, but we can also attend to an element for its sheer perceptual salience. Roland Barthes has spoken of a film's "third meaning," one lying beyond denotation and connotation: the realm in which casual lines, colors, expressions, and textures become "fellow travelers" of the story.[13] Kristin Thompson has identified these elements as "excess," materials which may stand out perceptually but which do not fit either narrative or stylistic patterns.[14] (See fig. 4.1.) As we have seen, the spectator's categories push her or him to construct objects and denotative meaning from the outset. The canonic story in particular favors the dominance of story-world factors. From this standpoint, it is as if nothing but narration matters. But in the first shot of *Rear Window*, we can choose not to construct a story world and instead savor random colors, gestures, and sounds. These "excessive" elements are utterly unjustified, even by aesthetic motivation. Now, this attitude is actually quite difficult to maintain over a long period, since it offers little perceptual and cognitive payoff. The *trouvailles* will never add up. Nonetheless, there may be aspects of a film that we cannot attribute to narration. In some cases, as Thompson shows with *Ivan the Terrible*, "excess" may offer a useful way into the film's overall formal work. "A perception of a film that includes its excess implies an awareness of the structures (including conventions) at work in the film, since excess is precisely those elements that escape unifying impulses. Such an approach to viewing films can allow us to look further into a film, renewing its ability to intrigue us by its strangeness."[15]

Whatever its suggestiveness as a critical concept, excess lies outside my concern here. The rest of this book is devoted to the process of narration. In the rest of this chapter and in all of the next, I will concentrate on basic principles of syuzhet patterning. We need to examine how a syuzhet may organize story material, how it may limit or expand our access to fabula information. We also need to understand overall narrational strategies, the broad aims that syuzhet tactics and film style may fulfill. Subsequent chapters will concentrate on how narration may render fabula time and space, and there we will take up specific stylistic procedures.

Tactics of Syuzhet Construction

The analysis of narration can begin with the syuzhet's tactics for presenting fabula information. We must grasp how the syuzhet manages its basic task—the presentation of story logic, time, and space—always recalling that in practice we never get ideally maximum access to the fabula. In general, the syuzhet shapes our perception of the fabula by controlling (1) the quantity of fabula information to which we have access; (2) the degree of pertinence we can attribute to the presented information; and (3) the formal correspondences between syuzhet presentation and fabula data.

Assume that an ideal syuzhet supplies information in the "correct" amount to permit coherent and steady construction of the fabula. Given this hypostatized reference point, we can distinguish a syuzhet which supplies too little information about the story and a syuzhet which supplies too much: in other words, a "rarefied" syuzhet versus an "overloaded" one.

Now at any given point an ordinary narrative may give us more or less information than the hypostatized ideal. A detective tale might bamboozle us with a plethora of clues and a paucity of motives. Our normal syuzhet, then, reduces to a demand for enough information for the construction of a fabula according to conventions of genre or mode. *Rear Window* holds back some data and sometimes gives us "too much" to assimilate at the moment, but eventually the quantity proves "just right" for generic needs. The momentarily overloaded or rarified approach of the mystery film is in fact normal for syuzhet construction in its genre. But our detective story would leap out of its genre if it were radically to pursue either strategy in its recounting of the detective's investigation or in its construction of the solution. For example, Antonioni's *Blow-Up* fails as a detective story: it presents too few pieces of information to enable the protagonist, or us, to solve the crime (or even to determine what the crime involves). Two conclusions follow. At local points, "ordinary" films can indulge in either overload or rarefaction tactics; and extraordinary films can indulge in either, or both, consistently and throughout.

Again, assume an ideal syuzhet which supplies information which is relevant to the coherent and steady construction of the fabula. Opposed to this, we can situate any syuzhet which indulges in information not relevant to such construction. Godard's films, for instance, are often peppered with citations, skewed allusions, and interruptions which cannot be clearly related to the story. We tend to take these as digressions. It is of course often difficult to judge the pertinence of a piece of information at the moment it emerges. Something which seems out of place may eventually slot itself neatly into the total fabula. (Here we touch on the problem of gaps, to be taken up shortly.) In any case, in judging the pertinence of information as in judging its quantity, the analyst will need to specify generic and other transtextual constraints. The criteria of relevance in a drama will not be appropriate to a farce. And some films, such as *L'année dernière á Marienbad* or *Not Reconciled,* make it hard to determine a main fabula path from which we could measure deviations—exactly a point which characterizes these films' formal operations.

The most analytically important variable is the set of formal correspondences between fabula and syuzhet. That is, to what extent does the unfolding syuzhet correspond to the logical, temporal, and spatial nature of the fabula we construct? Are there disparities, incompatibilities, lacks of synchronization? Any syuzhet selects what fabula events to present and combines them in particular ways. Selection creates gaps; combination creates composition.

No syuzhet explicitly presents all of the fabula events that we presume took place. A princess is born; in the next scene she is eighteen years old. In leaving a gap in the syuzhet, the narration implies that nothing extraordinary took place in those intervening years. We will assume that the princess had an infancy, a childhood, and an adolescence. (Knowing the conventions of fairy tales, we might also expect that she will soon meet a prince.) Temporal gaps are the most common sort, but any mystery or riddle narrative may also contain causal gaps. (Why is Mrs. Thorwald missing?) The syuzhet can present us with spatial gaps too, as when it withholds knowledge about a character's whereabouts or neglects to define the action's locales. Gaps are among the clearest cues for the viewer to act upon, since they evoke the entire process of schema formation and hypothesis testing.

Sternberg points out that gaps can be *temporary* or *permanent*.[16] That is, the informational hole in the fabula can be plugged (quickly or eventually) or never plugged. In our fairy tale, the gap is fleeting: we leave the princess's cradle and then see her as a young woman; we very rapidly fill in the gap. In a detective story, the crucial causal gap— e.g., what became of Mrs. Thorwald—is maintained much longer, but it too is eventually plugged. In some narratives, however, a gap remains open to the end; Iago's motive is the classic example. We can characterize syuzhet processes as working to open, prolong, or close gaps in fabula events.

We can also describe a gap as relatively *diffuse* or *focused*. How the princess passed those eighteen years is unspecified; we can fill the gap only with general and typical assumptions. But "Did Thorwald kill his wife?" is a clear-cut question demanding a precise answer. Sometimes a syuzhet will conjure up a diffuse gap only to bring it into focus later. For instance, a flashback might jump back to an otherwise unremarked interval and sharpen our sense of what information might fill the gap.

The syuzhet can also *flaunt* or *suppress* gaps in the fabula. A gap is flaunted when we know that there is something we need to know. Our fairy tale calls the temporal gap to our attention, demanding that we fill the eighteen years of the princess's life with the help of our conventional assumptions. A detective story also typically calls attention to its gaps, making us fret over our lack of certain data. Other syuzhets do not call attention to their gaps. That *Rear Window* does not show Thorwald's mistress enter his apartment is a striking case of a suppressed gap. At the time we see her leave, we do not know that her entry has been omitted.

It should be evident that selections of fabula events shape the constructive activities of the spectator. Temporary gaps point us forward and build up surprise; a permanent gap invites us to apply a "scanning" strategy, sorting back through single episodes looking for information we might have missed. A focused gap obviously tends to solicit exclu-

sive and homogeneous hypotheses, while a diffuse gap yields room for more open-ended inferential work. A flaunted gap may warn us to pay attention: either the omitted fabula information will become important later , or the narration is misleading us by stressing something that will prove insignificant. If a gap is suppressed, however, surprise is the likely result, especially if the omitted information ranks low on a scale of probabilities. These are only general indications, but they suggest the range of effects that "gapping" tactics can achieve. In each case, it must be remembered, the viewer will strive to justify the very presence of the gap by appeal to principles of compositional, realistic, transtextual, and artistic motivation.

Gaps are created by choosing to present certain pieces of fabula information and to hold back others. The pieces of information selected can be combined in a great variety of ways. In cinema, the narration can arrange fabula information temporally or spatially, as we shall see in Chapters 6 and 7. For now we can look at two general principles that govern syuzhet composition in any medium: retardation and redundancy. Both offer clear-cut instances of how textual form both triggers and constrains spectator activity.

We have already noted the overall importance of retardation in cueing the spectator's comprehension. Only by delaying the revelation of some information can the syuzhet arouse anticipation, curiosity, suspense, and surprise. For example, *Rear Window* lays out its fabula information so that (a) the crucial murder evidence emerges piecemeal and the case is not solved too quickly, and (b) the murder investigation suspends and (possibly) resolves Jeff and Lisa's romantic problems. The "God and Country" sequence of *October* breaks off from presenting the fabula and interpolates material that not only retards the outcome of the story action (how will the battle between Kornilov and Kerensky turn out?) but also has its own miniature retardatory curve: the point could have been made by an intertitle rather than dozens of shots which form, to say the least, a fairly difficult passage.

The very centrality of retardation as a principle demands that we make some distinctions. Meir Sternberg has shown that retardatory material can be considered from many angles: the nature of the material (action, description, commentary, etc.), the magnitude of it, its location (how annoying is it here?), its relation to what it retards, how it is motivated, how it functions, its relation to transtextual norms, and its relation to basic properties of the medium.[17] We could then characterize *Rear Window's* red herrings—the false leads of Thorwald's trunk and the zinnia garden—as retardatory material which is action centered, large-scale (each false lead takes several scenes to work out), positioned to maximize suspense, motivated compositionally and generically, and, because manifested in props and setting, conforming to a conception of the film medium as one suitable for revealing dramatic situations through significant objects (Hitchcock's well-known adherence to Pudovkin's dictum about "plastic material"). The "God and Country" sequence, on the other hand, represents commentary and not fabula action; though it is of relatively short duration, its nondiegetic motivation subscribes to different conventions of genre and mode (the Soviet montage film); it is more annoying in its placement and even more so in its cryptic working out; and its rebus-like syntax links it to a quite different conception of film (Eisenstein's "intellectual cinema"). In any given case, we can apply these distinctions to characterize how the syuzhet impedes the viewer's acquisition of fabula information.

Retardation may occur when the syuzhet postpones revealing certain items of fabula information. Because this postponement stands out most sharply in expositional passages, Sternberg has studied them most closely, and his efforts show how overall patterns of retardation have perceptual and cognitive consequences.

Exposition is measured with respect to what theorists of drama call the "point of attack," that juncture in the fabula that forms the initial "discriminated occasion" in the syuzhet. But the receiver of the narrative must be informed of the fabula events previous to this initial scene. The transmission of this information is the task of the exposition, and several choices present themselves. At some point in the syuzhet we might be given the prior fabula information in a lump, a practice Sternberg calls *concentrated* exposition. Or the narration might scatter the information through the syuzhet, interweaving it with ongoing present action. This is *distributed* exposition. *Rear Window* utilizes concentrated exposition in its first two scenes. We are provided, visually in the first sequence and both visually and sonically in the second, with the pertinent background to Jeff's situation. The exposition can also be put at any syuzhet point: in the beginning (*preliminary* exposition, as in *Rear Window*) or later (*delayed* exposition). We have then three general expositional possibilities. The classic fairy tale employs preliminary and concentrated exposition: "Once upon a time" usually signals it. Popular fiction and film typically weave all the exposition into the first scene or two, thus employing preliminary and fairly concentrated exposition. The crime plot in the detective tale is usually revealed through delayed and concentrated exposition, a long scene near the end of the syuzhet recounting the events leading up to the crime. And Ibsen's practice of "continuous exposition" constitutes an adherence to both delayed and distributed principles: prior fabula events come to light gradually throughout the entire play.

As Sternberg shows, each of these options triggers different inferential activities on the part of the spectator. Concentrated and preliminary exposition supplies a strong primacy effect, solid grounds for confident hypothesis formation. Distributed and delayed exposition encourages curiosity about prior events and can lead to a suspension of strong or absolute hypotheses. There is also that exposition peppered with warning signals, which Sternberg calls a "rhetoric of anticipatory caution."[18] In a limit case, our primacy effect might be completely undermined by the suppression of key fabula information; we would then be forced to revise our assumptions and hypotheses when the data come to light. Sternberg calls this "the rise and fall of first impressions."[19]

The syuzhet also repeats. In cinema, an intertitle may describe an action, and then we see that action; or scenes will be presented that allude, visually or sonically, to events already completed. Such repetitions reinforce assumptions, inferences, and hypotheses about story information. Let us call this sort of functional, significant repetition "redundancy."

The possibilities of redundancy in any narration have been exhaustively surveyed by Susan R. Suleiman; I abbreviate and modify her categories.

1. At the level of the fabula, any given event, character, quality, story function, environment, or character commentary may be redundant with respect to any other. For example, A may declare B to be a rake; that statement can be redundant in view of B's overt behavior (he tries to seduce women), or his story function (he is put there to seduce the heroine), or his name, or his surroundings, or other characters' judgments, or all of these.

2. At the level of the syuzhet, the narration can achieve redundancy by reiterating its relation to the perceiver; by repeating its own commentary about an event or character; or by adhering to a consistent point of view. In *October*, the mock-heroic comparison of Kerensky to historic figures achieves redundancy by all these means: reiteration of direct address; constant comparison between him and the statuary, architecture, and bric-a-brac of the Winter Palace; and adherence to a satiric omniscience throughout.

3. At the level of the relations between syuzhet and fabula, redundancy can be achieved by representing an event more than once (as Todorov puts it, "Each event is narrated at least twice"[20]), or by making any fabula event, character, quality, story function, environment, or character commentary redundant with respect to narrational commentary. At the start of *Rear Window*, the furnishings of Jeff's apartment tell us that he is adventurous; in the second scene, Jeff tells his editor (and us) the same thing.

In most narrative texts, redundancy operates so completely on all these levels that we scarcely notice it—until we encounter a text that is not so redundant, or not redundant in ways that we are used to. Suleiman's scheme lets us spell out exactly how a film can reinforce important information and thus guide our grasp of the syuzhet.

To sum up: In any narrative text in any medium, the syuzhet controls the amount and the degree of pertinence of the information we receive. The syuzhet creates various sorts of gaps in our construction of the fabula; it also combines information according to principles of retardation and redundancy. All of these procedures function to cue and guide the spectator's narrative activity.

Knowledge, Self-Consciousness, and Communicativeness

Choosing what to include in the syuzhet and what to leave tacit, deciding how to retard the syuzhet and where redundancy is needed—such particular syuzhet tactics depend on broad narrational strategies. How can we characterize these strategies? Meir Sternberg has suggested three categories that will prove helpful. Although his terms are ones usually reserved for conscious agents, they can be applied to narrative processes with the same legitimacy with which we call a picture "graceful." I should add that these characteristics are properly narrational in that they not only shape syuzhet processes but often involve stylistic options too.

A film's narration can be called more or less *knowledgeable* about the fabula it represents. Every film will employ norms of relevant knowledge for our construction of the fabula. In a mystery film, circumstantial information divulged about past events can have more structural centrality than information about a character's current state of mind. In a musical or melodrama, however, information about immediate states of mind might take priority. We know these norms through acquaintance with genre conventions and through qualitative and quantitative factors in the given film (placement of information in a highlighting context, repetition of information across the film). But knowledgeability has other aspects as well.

First, what *range* of knowledge does the narration have at its disposal? The narration can be more or less *restricted*. *Rear Window*, for instance, confines itself almost wholly to what Jeff knows (with a few significant exceptions). In *The Birth of a Nation*, on the other hand, the narration presents more information about the overall story action than any character has.

Unlike prose fiction, the fictional film seldom confines its narration to what only a single character knows. Most commonly, portions of the syuzhet will be organized around one character's knowledge and other portions will confine themselves to the knowledge held by another character. Such restrictions and divisions will inevitably create gaps in the fabula. We tend to motivate restricted narration realistically ("After all, we know as much as she plausibly could") but to motivate more unrestricted narration transtextually ("In films of this sort, you always know more. . ."). Both sorts of narration are, of course, fundamentally motivated by compositional requirements.

We can ask a second question. How profound is the knowledge available to the narration? This is a matter of *depth*, of degrees of subjectivity and objectivity. A narration may present the whole of a character's mental life, either conscious or unconscious; it may confine itself to the character's optical or auditory experience; it may eschew any but behavioral indications of psychological states; it may even minimize those. For example, although the narration of *The Birth of a Nation* is relatively unrestricted in range, it penetrates the characters' minds less deeply than does the narration of, say, *Secrets of a Soul*, which represents the protagonist's dreams. *The Maltese Falcon*, which contains one shot cued as being through Spade's eyes, is less subjective than *Rear Window*, with its many optical point-of-view shots. Again, depth of knowledge can be justified on compositional, realistic, and/or transtextual grounds.

Range and depth of information can be related in various ways. Restricted narration does not guarantee greater depth, nor does depth at any point guarantee that the narration will stay constantly limited. Hitchcock's films alternate between sequences of great subjectivity and sequences that flaunt the narration's unrestricted knowledge. In general, narrative films are constantly modulating the range and depth of the narration's knowledge. Such shifts provide strong cues for hypothesis formation.

Narration also relates "rhetorically" to the perceiver, and this opens up other areas of inquiry. To what extent does the narration display a recognition that it is addressing an audience? We can call this the degree of *self-consciousness*. For example, Eisenstein's films often intensify an emotional climax by having characters look at or gesture to the audience. Similarly, a retrospective voice-over commentary can push the narration toward a greater self-consciousness, especially if the addressee is not another fictional character. We can see many tactics of redundancy, such as repetition of fabula information by the syuzhet, as evidencing a degree of self-consciousness (e.g., Eisenstein's repeated intercutting of Kerensky with statues). At the beginning of *Rear Window*, the camera movement presents aspects of courtyard life for purposes of quick exposition. In contrast, the artificial but relatively inoffensive frontality of figure position we observed in figure 1.1 earlier is less self-conscious than these cases. When we speak of being "aware of manipulation" in a Lang film and "unaware" of such manipulation in a Hawks film, we are usually referring to the narration's greater or lesser acknowledgment that a tale is being presented for a perceiver.

The concept of self-consciousness offers distinct advantages over "enunciative" accounts of speaker-listener relations, such as the applications of Benveniste's grammatical theory. For one thing, self-consciousness is a matter of degree, not of absolutes (as, say, "first person" and "third person" are). All filmic narrations are self-conscious, but some are more so than others. Furthermore, "self-consciousness" varies in degree and function within different genres and modes of film practice. Groucho Marx's asides to the audience are more self-conscious than Popeye's muttered imprecations, but the patriotic voice-over of Capra's *Why We Fight* is more self-conscious than either. The staging of most Hollywood shots reveals a moderate self-consciousness by grouping characters for our best view (see figs. 1.1–1.3). In a musical, characters may sing directly to us—a moment of stronger narrational self-consciousness codified by the genre. By contrast, Antonioni will stage scenes with characters turned away from us, and the overt suppression of their expressions and reactions becomes in context a token of the narration's awareness of the viewer. In the celebrated filling station sequence of *Deux ou trois choses que je sais d'elle*,

Godard's voice-over commentator is so acutely aware of the audience that he is at a loss to decide what to show us next. As a critical category, self-consciousness helps us consider to what extent and with what effects the film lets a recognition of the audience's presence shape the syuzhet.

At one point in Hitchcock's *Shadow of a Doubt* (1943), the sinister Uncle Charlie settles down to read the evening paper. Earlier in the film our knowledge has occasionally been restricted to his knowledge (as in the first scene, when he learned that two men were shadowing him). There has even been some depth of subjectivity, with certain shots being framed from his optical point of view. Now, while he reads, he is filmed from a low angle, the outspread newspaper blocking his face. There is silence. A puff of cigar smoke. Slowly the paper is lowered, and Charlie is now frowning thoughtfully. He looks off right. Cut to his optical point of view of the opposite end of the room: no one notices him. Cut back to Uncle Charlie, who calls his niece Ann to him. He proceeds to make a toy house out of newspaper and, in tearing out a portion, folds it up and slips it into his pocket.

This short passage shows how a narration shifts its depth of knowledge (objective to more subjective) and how it can gain a degree of self-consciousness (the pause in telling us Uncle Charlie's reaction). The scene also illustrates another aspect of narration—what Sternberg calls its *communicativeness*. Although a narration has a particular range of knowledge available, the narration may or may not communicate all that information. In literature, for example, a diarist-narrator will have a very restricted ken, but she or he can be completely communicative about what she or he knows. In *Shadow of a Doubt,* the narration has established itself as restrictive (frequently limited to Charlie's knowledge) and potentially subjective (e.g., previous optical point-of-view shots). Now, however, the low-angle shot of Charlie reading does not reveal the newspaper article that he sees. It is not just that the narration flaunts this curiosity gap, though it certainly does. The narration holds back exactly the sort of information to which it has earlier claimed complete access. The suppressiveness of the newspaper shot is emphasized all the more when, after Charlie lowers the paper, the narration immediately switches to his optical point of view. If we had been permitted to share his vision an instant sooner, we would have seen the offending article. As it is, the film will make us wait some time to find out.

The degree of communicativeness can be judged by considering how willingly the narration shares the information to which its degree of knowledge entitles it. The unrestricted narration of *The Birth of a Nation* is highly communicative; the only information withheld is of a "suspense" variety (i.e., what will happen next). The sharply restricted narration of *Rear Window* is likewise generally communicative in that (on the whole) it tells us all that Jeff knows at any given moment. If *The Birth of a Nation* were suddenly to conceal the fact that the Little Colonel founds the Ku Klux Klan, or if *Rear Window* were to withhold some crucial action of Jeff's, the narration would tend toward a lesser degree of communicativeness. That a highly "omniscient" narration and a highly restricted narration may both be considered communicative shows the importance of context.

As with self-consciousness, every film is uncommunicative to at least a slight degree; there may be a fluctuating relation between the film's overall informational norm and the extent of concealment at various moments. In one sense, any deviation from a film's internal norm of communicativeness becomes a mark of suppressiveness. The narration could tell more, but it doesn't. Transtextual motivation, however, can make the suppression less overt. When Jeff is asleep, we see Thorwald leave his aparment with the woman in black. This violates the narration's restriction to Jeff's knowledge, and it might be seen as unmasking what the film suppresses all along (that is, what Thorwald is up to). But now generic norms take over. It is a convention of mystery and detective tales that the narration can inject hints, clues, and false leads which the detective does not recognize at the moment, as long as the detective eventually learns or infers the information and as long as the solution to the mystery is not given away prematurely. In *Rear Window,* both conditions are satisfied. To put it more technically, the detective tale tones down its occasional suppressive operations by realistic motivation (restricting the bulk of the narration to what the detective could plausibly know) and by generic convention. A different norm of communicativeness can be found in the melodrama, where more omniscient narration tends to emphasize communicativeness so as to play up ironic and pathetic twists of which the characters are unaware. In general, we must distinguish between generically codified shifts in the range or depth of knowledge and more or less overt indications of suppressiveness.

The best critical solution to the problem of communicativeness is to weigh transtextual norms against intrinsic structural demands. Withholding key pieces of information is a convention of the mystery film, so to some extent *Shadow of a Doubt* obeys generic rules in the scene we have considered. But the flagrancy with which the narration indicates its suppressiveness must be seen as playing a role within the film's overall form. The film begins by being restricted to Uncle Charlie's knowledge but soon starts to undermine that when he escapes from the police by means not shown to us. In the course of the film Little Charlie gradually replaces Uncle Charlie as the principal agent of knowledge; it is she who solves the mystery surrounding her uncle. The scene we have considered is pivotal here, marking another stage in the "weaning away" of the audience from Uncle Charlie's range of knowledge. Thereafter, the film will modulate quite carefully from restricted to unrestricted states, and from overt communicativeness to momentary but overt suppressiveness and back again. At certain moments our knowledge is greater than that of the characters, and the narration may call attention to the fact; at other moments (e.g., the newspaper scene), we know less than the character, and the narration points that out too. The final effect of these manipulations is double: to make the spectator play with simultaneous hypotheses about Uncle Charlie's past and motives; and to create in the viewer the shadow of a doubt about the narration's own trustworthiness. In at least some cases, then, overt marks of communicativeness or suppressiveness can also convey a degree of self-consciousness.

The categories of knowledgeability, self-consciousness, and communicativeness can be used to clarify two common but imprecise critical concepts. In cinema, the concept of "point of view" has usually been loosely employed, especially within the mimetic tradition. When critics speak of a character's point of view, they are usually referring to the range and/or depth of knowledge which the narration supplies. With respect to range, *Rear Window* comes close to Jeff's "point of view." With respect to depth, a film like *La guerre est finie,* which plunges us into the protagonist's inner life, may be considered to give us Diego's subjective "point of view." More broadly, when critics discuss narrational "point of view" (or the narrator's point of view), they are usually referring to any or all of the properties I have picked out— knowledgeability, self-consciousness, and communicativeness. Speaking of Hitchcock's "point of view" as intruding on a scene usually implies a great range of knowledge, a high degree of self-consciousness, and perhaps some overt manipulations of communicativeness. To avoid blurring these distinctions, I will use the term "point of view" only to refer to the optical or auditory vantage point of a character; thus "point-of-view shot" is synonymous with "optically subjective shot."

Similarly, these concepts can specify the term "unreliability" a little more. If "reliable" means "forthcoming," the more communicative the narration, the more reliable it is. In the *Shadow of a Doubt* scene, the suppression of Charlie's view of the newspaper article causes us to mistrust the narration to some degree; henceforth we must be on our guard for what it might withhold. "Reliability" can also imply objective accuracy, in which case the range and depth of knowledge can become factors. A narration which confined itself to a character's mental states might be highly communicative but it would not necessarily inspire confidence in its veracity. The framed story of *The Cabinet of Dr. Caligari* is a case in point. We also spot "unreliable" narration as it is occurring or recognize it only after the fact. In *Rashomon,* the flashbacks are motivated as representations of various character's court testimony; since we are warned at the outset (through an "anticipatory caution" in the exposition) that the accounts are incompatible, we view each flashback as at best an overall hypothesis and at worst a fabrication. The characters must take the responsibility for the "unreliability" of their narration. But in *Stage Fright,* probably the canonic case of unreliable narration in classical cinema, we are given a flashback putatively both trustworthy and accurate but which turns out to have been the visual and auditory representation of a lie. It is not just the character's yarn that is unreliable. The film's narration shows itself to be duplicitous by neglecting to suggest any inadequacies in Johnnie's account and by appearing to be highly communicative—not just reporting what the liar said but showing it as if it were indeed objectively true.

As categories of information transmission, knowledgeability, self-consciousness, and communicativeness all bear on how film style and syuzhet construction manipulate time, space, and narrative logic to enable the spectator to construct a particular unfolding fabula. I should add, however, that other, less central narrational factors may be present. These are *judgmental* factors, often called "tone" by literary critics. When we say that a film takes pity on its characters or has contempt for its audience, we are talking, however loosely, about ways in which a film's narration can strike an attitude with respect either to the fabula or to the perceiver. The "God and Country" sequence of *October* would exemplify a strikingly judgmental syuzhet passage. We cannot list such attitudes exhaustively, and many acts of narration probably do not possess them, but for our survey to be complete we should mention some clear cases.

We are most familiar with narrational judgment as a function of particular stylistic devices. In a silent film, an expository intertitle may make no bones about the narration's attitude. A title in *The Birth of a Nation* identifies an old man as "the kindly master of Cameron Hall."Music can indicate narrational attitude in a similarly direct way: sympathetic (the "Diane" tune in *Seventh Heaven*), ironic ("We'll Meet Again" at the close of *Dr. Strangelove*), or comic (Irish folk tunes in *The Quiet Man*). It is a cliché of some films that a distant high angle at the end connotes a compassionate, detached attitude. Within given styles and conventions, many devices can imply judgments on the story action.

It is generally more fruitful, though, to look for attitudes as emergent qualities of the systems at work within entire films. For instance, the narrational attitude toward Uncle Charlie in *Shadow of a Doubt* is less a matter of camera angle or figure placement at any one moment than a function of an overall narrational strategy that presents certain aspects of his conduct as both fascinating and inexplicable. In *The Birth of a Nation*, the narration's attitude toward the Cameron household is governed by its role in the film's total narrative economy: the family is the causal, spatial, and temporal center of the film. Similarly, any narration's "attitude" toward the perceiver usually emerges from the general properties of narration. A highly suppressive narration, as in Lang or Hitchcock, might be considered to look down on the audience. A more communicative narration, such as is found in Ford or Capra, makes more straightforward and "sincere" appeals. While our critical vocabulary for narrational judgment remains weak, we can usually ground our intuitions in the formal properties of narration I have indicated.

Narrator, Author

Throughout my discussion, one particular question may have nagged the reader. I have not referred to the narrator of a film. In what senses can we speak of a narrator as the source of narration?

If a character is presented as recounting story actions in some fashion (telling, recollecting, etc.), as Marlowe does during most of *Murder My Sweet,* the film possesses a character-narrator. Or a person not part of the story world may be identified as the source of parts of the narration. In *Jules and Jim,* a voice-over commentary points up the diegetic world; in *La ronde,* a *meneur de jeu* appears in flesh and blood to address the audience. Such films contain explicit, noncharacter narrators. But, as Edward Branigan has demonstrated, such personified narrators are invariably swallowed up in the overall narrational process of the film, which they do *not* produce.[21] So the interesting theoretical problem involves an implicit, nonpersonified narrator. Even if no voice or body gets identified as a locus of narration, can we still speak of a narrator as being present in a film? In other words, must we go beyond the process of narration to locate an entity which is its source?

Some theorists believe so. Diegetic theories often identify the narrator as the enunciator, the film's "speaker," but we have already seen that the analogy to speech fails because of the weak correspondences between verbal deixis and the techniques of cinema. Other theorists suggest that the source of narration is akin to Wayne Booth's "implied author." The implied author is the invisible puppeteer, not a speaker or visible presence but the omnipotent artistic figure behind the work.[22] In film, Albert Laffay speaks of *le grand imagier,* the master of images: a fictional and invisible personage who chooses and organizes what we shall perceive.[23] On Laffay's account, at the center of a narrative film stands a ghostly master of ceremonies, invisible twin of the *meneur de jeu* of *La ronde.*

Since any utterance can be construed with respect to a putative source, literary theory may be justified in looking for a speaking voice or narrator.[24] But in watching films, we are seldom aware of being told something by an entity resembling a human being. Even with the dissective attention of criticism, we cannot construct a narrator for Vidor's film *War and Peace* with the exactitude with which we can assign attributes to the narrator of Tolstoy's original novel. As for the implied author, this construct adds nothing to our understanding of filmic narration. No trait we could assign to an implied author of a film could not more simply be ascribed to the narration itself: it sometimes suppresses information, it often restricts our knowledge, it generates curiosity, it creates a tone, and so on. To give every film a narrator or implied author is to indulge in an anthropomorphic fiction.

There is a fairly important theoretical choice involved here. Literary theories of the implied author, such as Seymour Chatman's, take the process of narration to be grounded in the classic communication diagram: a message is passed from sender to receiver.[25] This has committed theorists to seeking out noncharacter narrators and implied authors, not to mention "narratees" and "implied readers." These entitites, especially the latter two, are sometimes very hard to find in a narrative text. I suggest, however, that narration is better understood as the organization of a set of cues for the construction of a story. This presupposes a perceiver, but not any sender, of a message. This scheme allows for the possibility that the *narrational process may sometimes mimic the communication situation more or less fully.* A text's narration may emit cues that suggest a narrator, or a "narratee," or it may not. This explains the range of examples, and the asymmetrical structures, that we often find: some texts do not signal a narrator, or a narratee; others signal one, but not the other. For instance, Robert Bresson's film *Pickpocket* starts with a prologue asserting that the "author" is presenting images and sounds to explain the story. As we shall see in Chapter 12, this is a way of marking stylistic factors as having an overt, dynamic relation to the syuzhet. Most films, however, do not provide anything like such a definable narrator, and there is no reason to expect they will. On the principle that we ought not to proliferate theoretical entities without need, there is no point in positing communication as the fundamental process of all narration, only to grant that most films "efface" or "conceal" this process. Far better, I think, to give the narrational process the power to signal under certain circumstances that the spectator should construct a narrator. When this occurs, we must recall that this narrator is the product of specific organizational principles, historical factors, and viewers' mental sets. Contrary to what the communication model implies, this sort of narrator does not create the narration; the narration, appealing to historical norms of viewing, creates the narrator. In Part 3, we will consider how this might work. For now, I need only signal that we need not build the narrator in on the ground floor of our theory. No purpose is served by assigning every film to a *deus absconditis.*

5. Sin, Murder, and Narration

The concepts and principles laid out in Chapter 4 can address the workings of entire films. This chapter shows how these narrational categories can be applied to three films: *The Big Sleep* (1946), *Murder My Sweet* (1944), and *In This Our Life* (1942). Moreover, my claims will be explanatory rather than simply descriptive. This theory of narration seeks to show *why* a syuzhet is constructed as it is and *how* style works in relation to it. This is one reason I have laid such stress on the dynamics of narrational processes and spectatorial activities.

The Detective Film

Detective films provide clear illustrations of how the syuzhet manipulates fabula information over an entire narrative. In fact, specific sorts of syuzhet tactics are the *differentia specifica* of the genre. Most basically, the viewer construes the fabula's causal chain as consisting of a crime and its investigation, which may be represented schematically in this way:

CRIME

cause of crime
commission of crime
concealment of crime
discovery of crime

INVESTIGATION

beginning of investigation
phases of investigation
eludication of crime
identification of criminal
consequences of identification

The fundamental narrational characteristic of the detective tale is that the syuzhet withholds crucial events occurring in the "crime" portion of the fabula. The syuzhet may conceal the motive, or the planning, or the commission of the crime (an act which includes the identity of the criminal), or aspects of several of these. The syuzhet may commence with the discovery of the crime, or it may start before the crime is committed and find other ways to conceal the crucial events. In either case, the syuzhet is principally structured by the progress of the detective's investigation. Thus the detective film creates gaps which are usually focused and flaunted by being posed as questions, such as "Who killed Arthur Geiger?" (*The Big Sleep*) or "What has become of Moose Malloy's girlfriend Velma?" (*Murder My Sweet*). The viewer creates a set of exclusive hypotheses—a closed set of suspects, a gradually defined range of outcomes. The genre promotes suspense with respect to the twists and turns of the

investigation and plays upon curiosity about the missing causal material.

Since the investigation is the basis of the syuzhet, there is obviously a more or less constant revelation of prior fabula information. The circumstances governing the investigation will typically be explained compactly: General Sternwood hires Marlowe (*The Big Sleep*), or Moose comes to his office (*Murder My Sweet*). But the most pertinent missing causes will emerge only gradually, often near the very end of the syuzhet. In other words, exposition about the investigation itself tends to be concentrated in preliminary portions of the syuzhet, while information about the motive, agent, and circumstances of the crime will be distributed and finally summed up clearly in later portions. Thus no gap will be permanent.

This tidy description is oversimplified, however. For one thing, the exposition tends to temper the primacy effect. This tempering is generically motivated, since the spectator knows that, in a detective film, almost anyone may turn out to be the culprit and that first impressions may therefore be misleading. On a larger scale, the investigation is usually complicated by retardatory material. In the detective tale, the syuzhet typically delays revelation of the criminal by inserting comedy (e.g., byplay with incompetent police), romance (a young couple falls under suspicion, or the detective is prey to romantic inclinations), and the commission of more crimes. This last retardatory device is especially useful since it generates new causal gaps and hypotheses. In *Murder My Sweet*, two lines of action—Moose Malloy's search for Velma, and the theft of Mrs. Grayle's jewels—alternately block one another until Marlow finally realizes that Mrs. Grayle *is* Velma.

The Big Sleep proffers such a mare's nest of retardations that it is not easy to reconstruct the crime fabula's causal chain. In fact, Hawks and some critics have talked as if the fabula could never be reconstructed: "I never could figure the story out. . . . They asked me who killed such and such a man—I didn't know."[1] One virtue of the theory that I suggest is that its categories can explain the viewer's difficulties here. *The Big Sleep* has an abnormally overloaded syuzhet;

many events occur offscreen or before the syuzhet opens, and one major character (Sean Regan) is never seen. There is also a low level of redundancy in the presentation of the fabula: characters and narration seldom repeat causal information about the crime. Perhaps only the analyst can come up with a coherent causal chain, but it certainly can be done.[2] *The Big Sleep* is a detective film in which the interest of constructing the investigation fabula takes precedence over the construction of a coherent crime fabula.

The detective film justifies its gaps and retardations by controlling knowledge, self-consciousness, and communicativeness. The genre aims to create curiosity about past story events (e.g., who killed whom), suspense about upcoming events, and surprise with respect to unexpected disclosures about either story or syuzhet. To promote all three emotional states, the narration must limit the viewer's knowledge. This can be motivated realistically by making us share the restricted knowledge possessed by the investigator; we learn what the detective learns, when she or he learns it. There can be brief marks of an unrestricted narration as well, as we shall see, but these function to enhance curiosity or suspense. By restricting the range of knowledge to that possessed by the detective, the narration can present information in a fairly unselfconscious way; we pick up fabula information by following the detective's inquiry. Again, the narration can signpost information more overtly, but this is occasional and codified. Most significant, of course, is the coded communicativeness of the detective genre. The demands of "fair play" have dictated a particular solution to the problem of how suppressive to be.

Both *The Big Sleep* and *Murder My Sweet* restrict our range of knowledge to that possessed by the detective. In *The Big Sleep*, for instance, when the butler asks Philip Marlowe to stop to see Vivian Sternwood, Marlowe asks: "How did she know I was here?" The butler responds: "She saw you through the window, sir, and I was obliged to tell her who you were." It would have been simple for the film to have shown Vivian looking out her window and observing Marlowe's entrance, but it would have made the narration more overtly knowledgeable. Similarly, in *Murder My Sweet*, Mar-

lowe is exploring a thicket when a sound catches his attention; he flashes his light; cut to his optical point of view on a terrified deer. In both films, we typically enter or leave a locale when Marlowe does; most if not all subjective shots are from his optical vantage point; and he is often placed so that we look over his shoulder at the action. The music often reflects his understanding of the scene: in *Murder My Sweet*, when Marlowe remembers a clue, the music announces it; and Max Steiner's score for *The Big Sleep* signals whether Marlowe judges the scene to be menacing, comic, or romantic. What surprises Marlowe often surprises us. He returns to a nightclub table, and at the moment he discovers that his companion has vanished, the camera reveals it to us (*Murder My Sweet*). Or he comes home to find Carmen in his armchair, disclosed when the camera pans with him tossing his hat onto a chair (*The Big Sleep*). In both films, the final scene confines itself to what Marlowe, inside a parlor with a killer, could perceive; the film never depicts action outside the house unless he sees it. To a great extent, our "identification" with a film's protagonist is created by exactly this systematic restriction of information.

Several stylistic conventions come into play to restrict our knowledge. Point-of-view shots are obvious examples, as is the voice-over commentary in *Murder My Sweet*. At certain moments in *The Big Sleep*, the narration needs to underscore our perception of what Marlowe hears rather than sees, and thus resorts to an image yielding limited information. For instance as he approaches Geiger's house, we cut to a shot of a man's feet sprinting away; the shot is a compromise between restriction to Marlowe and suppression of the killer's identity.

What this last convention reveals, though, is that the film is in fact constituted by an omniscient narration that "voluntarily" restricts itself for specific purposes (e.g., the need to conceal story events) but which can at any instant diverge from its confinement to character knowledge. Often, of course, Marlowe is a little ahead of us, spotting a detail we miss or making a discovery that a new shot then shares with us. But sometimes the film gives us a slight edge over him, and then we glimpse omniscient narration's work. In both films, Marlowe's head will turn for a moment and we will spy a gesture or expression he cannot see. In *The Big Sleep*, we see Joe Brody draw his gun before Marlowe does. Similar situations crop up in *Murder My Sweet*: we see Helen enter Marlowe's apartment before he glimpses her in the mirror, or we notice Moose strolling behind Marlowe's table before he does. True, our extra knowledge often turns out to be a fleeting satisfaction; in these instances, the detective gets the message very soon after we do. The point remains, though, that an omniscient narration can frame the detective's field of knowledge within a slightly wider compass for purposes of suspense, curiosity, or surprise.

Omniscience, in these films, is thus still paradoxically "limited"; it is that of the ideal-but-not-impossible observer praised in mainstream mimetic theory. This discreet omniscience often emerges in a rhetorical flourish. For instance, Canino fires into the car where he believes Marlowe to be hiding. The framing gives us the "point of view" of the car's nonexistent occupant before Marlowe shoots Canino, an action filmed from another angle. Such camera positions, while motivated by Marlowe's knowledge, could proceed only from an omniscient, or at least "omnipresent," narration.

We can watch this omniscience at work elsewhere. Credit sequences are very important narrational gestures. These extrafictional passages usually present information in highly self-conscious and omniscient fashion. Transitions between scenes also tend to play up knowledge which the detective doesn't yet have. The camera can begin on a sign and then crane down to the detective arriving beneath it (*Murder My Sweet*). Such expository shots—establishing shots of locales, signs, or other indices of location— can be attributed only to the omniscient narration, relatively self-conscious in its mounting of these images for our benefit. Usually, however, the film does not reinsert these images when later scenes return to the locale; the classical narrative cinema assumes that we will recall these earlier expository shots. For such reasons, we can best study the narration's omniscience when the expositional burden is heaviest: in the very first scene of the film.

The beginning of *The Big Sleep* might seem a paragon of the sober, "invisible" filmmaking for which Howard Hawks is famous, but scrutiny reveals a moderate self-consciousness and omniscience. A medium shot reveals a heavily carved door with the name "Sternwood"; the camera pans left to a hand pressing the doorbell. We are not shown the hand's owner. A dissolve takes us into the foyer as a butler goes to answer the door. But he does not swing the door wide enough for us to see the caller. A voice says: "My name's Marlowe. General Sternwood wanted to see me." The butler ushers Marlowe in; the camera tracks with him as he looks around the foyer and encounters Carmen. The visual ubiquity (from outside to inside, anticipating Marlowe's entrance) sets the knowledge limits of the film as a whole. The first two shots have also posited the narration as initially self-conscious, not only informing us where we are (via the sign) but delaying the revelation of our protagonist and creating a brief buildup of anticipation. Once Marlowe enters, however, the camera subordinates itself to his stride, and the degree of self-consciousness drops as the narration filters salient facts through his conversations with Carmen and the General. Within two shots, the narration glides smoothly into a restricted and comparatively communicative and unselfconscious presentation.

Murder My Sweet opens in a more flamboyant fashion, but the principles are the same. Under the credits we crane down toward a table around which several men are seated. Eventually all we see is a dazzling patch of light on the table's surface. After a dissolve, the camera tracks back from the lamp overhead while unattributed offscreen voices make cracks about Marlowe. Soon the framing reveals policemen around the table interrogating him, his eyes blindfolded. The camera movements, the geometrical arrangement of the men, and the smooth transitions (from light patch to light source) all mark out a narrational process addressed to the audience—opening gaps for the sake of intensifying curiosity and a sombre mood. Moreover, the film immediately sets up a potential disparity between Marlowe's knowledge of the situation and ours, since we can see the room and he can't. (As the last scene will reveal, we haven't seen everything important either, but we will still be one jump ahead of him.) Only after Marlowe begins his tale and the camera tracks to the window as a transition to the flashback does our range of knowledge begin to approximate his. When the transition is over, we slide into as restricted a narrational state as we had enjoyed in *The Big Sleep*.

Both films, then, motivate the withholding of certain story information by restricting the narration to what the investigator learns. This restricted narration is framed and interrupted by an omniscient narration that asserts itself chiefly in expository passages and during moments of localized suspense. The alternation of restriction and omniscience and the variations in self-consciousness that result are characteristic of classical narrative cinema, but the degree of restriction is specific to the mystery genre.

The two films are also similar in their need to respect yet another generic convention, and this leads to an interesting problem of communicativeness. One convention of detective fiction since the 1920s has been the rule of "fair play," in which the reader has as good a chance to discover the solution as the detective does. But this raises a difficulty, which Dorothy Sayers explains in this way: "The reader must be given every clue—but he must not be told, surely, all the detective's deductions, lest he should see the solution too far ahead. . . . How can we at the same time show the reader everything and yet legitimately obfuscate him as to its meaning?"[3] Put in our terms, how is the author to motivate a particular lack of communicativeness in the narration? The solution which Sayers indicates involves a play between various degrees of *depth* in representing the detective. She shows how prose in detective fiction modulates between a "purely external" description; a "middle viewpoint" in which "we see what the detective sees but are not told what he observes"; a "close intimacy" in which we see all the detective sees, and he then states his inferences; and "a complete mental identification with the detective," in which we follow his thoughts without the need of external report.[4] Through an analysis of a page from *Trent's Last Case*, Sayers shows that E. C. Bentley shifts three times among these different registers.

Despite the lack of close analogies between prose and cinema, syuzhet/fabula patterning—Sternberg's "preverbal compositional constructs"—can be homologous across media. Like the novel, the detective film employs the generic convention whereby we are not allowed access to the detective's inferences until he or she voices them (*unless*—Sayers also reminds us—the detective is baffled or turns out to be wrong). The detective film will utilize a restricted narration to justify gaps in our knowledge of the crime fabula, and when the detective is in the dark, we will be too; but the narration will make sure that we do not become privy to the investigator's solution until he or she states it at the proper time.

Hiding the detective's thinking poses no problem in *The Big Sleep*, for here Marlowe is a closed mouth. Until very late in the film, he takes no confidants and trusts no one. The narration is wholly external, yielding no access to any conclusions he has drawn until he speaks his mind. When Marlowe goes into Geiger's bookshop and asks for certain rare editions, the clerk Agnes replies that she hasn't any of them. He does not expose her, but leaves (after a little more banter). Only later will we learn that her answer revealed to him that Geiger's business is a front. This is Sayer's "middle viewpoint" in action. Compare the film with the novel. Even before Agnes gives her reply, Marlowe shares his thoughts with us: "She didn't say:'Huh?' but she wanted to." As soon as she answers, Marlowe draws a conclusion: "She knew about as much about rare books as I knew about handling a flea circus."[5] Here the narration is much more internal, providing the "mental indentification" Sayers mentions. In the film, the narration need never supply direct access to Marlowe's mind, so we must often figure out the clues and also try to figure out what Marlowe makes of them. This process is nicely laid bare by the film itself. After Vivian has tried to pump him, the impassive Marlowe says: "You're trying to find out what your father hired me to find out and I'm trying to find out why you want to find out—" Vivian interrupts: "You could go on forever, couldn't you? Anyway, it'll give us something to talk about next time we meet."

Murder My Sweet offers a more complex case. Unlike *The*

Big Sleep, the film presents the bulk of the syuzhet as a protracted flashback, with Marlowe's voice-over commentary supplying information and linking several scenes. The advantages of this presentation are great, since from the credits on we are curious. (What has led to this situation? Will Marlowe be freed? Why are his eyes bandaged?) But the syuzhet must now motivate the suppressiveness of not one but two narrations: Marlowe's telling and the film's overall narration. Marlowe's telling engenders a tension between knowledge after the fact (who is actually guilty, what it all means) and the ongoing communication in the present. He could, after all name the victims and killer in one sentence. But then the movie would be over. So he must hold back his knowledge of the killer's identity and recount the investigation chronologically. "Let's get it on the record," says Lieutenant Randall. *"From the beginning."* Marlowe consents. The official circumstances of his testimony conveniently justify his linear recounting.

As for the narration's overall rendition of the action, it too must steer the fair-play course between displaying all relevant information and concealing Marlowe's thoughts. This is especially difficult because Marlowe's voice-over commentary quickly loses its quality of being addressed to the cops at the table and comes close to stream of consciousness. At its giddiest moments, in the visual and verbal rendering of Marlowe's drug-induced dream, the narration plunges into extremes of mental process. But *Murder My Sweet* distinguishes carefully among sheer subjectivity (dreams), impaired functioning (the scene in the hospital), groggy but more or less coherent thought (theremin-style music, shots in hand-held point of view), deliberate activity with voice-over accompaniment, and deliberate activity without voice-over commentary (the situation of the whole of *The Big Sleep*). Thus the degree of subjective depth is usually inversely proportional to the extent of Marlowe's reasoning capacity. He is not about to solve the case in the throes of delirium, so the narration can safely present his hallucinations at that point. When he is more conscious, both his commentary and the overall narration must refrain from revealing all his inferences. He confines his voice-over re-

marks to snap judgments and to discrete pieces of information. As in *The Big Sleep*, most of the detective's inferences emerge from conversation, so the ability of the "first-person" commentary to share thoughts with us is hardly ever exploited. By the end of the flashback, Marlowe's voice can announce: "I had to know one more thing. I had to know how the jade figured." But his conclusions emerge from dialogue when he confronts the killer. Despite the voice-over commentary and flashback structure, the film fulfills generic demands by avoiding any subjectivity which would prematurely reveal Marlowe's conclusions.

Here again the omniscience underlying classical narration can be glimpsed in stylistic devices. In the scene in the private hospital, Marlowe wakes from a dream and we see him through superimposed cobwebs. "The window was open," the commentary explains, "but the smoke didn't move. It was a gray web woven by a thousand spiders." Throughout the scene, the cobwebs and the eerie music remain constant. In the course of the scene, a male nurse and Moose Malloy enter the room. Marlowe is initially unaware of their presence, so the framing and cutting here momentarily diverge from Marlowe's knowledge. Yet cobwebs are superimposed over the two men as well (fig. 5.1). The narration here combines our adherence to Marlowe's "deeper" mental state with a divergence from his perceptual awareness. The same sort of compromise appears more briefly whenever Marlowe gets knocked out, as he frequently does. His commentary speaks of a "black pool" opening up before him, but what we see is a swelling spot of darkness superimposed upon his prostrate body. Or, as Marlowe comes to on the road, the camera angle of Ann looking down at him does not replicate his optical point of view, but the image gradually comes into focus, a cue that he is refocusing his attention. Such conventional signals can be the product only of narration not wholly restricting itself to Marlowe's knowledge.

At the end of *Murder My Sweet* the divergence from Marlowe's range of knowledge is the greatest. The climactic scene ends abruptly, with Marlowe diving for a gun that goes off in his face. His passing out leaves the action suspended;

5.1. Murder My Sweet

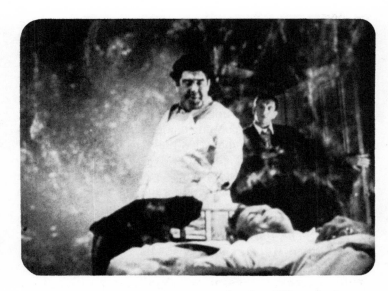

at this moment, our ignorance matches his. When the image fades up, we are back in the present and he is wrapping up his tale. He explains that he didn't see what finally happened because his eyes were scorched; now our initial question about the bandage is answered. But, Marlowe asks, did Ann get hit? The police assure him she did not. They release him; he asks who backed his story up. The camera pans right to reveal Ann, who, we now learn, has been sitting offscreen throughout the interrogation. The film's narration, then, has restricted us to Marlowe's standpoint in a way we didn't realize; Ann's presence is now revealed as a suppressed gap. This is not only retardation at work. The narration's aim was not to give away too much at the outset by ruling out a prime suspect.

This reticence must in turn be motivated within the story world: why doesn't Ann rush in to confirm Marlowe's version? The spectator is asked to motivate the delay realistically by taking Ann to be uncertain of Marlowe's integrity. Throughout the film, she judges him to be wholly mercenary and devoid of compassion. His telling of the story becomes a test of his honesty. As the still-unseeing Marlowe leaves the policemen, he is further tried: they offer him the valuable

jade necklace, which Ann has supposedly left for him. He refuses it. And, led out by a cop, he talks about how much he loved Ann—completely unaware that she is walking a few steps behind. At the film's close, Ann takes the cop's place and climbs into a cab with Marlowe. Only then does he sniff Ann's perfume and realize she has been there all along. In sum, an omniscient narration retrospectively reveals the sharp limits that have been imposed upon our knowledge throughout. Marlowe's recounting is set firmly in a frame that allows us to shift from limited to unlimited knowledge. As in *The Big Sleep*, a conversation lays bare the device. When Marlowe says, "I don't get it," the sinister Jules Amthor sneers, "You mean there are some things you do not understand. I've always credited the private detective with a high degree of omniscience. Or is that true only in rental fiction?"

The activity of piecing together cause and effect in the crime fabula constitutes the central formal convention of the detective tale. We have also seen that the narration displays a mixture of restriction and omniscience, communicativeness and suppressiveness, and varying degrees of self-consciousness. The ending of *Murder My Sweet* illustrates yet another way that this mixture is effected. One sign of the narration's omniscience and suppressiveness is that in the course of the investigation we not only discover more causal information but also learn more about the detective. Just as we do not share the detective's inferences, we often do not receive privileged access to his character and motives. This convention seems specific to the "hard-boiled" tale, wherein questions arise about the detective's degree of unselfishness, honor, integrity, and so on. In both films I am considering here, the detective eventually explains that professionalism functions as his principal motive: he is obligated to his client to see the job through. As the film goes on, romance becomes another factor. He is attracted to women, even if he suspects them of deception, betrayal, or worse. Thus the narration will take as part of its task the planting of hints and equivocations about the strength of the detective's professional and romantic allegiances. In *The Big Sleep*, Marlowe and Vivian exchange sexual banter before he shifts gears:

"Who told you to sugar me off this case?" In *Murder My Sweet*, we are asked to wonder if Marlowe's interest in Mrs. Grayle is feigned for investigative purposes; this is another aspect of his character which the final blindfold test in the police station will reveal to Ann and to us. Restricting us to the detective's range of knowledge while limiting how internalized the narration will be affects our judgments about the detective's personality as the syuzhet takes its course.

Detective films illustrate one way that classical cinema has solved problems that every narrative must face. But these solutions are not the only ones available. We can examine how another genre motivates a different approach.

The Melodrama

It is a critical commonplace that film melodrama as a genre subordinates virtually everything to broad emotional impact. Translated into the theoretical categories Chapter 4 outlined, this is to say that the narration will be highly communicative about fabula information—specifically, information pertaining to characters' emotional states. There will be fewer focused gaps in fabula information. The narration will also be quite unrestricted in range, closer to an omniscient survey, so that the film can engender pity, irony, and other "dissociated" emotions. Whereas the detective story emphasizes the act of unearthing what already occurred, the melodrama typically relies on a firm primacy effect, plays down curiosity about the past, and maximizes our urge to know what will happen next—and, especially, how any given character will react to what has happened. Viewer interest is maintained by retardation and carefully timed coincidences that produce surprise. All of these narrational strategies can be seen at work in *In This Our Life*.

The cause-effect chain of the film's fabula centers on Stanley Timberlake, an impetuous and selfish young woman from a declining Southern family. Stanley seduces Peter, her sister Roy's husband; drives him to alcoholism and suicide; and then makes a play for Craig, the man she had spurned to run off with Peter. When Craig avoids her attentions, prefer-

ring Roy instead, Stanley drives off in a rage. Her car runs over a mother and her child. She testifies, however, that Parry, a family servant, is guilty. After Craig forces Stanley to tell the truth, Stanley flees the police in a reckless chase. Her car crashes and she is killed. I have skipped over many details and some characters, such as Asa, the saintly but ineffectual father; Lavinia, the neurasthenic mother; and Uncle William, a vest-popping toper who at one point implies that he would like to make his niece his mistress; but the general outline is clear enough. (My reader will also have to accept the fact that the principal women characters have male names.) Given that Stanley's actions propel the fabula (not to mention that she is played by Bette Davis), it may seem odd that the film's range of knowledge is not restricted to her. If *The Big Sleep* and *Murder My Sweet* enhance identification with a single character by limiting our information to what he could know, *In This Our Life* shuttles us from person to person; we "identify" less with a single character than with a presentation of the emerging situation as a whole.

The emotional expressiveness of the film issues partly from the narration's tendency to be omnicommunicative. For one thing, characters usually speak their minds. When Craig mopes after losing Stanley, he declares: "I don't believe in anything." Later Roy's emotional numbness is exposed: "I don't want to hear anything or feel anything." After Peter kills himself, Stanley breaks down in a fit of remorse bordering on hysteria. The "big scenes" of melodrama, full of soul-bearing histrionics, bear witness to the narration's desire to communicate "everything." All the expressive resources of mise-en-scène—gesture, lighting, setting, costume—work to convey inner states. Dressed in a sexy frock, Stanley declares she won't wear widow's black, stamping her foot petulantly, stiffening her spine, and speaking what might be a slogan for the melodramatic character: "I'm fed up with pretending something I don't feel." When Roy and Craig see a forest fire in the distance, she draws the comparison to their intense but brief affair. And music, one of the foundations of "melodrama" as classically conceived, communicates characters' perceptions and attitudes. It is especially identified with the two sisters, punctuating major discoveries and underlining intense passages.

To wring every emotional drop out of fabula situations, the narration employs omniscience. This procedure is established during the first extended sequence of the film. While the family sit at home waiting for Stanley, we cut to Stanley and Peter making plans to run off that night. The primacy effect works fully: all of Stanley's subsequent behavior will be measured against her traits displayed here. Stanley comes home, followed soon by Peter. We know something crucial that the family does not, and the narration dwells on Roy's ignorance and confusion about the true state of affairs (the better to build up pity for her). When Craig calls for Stanley, we understand her "headache" as a pretext to stay home and sneak out with Peter. It might seem that our knowledge is restricted to Stanley's were it not for all the behavior (Roy's attraction to Craig, Uncle William's decision to control Stanley through his power of the purse, and so forth) which we witness but which Stanley does not. Thus the film's first big scene yields a range of knowledge far beyond that available to any single character.

One interesting consequence of this is that subsequent scenes often consist of little more than various characters' discovering what we already know. For instance, after Stanley and Peter have run off, the next scene shows Asa informing his in-laws, and the scene after that presents Roy's response. By shuttling from one character to another and giving us a comparatively wide field of view, the narration multiplies opportunities for our anticipating characters' reactions. How, for example, will Stanley respond when Roy confronts her with her lies? A scene is devoted to working this out. (The high number of scenes devoted solely to the playing out of reactions would seem to be a convention not only of film melodrama but of television soap opera.)

Unrestricted knowledge, then, is created in several ways. Cutaways to action nearby, crosscutting different plot lines, following several characters from one locale to another—all expand the range of knowledge in *In This Our Life*. As in the detective films, the omniscience of narration tends to become more overt in transitional passages, with signs, musical cues, and establishing shots all contributing to a degree of self-consciousness. The score can anticipate what will occur, as when over a shot of Stanley's car the dependable Max Steiner supplies the strains of "Here Comes the Bride." And the film as a whole can alternate lines of action, shifting us from a scene restricted to Stanley or Peter to one limited to Roy or Craig. Both specific film techniques and systematic principles of syuzhet presentation are used to enhance our range of knowledge.

An emphasis on omnicommunicativeness and omniscience does not imply that the film does not manipulate knowledge in as complicated a fashion as do *Murder My Sweet* and *The Big Sleep*. It is true that after the opening few scenes, very little of prior fabula information comes to light. (The sole instance involves Uncle William's confession to Stanley of how he bilked her father, which is not a major issue in the film.) The principal interest arises from the question of what will happen next. We have already seen that character reaction scenes are one case in point. The syuzhet also manipulates interest through unfocused temporal gaps. The melodrama's syuzhet will inform us of initiation of a chain of action and then skip over some time or move to another line of action; we will then wonder what happened in the interval. For example, after Stanley's hit-and-run, the scene ends abruptly. The next scene starts the following morning, when the police visit the family home. Only when the police reveal that they found the car abandoned do we get an answer to the question of what Stanley did after the accident. Another scene consists of a heated quarrel between Stanley and the drunken Peter. He slaps her, and the shot quickly fades out. We assume that the marriage will continue to deteriorate, but we see no more of it. Two sequences later we are told that Peter has killed himself. In general, the practice of parallel plotting retards the revelation of fabula information, compelling us to suspend questions about the progress of one line of action while another occupies our attention.

The detective film tends to presuppose a stable but concealed emotional nexus (A hates and kills B, but pretends that he did not hate or kill). The melodrama, however, assumes violent and overt changes of emotional attitudes.

When Peter leaves Roy, she vows to be "hard"; yet she later softens through love for Craig. Craig's loss of Stanley temporarily makes him cynical, but through Roy's love he recovers his old idealism. Even the apparently inflexible Stanley seems overcome by Peter's suicide. Another source of melodrama's typical syuzhet pattern is thus what we normally call character change; we try to anticipate how an event will alter a character's conduct. This inverts what a commonsensical account of viewing might lead us to posit. It is not that the world of the melodramatic film contains volatile characters which the narration faithfully records. Rather, if the viewer is to execute the inferential moves conventional in the genre, character behavior must trace an emotional zigzag. From a rhetorical standpoint, the characters' volatility is a structural necessity for the genre's narrational processes and effects.

There is one other way that the film maintains the forward course of its fabula despite being omniscient and highly communicative. Most commentators on the melodrama, in both theater and film, have observed the central role played by coincidence. As Daniel Gerould, paraphrasing the Russian critic Sergei Balukhatyi, puts it: "At those moments when separate phases of (the syuzhet) are united, 'chance' plays a key role as a cohesive element, combining and crossing lines of action and intrigue and producing sharp dramatic situations. . . . Thus 'chance' allows for new, unexpected plot twists."[6] Coincidence retains our interest in the unfolding syuzhet. Roy happens to encounter Craig in the park, a meeting which rehabilitates him and triggers their romance. At the moment Roy and Craig agree to marry, Asa tells them that Peter is dead. The evening that Stanley is out to pursue Craig, a mother and her little girl step in front of her car. And the night that Stanley begs Uncle William for help is also the night he has just learned that he has only six months to live. We get an overall knowledge of such events when they occur (cutaways to Asa in the house getting a phone call, crosscut shots of mother and child stepping into a street, a portentous composition showing the doctor's bag in Uncle William's home, etc.), but we could never have predicted the occurrence of these events, or at least their

occurrence at a particular moment. Coincidence in the melodrama serves one purpose of the investigation in the detective film: both provide generically conventional occasions for surprise.

Against the background of a general unrestrictedness and omnicommunicativeness, any sharp restrictions or suppressions stand out. In *In This Our Life*, these elements remain isolated moments, briefly intensifying our emotional investment. For instance, Peter angrily abandons Stanley at a bar and we follow him home. When he arrives, he—and we—discover that she is there ahead of him, waiting in a negligee; her tantrum in the bar was solely a lesson in who is boss. (This is a good example of successive hypothesis forming; one hypothesis simply replaces another.) At another point, Craig's plan to make Stanley confess to the hit-and-run accident is temporarily kept from us. But again, it gets quickly revealed. On the whole, restricted and suppressed knowledge cannot come to the fore without reducing our anticipation of those misalliances and fatal misunderstandings so central to the genre.

If I have said little about the depth of information available, it is because *In This Our Life* explains the characters' feelings squarely through speech, behavior, and other aspects of mise-en-scène. Other melodramas of the 1940s go deeper into characters' mental states; *Possessed*, for example, presents visual and acoustic hallucinations of the protagonist. The degree of internal information presented seems to vary within the genre, the basic demand being exposure of the critical emotional processes. Stanley's hysteria at Peter's death might have been rendered more subjectively than it is. This genre has no inherent need to suppress aspects of the protagonist's mental life, as in the detective film's "middle-viewpoint" convention. By the same token, the narration's degree of self-consciousness is not stipulated by genre. One could argue that certain patterns of staging— very frontal playing, the habit of making a scene end with a somewhat stylized reaction by Stanley, or the unusual angling of certain sets—all enhance the film's self-consciousness. So does the typically overwrought score. The "stylization" commonly remarked in melodrama stems from

5.2. In This Our Life

a considerable narrational self-consciousness allied to a high degree of communicativeness, especially about emotional conditions and effects. A shot like figure 5.2, in which the table at which the couple will sit stands waiting for them in the foreground, signals a recognition of what would be the audience's best view.

The Big Sleep, Murder My Sweet, and *In This Our Life* by no means exhaust the narrational options of genre-bound filmmaking, but perhaps two conclusions can be drawn from my brief analyses. First, the basic narrational properties are fulfilled through both syuzhet construction and stylistic embodiment—everything from gaps and retardation to figure movement and music, from the construction of space (e.g., Canino firing into the car in *The Big Sleep*) to the arrangement of temporal order (e.g., the flashback in *Murder My Sweet*). All film techniques, then, can function narrationally. Secondly, transtextual motivation is a strong factor in determining a film's narrational options. All films exploit disparities between fabula and syuzhet, but different genres do so in different ways. We should not expect any film to adhere to a single pitch of knowledge or self-consciousness or communicativeness. There will be shifts between omniscience and restriction, greater and lesser self-consciousness, more or less suppressive narration. It is the *patterns* and *purposes* of these shifts that become conventionalized. In the mystery film, the shifts promote that emphasis upon curiosity characteristic of the genre; the melodrama's insistence upon communicativeness justifies shifts that reveal a range of emotional experience. Each film operates, in its own way and with its own devices and systems, within a frame of reference codified by past practice. This will become evident again in Part 3, when we consider several conventional modes of narration.

Other theoretical regions still want exploring, however. This chapter and the previous one have concentrated on basic fabula/syuzhet strategies and overall narrational qualities. I have not done sufficient justice to the ways in which film style can serve narrational purposes. As a medium, cinema is particularly suitable for supporting the syuzhet's manipulation of time and space.

6. Narration and Time

In watching a film, the spectator submits to a programed temporal form. Under normal viewing circumstances, the film absolutely controls the order, frequency, and duration of the presentation of events. You cannot skip a dull spot or linger over a rich one, jump back to an earlier passage or start at the end of the film and work your way forward. Because of this, a narrative film works quite directly on the limits of the spectator's perceptual-cognitive abilites. A gap will be closed only when the syuzhet wants it that way; retarding material, however annoying, must be suffered through; a gap may be hidden so cunningly that the spectator cannot recall how the trick was pulled. It is evident that in cinema many processes of narration depend upon the manipulation of time.

Even at the level of the image, the programing of duration and order affects the viewer's experience. There appear to be distinct levels of processing. Some data, such as stroboscopically generated apparent motion, are processed very quickly (35–350 milliseconds), while the recognition of objects and the fitting of objects into some coherent spatial or narrative schema take longer (350–500 milliseconds per view).[1] A shot "dawns," it seems, in about half a second.

Thereafter, of course, the spectator continues to scan the image in search of meaning, and the shot can emit strong cues about its temporal development within its composition, as when in *The Birth of a Nation* empty foreground regions cue us to anticipate the trajectory of the Klan's ride (fig. 6.1). A more prolonged example occurs in *The End of St. Petersburg*, when Pudovkin stages a czarist march in a long shot (fig. 6.2) that prepares us for a compositional crescendo (fig. 6.3) and a climax (fig. 6.4). In contrast, the shock of one shot in *Dead Pigeon on Beethoven Street* issues from its refusal to "prime" the spectator for how it will develop (figs. 6.5–6.6).

In most synchronized sound cinema, our expectations about shot duration are also determined by the length of the spoken sentence. We are so accustomed to letting the speaker have his or her say (or nearly all of it) before a cut interrupts that we forget that any film could be edited like Marcel Hanoun's *Authentique procès de Carl Emmanuel Jung*, in which a short sentence may be chopped up into eight shots. And our absorption of a shot's information can also be prompted by camera movement, which can suggest a whole trajectory of interest contrary to that cued by figure

6.5. Dead Pigeon on Beethoven Street
6.6. Dead Pigeon on Beethoven Street

movement. I shall say more about scanning the image in the next chapter, but it is worth noting here the extent to which our comprehension of cinematic space depends upon cinema's ability to govern the rate of our viewing and thus the rate at which we propose, test, and confirm hypotheses.

The temporal constraints of the viewing situation also point directly to the central importance of "rhythm" in the cinema. Cognitive psychologists have suggested that the mind's induction operations can be limited by the speed at which the environment demands decisions.[2] Our anticipatory schemata are ready to pick up certain kinds of data, and the rate at which the information is presented can affect how we develop hypotheses. If narrative information is coming thick and fast, the viewer will opt for a "quick-elimination" strategy that discards many alternative hypotheses out of hand.[3] As we saw in the final sequence of *Rear Window*, a brief shot or sound compels the viewer to pick out salient features very quickly. At the climax of *The Birth of a Nation*, Griffith's alternating editing gives us a firm frame of reference—the Klan is riding to the rescue—that permits us to classify each syuzhet bit in gross terms (the beseiged/the rescuers). If a rapidly paced narrational passage does not trigger such clear formal patterns (as Godard's fast cutting often does not), the viewer will feel that there are too many decisions to be made simultaneously—an overload effect that may be just what the narration requires for the sake of ambiguity or unreliability. Alternatively, slowly paced narration may not confirm the schemata rapidly enough, forcing the specator to reassess the appropriateness of the initial expectation. Meir Sternberg shows that such features depend on the "qualitative indicator," the sense that the syuzhet span devoted to a fabula event lies in proportion to the event's contextual importance.[4] When Antonioni or Ozu dwells upon a locale that characters have left, or when Dreyer insists upon a character's slow walk across a parlor, the viewer must readjust his or her expectation, reset the scale of significance to be applied to the syuzhet, and perhaps play with a more open set of alternative schemata. Rhythm in narrative cinema comes down to this: by forcing the spectator to make inferences at a certain *rate*, the narration governs *what* and *how* we infer.

Features of Temporal Construction

Chapter 2 showed that film narration does not possess features akin to deixis, those linguistic signals of the context of utterance. This lack is especially notable with respect to time. As Jean-Paul Simon has remarked, "The cinematic signifier does not have formal marks which could characterize its temporality, not even equivalents of autonomous monemes, the specialized lexical items of language (yesterday, today, tomorrow, etc.)."[5] The temporal relations in the fabula are derived by inference; the viewer fits schemata to the cues proffered by the narration. This process affects three aspects of time: the order of events, their frequency, and their duration.[6]

Temporal Order

In the fabula, events take place either simultaneously (event 1 occurs while event 2 is occurring) or successively (event 2 occurs after event 1). Now, it is obvious that fabula events can be deployed in the syuzhet in any fashion whatever. This yields four general possibilities (each of which can be instantiated by various stylistic options):

FABULA	SYUZHET
A. simultaneous events	simultaneous presentation
B. successive events	simultaneous presentation
C. simultaneous events	successive presentation
D. successive events	successive presentation

Type A occurs when we presume that events simultaneously present in the syuzhet refer to simultaneous fabula events. A deep-space composition offers a clear case. Type A could also be presented by split-screen, offscreen sound, or other stylistic devices. Type B, simultaneity in the syuzhet but successivity in the fabula, is rare, but it can be observed in those cases when, say, characters watch a film or television program depicting prior fabula events: the act of watching and the past events are simultaneously represented in the syuzhet. More self-consciously, the narration can represent successive events as simultaneous by using split screen or "sound overlap"—letting the dialogue or effects from the upcoming scene creep up under the last few images of this one. Type C is obviously much more common; crosscutting is the principal device whereby simultaneous fabula events (Jones walks his dog while Smith flees the police) are spread out successively in the syuzhet (cut from Jones to Smith to Jones).

Usually successivity in the fabula is rendered as successivity in the syuzhet (type D). But even here the syuzhet can take many liberties. The fabula constitutes a chronological series of actions; the syuzhet can adhere to this chronology (1-2-3) or shuffle events (1-3-2, 2-1-3, 3-2-1, and so forth). The most vivid example is obviously the flashback, in which a prior fabula event (1) is positioned later in the syuzhet (yielding, say, 2-1-3). In *Sunrise*, the fabula chronology runs this way: the couple are initially happy; then the City Woman arrives; then the husband lets the farm deteriorate; then, one night, he has a rendezvous with the vamp. After an expository prologue, the syuzhet presents the husband going out to meet the City Woman; only then, through the conversation of two old villagers, are earlier fabula events revealed through brief flashbacks. The contrary case is that of the flashforward, in which the 1-2-3 fabula order gets recast in the syuzhet as something like 1-3-2. And it is evident that image and sound can diverge with respect to fabula order: the image can be in the syuzhet's present, while the sound can be in the past (e.g., the auditory flashback), or both image and sound can be in the past. Image and sound can even be presented as occurring at different moments in the fabula past, as in Francesco Rosi's *Illustrious Corpses*, when a flashback to a trial retains trial dialogue on the sound track while presenting images that go back to the commission of the crime.

It might seem that in most films the narration represents fabula events in chronological order throughout; flashbacks and flashforwards are, after all, not common. But now we can draw a distinction which Seymour Chatman has proposed.[7] When the syuzhet presents characters communicating information about prior events by any means (writing, speech, pantomime, tape recording, film clips, etc.), we have *recounting*. When the syuzhet presents prior events as if they were occurring at the moment, in direct representation, we have *enactment*. (A mixed case is the convention of "enacted recounting": a character tells about past events, and the syuzhet then presents the events in a flashback.) This distinction is an essential tool in describing the effects of a medium that can transmit fabula information "by report" or "by direct presentation."[8]

It is very common for a syuzhet to present fabula events out of order by recounting them. Most commonly, character dialogue does this. On the other hand, the flashback and the flashforward constitute enactment—we witness and/or hear the syuzhet dramatizing the significant fabula episode. The *Sunrise* scene is a mixed case: some prior events are enacted (e.g., the husband selling the cow), some are recounted (the arrival of the City Woman). We must say, then, that in most narrative films the narration does rearrange fabula order, principally through verbal recounting and in expository passages. It is more unusual to find the syuzhet *enacting* fabula events out of chronological sequence—that is, employing flashbacks or flashforwards.

Manipulations of fabula order offer obvious narrational possibilities. Adhering closely to fabula order focuses the viewer's attention on upcoming events—the suspense effect that is characteristic of most narrative films. This helps the viewer to form clear-cut hypotheses about the future, as when in *Sunrise* the farmer's conception of how he might kill his wife sharpens our projection of possible actions. By following fabula order the syuzhet also encourages the primacy effect, since each action can be measured as a change from the first one we see. Conversely, reshuffling fabula order can be used to break or qualify the primacy effect, forcing the viewer to evaluate early material in the light of new information about prior events (as in Bertolucci's *The Conformist*). Postponing the representation of some fabula events also tends to create curiosity, as *Sunrise* does at the beginning when the comparatively late point of attack leads us to ask what enabled the City Woman to break up the farmer's home. Reordering fabula events also

obviously creates narrational gaps, which may be temporary (*Sunrise*) or permanent (as some would argue is the case in *Citizen Kane*); focused (we may want to know exactly what happened at a specific point) or diffuse (a general sense that events are out of order); flaunted (e.g., the multifarious signals for a flashback) or suppressed (e.g., the absence of such signals). Manipulations of order may serve retardation and may also answer to requirements of narrational knowledgeability. In *The Big Sleep* and *Murder My Sweet*, we encounter information out of fabula sequence because our knowledge is principally restricted to that of the detective. Or a shift in order may be justified in the name of greater subjectivity; most flashback sequences are motivated to some degree as representing character memory. Note, however, the effect in *Sunrise* of confining the flashback to minor characters; they are little more than devices for revealing prior events in a way that is more "public" than either the husband's or the wife's recollections would be.

We can measure the effects of various narrational strategies by returning to two outstanding instances: the flashback and the flashforward. Though logically parallel, the procedures have quite different narrational implications. The flashback enacts events at a later point in the syuzhet than they occurred in the fabula. The flashback may display events that occur prior to the first event represented in the syuzhet; this is the *external* flashback. *Sunrise* furnishes an example: the couple were happy and the City Woman stopped at the village before the opening of the syuzhet. Alternatively, the flashback may be *internal*—that is, it may display events that occur within the temporal bounds of the syuzhet proper, after the initial event presented. In *The Birth of a Nation*, the Cameron sister spurns the young Stoneman, and there is a flashback to her brother dying on the battlefield—an event that we have in fact already witnessed once. Or, at the end of *The Joyless Street*, the mistress tells the police what occurred during an earlier gap, and a flashback clarifies her account. In either the external or the internal case, the flashback is usually motivated psychologically, as character recollection. When employed in this fashion, the flashback can create a relatively communicative narration with a small degree of self-consciousness. The narration motivates the presentation of the flashback realistically, letting us eavesdrop on the character's memory.

The flashforward, however, raises other problems. It would be impossible to find any external flashforwards, since the last fabula event necessarily sets one boundary of the syuzhet's time span. Moreover, the flashforward is very hard to motivate realistically. Consider *They Shoot Horses, Don't They?* The action of the dance marathon is punctuated by brief images of the protagonist's arrest and trial. It is not until the end of the film, when the hero shoots his dance partner, that we understand the images as flashforwards to his trial. But these flashforwards cannot be attributed to character subjectivity; they constitute self-conscious narrational asides to the spectator. The flashforward is thus communicative, but often in a teasing way: it lets us glimpse the outcome before we have grasped all the causal chains that lead up to it.

One might argue that a film could plausibly motivate a flashforward as subjectivity by making the character prophetic, as in *Don't Look Now*. But this is still not parallel to the psychological flashback, since we can never be as sure of a character's premonitions as we can be of a character's powers of memory. The forward movement of the syuzhet will inevitably involve the question "Will X be right about the future?" (indeed the case in *Don't Look Now*), whereas the psychologically motivated flashback does not necessarily raise the question "Was X right about the past?" The very rarity of this latter question is what permits a mendacious flashback like that in *Stage Fright*. In sum, because of the irrevocable forward movement of the syuzhet under normal viewing conditions, a flashforward tends to be highly self-conscious and ambiguously communicative. This is doubtless why classical narrative cinema has made no use of it and why the art cinema, with its emphasis on authorial intrusion, employs it so often.

Temporal Frequency

The viewer presumes that fabula events are unique occurrences, but each one can be represented in the syuzhet any number of times. For convenience let us say that the syuzhet can represent a fabula event once (1), more than once (1 +), or not at all (0). Using the recounting/enactment distinction, we arrive at nine possibilities for syuzhet representation of frequency (see chart).

Number of times fabula event is:	A	B	C	D	E	F	G	H	I
Recounted	0	0	0	1	1	1	1+	1+	1+
Enacted	0	1	1+	0	1	1+	0	1	1+

Case A points out the importance of story schemata. Even if a fabula event is neither recounted nor dramatized, we can still infer it as having occurred. In *The Big Sleep*, Marlowe makes an appointment to meet Harry Jones at Walgreen's office. A dissolve takes us to the lobby of an office building as Marlowe walks in and starts upstairs. The trip itself is not shown, but we infer it on the basis of earlier scenes (Marlowe drives a car) and general cultural knowledge. Typically, of course, the least "interesting" fabula events will be treated in this fashion. If something of causal consequence occurred during Marlowe's drive, it would usually be either enacted or recounted.

Case B, in which a fabula event is not recounted and enacted only once, can occur in any film, but some films, such as pre-1908 narrative cinema, eliminate recounting altogether and rely wholly on dramatization. In mainstream narrative cinema, many events are mentioned once or more than once without ever being enacted (cases D or G). This is especially common during expository passages. Classical narration also commonly dramatizes a significant fabula event once and recounts it one or more times (cases E and H); in *Sunrise*, the idyll of the married couple is recounted once in the old women's talk and enacted once in a shot of the family. In general, it is rare for an event to be enacted more than once, as in cases C, F, and I. When Eisenstein's narration repeats an action without having characters recount it, such as the fall of the czar's statue in *October*, we have case C. And an event may be recounted in character dialogue one or more times and still be enacted several times (cases F and I). Throughout *Pursued* the hero's childhood trauma is repeatedly discussed and shown through subjective imagery.

Because viewing time sets constraints on memory, the spectator's ability to construct a coherent fabula depends upon repeated reference to story events. To keep the main outlines of the action clear and to assure that proper hypotheses are launched, the narration must reiterate the salient causal, temporal, and spatial coordinates of the fabula. Repetition can heighten curiosity and suspense, open or close gaps, direct the viewer toward the most probable hypotheses or toward the least likely ones, retard the revelation of outcomes, and assure that the quantity of new fabula information does not become too great.

Yet only certain kinds of repetition are common in mainstream cinema. An event may be recounted any number of times, but it will typically be enacted only once (case H). This is to say that repetition chiefly occurs as a repetition *in the fabula world* that is relayed by the syuzhet (characters repeatedly discuss or mention the event). If the event does get "replayed," the repetition is subject to stringent narrational rules. It must be motivated realistically—typically through character subjectivity, as a memory. This was the case in the internal flashback in *The Birth of a Nation*, which repeats the death of one Cameron son. In some instances, the repeated dramatization can be justified as bringing to light information suppressed or ignored in the earlier occurrence, as in Donophon's flashback in *The Man Who Shot Liberty Valance*. To redramatize the story event without realistic motivation is to create a highly unrestricted, self-conscious narration, one which can override the fabula world's laws and rerun any portion of the action at will. Such is of course the case with the Soviet montage filmmakers of the 1920s; in Chapter 11 we shall see how a "spatial" conception of construction made it perfectly feasible for the narration to repeat a story action immediately or at intervals throughout the film.

Duration

Like order and frequency, duration is strictly governed by the conditions of normal viewing. Just as we cannot choose to skip around in a film or go back and rewatch a portion, so we cannot control how long the narration takes to unfold. This is of capital importance for filmic construction and comprehension.

We have three variables. *Fabula* duration is the time that the viewer presumes the story action to take—a decade or a day, hours or days or weeks or centuries. *Syuzhet* duration consists of the stretches of time which the film dramatizes. Of the ten years of presumed fabula action, the syuzhet might dramatize only a few months or weeks. The distinction is clearly exemplified in *High Noon*. Instead of enacting phases of Marshal Kane's struggle with Frank Miller or moments of Kane's courtship, the syuzhet dramatizes only the climactic point of those relationships, in the span of a few hours on one day. All the rest of fabula duration is cued through recounting.

Conventional means of signaling the relations between syuzhet and fabula duration would include clocks, calendars, verbal indications, intertitles or dialogue, and general cultural prototypes (shops opening up, roosters crowing). Generally, if the syuzhet duration focuses on one or a few portions of fabula duration, we tend to consider the story duration highlighted in a fashion reminiscent of post-Ibsen dramaturgy or of the twentieth-century short story. To the extent that syuzhet duration includes many and lengthy stretches of fabula duration, the plot construction seems more reminiscent of the "epic" novel of the nineteenth century. It should also go without saying that both fabula and syuzhet duration may be indeterminate, either through a paucity of cues (see the discussion of *Pickpocket*, p. 290), or through a radical refusal to conform to "normal" duration, as in Dreyer's *Passion de Jeanne d'Arc*.

Fabula duration and syuzhet duration are not embodied in

the film's stylistic system, but a third sort of duration is. We can call this *screen* duration, or "projection time." The story action may take ten years, the syuzhet may run from March to May of the final year, but the film may present these durations in the running time of two hours. Since screen duration is ingredient to the very medium of cinema, all film techniques—mise-en-scène, cinematography, editing, and sound—contribute to its creation.

So far I have taken the three sorts of duration as pertaining to the whole—the whole narrative, the entire running time. But duration also operates in important ways at a more local level: parts of the syuzhet (actions, scenes, episodes) and segments of screen time. The need to recognize this becomes clear if we consider the spectator's baseline assumptions about an "ordinary" film. At the level of the whole, the fabula duration is expected to be greater than the syuzhet duration, and syuzhet duration is assumed to be greater than projection time. This is because very few narratives represent the entirety of every action. At the level of various parts, however, the situation changes. Stylistic factors intervene decisively. In normal circumstances, the duration of a single shot is assumed to be equivalent to the duration of the action it represents. A man gets into a car: the shot presents a screen duration which equals both syuzhet and fabula duration. Scenes presented in spatiotemporal continuity are likewise comprehended as representing syuzhet and fabula duration faithfully. On the other hand, spectators understand that crosscutting, cutaways, and other techniques hold out possibilities of manipulating story duration. Chase sequences, montage sequences, and so forth are construed as cases when fabula duration will clearly exceed running time. In sum, the nature of the part shapes the spectator's construction of story duration.

I hasten to stress that all these durational assumptions are grounded in conventions of mainstream narrative cinema. They can be overridden by specific cues. It is possible, for instance, for a single shot to suggest a greater syuzhet and fabula duration than is present in projection time. In *The Red Shoes*, a shot of students in a balcony waiting for a ballet to begin is cued as being over forty-five minutes long. To convey this, the narration runs a caption ("Forty-five minutes later") over the shot. The sound track is also useful in challenging normal presuppositions: dialogue or voice-over commentary can suggest that an action taking moments on the screen took hours, or (the rarer case) vice versa. And the assumption of stylistic continuity as a cue for fabula duration can be undercut, as is shown in *Occurrence at Owl Creek Bridge*. Here, by suppressing a gap, the narration presents in several minutes events which occur in a few (subjective) seconds in the fabula. In the proper context, any film technique can modify or eliminate the spectator's tendency to assume that, at the level of the scene or shot, fabula time is either greater than or equal to projection time.

Given three possible durational relationships (equality, expansion, contraction), we could generate a set of nine possible relations among fabula, syuzhet, and style. Fortunately, these can be summarized informally. There is *equivalence*, in which fabula duration equals syuzhet and screen duration. There is what I shall call *reduction*, in which fabula duration is narrated in abridged or abbreviated fashion. And there is *expansion*, in which fabula duration is narrated in augmented fashion. Some possibilities are of course more common—and thus, from a spectator's viewpoint, more probable—than others.

At the level of the whole film, equivalence among syuzhet, fabula, and screen duration can be found in very simple narratives, such as "primitive" films. In *Pickpocket* (1903), a thief picks a man's pocket, is chased, and is caught: the end. The syuzhet asks us to construct no prior fabula events, so here syuzhet and fabula duration are identical. But this situation is very rare. Normally the fabula consists of more than the depicted action: it is the entire chain of story events. The fabula of *High Noon* includes not just the events in a two-hour space in Marshal Kane's life but also all their pertinent antecedents—sending Frank Miller to prison, promising his fiancée to quit his job, and so forth. Thus syuzhet duration may closely approximate screen time, but the entire fabula duration tends to outrun both.

At the level of any given part, however, equivalence among fabula, syuzhet, and screen duration is quite possible and is, as we saw, often taken for granted. An event represented on screen as taking one minute is usually assumed to have taken one minute in both the syuzhet and the fabula. This representation can be accomplished through a single shot, or continuity editing, or on the sound track—by any technical means.

The film's narration can also *reduce* fabula time. This is the most common procedure at the level of the whole: the syuzhet renders ten years as ten days, while screen duration makes the ten days two hours. Some parts of the film may also reduce story time, typically by positing a congruence of fabula and syuzhet duration but then rendering that span in a more abbreviated screen duration. A scene may be contextually cued to consume five minutes in the story and in the syuzhet, but by cutaways or other editing devices the action might be presented in three minutes on the screen. Fast motion is another technique that shortens screen duration without necessarily cueing the spectator to assume that syuzhet and fabula duration differ.

All such procedures are commonly called "ellipses," but our initial distinction reveals that actually there are two quite different ways of reducing story duration. One way, which we can call ellipsis proper, occurs when the syuzhet omits discrete segments of fabula time. This is normal operating procedure. In passing to scene B, the narration typically eliminates an interval of story action following scene A. Screen duration is here identical with syuzhet duration, and stylistic features (dissolves, music, and so forth) comprise conventional cues for the ellipsis. The Hollywood montage sequence is another example, in which portions of a process are rendered through emblematic images linked by dissolves or other forms of punctuation. The spectator is to take this as a brief summary of a longer string of events, and again discrete (if not always exactly measurable) portions of fabula time are skipped over.

Fabula time can also be reduced without any ellipses. Both fabula and syuzhet duration can be greater than screen time, but screen time presents a series of actions in such a way that no missing time can be detected. Since time is here not ellided but condensed, I shall call this procedure *compres-*

sion. A simple example is the *Red Shoes* shot ("Forty-five minutes later"). A less "literary" case occurs in Ozu's *The Only Son*. Here a shot which consumes less than ninety seconds of screen time moves the fabula from a moment around 10 P.M. to dawn. A "fast-motion" shot would also exemplify compression if we assume that through this technical device a "normal" fabula and syuzhet duration was presented in accelerated fashion. A more virtuosic case is the devastating (in every sense) restaurant sequence in Tati's *Play Time*. A night-to-dawn carouse in the prematurely opened Royal Garden is rendered in forty-five minutes of screen time. But there is no point at which we can isolate moments, let alone hours, as having been ellided by the syuzhet. Nearly every shot change is a continuity cut (an eyeline match, match on action, or whatever) that assures durational equivalences between syuzhet and fabula. More important, there is also diegetic music, played by bands performing at the Royal Garden and running almost without interruption throughout the sequence. (Continuous sound issuing from the diegetic world is a conventional cue for uninterrupted fabula duration.) Thus the sequence presents at least six hours of fabula and syuzhet time without, strictly speaking, omitting a second! We can only say that the sequence has concentrated, or compressed, those hours into about forty-five minutes of screen time.

Compression is probably not rare, but ellipsis is much more common, and its narrational functions are various. In analyzing a film's use of time we should consider the extent to which the ellided fabula time is determinable (what Noël Burch calls "definite" versus "indefinite" ellipses)[9] and the function of the ellipses for the syuzhet's goals. Obviously, ellipses leave gaps, and these may be permanent or temporary, focused or diffuse, flaunted or suppressed. Ellipses often work against retardation—time is skipped over in order to get to the next big moment—so a highly elliptical narration may require complicated plot lines to retard the action. (Lang's *Spione* is a good example.) If the omitted span contains significant information, the ellipsis can create a suppressive narration that shapes our hypothesis-forming activity.

Consider one of the most flagrant ellipses in the Hollywood cinema. In *Secret beyond the Door*, Celia Lamphere believes her husband Mark to be a murderer. One night she flees from the house, with Mark apparently in pursuit. She pauses in the foreground. A man's shape emerges behind her. The screen goes black and we hear her scream. The next scene fades up on Mark alone the next morning. His internal monologue reflects: "It'll be a curious trial. The People of the State of New York versus Mark Lamphere, charged with the murder of his wife, Celia. Exhibit A. What can I answer if I am asked if the murder was premeditated?" Thus juxtaposed, the two scenes lead us to infer that he has murdered her. But two scenes later, Celia enters his room and we learn that last night another man met her on the lawn and helped her escape. The narration has skipped over only a few moments and flaunted the gap, but then appeared to fill it satisfactorily. Now we learn that the narration has misled us. This is "unreliable" narration par excellence.

At the level of the whole film or of some part, the narration may also *expand* fabula duration. An event may be presumed to take one minute in the story but its syuzhet composition or its manifestation in running time may actually consume two minutes. As with reduction, we can distinguish two sorts of expansion. There is expansion by *insertion*, which roughly parallels ellipsis. Here fabula time is expanded by "padding": the syuzhet and the style wedge in foreign matter. If I film a man crossing a threshold and I cut to a shot of an action occurring a mile away and then cut back to him continuing to cross the threshold, I have expanded the action by insertion. *Occurrence at Owl Creek Bridge* offers a famous example, whereby a few seconds of story action—the last moments of a man about to be hanged—are prolonged to half an hour of screen time by the insertion of a prolonged subjective sequence. In Soviet silent cinema, it is not uncommon to find a concrete story action interrupted by an intertitle and then resuming from where it left off. My examples have stressed editing as the chief means of accomplishing insertion because that is the most frequent practice, but certainly other techniques could work as well. There is a curious instance in *Tout va bien* when, during the lengthy tracking shot in the supermarket, successive story events (e.g., the young rioters' disruptions) are treated as insertions into the chain of other story events, since occasionally the camera returns to supermarket customers at the checkout counters who are taking out of their shopping carts exactly the same packages they were taking out several minutes before. And expansion could also be accomplished through insertion of dialogue or sound effects insofar as a film's sound track cues fabula events.

The second sort of expansion is *dilation*. Somewhat parallel to compression, this tactic stretches out a continuously represented action. Here fabula and syuzhet duration are congruent; only screen duration expands time. The most common instance is slow-motion cinematography. The slow-motion death scenes in *Seven Samurai* are narrationally self-conscious prolongations of actions which in both fabula and syuzhet terms must be occupying a shorter time span. Overlapping editing is another technique for achieving the same end. Specific cues in the mise-en-scène (lighting or costume or setting shifts) or on the sound track (e.g., voice-over commentary, or Jean Epstein's experiments in "slow-motion" sound effects) could also override our normal assumption that a given event takes only as long in the fabula as it does on screen.

The fundamental ways in which narration can manipulate fabula duration can be summed up simply:

Equivalence: Fabula duration equals syuzhet duration equals screen duration.
Reduction: Fabula duration is reduced.
  A. Ellipsis: Fabula duration is greater than syuzhet duration, which is itself equal to screen duration. A discontinuity in the syuzhet marks an omitted portion of fabula duration.
  B. Compression: Fabula duration equals syuzhet duration, both of which are greater than screen duration. There is no discontinuity in the syuzhet, but screen duration condenses fabula and syuzhet duration.

6.7. His Girl Friday

Expansion: Fabula duration is expanded.
  A. Insertion: Fabula duration is less than syuzhet
      duration, which is itself equal to screen dura-
      tion. A discontinuity in the syuzhet marks added
      material.
  B. Dilation: Fabula duration equals syuzhet duration,
      both of which are less than screen duration. There is
      no discontinuity in the syuzhet, but screen duration
      stretches out both fabula and syuzhet duration.

All of these manipulations can be accomplished by various
film techniques.

These distinctions can help us analyze two outstanding
figures of film style, both operating in a more complex
fashion than is usually realized. Clarifying these figures also
sheds some new light on two films which have become
textbook examples of the creative use of time in cinema.

Crosscutting is one stylistic vehicle of temporal manipulation. Here the narration intercuts two or more distinct lines
of action. This raises questions of order, as we have seen: do
we understand the successively presented events as occurring successively or simultaneously in the fabula? But crosscutting raises questions of duration too. *The Birth of a Nation*, that old chestnut whose temporal construction
nonetheless remains inadequately analyzed, offers remarkable instances.

The climax of *The Birth of a Nation* crosscuts four distinct
lines of action: Silas Lynch imprisoning Elsie and Austin
Stoneman, the riot in the streets of Piedmont, the Cameron
family and friends besieged in a cabin outside town, and the
Klan riding to the rescue. In narrational terms, each cut to
another line of action creates a strong retarding effect. Overall, the actions are grasped as simultaneous: the family
fights while the Klan gallops to them. At a more microscopic
level, however, the editing's discontinuities create a curious
durational effect which no one, to my knowledge, has
pointed out. The crosscutting produces an *ellipsis* in some
lines of action and an *expansion* in others. For example, the
little band in the cabin is only moments from annihilation,
and the Klan must ride several miles to rescue them. Cutting
to the galloping rescuers prolongs the cabin seige (expan-

sion by insertion), while cutting back to the cabin motivates
the omission of very long stretches of the Klan's ride (ellipsis). This example, not at all extraordinary, shows how the
tension of crosscutting proceeds partly from the fact that
syuzhet and style have given each line of action a different
durational span.

A second canonic case of temporal manipulation in the
cinema is overlapping editing—cutting together shots of the
same action so as to expand screen duration. This is commonly used for emphasis. In *His Girl Friday*, Molly Malloy
has berated the callous reporters, and Hildy Johnson has
ushered her out. The chastened men remain uncomfortably
quiet. Hildy returns, slowly swinging the door open (fig.
6.7). Cut to a *plan américain* of her, still opening the door
and swinging it over a portion of the arc it has already
completed (fig. 6.8). Hildy stands poised in the doorway and
murmurs, "Gentlemen of the Press," before striding back to
her desk. The overlapped cut accentuates the pause and
Hildy's muted denunciation. This instance shows that manipulation of duration in editing often requires controlling
the frequency of the syuzhet event—repeating or not repeating a particular action. (Although most matches on action do

6.8. His Girl Friday

6.9. Potemkin, *shot 239*
6.10. Potemkin, *shot 240*

not replay lengthy portions of a movement, sometimes three or four frames of movement are repeated. This slight overlap makes the cut perceptually smoother.)

But some cases of temporal expansion are not so simple. It is common to cite the plate-smashing scene in *Potemkin* as simply stretching out time, but analysis of the sequence reveals powerful ambiguities. The sailor washing the dishes sees a plate labeled "Give Us This Day Our Daily Bread." He becomes enraged, and these shots follow (see figs. 6.9–6.18):

239. High-angle medium shot: The plate is lifted up out of frame.

240. Medium shot: Three sailors washing dishes. The sailor brings the plate into frame and upward.

241. Medium close-up: The sailor swings the plate back across his chest toward his left shoulder.

242. Medium shot: The sailor continues to swing the plate back and holds it an instant. Then he swings it downward, backhand, and it arcs just out of the lower frame line.

243. Medium close-up: The sailor is now raising his arm upward to his right; the plate is high, out of the top of the frame.

244. Extreme close-up: The sailor's furious face moves to and from the camera.

245. Medium shot, as (242): The sailor's right arm is up out of frame (as in 243); he swings the plate down into the shot overhand.

6.11. Potemkin, *shot 241*   6.13. Potemkin, *shot 243*
6.12. Potemkin, *shot 242*   6.14. Potemkin, *shot 244*

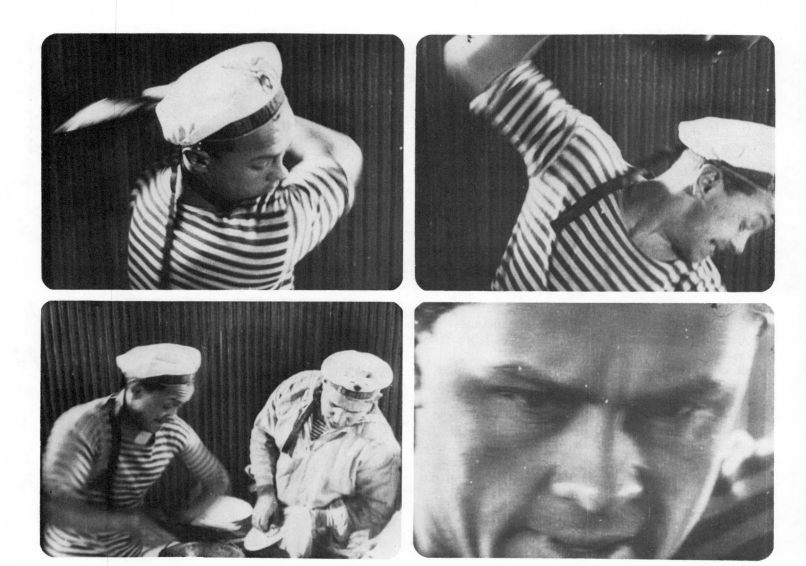

246. High-angle medium shot, as (239): The arm brings the plate down, and it smashes on the table.

247. Medium close-up, as (243): The sailor's back, shoulder, and left arm writhe, and the head starts back up into the shot.

248. High-angle medium shot, as (246): The table; the sailors' bodies start to move away. Fade out.

Overlapping editing requires some repetition of action, but here there is almost none. The only possible cue of this sort occurs in shot 244, when the movement of the face can be taken to suggest that the body is lunging forward, already bringing the plate down in the action that will start again in

6.15. Potemkin, *shot 245*
6.16. Potemkin. *shot 246*

6.17. Potemkin, *shot 247*   6.18. Potemkin, *shot 248*

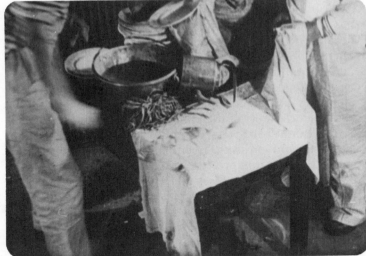

hand makes a *single* gesture of swinging the plate up (shots 239–242), swinging it across his chest, then raising it above his right shoulder (shots 243–245) before smashing it down (245–248). In this case, only shot 244 expands fabula duration. Shot 247, which shows recoiling musculature, cannot be said to expand duration either, since the smashing action has been completed; this is the follow-through. In fact, if the fabula action consists of a single movement, this passage offers an ellipsis. The cut from (242) to (243) omits showing the swing of the plate across the sailor's body. One or two seconds have been ellided, not expanded.

On the other hand, one could assume that the syuzhet violates the canonic fabula principle of noncontradiction by showing the sailor smashing the plate in two *different* gestures: bringing the plate down backhand (239–242) and bringing it down overhand (243, 245). The syuzhet would then be ambiguous with respect to how the plate was "actually" smashed. Either the backhand or the overhand blow would cut smoothly in with the shot of the shattering plate (246). On this account, screen duration would be lengthened by the insertion of the alternative gesture.

Strictly on the evidence in the sequence, the two accounts cannot be made compatible. *Potemkin*'s plate-smashing scene is not a clear case of durational expansion, for the syuzhet conjures up conflicting possibilities of what constitutes the fabula event (one complex gesture or two simple ones?). It is interesting, though, that most viewers and critics seem to take this sequence for an extensive expansion. This can be explained by two principles I have invoked earlier. First, the whole sequence goes by so quickly that the pressure of the viewing situation encourages the viewer to

the next shot. On the whole, the editing transitions are smooth and continuous matches on action, often "frame cuts" (from shot 239 to shot 242, and between shots 245 and 246).[10]

About the fabula event itself we can make one of two assumptions. Let us assume, first, that the sailor's right

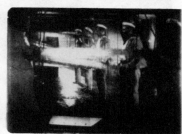

take the simplest explanation; an expansion of a single, simple gesture is cognitively more economical than other assumptions. Second, the film's context encourages us to read any durational discontinuity within physical movement as an expansion. Most of the cuts on action in *Potemkin* offer either smooth matches (equivalence of syuzhet duration and fabula duration) or joltingly overlapped cuts. A characteristic passage occurs when the mess orderlies lower the tables (figs. 6.19–6.22). The cuts alternate perfect matches on action (shots 141–142, 143–144) with jarring expansions (142–143, 144–145). The viewer comes to expect a nervous, vibrating treatment of fabula time as the film's internal norm, so that perplexing shots involving movement tend to be slotted into the most probable category.

Temporal Stratagems and Spoils

As Chapter 10 will show in more detail, the "serious" postwar European cinema can be characterized by its effort to structure a film around highly self-conscious narration. The film defines its narrational work with respect to certain external norms (as every film must), but it seeks to create unique internal norms by using devices and/or systems which generate an ambiguous, gamelike process of narrative construction. Taking one example, Bernardo Bertolucci's *The Spider's Stratagem*, I want to show how the theoretical principles of narration and the principles of temporal organization I have outlined can be used to trace this game across an entire film.

Up to a point, *The Spider's Stratagem* can be considered a detective story. Athos Magnani comes to the Po Valley village of Tara. His father, also named Athos Magnani, was murdered in 1936 during a performance of *Rigoletto* and has become sanctified as an antifascist hero. The father's mistress, Draifa, urges Athos to discover the killer. After talking with his father's old comrades and the mysterious landowner Beccaccia, Athos learns that Magnani was in fact a traitor who sold out to the fascist authorities. But since a dead hero is more politically useful than a living traitor, he arranged his

death to appear to be the work of the fascists. Although Athos has discovered the truth, he keeps silent, at least partly because he realizes that he too is "part of the story of Athos Magnani."

The film thus presents the characteristic double fabula-forming process of the detective tale: we construct the story of Athos's ongoing investigation, and we (along with Athos) construct the story of the crime itself, filling in causal gaps. To this extent *The Spider's Stratagem* appeals to processes of suspense and curiosity. Eventually, part of the mystery is solved. But the film presents two difficulties that we did not encounter in *The Big Sleep* and *Murder My Sweet*. One is a permanent causal gap. No explanation is offered for why the elder Magnani betrayed his friends and his cause. Like *Citizen Kane*, *The Spider's Stratagem* suggests a fundamental unfathomability in human action. The more pressing difficulty—and one that does not arise in *Citizen Kane*—has to do with the presentation of both the investigation and the crime. In this film, the narration is itself more ambiguous than in any of the Hollywood films we have considered. There are several permanent gaps, and these are flaunted; we are asked to form competing, nonexclusive hypotheses;

6.23   6.25
6.24

cues are inconsistent rather than redundant. *The Spider's Stratagem* utilizes an equivocal narration which compels us to form hypotheses about the narration's own operations, to live with the dissonance of withheld fabula information and incompatible cues.

The narration refuses to mark clear boundaries among character subjectivity, objective events, and narrational "commentary." Now, the classical film typically signals each of these unequivocally. In *Rear Window*, the narration begins with an image of the rising window blind, addressed wholly to us without any diegetic motivation; other images are marked as being from Jeffries's optical viewpoint; still other events are presented as occurring objectively, even if independently of Jeff's awareness. *The Spider's Stratagem*, however, conforms to the narrational mode characteristic of the European art film. Without rehearsing an argument to be developed later, I can say here that this narrational mode often asks us to treat the syuzhet as mixing subjectivity and objectivity with no promise of eventual choice between the two. The film's style supports this syuzhet strategy by making cues incomplete or inconsistent. We must therefore keep our hypotheses more open than in classical Hollywood narration.

Two quick examples may illustrate. The morning after Athos arrives, he wakes up to a knock at his door. He opens it (fig. 6.23). Cut to a shot of a man with his fist raised (fig. 6.24) who then punches it to the camera (fig. 6.25). There is a smack and a crash, and the screen goes dark. Athos has apparently been knocked cold. The stylistic cues for optical subjectivity are the man's posture and glance and the fist shoved to the camera. Yet one cue is inconsistent: when the smack is heard on the sound track, the fist is colliding with nothing at all. The shot thus also presents itself as a *non-subjective* construct, the narration's stylized representation of the assault—somewhat like the passage in *Potemkin* that refuses to communicate exactly how the plate was smashed.

Here is a more complex sequence. Off the Tara town square stands a white stone bust of the elder Magnani. In one scene Athos strolls around it, and we get shots of the statue as if from his optical point of view. However, the cues

pose problems. The bust is no longer pure white; now the kerchief and the eyes are painted. The camera travels in an arc around the statue, thus cueing us to Athos's movement; but the statue seems to rotate *with* the camera movement, always remaining frontal. And when Athos stops his pacing, turns, and walks in an opposite trajectory, the statue and the background continue their movement as if he had not reversed his course. Later, the shot of the bust that would have "properly" accompanied Athos's switch in direction is inserted into the scene of his speech to the populace. We are left with nonredundant cues and unconfirmed hypotheses. Has the statue been painted after Athos's arrival (an "objective" change in the fabula world)? Or is the statue's paint a cue that this shot depicts Athos's mental state (i.e., a subjective image)? The statue's unrealistic rotational movement could suggest either mental subjectivity or an external narration breaking the laws of the diegetic world. If the passage is subjective, why does the statue's rotation not change direction when Athos does? And is the last appearance of the statue a subjective flashback (Athos recalling what he saw) or a narrational aside that calls our attention to the juxtaposition of Magnani junior and senior? These questions cannot be conclusively answered. Even as we frame exclusive and simultaneous hypotheses about the crime fabula (did Beccaccia kill Magnani, or did someone else?), we must frame looser, more successive or "developmental," and less easily confirmed hypotheses *about the narrational process itself*. Why is this or that scene being shown? Is this event objective, or subjective, or something else?

Athos's inquiry consumes four days, but this concentrated syuzhet duration is opened up by a series of nine external flashbacks that dramatize events leading to the elder Magnani's death.

1. The elder Magnani and his three comrades stroll along at night, and he imitates a rooster's crowing.

2. At a village festival, Magnani defies the local blackshirts by dancing during the playing of a patriotic tune.

3. Magnani and his comrades discuss how to assassinate Mussolini.

4. Magnani and his comrades decide to kill Mussolini by a bomb during the performance of *Rigoletto*.

5. Draifa sees Magnani for the last time: while circus trainers pursue an escaped lion, she quarrels with him.

6. Magnani's comrades present him with a stuffed lion on a platter.

7. Magnani runs through a forest.

8. Magnani confesses his treachery, and with his friends he plots his own death.

9. Brief fragments from several of these appear when Athos dedicates Tara's memorial to his father.

Like any narrative film that utilizes flashbacks, *The Spider's Stratagem* asks us to slot these into one overall chronology. This presents no great difficulty, since most scenes are presented in chronological and causal sequence. There are admittedly some causal gaps: the lion banquet (6) and the shots of Magnani's running (7) remain hard to link up and may not even be flashbacks at all. But the real ambivalence of these flashbacks lies in their abnormal use of temporal cues, both of syuzhet and style.

There is, first, the problem of properly signaling a transition into or out of a flashback. In *Citizen Kane*, to take a counterexample, each flashback is carefully "framed" by a narrating situation. A teller in the present gives way to dramatized scenes set in the past, and when these are done we return, however briefly, to the narrating present. This is the "enacted recounting" discussed on p. 78. Now, the first flashback in *The Spider's Stratagem* sticks to this convention. Draifa tells Athos that his father was humorous; we then see Magnani, out with his cronies, mimicking a cock's crowing; and the narration returns to the situation that had introduced the flashback. As we work our way through the film, though, such standard cues fall away. In flashback 2, Gaibazzi tells Athos of the festival; cut to the festival and the confrontation with the blackshirts. But at the scene's end there is no return to the narrating situation—simply a cut to another old pal, Rasori, starting to tell Athos of another moment in the past. The narration leaves a gap, which we must fill in this way: after Gaibazzi completed his story, Athos left and came to visit Rasori.

A more disturbing problem comes up here. Conventional flashbacks, such as those in *Citizen Kane*, furnish an obvious cue for differentiating the two eras: characters surviving in the present are depicted as younger in the flashback. In *The Spider's Stratagem*, however, things are more complicated. In both the first and second flashbacks, Magnani is played by the actor who plays his son. This can be realistically motivated as family resemblance. But not only are Gaibazzi and the other comrades played by the same actors in both past and present; they are also presented as being *exactly the same age* in the 1936 scenes as in those taking place thirty-five years later. (This is not as apparent in the first flashback because it is a night scene and because we have not yet seen the men in the present.) The second flashback, then, initiates new hypotheses—the narrating present may not return at the end of a flashback, the other comrades will look the same in present and past—and these pertain as much to the narration itself as to the causal chain of fabula events.

In the short term, these hypotheses are confirmed. Flash-

6.26 *6.27*

back 3 begins with Rasori's telling Athos about the period, then moves to the past—in which Rasori looks no younger than in the present—and instead of closing on a return to the narrating frame, fades to Athos and the third comrade, Costa, resuming the story. The effect of running the three men's stories so closely together is to discourage us from looking for incompatibilities among them. (Contrast *Citizen Kane* in this regard.) Yet if we now expect that the film has a rule—no return to the narrating present—this expectation is foiled, for Costa's flashback, unlike the others, does conclude with a scene of Athos talking with him about what he has said. The playful quality of the narration emerges: of four flashbacks, two return to the framing situation and two do not. The spectator cannot confidently hypothesize that the narration will end a flashback in any definite way—which means that the viewer cannot exactly predict when a flashback will start. (As the cut to Rasori and the fade to Costa indicate, even punctuation will not afford a trustworthy cue.)

The ambiguity is increased when we consider the depth of knowledge we can assign to these four flashbacks. In the Hollywood film, a flashback functions principally to justify withholding or revealing fabula information at a specific moment. The flashback is typically not consistently "subjective"; often it tells us things that the narrating or recollecting character could not even know. In *The Spider's Stratagem*, the anomalies of presentation might lead us to ask whether the flashbacks might not be more pervasively subjective than in the Hollywood tradition. The first flashback, framed by Draifa's recounting, might then be attributed to her or to Athos. There are, though, no cues for taking it this way. If the scene is Draifa's memory, there is no explanation of why the three comrades are represented at their current age. If the scene is Athos's imagining, how could he visualize the men accurately before he has met them? The best hypothesis here is that the flashback is impersonally relayed by the narration in Hollywood fashion. Later, since the investigation is restricted to Athos's range of knowledge, the flashbacks might be considered subjective, but again, the first two involve portrayal of men whom Athos has not met.

Yet if all these flashbacks are impersonal, the fifth one challenges all the schemata and hypotheses we have cultivated so far.

As Draifa and Athos walk to her home, he asks about his father. "How was he intimately?" Draifa turns away, facing toward us in the foreground; Athos goes out of focus (fig. 6.26). Cut to Draifa winding a bandage around Athos's father. The couple start to quarrel. She calls him a coward and vows never to see him again. Cut back to the present, an extreme long-shot view of Draifa and Athos walking on the edge of a wood. Cut back to the past, continuing the scene we have watched. Draifa looks out the window and calls Magnani over. Cut to the present again: Draifa and Athos stop by a cornfield and she falls backward, as if fainting. Athos bends over her; she opens her eyes. Cut back to the past: Magnani is looking out the window, perhaps at the escaped lion. After some shots of the lion and Magnani, track back from the window to Draifa in the foreground (fig. 6.27), as we have seen in her the present (fig. 6.26). She speaks: "It might have been fear, or because his back was to me so that I couldn't see his face, but I realized it was all over. It was the last time I saw him alive." She turns from us, and the camera tracks in, past her, to Magnani looking out the window. Cut back to the present, as she still looks up at the young Athos.

The flashback is the first one in which a narrating situation is not created. There is no evidence whatever that Draifa tells Athos of these events. Therefore the flashback cannot represent Athos's mental subjectivity. But the scene maintains the anomaly of the first four flashbacks by presenting Draifa as the same age in the past as in the present, so we can no longer take that as a consistent cue for Athos's imagination. Moreover, although there is no framing narrating situation, Draifa's final monologue violates the integrity of the fictional world—she speaks of Magnani's current behavior in the past tense, and to no defined addressee. That is, her final lines would be appropriate only if they were spoken in a framing situation like those of flashbacks 1 through 3. As they stand, her lines could suggest the overt intervention of a narration that breaks with verisimilitude in the staging of the profilmic event for the sake of self-conscious transmission of information. This sequence is a good example of how conventional cues can become ambiguous if they are shaken out of redundant relations with one another. To add to the ambiguity, one shot from Draifa's flashback will appear in the last flashback passage (9), which we might otherwise be inclined to attribute to Athos; yet since she has told him nothing of these events, there is no causally realistic way it could reappear in his memory. Again some cues point to character subjectivity, others to omniscient narrational commentary.

The result of the first five flashbacks is to create a consistent play against any solid predictions about the film's narrational procedures. If we assume the narration to be restricted to Athos, Draifa's flashback violates this. If we assume this scene to be her private musings, then we will not later be able to explain how it crops up in Athos's memory. And we still have no explanation for the representation of characters' ages in the past. Or rather we have an overall hypothesis: that we are engaging with a highly self-conscious, ambiguously communicative narration that, within certain limits, changes cues in order to catch us off guard. Only a playful narration could keep shifting the ground under our feet.

The remaining flashbacks maintain the unpredictability. In a deck chair on Draifa's terrace, Athos watches the three old friends confront the sinister Beccaccia. When they mention the lion, a dissolve takes us to a mock funeral procession. Stretched out on a platter, the big cat is set before the elder Magnani. Here there is no explicit framing, no one telling Athos of the event at all; he simply overhears an oblique reference. The sequence also lacks sheer surface plausibility: why feast on a lion carcass? The scene can then be either a flashback or a fantasy, and in either case attributable to the comrades, Athos, or the omniscient narration. The sequence becomes much more questionable in its mental status than earlier, more firmly grounded flashbacks.

Something similar occurs in the seventh flashback. Here Athos is taken to the riverbank, where the three old men wait threateningly for him. Frightened, he flees, and his run through the forest is paralleled, via editing, to his father's running through the same terrain. Is it subjective, Athos imagining himself as his father? Is it an "objective" intercalation of past and present, in which Athos repeats the gesture of Magnani years before? Or is it an analogy drawn by narrational commentary and suggesting the increasing resemblance of father and son? Magnani's run never gets contextualized in fabula terms, so here, as with the lion feast, our hypotheses are vague, and the paucity of cues never lets us settle on one construction.

After these oscillations among subjectivity, objectivity, and narrational interjection, the penultimate flashback appears quite traditional. Athos infers that his father connived at his own death, and the three comrades confirm it in a flashback that details Magnani's confession and his proposal for staging the murder. And now the flashback is completely enclosed within narrating frames. The clarity is necessary if we are to plug gaps in the crime fabula; however equivocal the narration becomes in other respects, we are at last allowed some definite answers, and the tidy flashback offers the comfort of achieved truth. Nonetheless, Athos broods on a causal gap. Why did his father betray? "What was the story of Athos Magnani?" This provides the impetus for the last flashback scene.

At the town square Athos dedicates a memoral to his father. As he gropes for words, the narration springs a new cue on us: character voice-over. The band strikes up, and over a close-up of Athos we hear his voice ask: "Who is Athos Magnani—a traitor or a hero?" Voice-over questions mix with images previously shown: Magnani running through the forest, Draifa calling him a coward, Magnani designing his own murder, the rotating statue. Even Athos's speech to the townspeople picks up phrases we have heard earlier in the film. This play with frequency, repeating elements dramatized at earlier points in the syuzhet, is conventionally readable as character memory, but we have already seen that some of these images are equivocal: Athos cannot know of Draifa's recollection, and the bust shot is out of place. Yet if we take these repetitions as narrational commentary distinct from Athos's memory, the voice-over monologue remains a powerfully codified cue for subjectivity. The problem is exacerbated by a brief image of boys marching through a Tara street; this could be either a flashback or a cutaway to a simultaneous event. In sum, this last scene is no less equivocal than the earlier passages.

The film's play with order, then, engages us in a process of curiosity and suspense that involves not only the syuzhet's manipulation of the fabula but the syuzhet's own working out. This is accomplished by blocking normal access to the fabula through incompatible and insufficient cues. In general, what Hitchcock accomplished with Uncle Charlie's newspaper in a single scene of *Shadow of a Doubt*, Bertolucci does repeatedly throughout *The Spider's Stratagem*. The narration becomes overtly omniscient, alternately communicative and suppressive, and self-conscious to a very great degree.

This process reaches down to the stylistic tissue of the film. Mise-en-scène and camera movement are often used to signal self-consciousness and an omniscient range of knowledge, as well as to perpetuate the game of hypothesis testing. When Athos strides back to the opera house, his progress is shown in a series of long shots, some of which "inscribe" his trajectory into their composition, others of which trick us to expect him to emerge at the wrong point. The film's camera movements are striking in their insistence on making the camera a distinct entity with respect to the action filmed. A shot will lag behind a character's walk, dwelling on a portion of setting. Near the end of the film, Draifa bustles Athos into an adjoining room, and the camera loses sight of them. When it catches up, she has already fitted him into his father's jacket. The (quite Hitchcockian) delay in revealing Draifa's plan underlines the self-consciousness of the narration. At an earlier point, a camera

movement follows Draifa and Athos from room to room, and even though she faints, the camera continues on a rigidly lateral path, overtly withholding details of the situation. Most striking of all, perhaps, is the omniscient camera movement that "loses" Athos (fig. 6.28) in order to dwell on a sign bearing his name (fig. 6.29), and then moves on to catch up with him, only to frame him as exactly occluding his father's bust (fig.6.30). He moves off down the street (fig. 6.31), and his father's bust then occludes him (fig. 6.32). The tracking shot and the compositions flaunt the prophetic powers of the narration, foreshadowing the ambiguous parallels that will operate between father and son.

6.33
6.34

6.35
6.36

6.37

From a temporal perspective, the most important technique is editing, which not only governs the presentation of syuzhet order, as in the flashbacks, but also sets up a play with duration. In only one passage does the film expand fabula time, and in only one other is there compression. More often, each shot change offers either equivalence of syuzhet and fabula duration; or ellipsis; or an ambiguous case. A simple example of ellipsis is the cut from Draifa and Athos on the street to a shot of them climbing a hill (figs. 6.33–6.34). The discontinuity of figures and setting marks an omitted piece of fabula duration. An ambiguous case is afforded by a very early cut in the film. A sailor outside the train station points off and says, "Tara." Athos turns and looks up right (fig. 6.35). Cut to a long shot of the village (fig. 6.36). We might be inclined to take this as Athos's optical point of view, except that there is no cue for optical subjectivity in the framing of figure 6.36, and the next shot shows him walking down a Tara street (fig. 6.37). Thus the landscape shot could also be taken as an "objective" establishing shot, leading in to the shot of Athos in town. How we construct the space will affect duration: if figure 6.36 is a point-of-view shot, the cut will be seen as presenting continuous fabula duration, but if it is not, it can be taken as elliding part of the time of Athos's walk to town. Of course, a judgment of equivalence, ellipsis, or ambiguity cannot always be made instantly; often the development of a shot will retrospectively reveal the cut's effect on duration. But in this case we are never able to answer with certitude; the cut is permanently ambiguous.

6.38
6.39

Remarkably, *The Spider's Stratagem* contains almost exactly as many elliptical or ambiguous shot changes (138, by my count) as continuity cuts (137). Some of the ellipses, of course, are shot changes that link sequences (cuts, fades, dissolves), but most of the cuts set up an unusual play with duration. Put in terms of the viewer's activity, the many cuts that clearly skip over time or that *may* skip over time generate hypotheses about duration that are as contextually controlled and open-ended as those about fabula order. And the flashbacks' trick of playing with expectations also lurks behind the development of durational cues across the film.

The early passages of the film, which expose the premises of Athos's investigation, make heavy use of elliptical and ambiguous cues. Athos's arrival at the station and at Tara (e.g., figs. 6.35–6.37), his visit to Draifa, the evening during which he sits in the cafe and is locked in a stable, and the assault on him the next morning (figs. 6.23–6.25)—in each scene, almost every cut is equally likely to present either durational continuity or ellipsis/ambiguity. In these scenes, the film is establishing what I shall call later an internal narrational norm, a primacy effect pertaining not to the fabula events (e.g., what a character is initially like) but to schemata that the narration will employ. After the assault, Athos talks with the innkeeper's grandson, and here the narration for the first time cues us to construct a conventionally continuous time. Correct shot/reverse-shot cutting here suggests the durational equivalence of fabula and syuzhet (figs. 6.38–6.39). A device that is taken for granted in most films is *achieved* by this film's unique stylistic work.

Athos's second visit to Draifa recasts the film's use of temporal cues. This is the first scene in which a flashback appears, so our hypotheses must now widen to include the possibility that a shot change may manipulate order as well as duration. As we have seen, however, the first flashback is conventionally framed and does not pose a problem for constructing the fabula. But once the flashback has ended, the narration complicates matters by offering a barrage of ambiguous temporal (and spatial) cues. There is no establishing shot, only a series of medium shots of Athos and Draifa (figs. 6.40–6.49). She is arranging flowers while they

6.40   *6.44*   *6.48*   *6.49*
6.41   *6.45*
6.42   *6.46*
6.43   *6.47*

talk about Magnani's old friends and enemies. The sequence
stands in contrast to Athos's shot/reverse shot talk with the
boy because the characters' eyelines are inconsistent and
the settings change from shot to shot. Furthermore, Draifa is
constantly arranging different sprays of flowers at various
points in one (or more) rooms. We might attribute the discontinuities to ellipses, but on the sound track the conversation continues without apparent omission. Still, no diegetic
sound bleeds over the cuts, so we cannot be sure whether
continuity or compression is at work. With the exceptions of
the shots shown in figures 6.43–6.45, the narration presents
insufficient cues to allow us to pinpoint fabula duration.

If the cut thus suggests an indefinite ellipsis, the narration
shortly reverses itself. While Athos questions Gaibazzi, the
older man sniffs the pork rumps hanging in his curing room.
In mainstream cinema, the fade-in and -out links entire
sequences and indicates that a lengthy passage of time is
omitted. Here, however, fades link brief shots, and the duration skipped over is negligible—no more than a minute or so,
possibly only a few seconds. The fades here not only contex-
tualize yet another cue in unique fashion but also make it
difficult to predict how the sequence will signal its end. Thus
the narration freshens up its game with the spectator by
introducing new gambits as the film goes along.

In general, as the narration presents more flashbacks, the
play with durational ambiguity diminishes. Manipulation of
order assumes greater importance. Each old comrade tells
his story, and both the narrating present and the flashbacks
use cuts that are clearly continuous or clearly elliptical. Even
Draifa's equivocal flashback contains very few cuts that are

durationally problematic. And after the flashbacks, the film settles for some time into a more conventional approach, relying almost entirely upon the equivalence of syuzhet and fabula duration and using even ellipses sparingly. Nonetheless, our progress through the syuzhet has taught us that no stability lasts forever. A very striking scene in the theater, when Athos talks with Beccaccia, alternates ellipses and continuity in ways that ask us to keep our guard up. At the film's climax and in its last two sequences, a play with duration returns reinvigorated.

Athos is at the train station, about to leave town, when he hears over the village loudspeaker the opening bars of *Rigoletto*, broadcast from the Tara theater. He strides back to town as the performance begins, and after interrogating some old women in a cart outside the theater, he goes in. From the moment he leaves the train station, the narration employs that convention of compression whereby diegetic sound continues across the cuts while the images present ellipses between shots. (*Play Time* was our chief example earlier.) Athos's walk, his conversation with the women, and his entry into the theater are cut elliptically, but the offscreen music signals durational continuity. Once he enters the theater, however, there is a cut on the sound track as well, elliding a portion of the score. Then, as we see him in a box watching his father's old cronies, the music resumes and continues to the climactic moment ("Ah! Maledizione!") at which his father was shot. In building up to this, the narration provides a virtuosic series of cuts that shows the cronies disappearing from the box one by one as the music runs on without break. Such flaunted gaps on the image track effectively render the conventional schema inoperative: we have to posit two separate durations, one continuous for the sound, one discontinuous for the image. Like the flashback scenes, this sequence shows the power of a context to "estrange" ordinary schemata and cues.

And now the ambiguity that has informed shot changes in the present moves squarely into the past. A flashback shows Magnani confessing his treachery while his pals rough him up. As he cries out, the narration cuts very quickly between the fight and landscape views of Tara similar to that seen when Athos arrived (fig. 6.36). The landscape shots are ambiguous in two respects. They may be construed as being in the present (like the Tara view seen when Athos arrived) or in the past (cutaways from the scene of the fight). Second, the landscape shots may be taken as durationally continuous (cue: the offscreen cries of Magnani) or as expansions by insertion, stretching out the moment of violence (cue: the cuts back to similar positions in the fight). This last full-scale flashback thus poses problems of duration congruent with those raised in the "present-tense" sequences.

The film's last scene testifies to the importance of durational manipulation for the narration's overall goals. Athos waits at the station platform. A loudspeaker announces that the Parma train will be twenty minutes late. He sits down on a bench as another announcement intones that the train will now be thirty-five minutes late. He asks for today's *Oggi*, but it hasn't arrived: "Sometimes they forget we exist." Athos idly watches passing trackmen. Cut to a shot which recalls the durational split of image and sound in the opera scene. Athos is now sitting on the edge of the platform (visual ellipsis) while the strokes of the passing handcar are still audible (sonic continuity). The camera tracks right as he looks down, and we tilt down to weedy, overgrown tracks. Inference: an unrealistically long span of time has passed, and no train has come. Athos reenters the shot and kneels by the rails, then looks up (fig. 6.50). Cut to a long shot of Tara (fig. 6.51), much as we had seen it in the first scene (fig. 6.36); the image is just as ambiguous by its placement here. Cut back to the rails; the camera tracks right until undergrowth has blotted out the rails altogether. With these final three cuts, the editing has claimed its right to ambiguate duration indefinitely. We can take the cuts as temporally continuous or as containing ellipses that last as long as we like. Moreover, the final camera movement eliminates Athos to reveal more and more overgrown tracks, as if the duration of the shot were recording the foliage's creeping growth. What happens to Athos? Is he trapped in Tara forever? Instead of the exclusive hypotheses which characterize the climax and epilogue of the classical Hollywood film, the "open" ending of the art film offers a heterogeneous mixture

6.50   *6.51*

of unresolvable hypotheses. The last shot of *The Spider's Stratagem*, in emphasizing the ambiguity of duration itself, thus extends the play with time beyond the close of the film.

From the temporal standpoint, *The Spider's Stratagem* can be seen as working with and against dominant schemata to loosen up classical bonds among syuzhet, style, and fabula. The critic's task becomes the explanation of how the narration generates an ambivalent denotation by blocking access to a coherent chain of cause and effect, by deploying incomplete and inconsistent cues, and by making the very process of narration an object of self-conscious suspense and curiosity. Chapter 10 will show that this approach is itself conventionalized within an entire mode of narration. For now, let us simply recall how the film's title offers a provocative analogy. Connotatively, it can be read as applying to Draifa's ploys to entrap Athos in Tara or to Magnani's scenario for his own death; but in my terms here, "the spider's stratagem" aptly characterizes a narration that lures us with the promise of an intelligible fabula and then enmeshes us in elusive but tenacious formal processes.

7. Narration and Space

A single concept has dominated reflection on filmic space—position. For mainstream mimetic theories, each image is attributed to an invisible observer incarnated in the camera; this observer is at once narrator and spectator. The totalized space built up from editing is then attributed to an idealized invisible witness, the occupant of an absolute position, Pudovkin's "observer ideally mobile in space and time." Diegetic theories are no different in this regard. Here space is said to be "enunciated" by the film, but since no entity can speak space, theorists tend to slip back into mimetic assumptions. Discourse becomes a series of views, having their source in the viewer's positions.

Just as there is more to narration than the camera, so there is more to cinematic space than effects of position. Rather than conceive of the spectator as the apex of a literal or metaphorical pyramid of vision, we can treat the construction of space dynamically. The syuzhet's presentation of information can be facilitated or blocked by the style's representation of space. No theory of narration can simply omit questions of position, but they need to be integrated into a broader account of how films mobilize spatial perception and cognition for storytelling ends.

Constructing Space

The account I propose distinguishes itself from two principal trends in the psychology of visual representation.[1] One trend, close in spirit to that of traditional approaches to narration, has been called the "perspectivist" theory. Its principal exponent, James J. Gibson, has argued that the perceiver's understanding of a visual field is uniquely determined, or "specified," by the laws of geometrical optics. Under normal conditions, the psychophysical stimulus suffices to produce accurate perception; there is no need to reckon in mental processes. According to this theory, a picture can, if it obeys the laws of linear perspective, correctly depict the invariant structure of a viewer's optic array. A film can go beyond this arrested image and *specify* the invariants, thus achieving a delimited array "analogous to the temporary field of view of a human observer in a natural environment surrounding the observer."[2]

The second trend is the Gestaltist one, usually associated with Rudolf Arnheim's work. Here mental operations play a much larger role. The mind is assumed to structure vision through *Gestalten* or what Arnheim calls "visual concepts." Laws of simplicity, good continuation, and so forth govern the structure we "read out" of the world. No picture, therefore, faithfully copies nature in the empirical manner perspectivism assumes. Arnheim sees all pictures as equally artificial in that they rely on the two-dimensional conditions of the medium to convey and express meaning. Perspective is no more faithful to everyday perception than is any other system. "The rule that controls the rendering of depth in the plane prescribes that no aspect of visual structure will be deformed unless space perception requires it—regardless of what a mechanically correct projection would call for."[3] To produce a convincing picture, expressiveness and formal clarity come first, and the mathematics of perspective must be adjusted to fit these demands. As is generally known, Arnheim applied these assumptions to film in order to show that "art begins where mechanical reproduction leaves off."[4]

To some extent, the perspectivist and the Gestaltist views can be reconciled, at least as far as pictorial perception is concerned. Often Gibson and Arnheim aim to explain different things. Gibson likes likeness, Arnheim loves liveliness. Gibson is drawn to representational art, good or bad, while Arnheim favors abstract art and works of quality. Both views offer a wealth of suggestions for analyzing spatial representation in film, but from the theoretical standpoint of this book, the most appropriate theory of spatial perception is that afforded by the "Constructivist" trend.

Chapter 3 has already maintained that a Constructivist theory can explain crucial aspects of spectatorial activity. The film proffers cues upon which the spectator works by applying those knowledge clusters called schemata. Guided by schemata, the spectator makes assumptions and inferences and casts hypotheses about story events. These assumptions, inferences, and hypotheses are checked against material presented to the perceiver. In Chapters 4 and 5, I suggested that this material is organized into a syuzhet which cues the spectator to construct a fabula according to schemata of logic, time, and space. Film style usually supports the construction of the fabula, principally by being compositionally motivated. The Constructivist approach treats the perceiver as constantly active—applying prototypes, slotting items into evolving templatelike macrostructures, testing and revising procedures for making sense of the material. Crucial points in the process are the syuzhet's presentation of gaps in fabula information. The previous chapter adduced some major temporal schemata in narrative cinema, such as 1-2-3 order and conventional relations of syuzhet and fabula duration. Space can also be considered from a Constructivist standpoint, and here we can draw on the rich body of work produced by E. H. Gombrich, R. L. Gregory, and Julian Hochberg.

The perspectivist insists that the stimulus specifies the percept, but the Constructivist believes that the stimulus is insufficient to dictate perceptual experience.[5] Perspectivist theory treats perception as essentially a filtered selection of invariants from the range of available stimuli; on the Constructivist theory, perception is an inferential process which

7.1

reworks stimuli. For the Gestaltist, perception is the imposition of a mental order upon the world, but these *Gestalten* operate in a static, absolute manner. For Constructivist theory, perception is a temporal process of building the percept in a probabilistic fashion.

This is not to say that spatial perception is wholly a "top-down" process. (See Chapter 3.) It seems evident that even though the visual stimulus insufficiently determines the percept, some perceptual inferences are drawn in an involuntary, virtually instantaneous manner.[6] Yet this does not invalidate the exploratory, trial-and-error quality of the operations. Visual perception, for instance, "automatically" treats an array as representing a three-dimensional layout. The perceiver might be wrong in this inference, but it is of evolutionary advantage to an organism to incline toward this sort of error rather than its opposite.

Art, I suggested in Chapter 3, involves both bottom-up and top-down perceptual processes. To the extent that a painting or a film image can create equivalent cues for real-world stimuli, the sensory system infers a state of affairs "automatically." For example, contours or variations in color intensity are reliable cues for inferring the edges of objects. At the same time, expectations, memory, recognition, attention, and other top-down processes are also crucial in our grasping of pictorial space. Prior knowledge of the picture's purpose, its medium, and its stylistic traditions shapes how we construct the spatial percept.

We can start our analysis of spatial representation by assuming that the spectator works upon cues supplied by the medium and by stylistic conventions. For instance, the medium of painting lacks certain cues for depth, such as movement parallax (the sense that movement of the spectator induces corresponding changes in the internal relations of elements in the optic array). At various points in the history of painting, different cues available within the medium have been deployed to suggest pictorial depth: the use of overlapping contours, various perspective systems, treatments of light and shade, and so forth. What is important about the notion of "cue" is that it implies that any

pictorial representation is inherently incomplete and potentially ambiguous. The image does not in itself uniquely determine the kind of objects represented or the depth relations among them.

This is dramatized in the celebrated experiments of Adelbert Ames. He constructed ingenious peepshow views in which apparently solid bars cut through equally solid trapezoids, in which objects moving away from the viewer appeared to get larger, in which a tangle of wires and sticks seemed unequivocally to be a chair, and most notoriously in which an ordinary person could become a giant or a dwarf in an apparently normal room (fig. 7.1). Ames's experiments raised two points which are important for Constructivist theory. First, they showed that an unlimited number of objects can create the same percept.[7] The Ames chair was visible as such only from the peephole; from any other position it was a Tatlinesque assemblage. But this entails that an infinite number of other combinations of sticks and wire could provoke the same percept at the station point. Now, many theorists would deny that this finding has much to do with ordinary experience; Gibson, for one, has insisted on the binocular and ambulatory nature of real perception. But the Ames demonstrations do interestingly approximate the conditions of pictorial experience. As Gombrich points out, all images are inherently ambiguous in the way that the Ames illusions are. A great many possible configurations of objects, of any size or shape or distance apart, could be imagined "behind" the picture plane. Instead of a receding pavement of uniformly square tiles, there could be a sloping ramp of irregular ones. Instead of a costumed man, a scatter of garments flung up and frozen, with a huge head miles off that happens to coincide, on our view, with the top edge of a collar. That we do not comprehend pictures in this outlandish way suggests that we infer "probable worlds" on cognitive grounds, not purely perceptual ones.

The Ames exhibits also illustrate the stubborn insistence with which we cling to familiar assumptions about our world of regular shapes, right angles, and consistency in depth. The room illusion, for example, fools us partly because we expect a room's corners to form right angles and we expect perspective diminution when walls recede from us. Because of these assumptions, we hypothesize a world of giants and dwarfs. In fact, the room is systematically distorted, a fact which is visible from other vantage points. Ames's demonstrations show the importance of our expectations about familiar size, overlap, perspectival relations, and the "carpentered world" we inhabit. Interestingly, even when we know how the illusion was rigged, we still have difficulty seeing the space as it is; we cannot, it seems, perceive spaces so radically unlike those we have learned.

What overcomes the incomplete and ambiguous cues that pictures offer is a process of schema-driven perception. In confronting a picture, we frame hypotheses about what the medium can represent and about how to interpret the cues we are given. In representational art, the principal spatial schemata are those which construe pictorial cues as representing a layout of objects in an environment. Constructivist psychology emphasizes the priority of object perception in our everyday world. "Perception," R. L. Gregory writes, "involves betting on the most probable interpretation of sensory data, in terms of the world of objects. Perception involves a kind of inference from sensory data to object-reality."[8] Attri-

butes of size, shape, and distance depend upon object hypotheses, as Ames's enterprise vividly shows. Gombrich puts it well: "We are blind to the other possible configurations because we literally 'cannot imagine' these unlikely objects. They have no name and no habitation in the universe of our experience."[9] Representational pictures do not portray space as such, only recognizable things in recognizable situations.[10] Across the history of visual art, artists create conventions, pictorial schemata, which viewers learn to tally with their ordinary schemata for recognizing objects in space.

The priority of object perception does not mean that the picture "as a picture" is unimportant. For one thing, the limits of the medium invite us to notice the difference between, say, how oil paint and watercolor suggest texture. And at any moment the perceiver can switch attention from the depicted object to the picture plane itself. Pictorial styles invite this switch by their handling of depth, composition, color, and surface treatment. Moreover, the perceiver's knowledge of other pictures yields a storehouse of traditional schemata which can be compared to this work. Gombrich stresses that an interplay of stereotype and novelty informs both artistic creation and pictorial perception. Each schema is like a notation system that lets some information escape, and the spectator is often expected to imagine what is absent. There is, in short, a continual give-and-take between the recognition of the depicted space and the awareness of visual style.

The Constructivist approach stresses the dynamic quality of perception. Armed with hypotheses about how to make sense of what is presented, the spectator tests them over time. For instance, in viewing pictures people act the way a cognitive theory would predict. The perceptual act is not a kind of snapshot of the whole picture. Viewers search the composition, fixating briefly but repeatedly on certain regions: sharp contours, points of juncture, angles, unusually bright or dark patches. These are areas most likely to provide information about objects' identities and depth relationships. These are also areas that could quickly disconfirm any hypotheses about the represented space. Moreover, the

7.2
7.3

viewer's scan paths are shaped by a search for information of a specific sort, and this can be governed by a prior "mental set"—the picture's title, a hypothesis about the action represented.

Julian Hochberg has proposed visual search as a paramount instance of how perception involves knowledge, anticipations, and decisions. He argues that scanning a picture includes predictions about what visual edges depict surfaces, and these predictions are tested by successive saccadic movements guided by peripheral vision. Presented with a picture, my scanning will be driven by schemata which pose questions (Is this a cat?), guide visual sampling (If it is a cat, there should be an ear here), and store the results in memory.[11] These schemata are likely to be based upon the most probable characteristics of the world and upon general hypotheses which resemble the Gestalt "laws." Thus the figure/ground relation may not be a form wired into our brain fields, as Gestaltists believed, but a learned expectation about likely consequences of eye movements.[12] Picture perception will then consist of adapting a schema to what each glance supplies.[13] How then do we arrive at a sense of the image as a whole? Hochberg suggests that thanks to preattentive processes (e.g., knowledge about what to expect) and to the fact that each glance is a test for consistency, the spectator creates a schematic "map" of the picture in memory. This map is not necessarily passive or imagistic, since the viewer can store spatial information in a schematic or skeletal form.[14]

The Constructivist theory of pictorial perception is still being tested and revised, but it already holds great promise for the study of filmic space. On this account, a representational film provides a range of spatial cues for objects, depth, and contiguity. These cues are "coded" in terms of a specific medium. Compared with painting and photography, cinema might seem to deploy more cues and thus be more "realistic" in its spatial possibilities. Even film, however, cannot be free of the ambiguity and incompleteness of all pictorial representation. Apparent movement is "bottom-up" and mandatory. No one can choose *not* to see movement in a film. Yet these effects are still the product of the organism's inferential activity, here at a psychophysical level. Similarly, the

Ames illusions work as well on film as in the still photo. Watching two people move about the distorted room does not destroy the illusion (figs. 7.2–7.3). It is also evident that creating space for a film makes use of expectancies, decisions, and prior knowledge in a way compatible with the

Constructivist scenario. If we usually "lose" the screen surface, that is because we search for a recognizable world of
objects beyond it.[15] We also scan the image and fixate on
spots of likely information—faces, eyes, hands; what
Arnheim calls the visual "nodes" formed by compositional
vectors.[16] Film editing, as Hochberg himself has begun to
show, can be integrated into a "cognitive map" account of
how we construct a total space. Most pertinent to our purposes here, in a narrative film the drive to construct a coherent fabula out of what we see and hear will lead us to seek
particular spatial cues and rely upon particular spatial schemata.

We can now usefully return to the problems of spatial
"position" emphasized in mimetic and diegetic theories.
How would the theory I propose counter an explanation of
the image in terms of "perspectival positioning"? How would
it counter an appeal to the "ideal observer" formed by the
passage from shot to shot?

Perspective and the Spectator

"Perspective" is not a unitary phenomenon. As Chapter 1
mentioned, Renaissance artists and thinkers theorized two
principal "scientific" systems. The first is linear perspective,
the most famous type being *central* or "Albertian" perspective. Here, orthogonals converge to a single, central
vanishing point (fig. 7.4). Other sorts of linear perspective
include *angular* or oblique perspective, which utilizes two
compatible vanishing points; and *inclined* perspective,
which creates three consistent vanishing points and makes
no sides of the object parallel to the picture plane. Besides
these variants of linear perspective, Leonardo da Vinci proposed a second system, since known as *synthetic* perspective. This system renders some parallel edges as curves on
the picture plane, in order to respect the curvature of the
ocular image. Both "scientific" systems offer a mathematically measurable scenic space.

Other perspective systems are capable of organizing the
fictive space of the picture, but they do so without benefit of a
theory of the behavior of light. In *parallel* perspective, a
schema common in Asian art, parallel edges running into
depth are rendered as such on the picture plane. (See fig.
7.5.) Here, orthogonals never converge. In so-called *in-*
verted perspective, parallel edges in the three-dimensional
space are rendered as converging in front of the picture

7.5. *Parallel perspective in the treatment of orthogonals. Ippitsusai Bunchō,* The Actor Sanogawa Ichimatsu as the Dancer Chūshō in Imayō dōjōji,

Ichimura Theater (*1769*). *Elvehjem Museum of Art, University of Wisconsin– Madison; bequest of John Hasbrouck Van Vleck.*

7.6. *Inverted perspective in an Indian miniature.* A Lady Waiting for her Lover (*late 18th century*). *Elvehjem Museum of Art, University of Wisconsin–*

Madison; lent by Mrs. Earnest C. Watson.

plane (fig. 7.6). In *vanishing area* perspective, orthogonals converge into depth, but only at a general region of the picture. *Axial* or "vanishing axis" perspective makes the orthogonals meet at a vertical axis, creating a herringbone pattern. Both vanishing area and axial perspective can be found in medieval and Gothic art. B. A. Carter identifies yet another variety practiced in the early Renaissance: *bifocal* perspective, in which orthogonal edges of different objects converge at two incompatible vanishing points.[17]

Perspective, of whatever sort, is not the only way a picture conveys depth. There are many sorts of depth cues, such as overlap, familiar size, and others we shall examine. The viewer thus has a great many data with which to infer objects and spatial relations, and these data do not all entail assuming a Euclidean vantage point onto the depicted space.

It is nevertheless the case that scientific perspective offers very strong and internally consistent depth cues, especially ones involving the behavior of parallel lines in depth. But it does not follow that spectators take an image constructed in scientific perspective as creating an illusion of phenomenal reality. A picture constructed in accord with Albertian or Leonardian precepts will approach such absolute realism only if viewed monocularly from a fixed vantage point. Normally our movement around a picture creates marginal distortions and an awareness of the picture's surface. Even during the Renaissance, there was a recognition that scientific perspective was not to be understood as a kind of *trompe l'oeil*. Many theorists knew that linear perspective did not properly foreshorten vertical dimensions, and artists often broke mathematical rules to achieve particular effects. Pictures were placed in architectural sites that forebade visitors to stand at the "correct" point.[18] There is also good evidence that for the Renaissance perceiver optical verisimilitude was only one of many criteria for judging a painting. Michael Baxandall has shown that the connoisseur was not to feel lost in an illusory scene but to admire the virtuosity of a painter who could use perspective to call forth the viewer's skills of inference, memory, and imagination. According to Brunelleschi's biographer, even he deliberately stopped short of perfect illusion in his mirrors-and-peephole setup: "He left it up to the spectator's judgment, as is done in paintings by other artists."[19]

In fact, an illusionist notion of perspective forgets that true *trompe l'oeil* operates only when we cannot locate the painting's surface at all. Pozzo accomplished this in his St. Ignazio ceiling, which is so far from the spectator that binocularity and movement do not call attention to the painted surface. Or the painter can depict very thin objects—postage stamps, letters tacked to a board, a flattened paper sack. Before such figures, we may move around and use both eyes all we want, and we will still find it hard to see the configura-

tion as a painting. Under normal viewing conditions, the greater a picture's perspectival depth, the *less* likely we are to be fooled.

Scientific perspective, it might be claimed, does not create optical illusions, but it does present an ideal vision. Stephen Heath attributes this to "the confirmed and central master-spectator," owner of a "sure and centrally embracing view," "the detached, untroubled eye . . . free from the body, outside process, purely looking."[20] But this is too general a description of the matter. There is nothing unique to scientific perspective about a unified subject position. Pictures done in nonscientific perspective, such as figures 7.5–7.6, present as detached and untroubled a view as one could ask for. Our position cannot be defined by Euclidean coordinates, but it is no less that of a "master-spectator, serenely 'present.' "[21] Thus the ideology of the visible, and the unity of self which it is said to promote, occur in many other pictorial systems. Scientific perspective answers to more specific ideological needs. Alberti and his successors used their invention to demonstrate the rational nature of space, the power of measurement and prediction, and the beauty of harmonious relation among parts. Linear perspective, Panofsky notes, "is a mathematical method of organizing space so as to meet the requirements of both 'correctness' and 'harmony' and is thus fundamentally akin to a discipline which sought to achieve precisely the same thing with respect to the human and animal body: the theory of proportions."[22] The master-spectator of perspective is the scientific mind, realizing the underlying beauty and system in the world. Linear perspective was, in this sense, a kind of experimental demonstration of scientific principles; or, as Samuel Edgerton puts it, "a means of —literally—squaring what was seen empirically with the traditional medieval belief that God spreads his grace through the universe according to the laws of geometric optics."[23]

Because scientific perspective portrays things as they are believed to be, there has been a tendency to consider it as being no less "conventional" and "arbitrary" than other pictorial systems. This relativistic position has been bolstered by reference to several assumptions. Scientific perspective is said to have no claim to truth because (1) historical circumstances brought it about; (2) artists and perceivers have to learn it as a system; and (3) it falls short of complete replication of phenomenal reality. The literature of this controversy is enormous; here I can only indicate how each claim could be refuted from a Constructivist stance.

1. Of course there are historical causes for the discovery of scientific perspective, including the clichéd "Renaissance humanism" as well as concrete practices: cartography, surveying, architectural theory, rhetorical theory, and terraced agriculture. But all this does not invalidate scientific perspective's claims to superior accuracy. The telescope and the microscope also spring from social demands, but we still believe in each tool's objective power to reveal asteroids and microbes.

2. As for having to learn perspective: There is, Gombrich points out, a continuum between natural skills and acquired ones. It seems evident that the ability to comprehend "scientific" perspectival images is much more easily acquired than, say, the ability to read a language. Perhaps perspectival cues build upon some natural skills, such as the organism's ability to detect surfaces and edges.[24]

3. No pictorial system can completely copy empirical space. A Constructivist theory emphasizes that every pictorial system aims to serve certain functions. Linear perspective would add nothing to a placard warning us to beware the dog; here you want a caricature of salient expressive features. But if you want your picture to convey information about the relative locations, sizes, and dimensions of objects in a measurable space as seen from one spot, then scientific perspective is not as "arbitrary" as other systems. For this purpose, scientific perspective yields the most and the most accurate information about what can be seen and, just as important, it yields no false information. If geometrical perspective did not work in this way, cartographers and architectural designers would be able to use any representational system they pleased, to the grief of us all.

The motion picture camera is constructed to produce an image by virtue of the central projection of light rays. Many film theorists have taken this to imply that the film image is condemned to repeat the single spatial schema, and thus the "positionality," of Albertian linear perspective. This conclusion is utterly unwarranted. Like photographers, filmmakers transform the light that enters the camera. One way they do this is by arranging the objects to be filmed, and this procedure can counter the perspective effect. Although the camera is committed to the central projection of light rays, the composition of the scene can contain two or three vanishing points (as in figs. 7.7 and 7.8). The filmmaker can go further, as in figure 7.9. If linear perspective is defined by vanishing points and the regular recession of planes, figure 7.9 is not in linear perspective. This is not to say that such a shot lacks depth cues, but the depth depicted here owes nothing to the schemata of scientific perspective. The same holds true for the Expressionist landscape of figure 7.10. German Expressionist cinema's use of false perspective presents us with many "Ames rooms."

Theorists who see the camera as doomed to replicate central perspective tend to wave aside variations in lens lengths, but these too can override Albertian schemata. In figure 7.11, the photographer's telephoto lens has flattened the stage space, creating a curious effect on the upturned surfaces. The nearer edges of the bench and the table look shorter than the more distant ones, creating a mixture of inverted perspective (the table) and parallel perspective (the bench). Brecht, the second figure from the right, might have enjoyed being portrayed in perspectival systems usually associated with Asian art. Measurement reveals that the nearer edges are in fact longer than the rear ones and that the orthogonals will eventually converge to a vanishing point. But knowing this does not change the illusion; the objects still look wrong. This is because long focal length lenses decrease apparent depth and make any slanted, foreshortened surface more parallel and less receding. (See fig. 7.12.) Telephoto lenses can violate other laws of linear perspective, such as mathematical diminution of scale; with very long lenses, the more distant of two identical objects may appear larger—an effect Kurosawa frequently exploits in *Red Beard*.[25] (See fig. 7.13.) If lens length has the capacity to create effects of "nonscientific" perspective systems, it

7.7. *Angular perspective yields two vanishing points in this shot from* Manhandled: *the figures are arranged to recede toward the door, but the lines of the architecture create another vanishing point off right.*

7.8. *The lines of trees provide three vanishing points—one central, one on each side—in this shot from* The Spider's Stratagem.

7.9. The Goldwyn Follies

7.10. Raskolnikov

7.11. *Bertolt Brecht in rehearsal with the Berliner Ensemble.*

7.12. *The telephoto lens creates parallel perspective in* Dead Pigeon on Beethoven Street; *compare fig. 7.5.*

7.13. *The young intern stands at the woman's waist, yet the telephoto lens pulls him nearly as far forward as her head is; from* Red Beard.

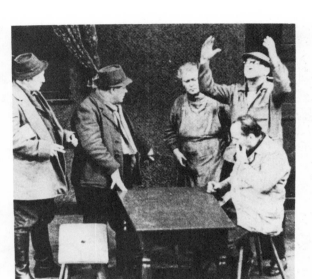

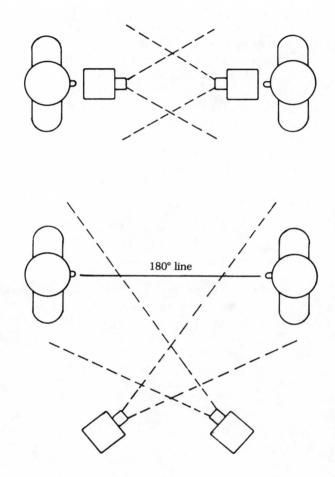

does not matter that the camera is built on the Albertian model. The Renaissance masters of perspective knew that the mechanical projection of light rays was something quite apart from the perceptual experience of the picture.

Ideal Positionality: Shot/reverse Shot

In recent film literature, the problem of the viewer's totalized view in the mind's eye has been most sharply posed with respect to the stylistic figure known as shot/reverse shot. In many films there occurs a pair of shots depicting complementary areas of space. The clearest case follows this pattern:

1. A character looks offscreen.
2. A second character looks offscreen in the opposite direction.

From this pair of shots, the spectator typically infers that the two areas are more or less contiguous and that the characters are looking at each other. How are we to explain these inferences? Before we consider Jean-Pierre Oudart's account of "suture," we should quickly clear away some misreadings it has undergone.

A terminological ambiguity surrounds "shot/reverse shot" (or *champ-contrechamp*, "field-counterfield"). Many commentators have assumed that this necessarily depicts one segment of space and then depicts a segment exactly opposed to it, a 180-degree "reverse" or "counterfield" as in figure 7.14. Typically, however, the shot/reverse-shot device posits that each shot represents, from a more or less oblique angle, one endpoint of an imaginary 180-degree line running through the scenographic space, as in figure 7.15. The layout of figure 7.14 is an exceptional variant of shot/reverse shot, since it puts each camera position exactly on the 180-degree axis; this is conventional for subjective point-of-view cutting. On the other hand, note that the conventional schema depicted in the second figure (7.15) does *not* represent either character from the other's optical standpoint.

Oudart specifically rules out of his province cases like figure 7.14. What he calls the suture does *not* operate in that "subjective" cinema which puts the camera in the character's "optical" place.[26] Oudart's commentators have misunderstood this. Daniel Dayan, claiming to paraphrase Oudart's argument, treats the suture as applying to point-of-view cutting, whereby shot 1 asks the question "Who is seeing this?" and shot 2 answers by revealing the character who owns the view of the space presented just before. As an

account of typical shot/reverse-shot cutting this is inaccurate, and as an account of subjective cutting it is incomplete.[27] Nick Browne follows Dayan's account and
claims that a conventional shot/reverse-shot passage reveals
one character as "the owner of the glance that corresponds to
the first shot."[28] In fact, Oudart finds such cases disturbing:
the viewer becomes "uneasy" when the camera "actually
occupies the place of the character in that position."[29]

Oudart's account of suture is subtler and more interesting
than his commentators' version. The suture does not operate
when there is what he calls a "mutual articulation of images"—e.g., an analytical cut which enlarges a portion of a
long shot. He claims that in the shot/reverse-shot figure, the
first shot entails a space offscreen, behind the camera, "the
fourth side, a pure field of absence."[30] The next shot in the
series reveals that something occupies that offscreen space.
The spectator must anticipate and recall: the first image
foreshadows what could replace it, while the second image
makes sense only as an answer to its predecessor. There are,
Oudart adds, two requirements for the suturing effect. First,
the camera angles must be oblique to the filmed material
(i.e., not perpendicular or straight-on). Second, the same
portion of space must be represented at least twice, once in
the visual field and once as an offscreen presence. Thus the
suture operates by creating gaps and then filling them, im-
plying an imaginary space immediately shown in the next
shot.

Oudart wants to prove that this backing-and-filling movement, this process of stitching across a gap, helps narration
construct space. The first shot implies an offscreen area
which is occupied by a presence which Oudart calls the
Absent One. Note that the shot does not suggest a perspectival *point of vision*, only an offscreen *field* or *zone*. The shot
is not the record of a glance but the sign of an absence. The
Absent One is not a character, only an offscreen presence
constructed by the viewer. In sutured cinema, Oudart
claims, not a character but the *author or narrator* can be
identified with the Absent One.[31] The suture operates when,
in shot/reverse shot, "the appearance of a lack perceived as a
Someone (the Absent One) is followed by its abolition by

someone (or something) placed within the same field."[32] All
that is necessary is that the Absent One's field be shown to
contain objects or characters. Shot/reverse-shot cutting
plays down narration by creating the sense that no scenographic space remains unaccounted for. If shot 2 shows that
something is "on the other side" of shot 1, there is no place
for the narrator to hide.

Oudart's argument is suggestive on many counts. He
indicates some ways that the filmmaker can foreground the
suture—by flaunting the oblique camera angle, by denying
us an establishing shot, by slowing the rhythm of shot/
reverse-shot cutting. He also sketches some alternatives to
sutured cinema (e.g., a film practice which fetishizes the
very framing effects and shifts in camera position that sutured cinema closes off). Most important, he makes a start
toward characterizing the viewing activities that the spectator often engages in—anticipation, recollection, and recognition of the spaces which narration presents. His explanation nonetheless remains cumbersome and imprecise.

To posit a phantom narrator as the creator of shot 1 is to fall
back into the invisible-observer account, whereby the
camera is the eye of a witness. A shot is not necessarily
grasped as a record of anyone's absence. A shot is attributed
to a narrator only in the presence of specific cues and
through the application of certain schemata. The shot/re-
verse shot affords Oudart a privileged example; he would
have had much more trouble showing that an analytical cut
or a cutaway involves a hide-and-seek game with the narrator in any related sense.

Oudart is hampered by an inadequate conception of spectatorial activity. He claims that the suture channels energies
that the appearance of the shot itself releases. The spectator
reads the isolated image in several stages: (1) object recognition; (2) discovery of the elasticity of cinematic space;
(3) discovery of the frame and realization that the image has
been created to have an effect; (4) realization of the objects
as signifiers of the absent creator; and (5) unification of the
image around a semantic meaning, a "signifying sum."[33]
The suture then contains this discovery by attributing the
space to the narrator in the offscreen zone. Yet this explana-

7.16. To Be or Not To Be
7.17. To Be or Not To Be

tion suggests that the viewer builds the meaning of each shot from the ground up (an oddly empiricist notion, given Oudart's emphasis on the role of anticipation and memory). In the absence of suture, Oudart's spectator learns nothing and must repeat the same cycle every time the shot changes. Furthermore, Oudart appears to claim the suture as an unconscious process (he borrows the term from Lacanian psychoanalysis). Yet all the operations he describes must occur in what Freud calls the "preconscious," since they are not repressed and there is no resistance to an analyst's bringing them to light.

A Constructivist account would propose that we come to the image already "tuned," prepared to test spatial, temporal, and "logical" schemata against what the shot presents. In this sense, the "signifying sum" often *precedes*, as a hypothesis, the perception of the object. We can thus locate "suture" within the general repertoire of editing schemata that govern mainstream filmmaking. For instance, classical narrative cinema establishes conventional, more or less probable alternatives for spatial representation. A long shot can plausibly be followed by a long shot of a different locale, another long shot of the same locale, or a closer view of the space; the last alternative is the most likely. Cutting within a locale is most likely to base itself upon shot/reverse-shot patterns, typically motivated by eyelines. Contrary to Oudart, the viewer checks the shot against what he or she expected to see and adjusts hypotheses accordingly. By using conventional schemata to produce and test hypotheses about a string of shots, the viewer often knows each shot's salient spatial information *before* it appears.

Schemata and hypotheses work with cues, and here Oudart misses not only particular elements but the underlying purposes they fulfill. Camera angle and an implicit space offscreen can, as he says, be significant cues; but so can dialogue, eyelines, landmarks in the setting, figure orientation, and shot scale. Take a conventional shot/reverse-shot exchange such as figures 7.16–7.17. Firm spatial hypotheses are encouraged by redundant cues: the shoulders in the foregrounds present strong landmarks, while complementary body positions and eyelines enable the spec-

tator to assume that an imaginary axis of action, or 180-degree line, connects the characters. Even shot scale is commensurate for each figure, creating symmetrical mirror image framings. Thus the specific cues presented by the shot, emphasized by the narrative context and rendered likely by stylistic conventions, will affect whether we construct an offscreen space or a self-conscious narration. That is, the spatial representation is assumed to be adequate *for its narrational purpose* (which can of course vary). No need to posit a phantom presence offscreen; Oudart's absent field goes unremarked as long as it is presumed consistent with what we see and as long as the salient features of what is on screen confirm our spatial and causal hypotheses. Only when cues become inconsistent does the spectator start to notice narrational interventions. Recall our deviant shot/reverse-shot scene from *The Spider's Stratagem* (figs. 6.40–6.49). Here, *non*-redundant cues of setting, figure movement, and eyelines forbid us to settle on a satisfactory hypothesis about the scene. (One room? Many rooms? Continuous duration? Ellipsis?)

One factor that permits this play is the absence of any shot which would define the relative positions of Athos and Draifa. Establishing shots are ignored by Oudart, who is concerned only with the two "sutured" images and not what comes before or after. In his privileged example, Bresson's *Procès de Jeanne d'Arc*, it is no wonder that shot/reverse shot stands out: the film's dialogue scenes scrupulously exclude establishing shots. In most films, however, "suture" furnishes redundant cues, confirming our construction of a space that we have seen or will see in a more comprehensive view. As Julian Hochberg suggests, it seems likely that the spectator makes sense of a string of shots by fitting each cue into a cognitive map of the locale, and this is facilitated by an establishing shot.[34]

This is not, I should add, to resuscitate the ideal observer, since the cognitive map does not exactly duplicate the locale in the "mind's eye." The map is rather a selective codification and storage of narratively and spatially salient elements. The spectator cannot summon up a detailed replica of the space. He or she can do something much more appropriate: locate the most important figures and objects in relation to one another, hypothesize what actions and views are likely to follow currently visible ones, and compare what ensues with what went before.

Most broadly, film editing draws upon the spectator's knowledge of the narrative context, generic conventions, schemata of human behavior, and the historical context of filmmaking and film viewing. As a description, "suture" designates simply some aspects of schemata which we mobilize in order to make spatial and causal sense of a scene's total space. As a theoretical concept, "suture" is not an adequate explanation of how this process occurs.

Cues, Features, and Functions

It is possible to consider filmic space only in its *graphic* aspects. We can treat space as nonrepresentational matter, analyzing it as compositional design and acoustical form and texture. Some films, such as abstract ones, encourage us to limit ourselves to graphic aspects.[35] My concern here, however, is with *scenographic* space: the imaginary space of fiction, the "world" in which the narration suggests that fabula events occur. On the basis of visual and auditory cues, we act to construct a space of figures, objects, and fields—a space of greater or lesser depth, scope, coherence, and solidity.

The scenographic space of a film is built out of three sorts of cues: shot space, editing space, and sonic space. Each of these groupings also involves representing space on screen or offscreen.

Shot Space

Several cues are at work when we construct the objects and spatial relations represented in a shot. In most cases, these work in an involuntary, "bottom-up" manner, but any film can make these cues inconsistent or equivocal in a way that renders them the targets of more deliberate hypothesis testing. (We have seen cases of the latter in those shots that defy linear perspective, as in figs. 7.12–7.13.)

Overlapping contours (partial masking). When one contour occludes another, we attribute the occluding edge to a near object (figure) and the other edge to a distant one (another figure, or the ground).

Texture differences. The rougher or more dense the texture of a surface, the more it comes forward; smoother and less dense surfaces tend to recede.

Atmospheric perspective. All other things being equal, the more indistinct the surface, shape, color, or mass of an object is, the more distant we assume that object to be. Photography and cinema can manipulate aperture, depth of field, lens focus, or interposed translucent materials (gauze, smoke) to create effects of atmospheric perspective.

Familiar size. We tend to base object hypotheses on what we know of the class of objects represented. Prototype schemata for the normal size of people, animals, and things help us decide what is nearer or farther away.

Light and shade. Lighting can suggest planes, as classical backlighting does by reinforcing figure/ground differentials. Lighting can also model the object's form, rounding off planes to create volumes. Highlights tend to suggest surface texture and the direction of the light sources.

Shadows are of two sorts. Attached shadows, or shading, are caused by portions of the object casting shadows on the object itself. Shading tends to suggest texture, form, and relief. Cast shadows may define the object's form, often in distorted ways, or cue us to infer spatial relations within the milieu. Such inferences can throw us off course, as in *India Song.* Here many shots frame a mirror which purportedly reflects the scene before it. Yet the reflections in the mirror cast shadows *into* the space inhabited by the characters—an optical impossibility. (See figs. 7.18–7.19.) This incompatible cue suggests a duplicate world of solid persons and objects behind the mirror's surface.

Illumination and shadows present the same problem as perspective in the Ames room, since any intensity of light could result from an infinity of possible sources and surfaces. The visual system simplifies by assuming that the light comes from a specified direction (usually from above) and is unvarying in its intensity.[36]

Color. Regardless of object, lighter, warmer, and more intense colors tend to seem closer than do darker, cooler, and less saturated ones. For example, pure reds and yellows come forward, pure blues retreat.

Perspective. All the perspective systems we have considered (pp. 104–10) suggest depth on the basis of how straight lines behave. In linear perspective, orthogonal lines converge to one or more vanishing points. Synthetic perspective treats orthogonals as curves. Nonscientific perspective systems can also produce consistent depth cues. For instance, in the inverted perspective of figure 7.12, we can still make hypotheses about what is nearer or farther off. We have already seen how photography and cinema can employ mise-en-scène and lenses of different lengths to create various perspective cues.

Figure movement. One of the cinema's most important cues for object identification and spatial relations is the fact that figures move in the frame. This creates a continuous flow of overlapping contours, strengthening figure/ground hypotheses and often generating transformations of illumination (movement into shadow or light, glitter as highlights play across a moving surface). Movement helps concretize the space, reinforcing object and depth hypotheses. To some degree, as I mentioned in Chapter 3, the construction of objects, their three-dimensional shapes and layout, and their movements call upon bottom-up, involuntary perceptual processes.[37] Still, more strictly cognitive activities, such as prior acquaintance with representational traditions, doubtless also play a role.

Monocular movement parallax. Another very powerful spatial cue is the ability of the camera itself to move. Panning and tilting (i.e., swiveling the camera horizontally or vertically) significantly modify the perceived layout of surfaces and the apparent distances among objects. Tracking or craning the camera in any direction can yield even more information about the field. (Zoom shots, which simply magnify or demagnify the field, do not supply motion parallax.)

Usually, the film viewer constructs monocular movement parallax in bottom-up fashion. This is not to say, however, that Gibson is right to think that camera movement "specifies" both a unique field and a continuous observation point.[38] Bottom-up processes are inferential and probabilistic, however mandatory; the data could be otherwise than the system takes them to be. That this is so in cinema is

7.18. India Song
7.19. India Song

shown by the fact that any camera movement can control its trajectory so that we are prevented from testing the objects' shapes and spatial relations. The potential ambiguity of the actual spatial layout traversed by a camera movement is exploited in the filming of back projections and of sets in false perspective.

At this point we might well agree with Donald Weismann's claim that representational space can never be strictly flat. As soon as one line or patch appears, there will be cues for figure and ground, near edge and distant surface. Instead, Weismann distinguishes various sorts of depth. There is shallow space, as in Egyptian art, which uses overlapping as the primary depth cue.[39] There are varieties of cubical space, such as those obtained in Japanese angular-isometic perspective, Indian cubical space, and Western linear perspective.[40] Here various cues are integrated into more or less consistent systems. And there is ambiguous space, in which cues come into conflict; the work of El Greco, Cézanne, and the Cubists furnishes many examples. These sorts of space can all be achieved in cinema: the shallow space of primitive film, of *La Passion de Jeanne d'Arc* and *La Chinoise*, and of many shots in mainstream cinema; the cubical space of long-shot views in Hollywood film, brought to its apogee by Welles's baroque effects; the ambiguous space of the Expressionists and films like *Red Beard*. It is up to the analyst to discover the different factors that cue the spectator to construe the shot's space.

Depth is also a matter of degree. As an example, we might examine how Godard's *Weekend* utilizes depth in depicting an outlandish traffic jam on a rural highway. The action is rendered in four shots and interrupted by titles. Each shot offers an abundance of depth cues. (See figs. 7.20–7.22 for specimen frames.) Foreground planes are picked out clearly, haze diffuses the trees and fields at the horizon (atmospheric perspective), trees and cars overlap and occlude one another, assumptions of familiar size are confirmed, and the movements of vehicles and humans offer straightforward figure/ground cues. Colors bring objects forward by virtue of warmth (red cars or clothes, a red-and-yellow Shell truck), intensity (the foreground colors are more saturated), and brightness (a white horse, white vehicles). Since the day is overcast, there are no strong shadows, but the diffused daylight casts soft shadows onto the road and creates highlights that indicate the curvature of fenders and windshields. The camera's high angle and oblique orientation make the road dash off at an angle, its edges suggesting offscreen perspec-

7.20. Weekend
7.21. Weekend   *7.22.* Weekend

the significant action is confined to the roadway in the foreground, the scene employs many cues to articulate planes and volumes.[41]

In contrast, consider a shot of the galloping Teutonic knights in *Alexander Nevsky* (fig. 7.23). There are no cues of cast shadow, color, perspective, or haze. The space is thus relatively shallow. We must rely on overlapping contours and familiar size to place the knights in relative (if vague) depth against the sky. The knights rise and fall, the foreground rider occasionally occluding his mate. But the shot is a very unconvincing depiction of riding a horse. The men's metronomic lungings are implausible as a cue for the thudding and swaying of a horseback ride. And if this is a tracking shot following subject movement, there need to be some cues for relative displacement of figure and background: shifting highlights, slight changes in the knights' positions in the frame, and some background features that by their changing aspects suggest motion parallax. In the absence of such cues, the shot is more easily construed as a static image of two knights rocking to and fro against a backdrop. This seems to me the reason that the shot often raises a guffaw from the audience.

tival convergence. And there is, in all these shots, a steady tracking movement from left to right. Although the movement does not penetrate the cars' area, it maintains the diagonal orientation of the road and constantly suggests the relative distances of objects and figures. In sum, although

7.23. Alexander Nevsky

7.24. Jezebel: *In the first shot,*
Jezebel stands only at Pres's
chest . . .
7.25. . . . *but in the closer view,*
she has risen to his chin.

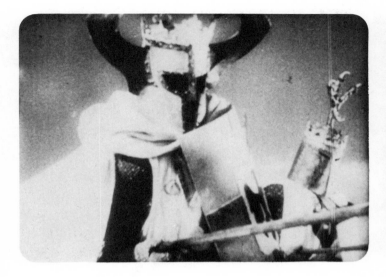

Editing Space

The perceiver constructs intershot space on the basis of anticipation and memory, favoring cause-effect schemata and creating a "cognitive map" of the pertinent terrain. For any series of shots, we can always ask how complete and consistent its layout of space is and what areas tend to be favored. For example, in most Hollywood scenes, the editing leaves some areas unshown (the "fourth wall" of interiors) and makes those irrelevant to constructing the fabula. The 180-degree principle of filming and cutting assures that vantage points on the same side of the axis of action are privileged. And the spatial cues tend to be consistent across the cuts.

Interestingly, though, features of figure position often vary markedly from shot to shot without the spectator's noticing (for example, figs. 7.24–7.25). Often such "cheat cuts" affect only peripheral details that never receive foveal attention anyhow. More generally, the cheat cut illustrates how hypotheses favor object recognition and narrative factors and how schemata work "from the top down." Gross cues for objects and relative spatial position fit more quickly into a pattern of causal inference and a general cognitive map than does exact measurement of the placement of a lamp or the precise distance between figures. Noël Carroll remarks: "The ability to postulate a coherent unity of action rather than the spatial continuity associated with matching

7.26. Earth   7.27. Earth

is more fundamental to the flow of the narrative."[42] It also seems likely that shifts in camera position and lens length across the cut make detailed retrospective comparison of two successive shots very difficult. It is simpler to assume consistency and block out minor deviations as "noise." In our shot/reverse shot from *The Spider's Stratagem*, the incompatibilities of background would escape notice were not the ambiguities of Draifa's constantly changing bouquet so compositionally central.

Other films, of course, will challenge the viewer's assumptions about spatial clarity, completeness, and consistency. One scene of Dovzhenko's *Earth* shows a father and son quarreling. The narration withholds any establishing shot (a typical procedure in Soviet montage). Shots of the father alternate with shots of the son. But each man has his back turned to us, and the camera takes up a perpendicular line of view, so that initially the men's relative locations are indeterminate (figs. 7.26–7.27). The men could be facing in any of several different directions. We have too few cues—no eyelines, no overall orientation, no symmetrically oblique setups. Eventually, however, the men's heads turn slightly left or right, and we grasp gratefully at one cue. This proves consistent: father and son are most likely standing side by side, not back to back.

The space of a series of shots can extend over great distances, as in passages of crosscutting, and here the codified cues do not favor completeness. Why would one show every mile between the galloping Klan and the beseiged town in *The Birth of a Nation*? Often, however, constant screen direction becomes an important cue. If the Klan rides from the right, Piedmont must be somewhere off "left" on some grand cognitive map. Many intervening stretches will be hazy, but the end points of this extensive axis of action remain consistent.

Sonic Space

Like visual factors, auditory ones can solicit us to construct space. "Figure" and "ground" exist in sound as well, as when a high-pitched tone tends to emerge from a welter of lower ones. In most films, speech appears to occupy the foreground, noise the background. Volume and acoustic texture can create what engineers for early talking films called "sound perspective." At first they believed that for maximum realism the microphone should be placed as close to the camera as possible, so that in long shot there would be appropriately distant sound.[43] It soon appeared, however, that more compelling cues would be furnished by a microphone placed fairly close to the players, even when filming long shots. The result was only a slight change in reverberation and volume when cutting from long shot to closer view—certainly nothing as acoustically drastic as the shot change was visually. This ploy succeeds because, for spatial information, sight outranks hearing in the human sensory system. While auditory frequency, amplitude, and timbre can approximately locate a sound source, determining exact distance and position is more difficult than with vision.[44] Under most circumstances, seeing is believing, and so when our vision tells us that a long shot portrays a distant figure, we trust that information more than we trust acoustic cues that suggest that we are somewhat "closer."

Sometimes, of course, sound perspective will be emphasized, as when in *The Big Sleep* the muffled sound from inside Walgreen's office becomes clearer as Marlowe approaches. But even here we are not dealing with direct fidelity. What must be remembered is that the "spatiality" of sound on film is as manipulated as the image. Sound recording, mixing, and reproduction rework the raw material of acoustic phenomena to construct cues. For example, simply recording in a busy environment produces a distressing jumble of sound. Ordinary perception and cognition select certain sonic information and screen out the rest. Conventional film sound does much of this work for us by recording on separate tracks, mixing so as to highlight the important information, eliminating much ambient noise, and smoothly modulating from a dense mix to a thin one. Stereophonic sound exemplifies a more recent attempt to fuse sonic realism with schematic clarity. The spectator falls back on the simplicity hypothesis and assumes a direct link between acoustic clarity, narrative relevance, and spatial coherence. When a filmmaker refuses to construct such redundant cues, as Godard does in his notorious single-miked cafe scenes, the spectator must be more attentive to pick out the narratively pertinent and spatially informative sound events.[45]

Offscreen Space

Shot space, editing space, and sonic space can all engage the viewer's spatial hypothesis forming by guiding his or her construction of offscreen areas. Such areas are of two sorts: *nondiegetic* offscreen zones and *diegetic* ones.

Nondiegetic offscreen space is space which is not part of the fictional world. The principal example of this is a schema all critics invoke: the camera. In our construction of the fabula world, the "camera" is not a physical machine (weighing a lot or a little, bearing a brand name) but a hypostatized offscreen narrational agency that puts certain material on display. This camera is a purely mental construct, a schema for explaining certain spatial qualities and transformations. Of course this schema plays the starring role in invisible observer accounts, which make the camera an anthropomorphic entity. We must recall, however, that this "camera" is not the *creator* of the narration's spatial qualities but the *product* of them.[46] To a design of diagonal lines and upward-tapering human forms there corresponds the schema-driven hypothesis "The camera is at a low angle." To a stream of continually altering aspects and objects there corresponds: "The camera tracks left." Images can cue such hypotheses without the real camera's ever having been in any such position, as animators have known for decades. All that people need in order to construct the schema called "camera," it seems, are some assumptions about how photographic images are produced. The analogy to photography, however, tends to objectify the fictional world as the profilmic event, whereas the critic's task is to treat this camera as the most economical way to integrate many cues about space.

In most films the viewer makes the Bazinian assumption that outside the frame edges lie more regions of the fictional world: these regions comprise diegetic offscreen space. Noël Burch has itemized them: the spaces beyond the four frame lines, the area behind the camera, the space "beyond" the horizon.[47] It is evident that editing and sound contribute to the construction of offscreen space. Shot 2 will usually show something that was offscreen in shot 1, while diegetic sound will characteristically continue when its source is no longer in the frame.

As a schema, diegetic offscreen space has what Burch calls a "fluctuating" existence.[48] A Constructivist theory can explain why. From a psychological point of view, it would be extremely inefficient—that is, it would call up a cumbersome number of schemata and hypotheses—to project and recall all areas of offscreen space at every moment. Therefore the viewer bets that only certain offscreen areas will become narratively significant and she or he attends to cues that reinforce or disprove that. Thus if a framing leaves some space on the right, it is more likely that a character previously established as being offscreen right will enter the shot. Offscreen space modulates in importance because the viewer's hypotheses make it more or less salient or concrete. Needless to say, the narration can also emit ambiguous or contradictory cues about offscreen locations, as the examples from *The Spider's Stratagem* and *Earth* suggest. In such cases we must revise our spatial hypotheses, and perhaps our causal and temporal ones as well.

One such ambiguity may appear when the narration treats the camera as if it occupied offscreen diegetic space. An amusing example occurs in *The Gold Rush*, when the amnesia-crazed Big Jim lumbers into the lens just as the shot fades out. This usually evokes a laugh because we assume that he is about to collide with that apparatus we call a camera. We shall see shortly how a famous shot from *Sunrise* plays upon a similar shift. At any moment, the narration can evoke the camera as an entity within either nondiegetic or diegetic offscreen space.

Sound has a particularly strong potential for cueing us about offscreen space. The ordinary film often includes ambient noise to suggest a vague but consistent world offscreen. The locality of sound can play subtly between the fabula world and an indefinite spot we call "sound over,"

from which nondiegetic music and commentary issue.[49] Thus the viewer senses an important difference between the sound montage in *Made in USA* (mixing nondiegetic and diegetic sound into an ambiguously equal "presence") and the cacophony of TV sets, radios, and character speech within the diegetic space of Fassbinder's *Third Generation*.

Given all these factors, how can we theorize the narrational functions of space? Everything we have considered as part of the spectator's activity and of syuzhet/fabula relations—gaps and retardations; matters of knowledge, self-consciousness, and communicativeness—all structure spatial representation. Before we consider one film in detail, a few illustrations may be suggestive.

No single shot is more famous than the one in *Sunrise* which tracks the husband trudging through the marshes to meet the City Woman. The context, pertinent perceptual factors, and narrational functions all contribute to the force that space assumes in this passage.

The shot gathers its effect partly by contrast with another tracking shot that precedes it by a few minutes. The City Woman leaves her cottage and walks through the village to the husband's home to lure him out. A composition in one-point perspective shows her leaving the cottage, with orthogonals and empty space on the left anticipating her trajectory through the shot (fig. 7.28). As she passes, the camera pans left to keep her centered, discovering more offscreen space and strengthening the cues for depth (fig. 7.29). The panning shot is redundant with the narrative schema; she, not the old man and woman in the right foreground, is the important figure. As the pan reaches its apex (fig. 7.30), the camera starts to move with the City Woman, tracking along behind her at her pace (fig. 7.31). She passes a house, to which monocular movement parallax attributes strong effects of volume. The sloping path continues to create cues for linear perspective, eventually revealed as culminating in her target, the family's cottage (fig. 7.32). By tracking behind her, the camera movement plays down the figure and plays up our anticipation of her destination: her size and aspect remain constant, and the greatest spatial transformations occur in the setting. Thus the shot, which begins with her leaving one cottage, points us toward the end point of her

walk, creating a mild crescendo somewhat like that in *The End of St. Petersburg* (p. 74). But here the effect is less self-conscious than in Pudovkin's film because the shot seems "unobtrusively" to follow the City Woman's movement.

In the more celebrated shot—of the husband's rendezvous with the City Woman, the perceptual and narrational cues are quite different. The man walks away from the camera (fig. 7.33); then, having crossed a little bridge, he turns right and passes around behind a hillock (fig. 7.34). The camera follows at a distance, traveling leftward. He emerges from behind the hillock (fig. 7.35) and climbs over a fence (fig. 7.36). Unexpectedly, the man comes straight toward us (fig. 7.37). The camera pans leftward, losing him (fig. 7.38) and glides on through willow branches (fig. 7.39) to reveal the City Woman standing by the marsh waiting for him (fig. 7.40).

The depth cues differ significantly from those in the earlier shot. There is little linear perspective (fragmentary recessions provided by the bridge and the fencelines), and the total space is quite undifferentiated. Atmospheric perspective is a more significant cue because of the mist shrouding the landscape, and familiar size helps pick out objects as

well. The camera movement is crucial in endowing trees and slopes with volume. The most sharply articulated space, though, is that occupied by the City Woman (fig. 7.40), with its zones of figure, marsh, and sky: an oasis of clear vision in a vast murk.

7.31. Sunrise
7.32. Sunrise

7.33. Sunrise
7.34. Sunrise

7.35. Sunrise
7.36. Sunrise

7.37. Sunrise
7.38. Sunrise

7.39. Sunrise
7.40. Sunrise

keep him in frame, sometimes hastening, as when he climbs over the fence. How many viewers would realize that "objectively" the camera pursues an almost perfectly straight path? It is the convoluted terrain and the man's roundabout path that create the sense of serpentine movement. Of course, the fact that the camera does not follow his footsteps but strikes out on its own (fig. 7.38) cues us to read the mobile framing as an independent narrating agency; this is confirmed when we lose the husband altogether (fig. 7.39) and move on to disclose the City Woman (fig 7.40). But there is a cognitive inconsistency in the camera movement that perhaps supplies some of its fascination. The camera becomes an independent presence when it departs from the husband, but in stalking up to us, the man betrays no recognition of the camera's presence; we might be tempted to identify it with our old friend, the invisible observer. Yet immediately the camera moves leftward, and it brushes away the willow branches in our path (fig. 7.39). This invisible observer leaves physical traces of its passing. Unlike the shot following the City Woman, this camera movement heightens the narration's self-consciousness, even at the expense of creating a logical incompatibility.

The camera movement heightens communicativeness as well, taking a shortcut through the foliage to anticipate the target of the husband's walk (with far more overtness than the anticipation of the City Woman's destination earlier). No longer restricted to either character's range of knowledge, we are presented with nearly all the factors of the situation before the characters meet. In fact, our knowlege is as much spatial as causal. The husband has gone out of the shot and the camera moves left, creating a spatial gap: where did he go? The answer is supplied when the camera frames the woman so as to leave a vacancy on frame left (fig. 7.40). She is looking off right, but because of the unbalanced framing and the fact that we have seen the husband leave the frame diagonally on the right, we hypothesize that he is probably circling around to our left. She starts, looks slightly off left (fig. 7.41), tosses her flower away, and starts making up for his arrival (fig. 7.42). Now she looks sharply left and he comes into the shot, balancing the frame at last (fig. 7.43).

The action here is also much less rectilinear than in the village shot. The husband moves at a constant pace, but because he moves to and from the camera, we see him from many aspects and distances. The velocity of the camera movement must also vary—sometimes slowing down to

7.41. Sunrise
7.42. Sunrise

7.43. Sunrise

She steps to him and they embrace. The off-centered framing and the presumption that the husband was somewhere "off left and behind the camera" furnish a strong hypothesis about the development of the shot's space—one which of course supports the developing action schema (the husband has an assignation with his lover). The climax of the shot is at once causal and spatial.

The *Sunrise* shot glories in the ability of narration to go anywhere at will. In general the classical film translates narrational omniscience into spatial omnipresence.[50] The narration freely acknowledges, we might say, its ability to take us wherever it wants. This omnipresence is usually deployed more discreetly than in Murnau's film, with greater redundancy and fewer flaunted gaps. Most obviously, space can be limited by setting bounds on a character's knowledge. In *Rear Window*, with the exception of only two sequences, the exterior spaces we see are justified as what could be seen from Jeff's apartment. Yet strict confinement to a character's spatial locus can create new sorts of gaps. Take *Dark Passage*, which presents its first several scenes through the protagonist's eyes (subjective camera, "hidden" cuts, to-camera address by other characters, etc.). Instead of enhancing audience identification, this tactic actually conceals a crucial piece of information: the protagonist's appearance. Later, after he undergoes plastic surgery (and acquires Humphrey Bogart's face), the film resumes a normal spatial style.

7.44. The Big Sleep
7.45. The Big Sleep

This more "normal" style affords a fluid set of guidelines for regulating subjectivity and spatial representation. Edward Branigan has studied these principles in admirable detail; I would add only that the structural features he discerns operate as more or less salient cues for hypothesis building. For example, in analyzing optical point-of-view structures, Branigan isolates six elements: a point in space, an offscreen glance, a transition, a camera position from the initial point, an object, and a character. In *Rear Window*, Jeff (point) looks off (glance); cut (transition) to a distant view ("his" position) of what (object) he (character) sees. Each of these factors functions as a cue, and together they allow the spectator to make a strongly grounded inference about character subjectivity.[51] William Simon points out one more cue: an expressive reaction on the part of the character, which can clinch the previous shot as a subjective view.[52] And some cues are stronger than others; in the point-of-view structure, camera angle is a more critical variable than camera distance.

Mainstream narration's treatment of space remains fluid because narrative context can set limits on the tendency toward omnipresence. In *The Big Sleep*, Marlowe goes to a rendezvous with Harry Jones only to find that Canino has gotten there first. Here, for the sake of creating unequivocal cues, classical narration violates strict adherence to optical subjectivity, but it still confines itself within narrow bounds.

After hearing muffled voices inside Walgreen's office (fig. 7.44), Marlowe enters the waiting room. The sound texture clarifies, and an establishing shot shows him halt behind a filing cabinet, eyes right, while Canino interrogates Jones next door (fig. 7.45). There is a cut to a view of Jones and Canino through the office doorway (fig. 7.46). Now, this cannot be Marlowe's optical point of view, since the angle varies markedly from his vantage point. The shot indicates not what Marlowe sees but what he is trying to see, and the half-open door emphasizes the barriers to vision from his station point. When Jones mentions Marlowe's name, cut back to a reaction shot of Marlowe (fig. 7.47), who looks down reflectively as offscreen dialogue continues. He then appears to listen more intently. This frees the narration from any attempt to render Marlowe's vision. We cut back to Jones and Canino, but now seen from a position inside the office (fig. 7.48), followed by a reverse shot (fig. 7.49). These shots cannot be attributed to Marlowe's point of view. They are instead visual accompaniment to what he *hears*. Thus the narration confines itself to what Marlowe learns, but its

7.46. The Big Sleep
7.47. The Big Sleep

7.48. The Big Sleep
7.49. The Big Sleep

spatial system interprets that constraint generously, refusing to let the protagonist's immobility hog-tie the camera.
This tactic remains less self-conscious than the camera's
shortcut through the willows in *Sunrise* because the redundancy of action and spatial areas is very great and the cutting
is less independent of the character. Had the narration cut to
a high-angle shot of Jones and Canino with Canino's fateful
bottle of poison in the foreground, we could posit a disparity
between viewer knowledge and character knowledge comparable to that of the *Sunrise* shot. But the actual exchange

7.50. The End of St. Petersburg
7.51. The End of St. Petersburg

takes only slight liberties by using the most conventional spatial schemata (from establishing shot to medium shot through shot/reverse shot) to clarify and emphasize the dialogue. Here we encounter that muted, discreet omniscience which Chapter 5 has already discussed in relation to the detective film.

A less realistically motivated narration can flaunt spatial omnipresence, even using it to feed us false or ambiguous cues. In *The End of St. Petersburg,* a worker and a peasant come forward to ask government troops to join the revolution. The troops and the two Bolsheviks are never seen in the same shot, and the latter are in fact presented in an abstract, unlocalized space (fig. 7.50). A general (fig. 7.51) orders a squadron forward to fire on the men. The eyelines and the orientation of the rifles (fig. 7.52) suggest that the squad is on the left, aiming at the two men on the right, with the general somewhere in between (in a purified space like that of the Bolsheviks). The general shouts, "Fire!" Suddenly there is a brief shot of the general, now looking *right* (fig. 7.53) and then a shot of rifles firing to the *left* (fig. 7.54). This pair of shots disrupts our cognitive map of the scene. The general flinches in a head-on view (fig. 7.55). The rifles are now in their previous position, firing to the right. The general topples rightward, obviously stricken. The crossing of the imaginary axis of action in figures 7.52–7.54 throws momentary doubt on exactly whom the soldiers are firing at; the alternating shots of the general and the rifles at various angles suggests the hypothesis that he is the target. This is confirmed when he topples and another shot shows the peasant and worker unharmed. The nonredundant, overtly self-conscious manipulation of space recalls the passage from *Earth* mentioned above.

All these examples recall a point made throughout the previous chapters. In narrative cinema, syuzhet-centered schemata usually control stylistic ones. Once grasped as three-dimensional and furnished with recognizable objects, cinematic space is typically subordinated to narrational ends. The *Sunrise* shots function to match ongoing stylistic hypotheses with macrostructural syuzhet ones—delineating setting, shaping suspense, and forwarding the fabula chain.

The scene from *The Big Sleep* obviously asks us to slot spatial information into the syuzhet's larger pattern of information dissemination. Even the transgressive spaces of *Earth* and *The End of St. Petersburg* fulfill such purposes. When confronted by such deviant spatial features, we fall back onto

7.52. The End of St. Petersburg
7.53. The End of St. Petersburg

7.54. The End of St. Petersburg
7.55. The End of St. Petersburg

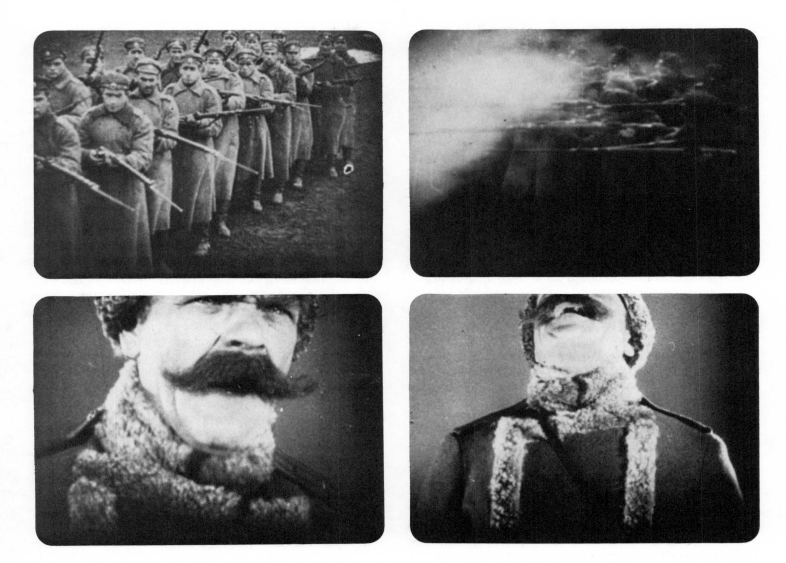

action-based schemata (e.g., soldiers turning on their superior) and then test those on the cues. Stylistic originality in film thus often consists of finding novel devices which the spectator can match to broad syuzhet schemata or hypotheses. Thus the back-to-the-camera compositions in *Earth* are a striking way of expressing the stereotype "fierce opposition," while the violation of conventional eyelines and orientations in *The End of St. Petersburg* vividly embodies the idea of a commander figuratively surrounded by his own troops. Yet the same instances show that, however functional film style may be, it can still powerfully shape our construction of space and narrative. It is to a remarkable example of this process that I now turn.

Space in *The Confrontation*

The films of Miklós Jancsó invite description even as they elude analysis. Every critic who writes on a Jancsó film is tempted to count the shots, plot the camera's gyrations, or try to render the mixture of fascination, apprehension, and exhilaration his scenes evoke. Yet I know of no attempt to show how Jancsó's style works, especially in narrational terms. Because his work relies so patently upon the construction of filmic space, I will use one of his films, *The Confrontation* (1969; the Hungarian title should be translated as "Sparkling Winds"), to illustrate how a critic could analyze principles of spatial construction.

Simply at the level of story action, *The Confrontation* is one of the most comprehensible of Jancsó's films. After World War II, a group of youths invade a seminary to turn it into a people's college. Laszlo, an idealistic moderate, tries to win over the priests and students through persuasion, debate, and fraternization. When this proves ineffective, his group votes him out as leader and installs two women, Jutka and Terez, in his place. Jutka embarks on a campaign of terror that leads to vandalism and animosity. Party officials intervene and order Jutka punished. Unrepentant, she breaks away and leads a small cadre; but at the end of the film, her group is rounded back up into the student ranks. The police official who has been observing the whole affair suggests wryly that Jutka may yet become a government minister some day. The syuzhet concentrates this action into only a few locales—the seminary, a riverbank, and adjacent fields—and limits dramatic duration to two days, with the first day containing nearly all the action.

To understand how the fairly simple fabula actually gets narrated, it is convenient to start with the spatial patterns of film style. Roughly, we can say that *The Confrontation*

exploits a tension between abnormally predictable and abnormally unpredictable stylistic features.

As is generally known, Jancsó employs very long takes—here, thirty-one shots for eighty-two minutes of screen time. Most scenes consist of one shot. Characters enter a locale, they interact there, and the action will conclude in some fashion. Cut to a new space and a later time. Because the long take makes a stylistic unit (a shot) also a syuzhet unit (a scene), there is an unusually tight connection between narrative comprehension and spatial perception. If the classical film establishes the space before the action gets going, Jancsó's film synchronizes the presentation of action with the revelation of space. In this film, retardation operates both with respect to the syuzhet and with respect to the stylistic patterning. Most shots begin on a detail—a face, a portion of scenery—so that the development of the action gradually unfurls the scene's locale as well. At the close of the shot/scene, if the characters simply leave the locale, the camera dwells on the empty space, emphasizing that the locale's possibilities have been exhausted and that a new scene will start. In other instances, a camera movement into a close-up of a solitary character reacting to what has occurred becomes a cue for the end of the scene and the shot. All these tactics for handling space create a set of general but strong stylistic expectations.

At a more local level, however, Jancsó's construction of space works against the reinforcement of spectator hypotheses. Although the long take offers a powerful stylistic norm, the moment-by-moment evolution of the shot is not at all predictable. Shot 4 offers a summary example which is laid out in stills and captions on the following pages. At various points I will compare this shot to later moments in the film.

Much of narrative moment is accomplished during the four minutes and ten seconds of this shot. Several characters are introduced, and later confrontations are foreshadowed. Graham Petrie points to major issues broached here: "the oscillation between confrontation and fraternization on a tactical level; the question of loyalty and divided commitment on a personal level; the sense that, for these young

Fig. 7.56. *The scene begins with Jutka turned from us, looking across the river.*

Fig. 7.60. *She tells him to hurry up. The camera tracks with them as they walk right to a road and Jutka goes out frame right.*

Fig. 7.57. *As she walks right, the reflection of a jeep is visible in the water.*

Fig. 7.61. *Other young men come into the shot from offscreen right . . .*

Fig. 7.58. *She turns and walks to the edge of the river . . .*

Fig. 7.62. *. . . and they race down the road as the camera zooms back.*

Fig. 7.59. *. . . as a boy walks in from frame right.*

Fig. 7.63. *The boys take cover . . .*

Fig. 7.64. . . . and when the jeep passes, they run out behind it.

Fig. 7.65. The police official climbs out and sends the jeep away.

Fig. 7.66. Behind him, the boys form a chain to block the road . . .

Fig. 7.67. . . . and they swivel to block the next jeep.

Fig. 7.68. Laszlo emerges in the right foreground . . .

Fig. 7.69. . . . and strides to the official as the camera zooms in and tracks right.

Fig. 7.70. Jutka comes in from the foreground and the official expostulates with both of them.

Fig. 7.71. As more students pour into the frame from off right . . .

Fig. 7.72. . . . the official strides about, urging his men to put away their weapons.

Fig. 7.73. The frame fills with students, the camera zooms and tracks back, and the police are revealed to be surrounded.

Fig. 7.74. The students join hands threateningly . . .

Fig. 7.75. . . . then fall to the ground singing a song about the Spanish Civil War.

Fig. 7.76. Zoom in on the official as he walks to Laszlo . . .

Fig. 7.77. . . . and in a gesture of solidarity lies down and joins the students.

Fig. 7.78. He rises and as the camera pans and zooms back . . .

Fig. 7.79. . . . he walks left and orders his officers to remove the students.

Fig. 7.80. *The camera pans and tilts with one officer as he comes forward to pull one boy . . .*

Fig. 7.81. *. . . but failing he runs off to the left to try another.*

Fig. 7.82. *. . . Suddenly students grab the policeman . . .*

Fig. 7.83. *. . . carry him to the river bank . . .*

Fig. 7.84. *. . . and toss him in.*

Fig. 7.85. *Other students rush in from the right bearing policemen . . .*

Fig. 7.86. *. . . whom they dunk.*

Fig. 7.87. *Pan and track left as other youths begin to strip and jump into the river.*

Fig. 7.88. *As the camera continues to move leftward, the official backs into the frame . . .*

Fig. 7.89. *. . . and moves leftward, arms upraised as if facing a weapon.*

Fig. 7.90. *Laszlo eventually appears at frame right.*

Fig. 7.91. *The camera tracks with them to the corner of a lock . . .*

Fig. 7.92. *. . . and it is revealed that Laszlo has no weapon.*

Fig. 7.93. *The camera arcs leftward as Laszlo takes the official's pistol.*

Fig. 7.94. *Laszlo goes around to face the official . . .*

Fig. 7.95. *. . . who runs to the rear, picks up the bathers' clothes . . .*

Fig. 7.96. . . . and tosses them into the water.

Fig. 7.97. Laszlo asks to examine the gun.

Fig. 7.98. Zoom in on them as they sit and Laszlo examines the pistol.

Fig. 7.99. As Laszlo remarks that the gun is not loaded, the official looks off right. End of shot.

people, politics is a game whose deeper and darker implications they are still incapable of sensing."[53] Such general implications, however, do not account for the film's spatial style. The same information could be extracted from a film staged and cut in traditional fashion. Jancsó's shot presents an evolving narrative situation in a way that makes the viewer engage in a process of framing and testing purely spatial hypotheses.

Shot 4 presents a space in continuous transformation. Figures are constantly moving in many directions and showing all aspects. Even when characters pause, the frame keeps moving , as the camera pans, tilts, and tracks or as the lens zooms or racks focus. The interaction of figure and camera varies throughout: when the camera tracks in a linear path, the characters may turn around or walk in circles (figs. 7.70–7.73); when the figure is moving straightforwardly, the camera may arc around to reveal fresh aspects (figs. 7.90–7.94). If the long take functions to limit our spatial assumptions and hypotheses (no change of space unless change of scene), figure movement and camera movement work against this by presenting a spatial flux that is never predictable, either in its overall trajectory or in its moment-by-moment oscillations.

The constant camera movements and optical transformations tend to be motivated by current or immediately upcoming figure movements. Seldom does the camera move independently of any figure. This might help guide our spatial hypotheses were it not for two crucial factors. First is the considerable number of people in the scene. Here the syuzhet/fabula requirements of depicting a group revolutionary activity coincide with the stylistic treatment. Jancsó has cited Antonioni as the decisive influence on his work, and clearly *Cronaca di un Amore* serves as a precedent for the camera's tendency to follow one character for a while before picking up another just as the figure crosses our path. Jutka is walking right and a boy comes in (figs. 7.58–7.59); track with the two of them, but Jutka goes out frame right and we continue to follow the boy. Or we follow the official striding to his officers, but then the camera picks up the policeman in the foreground and we stay with him for a bit.

The possibilities of this technique are intensified by the widescreen format. The width of the display multiplies the possible trajectories that can cross and redirect figure and frame movement.

A second device that increases the unpredictability of frame and figure mobility is the narration's tendency to avoid absolute points of rest within a shot. Seldom do characters sit or stand still; even during the pause for the song (figs. 7.75–7.78), the camera frames the most constantly moving figure in the scene. Moreover, by having characters circle each other while they speak, the style makes it difficult to guess where in the frame anyone will stop. Jancsó speaks of how most directors' long takes are composed of static "nuclei" and mobile "passages" that link them.[54] In *The Confrontation*, we cannot break a shot into nodes of story action connected by transitional movement. This is one source of the fascination I noted at the outset: because each instant of spatial transformation becomes potentially significant, there is no filler material in the shot.

Frame mobility, whether achieved through camera movement or zoom, inevitably sets up a play between offscreen and onscreen space. This is especially true in *The Confrontation*, in which the opening moments of a scene do not supply a comprehensive view of the locale. Most of the shots begin on a portion of the space and only very gradually reveal other areas. The practice would not necessarily be disorienting if the narration did not consistently exploit unexpected frame entrances and exits. Early in shot 4, the boy calls his comrades down from the hillside (fig. 7.61). Later, the jeep drives off left (fig. 7.65), eventually to be revealed as parked just out of frame (fig. 7.82). Laszlo pops into the foreground (fig. 7.68), students gradually surround the police official (fig. 7.72), and most strikingly, the official backs slowly into the frame with his arms upraised, apparently threatened by an offscreen force (fig. 7.88). In this last instance, we cannot tell if Laszlo is holding a weapon because the lower frame line is concealing information (figs. 7.90–7.92). Throughout the film the style will utilize this freedom of frame entrances and exits, and in at least one shot we will be taken by surprise when a figure walks out of frame screen right and reenters the frame from the left—having gone around behind the camera.[55]

Highly unpredictable frame entrances and exits, combined with the proliferation of characters, produce unexpected dialogue exchanges. The best example in shot 4 occurs when, as Laszlo addresses the official (fig. 7.69), the latter asks Jutka a question at the moment she enters the frame (fig. 7.70). Even more vivid is a later scene in which students debate with a priest. The shot begins with Laszlo walking left to the priest (fig. 7.100) and turning as the dialogue begins (fig. 7.101). Suddenly another boy strides into the frame from the left (fig. 7.102) and begins to interrogate the priest (fig. 7.103), who answers (fig. 7.104). At this moment (fig. 7.105), we might expect either a reply from the boy on the far right or something from the bespectacled boy in the rear. We cannot expect that Jutka will stride into the shot (fig. 7.106) exactly at the instant she demands a debate (fig. 7.107). The figures offer good examples of how depth can be summoned up without linear perspective: cues of overlap, familiar size, attached shadow, and atmospheric perspective create strips of figures lined up in depth. Yet the space of figure 7.105 seems so crammed (partly due to the telephoto lens) that no one else could possibly be added—let alone articulate yet another plane, as Jutka does. In *The Confrontation*, this "frieze" technique takes the place of traditional shot/reverse shot; characters enter or swivel to present the oblique or profiled aspects typical of the more normal stylistic schema. But the constant movement of camera and figures and the unexpected frame entrances prevent that cognitive mapping that the shot/reverse-shot schema redundantly guarantees.

Having characters step in to carry part of a dialogue exchange is so common in the film that in some scenes the narration can play upon our expectation that the device will occur. When Laszlo confront the party leaders who want to drum Jutka and Terez out, the narration presents the characteristic to-and-fro circling of the figures as they speak in close-up (fig. 7.108). But here many characters walk through in the background, and even though they pause as if about to speak, they never do (fig. 7.109). To the extent that

7.100   7.104
7.101   7.105
7.102   7.106
7.103   7.107

this stylistic device becomes a norm intrinsic to the film, the narration can assume we will get used to it; it is then that the norm can itself be violated, in the name of maintaining unpredictability.

The sound track could give this game away, so the narration usually avoids cueing events with offscreen noise. When, in shot 4, the official backs abruptly into the frame (fig. 7.88), no offscreen sound lets us anticipate his arrival. After the jeep pulls away (fig. 7.65), its motor dies out quickly and is not heard again; nothing prepares us to see it parked so close to where it had let out the official (fig. 7.82). When offscreen sound does cue a figure's entrance, it does so only just before the figure appears, as when between figures 7.61 and 7.62 the boys can be heard rustling down the hill. In a later shot, a troop of marching students is heard only a second or so before it enters the frame, not "realistically" far in advance. Unlike the party scene in Renoir's *La règle du jeu*, which uses variously "present" offscreen music and noise to remind us of a world beyond the frame, Jancsó's narration withholds sonic cues about offscreen action. Even the most flamboyant use of offscreen sound in the film manages to be ambiguous. In the courtyard of the seminary, Laszlo has gathered a group of peasant dancers to entertain the seminarians. The camera glides leftward with Laszlo, past the central pedestal, to a group of dancers. Suddenly, as they start to dance, there is a burst of music. The sound could be taken as nondiegetic until the camera arcs right with Laszlo to reveal what the leftward camera movement had concealed—an ensemble of musicians lined up on the pedestal. The abrupt entry of offscreen sound only empha-

sizes how the narration could have cued us aurally or visually to the musicians' presence much earlier.

So much frame and figure movement should produce great effects of depth, and that does often happen. Volumes leap into prominence when the camera arcs around figures or when characters circle one another. Color also functions as a depth cue: in shot 4, the pale sky and water are pushed to the background, while the carroty hue of Jutka's hair (figs. 7.56–7.60) and the bright red of Laszlo's shirt (figs. 7.68 ff.) make the characters stand out. In shot 4, sharp diagonals of riverbank and road and the "carpentered-world" lock generate perspectival cues. It would be wrong, however, to think that the narration did not qualify scenographic depth with factors tending toward flatness. Jancsó has remarked that he works in the widescreen ratio because it minimizes distance between near and distant planes.[56] (He may be thinking of the long focal lengths of many anamorphic lenses.) As for countering the effects of color, one of the rare moments when characters and camera stop moving occurs when Laszlo and the Jewish student pause outside a chapel. As they speak, what had initially appeared to be purely empty black space springs into relief as, one by one, nuns' faces turn round to look at them (figs. 7.110–7.111). More pervasively, the camera is both tracking forward and zooming in. The same process occurs in figures 7.75–7.78. Such movements create a plastically "stretched" space: the flatness yielded by the long lens is countered by volumetric effects of monocular movement parallax.

As a whole, *The Confrontation* encloses the scenographic depth achieved by movement and other cues within a more

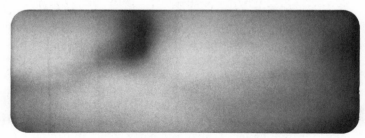

abstract frame that reminds us of sheerly graphic space. The film's credits appear against two shots, each a variant of a blurred and unidentifiable composition. The first of these variants recurs as a third shot (fig. 7.112), held for about twenty-two seconds. After a half second of blackness, the opening of shot 4 appears (fig. 7.56). We now recognize this as shot 3, but sharply focused. The narration asks us to decipher shot 3, to project spatial configurations onto it, and then allows us to check our (very heterogeneous) hypotheses when shot 4 supplies denotative specification. At other points in the film, a shot will end with an explosion of purely graphic space, as when a Carmagnole crack-the-whip ends with faces bobbing and blurring through the frame. The film closes with Jutka assuming a position almost identical to that she took in shot 4. There is a cut to a repetition of the second unfocused view, but now this is held almost two minutes. Apart from providing time to rethink the events of the film, this last image returns us to the purely graphic realm and completes the alternation of deep and shallow space that has run through the film's stylistic texture.

In this chapter we have seen how cues to the development of the shot are very often inscribed in the visual composition. The traveling shots in *Sunrise* anticipate the character's destination or suggest the emergence of an offscreen figure. The style of *The Confrontation* swings between feeding our expectations in this way and running counter to them. Returning to shot 4, we can see that framings like figures 7.82–7.83 anticipate the trajectory of figure movement. A good example is figure 7.56, in which the unbalanced framing anticipates the path that the action will follow in figures 7.57–7.59. And this is frequently the case throughout the film. To this extent, the reframings and figure movements are "easy to watch," that is, conforming to the hypotheses cued up. But often offscreen space works against the anticipations built up by composition. The police official's trajectory of movement established in figure 7.67 is broken by Laszlo's unexpected entry in the foreground (fig. 7.68), and the official swerves from his path to talk to him (fig. 7.69). A similar situation occurs in figure 7.88, when the official backs leftward into a shot that has reserved space for a

rightward entrance. More powerfully uncertain cases occur during the moments of interjected dialogue from characters who abruptly enter the frame, as in the exchange among Laszlo, the priest, the other boy, and Jutka (figs. 7.100–7.107). Here the narration does not inscribe any particular spatial development into the composition.

The absence of an establishing view can also make each moment compositionally indeterminate. A high angle shows the students in the courtyard (fig. 7.113). Tilt down with the boys running to the lower foreground (fig. 7.114) and follow one boy running to the right (fig. 7.115), who scoops up

7.113
7.114
7.115

7.116
7.117
7.118

something (fig. 7.116) and runs back leftward (fig. 7.117). The camera pans with him to reveal—at last—the boys throwing stones at windows (fig. 7.118). Since the target of the students' anger was offscreen in the initial framing (fig. 7.114), the viewer cannot predict the spatial development of the shot. And of course these effects of "indeterminate inscription" are exacerbated by the 1:2.35 widescreen format. At the film's end, the police official walks away from Jutka. He starts leftward (fig. 7.119), swings abruptly right (fig. 7.120), and then the unbalanced reframings trigger a guessing game as to whether she will enter from the left (fig. 7.121)? from the right (fig. 7.122)? or from the left (fig. 7.123)?

One effect of justifying every camera movement by figure movement is to make the scene not at all homologous with a traditional decoupage. The camera's gyrations almost never replicate cut-ins or eyeline matches in the way Hitchcock's independently traveling camera does in *Rope*. Only the circling figures in dialogue (e.g., in shot 4, figs. 7.69–7.71) somewhat parallel the results of orthodox shot/reverse shot; but, as we have seen, the instability of offscreen space renders such a schema inappropriate. There is thus virtually no

7.119
7.120
7.121

7.122
7.123
7.124

"editing within the shot" in *The Confrontation*. But we must also consider the real editing that occurs, since that too affects the spectator's construction of space.

The general rule is that when the cut comes, we are shifted to a new time and place; and this usually holds good. Yet the narration employs cues which are incompatible with this rule. For example, a shot will characteristically end with a character looking distinctly offscreen, as the official is doing at the end of shot 4 (fig. 7.99). The new shot will present something that appears at first to be the object of vision. (Shot 5, for instance, shows the group of swimmers now dancing in a circle with the police.) As the next shot develops, though, it usually becomes clear that there has been some ellipsis at the cut. Thus the gaps created in the scene's space by figure movement, camera movement, and offscreen action find their equivalents in the diffuse spatial and temporal gaps between shots. To take a stronger example, one shot ends with Jutka leaving the frame and with the official on a hillside looking after her (fig. 7.124). Cut to what appears to be a correct eyeline match of her returning his look (fig. 7.125). But this shot soon reveals that she is in an entirely new locale, the riverbank of the film's opening, and

7.125
7.126
7.127

medium-long shot of the students below. This deviation is relatively unforegrounded (and might even be missed) because the spaces in the two shots are adjacent, and shot scale and composition hardly vary. But at the climax of the film, when Jutka is dismissed from the group, the narration flagrantly breaks its own rule with a cut from a high angle of the scene (fig. 7.126) to an extreme close-up of Jutka defiantly refusing to accept their criticism (fig. 7.127). This blatant shot change, for once clearly subordinating spatial demands to psychological causality, stands out against the film's normal operating procedure. There follows a cut back to the long-shot view as Jutka turns and runs off. Near the very end of the film, the narration thus cites a standard stylistic option, throwing open new hypotheses about the editing of the final scenes.

Jancsó has remarked that another of his films, *Sirocco* (1969), was shot in ordinary locales, yet "when you see the film, you understand that you are not in a preexistent space, but in an abstract, completely recreated space. The space exists only on the screen."[58] The film techniques we have considered—filmed action that refuses to create fixed dramatic nodes, the multiplication of characters and unpredictable movements, the unexpected frame entrances and exits, the elimination of offscreen sound cues, the interaction of deeper and more shallow space, the refusal to inscribe each action's trajectory into the composition, editing by "enjambment"—all function generally to "derealize" the total space of the scene, working toward that abstraction of which Jancsó speaks. Because what is offscreen is ever-changing and because we never get an all-embracing view, we cannot situate figures on a cognitive map. At any moment a relatively strong cue, such as the inscription of a movement's direction into the composition, may war with a contrary datum, such as the unexpected entry of a character from another offscreen zone. If a shot ends with a character looking off left and the next begins with a character looking off right, breaks in the fictional space stand out against continuity cues at the stylistic level. In any event, the viewer can never predict very far in advance how the space will develop. The narration, not notably redundant with respect

some time has elapsed since the last shot. Most cuts thus initially negate our assumptions that the space is exhausted and that there will be an ellipsis; the cuts initially suggest that we are in the same place and that no time has been omitted. Yvette Biró describes Jancsó's cuts as "enjambments," a fine term for that mixture of sharp break and apparent continuity characteristic of his shot-changes.[57]

Like other internal norms, the one-shot-per-scene rule gets challenged. About halfway through the film, there is one cut-in that is purely gratuitous—a shot zooming in to women on a balcony dancing in priests' vestments cuts to a

7.128

to character identity or causality, is even less so with respect to the concrete unfolding of space within and between shots. Thus the curiosity, suspense, and surprise characteristic of *The Confrontation* bear on not only the syuzhet patterns but the moment-by-moment stylistic suppressions and revelations.

To some extent, this style can be considered as distinct from any syuzhet-centered needs it might fulfill. We can imagine Jancsó's style as being "preformed," able to "process" many sorts of stories (as indeed it has in the course of his career). Yet these stylistic manipulations serve at least some general syuzhet ends. They are properly narrational in that the gaps they create, the schemata they invoke and manipulate, affect the spectator's ongoing construction of the syuzhet according to principles of knowledge, self-consciousness, and communicativeness.

The key to the narration of *The Confrontation* is its great degree of uncommunicativeness. Rendering almost every scene in a single shot effectively denies us the spatial ubiquity of a more editing-centered style. Within the scene, this narration refuses to show us anything that is not within the ken of a traveling camera; no instantaneous changes of angle, no crosscutting. Yet this restriction is not motivated by the limits on a character's knowledge. There are no optical point-of-view shots, and the frame's movements never adhere wholly to what a single character knows.

Now, the continuously moving camera and the refusal to cut might seem easy meat for an invisible-observer explanation. "It's as if we were a bystander witnessing the event." But this is to ignore how the narration limits our knowledge. In shot 4, no witness could fail to look a little more to the right in figure 7.89 to see Laszlo backing the official up; but the narration withholds this information for some time. It is common for the camera to frame what appears to be random figure movement before withdrawing to a long shot that reveals the figures to have formed a patterned ensemble— dance, march, military formation. In shot 4, students seem just to be moving through the frame (figs. 7.71–7.72), but a slight track and zoom back reveals that the official is trapped in a ring of them (fig. 7.73). Or consider figure 7.128, from the scene in which Jutka faces her accusers: the framing excludes their reactions. So much information is offscreen that we in fact know *less* than an imaginary observer would. Bazin believed that in the party scene of *La règle du jeu* the camera became "an invisible guest . . . not noticeably any more mobile than a man would be"; but even he had to admit that Renoir's use of offscreen space limits the guest's powers: "this invisible witness is inevitably made to wear blinders; its ideal ubiquity is restrained by framing, just as tyranny is often restrained by assassination."[59] Renoir's style, like Jancsó's, should lead us to drop the invisible observer metaphor altogether. All the devices in *The Confrontation* that make the flow of information unpredictable—multiplication of figures, avoidance of points of rest, and the like—become the traces of an uncommonly suppressive narration. Much of the frustration and anxiety of Jancsó's narration is produced by an approach in which we should be able to see and know more than we do.

Suppressiveness applies not only to the shot. Considered as the product of our viewing activity, my summary of the story at the outset looks unproblematic. There are no jugglings of story order, no play between objectivity and subjectivity. Little information is supplied about the characters as individuals, but this would not be pertinent anyhow: the syuzhet aims to reveal group dynamics in a political process—what Jancsó and his scenarist Gyula Hernadi call a "model" that delineates the essentials of a historical situation.[60] (In this respect, the group-centered syuzhet of *The Confrontation* recalls Soviet cinema of the 1920s.) But just as we must infer each shot's locale and population bit by bit, so does the film's narration force us to piece this fabula together retrospectively.

Most scenes begin in medias res. As Graham Petrie notes, "We are introduced to an already fully developed situation and are left to put together the details, and assemble the overall context, as the film proceeds. Shifts of time and place are often arbitrary and apparently unmotivated."[61] In shot 4, for instance, the narration withholds exposition almost entirely. We do not know who the students are, who will be the protagonists, or what goals or issues are at stake in the confrontation with the jeeps. We cannot even be sure of the historical period; although the epoch depicted is the late 1940s, the police official and the students wear 1960s clothes. Prior affiliations between Laszlo and the official are implied, but we never learn what they are. There will be no flashbacks, no voice-over explanation, and precious few mentions of what has happened before the syuzhet began. The result is a unique blend of curiosity and suspense: at almost every scene we must gradually infer what is transpiring in the story action while the style creates a spatial suspense (what will be revealed next?). As the film goes on, we gain more ability to hypothesize and predict: we learn of Jutka's terrorist plan before she applies it, we hear of the college governors' plan to drum her out before the student group does. But this brings us back to the determining stylistic choice of the long take, since we pick up these data only by virtue of their occurring in the scene's locus. Where another film would have crosscut the students' vandalism with the party officials elsewhere learning of the disturbance, here the rock throwing is followed immediately by the arrival of the displeased governors. How they learned of it we will never know. Like the framing that withholds the target of the rock throwing until the moment the action occurs (figs. 7.113–7.118), the syuzhet works to withhold the next event until it enters the arena we already inhabit. And we have already seen that we have no perfect access to all that will occur there.

The limitations upon our sight, hearing, and knowledge are frankly imposed from without, by stylistic fiat. As our example from *Shadow of a Doubt* back in Chapter 4 suggested, overt suppression creates a strongly self-conscious narration. Jancsó's narration could be more forthcoming about the characters; it could employ more concentrated exposition; it could include establishing shots. Choosing to construct the syuzhet as a series of pageantlike, often cryptic encounters and utilizing the long take to limit our knowledge signal a narration addressed to the spectator. An invisible-observer account would have to treat the action as occurring independently of the act of filming (as in Bazin's discussion of *La règle du jeu*), but we cannot fail to recognize that the self-consciousness of Jancsó's narration derives both from camera operations and from the manipulation of figures and setting. Jancsó's famous "choreography" flaunts the power of narration wholly to synchronize the profilmic event with its cinematic rendition.

Suppressiveness and self-consciousness could not work without omniscience. The classical film tends to conceal narrational omniscience behind spatial omnipresence, and even the latter usually gets curtailed in the interests of discretion and predictability, as our scene from *The Big Sleep* showed. *The Confrontation* works in opposite fashion. It refuses omnipresence but flaunts omniscience. At the level of the scene, the narration adheres to the rule that only what occurs in this locale, within a space the camera can traverse, is available for presentation. Yet however strong the self-imposed constraints, the narration knows all that happens or will happen. Often, when following a character, the camera is also anticipating a subsequent action. In shot 4, the camera pans left to follow students tossing policemen into the river (figs. 7.85–7.87), but it also tracks left at exactly the rate appropriate to the eventual entry of the police official (fig. 7.88). As in the films of Antonioni and Dreyer, the framing, so apparently subservient to the characters, in fact follows only those who the narration "knows" will lead to the next piece of information.[62] The inscription of an upcoming movement within the frame has similar anticipatory effects. Most often the framing is at a straight-on position, but when the camera assumes a high angle, this foreshadows the fact that the characters will eventually climb to a spot level with the camera. Here again, the narration's power over the profilmic event emerges. Omnipresence is unnecessary when the narration flaunts its ability to parade events through the frame.

The beginning and ending of the film reveal the narration's capacity for omniscience. Jutka will play no distinctive part in the action until several scenes into the film; but shots 1–3 present her out of focus (fig. 7.112), and shot 4 begins by singling her out, thus foreshadowing her eventual emergence as a major character. Similarly, the penultimate shot perfectly frames the overall syuzhet action by beginning at the geographical point where shot 4 had ended and by itself ending with a framing that repeats the film's opening composition. In other words, the narration "knew" that Jutka would be significant in the film's second half and so by a stylistic device made her presence symmetrically open and close the film.

Taken together, the film's style and its syuzhet present the fabula as an exemplary fiction: pretending to no real existence, wholly enacted through the narration, presented simply as what Jancsó and Hernadi call a "model."[63] Omniscience, self-consciousness, and suppressiveness create a highly overt narration that turns the world of the fiction into a derealized representation of various political positions, strategies, and tactics. *The Confrontation* does not present the unresolvable narrational ambiguities of *The Spider's Stratagem*; here there is a stark political allegory, overtly didactic even when its lessons are equivocal. This narration thus pushes us toward a reflection and interpretation that go beyond story comprehension. This effect becomes salient in the last shot, whose protracted length and adamant silence announce that the fabula is over but the film is not. The "empty" screen thus invites the viewer to think over the spectacle just past. The strategy of representing a story in a fashion that is at once politically significant, objectively referential, and self-consciously abstract has its origins in Soviet historical-materialist cinema of the 1920s, and during the 1960s this mode often took the "interrogative" shape it assumes here. (Chapter 11 will discuss this in more detail.) But the role of Jancsó's "stylistics of space" is to carry the qualities of omniscience, self-consciousness, and suppressiveness down to the moment-by-moment development of the film's texture, to make the spectator's testing of hypotheses no less active and interrogative at the level of figures and framing than at the level of psychology and plot. Jancsó's style has seldom been compared to Soviet montage, but it is functionally similar in its ability to structure the narration and in its power to jostle the spectator's perception.

This consideration of *The Confrontation* has not sought exhaustive analysis. I have simply tried to show how, in constructing cues for scenographic space, film style contributes to viewing activities and narrational processes. In this respect, the chapter completes my general survey of the theory of narration I have been proposing. This theory, I suggest, overcomes the deficiencies of mimetic and diegetic theories. It is coherent; it applies to a broad range of films; it discriminates among films that intuitively seem different. It does not privilege certain techniques: any device can function narrationally. And it can be applied to entire films, helping us explain how processes of syuzhet and style solicit particular spectator activities in the viewing process.

Yet more remains to be done. We should, I suggested back in the introduction, be able to demonstrate the *historicity* of film narration. The films I have used as illustrations exemplify a variety of norms: the classical assumptions about syuzhet and style governing *Rear Window, The Big Sleep, Murder My Sweet,* and *In This Our Life;* the ambiguous interplay of subjectivity and objectivity in *The Spider's Stratagem;* the self-consciously didactic narration of *The Confrontation.* Although many theoretical alternatives could be spelled out, only certain narrational options have become historically dominant, and these are the subject of the last portion of this book.

PART THREE

Historical Modes of Narration

*A little formalism turns one away from
History, but a lot brings one back
to it.*

Roland Barthes

8. Modes and Norms

Part 2 treated narration as involving hollow forms, fairly abstract principles. It is evident, though, that however much the ability to form schemata relies upon innate mental capacities, viewers acquire particular prototypes, templates, and procedures *socially*. "Realistic" motivation depends on what seems lifelike to someone versed in specific conventions. The canonic story format (exposition, state of affairs, introduction of protagonist, and so forth) is apparently learned from one's experience of stories. Expectations about how the narration may manipulate time and space are circumscribed by the possibilities and probabilities of particular traditions. To lay out the overall principles and processes of filmic narration, it was necessary for me to hold at bay the messy contingencies of history.

Now there comes a methodological choice. On the one hand, the analyst could describe the various schemata that are available to a viewer at a given historical moment. This synchronic approach would inventory the possible ways that spectators may comprehend a particular passage. For instance, one contemporary procedural schema might be: "If an image or sound is not justifiable as objectively realistic, treat it as representing a character's mental state." This schema could be illustrated by cues found in Hollywood films, Soviet films of the 1920s, European films of the 1960s, films of the American avant-garde of the 1950s, and so on. The analyst could reconstruct the range of options by which the spectator may build a story out of any film.

The alternative approach is more diachronic and text-centered. Here the analyst describes the fairly stable and consistent narrational principles employed in a historically defined group of films. The group might be constrained by genre, school, movement, nation, or some other feature.

In this part of the book, I have chosen the diachronic approach because I am interested in revealing certain formal changes and alternatives within the history of narrative filmmaking. It seems intuitively apparent that different types of films call forth different rules and procedures of sense-making. We ought to be able to specify the kinds of textual cues and structures which solicit particular viewing acitivites. It will be useful, then, to study how some distinct narrational options have emerged within various filmmaking traditions. I have selected the concept of *mode* as one which will reveal, at a certain level of generality, significant unity among historically specific narrational strategies. The foray into descriptive poetics that occupies Part 3 will show how various bodies of films have actualized the abstract principles considered in Part 2.

The term "mode" demands a quick gloss. Etymologically, it derives from *modus*, or "measure"; since the seventeenth century, English speakers have included among its meanings that of conventional or habitual usage, as in "mode of behavior." Theoretically, the term connects with Aristotle's "mode of imitation" in the *Poetics*, where he distinguishes among various ways in which the poet can present the fable. To some extent, I also intend to signal the widely accepted difference between mode and genre. A genre varies significantly between periods and social formations; a mode tends to be more fundamental, less transient, and more pervasive. In this spirit, I will consider modes of narration to transcend genres, schools, movements, and entire national cinemas. Finally, the notion of a plurality of modes allows us to grasp different systems of conventions. It is uninformative to call a film "unconventional," for its peculiarity may itself be law-abiding according to another set of conventions.

A narrational mode is a historically distinct set of norms of narrational construction and comprehension. The notion of norm is straightforward: any film can be seen as seeking to meet or not to meet a coherent standard established by fiat or by previous practice. *Rear Window*, *In This Our Life*, and *The Big Sleep* are made and understood within terms canonized by many years of Hollywood filmmaking.

"The history of art, if we examine it from the standpoint of the aesthetic norm, is the history of revolts against reigning norms."[1] Jan Mukařovský thus posits an initial distinction between the reigning norm—the canonized style, the mainstream practice—and deviations from that. In fictional cinema, the split would correspond to the average viewer's distinction between ordinary movies and offbeat stuff. We can go further, however. For one thing, *within* the reigning norm there is always a range of differentiation. Moreover, *outside* the reigning norm, all is not sheer heterogeneity. A deviation from mainstream practice tends itself to be organized with respect to another extrinsic norm, however much a minority affair it may be. Films like *The Spider's Stratagem* and *The Confrontation* clearly deviate from the narrational canons of classical Hollywood cinema, but they are constructed in line with other norms.

We are left with the possibility that a film may be analyzed as norm-breaking, norm-affirming, or both. A film may accede (differentially) to a reigning set of norms: nearly all Hollywood films do this. A film may challenge the reigning set of norms, as, for instance, *The Spider's Stratagem* and *The Confrontation* challenge classical filmmaking; but that challenge will itself be codified with respect to more pertinent and proximate norms. It is the relative stability and coherence of these sets of norms that enable viewers to learn and apply various schemata of narrative comprehension. These norms also provide filmmakers with patterns of construction. To treat sets of norms as supplying concrete historical bases for the acts of viewing and filmmaking is to consider them as what I am calling modes of narration.

There are also what stylisticians of literature call "secondary" or *intrinsic* norms. These are the standards attained within the text itself. Intrinsic narrational norms obviously constitute a central source for our stable and ongoing expectations as we move through a particular film. Because of the primacy effect and the durational control that the viewing situation exercises, the viewer tends to base conclusions about the narrational norm upon the earliest portions of the syuzhet. The first few scenes in *Rear Window* imply that we will be confined to what can be seen from within Jeff's apartment. In *The Spider's Stratagem*, the narration quickly establishes the norm that shot changes will likely involve ellipses or durational ambiguities. The first scene of *The Confrontation*, as we saw, sets up the expectation that each subsequent scene will deploy a very limited number of stylistic possibilities.

Like all norms, intrinsic norms can be transgressed or modified. The narration can deviate from its own most likely patterns of construction. We saw in Chapter 3 how *Rear Window* swerved from its spatial norm during the scene of the dog's death. In later portions of *The Spider's Stratagem*, ellipsis and durational ambiguities become much less common, thus modifying the film's own "rule." Perhaps most drastic of all is the way that the narration of *The Confrontation* violates its intrinsic norm by suddenly cutting in to a huge close-up of Jutka as she is discharged from the group.

The concept of the intrinsic norm lets us study narration as a dynamic phenomenon, capable of developing through the film and shaping or challenging expectations in the process. It should be noted, however, that a film's intrinsic norms may be more or less idiosyncratic. *Murder My Sweet* restricts the syuzhet to what Marlowe knows; as one basis for our continuous hypothesis-forming activity, this constitutes an intrinsic norm of the film's narration. But the restriction of the syuzhet is a convention of the detective genre. (We saw it in *The Big Sleep* too.) Here the norm that the film attains matches one already canonized extrinsically. Another work might create rare or unique intrinsic norms. Moreover, the individual film's *deviation* from its intrinsic norm can be a perfectly acceptable *fulfillment* of an extrinsic one. In *Murder My Sweet*, the scene in which Marlowe awakes to find himself drugged violates the film's intrinsic norm in that we learn more than he knows. (See p. 68.) But the brief violation of restricted narration obeys one extrinsic norm of the classical detective film, which periodically punctuates the narration with more unrestricted access for the

sake of whetting suspense or curiosity (pp. 65–66). Thus, of any momentary deviation, we must ask: Does the breaking of the film's intrinsic norm still fulfill norms of the general narrational mode to which the film belongs?

Any norm, extrinsic or intrinsic, gets unified by setting limits to what is possible. If every card is wild you can't play cards at all. The norm thus damns a great many practices as nonpertinent. But the unity of a norm should not be construed as stringent uniformity. Most differences are not deviations. What makes a norm diversified is that it creates a range of compositional *options*. In Hollywood film style, for instance, there are several ways to make spatial arrangement stress an important point: instead of a cut-in to a close-up, we can get a track-in, or a shift in lighting, or a character's movement into the foreground. A norm is usefully considered as what semiologists call a paradigm—a bounded set of alternatives which at some level serve equivalent functions. We shall find that each narrational mode allows a range of paradigmatic options. (Some modes, such as that of art-cinema narration, vigorously encourage the development of new devices for normalized functions.) A film's narration will differentiate between what is a likely alternative, what is improbable but still within the norm, and what is improbable because distinctly outside the paradigm. One can underscore a point in a classical film by all the means I mentioned but not, say, by the filmmaker's voice-over commentary exhorting us to notice something; that is ruled out in this paradigm. In any instance, the analyst can always shift focus from the possible variants (why x in this text rather than y or z?) to the normalized boundaries set on them (why are x, y, and z the only options in this film or in this mode?).

Insofar as a spectator comprehends a film, he or she must relate it to some schemata. Narrational norms, especially extrinsic ones, appeal to the spectator's schemata. Not all schemata are norm-derived, however. My expectations about what a fictional dog will do may be based on a schema derived from the behavior of my faithful Shep. We must limit ourselves, as I have from the outset, to those schemata which are historically intersubjective and characteristic of the formal process of narrative comprehension. Narrational norms satisfy both conditions: they underlie the viewing activities of spectators, and they constitute the principal source of formal expectations. Felix Vodička says of literary history: "All the possible concretizations of an individual reader cannot become the goal of understanding, but only those that reflect the encounters between the structure of the work and the structure of the literary norms of a period."[2] As for the question of which "comes first"—extrinsic norms or spectator schemata—there can be no sweeping answer. Some norms seem to follow already-acquired schemata in the audience. In early cinema, filmmakers drew upon the narrational conventions of dominant forms of storytelling. Similarly, the norms of the international "art cinema" objectify template schemata (e.g., alternatives to the canonic story format) which educated audiences had already constructed for comprehending early modernist literature and theater. In other cases, the filmic norm may be formulated before very many viewers have appropriate schemata ready to hand. This occurs in avant-garde movements, which often teach viewers how to construe the movement's films.

How does the spectator recognize norms and deviations in watching a film? Quantitative grounds play some part. Generally speaking, the more an element recurs within a film or body of films, the more it is taken for granted by the spectator and the more it contributes to forming a tacit standard. If every scene is presented in a comparable fashion—e.g., restricted syuzhet handling, spatial continuity, and so forth—this will constitute an intrinsic norm. There is thus some justification for statistical study, especially of stylistic features. This method could supply a more exact sense of how frequent some devices are within a film or within a mode. This is not to say, however, that quantitative measures can be divorced from a spectator's or critic's recognition of the significance and relevance of a device. For one thing, the most narrationally perceptible factors are often not easily quantifiable. How could one statistically study the minimization of psychological motivation in a film like *The Confrontation*? The viewer's expectations, however probabilistic, are only approximate and not reducible to statistical

measures. Furthermore, a negligible element (e.g., a patch of color in the upper-right corner of the frame) may recur as often as a narrationally important factor (e.g., the presence of the protagonist in the shot).[3] Quantitative measures cannot alone determine narrational salience, though they can be useful when guided by theoretically defined qualitative concepts.

Of these qualitative concepts, two are especially important for our purposes. *Prominence* refers to the perceived highlighting of a narrational tactic with respect to an extrinsic norm. In the art cinema, for instance, shifts between "objective" action and "subjective" moments are often not signaled by the narration. This creates a suppressed gap which we retrospectively try to fill, as when we supply the missing "frames" around the flashbacks of *The Spider's Stratagem*. These suppressed gaps leap into prominence against the background of the classical narrative mode, which provides explicit signals for the transitions between objectivity and subjectivity. Jancsó's use of the long take in *The Confrontation* is an instance of stylistic prominence, since it deviates sharply from normal decoupage practice.

Foregrounding, in the sense I shall use it in this book, refers to the salience of a narrational tactic with respect to intrinsic norms. If a film typically signals the transition from objective to subjective states but then on one occasion does *not*, that occasion becomes foregrounded. In *The Spider's Stratagem*, the absence of a framing "recounting" situation foregrounds Draifa's flashback as a significant deviation from the others. In *The Confrontation*, the cut-in to Jutka's close-up is a foregrounded device.

In both prominence and foregrounding, deviations include not only violations of normal patterns but exceptional *regularities* of pattern. For example, in *The Confrontation*, the framing of the syuzhet action within out-of-focus shots at the beginning and the end of the film achieves a degree of stylistic symmetry not specified by extrinsic norms (thus achieving prominence) but also not achieved elsewhere in the film (thus becoming foregrounded too).

Prominence and foregrounding are structured and functional. The salient features must stand in some relevant relation to the film as a whole. The feature may be motivated in various ways, it may connect with other normal or deviant features, it may contribute to modifying the viewer's hypotheses, and so forth. To take our earlier example: if the single suppressed transition from an objective state to a subjective state coincides with a central causal event or is justified by reference to a notion of realism or makes us rethink fabula information we had taken for granted, then the foregrounding of the device has a function within the film's narration. As we saw, *The Spider's Stratagem* varies its treatment of flashback cues so as to make the line between mental subjectivity and narrational commentary difficult to draw. What Mukařovský says of foregrounding applies to prominence as well: it has "consistency and a systematic character."[4] That is, incidentally, another reason why a sheerly quantitative approach misses the point: any aberration is not ipso facto a case of prominence or foregrounding.

Prominence and foregrounding may be present in varying degrees. In general, the degree of prominence is proportional to the historical probability that the film will manifest this intrinsic norm. *Citizen Kane*'s long takes gain some prominence with respect to classical norms of editing, but against those same norms *The Confrontation*, with its constant use of long takes, emerges as having far greater prominence. As for foregrounding, it is usually strengthened insofar as the disparities between the salient passage and the film's intrinsic norm spread over several dimensions of syuzhet composition, stylistic patterning, or both. In *The Confrontation*, the first cut-in, to women on a balcony, is less foregrounded than the cut-in to Jutka later. The latter presents a greater change in shot-scale, comes at a more critical point in the scene, and so forth.

To sum up: The spectator comes to a film with schemata, and these are derived in part from experience with extrinsic norms. The viewer applies these schemata to the film, matching the expectations appropriate to the norms with their fulfillment within the film. Greater or lesser deviations from these norms stand out as prominent. At the same time, the viewer is alert for any norms set up by the film itself; these intrinsic norms may coincide with or deviate from the conventions of the extrinsic set. Finally, the spectator may encounter foregrounded elements, the moments when the film diverges to some degree from intrinsic norms. In a sort of feedback process, these deviations may then be compared with pertinent extrinsic norms. Throughout this process, both intrinsic and extrinsic norms set up paradigms, or rough sets of alternatives which form the basis of spectators' schemata, assumptions, inferences, and hypotheses.

All this sounds more complicated than it is in practice, but parsing out the factors involved shows the central importance of extrinsic norms. Organized into narrational modes, these norms supply the most "naive" viewer and the most sophisticated critic with primary tools for constructing a film's narrative.

Although one could generate an abstract deductive taxonomy of narrational modes, it would be a colossal task. Since any narrational parameter (e.g., temporary/permanent gaps, restricted/unrestricted narration) can be varied with respect to any other, we could wind up with a menagerie of combinations that achieves logical exhaustiveness at the expense of critical incisiveness. Moreover, it is not simply the particular combination of factors that characterizes a narrational mode. Often two modes will weight the same organizing principle differently. In art-cinema narration, for example, authorial commentary counts for more than it does in the classical narrative cinema. Parametric narration makes stylistic patterning more significant than it is in other modes. In order to recognize how different films utilize such varying "dominants," we need to be able to describe some historically salient modes without demanding that the descriptions be exclusive or exhaustive. I therefore claim only that the modes discussed in the chapters that follow differ significantly in their deployment of narrational principles. There could be, and probably have been, other modes of fictional filmmaking than the ones I pick out.

Treating norms historically lets us fill in those hollow forms that I have plotted in Part 2. Now we can see, for instance, that the various sorts of motivation that the spectator supplies will gain concrete substance from pertinent extrinsic norms. "Realistic" motivation will be applied according to what the given narrational mode defines as realistic. In other words, verisimilitude in a classical narrative film is quite different from verisimilitude in the art cinema. Compositional motivation is likewise bound to extrinsic norms in that they will shape what counts as essential to the fabula's causal scheme. What I have called "transtextual" motivation obviously presupposes a bounded set of other films within a mode. One cannot say that Groucho Marx's jokes addressed to the camera are motivated by transtextual citation of the work of Godard. Even artistic motivation—the calling of attention to a device or pattern for its own sake—will vary according to the demands of extrinsic norms.

Another advantage of a historical scheme is that it may help us realize how we intuitively make sense of films. What goes on when children learn to construct the story of *Snow White* or (to go down several notches in subtlety) *E.T.*? What is happening when someone gradually learns to make some sense of a film by Fellini or Oshima or Bresson? Those of us involved in film criticism and pedagogy must confront still other questions. What is V. F. Perkins assuming when he suggests that Nicholas Ray's editing reflects the dislocated lives of his characters?[5] What are film teachers doing when they teach students to analyze, interpret, and judge films? My answers should be apparent, although still general. Children learn to follow ordinary films by learning schemata and norms, by discovering what notions of causality, time, and space are permitted within the dominant mode and are appropriate to the cues supplied. People come to appreciate a range of films by acquiring schemata and by sensing what is normative within given modes. The critic is often concerned with showing how a film's narrational operations conform to a given mode, or with persuading us that a film commonly construed according to one mode can be fruitfully studied in relation to another one. (So Perkins suggests that we take Ray's films as instances not of classical narration but of art-cinema narration.) And film teaching consists to a great extent of exploring norms which the student already knows (e.g., analyzing an MGM musical) or introducing the student to new norms. I think it evident, for instance, that most college courses in film seek to promote the mode of the art cinema at the expense of classical narrative film, and this involves demonstrating new viewing activities which the student is expected to master. If the chapters that follow had no other consequence, I would be happy if they could spur viewers, critics, and teachers to consider how their activities operate within tacit, conventional frameworks that are social and historical.

We can construct narrational norms by drawing upon several bodies of data. There are, most obviously, the films themselves. Our analysis will distinguish systematic differences of syuzhet and style according to mode. Other evidence is furnished by viewers' recognition of differences. That most spectators will intuitively judge *Rear Window* as more like *The Big Sleep* than *The Confrontation* is not an explanation, but it is a clue to normative differences. Another source of data is that body of discourse which states guidelines for producing or consuming the films—manifestos, rule books, technical manuals, theoretical treatises, and educational practices. (How many viewers of today's art cinema were initiated by college textbooks explicating the personal vision of Bergman or Truffaut?) There are also the writings of critics who, as Felix Vodička suggests, tend to "place" the artwork with respect to norms that are presumed to be widely shared by the critic's audience.[6] Much the same sources will furnish some help in locating intrinsic norms, though here of course close analysis is the principal tool.

Accepting a historical basis for narrational norms requires recognizing that every mode of narration is tied to a mode of film production and reception. It would be naive to think that, in a mass medium like cinema, norms rise and fall of their own accord. One can link conservative, norm-abiding aspects of Hollywood filmmaking to the studio system's standardized division of labor and production practices.[7] The art cinema's insistence upon modifying both extrinsic and intrinsic norms operates within a marketing system in which authorial differentiation and intracareer development have exchange value. This is not a book of social or economic history, but "historicizing" narration demands that I suggest, if only in passing, some concrete causes and consequences of these modes.

The narrational modes I will examine in the next four chapters are these: classical narrative cinema (exemplified by Hollywood); the international art cinema; historical-materialist cinema (exemplified by Soviet montage films of the 1920s and some 1960s European work); and what I shall call "parametric" cinema. Each constitutes a distinct and coherent set of conventions of syuzhet construction and film style, and these conventions are actually used in creating and understanding fictional films. This is not to say that the conventions are immutable—indeed, one of my subsidiary concerns will be to show that most modes have changed across time. Nor am I suggesting that every film stands in strict accord with one mode. For many reasons, a particular

film may be made or understood with respect to several modes; it becomes, in Mukařovský's words, "a complex tangle of norms. Being full of internal harmonies and disharmonies, it represents a dynamic equilibrium of heterogeneous norms applied in part positively, in part negatively."[8] Chapter 13 will consider how the work of Jean-Luc Godard affords vivid examples of such heterogeneity.

Finally, I should mention that my categories are not intended as evaluative ones. I do not prefer one narrational mode to another, although I believe that in some circumstances certain modes have a better claim on our attention than others do. My chief concern here is analytical. By spelling out the norms constituting each mode, we can begin to show how the construction and comprehension of film narration have operated in history.

9. Classical Narration
The Hollywood Example

In fictional filmmaking, one mode of narration has achieved predominance. Whether we call it mainstream, dominant, or classical cinema, we intuitively recognize an ordinary, easily comprehensible movie when we see it. Our survey of narrational modes can properly start with this classical tradition, since it relies on the strongest schemata and the most prevalent extrinsic norms. Our example will be the most historically influential classicism: Hollywood studio filmmaking of the years 1917 to 1960. The concepts developed so far in this book allow us to analyze classical Hollywood narration with considerable precision. We do not need to fall back on clichés like "transparency," "seamlessness," "invisibility," "concealment of production," or "*discours* posing as *histoire*." We can define classical narration as a particular configuration of normalized options for representing the fabula and for manipulating the possibilities of syuzhet and style. This approach will also enable us to suggest a more dynamic account of the spectator's role.[1]

Canonic Narration

The classical Hollywood film presents psychologically defined individuals who struggle to solve a clear-cut problem or to attain specific goals. In the course of this struggle, the characters enter into conflict with others or with external circumstances. The story ends with a decisive victory or defeat, a resolution of the problem and a clear achievement or nonachievement of the goals. The principal causal agency is thus the character, a discriminated individual endowed with a consistent batch of evident traits, qualities, and behaviors. Although the cinema inherits many conventions of portrayal from theater and literature, the character types of melodrama and popular fiction get fleshed out by the addition of unique motifs, habits, or behavioral tics. In parallel fashion, the star system has as one of its functions the creation of a rough character prototype for each star which is then adjusted to the particular needs of the role. The most "specified" character is usually the protagonist, who becomes the principal causal agent, the target of any narrational restriction, and the chief object of audience identification. These features of the syuzhet will come as no surprise, though already there are important differences from other narrational modes (e.g., the comparative absence of consistent and goal-oriented characters in art-cinema narration).

Of all modes, the classical one conforms most closely to the "canonic story" which story-comprehension researchers posit as normal for our culture. In fabula terms, the reliance upon character-centered causality and the definition of the action as the attempt to achieve a goal are both salient features of the canonic format.[2] At the level of the syuzhet, the classical film respects the canonic pattern of establishing an initial state of affairs which gets violated and which must then be set right. Indeed, Hollywood screenplay-writing manuals have long insisted on a formula which has been revived in recent structural analysis: the plot consists of an undisturbed stage, the disturbance, the struggle, and the elimination of the disturbance.[3] Such a syuzhet pattern is the inheritance not of some monolithic construct called the "novelistic" but of specific historical forms: the well-made play, the popular romance, and, crucially, the late-nineteenth-century short story.[4] The characters' causal interactions are thus to a great extent functions of such overarching syuzhet/fabula patterns.

In classical fabula construction, causality is the prime unifying principle. Analogies between characters, settings, and situations are certainly present, but at the denotative level any parallelism is subordinated to the movement of cause and effect.[5] Spatial configurations are motivated by realism (a newspaper office must contain desks, typewriters, phones) and, chiefly, by compositional necessity (the desk and typewriter will be used to write causally significant news stories; the phones form crucial links among characters). Causality also motivates temporal principles of organization: the syuzhet represents the order, frequency, and duration of fabula events in ways which bring out the salient causal relations. This process is especially evident in a device highly characteristic of classical narration—the deadline. A deadline can be measured by calendars (*Around the World in Eighty Days*), by clocks (*High Noon*), by stipulation ("You've got a week but not a minute longer"), or simply by cues that time is running out (the last-minute rescue). That the climax of a classical film is often a deadline shows the structural power of defining dramatic duration as the time it takes to achieve or fail to achieve a goal.

Usually the classical syuzhet presents a double causal structure, two plot lines: one involving heterosexual romance (boy/girl, husband/wife), the other line involving another sphere—work, war, a mission or quest, other personal relationships. Each line will possess a goal, obstacles, and a climax. In *Wild and Woolly* (1917), the hero, Jeff, has two goals—to live a wild Western life and to court Nell, the woman of his dreams. The plot can be complicated by several lines, such as countervailing goals (the people of Bitter Creek want Jeff to get them a railroad spur, a crooked Indian agent wants to pull a robbery) or multiple romances (as in *Footlight Parade* and *Meet Me in St. Louis*). In most cases, the romance sphere and the other sphere of action are distinct but interdependent. The plot may close off one line before the other, but often the two lines coincide at the climax: resolving one triggers the resolution of the other. In *His Girl Friday*, the reprieve of Earl Williams precedes the reconciliation of Walter and Hildy, but it is also the condition of the couple's reunion.

The syuzhet is always broken up into segments. In the silent era, the typical Hollywood film would contain between nine and eighteen sequences; in the sound era, between fourteen and thirty-five (with postwar films tending to have more sequences). Speaking roughly, there are only two types of Hollywood segments: "montage sequences" (compromising Metz's third, fourth, and eighth syntagmatic types) and "scenes" (Metz's fifth, sixth, seventh, and eighth types).[6] Hollywood narration clearly demarcates its scenes by neoclassical criteria—unity of time (continuous or consistently intermittent duration), space (a definable locale), and action (a distinct cause-effect phase). The bounds of the sequence will be marked by some standardized punctuations (dissolve, fade, wipe, sound bridge).[7] Raymond Bellour points out that the classical segment tends also to define itself microcosmically (through internal repetitions of style or story material) and macrocosmically (by parallels with other segments of the same magnitude).[8] We must also remember that each film establishes its own scale of segmentation. A syuzhet which concentrates on a single locale over a limited dramatic duration (e.g., the one-night-in-a-haunted-house film) may create segments by character entrances or exits, a theatrical *liaison des scènes*. In a film which spans decades and many locales, a series of dissolves from one small action to another will not necessarily constitute distinct sequences.

The classical segment is not a sealed entity. Spatially and temporally it is closed, but causally it is open. It works to advance the causal progression and open up new developments.[9] The pattern of this forward momentum is quite codified. The montage sequence tends to function as a transitional summary, condensing a single causal development, but the scene of character action—the building block of classical Hollywood dramaturgy—is more intricately con-

structed. Each scene displays distinct phases. First comes the exposition, which specifies the time, place, and relevant characters—their spatial positions and their current states of mind (usually as a result of previous scenes). In the middle of the scene, characters act toward their goals: they struggle, make choices, make appointments, set deadlines, and plan future events. In the course of this, the classical scene continues or closes off cause-effect developments left dangling in prior scenes while also opening up new causal lines for future development. At least one line of action must be left suspended, in order to motivate the shifts to the next scene, which picks up the suspended line (often via a "dialogue hook"). Hence the famous "linearity" of classical construction—a trait not characteristic of Soviet montage films (which often refuse to demarcate scenes clearly) or of art-cinema narration (with its ambiguous interplay of subjectivity and objectivity).

Here is a simple example. In *The Killers* (1946), the insurance investigator Riordan has been hearing Lieutenant Lubinsky's account of Ole Anderson's early life. At the end of the scene, Lubinsky tells Riordan that they're burying Ole today. This dangling cause leads to the next scene, set in the cemetery. An establishing shot provides spatial exposition. While the clergyman intones the funeral oration, Riordan asks Lubinsky the identity of various mourners. The last, a solitary old man, is identified as "an old-time hoodlum named Charleston." Dissolve to a pool hall, with Charleston and Riordan at a table drinking and talking about Ole. During the burial scene, the Lubinsky line of inquiry is closed off and the Charleston line is initiated. When the scene halts, Charleston is left suspended, but he is picked up immediately in the exposition of the next scene. Instead of a complex braiding of causal lines (as in the films of Rivette) or an abrupt breaking of them (as in Antonioni, Godard, or Bresson), the classical Hollywood film spins them out in smooth, careful linearity.

Something else contributes to this linearity. The mystery film, with its resolved enigma at the end, is only the most apparent instance of the tendency of the classical syuzhet to develop toward full and adequate knowledge. Whether a protagonist learns a moral lesson or only the spectator knows the whole story, the classical film moves steadily toward a growing awareness of absolute truth.

The linkage of causal lines must eventually terminate. How to conclude the syuzhet? There are two ways of regarding the classical ending. We can see it as the crowning of the structure, the logical conclusion of the string of events, the final effect of the initial cause, the revelation of the truth. This view has some validity, not only in the light of the tight construction that we frequently encounter in Hollywood films but also given the precepts of Hollywood screenwriting. Rule books tirelessly bemoan the pressures for a happy ending and emphasize the need for a logical wrap-up. Still, there are enough instances of unmotivated or inadequate plot resolutions to suggest a second hypothesis: that the classical ending is not all that structurally decisive, being a more or less arbitrary readjustment of that world knocked awry in the previous eighty minutes. Parker Tyler suggests that Hollywood regards all endings as "purely conventional, formal, and often, like the charade, of an infantile logic."[10] Here again we see the importance of the plot line involving heterosexual romance. It is significant that of one hundred randomly sampled Hollywood films, over sixty ended with a display of the united romantic couple—the cliché happy ending, often with a "clinch"—and many more could be said to end happily. Thus an extrinsic norm, the need to resolve the plot in a way that yields "poetic justice," provides a structural constant, inserted with more or less motivation into its proper slot, the epilogue. In any narrative, as Meir Sternberg points out, when the syuzhet's end is strongly precast by convention, the compositional attention falls on the retardation accomplished by the middle portions; the text will then "account for the necessary retardation in quasi-mimetic terms by placing the causes for delay within the fictive world itself and turning the middle into the bulk of the represented action."[11] At times, however, the motivation fails, and a discordance between preceding causality and happy denouement may become noticeable as an ideological difficulty; such is the case with films like *You Only Live Once, Suspicion, The Woman in the Window,* and *The Wrong Man.*[12] We ought, then, to be prepared for either a skillful tying up of all loose ends or a more or less miraculous appearance of what Brecht called bourgeois literature's mounted messenger. "The mounted messenger guarantees you a truly undisturbed appreciation of even the most intolerable conditions, so it is a sine qua non for a literature whose sine qua non is that it leads nowhere."[13]

The classical ending may be a sore spot in another respect. Even if the ending resolves the two principal causal lines, some comparatively minor issues may still be left dangling. For example, the fates of secondary characters may go unsettled. In *His Girl Friday,* Earl Williams is reprieved, the corrupt administration will be thrown out of office, and Walter and Hildy are reunited, but we never learn what happens to Molly Malloy, who jumped out a window to distract the reporters. (We know only that she was alive after the fall.) One could argue that in the resolution of the main problem we forget minor matters, but this is only a partial explanation. Our forgetting is promoted by the device of closing the film with an *epilogue,* a brief celebration of the stable state achieved by the main characters. Not only does the epilogue reinforce the tendency toward a happy ending; it also repeats connotative motifs that have run throughout the film. *His Girl Friday* closes on a brief epilogue of Walter and Hildy calling the newspaper office to announce their remarriage. They learn that a strike has started in Albany, and Walter proposes stopping off to cover it on their honeymoon. This plot twist announces a repetition of what happened on their first honeymoon and recalls that Hildy was going to marry Bruce and live in Albany. As the couple leave, Hildy carrying her suitcase, Walter suggests that Bruce might put them up. The neat recurrence of these motifs gives the narration a strong unity; when such details are so tightly bound together, Molly Malloy's fate is more likely to be overlooked. Perhaps instead of "closure" it would be better to speak of a "closure effect," or even, if the strain of resolved and unresolved issues seems strong, of "pseudoclosure." At the level of extrinsic norms, though, the most coherent possible epilogue remains the standard to be aimed at.

Commonplaces like "transparency" and "invisibility" are

on the whole unhelpful in specifying the narrational properties of the classical film. Very generally, we can say that classical narration tends to be omniscient, highly communicative, and only moderately self-conscious. That is, the narration knows more than all the characters, conceals relatively little (chiefly "what will happen next"), and seldom acknowledges its own address to the audience. But we must qualify this characterization in two respects. First, generic factors often create variations upon these precepts. A detective film will be quite restricted in its range of knowledge and highly suppressive in concealing causal information. A melodrama like *In This Our Life* can be slightly more self-conscious than *The Big Sleep*, especially in its use of acting and music. A musical will contain codified moments of self-consciousness (e.g., when characters sing directly out at the viewer). Second, the temporal progression of the syuzhet makes narrational properties fluctuate across the film, and these fluctuations too are codified. Typically, the opening and closing of the film are the most self-conscious, omniscient, and communicative passages. The credit sequence and the first few shots usually bear traces of an overt narration. Once the action has started, however, the narration becomes more covert, letting the characters and their interaction take over the transmission of information. Overt narrational activity returns at certain conventional moments: the beginnings and endings of scenes (e.g., establishing shots, shots of signs, camera movements out from or in to significant objects, symbolic dissolves), and summary passages known as "montage sequences." At the very close of the syuzhet, the narration may again acknowledge its awareness of the audience (nondiegetic music reappears, characters look to the camera or close a door in our face), its omniscience (e.g., the camera retreats to a long shot), and its communicativeness (now we know all). Classical narration is thus not equally "invisible" in every type of film or throughout any one film.

The communicativeness of classical narration is evident in the way that the syuzhet handles gaps. If time is skipped over, a montage sequence or a bit of character dialogue informs us; if a cause is missing, we will typically be informed that something isn't there. And gaps will seldom be permanent. "In the beginning of the motion picture," writes one scenarist, "we don't know anything. During the course of the story, information is accumulated, until at the end we know everything."[14] Again, these principles can be mitigated by generic motivation. A mystery might suppress a gap (e.g., the opening of *Mildred Pierce*), a fantasy might leave a cause still questionable at the end (e.g., *The Enchanted Cottage*). In this respect, *Citizen Kane* remains somewhat "unclassical": the narration supplies the answer to the "Rosebud" mystery, but the central traits of Kane's character remain partly undetermined, and no generic motivation justifies this.

The syuzhet's construction of time powerfully shapes the fluctuating overtness of narration. When the syuzhet adheres to chronological order and omits the causally unimportant periods of time, the narration becomes highly communicative and unselfconscious. On the other hand, when a montage sequence compresses a political campaign, a murder trial, or the effects of Prohibition into moments, the narration becomes overtly omniscient. A flashback can quickly and covertly fill a causal gap. Redundancy can be achieved without violating the fabula world if the narration represents each story event several times in the syuzhet, through one enactment and several recountings in character dialogue. Deadlines neatly let the syuzhet unselfconsciously respect the durational limits that the fabula world sets for its action. When it is necessary to suggest repeated or habitual actions, the montage sequence will again do nicely, as Sartre noted when he praised *Citizen Kane*'s montages for achieving the equivalent of the "frequentative" tense: "He made his wife sing in every theatre in America."[15] When the syuzhet uses a newspaper headline to cover gaps of time, we recognize both the narration's omniscience and its relatively low profile. (The public record is less self-conscious than an intertitle "coming straight from" the narration.) More generally, classical narration reveals its discretion by posing as an *editorial* intelligence that selects certain stretches of time for full-scale treatment (the scenes), pares down others a little, presents others in highly compressed fashion (the montage sequences), and simply scissors out events that are inconsequential. When fabula duration is expanded, it is done through crosscutting, as we have seen in our consideration of *The Birth of a Nation* (p. 84).

Overall narrational qualities also get manifested in the film's manipulation of space. Figures are adjusted for moderate self-consciousness by angling the bodies more or less frontally but avoiding to-camera gazes (except, of course, in optical point-of-view passages). That no causally significant cues in a scene are left unknown testifies to the communicativeness of the narration. Most important is the tendency of the classical film to render narrational omniscience as spatial *omnipresence*.[16] If the narration plays down its knowledge of upcoming events, it does not hesitate to reveal its ability to change views at will by cutting within a scene and crosscutting between various locales. Writing in 1935, a critic claims that the camera is omniscient in that it "stimulates, through correct choice of subject matter and set-up, the sense within the percipient of 'being at the most vital part of the experience—at the most advantageous point of perception' throughout the picture."[17] Whereas Miklós Jancsó's long takes create spatial patterns that refuse omnipresence and thus drastically restrict the spectator's knowledge of story information, classical omnipresence makes the cognitive schema we call "the camera" into an *ideal* invisible observer, freed from the contingencies of space and time but discreetly confining itself to codified patterns for the sake of story intelligibility.

By virtue of its handling of space and time, classical narration makes the fabula world an internally consistent construct into which narration seems to step from the outside. Manipulation of mise-en-scène (figure behavior, lighting, setting, costume) creates an apparently independent profilmic event, which becomes the tangible story world framed and recorded from without. This framing and recording tends to be taken as the narration itself, which can in turn be more or less overt, more or less "intrusive" upon the posited homogeneity of the story world. Classical narration thus depends upon the notion of the invisible observer.[18] Bazin, for instance, portrays the classical scene as existing independently of narration, as if on a stage.[19] The same quality is named by the notion of "concealment of production": the fabula seems not to have been constructed; it appears to have preexisted its narrational representation. (In production, in some sense, it often did: for major films of the 1930s and thereafter, Hollywood set designers created toy sets within which model cameras, actors, and lighting units could be placed to predetermine filming procedures.)[20]

This "invisible-observer" narration is itself often fairly effaced, for stylistic causes that I shall examine shortly. But we can already see that classical narration quickly cues us to construct story logic (causality, parallelisms), time, and space in ways that make the events "before the camera" our principal source of information. For example, it is obvious that Hollywood narratives are highly redundant, but this effect is achieved principally by patterns attributable to the story world. Following Susan Suleiman's taxonomy,[21] we can see that the narration assigns the same traits and functions to each character on her or his appearance; different characters present the same interpretive commentary on the same character or situation; similar events involve different characters; and so on. Information is for the most part repeated by characters' dialogue or demeanor. There is also some redundancy between narrational commentary and depicted fabula action, as when silent film expository intertitles convey crucial information or when nondiegetic music is pleonastic with the action (e.g., "Here Comes the Bride" in *In This Our Life*). But, in general, the narration is so constructed that characters and their behavior produce and reiterate the necessary story data. (The Soviet montage cinema makes much stronger use of redundancies between narrational commentary and fabula action.) Retardation operates in analogous fashion: the construction of the total fabula is delayed principally by inserted lines of action, such as causally relevant subplots, interpolated comedy bits, and musical numbers (rather than by narrational digressions of the sort found in the "God and Country" sequence of *October*). Similarly, causal gaps in the fabula are usually signaled by character actions (e.g., the discovery of clues in detective films). The viewer concentrates on constructing the fabula, not on asking why the narration is representing the fabula in this particular way—a question more typical of art-cinema narration.

The priority of causality within an integral fabula world commits classical narration to unambiguous presentation. Whereas art-cinema narration can blur the lines separating objective diegetic reality, characters' mental states, and inserted narrational commentary, the classical film asks us to assume clear distinctions among these states. When the classical film restricts knowledge to a character, as in most of *The Big Sleep* and *Murder My Sweet*, there is nonetheless a firm borderline between subjective and objective depiction. Of course the narration can set traps for us, as in *Possessed*, when a murder that appears to be objective is revealed to have been subjective (a generically motivated switch, incidentally); but the hoax is revealed immediately and unequivocally. The classical flashback is revealing in this connection. Its *presence* is almost invariably motivated subjectively, since a character's recollection triggers the enacted representation of a prior event. But the *range of knowledge* in the flashback portion is often not identical with that of the character doing the remembering. It is common for the flashback to show us more than the character can know (e.g., scenes in which she or he is not present). An amusing example occurs in *Ten North Frederick*. The bulk of the film is presented as the daughter's flashback, but at the end of the syuzhet, back in the present, she learns for the first time information we had encountered in "her" flashback! Classical flashbacks are typically "objective": character memory is a pretext for a nonchronological syuzhet arrangement. Similarly, optically subjective shots become anchored in an objective context. One writer notes that a point-of-view shot "must be motivated by, and definitely linked to, the objective scenes [shots] that precede and follow it."[22] This is one source of the power of the invisible-observer effect: the camera seems always to include character subjectivity within a broader and definite objectivity.

Classical Style

Even if the naive spectator takes the style of the classical Hollywood film to be invisible or seamless, this is not much critical help. What makes the style so self-effacing? The question cannot be completely answered until we consider the spectator's activity, but we may start with Yuri Tynianov's suggestion: "Pointing to the 'restraint' or 'naturalism' of the style in the case of some film or some director is not the same as sweeping away the role of style. Quite simply, there are a variety of styles and they have various roles, according to their relationship to the development of the syuzhet."[23] Three general propositions, then.

1. *On the whole, classical narration treats film technique as a vehicle for the syuzhet's transmission of fabula information*. Of all modes of narration, the classical is most concerned to motivate style compositionally, as a function of syuzhet patterning. Consider the very notion of what we now call a shot. For decades, Hollywood practice called a shot a "scene," thus conflating a material stylistic unit with a dramaturgical one. In classical filmmaking, the overriding principle is to make every instantiation of technique obedient to the character's transmission of fabula information, with the result that bodies and faces become the focal points of attention. Film techniques are patterned to fit the causal structure of the classical scene (exposition, closing off of an old causal factor, introduction of new causal factors, suspension of a new factor). The introduction phase typically includes a shot which establishes the characters in space and time. As the characters interact, the scene is broken up into closer views of action and reaction, while setting, lighting, music, composition, and camera movement enhance the process of goal formulation, struggle, and decision. The scene usually closes on a portion of the space—a facial reaction, a significant object—that provides a transition to the next scene.

While it is true that sometimes a classical film's style becomes "excessive," decoratively supplementing denotative syuzhet demands, the use of technique must be minimally motivated by the characters' interactions. "Excess," such as we find in Minnelli or Sirk, is often initially justified by generic convention. The same holds true for even the most eccentric stylists in Hollywood, Busby Berkeley and Josef von Sternberg, each of whom required a core of generic motivation (musical fantasy and exotic romance, respectively) for his experiments.

2. *In classical narration, style typically encourages the spectator to construct a coherent, consistent time and space for the fabula action.* Many other narrational norms value disorienting the spectator, albeit for different purposes. Only classical narration favors a style which strives for utmost denotative clarity from moment to moment. Each scene's temporal relation to its predecessor will be signaled early and unequivocally (by intertitles, conventional cues, a line of dialogue). Lighting must pick out figure from ground; color must define planes; in each shot, the center of story interest will be near the center of the frame. Sound recording is perfected so as to allow for maximum clarity of dialogue. Camera movements aim to create an unambiguous, voluminous space. "In dollying," remarks Allan Dwan, "as a rule we find it's a good idea to *pass* things . . . . We always noticed that if we dollied past a tree, it became solid and round, instead of flat."[24] Hollywood makes much use of the *anticipatory* composition or camera movement, leaving space in the frame for the action or tracking so as to prepare for another character's entrance. Compare Godard's tendency to make framing wholly subservient to the actor's immediate movement with this comment of Raoul Walsh's: "There is only one way in which to shoot a scene, and that's the way which shows the audience what's happening next."[25] Classical editing aims at making each shot the logical outcome of its predecessor and at reorienting the spectator through repeated setups. Momentary disorientation is permissible only if motivated realistically. The hallucinatory murder in *Possessed* that at first appears to have objectively occurred is justified retrospectively by the protagonist's increasing madness. Discontinuous editing, as in Slavko Vorkapich's montage sequence depicting the earthquake in *San Francisco*, gets motivated by the chaos of the action depicted. Stylistic disorientation, in short, is permissible when it conveys disorienting story situations.

3. *Classical style consists of a strictly limited number of particular technical devices organized into a stable paradigm and ranked probabilistically according to syuzhet demands.* The stylistic conventions of Hollywood narration, ranging from shot composition to sound mixing, are intuitively recognizable to most viewers. This is because the style deploys a limited number of devices and these devices are regulated as alternative depictive options. Lighting offers a simple example. A scene may be lit "high-key" or "low-key." There is three-point lighting (key, fill, and backlighting on figure, plus background lighting) versus single-source lighting. The cinematographer also has several degrees of diffusion available. Now, in the abstract all choices are equiprobable, but in a given context, one alternative is more likely than its mates. In a comedy, high-key lighting is more probable; a dark street will realistically motivate single-source lighting; the close-up of a woman will be more heavily diffused than that of a man. The "invisibility" of the classical style in Hollywood relies not only on highly codified stylistic devices but also upon their codified functions in context.

A similarly restricted paradigm controls the framing of the human figure. Most often, a character will be framed between *plan américain* (the knees-up framing) and medium close-up (the chest-up framing); the angle will be straight on, at shoulder or chin level. The framing is less likely to be an extreme long shot or an extreme close-up, a high or low angle. And a bird's eye view or a view from straight below is very improbable and would require compositional or generic motivation (e.g., as an optical point of view or as a view of a dance ensemble in a musical).

Most explicitly codified into rules is the system of classical continuity editing. The reliance upon an axis of action orients the spectator to the space, and the subsequent cutting presents clear paradigmatic choices among different kinds of "matches." That these are weighted probabilistically is shown by the fact that most Hollywood scenes begin with establishing shots, break the space into closer views linked by eyeline matches and/or shot/reverse shots, and return to more distant views only when character movement or the entry of a new character requires the viewer to be reoriented. An entire scene without an establishing shot is unlikely but permissible (especially if stock or location footage or special effects are employed); mismatched screen direction and inconsistently angled eyelines are less likely; perceptible jump cuts and unmotivated cutaways are flatly forbidden. This paradigmatic aspect makes the classical style, for all its "rules," not a timeless formula or recipe but a historically constrained set of more or less likely options.[26]

These three factors go some way to explaining why the classical Hollywood style passes relatively unnoticed. Each film will recombine familiar devices within fairly predictable patterns and according to the demands of the syuzhet. The spectator will amost never be at a loss to grasp a stylistic feature because he or she is oriented in time and space and because stylistic figures will be interpretable in the light of a paradigm.

When we consider the relation of syuzhet and style, we can say that the classical film is characterized by its obedience to a set of extrinsic norms which govern both syuzhet construction and stylistic patterning. The classical cinema does not encourage the film to cultivate idiosyncratic intrinsic norms; style and syuzhet seldom enjoy prominence. A film's principal innovations occur at the level of the fabula—i.e., "new stories." Of course, syuzhet devices and stylistic features have changed over time. But the fundamental principles of syuzhet construction (preeminence of causality, goal-oriented protagonist, deadlines, etc.) have remained in force since 1917. The stability and uniformity of Hollywood narration yield one reason to call it classical, at least insofar as classicism in any art is traditionally characterized by obedience to extrinsic norms.[27]

The Classical Spectator

The stability of syuzhet processes and stylistic configurations in the classical film should not make us treat the classical spectator as passive material for a totalizing machine. The spectator performs particular cognitive operations which are no less active for being habitual and familiar. The Hollywood fabula is the product of a series of particular schemata, hypotheses, and inferences.

The spectator comes to a classical film very well prepared. The rough shape of syuzhet and fabula is likely to conform to the canonic story of an individual's goal-oriented, causally determined activity. The spectator knows the most likely stylistic figures and functions. He or she has internalized the scenic norm of exposition, development of old causal line, and so forth. The viewer also knows the pertinent ways to motivate what is presented. "Realistic" motivation, in this mode, consists of making connections recognized as plausible by common opinion. (A man like this would naturally . . .) Compositional motivation consists of picking out the important links of cause to effect. The most important forms of transtextual motivation are recognizing the recurrence of a star's persona from film to film and recognizing generic conventions. Generic motivation, as we have seen, has a particularly strong effect on narrational procedures. Finally, artistic motivation—taking an element as being present for its own sake—is not unknown in the classical film. A moment of spectacle or technical virtuosity, a thrown-in musical number or comic interlude: the Hollywood cinema intermittently welcomes the possibility of sheer self-absorption. Such moments may be highly reflexive, "baring the device" of the narration's own work, as when in *Angels over Broadway* a destitute playwright reflects, "Our present plot problem is money."

On the basis of such schemata the viewer projects hypotheses. Hypotheses tend to be probable (validated at several points), sharply exclusive (rendered as either/or alternatives), and aimed at suspense (positing a future outcome). In *Roaring Timber*, a landowner enters a saloon in which our hero is sitting. The owner is looking for a tough foreman. Hypothesis; he will ask the hero to take the job. This hypothesis is probable, future-oriented, and exclusive (either the man will ask our hero or he won't). The viewer is helped in framing such hypotheses by several processes. Repetition reaffirms the data on which hypotheses should be grounded. "State every important fact three times," suggests scenarist Frances Marion, "for the play is lost if the audience fails to understand the premises on which it is based."[28] The exposition of past fabula action will characteristically be placed within the early scenes of the syuzhet, thus supplying a firm basis for our hypothesis-forming. Except in a mystery film, the exposition neither sounds warning signals nor actively misleads us; the primacy effect is given full sway. Characters will be introduced in typical behavior, while the star system reaffirms first impressions. ("The moment you see Walter Pidgeon in a film you know he could not do a mean or petty thing."[29]) The device of the deadline asks the viewer to construct forward-aiming, all-or-nothing causal hypotheses: either the protagonist will achieve the goal in time or he will not. And if information is unobtrusively "planted" early on, later hypotheses will become more probable by taking "insignificant" foreshadowing material for granted.

This process holds at the stylistic level as well. The spectator constructs fabula time and space according to schemata, cues, and hypothesis-framing. Hollywood's extrinsic norms, with their fixed devices and paradigmatic organization, supply the viewer with firm expectations that can be measured against the concrete cues emitted by the film. In making sense of a scene's space, the spectator need not mentally replicate every detail of the space but only construct a rough relational map of the principal dramatic factors. Thus a "cheat cut" is easily ignored because the spectator's cognitive processes rank cues by their pertinence to constructing the ongoing causal chain of the fabula, and on this scale, the changes in speaker, camera position, and facial expression are more noteworthy than, say, a slight shift in hand positions.[30] The same goes for temporal mismatches.

What is rare in the classical film, then, is Henry James's "crooked corridor," the use of narration to make us jump to invalid conclusions.[31] The avoidance of disorientation we saw at work in classical style holds true for syuzhet construction as well. Future-oriented "suspense" hypotheses are more important than past-oriented "curiosity" ones, and surprise is less important than either. In *Roaring Timber*, imagine if the landowner had entered the bar seeking a tough foreman, offered the job to our hero, and he had replied in a fashion that showed he was not tough. Indeed, one purpose of foreshadowing and repetition is exactly to avoid surprises later on. Of course, if all hypotheses were steadily and immediately confirmed, the viewer would quickly lose interest.

Several factors intervene to complicate the process. Most generally, schemata are by definition abstract prototypes, structures, and procedures, and these never specify all the properties of the text. Many long-range hypotheses must await confirmation. Retardation devices, being unpredictable to a great degree, can introduce objects of immediate attention as well as delay satisfaction of overall expectation. The primacy effect can be countered by a "recency effect" which qualifies and perhaps even appears to negate our first impression of a character or situation. Furthermore, the structure of the Hollywood scene, which almost invariably ends with an unresolved issue, assures that an event-centered hypothesis carries interest over to the next sequence. Finally, we should not underestimate the role of rapid rhythm in the classical film; more than one practitioner has stressed the need to move the construction of story action along so quickly that the audience has no time to reflect—or get bored. It is the task of classical narration to solicit strongly probable and exclusive hypotheses and then confirm them while still maintaining variety in the concrete working out of the action.

The classical system is not simpleminded. Recall that under normal exhibition circumstances the film viewer's rate of comprehension is absolutely controlled. The cueing of probable, exclusive, and suspense-oriented hypotheses is a way of adjusting dramaturgy to the demands of the viewing situation. The spectator need not rummage very far back into the film, since his or her expectations are aimed at the future. Preliminary exposition locks schemata into place quickly, and the all-or-nothing nature of most hypotheses allows rapid assimilation of information. Redundancy keeps attention on the issue of immediate moment, while judicious lacks of redundancy allow for minor surprises later. In all, classical narration manages the controlled pace of film viewing by asking the spectator to construe the syuzhet and the stylistic system in a single way: construct a denotative, univocal, integral fabula.

By virtue of its centrality within international film commerce, Hollywood cinema has crucially influenced most other national cinemas. After 1917, the dominant forms of filmmaking abroad were deeply affected by the models of storytelling presented by the American studios. Yet the Hollywood cinema cannot be identified with classicism *tout court*. The "classicism" of 1930s Italy or 1950s Poland may mobilize quite different narrational devices. (For instance, the happy ending seems more characteristic of Hollywood than of other classicisms.) But most of classical narration's *principles* and *functions* can be considered congruent with those outlined here. A group of Parisian researchers has come to comparable, if preliminary, conclusions about French films of the 1930s.[32] Noël Burch has shown that in the German cinema, a mastery of classical style is displayed as early as 1922, in Lang's *Dr. Mabuse der Spieler*.[33] As a narrational mode, classicism clearly corresponds to the idea of an "ordinary film" in most cinema-consuming countries of the world.

Seven Films, Eight Segments

The many variants of classicism make any overall periodization of the mode very difficult. Even the history of Hollywood norms is notoriously hard to delineate. This is partly because significant periods in the history of studios or technology will not necessarily coincide with changes in stylistic or syuzhet processes. Broadly speaking, we could periodize classical Hollywood narration on two levels. With respect to *procedures*, we could trace changes within classical narrational paradigms, according to what options come into favor at certain periods. Here we should look not only for innovations but for normalization, majority or customary practice. Connecting scenes by dissolves is possible but rare in the silent cinema, yet it is the favored transition between 1929 and the late 1960s. With respect to narrational *principles*, we could study how classical films assume narrative causality, time, and space to be constructed. Spatial continuity within a scene can be achieved by selecting from several functionally equivalent techniques, but such continuity rests on broader principles too, such as the positing of the 180-degree line, or axis of action; and changes in this postulate can be traced across the Hollywood cinema. Also within the domain of principles are the fluctuations of broader narrational prop-

erties. For instance, narration in the silent cinema tends to be somewhat more self-conscious than in the sound cinema, if only because of expository intertitles. Similarly, an insistent suppressiveness emerges in many films associated with the grouping known as *film noir*.

No single film, or even a dozen films, can exhaustively characterize a narrational mode. Because particular devices vary across periods, and because norms tend to be organized paradigmatically, any film must choose only a few possibilities to actualize. Part 1 has already considered four classical Hollywood films in some detail: *Rear Window, The Big Sleep, Murder My Sweet,* and *In This Our Life*. These have exemplified the viewer's role, the patterned fluctuations of narrational processes, and the effect of genre on narration. Rather than analyze yet another classical film in depth, we can more usefully broaden our scope to survey the breadth of the Hollywood paradigm and to map, however roughly, historical changes in syuzhet construction and stylistic composition. Let us, then, consider eight segments from seven films, arranged chronologically from 1917 to 1957. The seven films represent different studios, various genres, a range of directorial renown (from Lubitsch and Hawks to John Emerson and Lloyd Bacon), and a spectrum of stylistic trends (early talkie, *film noir*, wide screen). The segments are also laid out in syuzhet sequence, as if this were all one macrofilm running from prologue and opening scene to climax and epilogue.

Wild and Woolly (Artcraft, 1917)

A prologue establishes the romance of the Old West and contrasts it with the West today. The story proper begins in the mansion of Collis J. Hillington, a railroad tycoon. His son Jeff is obsessed with the Old West: he has a tepee in his room, dresses cowboy style, and is an expert roper and pistol shot. At breakfast Hillington tells his butler, Judson, to fetch Jeff to leave for the office. After Jeff playfully ropes Judson to a chair, demonstrates his marksmanship, and rides Judson downstairs like a rodeo star, Jeff leaves with his father.

The prologue introduces an omniscient and frankly communicative narration that employs expository intertitles and shots to alternate the Old West of covered wagons, stagecoaches, and rip-roaring cowboys with a modern land of trains, trolleys, and paved streets. The antithetical structure is carefully mapped by linguistic parallels ("In those days . . ."/"But today . . ."), editing patterns (one shot of the old, one shot of the new), and mirrored compositions (the screen direction of covered wagon and train). This title follows:

> Has this march of progress killed all the romance— all the thrills? Well, we shall see. In the meantime let us cross the continent to the New York home of Collis J. Hillington, the railroad king, who helped make the West what it is today.

At the denotative level, the title is a transition from the rhetorical antithesis (Old West/modern West) to a discriminated occasion and the beginnings of narrative causality.[34] The narration asks the audience a question that can be answered either/or fashion and explicitly promises but postpones the answer. Connotatively, to the old/new split is added an East/West one ("Let us cross the continent . . ."). Such a high degree of narrational presence is conventional in the opening of the classical film.

Once the fabula begins to be narrated, strong self-consciousness and omniscience become rarer. In the first scene, there is only one expository title (echoing the description of Hillington by characterizing Jeff as a fellow who imagines "a Wild and Woolly West as it *isn't* today") but seven dialogue titles. Thus the characters take up the narrational task of informing the audience of important data. Omniscience is rendered as omnipresence, chiefly through editing. For instance, after Hillington sends the butler for Jeff, crosscutting enables us to anticipate what will happen. Judson knocks timidly at the door; cut to Jeff inside preparing to lasso Judson when he enters; cut back to Judson opening the door. Through camera placement and editing, we always occupy what Lane called "the most advantageous point of perception."

Apart from the very explicit title describing Jeff, the narration relies principally upon characters to emit story informa-

tion. Depicting Jeff as nutty about the West is the chief task here, and this is accomplished through several means: setting (a tepee, photographs, and relics), costume, behavior (reading a dime novel, riding, roping, shooting), subjective point-of-view shots (Jeff imagines himself in the scene portrayed in the picture on the wall), and dialogue (Hillington to Judson: "Tell that Comanche Indian that we are due at the office in ten minutes"). Needless to say, the primacy effect is overpowering. The redundancy is so great, in fact, that we must motivate it generically, as an excessive portrayal appropriate to a comedy. But this scene is not here simply to delineate Jeff's character traits. It establishes his father's profession, since it will be to him that the citizens of Bitter Creek appeal for a railroad spur. The scene also displays Jeff's genuine cowboy skills, which will be of causal importance when he gets out west and the narration begins to answer its own question about the degree to which thrills are still available. In addition, the scene foreshadows Jeff's two goals. Jeff tells Judson he is sick of the East: "I want to be out in the West, where there's room to breathe—where the blood runs red in one's veins—where a six-shooter is a man's best friend." The goal of living the authentic cowboy life provides causal impetus for the rest of the film. Shortly afterward, as Jeff comes downstairs, he encounters the maid delivering flowers from his sister's suitor. Jeff remarks: "That's the way the effete Easterner woos his woman. When I find my mate I'll carry her off with my two bare arms." The classical dual structure, a romance line of action and a nonromance line, is locked firmly in place. Even the importance of deadlines is signaled early on, when Hillington announces that they are due at the office. Overall, this scene perfectly exemplifies how the classical opening establishes the place and time of the story action, introduces characters and tags them with specific motifs, marks out the protagonist, and introduces the principal conflicts. Taken together with the prologue, does the scene also establish the terms of the ending? Well, we shall see.

This scene does not tell us all we need to know about prior fabula events; soon we will learn about what is going on at Bitter Creek. But within a few minutes we will be in possession of all relevant information. *Wild and Woolly*, then, ex-

9.1
9.2

hibits concentrated and preliminary exposition, and the narration is highly communicative. Here there is little curiosity about past material. We are never told how Jeff became so passionately keen on the Old West. The viewer's interest is almost entirely suspense oriented. We want to know if Jeff will get to the West, or even get to his father's office; we want to know if he will meet his mate and will indeed take her in his arms. The forward-pointing quality of the prologue is thus confirmed in the first scene.

All these syuzhet maneuvers are assisted by a repertoire of stylistic devices. These are not identical with ones that would emerge at later periods, but they do fulfill comparable functions. One or two shots may strike the contemporary viewer as anachronistic, such as the abnormally low framings of Hillington at breakfast (fig. 9.1), though even these are motivated to leave room for the butler's entry. Camera movement is used to play a narrational joke: from a medium shot of Jeff squatting by a campfire and tepee, we track back to reveal that this landscape is really a bedroom (figs. 9.2–9.3). Yet in general there is little camera movement, with none of the reframing that would become common later. Instead, character action is kept in frame by heavy use of cutting; the prologue and the first scene contain seventy-eight shots, of which fifteen are intertitles. Now, films of the 1917–1928 period generally display much more editing than those of previous years. (The typical silent feature of 1915 or 1916 contains between 275 and 325 shots per hour, while films made between 1917 and 1928 usually contain between 500 and 800 shots per hour.) With respect to this extrinsic norm, *Wild and Woolly*'s editing achieves some prominence: the film's average shot length is between three and four seconds, quite fast even for this period. The film obeys all the rules of matching. The 180-degree system is fully adhered to, and there are some superb matches on action. (Others, though, are strikingly elliptical or expansionary; see figs. 9.4–9.5. No wonder Kuleshov and his pupils closely studied this film.) And if *Wild and Woolly* strikes an audience today as remarkably "classical," it is not an isolated case. The same year produced *Straight Shooting, The Narrow Trail*, and a

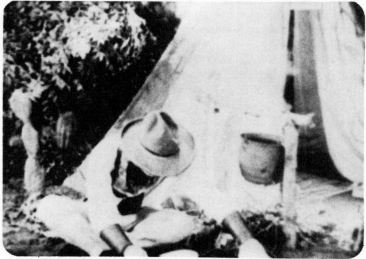

host of lesser-known films that demonstrate that by 1917 the classical paradigm had become the dominant one for Hollywood feature filmmaking.

9.3
9.4   *9.5*

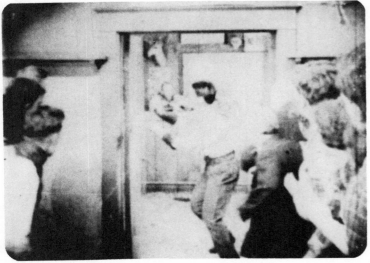

Miss Lulu Bett (Paramount, 1921)

The middle-class Deacon family assembles for dinner, and the customary quarreling starts, most of it triggered by the domineering father, Dwight. His sarcasm causes his

mother-in-law to absent herself from the table. Because the younger Deacon daughter refuses to eat, Lulu Bett, the sister-in-law who does the cooking and cleaning, returns to the kitchen to fix the child milk toast. The scene in question opens with the family's finishing its meal before Lulu has had a chance to start hers.

Unlike *Wild and Woolly*, the film has no need of an illustrated prologue. Two expository titles will suffice to introduce the story's theme: the way that an unhappy family can imprison its members. The expository titles initially provide one overt guideline to the story: one title enjoins us to look at the dining room (this is followed by a series of shots of the empty room and its furnishings), and others introduce the characters to us as they enter one by one. The redundancy level is immediately high. A 1921 screenplay manual points out that one may introduce a character by a title, by significant dress or appearance, by environment, or by actions: the opening of *Miss Lulu Bett* uses all four for each family member.[35] The narration is thus established as omniscient, reliable, and self-conscious. In later scenes, the expository phase will typically be fulfilled by an intertitle, followed by an establishing shot.

9.6
9.7

As the film develops, the narration becomes somewhat less self-conscious while remaining fully communicative and omniscient. Crosscutting one line of action with another, such as the daughter Diane's romance intercut with the father and mother inside the house, is a characteristic case of presenting omniscience as omnipresence. Striking deep-space compositions such as figure 9.6 cue the simultaneity which crosscutting could also signal. The film's subtle use of optical point of view, as in the series rendering Diane's vision of the scene downstairs (figs. 9.7–9.8), lets characters take up the narrational burden. There are unobtrusive "hooks" between scenes (as in the sequence we will examine) and careful foreshadowing. A 1921 screenplay manual links the need for clear "planting" to the durational fact of film viewing ("What has passed has passed").[36] A good example of planting occurs when the paterfamilias enters in scene 1. An intertitle introduces him as "Dwight Deacon, Dentist and Justice of the Peace." The latter attribute will become important many scenes later, when in a mock ceremony he accidentally marries Lulu Bett to his brother. Similarly, Diane's eventual elopement is prepared by an early title that describes her as eager to leave the family. As a result, the viewer is given extensive knowledge—a state maintained when we eventually learn that Miss Lulu has sacrificed her reputation to conceal Diane's attempted elopement, while the family and the townspeople remain ignorant to the end.

Many of these passages show the extent to which expository intertitles relay story information to us. Like most silent films, *Miss Lulu Bett* is reluctant to relinquish such traces of self-conscious narration, even though the number of such titles diminishes sharply across the film (ten in the first scene, two each in the second and third scenes, one per scene thereafter). A film from later in the decade will typically have a higher proportion of dialogue titles to expository titles, but it is the rare film that does without the latter. Such titles, usually placed at the start of a segment, accord with the greater self-consciousness of the scene's expository phase. In the sound era, these titles would be replaced by less overt devices like signs, establishing shots, and other transitional material.

It is instructive to concentrate on the second scene of *Miss Lulu Bett*. The previous scene has ended with Lulu's starting to make milk toast for Monona—a suspended action picked up and settled at the start of this scene when the family is shown having finished its meal and Monona rises

9.8

from the table to run out. The twenty shots, six of which are titles , reveal the flexibility of choice available in the classical paradigm as relatively early as 1921.

1. *Expository title: "Thus Lulu's supper grows cold."* The "thus" is a link to the previous action—Lulu's kitchen duties—creating the tight cause-effect linkage characteristic of classical narration. The title also covers an ellipsis in story duration. The phrase leads us to expect some outcome, defined by real-world schemata: Will Lulu eat her cold supper? The sampler background, characteristic of the "art title" of the period, provides ironic commentary.

2. *Long shot: Dinner table. Family finishes the meal. Diane and Monona leave. Lulu enters and prepares to eat.* (Fig. 9.9.) The establishing shot reveals not only a familial space but a familiar one. As is often the case, when a classical film returns to a locale shown earlier, the narration helps us recall the spatial arrangement by repeating the vantage point. This framing is identical or nearly identical with no fewer than ten shots in the prior scene (or fifteen percent of the images in the scene). Yet we should also note the extent to which this arrangement is an enrichment of that in *Wild and Woolly*. Unlike the comparatively flat frontality of Hillington at breakfast (fig. 9.1), here there emerges a more volumetric space, furnished by the orientation of the table and, as we shall see, the use of offscreen areas. In this connection, note that Ina, the wife, remains in the foreground.

3. *Medium shot: Deacon rises as Lulu fills a plate for herself. Noticing something offscreen left, he goes out of frame. She looks off, concerned.* (Fig. 9.10.) The analytical cut, smoothed down by a flawless match on action, provides a new framing of the two characters. The slight angularity of such framings would become the most favored choice in the ensuing decades.

4a. *Medium shot: Deacon strides to the potted plant on the table.* (Fig. 9.11.) Screen direction is maintained, and the angle of the framing consistently opposes that of shot 3, as if an invisible observer had simply turned his head. We should also note the mastery of the timing of the cut: by dwelling on Lulu after Deacon has left shot 3, the narration gives him time to get to the plant, so he can be already entering shot 4.

It is significant that the plant and its table have not previously been shown in an establishing shot. At the start of the previous scene, a series of shots made a leftward circuit of the room, showing the plant in close-up but never integrating it firmly within an overall view. Later in the first scene, the plant is in the background of seven medium shots of the characters. It is thus very unobtrusively "primed" for exploitation here.

b. *Deacon frowns at the plant and summons his wife.* (Fig. 9.12.) Deacon's leftward look calls up the offscreen space of the table, confirming that his wife is still sitting there.

c. *Ina enters the shot and says the plant is not hers.* (Fig. 9.13.) When Ina enters the shot diagonally from frame left, this reinforces the eyeline cue given in 4b, but more: it shows conclusively that Nina was "behind" us earlier in the shot. The camera is within a volumetric space, with pertinent offscreen areas on many sides.

d. *Ina indicates Lulu, off right, and Deacon looks off as well.* (Fig. 9.14.) The eyelines reactivate Lulu's space; we expect a reverse shot. Given the asymmetry of the composition, we also expect Lulu eventually to come join them.

5. *Medium shot, as (3): Lulu looks off left, reacting to them.* (Fig. 9.15.) This is the countershot, answering the end of (4). It reaffirms that a coherent axis of action exists between Lulu and the Deacons. In addition, if we superimpose shots 4 and 5, we clearly see how classical composition repeats the same significant areas with enough asymmetry to avoid "graphic matches."

6. Plan américain: *The Deacons still looking off right. Lulu comes to them as Deacon speaks.* (Fig. 9.16.) As a variant of shot 4, the shot reveals how finely classical narra-

tion can judge its tasks. Shot 4 gives a better play to facial expression, while this shot anchors Lulu more firmly in the locale. There is still space reserved for her entrance. In the film as a whole, there is an intrinsic norm established whereby two characters start in the same shot and one leaves (our fig. 9.10); there follows a shot/reverse-shot passage (figs. 9.11–9.15); then one character enters another's shot and the action resumes in two-shot (fig. 9.16). This norm, of course, wholly conforms with extrinsic norms of staging and cutting.

9.17
9.18

7. *Dialogue title: "Suitors?"* Deacon's sarcasm is heavily redundant with his characterization so far; it also prepares for Diane's refusal to go home after her abortive elopement, when she says she could not face his teasing.

8. *Medium shot: Lulu shakes her head.* (Fig. 9.17.) A dialogue title can cover a change of setup from shot to shot; if framing and angle are kept roughly constant, the spectator will be unlikely to notice the subtle manipulation of attention.

9. *Dialogue title: "It was only a quarter—and it looked so pretty."*

10. *Medium shot, as (8): Deacon becomes angry.* (Fig. 9.18.) Again the repetition of camera setup. Such redundancy of framing allows us to ignore framing and concentrate on what is most important in the classical scene: the human face and body. In the entire scene, there are only seven camera setups, and three of these are simply closer or more distant variants of others.

11. *Dialogue title: "Yet I give you a home because you have no money to spend even for the necessities."* Through this recounting, the spectator constructs prior fabula events: after marrying, Ina and Deacon took Lulu in.

12. *Medium shot, as (10): Lulu furiously leaves the shot and goes diagonally right. They stare after her.* (Fig. 9.19.) Lulu's anger foreshadows her final outburst at the film's climax: she is not simply a doormat. Screen direction leads us to expect that she will next be seen at her earlier point of departure, the table (shots 3, 5).

13. *Medium long shot: Lulu comes in left and sits down to eat in the far-right chair.* (Fig. 9.20.) Once more, delaying the cut gives Lulu time to get back to the table (about as much time as Deacon took to stride to the plant). The choice of this seat rather than her earlier one reveals both psychological reactions (she gets as far from him as possible) and new opportunities for spatial manipulation.

14a. *Plan américain, as (6): In disgust, Deacon replaces the plant. Ina goes out sharply right.* (Fig. 9.21.) The main doorway has been established in shot 1 when the children left, so Ina's straight exit from the window area implies an exit out the main doorway. This is confirmed when we no longer see her again in this scene.

b. Deacon glares off diagonally right and wipes his hands distastefully. (Fig. 9.22.) Deacon's glare again creates a volumetric space: Lulu's new seating in shot 13 is here confirmed by his eyeline. (Compare shot 4d.) A new axis of action is established.

c. *He walks out sharply right*. (Fig. 9.23.) Like Ina, Deacon leaves the frame in a fashion that implies he is leaving the room.

15. *Medium long shot: Lulu at the table, distraught. Her mother comes in the background. Pan right with her as she*

comes to sit by Lulu. (Fig. 9.24.) This is the boldest cut in the scene, but it is perfectly comprehensible. The shot change is slightly more than the 180-degree line between Deacon and Lulu might lead one to expect. Yet once Deacon has left the room, the axis of action is gone and a new establishing shot

match-on-action cut smoothly enlarges the significant portion of the space in order to control our attention.

17. *Dialogue title: "I know I'm not a charmer—that I've got no suitors, but I'm sick of Dwight's rubbing it in all the time."* Repetition of salient information already presented or inferred.

18. *Medium shot, as (16): Mother pours coffee.* (Fig. 9.26.) Again, repetition of a setup facilitates concentration on actors' gestures and expressions.

19. *Dialogue title: "Well, you got a home here, ain't you?"* The question is strongly narrational, motivated realistically through the mouth of a character but connoting the irony of the expository titles' discussion of "home."

20. *Medium shot, as (18): Lulu nods, desperately holding her head. Fade out.* (Fig. 9.27.) The progress of the classical scene is spatially asymmetrical. The scene typically begins with an establishing shot, but it usually ends by emphasizing a portion of that space containing a significant gesture or reaction. Lulu's response to her mother's question leaves a causal line dangling: How long will she endure this?

Not all the stylistic procedures we will associate with 1930s classical film are present here. Two- and three-shot

can be presented. The panning movement is a comparatively rare option in the 1920s paradigm, but it is here motivated as following a character.

16. *Medium shot: Mother asks what's wrong, and Lulu responds.* (Fig. 9.25.) Like the cut between (1) and (2), this

compositions like shots 2, 4, 6, and the like would later be staged less frontally and broken up into over-the-shoulder shot/reverse shots. But this device already existed as a lesser option in *Miss Lulu Bett*'s time. (See figs. 9.28–9.29.) The camera movements of the sound era are more uncommon

here, though the pan in shot 15 operates somewhat as a reframing. In all, *Miss Lulu Bett* exemplifies how early all the principles and many of the procedures of classical style were already codified, and how a director like William C. deMille could manipulate them skillfully.

Lady Windermere's Fan (Warner Bros., 1925)

While Lady Windermere is being pursued by Lord Darlington, her husband is paying hush money to Mrs. Erlynne, a woman of dubious virtue who is actually Lady Windermere's mother. Lord Darlington, assuming that Lord Windermere is having an affair with Mrs. Erlynne, informs Lady Windermere that she will find canceled checks to Mrs. Erlynne in her husband's possession. Lady Windermere enters her husband's study to investigate.

What François Truffaut calls the "mischievous charm" of Lubitsch's films stems principally from the manipulation of narration, and *Lady Windermere's Fan* is no exception.[37] It is easy to point out the droll expository titles, the sidelong glances, and the underlining of objects. But the film's playfulness stems from less evident narrational factors as well: the use of omniscience and a play with space that amplifies extrinsic norms in unexpected ways.

The film's narration generally adheres to the classical tenet of omniscience in that the spectator is given much more information than any one character possesses. We know, as most of the characters do not, that Mrs. Erlynne is Lady Windermere's mother. We know, as most characters do not, that Lady Windermere is attracted to Lord Darlington and that he has declared his love for her. We also know that Lord Windermere's defense of Mrs. Erlynne during the racetrack scene does not reflect romantic interest on his part. And so it goes, to the very climax: we know that Lady Windermere has come to Lord Darlington's flat to yield to him, but Mrs. Erlynne helps Lady Windermere escape and pretends to have been Darlington's paramour. One source of the wit of Lubitsch's films is thus an unrestricted narration which permits us to watch characters concealing the truth, half concealing it, or making false inferences about it.

This process is aided by classical "omnipresence" of the sort we have already seen in *Wild and Woolly* and *Miss Lulu Bett*. While Lady Windermere is visited by Lord Darlington, the narration cuts away to show us Lord Windermere in his study, pondering over the letter Mrs. Erlynne has sent. While Lord and Lady Windermere celebrate her birthday, Mrs. Erlynne plans to get invited to the party. Crosscutting

and cutaways thus create an omniscient range of knowledge. The narration goes further, though, and uses shifting optical subjectivity to intensify the disparities among various characters' knowledge. The celebrated racetrack scene provides the sharpest example.

When Mrs. Erlynne arrives, men all over the grandstand train their binoculars on her, and point-of-view shots reveal her from almost every angle. At one point, the narration begins to withhold information about who is looking and simply presents shots of her seen through different pairs of binoculars, making her the target of all eyes. Mrs. Erlynne looks toward the Windermere box, fixating on her daughter, who does not notice her; but Lord Windermere sees her, and Lord Darlington sees him seeing. We can infer and compare characters' reactions: Mrs. Erlynne would like to speak to Lady Windermere, Lord Windermere is anxious about her presence, and Lord Darlington begins to suspect a liaison between his friend and the mysterious Mrs. Erlynne. Then Lord Augustus Lorton notices Mrs. Erlynne and, inferring that she is flirting with him, gives her a sly smile. When Mrs. Erlynne sits, three gossips in the Windermere party start to spy on her through binoculars. They tell Lady Windermere to have a look, but then we see, from her vantage point, that two other spectators block the view. The narration thus distinguishes precisely what can and cannot be seen from adjoining seats. Then the gossips use their binoculars to scrutinize Mrs. Erlynne's one stray gray hair and her expensive ring. When Lord Windermere urges the women not to slander Mrs. Erlynne, all members of the party look studiously down at their racing cards, at the cost of ignoring the race itself. Throughout this virtuosic sequence, our superior degree of knowledge allows us to follow the processes of attention and faulty inference through the shifting point-of-view patterns.

Such optical subjectivity can become quite rigorously structured across the whole film. There is a pattern of characters glancing out windows. The first time, Lady Windermere and Lord Darlington watch Lord Windermere hire a cab. Still later, Lady Windermere and Mrs. Erlynne look out another window to watch Lord Windermere and Lord Darlington drive up outside. Furthermore, one turning point of

9.30
9.31

the narrative depends on a crucial mistake of optical point of view. Standing in the garden, Lady Windermere sees Mrs. Erlynne on the terrace with a gentleman. She believes the man screened by the shrubbery to be Lord Windermere, but a cut shows that it is Lord Augustus. As usual, we are several jumps ahead of the characters. Then Mrs. Erlynne notices Lady Windermere, but it is too late. Lady Windermere is resolved to leave her husband.

The narration's reliance on point-of-view shots to compare reactions creates complex patterns. In the reception scene, Lady Windermere greets Mrs. Erlynne frostily: "I have heard so much about you—from every side." The line, recalling the multiple-angle point-of-view barrage at the racetrack, also signals the circular construction of point of view that is to come. Lady Windermere excuses herself and passes through various groups of guests on her way to the terrace. Men descend upon Mrs. Erlynne. Then comes a series of six shots, in each of which the gossipy duchess moves to whisper to a different cluster of guests, each group staring off at Mrs. Erlynne. The various angles at which the bystanders glance fulfill Lady Windermere's description of a woman discussed "from every side," while the emphasis upon characters looking offscreen forms a counterpart to all the binocular shots of Mrs. Erlynne in the racetrack sequence: just as earlier we were to infer the offscreen lookers, so now the narration asks us to infer the offscreen object of all these glances.

As the manipulation of point of view shows, the narration employs space for syuzhet ends in a way that closely conforms to the principles of classical cinema. Other instances abound. Screen direction and eyeline matching are very exact. The space is "volumetric" in the way we saw the dining room to be in *Miss Lulu Bett*: the camera is "inside" the characters' space. Doors will often not be included in an establishing shot, but the angle of character movement will suggest them as located somewhere offscreen near the camera. The film is especially precise in its composition of the frame. Again and again, the shot creates strong symmetry of the sort we have seen in William deMille's film. If the frame is unbalanced, sooner or later a character will enter to fill the vacancy. (See figs. 9.30–9.31.)

Yet the film goes beyond simple obedience to extrinsic norms. Lubitsch's narration gains in wit by creating a margin of playful ambiguity with respect to selected classical devices. There is, for instance, a game with the film's norm of composition. A startlingly asymmetrical framing gets fore-

grounded (fig. 9.32), as does a series of jokes on symmetry: when the Duchess rushes from group to group, she encounters virtually identical women (fig. 9.33) and meets another woman in a mirror image (fig. 9.34). The frame-within-a-frame of the garden hedge has it both ways: rigid symmetry outside the frame, asymmetry reminiscent of figure 9.32 within it (fig. 9.35). A similar playfulness informs the treatment of servants' entrances and exits. In early scenes, the norm is established: the butler shows in Lord Darlington, and Mrs. Erlynne's maid shows in Lord Windermere. These resemble the careful setting up of entrances we saw in *Wild and Woolly*. But soon the narration starts to remove some conventional cues. The maid knocks; cut to Mrs. Erlynne saying, "Come in," and shortly a hand offers her a salver. The maid then leaves the room, but no shot shows her doing so. Later, when Lady Windermere and Mrs. Erlynne each call on Lord Darlington, a completely unseen servant opens the door and shows each woman in. (Such ellipticality is made possible by the sort of exits seen in figs. 9.21–9.23 of our analysis of *Miss Lulu Bett*.) Lubitsch's fundamental commitment to the redundancy favored by classical norms, however, reemerges when, in the last scene, the butler ushers Mrs. Erlynne in to Lord and Lady Windermere: all the cues for entry and exit are back.

Such moments also suggest the rich treatment of doors throughout the film. Characters pass through them, pause before them, peep past them, squint through their keyholes, are halted before reaching them, and are trapped by them. The film's climax pivots on the opening of a door, the revelation that Mrs. Erlynne is in Lord Darlington's study. Doorways are of course key spots in all classical films—this is a doorknob cinema—but as with the use of symmetry and the entrance and exit of functionaries, the variations on the theme reveal Lubitsch's innovative treatments of the normalized device.

A scene I shall now consider forms a nice contrast with the specimen from *Miss Lulu Bett*, for here similar devices are used to deviate from the film's intrinsic spatial norms. Lord Darlington has suggested that Lady Windermere look for a check written to Mrs. Erlynne. He departs. Lady Windermere goes into her husband's study and approaches the desk (fig. 9.36). But she does not look inside, continuing out of the frame (fig. 9.37). Cut to an armchair; she approaches (fig. 9.38) and sits in it. But she looks nervously off right at the desk (fig. 9.39). Given the prevalence of optical point of view, we expect the cut to show us the drawer, and it does—but from an angle that is opposed to her vantage point (fig. 9.40). We may brush the deviation aside, but the precision of optical subjectivity in the racetrack scene suggests that this may be a crafted discrepancy. Cut back to the chair, and

Lady Windermere rises and goes out right (fig. 9.41). The direction of exit from the first shot, the eyeline, and the exit from this shot all redundantly emphasize that the desk is offscreen right. So does the next shot of the desk, which shows her entering from frame left (fig. 9.42). Again she

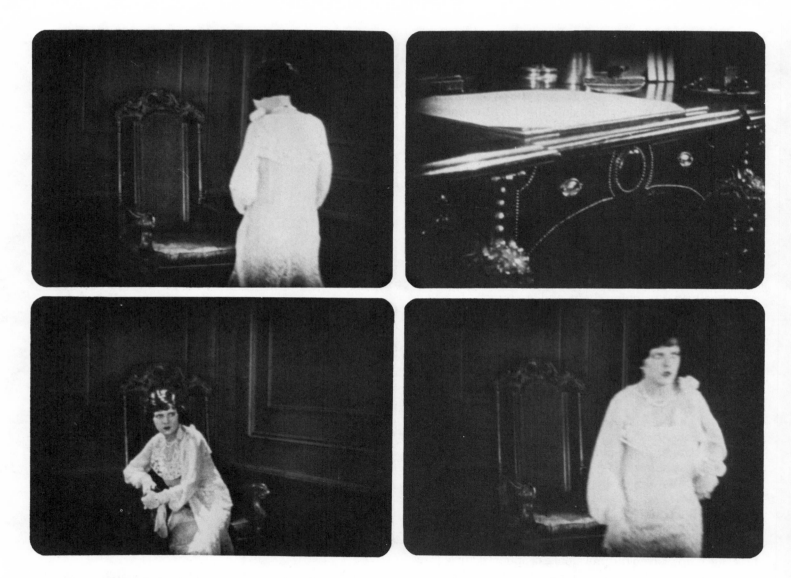

turns back and goes out left (fig. 9.43), toward the offscreen chair. Her to-and-fro movement expresses her hesitation and doubt. But instead of cutting away, the narration holds on the framing of the desk and chair (fig. 9.44).

Let us spell out the most likely hypotheses here. With respect to syuzhet development, we have a clear case of stairstep construction. Since the narration has chosen to present the scene in detail, and since causal complications will ensue if Lady Windermere looks in the drawer, the likelihood is that she will try. Her hesitation is thus pure

9.42
9.43

9.44

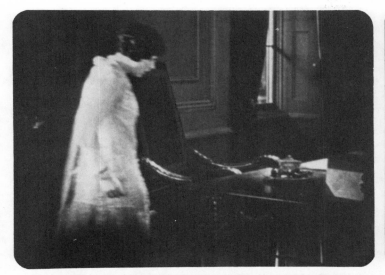

But the longer the empty shot lasts, the less likely we are to get a shot of the armchair. The most probable hypothesis is that Lady Windermere will reenter the frame: we attribute the shot to an omniscient narration which "knows" that she will return to the desk. We also expect Lady Windermere to enter from the foreground left—the area toward which she has gone off, and the one from which she has previously entered. Suddenly Lady Windermere darts into the shot—at the *rear*, from offscreen *right* (fig. 9.45). This is one of the least likely alternatives. Scenographically, it means that she has passed around "behind the camera" while it has trained on the desk and chair, a highly irregular option.[38] (So much for the ideal observer, if the characters can sneak behind its back.) Graphically, the framing is unlikely because it creates an asymmetrical composition in a film committed to an almost maniacal symmetry. The charming mischief of this shot is a fine example of foregrounding, of a narration violating its own "rules."

retardation, motivated realistically as psychological uncertainty. Once this motivation is supplied, hypotheses about space come into play. For an instant after Lady Windermere leaves the frame, a cut back to the armchair seems the most likely occurrence, since we have been primed for it earlier.

Now we can see that the odd angle on the drawer (fig. 9.40) prepares for the later violation of the desk's space. As if to flaunt the deviance of the earlier shot, the narration supplies a "correctly" angled close-up of Lady Windermere's

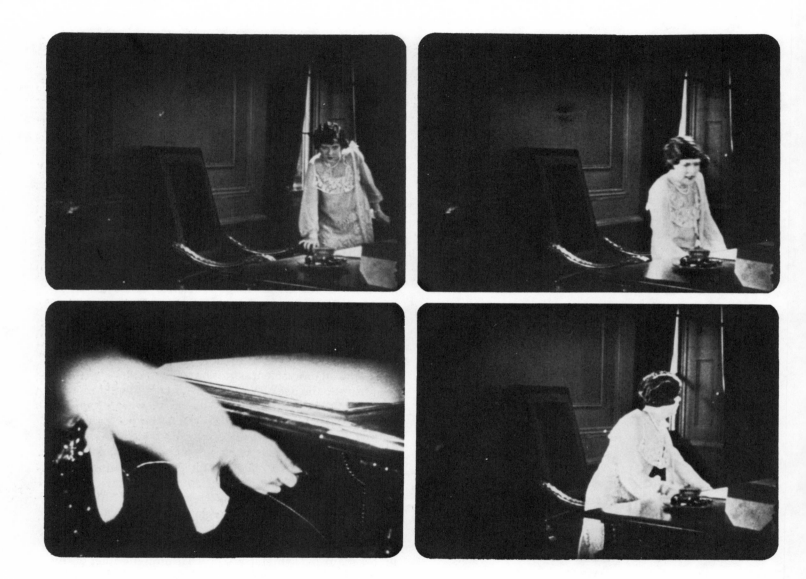

hand struggling to open the drawer (fig. 9.46). A return to the asymmetrical setup of her at the desk (fig. 9.47) gets smoothly normalized as the camera reframes right to center her (fig. 9.48) and brings the whole construction into line

with the film's intrinsic norm. The foregrounded moment is reabsorbed as an exception, and we are reoriented.

The playful manipulation of space is soon accompanied by the film's longest suppressive passage. Lady Windermere is

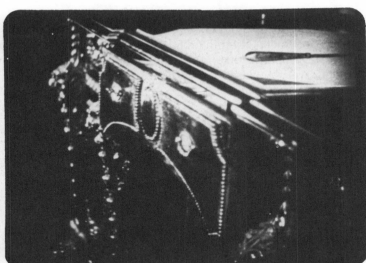

interrupted by the Duchess, and we fade out on the two women's conversation. At Mrs. Erlynne's, Lord Windermere agrees to invite her to the reception. He returns home, just as the Duchess is leaving. Lord Windermere goes in to his wife, who is somewhat cool to him. We now have two exclusive, simultaneous hypotheses: Lady Windermere has had time to discover the check, or she has not. The narration prolongs our uncertainty with shots of him nervously working up to suggesting inviting Mrs. Erlynne and shots of her, eyes lowered inscrutably. Suddenly Lord Windermere glances off right (fig. 9.49); cut to a perfectly correct point-of-view shot of the drawer, now ajar (fig. 9.50). He goes to investigate, in a framing reminiscent of the earlier ones but which now exhibits correct centering (fig. 9.51). He discovers his checks littering his drawer. When Lady Windermere confronts him, she shows him the telltale check she has discovered. Many critics have likened Lubitsch to Hitchcock, but here the formal processes contrast. Whereas *Rear Window* utilizes a restricted and uncommunicative narration peppered with more unrestricted moments that create the shadow of a doubt, *Lady Windermere*'s predominantly unre-

stricted and communicative handling is accentuated by a single scene that reduces the audience's knowledge to the ken of one character.

Lady Windermere's Fan is atypical in its deviations from

normal procedures, but it does conform to overall classical principles. Its foregrounded moments are justified as comic or suspenseful heightenings of the story. But they also testify to the law-abiding ingenuity of a certain director and the flexibility of the classical paradigm.

Say It with Songs (Warner Bros., 1929)

Radio singer Joe Lane (Al Jolson) is inclined toward irresponsibility but remains an adoring father and loving husband. After the manager of a radio station makes advances to Joe's wife, Kitty, Joe assaults him and accidentally kills him. Joe is sent to prison for manslaughter.

It is a commonplace that synchronized sound filmmaking and exhibition created some sort of revolution. Even though experiments in talking pictures go back to Edison's work, certainly talkies offered a perceptible degree of novelty. This novelty is nowhere more visible than in new narrative material, such as the use of radio in Say It with Songs. Yet in most films sound techniques were inserted into already-constituted narrational functions. Audible speech replaced mimicry, lip movements, and dialogue titles; nondiegetic music was no less pleonastic than that of the piano or orchestra in the silent film theater; even sound effects were not unknown to silent-film accompaniment. Omniscience, communicativeness, and self-consciousness could be as easily achieved on the sound track as on the image track. An anticipatory cut could be echoed by a slight modulation on the sound track. Shifts in camera position could be accompanied by shifts in "aural perspective" (chiefly a matter of volume and timbre). The most innovative uses of the new technology expanded the number of cues for fabula construction. For instance, synchronized sound made syuzhet duration potentially more concrete, as when uninterrupted diegetic music specifies durational continuity. (See p. 82.) And offscreen sound could supply cues for offscreen space—ambient noise or an unseen speaker. Sound created new techniques, but these were principally used in ways that replicated or extended the basic qualities and procedures of classical narration.

Hollywood filmmaking's use of sound technology altered the stylistic paradigm by making new visual devices more probable. Because of a complex of engineering and editing decisions, most scenes in 1928–1930 talkies were filmed with multiple cameras arranged in booths around the action. The entire scene would be recorded by three or more cameras—one giving a long-shot view, others supplying reverse angles or closer framings. Multiple-camera shooting assured sound synchronization and preserved the 180-degree rule and other classical editing options. The image took on a new look. The camera tended not to penetrate the area of the action, as in Miss Lulu Bett and Lady Windermere's Fan; the glass panes of the booths cut down contrast; close-ups became rare; and telephoto lenses exaggerated cues for the relative flatness of shot space. (See figs. 9.52–53.) Reframings, relatively uncommon in the mid-1920s, became far more frequent, as cinematographers panned to follow character's movements. Shot length also increased, though not dramatically. In the 1917–1927 era, shots averaged five to seven seconds, while in the early talkie era, average shot lengths clustered around eleven seconds; but this still produces over three hundred cuts per hour. (Say It with Songs has an average shot length of 8.7 seconds, only a little longer than a silent film might.) Multiple-camera shooting became rare after 1931, but it had important stylistic consequences, as we shall see later. Sound affected the visual properties of narration in another way, by endorsing widespread use of what became known as the Hollywood "montage" sequence.

Functionally, the montage sequence can be thought of as the rhetorical amplification of an implicit intertitle: "The world erupts in war," or "After two years in prison—" or "Her singing career rapidly declined." In this respect, the silent film had already mapped out a role for montage sequences. By the end of the silent era, many American feature films were inserting footage depicting the sort of stereotyped symbols that might also illustrate an "art title": a turning clock dial, wafting calendar pages, and so forth. The sound cinema began to eliminate expository intertitles and quickly expanded symbolic passages into full-fledged sequences. Shots, often of an emblematic or universalizing nature, would be linked by dissolves or superimpositions in order to

Lights of New York (1928) with a montage of Broadway life. The montage sequence could also be a vehicle for extensive musical treatment, as in *Glorifying the American Girl* (1929), in which an allegorical montage depicts women from hamlets all over the country descending on Manhattan while an offscreen chorus sings the title song.

Of the twenty-four segments in *Say It with Songs*, six could be called montage sequences. Two compress the passage of time by means of clichéd symbols. While Kitty waits for Joe, a clock striking 11:30, an hourglass, and a clock striking 7:00 are superimposed over her. At another point, Joe's stay in prison is evoked through flipping calendar leaves over which a pendulum's shadow falls. The ability to signal such ellipses earned the montage sequence another name—the "time lapse." In two other sequences, newspapers—those convenient vehicles of a communicative, omniscient narration—inform us of the inquest and, shortly, the jury's verdict. The opening of the film is a little less banal: a montage of dreadful radio acts. Not only does this sequence establish the radio station as a locale, but it makes Joe's aggressively jittery performances seem even more dynamic.

The most elaborate montage sequence is an extension of a musical number. In prison, Joe has tried to cheer up the doleful cons by a song exhorting them to struggle for happiness—"Why Can't You?" As the men file into their cells, Joe resumes singing, and the camera tracks down the corridor, revealing men in adjacent cells listening to him. Cut to Joe in frontal medium close-up at his cell door, singing. There appear, in quick succession, several superimposed images—prisoners marching, a canted angle of a cell door opening, an oppositely canted view of a door closing, a cell number, guards' hands, convicts' trudging feet, and men in cells. All this while Joe continues to sing: "Birdies sing in cages too, they know that's the thing to do." The superimpositions fade out, leaving Joe in the same shot to conclude: "Little birds can do it, why can't you?" Fade out. The whole superimposed sequence lasts less than thirty seconds, but by violating the coherence of fabula space and time, the passage invites us to construe it as representing routine series of actions and the dreariness of prison life. This is the sort of

cue a temporal ellipsis, phases of a repeated process, or a general state of affairs. The montage sequence could be transitional or expository, establishing a period or locale. *The Jazz Singer* (1927) opens with a montage of the ghetto, *The* heavily saturated symbolism that Parker Tyler calls the "pedantic" side of Hollywood.[39]

The six sequences in *Say It with Songs* constitute a convenient anthology of most of the montage devices and functions that would dominate Hollywood narration after 1930. The chief absence is a strongly *subjective* montage, such as the delirious ones in *Blues in the Night* (1941). "In a film based on a psychological theme," one writer suggests in 1949, "montage is quite often used to portray the confused or abnormal state of mind of one of the characters."[40] By the early 1930s, montage sequences became so common that we can say that the classical Hollywood film consisted of only two types of decoupage units: *scenes* and *summaries*.[41] The montage sequences may become slightly foregrounded as deviations from the film's normal scenes, but their very difference is inevitably relocated as the principal alternative within the extrinsic norm. Someone like Slavko Vorkapich could make a career as a montage "specialist" by subjecting clichéd montage tropes to visual hyperbole: canted angles, slow and fast motion, diagrammatically bold compositions, snazzy wipes, and so forth. Always an overtly rhetorical moment, the montage sequence became codified as a likely site of spectacle and a self-conscious narrational gesture.

His Girl Friday (Columbia, 1939)

Reporter Hildy Johnson has agreed with her ex-husband and ex-editor, Walter Burns, to write one last article before she marries her fiancé, Bruce Baldwin. The assignment involves interviewing Earl Williams, who awaits execution for shooting a policeman. Meanwhile, Walter schemes to thwart Hildy's marriage by having Bruce arrested on a trumped-up robbery charge. While Hildy has gone to get Bruce out of jail, her fellow reporters read the opening of her story, still in her typewriter carriage.

Louis Marcorelles has called *His Girl Friday* "le film américain par excellence,"[42] and indeed wherever one looks one finds evidence of pristine classicism: deadlines, narrational covertness, interdependent plotting of romance and nonromance lines.[43] The scene I have picked out is of interest in two chief respects: its exemplary stylistic patterning and its frank "laying bare" of principles of classical causality.

In the silent cinema, each piece of a scene's action would be filmed in a separate take, to be combined with other shots in the editing. With the multiple-camera shooting procedures of early talkies like *Say It with Songs*, however, one camera filmed the entire scene in long shot or medium long shot; this "master shot" provided a complete, synchronized sound record of the scene and allowed the editor to cut back to a reestablishing shot at any time. By 1933, multiple-camera shooting became rare, reserved for spectacle (a mammoth musical number) or unrepeatable actions (a fire, a car tumbling down a precipice). But the master shot hung on. It became conventional to film the entire scene once in establishing shot (the master shot) and then reshoot portions in medium shot and close-up. Some studios, directors, and producers adhered to this work plan quite rigidly: Darryl Zanuck was famous for insisting on having many different shots to juggle in the editing.[44] While in certain respects the master shot scheme encouraged a more formulaic shooting and cutting, some directors, such as Howard Hawks, seem to have used it to allow decisions at the moment of filming. When Leigh Brackett began to script *the Big Sleep,* she was told: "Just master scenes, do it all in master scenes."[45]

The style of *His Girl Friday* is an example of the complexity available within master shot procedures. The film's average shot duration (15 seconds) is quite long for its period, creating an intrinsic norm that is signaled in the very first scene, Hildy's visit to Walter's office. The shots also display a dense organization of characters within the frame. The scenes in the pressroom of the Criminal Courts Building are particularly striking in this regard. Compared with shots in *Wild and Woolly, Lady Windermere's Fan*, or *Say It with Songs*, a medium long shot around the card table in *His Girl Friday,* such as figure 9.54, packs its figures on various planes and in varying degrees of lighting. The shots use most of the screen space; even a small hole is a cue for us that a character will enter to fill the spot (figs. 9.55–9.56). The lateral pans across the action, initiated by the master shot camera of early talkies, has become a fluid reframing that

sequence: since the long takes refuse to cue the spectator by cuts, sound guides the viewer to look at one speaker, in one portion of the frame, then shift his/her attention to another spot. Of course, figure placement allows us to make some plausible hypotheses, so that in figure 9.54, the most prominent figures (Hildy and McCue are highest in the frame and most clearly lit) become the most probable sources of principal dialogue, while the chatter of the cardplayers becomes secondary. This hierarchy of attention can be seen even more vividly when Molly Malloy, Earl Williams's friend, confronts the reporters.

In the scene that occupies us here, the reporters are gathered around Hildy's typewriter and Sanders reads out her story.

1. The first shot begins with a characteristically packed composition (fig. 9.57) while the camera tracks back to establish the group (fig. 9.58). After Sanders has finished reading, he straightens and remarks, "But I ask you guys, can that girl write an interview?" The dialogue starts to ricochet around the frame, from McCue (standing on the right) to Bensiger (seated foreground left, turned away from us) to Sanders (seated middle-ground right). Bensiger rises

glides from one dense composition to the next. Accompanying this saturation of shot space is an emphasis on spreading the sources of sound across the frame. In figure 9.54, for instance, the dialogue is carried by figures dotted around the shot; conversation ricochets. This has an important con-

9.57
9.58

9.59
9.60

in disgust, and this motivates the camera's reframing to leave a bit of vacant space in the right middle ground (fig. 9.59). Sanders continues his comments, ending: "Now I give that marriage three months, and I'm laying three to one.

Any takers?" Hildy's voice rings sharply from offscreen— "I'll take that bet"—and the men look right.

2. Viewed from a new angle, the space reserved for Hildy is filled as she strides in (figs. 9.60–9.61). Hildy chides the

9.61
9.62

9.63

men and dials Walter at the *Morning Post*, using a phone that has been established long in advance.

3. A *plan-américain* of Bensiger, Sanders, and McCue (fig. 9.62). Sanders says she can't quit so easily. There is an evident "cheating" at this and the next cut: Sanders is so close to McCue here that he should be visible in shots 2 and 4. But the disparities pass unperceived because (*a*) in shots 2 and 4 he is on the left margin of the frame, and our attention is concentrated on the right center, where Hildy is moving and speaking; and (*b*) Sanders's *relation* to McCue is consistent even if the distances are not, and as we saw in Chapter 7, the spectator's spatial schemata are, within limits, tolerant of variations in distance, especially if the camera angle changes.

4. As (2). Hildy insists that she is quitting and phones Walter. She tells him off. Her fixed posture throws any other movement into relief, so the reporters' small grins and raised eyebrows emerge as a silent accompaniment to her jeremiad (fig. 9.63). A series of rapid reframings left and right makes Hildy the central carrier of narrative meaning. She grabs her story, carries it to the phone, rips the article up, returns to get her coat (fig. 9.64), dives for her purse, swings back to her desk, and, when the phone rings offscreen, strides back right to yank it out (fig. 9.65) and dump it in the very depth of the frame (fig. 9.66)—virtually the only zone of the shot not

occupied by narrative information! The growing momentum of the shot depends on an accelerating number of spatial assumptions guided and reinforced by physical movement and dialogue.

One point should be clear. It is not that *His Girl Friday*

"looks forward" to Orson Welles's use of deep-space compositions or sonic cues. Rather, we should say that these practices were somewhat uncommon but still permissible options within the extrinsic norms of the late 1930s, and Welles's work (like Wyler's) exploited and amplified them in ways that would become influential later. It is a matter not of a drastic change in style but of the promotion of particular stylistic options to a more prominent position.

The scene is of interest from another angle. From the outset of *His Girl Friday*, Earl Williams's killing of the policeman functions as a founding cause, triggering Walter's campaign to win Hildy back. But throughout the early scenes, there is a gap in the account of Williams's crime: what made him do it? Most of the "positive" characters assume that Earl went temporarily insane. Walter says that the "poor little guy" went berserk as a result of losing his job. One of the reporters tells Hildy that they do not believe that Williams knew what he was doing. Even Earl says he did not mean to kill the cop. To win payment from Walter, Hildy must write a story that supplies a plausible causal link. The reporters tell her that after Earl lost his job he began hanging about the park, listening to rabble-rousers. Interviewing Earl, she asks him if he remembers anything the speakers said. Earl recalls a phrase: "Production for use." Hildy pounces on this. "Now, look, Earl. When you found yourself with that gun in your hand and that policeman coming at you, what did you think about? . . . Could it have been 'production for use'? . . . What's a gun for, Earl?. . . Maybe that's why you used it. . . . Seems reasonable." Earl gratefully accepts this as what he had in mind. "Why, it's simple, isn't it?" "Very simple," Hildy answers softly. She now has a smooth account, at one end Earl's unemployment, at the other a dead policeman, with a series of causal links: jobless man hangs around park, hears a phrase, remembers the phrase, and acts upon his memory.

It is this account that Sanders reads from Hildy's typescript:

> And so into this little tortured mind came the idea that that gun had been produced for use, and use it he did. But the state has a production-for-use plan, too. It has a gallows. And at 7 A.M., unless a miracle occurs, that gallows will be used to separate the soul of Earl Williams from his body. And out of Molly Malloy's life will go the one kindly soul she ever knew.

Like a good classical storyteller, Hildy has filled the gap. She has also hooked one causal chain to another, a future-oriented one. She has satisfied curiosity but will not minimize suspense: Will Earl be executed? She stresses the deadline, 7 A.M. She introduces a romance subplot involving Molly. And she holds out the possibility of a miracle that may yet furnish a happy ending. In sum, Hildy's article is indeed what she calls it, a "story," a "yarn," and it duplicates, structurally and microcosmically, the conventions of classical syuzhet construction.

The film, of course, insists that Hildy's yarn is only a pretext, like Earl himself. Walter uses Earl's plight to chivvy a corrupt administration and to lure Hildy back. Hildy uses Earl and the story to extract a nest egg from Walter. Hildy's disclosed cause, "production for use," is frankly displayed as her invention. Any other phrase which Earl supplied could

have been twisted into an explanation of his case. And Hildy's story is never in fact printed; she tears it up. Earl's psychological impulse is only something to motivate her story realistically and compositionally, and by flaunting this the film's own narration lays bare, in a manner typical of "artistic" motivation, the arbitrariness of classical causality generally. Such devices, as Earl would say, are produced to be used.

The Killers (Universal, 1946)

In Brentwood, Ole the Swede is murdered by two unknown gunmen. This triggers an inquiry by insurance investigator Riordan. Interviewing Ole's acquaintances and tracing his career, Riordan discloses that Ole took part in a $250,000 robbery and then cheated the gang by running off with the loot and with the boss's girlfriend, Kitty Collins. But Kitty soon left Ole, and Ole settled down in Brentwood, apparently penniless. In Philadelphia, Riordan meets Kitty Collins and asks her to fill in the gaps. Who planned the robbery? Was Ole in love with her? What impelled him to double-cross the gang? What happened to the money? And who ordered Ole killed?

A character in Michel Butor's *Passing Time* notes that every detective story "superimposes two temporal sequences, the days of the inquiry which start at the crime and the days of the drama which lead up to it."[46] This remark is especially appropriate to *The Killers*. The murder of Ole is a hinge between the crime fabula and the investigation fabula; Riordan must search Ole's past for causes of the killing. In *The Big Sleep* and *Murder My Sweet*, the syuzhet uses the detective's investigation to expose prior fabula information through characters' recountings. But *The Killers* goes a step further: many past events are *enacted*, in flashbacks. This leads to a true "superimposition" of two dramatized sequences, Ole's past (1935–1946) and Riordan's investigation (eight successive days in 1946). Or rather, because of the flashbacks' complex insertion within Riordan's inquiry, the syuzhet interweaves one temporal sequence with another, linking the two series by transitional scenes of characters recalling or reciting the past.

The result is a splintered syuzhet containing no fewer than eleven self-contained external flashbacks, several of those consisting of still briefer scenes. (See the chart on pp. 195–96.) In the silent era, the predominance of crosscutting tended to create lengthy sequences within which alternation and parallelism came to the fore. With the coming of sound, the classical syuzhet became less reliant on crosscutting and took on a more "linear" quality, and the syuzhet was broken into several shorter but more self-contained scenes. *His Girl Friday*, because of its theatrical origins, is less characteristic of this trend than is *The Killers*, which contains forty-three distinct segments. Many of these are brief lead-ins to flashback passages. The effect is to create a rapid pace that somewhat mitigates the slowing of editing tempo (in *The Killers*, an average shot duration of 12.5 seconds).

Breaking the syuzhet into flashbacks is of course now commonly identified with Hollywood films of the 1940s, although brief expository flashbacks were not rare in the silent era. After the coming of sound, the short vogue for courtroom dramas led to some use of flashbacks for enacting testimony, as in *Through Different Eyes* (1929) and *The Trial of Vivienne Ware* (1932). The most famous and intricate use of flashbacks in the 1930s seems to have been the William K. Howard–Preston Sturges film *The Power and the Glory* (1933). No doubt, however, the growing popularity of flashback construction in the 1940s owed most to *Citizen Kane* (1941). Rearrangements of temporal order came into fashion. A framing story might treat the bulk of the film as one long flashback (*How Green Was My Valley*, 1941; *Double Indemnity*, 1942; *Murder My Sweet*, 1944). An opening scene might flash back for exposition before the syuzhet resumes in the present (*Pursued*, 1947). The syuzhet might be studded with flashbacks (*Brute Force*, 1947; *Letter to Three Wives*, 1948). Different flashbacks might even supply discrepant versions of fabula events (*The Grand Central Murder*, 1942; *Crossfire*, 1947).

The Killers works its own variations. Not only does it intersperse flashbacks with present action, it shuffles the flashbacks out of their fabula sequence. This tactic is motivated by adhering to the "natural" order in which Riordan turns up clues. For instance, after Ole's murder, he questions Nick Adams, who worked with Ole in Brentwood (3A). Nick tells him of an event occurring a week before Ole's death (3B). Riordan's next witness, a hotel maid to whom Ole has left his death benefits, recalls an incident in 1940 (5A–B). Then Riordan contacts Sam Lubinsky, the police lieutenant who had known Ole for years and who commences his tale in 1935 (7A–D). Riordan's investigation thus becomes a backing-and-filling process. The outline shows the crucial past fabula events in sequential order (a–o) and then notes when the event is dramatized in a syuzhet flashback. A glance down the "Past" column shows the extensive rearrangement of fabula order.

What unifies the information dispersed across the syuzhet? A strong causal logic and numerous motifs bind together the phases of Riordan's inquiry. Physical clues such as Ole's handkerchief and strong dialogue hooks from segment to segment keep the spectator oriented within the ongoing investigation. Riordan calls his office and says he's going to the Atlantic Hotel; next scene, he's there. Often the hooks are just as strong between a witness's recounting and the flashback itself. Finally, at three distinct points, the narration thoughtfully provides a summary of fabula events in proper order. In scene 6, a secretary reads to Riordan a chronology of Ole's life to 1940. In scene 10, Kenyon and Riordan sum up the story they have pieced together. And in the epilogue (scene 19), Riordan and Kenyon fill in the remaining pieces.

The Spider's Stratagem has a fairly "linear" arrangement of flashbacks, but its equivocations about subjectivity and objectivity make its fabula quite indeterminate. *The Killers*, despite its serpentine twistings of order, leaves no permanent gaps. The flashbacks are so arranged as to lead us steadily toward a reconstruction of the missing causes: Why was Ole killed? Who got away with the stolen money? Who ordered Ole's death? The flashbacks keep a balance between a "subjectivity" necessary to maintain mystery and that "ob-

The Killers

CRIME FABULA

a. 1935: Ole fights his last fight.
b. 1935: Ole takes Lily to Jake's party; he meets Kitty.
c. 1938: Ole is arrested covering up for Kitty.
d. 1938–1940: Ole is in prison with Charleston.
e. 1940: Big Jim devises plan to frame Ole.
f. 1940: Big Jim calls meeting to propose robbery; Ole joins the gang.
g. 1940: The night before the robbery; Ole and Big Jim quarrel.
h. 1940: The night before the robbery; Big Jim sends Kitty to lie to Ole.
i. 1940: The night before the robbery; Kitty comes and lies to Ole.
j. 1940: The next day; the gang robs the shoe company.
k. 1940: The same day; after the robbery, the men meet to split the loot. Ole steals it.
l. 1940: At the Atlantic Hotel, Ole discovers Kitty has left him.
m. 1940–1946: Big Jim and Kitty marry and lead a prosperous life.
n. 1946: Big Jim sees Ole in Brentwood.
o. 1946: Big Jim sends killers to murder Ole.

SYUZHET SEGMENTS

Present

1. Ole is killed.
2. At the police station: Riordan begins the search.
3. The morgue:
    A. Nick Adams recalls the Swede.
    C. Nick asks if he can leave.

Past

    B. Flashback: Big Jim sees Ole (*n*).

Present

4. Phone booth: Riordan calls his company.
5. Atlantic Hotel:
    A. Riordan questions maid.

6. Insurance company: Riordan meets with his boss, Kenyon.
7. Rooftop of apartment house:
    A. Riordan questions Lieutenant Lubinsky.

    E. Lubinsky wraps up. Lily, now his wife, picks up story.
    G. Lily finishes. Lubinsky resumes.

    I. Lubinsky concludes.
8. Ole is buried.
9. Pool hall:
    A. Riordan questions Charleston.

    C. Charleston continues.
    E. Charleston finishes.

Past

    B. Flashback: Maid stops Ole from committing suicide (*l*).

    B. Flashback: Ole's last fight (*a*).
    C. Flashback: Dressing room; Ole defeated (*a*).
    D. Flashback: Ole won't go out with Lily (*a*).
    F. Flashback: Ole takes Lily to party and meets Kitty (*b*).

    H. Flashback: Lubinsky catches Ole, covering up for Kitty (*c*).

    B. Flashback: Charleston in prison with Ole (*d*).

    D. Flashback: Big Jim's meeting (*f*).

Present	Past	Present	Past

10. Insurance company:
  A. Riordan brings Kenyon the news clipping.
  C. Kenyon allows Riordan to continue.
	B. Flashback: The gang robs the shoe factory (*j*).	15. Hotel room: Riordan and Lubinsky wait for Kitty's call.
		16. Adelphi Theatre and the Green Cat Cafe:
		  A. Riordan meets Kitty and is tailed.	

11. Prison hospital:
  A. Lubinsky brings Riordan to Blinky.
  C. Blinky dying.
  E. Blinky dies. Riordan makes plans.
	B. Flashback: Ole and Big Jim quarrel on the night before the robbery (*g*).
	D. Flashback: The gang meets after the robbery (*k*).
		B. In the cafe, Riordan questions Kitty.
		  D. The killers, tailing Riordan, are shot, but Kitty escapes.
			C. Flashback: Kitty goes to Ole on the night before the robbery (*i*).

12. Ole's room: Riordan sets trap for Dumdum, who arrives but escapes. 13. Train: Lubinsky joins Riordan. 14. Contractor's office: Riordan visits Big Jim, now respectable, and tells him he seeks Kitty.		17. Street: In a police car, Riordan and Lubinsky race to Colfax's mansion. 18. Mansion: Dumdum is shot firing at Colfax. Dying, Colfax admits the truth, damning Kitty. Events *e*, *h*, *n*, and *o* come to light. 19. Insurance company: Riordan and Kenyon wrap it up.	

jectivity" characteristic of classical syuzhet presentation. Subjectivity here consists not of the representation of psychological depth—no flashbacks are revealed to be hallucinatory, duplicitous, or whatever—but of an unusual restriction of each flashback to what the recounting character knows. Each character's recollected flashback consists only of events which the character has been present to witness; once the character has left a scene, the flashback's narration breaks off. There is even some spatial restrictiveness here, as when after the old thief Charleston walks out of the gang's meeting (9D) and waits for Ole in the hall; the narration presents his wait and refuses to show what is occurring inside.

Despite this restrictiveness, the flashbacks have as their

chief function the manipulation of causal information. Character revelation is secondary to syuzhet retardation. That the recounting characters are little more than mouthpieces for story events is shown by the perfunctory treatment of the narrating situations: Queenie the maid is dropped without even a return to her narrating situation (note that there is no 5C), and the dying Blinky's delirious chatter exists only to supply new data (11B, D). The "objectivity" of the flashbacks is epitomized in one scene in Kenyon's office (10). Riordan brings his chief the news story about the robbery, and as Kenyon reads it aloud the narration flashes back six years to enact the heist. Like the impersonal commentator of *Naked City* (1947, also produced by Mark Hellinger), Kenyon gives the rendition of the robbery the stamp of objective verisimilitude. In this film, character recounting is only a means to a syuzhet end: creating or plugging gaps.

In discussing *The Big Sleep* and *Murder My Sweet*, I argued that our range of knowledge closely conformed to that of the detective: Marlowe becomes the means of restricting spectator knowledge. Because of the alternating flashback construction, something more complicated is going on in *The Killers*. Our knowledge tends to be greater than Riordan's because the narration presents past events in ways that he is not permitted to grasp. For instance, in Nick Adams's flashback (3B), we see the driver who recognizes Ole; in later scenes we will identify him as Big Jim Colfax, the leader of the gang. Long before Riordan suspects Colfax, we find him a probable candidate for hiring the killers. The film thus splits our knowledge from Riordan's, so much so that he is often asking questions to which we know the answers. When Charleston recounts his tale to Riordan, he insists he won't specify who was present during the planning of the caper, but in the enactment (9D) we see Colfax, Blinky, Dumdum, and Kitty all there. Later Riordan will continue to ask others who was in on the caper. Blinky's flashbacks are even less clearly delineated as tellings; the omniscient narration gives us far more information than Riordan could get from Blinky's disjointed phrases. Thus the nodal points of summary already mentioned do more than reiterate the fundamental fabula. They also clarify the differences between Riordan's state of knowledge and ours.

As the syuzhet moves along, the causal gaps narrow down to three. In 1940, the gang has plotted to meet after the robbery. But Blinky's flashback (11D) reveals that the gang meets at a different hideout to divide the spoils. Ole sneaks in to steal all the cash. He claims he was not told of the new meeting place, but Colfax asks how then he knew where to find them. This becomes Riordan's question as well. Second, Riordan knows that the Swede and Kitty ran off to the Atlantic Hotel together after the robbery, but she fled, probably with the spoils. Why did she leave Ole, and where did she go? Finally, Riordan must assume that Ole was killed on the orders of a fellow gang member; but who? Blinky and Dumdum have learned of Ole's whereabouts only after the murder. This leaves Big Jim Colfax and Kitty Collins. These three gaps are apparently filled during the scene in which Riordan interrogates Kitty (16). Here the narration presents its last flashback.

In the Green Cat Cafe, Riordan asks Kitty about the robbery money, and she virtually admits that she took it. She claims she has made a fresh start and now has a home and husband. Riordan proceeds to ask questions that reveal the gaps in his knowledge (though they are not all gaps in ours). Then Kitty starts to explain her motives. She wanted to quit crime, and Ole would be her tool. The night before the robbery, she says, Big Jim sent her to tell the gang that the rendezvous point would be changed. "I saved the Swede for last." Dissolve to her flashback. She tells Ole that Colfax is planning to double-cross him and meet elsewhere. She tells him the real meeting place and promises to run off with him afterward. They embrace. Dissolve back to her and Riordan in the cafe, as she assures him that this is "the whole story." And indeed the gaps seem to be plugged. Kitty's lie about the double cross caused Ole to steal the money. She told him the real rendezvous point. After a few days in Atlantic City, she abandoned him. And now she has fled the gang and is safe, enjoying the money.

Like the other flashbacks, Kitty's is accurate; it is not the visual representation of a lie, as in *Crossfire* or *Stage Fright* (1950). But we soon learn that it is not the whole story. After a shootout at Colfax's mansion, Riordan will reveal that Ole's theft of the gang's haul was planned far in advance by Colfax

9.67   *9.68*

(event *e* in my chart). Colfax brought Ole into the theft, let Kitty seduce him, and then sent Kitty to lie about the double cross (event *h*). Once Ole stole the money, the other gang members would pursue him. And after Kitty abandoned Ole, she brought the money back to Colfax. They married and set up a respectable life (event *n*). Thus Kitty did use Ole, but not to escape the gang; she and Colfax were in league from the start. Note that here Riordan's knowledge is revealed as superior to ours. (He is able to solve the case because of temporal discrepancies in characters' stories.) The gaps in Kitty's account were suppressed. The intricacy of the flashback construction is now revealed as serving another purpose—concealing the crucial bargain between Kitty and Colfax, an event no outsider could witness. Thus the film conforms to a generic rule: at the end, the detective should disclose an unexpected causal link.

The convoluted syuzhet order and the suppressive narration make *The Killers* conform to another set of transtextual conventions, that known to critics as *film noir*. The film's style does the same. The use of deep space and deep-focus cinematography develops the compositional principles of *His Girl Friday* in a way that shows the clear influence of

Citizen Kane. (See figs. 9.67–9.68.) Nevertheless, as in Welles's film, such compositions are integrated into classical editing patterns. The use of hard, single-source, low-key lighting was linked to the crime and mystery film long before the 1940s thriller exploited it. The film's employment of the long take, particularly in the robbery scene (a two-minute shot), is a common sort of self-conscious virtuosity of the period. There is, for example, a three-and-a-half minute take, with intricate camera movements, at the beginning of *Ride the Pink Horse* (1947). In sum, *film noir* is not outside the pale, as many of its admirers prefer to think. It is a clearly codified option within classicism, a unified set of syuzhet tactics and stylistic features no more disruptive of classical principles than the conventions of genres like the musical or the melodrama. *The Killers'* narrational operations make it typical of one set of choices available in the classical paradigm at a particular period.

Heaven Knows, Mr. Allison
(Twentieth Century-Fox, 1957)

Marine Sergeant Allison is stranded on an island with a nun, Sister Angela, during World War II. Their plan to sail to safety is thwarted when invading Japanese capture the island, forcing them into hiding. Eventually the Japanese flee American forces, and during this lull Allison asks Sister Angela not to take her final vows. He proposes marriage. She declines. That night, frightened by Allison's drunken frustration, she runs into the jungle and contracts chill. The Japanese retake the island, and Allison risks his life to keep Sister Angela warm. When she emerges from her delirium, she expresses affection for him: "Perhaps God doesn't intend me to take my final vows." American shelling resumes, and Allison predicts that the marines will land tomorrow. To spare lives, he sneaks out during the night and removes the breech blocks from the Japanese howitzers. He returns to Sister Angela at dawn.

The construction of the narrative obviously conforms to extrinsically codified qualities, principles, and devices. There are two main lines of action—the tentative romance and the progress of the war, each of which has a deadline: Sister Angela has only a month to decide to take her final vows, and the couple must survive the war until the Americans land. Suspense gaps predominate; after the concentrated preliminary exposition, we have no curiosity about the characters' pasts. The narration is restricted to what Allison and Sister Angela could know, but when they are apart, the narration widens its range by alternating between them. A series of precise dialogue hooks unifies the separate scenes, and each segment obeys the pattern of exposing the situation, closing off old causal lines, and opening up new ones. The classical norms thus continued to function as a model in the 1950s, even as the studio system of production was breaking down. The classical mode also determined how film style absorbed the technological novelty of widescreen filmmaking.

The most widely adopted widescreen process was CinemaScope, an anamorphic system that yielded a ratio of 2.55:1 (magnetic sound) or, more commonly, 2.35:1 (optical sound). To a great extent, the debates around CinemaScope condense discussion about widescreen processes generally (the others including Todd-AO, Panavision, Techniscope, et al.). CinemaScope, many felt, would call for a revision of norms of staging and cutting. CinemaScope would eliminate close-ups, slow down cutting, decrease depth of field, reduce camera movements, and increase the distortion of wide-angle lenses.[47] This tendency was greeted by many *Cahiers du cinéma* critics as a step toward realism: longer takes and wider views would lead to a better "window on the world."[48] But in practice, Hollywood filmmaking quickly adapted the new screen shape to classical stylistic norms.

In classical widescreen filming, compositional centering becomes a function of camera distance: the longer the shot, the more centered the composition, as when, at the start of *Heaven Knows, Mr. Allison*, Allison's life raft bobs around in the center of a series of distant framings. Closer shots, however, will avoid centering the figure perfectly, and will usually include some dead space. But this empty area is typically impregnated by the character's glance or filled in by an object or a body. (See figs. 9.69–9.70.) The shot/reverse-shot schema is easily adopted to widescreen filming; the shoulder of an interlocutor can block off an unbalanced area (figs. 9.71–9.72). Wrote one cinematographer: "The figure size of the 'two-shot' is larger on the modern screen than was the 'big head' on the older, smaller screen. I personally prefer to use the 'over-shoulder' shot when closeups are required."[49] More outré directors such as Nicholas Ray and Samuel Fuller were able to use as many steep angles in Scope as they would have used in the regular format. The new widescreen process could also absorb conventional camera movements, although some processes (e.g., Ultra Panavision 70) tended to distort space during panning shots. By 1957, as *Heaven Knows, Mr. Allison* shows, even quite shaky camera movements taken in a choppy sea could be employed.

In 1953, Leon Shamroy, cinematographer for *The Robe*, declared that the new process encouraged longer takes.[50] Eighteen months later, cinematographer Charles G. Clarke agreed: long takes were more natural, and besides, "a vast

9.69   9.71
9.70   9.72

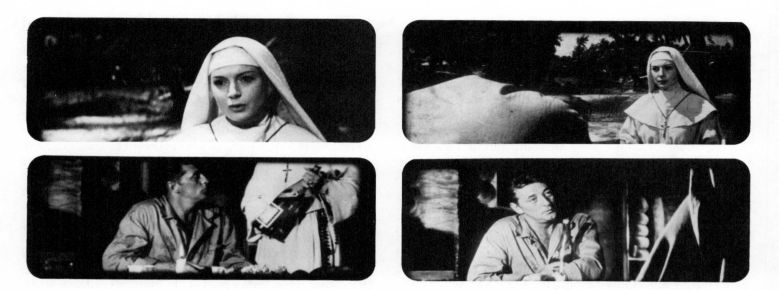

screen area approaching the periphery of vision requires new adjustment of the eyes each time the scene [shot] changed."[51] Nonetheless, although initially the cutting rate of widescreen films slowed somewhat, very soon a widescreen film enjoyed the same range of options available in the standard format. A CinemaScope film might have an average shot length of 23 seconds (*Bonjour Tristesse*, 1957), 18 seconds (*Young and Dangerous*, 1957), 14 seconds (*Jailhouse Rock*, 1957), 11 seconds (*Gidget*, 1959), 8 seconds (*Fire Down Below*, 1957), or about 6 seconds (*Journey to the Center of the Earth*, 1959). In this respect, *Heaven Knows, Mr. Allison*'s average shot length of 7.5 seconds shows how closely widescreen decoupage rates matched those of pre-1953 norms. More important, widescreen cutting would draw on all the existing procedures of analytical cutting—eyeline matching, shot/reverse shot, and so forth. As in the 1940s, the establishing shot could become a detail shot as well: a judicious framing or a panning movement could lay out the scene's space while initiating the story action. Unlike *The Confrontation*, which uses the widescreen ratio in ways that deviate from classicism, *Heaven Knows, Mr. Allison*

relies on intrinsic norms which conform closely to the most probable options in the classical stylistic paradigm.

Allison has spent the night disarming the Japanese guns, but he has been wounded in the shellfire. Now, while the marines are landing, he staggers out of the smoke to Sister Angela. It is the climax of the film, the point of resolution for both the romance and the battle. As the marines fight below them, Allison lies down on the hillside and Sister Angela comforts him. Here the narration continues to respect the restrictions upon narration that have operated throughout: with no attempt at omnipresence, the invasion is rendered by offscreen sound. In a classical film, the climax of a line of action is at once a turn toward a resolution and the meeting of a deadline, so when Allison speaks he begins: "Well, ma'am, we're coming to the end of our time together . . ." He then wishes her happiness. In her turn, Sister Angela confirms that she has decided to take her final vows. "Goodbye, Mr. Allison. No matter how many miles apart we are, or whether I ever get to see your face again, you will be my dear companion always—always." The romance is resolved. This exchange is played in a variant of shot/reverse shot (figs.

9.73
9.74

hold the townspeople at bay in the saloon. Jeff captures Steve, saves Nell, and rescues the townsfolk.

The skills of riding, roping, and shooting so amply demonstrated in the film's opening scene find their spectacular fulfillment when Jeff single-handedly foils Shelby and his gang. In the penultimate sequence, Jeff sits astride his horse and receives the plaudits of Bitter Creek's residents. But he hangs his head. "I know I've been a fool, and I've brought a lot of trouble on you boys, but there's no great harm done and I've learned my lesson. So I guess I'd better go back east to my dad's office where I belong. Good-bye." Jeff rides off to the station, followed by a posse of townspeople, and he hops on a train. Nell tearfully watches the train vanish in the distance. Throughout the film, the spectator has been asked to motivate events generically. The film uses the protagonist's naive fantasies to justify the admittedly stylized conventions of the Western. But the excessiveness of his expectations is motivated by comedy. Both the characters and the narration mock the corniness of barroom confrontations, square dances, and cowpoke lingo. True, Jeff has the next-to-last laugh, since his cowboy expertise saves the day and answers the film's initial question as to whether thrills are still possible in the West. But as Jeff's final speech acknowledges, he would not have needed his skills had not his fantasy created the problem. He now knows the real West. The causal chain is virtually complete. Having obtained the goal of the old-fashioned cowboy life, Jeff throws it aside. Yet after Jeff boards the train the narration intervenes overtly:

9.73–9.74) which motivates Allison's slightly low placement in the frame by his prone position. He turns and looks off left, and an eyeline match cut presents a shot of marines trudging up the hill. The second line of action is resolved: the island has been taken. All that remains is the epilogue. Throughout the scene, and throughout the film, the widescreen process has been used in ways which suggest that in Hollywood filmmaking, the classical norms poured old wine into new, narrow bottles.

> But wait a minute, this will never do! We can't end a Western romance without a wedding. Yet—after they're married, where shall they live?
>   For Nell likes the East,
>   And Jeff likes the West,
>   So where are the twain to meet?

Wild and Woolly

Once Jeff Hillington has been assigned to Bitter Creek to investigate building a railroad spur, the townspeople decide to win his support by turning their modern town into the Old West of his dreams. They stage gunfights and a town dance to fool him, and he protects the honor of Nell Larrabee, the hotel keeper's daughter. But a crooked Indian agent, Steve Shelby, takes advantage of the hoax to pull a real holdup and stir up an Indian attack. Nell is captured, and the Indians

The narration flaunts the generic basis of the syuzhet and announces the need to close off the romance line of action. Extrinsic norms permit such self-conscious interjection at the beginning and ending of the syuzhet (cf. the prologue). Any particular causal gaps (Does Jeff change his mind and return? Does the posse pursue the train and bring him back?) are plugged by fiat, the narration claiming full authority to wrap things up. Here is a good example of a causally unexplained happy ending, justified by transtextual motivation. And just as this omniscient narration could retard the answer to the initial question of whether there are still thrills in the Old West, so now the ending is postponed long enough to pose, prolong, and answer another question: Do Jeff and Nell settle in the East or the West?

A classical film often includes an epilogue, a coda reaffirming the stability of the state arrived at through the preceding causal chain. The unity sought by classical narration encourages this epilogue to reiterate connotative motifs highlighted at previous points in the film. For example, after a bigamous marriage to Deacon's brother, Miss Lulu Bett returns to her town in disgrace. When she stops Diane from eloping and pretends that she was about to run off with the town schoolteacher, her family flies into high dudgeon. She rages at them, smashes the kitchen that has been her prison, and leaves. In the epilogue, she is now employed at a bakery. She visits the schoolteacher and they declare their love while children (reminiscent of the two prying Deacon daughters) peer in at them. In *Lady Windermere's Fan*, Mrs. Erlynne visits Lady Windermere to say good-bye, having sacrificed her reputation and her marriage chances in order to save her. As Mrs. Erlynne leaves, she encounters Lord Augustus, who turned from her when he saw her in flagrante delicto at Darlington's flat. But she seizes her advantage, announces that she will not marry him, and instantly wins him back. The scene recalls an earlier moment when she charmed him out of a jealous funk. The film ends, fittingly, with a door closing as he follows her into a cab.

Say It with Songs concludes with the family reunited—mother and son at home before the radio, Joe crooning in the studio. His song is "I'm in a Seventh Heaven," sung in an earlier scene just before he was arrested. In *His Girl Friday*, once Hildy agrees to send Bruce Baldwin back home, Walter proudly announces to Duffy that they're remarrying. It is then that they learn of the strike in Albany, and the coda echoes their earlier honeymoon. The epilogue of *The Killers* depicts the insurance boss, Kenyon, summarizing the causes that plugged the story gaps. ("Have I got it all right?" he asks Riordan.) He then tells Riordan to take a rest: "Don't come in 'till Monday." Since it is apparently Friday, the joke ties up the motif of his giving Riordan only short intervals in which to pursue the case. And in the last scene of *Heaven Knows, Mr. Allison*, marines stare down at the dismantled Japanese guns, wondering how they were put out of commission; the film's title is thus revealed as an answer to their question. When a stretcher bears Allison down to the shore, Sister Angela walking proudly at his side, three motifs get completed. Allison is smoking a cigarette, an act which echoes his search for one early in the film. The nun is carrying a crucifix which Allison rescued from the church rubble and to which she has prayed throughout the film. She is also carrying the comb Allison has carved for her. The two objects, cradled in her arms and framed in a panning close-up as she passes, emblematically underscore her commitment to the church and her fondness for Allison: "You will be my dear companion always."

The epilogue of *Wild and Woolly* creates a false hypothesis by virtue of "rhymes" with the first scene. Fade in on the staircase of a luxurious mansion, with butlers standing at attention (fig. 9.75). The locale, the staff, and the strikingly symmetrical composition all hark back to Jeff's father's mansion at the very beginning. Nell and Jeff meet on the staircase and kiss. She is wearing the riding garb she wore before she posed as the simple ranch girl; he has on the Western suit he wore to work in scene 1. The probable hypothesis is that, like the opening sequence, this takes place in the East. Jeff and Nell run forward; cut 180 degrees to a heavy steel doorway, which they reach and two other butlers open—to reveal that this Eastern mansion looks out onto the prairie (fig. 9.76). In another symmetrical framing, Jeff and Nell ride off with the cowboys (fig. 9.77). Just as scene 1 had revealed Jeff with his tepee and campfire creating the-West-in-the-East, now the epilogue shows how he and Nell have achieved the-East-in-the-West. Moreover, the prologue had contrasted the Old West and the modern West, then had contrasted the West with the East. The last shot, with its

butlers, romantic couple, buckaroos, riding habit, and gen-
trified cowboy clothes, synthesizes Old West, new West, and
East. The classical epilogue can afford such self-conscious
play with expectations; overtness is permitted at the end.

Only by investigating norms historically can we grasp the
extent and limits of "authorship" in Hollywood cinema. For
the early *auteur* theory, a director's uniqueness was defined
principally by recurrent themes or generic innovations. Only
rarely was narration discussed. Behind *auteur* theory,
however, there lay the assumption that ordinary cinema
constituted a norm of simplicity, efficiency, and "invisibility." Virtually any film that varied from this could be considered of interest. By 1965, the *Cahiers* writers had recognized
that this distinction was too simple. As Michel Mardore
pointed out:

> The American cinema contented itself, in the view of the
> *politique des auteurs*, with a negation of all spectacular,
> "demiurgic"—that is, *authorial*—intervention. This en-
> forced simplicity condemned *a priori* all forms which
> were precious, baroque, in the last analysis unconvention-
> al (because simplicity and self-effacement are variants of

conventionality). . . . It is necessary to defend the idea of a
pluralism of forms, of styles, against a withered classicism
which had never existed in the minds of American
filmmakers.[52]

Classical narration, in other words, was not a recipe but a range of choice, a paradigm. It seems possible, therefore, to identify various auteurs' work by their characteristic narrational strategies and patterns. Hitchcock's and Fuller's films are more self-conscious than, say, those of Hawks and Preminger. We can also associate consistent stylistic choices with directorial signatures, such as Lubitsch's reliance upon frame entrances and exits. ("A director of doors," Mary Pickford called him.)[53] True, any Hollywood director's distinct approach to narration typically remains within classical bounds, creating intrinsic norms that fulfill extrinsic ones in fresh ways. But a group style can never be literally exhausted: even if a style possesses a body of rules, there is an indefinitely large number of strategies for realizing them.[54] Authorial difference in Hollywood thus dramatizes both the range and the limits of the classical paradigm.

Focus on the author or the extrinsic norms should not make us overlook the fact that even in this most ordinary cinema, the spectator constructs form and meaning according to a process of knowledge, memory, and inference. No matter how routine and "transparent" classical film viewing seems to have become, it remains an activity. Any alternative or oppositional cinema will mobilize narration to call forth activities of a different sort.

10. Art-Cinema Narration

The predominance of classical Hollywood films, and consequently classical narration, is a historical fact, but film history is not a monolith. Under various circumstances, there have appeared alternative modes of narration, the most prominent one of which I shall consider in this chapter. As a start, ostensive definition might be best. *L'Eclisse, The Green Room, Rocco and His Brothers, Repulsion, Scenes from a Marriage, Accident, Teorema, Ma nuit chez Maude, Rome Open City, Love and Anarchy*: whatever you think of these films, they form a class that filmmakers and film viewers distinguish from *Rio Bravo* on the one hand and *Mothlight* on the other. Not all films shown in "art theaters" utilize distinct narrational procedures, but many do. Within a machinery of production, distribution, and consumption—the "international art cinema," as it is generally known—there exists a body of films which appeal to norms of syuzhet and style which I shall call art-cinema narration.

We could characterize this mode by simply inventorying our theoretical categories. We could say that the syuzhet here is not as redundant as in the classical film; that there are permanent and suppressed gaps; that exposition is delayed and distributed to a greater degree; that the narration tends to be less generically motivated; and several other things. Such an atomistic list, while informative, would not get at the underlying principles that enable the viewer to comprehend the film. Our study of *The Spider's Stratagem* in Chapter 6 has already shown how its temporal manipulations are based on three broader interlocking procedural schemata—"objective" realism, "expressive" or subjective realism, and narrational commentary. The same schemata explain the various narrational strategies, and their instantiation in syuzhet and style, characteristic of this mode of filmmaking.

Objectivity, Subjectivity, Authority

The Russian Formalist critics pointed out that artists often justify novelty as a new realism, and this observation is borne out by art-cinema narration. For the classical cinema, rooted in the popular novel, short story, and well-made drama of the late nineteenth century, "reality" is assumed to be a tacit coherence among events, a consistency and clarity of individual identity. Realistic motivation corroborates the compositional motivation achieved through cause and effect. But art-cinema narration, taking its cue from literary modernism, questions such a definition of the real: the world's laws may not be knowable, personal psychology may be indeterminate. Here new aesthetic conventions claim to seize other "realities": the aleatoric world of "objective" reality and the fleeting states that characterize "subjective" reality. In 1966, Marcel Martin summed up these two new sorts of verisimilitude. The contemporary cinema, he claimed, follows Neorealism in seeking to depict the vagaries of real life, to "dedramatize" the narrative by showing both climaxes and trivial moments, and to use new techniques (abrupt cutting, long takes) not as fixed conventions but as flexible means of expression. Martin added that this new cinema deals with the reality of the imagination as well, but treats this as if it were as objective as the world before us.[1] Of course the realism of the art cinema is no more "real" than that of the classical film; it is simply a different canon of realistic motivation, a new *vraisemblance*, justifying particular compositional options and effects. Specific sorts of realism motivate a loosening of cause and effect, an episodic construction of the syuzhet, and an enhancement of the film's symbolic dimension through an emphasis on the fluctuations of character psychology.

The art film's "reality" is multifaceted. The film will deal with "real" subject matter, current psychological problems such as contemporary "alienation" and "lack of communication." The mise-en-scène may emphasize verisimilitude of behavior as well as verisimilitude of space (e.g., location shooting, non-Hollywood lighting schemes) or time (e.g., the *temps mort* in a conversation). André Bazin emphasized such aspects of the art cinema when he praised Neorealist films for employing nonactors to achieve a behavioral concreteness. Bazin also analyzed how specific stylistic devices, such as deep focus and the long take, could record the phenomenal continuum of space and time.

Such localized aspects do not, however, do justice to the extent to which an "objective" realism becomes a pervasive formal principle. In the name of verisimilitude, the tight causality of classical Hollywood construction is replaced by a more tenuous linking of events. In *L'Avventura*, for instance, Anna is lost and never found; in *Bicycle Thieves*, the future of Antonio and his son remains uncertain. We find calculated gaps in the syuzhet, as Bazin writes of *Paisà*: "This fragment of the story reveals enormous ellipses—or rather, great holes. A complex train of action is reduced to three or four brief fragments, in themselves already elliptical enough in comparison with the reality they are unfolding."[2] The viewer must therefore tolerate more permanent causal gaps than would be normal in a classical film.

Gapping the syuzhet's presentation of the fabula is not the only way that art-cinema narration loosens up cause and effect. Another factor is chance. Contingency can create transitory, peripheral incidents—the locus classicus is the unexpected rainstorm and the chattering priests in *Bicycle Thieves*—or it can be more structurally central. It is by chance that Anna is not found in *L'Avventura*; and by chance that Antonio discovers, then again loses, his bicycle. It is only coincidence that in *Wild Strawberries* Isak Borg's path crosses that of young people who trigger such significant memories. In this mode of narration, scenes are built around chance encounters, and the entire film may consist of nothing more than a series of them, linked by a trip (*The Silence, La Strada, Alice in the Cities*) or aimless wanderings (*La Dolce Vita, Cleo from 5 to 7, Alfie*). The art film can thus become episodic, akin to picaresque and processional forms, or it can pattern coincidence to suggest the workings of an impersonal and unknown causality. Here is Bazin on *Diary of a Country Priest*:

If, nevertheless, the concatenation of events and the causal efficiency of the characters involved appear to operate just as rigidly as in a traditional dramatic structure, it is because they are responding to an order, that of prophecy (or perhaps one should say of Kierkegaardian "repetition") that is as different from fatality as causality is from analogy.[3]

After working to open gaps, chance can also close off the syuzhet. When, at the end of *Nights of Cabiria*, the youths miraculously materialize to save Cabiria from despondency; or when the mimes make their calculatedly unexpected reappearance at the close of *Blow-Up*; or when two thugs emerge to rob and kill Fox at the close of *Fox and His Friends*—in each case, the narration asks us to unify the fabula by appeal to the plausible improbabilities of "real life."

We have seen that the classical film focuses the spectator's expectations upon the ongoing causal chain by shaping the syuzhet's dramatic duration around explicit deadlines. But the art film typically lacks such devices. How long do the searchers in *L'Avventura* have before Anna's fate is sealed? What could limit the time span of Marcello's adventures in *La Dolce Vita* or Alma's disintegration in *Persona*? By removing or minimizing deadlines, not only does the art film create unfocused gaps and less stringent hypotheses about upcoming actions; it also facilitates an open-ended approach to causality in general. While motivated as "objectively" realistic, this open-endedness is no less a formal effect than is the more tightly "economical" Hollywood dramaturgy.

The loosening of causal relations is aided by a second sort of schema, that of a subjective or "expressive" notion of realism. The art film aims to "exhibit character." But what kind of character, and how to exhibit it?

Certainly the art film relies upon psychological causation no less than does the classical narrative. But the prototypical characters of the art cinema tend to lack clear-cut traits, motives, and goals. Protagonists may act inconsistently (e.g., Lidia in *La Notte*) or they may question themselves about their purposes (Borg in *Wild Strawberries*, Anna in *Les rendezvous d'Anna*). This is evidently an effect of the narration, which can play down characters' causal projects, keep silent about their motives, emphasize "insignificant" actions and intervals, and never reveal effects of actions. Again

consider *L'Avventura*. Anna's disappearance is motivated to some degree: she is dissatisfied with Sandro, she is capricious, and she yearns for solitude. But once she vanishes, all our hypotheses become equally probable: she has died (by accident? by suicide?) or fled (in a passing boat). In the second half of the film, Claudia and Sandro take as their putative goal the tracing of clues to Anna's whereabouts. But the film's syuzhet devotes so much time to the couple's emotional reactions and to the other people they encounter that their objective starts to collapse. The recovery of Anna is no longer the causal nexus of the action, and our hypotheses turn to the development of the Claudia-Sandro affair.

Equivocating about character causality supports a construction based on a more or less episodic series of events. If the Hollywood protagonist speeds toward the target, the art-film protagonist is presented as sliding passively from one situation to another. Especially apt for the art-film fabula is the biography of the individual (Ray's Apu trilogy, Truffaut's Antoine Doinel series) or the slice-of-life chronicle (*Alfie, Cleo from 5 to 7*). If the classical protagonist struggles, the drifting protagonist traces out an itinerary which surveys the film's social world. Certain occupations (e.g., journalism, prostitution) favor an encyclopedic, "cross-sectional" syuzhet pattern. In general, as causal connections in the fabula are weakened, parallelisms come to the fore. The films sharpen character delineation by impelling us to compare agents, attitudes, and situations. In *The Seventh Seal*, the Knight's tour of medieval society is enhanced by the juxtaposition of flagellants and buskers; Watanabe, the protagonist of *Ikiru*, must encounter the denizens of nighttown and the kindly factory girl Toyo. At its limit, the device of parallellism can form the explicit basis of the film, as in Chytilova's *Something Different* and Pasolini's *Pigpen*. The art film's thematic crux, its attempt to pronounce judgments upon modern life and *la condition humaine*, depends upon its formal organization.

It is only in this sense that the art cinema counters Hollywood's interest in "plot" by an interest in "character." If the classical film resembles a short story by Poe, the art cinema is closer to Chekhov. Indeed, early-twentieth-century literature is a central source for art-cinema models of character causality and syuzhet construction. Horst Ruthrof points to the emergence of a new sort of short story in the modern period, one which is "organized towards pointed situations in which a presented persona, a narrator, or the implied reader in a flash of insight becomes aware of meaningful as against meaningless existence."[4] Typical of this is what Ruthrof calls the "boundary-situation" story, in which the causal chain leads up to an episode of the private individual's awareness of fundamental human issues. Examples would be Joyce's "Araby" and Hemingway's "Snows of Kilimanjaro." The boundary situation is common in art-cinema narration; the film's causal impetus often derives from the protagonist's recognition that she or he faces a crisis of existential significance.

A simple instance is Fellini's *8½* (1963). Guido, the womanizing film director, has coaxed cast and crew out on location to make a film whose point and script he cannot articulate. He also brings his mistress, thus creating marital problems for himself. And he is plagued by memories of his childhood, guilty feelings toward his family, fantasies of his dominance over women, and the vision of an idealized muse. As the film progresses, Guido becomes trapped in the world of his problems until a press conference called by his producer forces him to choose some course of action. What he chooses remains uncertain (he may kill himself), but that Guido reaches a boundary situation with respect to the purpose of his life is beyond doubt. A different sort of boundary situation can be found in *The Spider's Stratagem*, when Athos Magnani discovers that his father was a traitor.

How heavily the film weights the boundary situation depends partly on the syuzhet's expositional procedures. The syuzhet can lead up to the situation by dramatizing the pertinent causal chain, as in *The World of Apu* when the hero's youth gradually prepares us for his recognition of the meaninglessness of art after his wife's death. Or the syuzhet can confine itself more stringently to the boundary situation itself, providing prior fabula information by exposition. Ruthrof points out the tendency of modern literature to focus on the boundary situation by compressing duration and restricting space. In theater, the *Kammerspiel* tradition achieved a comparable end. The habit of confining the syuzhet to the boundary situation and then revealing prior events to us through recounting or enactment became a dominant convention of the art film, seen in *Rashomon, Ikiru, Death in Venice, The Go-between, The Model Shop, The Immortal Story*, and most of Rohmer's films. Bergman, with his strong affinities with *Kammerspiel*, provides perhaps the most obvious examples.

The boundary situation provides a formal center within which conventions of psychological realism can take over. Focus on a situation's existential import motivates characters' expressing and explaining their mental states. Concerned less with action than reaction, the art cinema presents psychological effects in search of their causes. The dissection of feeling is often represented as therapy and cure (e.g., many of Bergman's films), but even when it is not, causation is often braked and the more introspective characters pause to seek the etiology of their feelings. Characters retard the movement of the syuzhet by telling stories—autobiographical events (especially from childhood), fantasies, and dreams. Even if a character remains unaware of or inarticulate about his or her mental state, the viewer must be prepared to notice how behavior and setting can give the character away. The art cinema developed a range of mise-en-scène cues for expressing character mood: static postures, covert glances, smiles that fade, aimless walks, emotion-filled landscapes, and associated objects (e.g., Valentina's wire toy in *La Notte* or Catherine's hourglass in *Jules and Jim*). Within the fabula world—one that is usually as autonomous and internally consistent as that of the Hollywood film—psychological realism consists of permitting a character to reveal the self to others and, inadvertently, to us.

This is a fully expressive realism in that the syuzhet can employ film techniques to dramatize private mental processes. Art-cinema narration employs all the sorts of subjectivity charted by Edward Branigan.[5] Dreams, memories, hallucinations, daydreams, fantasies, and other mental activities can find embodiment in the image or on the sound track. Consequently, the behavior of the characters within the fabula world and the syuzhet's dramatization both focus on the character's problems of action and feeling; which is to say that "inquiry into character" becomes not only the prime thematic material but a central source of expectation, curiosity, suspense, and surprise.

Conventions of expressive realism can shape spatial representation: optical point-of-view shots, flash frames of a glimpsed or recalled event, editing patterns, modulations of light and color and sound—all are often motivated by character psychology. In *Repulsion, Belle de Jour, Juliet of the Spirits,* and many other films, the surroundings may be construed as the projections of a character's mind. Similarly, the syuzhet may use psychology to justify the manipulation of time. The flashback is the most obvious instance (*Hiroshima mon amour, Wild Strawberries, A Man and a Woman*). Subjectivity can also justify the distension of time (slow motion or freeze frames) and manipulations of frequency, such as the repetition of images. (*Hiroshima mon amour, The Spider's Stratagem*). As V. V. Ivanov notes, the distortions in modern cinema are often motivated not by "Newtonian" time but rather by "psychological" time of the sort discussed by Bergson.[6]

One major consequence of the goal-bereft protagonist, the episodic format, the central boundary situation, and the spatiotemporal "expressive" effects is to focus on the limitations upon character knowledge. Unlike most classical films, the art film is apt to be quite restricted in its range of knowledge. Such restriction may enhance identification (character knowledge matches ours), but it may also make the narration less reliable (we cannot always be sure of the character's access to the total fabula). Sometimes the syuzhet will confine itself to what only one character knows, as in *Blow-Up* or *The Wrong Move*; sometimes the syuzhet splits knowledge between two central characters, as in Antonioni's trilogy. The narrow focus is complemented by psychological depth; art-film narration is more subjective more often than is classical narration. For this reason, the art film has been a principal source of experiments in representing psychological activity in the fiction film.

To "objective" and "subjective" verisimilitude we may add a third broad schema, that of overt narrational "commentary." In applying this schema, the viewer looks for those moments in which the narrational act interrupts the transmission of fabula information and highlights its own role. Stylistic devices that gain prominence with respect to classical norms—an unusual angle, a stressed bit of cutting, a striking camera movement, an unrealistic shift in lighting or setting, a disjunction on the sound track, or any other breakdown of objective realism which is not motivated as subjectivity—can be taken as the narration's commentary. Recall the "prophetic" camera movement in *The Spider's Stratagem* (figs. 6.28–6.32), or the satiric freeze frame in *Viridiana* that invites the spectator to compare the beggars' feast to the Last Supper. The marked self-consciousness of art-cinema narration creates both a coherent fabula world and an intermittently present but highly noticeable external authority through which we gain access to it.

Thanks to the intrusive commentary, the self-conscious points in the classical text (the beginning and ending of a scene, of the film) become foregrounded in the art film. The credits of *Persona* and *Blow-Up* can tease us with fragmentary, indecipherable images that announce the power of the author to control what we know. The narrator can begin a scene in a fashion that cuts us adrift or can linger on a scene after its causally significant action has been completed. In particular, the "open" ending characteristic of the art cinema can be seen as proceeding from a narration which will not divulge the outcome of the causal chain. V. F. Perkins objects to the ending of *La Notte* on the grounds that "the 'real ending' is knowable but has been withheld. . . . The story is abandoned when it has served the director's purpose but before it has satisfied the spectator's requirements."[7] To complain about the arbitrary suppression of the story's outcome is to reject one convention of the art film. A banal remark of the 1960s, that such films make you leave the theater thinking, is not far from the mark: the ambiguity, the play of alternative schemata, must not be halted. Thus the unexpected freeze frame becomes the most explicit figure of narrative irresolution. Furthermore, the pensive ending acknowledges the narration as not simply powerful but humble; the narration knows that life is more complex than art can ever be, and—a new twist of the realistic screw—the only way to respect this complexity is to leave causes dangling and questions unanswered. Like many art films, *La Notte* bares the device of the unresolved ending when a woman at the party asks the writer Giovanni how a certain story should end. He answers: "In so many ways."

Art-film narration goes beyond such codified moments of overt intervention. At any point in the film we must be ready to engage with the shaping process of an overt narration. A scene may end in medias res; gaps are created that are not explicable by reference to character psychology; retardation may result from the withholding of information or from overloaded passages that require unpacking later. Lacking the "dialogue hooks" of classical construction, the film will exploit more connotative, symbolic linkages between episodes. Scenes will not obey the Hollywood pattern of exposition, pickup of old line of action, and start of new line. Irony may burst out: in *The Loneliness of the Long-Distance Runner*, Richardson cuts between a borstal choir singing "Jerusalem" and a captured boy being beaten. More generally, the canonic story schema we bring to the film may be disarrayed. There may be little or no exposition of prior fabula events, and even what is occurring at the moment may require subsequent rethinking (Sternberg's "rise and fall of first impressions"). Exposition will tend to be delayed and widely distributed; often we will learn the most important causal factors only at the film's end. Like classical narration, art-film narration poses questions that guide us in fitting material into an ongoing structure. But these questions do not simply involve causal links among fabula events, such as "What became of Sean Regan?" (*The Big Sleep*) or "Will Stanley seduce Roy's husband?" (*In This Our Life*). In the art film, as we saw in our analysis of *The Spider's Stratagem*, the very construction of the narration becomes the object of spectator hypotheses: how is the story being told? why tell the story in this way?

Obvious examples of such manipulation are disjunctions in temporal order. One common strategy is to use flashbacks in ways that only gradually reveal a prior event, so as to tantalize the viewer with reminders of his or her limited knowledge. *The Conformist* is a good example. Such a flashback is also usefully equivocal; it might be attributable to the character's spasms of memory rather than to the narration's overt suppressiveness. A more striking device is the flashforward—the syuzhet's representation of a "future" fabula action. The flashforward is unthinkable in the classical narrative cinema, which seeks to retard the ending, emphasize communicativeness, and play down self-consciousness. But in the art film, the flashforward flaunts the narration's range of knowledge (no character can know the future), the narration's recognition of the viewer (the flashforward is addressed to us, not to the characters), and the narration's limited communicativeness (telling a little while withholding a lot).

What the flashback and flashforward do in time can also take place in space. Odd ("arty") camera angles or camera movements independent of the action can register the presence of self-conscious narration. The "invisible witness" canonized by Hollywood precept becomes overt. In *La Notte*, for example, the bored wife Lidia leaves a party with the roué Roberto. As they drive in his car down a rainy street, they talk and laugh animatedly. But we never hear the conversation, and we see only bits of it, because the camera remains obstinately outside the closed car, tracking along with it as it passes through pools of light. The narration has "chosen" to "dedramatize" the most vivacious interpersonal exchange in the film. Such procedures tend to set an omniscient narration's range of knowledge in opposition to the character's; effects of irony and anticipation are especially prominent. In the *La Notte* example, the camera position deflating the scene foreshadows the sombre turn the action will take when Roberto soon tries to seduce Lidia. Unlike the classical film, however, which usually makes the profilmic event only moderately self-conscious, art-cinema narration often signals that the profilmic event is also a construct. This can be accomplished by means of unmotivated elements in the mise-en-scène, such as the sourceless strips of pink and blue light sliding through Fassbinder's *Lola*. Alternatively, stylized treatment of situations, settings, or props, or of an era or milieu, can seem to proceed from the narration. In *Senso* and *1900*, events are presented with an operatic opulence that invites us to consider the profilmic event itself as the narration's restaging of history.

The result is that a highly self-conscious narration weaves through the film, stressing the act of presenting this fabula in just this way. Deviations from classical norms can be grasped as commentary upon the story action. More generally, the degree of deviation from the canonic story becomes a trace of the narrational process. Syuzhet and style constantly remind us of an invisible intermediary that structures what we see. Marie-Claire Ropars's discussion of *écriture*—the tendency of directors like Resnais and Duras to bar direct access to a profilmic reality—emphasizes the general tendency of the art film to flaunt narrational procedures.[8] When these flauntings are repeated systematically, convention asks us to unify them as proceeding from an "author."

In Chapter 4, I argued that there was no good reason to identify the narrational process with a fictive narrator. In the art cinema, however, the overt self-consciousness of the narration is often paralleled by an extratextual emphasis on the filmmaker as source. Within the art cinema's mode of production and reception, the concept of the *author* has a formal function it did not possess in the Hollywood studio system. Film journalism and criticism promote authors, as do film festivals, retrospectives, and academic film study. Directors' statements of intent guide comprehension of the film, while a body of work linked by an authorial signature encourages viewers to read each film as a chapter of an oeuvre. Thus the institutional "author" is available as a source of the formal operation of the film. Sometimes the film asks to be taken as autobiography, the filmmaker's confession (e.g., *8½*, *The 400 Blows*, many of Fassbinder's works). More broadly, the author becomes the real-world parallel to the narrational presence "who" communicates (what is the filmmaker *saying*?) and "who" expresses (what is the artist's personal vision?).

The consistency of an authorial signature across an oeuvre constitutes an economically exploitable trademark. The signature depends partly on institutional processes (e.g., advertising a film as "Fellini's *Orchestra Rehearsal*") and partly upon recognizably recurring devices from one film to another. One could distinguish filmmakers by motifs (Buñuel's cripples, Fellini's parades, Bergman's theater performances) and by camera technique (Truffaut's pan-and-zoom, Ophuls's sinuous tracks, Chabrol's high angles, Antonioni's long shots). The trademark signature can depend upon narrational qualities as well. There are the "baroque" narrators in the films of Cocteau, Ophuls, Visconti, Welles, Fellini, and Ken Russell—narrators who stress a spectacular concatenation of music and mise-en-scène. More "realist" narrators can be found in the films of Rossellini, Olmi, Forman, and others. The art cinema has made a place for satiric narration (e.g., Buñuel's) and for pastiche (e.g., the many homages to Hitchcock). The author-as-narrator can be explicit, as in *Le plaisir* or *The Immortal Story*; or the narrator can simply be the presence that accompanies the story action with a discreet but insistent obbligato of visual and sonic commentary. The popularity of R. W. Fassbinder in recent years may owe something to his ability to change narrational personae from film to film so that there is a "realist" Fassbinder, a "literary" Fassbinder, a "pastiche" Fassbinder, a "frenzied" Fassbinder, and so on.

The authorial trademark requires that the spectator see this film as fitting into a body of work. From this it is only a short step to explicit allusion and citation. A film may "quote," as Resnais does when he includes classic footage in *Mon oncle d'Amérique*; it may be "dedicated," as *La sirène du Mississipi* is dedicated to Renoir; or it may cite, as when Antoine Doinel steals a production still from *Monika*. The film can allude to classical genre conventions (Fassbinder recalling the Universal melodrama, Demy the MGM musical). The art film often rests upon a cinephilia as intense as Hollywood's: full understanding of one film requires a knowledge of and a fascination with other films. At its limit, this tendency is seen in those numerous art films about filmmaking: *8½*, *Day for Night*, *Everything for Sale*, *Beware of a Holy Whore*, *Identification of a Woman*, *The Clowns*, and many more. A film-within-a-film structure realistically motivates references to other works; it allows unexpected shifts between levels of fictionality; it can occasionally trigger parody of the art cinema itself. In *La Ricotta*, Pasolini's episode of *RoGoPaG*, Orson Welles plays a director filming the Christ story; he is pestered by a journalist who asks him about his vision of life and his opinion of Italian society. Antonioni's *Lady without the Camellias* portrays a vacuous starlet who marries a scriptwriter. He immediately forbids her to play in any of the cheap romances that were her forte and instead puts her in a biopic of Jeanne d'Arc: "An art film, something that will sell abroad!"

The art cinema's spectator, then, grasps the film by applying conventions of objective and expressive realism and of authorial address. Yet are these schemata not incompatible? Verisimilitude, objective or subjective, is inconsistent with an intrusive author. The surest signs of narrational omniscience—the flashforward, the doubled scene in *Persona*, the shifts from black-and-white to color in *A Man and a Woman* and *If*—are the least capable of realistic justification. Contrariwise, to push the realism of chance and psychological indefiniteness to its limit is to create a haphazard narrative in which an author's shaping hand would not be visible. In short, a realistic aesthetic and an expressionist aesthetic are hard to merge. The art cinema seeks to solve the problem in a sophisticated way: through ambiguity.

Within some traditional aesthetic positions, ambiguity is what philosophers call a "good-making property." Therefore, Hollywood films would be judged bad because they are denotatively unequivocal, while art films become good because they ask to be puzzled over. Within the framework of this book, however, ambiguity is only one aesthetic strategy among many, all of potentially equal interest. What is significant is that art-cinema narration announces its debt to the arts of the early twentieth century by making ambiguity, either of tale or telling, central.

The syuzhet of classical narration tends to move toward absolute certainty, but the art film, like early modernist fiction, holds a relativistic notion of truth. This effect is achieved by means of a specific strategy. The three principal schemata provide norms, but the puzzling passages of the film will be explained equally well by alternative conven-

tions. We have already seen this ambiguity at work in our analysis of *The Spider's Stratagem*, where we found contrary cues for whether to assign flashbacks to characters or to the narrational commentary. Antonioni's *Red Desert* offers another example. Putting aside the island fantasy, we can motivate any scene's color scheme on grounds of subjective verisimilitude (Giulietta sees her life in this way) or of authorial commentary (the narration shows her life as being this way). That these schemata are mutually exclusive creates the ambiguity. Or recall *Rashomon*, in which any character's account of the rape and murder may be objectively accurate or warped by subjective interests. In Herzog's *Kaspar Hauser*, the interpolated desert footage may be ascribed to Kaspar's visions or to the narrational commentary.

The art film is nonclassical in that it creates permanent narrational gaps and calls attention to processes of fabula construction. But these very deviations are placed within new extrinsic norms, resituated as realism or authorial commentary. Eventually, the art-film narration solicits not only denotative comprehension but connotative reading, a higher-level interpretation. Whenever confronted with a problem in causality, time, or space, we tend to seek realistic motivation. Is a character's mental state creating the difficulty? Is "life" just leaving loose ends? If we are thwarted, we appeal to the narration, and perhaps also to the author. Is the narrator violating the norm to achieve a specific effect? In particular, what thematic significance justifies the deviation? What range of judgmental connotations or symbolic meanings can be produced from this point or pattern? Ideally, the film hesitates, hovering between realistic and authorial rationales. Uncertainties persist but are understood as such, as *obvious* uncertainties. Put crudely, the procedural slogan of art-cinema narration might be: "Interpret this film, and interpret it so as to maximize ambiguity."

As I have described it, art-cinema narration might seem to encourage what Veronica Forrest-Thomson calls "bad naturalization." She observes of Wallace Stevens, "His obscurity is a kind of coyness, an attempt to stay one step ahead of the reader and so gain a reputation for daring while ensuring that the reader knows exactly where the poet is and how he can take that one step to reach him.'"[9] And it is true that at its most banal, art-cinema narration promises complexity and profundity only to settle our attention on stereotyped figures: "reality," neurotic characters, the author as puppeteer. But in many of these films, the narration sustains a complex play within the conventions of the mode. There is the possibility of exploring nonredundant cues and devising new, wholly contextual narrational devices. The film can build up curiosity about its own narrational procedures, thus intensifying the viewer's interest in the unfolding patterns of syuzhet and style. Uncertainty about story events, generated by causal looseness and gaps, can create what Sternberg calls "anticipatory caution," a thwarting of the primacy effect and a discouraging of exclusive and likely hypotheses. The narration can warn us or mislead us. By alternating overloaded with sparse passages, the narration can demand intense attention; and by creating ambiguous organizational patterns, the narration can make such great demands on memory that it may be necessary to see the film more than once (a formal effect not without economic value). Finally, the film can undermine norms far more frequently than can a classical film. The art film plays among several tendencies: deviation from classical norms, adherence to art-cinema norms, creation of innovative intrinsic norms, and the greater or lesser foregrounding of deviations from those intrinsic norms. To see how the game can go, let us look at one film in detail.

The Game of Form

The career of Alain Resnais offers a good instance of how the art cinema as an institution encourages a filmmaker to formulate a discernible "project" running from one film to another. Resnais's recurrent concern has, of course, been the representation of time. In its day, *Hiroshima mon amour* (1959) caused considerable surprise for its minimal cueing of flashbacks, and *L'année dernière à Marienbad* (1961) was widely understood as blurring the line between memory and fantasy. *Muriel* (1963) contained no flashbacks or hallucina-

tion sequences but did exploit a highly elliptical approach to the moment-by-moment unfurling of the syuzhet. I mention these well-known facts because the average spectator of *La guerre est finie* (1968) is likely to approach the film with some expectations about the principal narrational manipulations the film will offer and to attribute those to an authorial intelligence. In such ways, the creation of a distinct formal project can lead the filmmaker to innovate fresh intrinsic norms from film to film. No two Resnais films treat the same aspects of narrative time, or handle time in quite the same way. The spectator will thus be asked to plot *La guerre est finie*'s particular work against the extrinsic norms of the mode, and the achieving of prominence will have an undeniable ludic component. So will the subsequent deviations from the intrinsic norms. The viewer must draw upon tacit conventions of comprehension characteristic of the art film—objective verisimilitude, expressive realism, overt narrational intervention—in order to construct the fabula and identify the rules unique to this film's narrational work.

The first nineteen shots of *La guerre est finie* introduce us to its intrinsic norm. The story is this: The agitator Diego is driving back across the Spanish border with Jude, a bookseller who occasionally assists anti-Franco leftists. As they approach the checkpoint, Diego looks forward to safe passage while Jude chats about how the sudden trip spoiled his vacation. But this fabula episode is made difficult by many procedures.

The "objective" verisimilitude of the action is evident—location shooting, the general fidelity to the political situation—but it gets overridden by the strongly subjective cast of the narration. The very first shot of the film (fig. 10.1) is from a passenger's optical point of view. Shot 2 (fig. 10.2) enables us to locate the source of the point of view (the character we will later learn to call Diego). The cues for subjectivity are reinforced by the next shot (fig. 10.3), another optical point of view, and by the sound track, for as the camera pans right to show the distant town, a nondiegetic voice is heard: "You're past the border. Again you see the hill of Biratou." The objective specificity of locale is secondary to the subjective depth, whereby the gaze is linked to a character's reac-

tion. At this point harpsichord music creeps onto the sound track, contributing to the emphasis upon subjective affect. As the camera pans left and the car drives forward, the voice-over asserts: "Once again, you'll get over."

There is now a shift into a slightly less restricted narra-

tional presentation. In shots 4–7 (figs. 10.4–10.7), Jude and Diego exchange patient glances. Despite the angle of Jude's look, neither man is filmed from the other's optical point of view. In addition, the timing of the glances presents a greater range of narrational knowledge: the camera antici-

pates each man's look by several moments. The unrestricted presentation in this suite of shots is of course highly conventional.

Diego's optical point of view returns (shot 8; fig. 10.8) as the car approaches the checkpoint. But now the accompanying sound is Jude's voice offscreen, confessing his worry that the car might have broken down en route. Midway through the sentence, the image track starts to diverge significantly from Jude's chatter. We see several images, rapidly cut. (See figs. 10.9–10.18.) Diego runs out of a train station to catch a

10.9
10.10   10.11
                                                         10.12

cab (shot 9). An apartment door opens to reveal a man and a woman coming forward (10). Diego enters an elevator as the same man strides out of an adjacent one (11). Diego runs out of the station but must wait in line for a cab (12). Diego walks down a train corridor (13). Diego hops onto a train as it pulls out (14). Diego runs to a train but misses it (15). Diego leaps from a car as it pulls up to a train station (16). The same unknown man comes into his apartment and greets Diego, who appears to have been waiting for him (17). And all this occurs while Jude's voice continues on the sound track. At

shot 18, we are back in the car, with Jude still behind the
wheel.

Later, certain questions raised by this sequence will be
answered. The man is Juan, whom Diego is coming to warn
against returning to Spain. But the mode of presentation
must give the spectator pause. Seeing that shots 9–17 rupture the spatiotemporal continuum of the scene in the car
and hearing Jude's chatter continuing in voice-over, the
viewer versed in the conventions of the art cinema hypothesizes a temporal disjunction between sound (the present)

might be an effort to fit the images into some chronology, on the assumption that arriving at the station (16) preceded catching the train (14) and riding it (13). But all of the shots are not easily explicable as events in any temporal string. Most of them present mutually exclusive alternatives:

1. Diego catches a cab quickly (9); or he has to wait in line (12).

2. Diego calls on Juan and he is home (10); or Diego misses him (11); or Diego calls and Juan arrives later (17).

3. Diego catches the train (14); or he misses it (15).

The all-or-nothing nature of the alternatives is strengthened by the immediate juxtapositions of extremes: Diego finds Juan or misses him (10/11), he catches the train or misses it (14/15). Whatever the spectator eventually makes of this sequence, there are strong cues that it probably does not represent a single stretch of past fabula events.

If this is not a single action in the past, the shots might be construed as an elliptical montage sequence of the "frequentative" type. That is, Diego's regular routine is to take cabs, visit contacts, catch or miss trains, and so forth. This hypothesis is strengthened by the voice-over's insistence upon repeated action ("Again you see the hill of Biratou . . ."). Yet Diego wears the same clothes in every shot—hardly a helpful cue for construing these actions as habitual repetitions in the past.

Only one construction accounts for everything in these shots. It is an unlikely one, but it is the one that later passages will confirm. These shots may be taken to represent various possible *future* events. Put in simple fashion: "I might grab a cab right away or have to wait in line," "I might miss Juan," "What if I can't catch my train?" *La guerre est finie* will explore character subjectivity according to one principle of the art film; we justify what we see and hear by reference to psychological motivation. The narration creates a unique intrinsic norm by supplying neither flashbacks nor fantasies in the usual sense. We are to share the character's *anticipation* of events. This also realistically justifies the lack of chronological order in the images. Diego might think

and image (not the present). But the ambiguities of the sequence thwart an easy comprehension. The most probable hypothesis based on extrinsic norms would be that the image is in the past. Yet this creates a new problem. It is difficult to grasp the series of shots as presenting a *single* event chain. True, nothing prevents our construing shot 9 this way. (Perhaps Diego caught a train earlier.) And there of meeting or missing Juan, then of how he will get to Juan's apartment, then of missing the train, and so forth. In a 1966 interview, Resnais asserted that his treatment of anticipation was "realistic" in showing the mind's tendency to leap ahead to a goal and only later speculate on what might happen on the way. Of course, this "realism" is wholly arbitrary. (One could just as easily argue that it's more plausible for the mind to plan its moves in chronological order.) Nonetheless, Resnais opens up a new category of psychological experience for narration to dramatize.

Resnais also doubted that all the implications of his treatment would get across. "I do not think that it is understandable to spectators, but they can feel a sort of uneasiness in the fact that the images are in the future."[10] One can certainly argue that shots 9–17, swiftly cut and referring to characters and places of whom we yet know nothing, are comprehended by most first-time spectators as little more than "images which are probably subjective." This initial difficulty is very important. First, it is typical of the art film to acclimate us gradually to its intrinsic norms. (Recall the cues for flashbacks in *The Spider's Stratagem*.) Much of the art film's appeal rests upon a tantalizing narration that plays a game of gaps with the viewer, and *La guerre*'s opening quickly sets that game in motion. We become keen to know not only whether Diego will get through the border (suspense) and what his past is (curiosity) but also what this flurry of interspersed images represents, and what the film's own "rules" are. Second, the mutual exclusiveness of the juxtaposed shots maximizes indeterminacy. We are not sure exactly what story event, in what place in the action sequence, we're seeing. Finally, such a striking opening cries out for critical discussion. In reviews and interviews, a commentator or indeed the director himself can call our attention to the difficulty of the device.

Once the sequence returns to Jude (shot 18), we are back in the present, and the next shot of Diego (19) confirms the subjective, digressive nature of the anticipatory images. It is reassuring, at the formal level, to discover that, however puzzling the excursions become, we will return to an "objective" frame of reference. We thus grasp the entire first sequence (in all, twenty-five shots) as a generally and "objectively" coherent scene (durationally continuous and primarily restricted to Diego's knowledge) which a subjective passage interrupts.

Against the overall narrative unity of the sequence must be set certain ambiguities and lacks of redundancy. What about the voice-over that speaks "to" Diego? It is not wholly subjective: it is not his voice, and it uses "you" rather than "I." Is it then the voice of some "authorial" narrator? Or is it a "subjective other," an impersonal objectification of his thoughts? Later scenes will play with possible sources of this voice. And the handling of point-of-view découpage is somewhat different from the normalized *ABA* cutting pattern of *Rear Window* (Jeff looks / shot of what he sees / back to him looking). Here we see through the character's eyes before we see the character (shot 1). Or we have shots *A* and *B*, but instead of a return to the looker we cut to another person (shots 2–4). Or a passage involving mental subjectivity begins on the musing character (shot 8) but ends on the other character (shot 18). Or we have mentally subjective images that work against consistent optical subjectivity (shot 11). Not that any of these tactics is fundamentally disquieting, but they do bring out how the classical paradigm uses many redundant cues; our comprehension does not necessarily flag if some are withheld.

As in this sequence, the whole film's syuzhet coheres around Diego, as both agent and psychological subject. Our range of knowledge is almost completely restricted to his. In this respect he resembles Philip Marlowe in *The Big Sleep* or *Murder My Sweet*: the syuzhet is constructed around gaps in the hero's knowledge. More to the point for art-cinema norms, however, is that restriction to Diego's range of knowledge is necessary for the central device—the anticipatory flashforward—to work. If we should learn Juan's fate or witness events of which Diego is ignorant, his visions would register simply as narrational irony. (He's right about this, wrong about that.) Confinement to what Diego knows not only justifies withholding information, as in the detective tale, but also increases the indeterminacies of "expressive realism" and permits the plumbing of elusive states of mind for their own sake. How much less confident would we feel about Marlowe's inferential powers if *The Big Sleep* dramatized, in abrupt flashes, all the alternative hypotheses that flit through his mind!

Later we will not be completely restricted to Diego's range of knowledge. There are brief, patterned violations that function to prepare the female characters to take over his role at the film's end. In scene 17, while Diego sleeps, there is a brief shot of his lover, Marianne, looking in on him. Five sequences later, Nadine Sallanches comes down the steps of a cafe while Diego's back is turned. In scene 27, when Diego goes into a drugstore to phone Nadine, the camera holds on Marianne. At the film's climax, the narration has recourse to crosscutting among these three characters: while Diego drives to Spain, Nadine is visited by a policeman and Marianne prepares to cross the border to warn him. The very last shots of the film identify Marianne and Diego, making her our new (and limited) protagonist; she now obtains, perhaps, a depth of subjectivity commensurate with that earlier assigned to Diego.

If Diego is our virtually constant point of reference, the overall composition of the film assures that we do not lose our bearings in a morass of subjectivity. For one thing, each gap is flaunted; we may be in the dark about the narration's goal, but we can pinpoint where we lose our bearings. (Contrast in this respect the suppressed gaps of *L'année dernière à Marienbad.*) Moreover, just as the first sequence framed Diego's anticipations within the "objective" action of crossing the border, so the narration always takes care to include stable expository portions. After the disorienting series of shots we have already considered, the narration goes objective for three scenes. Diego is questioned at the border and his false identity is tested. He escapes because the young woman who answers the phone at "his" address backs up his story. Here the restriction to Diego's range of knowledge yields orthodox results, a curiosity gap: why would Nadine Sallanches lie to protect a stranger who has apparently stolen her father's passport? In the next scene, Diego's discussions with Jude and Jude's wife explain to us the faked passport, his bluff before the border officer, and so on. Just as

important, it is during the stay at Jude's shop that clear cues are supplied about the nature of the subjective passages. If the flurry of Diego's anticipations in scene 1 was graspable only as "perhaps not flashbacks," the narration now takes pains to explain the device.

Over a medium shot of Diego, Jude's voice-off asks if Diego knows the Sallanches family. Nondiegetic piano music comes softly up. Diego responds: "No, none of them." This creates a primacy effect: we will evaluate what we see in the light of this statement. Ten shots follow, all but the last accompanied by the piano music. Each of the first five shots shows a young woman walking in medium shot away from the camera as it tracks to follow her. Similarity balances difference: graphically matched compositions and figure/camera movements play against the fact that each young woman is unique. (See figs. 10.19–10.21.) The next two shots show, again in graphically matched fashion, two different women entering a building. The eighth shot tracks in on yet another young woman talking on the phone. As in the first sequence, the "objective" conversation continues on the sound track, signaling that the series of shots is Diego's mental event. But instead of the several either/or pairings presented in the overloaded first passage, here a single piece of information—Diego's musing on what Nadine looks like—is reinforced by the musical cue, by his verbal declaration, and by a series of shots that reiterate ten alternatives. The same sort of point is made in the last two shots: on the sound track Diego says he's never seen their house, and the narration immediately supplies images of a street and a house number.

The viewer's prevailing hypothesis about the film's intrinsic narrational norm emerges: any images or sounds that cannot be related to an "objective" construction of the scene are then most likely Diego's subjective anticipation. Scene 5 reinforces this hypothesis immediately. After more conversation, Jude remarks to Diego that Antoine must be at the station. Cut to a man at a railway bookstall turning to look at the camera. Cut to the same man, now at the ticket window, turning to the camera. Cut to the same man in another spot, again turning to look at the camera. And cut to a long shot of

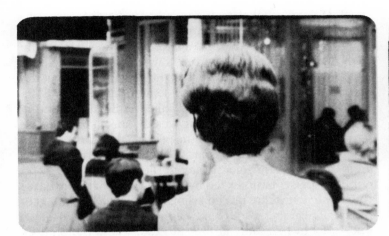

Jude and Diego coming downstairs, their footsteps having sounded over the three interpolated shots. Finally, this scene links the device to the first, most puzzling subjective passage. After Diego says that Juan can't be across the border, the narration cuts to a shot of the man we saw in the first sequence, riding in a car. From ten inserted shots to three

shots to one: after a trio of interpolations, we are primed to construe even a single disparate image as Diego's projection. By the end of scene 5, not only have we received a major portion of expository material about Diego's mission and his tactics, we have also found the key to the film's narrational method. This key, however, will not unlock anything unless the spectator is prepared to apply the art cinema's conventional schemata.

It is worth stressing just how redundant all this is. At the level of the fabula, characters' traits and functions are mutually compatible. At the level of the syuzhet, the narration's repeated alternation of subjective passages with objective ones and its adherence to a consistent point of view guarantee considerable predictability. And the narration presents the fabula so that we have ample opportunity to pick up information, especially in the expository conversation scenes. In scene 5, we not only understand what transpired in scene 2, when Diego was challenged by the border chief, but also learn the background to his underground activities. Even the content of Diego's anticipations is eventually clarified through repetition. Only certain aspects of the narration are not redundant, some bearing chiefly on a key plot point—what has become of Juan?—and some bearing on how certain narrational devices are to be interpreted, as we shall see. The ambiguity of the art cinema is of a highly controlled and limited sort, standing out against a background of narrational coherence not fundamentally different from that of the classical cinema.

La guerre est finie builds its story upon the base established in the opening scenes. The principal fabula lines involve Diego's mission to convince his leftist compatriots that the Spanish police have discovered Juan's plans; his love affair with Marianne, a book designer; and his involvement with Nadine, daughter of the man whose passport he carries and member of a youthful leftist group which is hoarding explosives for terrorist ends. These lines of action interweave across a syuzhet duration of four days (18–21 April 1968), each strand serving to retard resolution of the others. To this calendric verisimilitude the film adds other realistic touches: mishaps and coincidences (warning Juan, Diego's encounter with a cop in a cafe), real locations, allusions to political events, and a general depiction of debates within the French left (Old Left patience versus terrorism, etc.). There is also the convention of expressive realism, incarnated here as Diego's psychological crisis. Is he right to insist on warning Juan? Has he lost track of the political game he plays? His colleagues charge him with being blinded by the daily trivia of his job; he begins to doubt his judgment. "We're finicky about details," he tells Nadine. "It's the total picture we lose sight of." Marianne notices as well, asking him whether he is not confused about where he's going. Diego makes slips: he may have betrayed himself to the Spanish police, he forgets to turn on his headlights and is stopped by a policeman, and after a heated quarrel with Nadine's cadre, he realizes that he has led the police to them. His boundary situation is as much personal and political, since he desires Nadine but comes to realize that he wants to clear a place for Marianne in his life. All of these factors work to ensure that the film is unified by realistic motivation of an art-cinema stripe.

The realism of Diego's comportment also justifies the syuzhet's expositional tactics. The narration gives us information piecemeal and retards our complete understanding of the situation. Not until a later scene do we learn the basis for Diego's belief that Juan is walking into a trap. Still later, we learn that Diego has some relation to a woman named Marianne, and we see her somewhat after that. The narration also delays revealing Nadine's affiliation with the young leftists. Thus the film engages the spectator's interest with suspense gaps (e.g., will the police nab Diego?) as well as many curiosity gaps (what is Diego's relation to Marianne? how is Nadine connected to Diego's activities?). The curiosity gaps are motivated by Diego's state of mind in two ways: the restriction placed on his knowledge and the very nature of his mental activities. For instance, of course Diego knows about Marianne at the start, but the narration does not inform us of her existence for some time. This omission is justified by the way his mind is shown to work. He is characterized as cautious, so he is unlikely to volunteer information about Marianne in scenes with other characters. Since he is preoccupied with the mechanics of his border crossing and the possible peril to Juan, none of his anticipations involve Marianne until he approaches her apartment. The narration justifies its distributed and delayed exposition by making its central character ignorant, closemouthed, and so perpetually focused on the future that he does not occupy himself with the past. Hence the need for several lengthy scenes in which Diego and other characters pass expositional information along to the viewer.

La guerre est finie, then, appeals to conventional structures and cues while at the same time introducing significant innovations. The narration employs art-cinema principles of psychological verisimilitude but finds a new domain for them (the anticipatory flashforward). The film fulfills our expectations about ambiguity (e.g., the opening sequence) while also defining the range of permissible constructions (e.g., "probably not flashbacks"). Early on, the film tutors us in its methods, giving us a unique but comprehensible hypothesis to help us construct the story action. The film's problem now is to maintain psychological coherence—the focus on Diego's political and personal experience—while varying the narrational ploys. Once we have the key, the narration could become wholly predictable. How is the narration to engage that overt play with expectation characteristic of the art film?

One way that the game is sustained involves marking each subjective sequence unequivocally but also varying the particular filmic devices employed. In this film, two stylistic cues are necessary for a sequence to be identifiable as imaginary: a cut (visual cue) to images from which no diegetic sound is forthcoming (auditory cue). Thus the first sequence cuts to Juan leaving his apartment, Diego missing a train, and so on, but we do not hear voices, the throb of the train, or other diegetic sounds. These cues are accompanied by more contextual ones. Diego must be present, and the anticipation must be plausibly triggered by something in the current scene. Otherwise the flashforwards display great freedom in their sylistic figures. On the image track, the subjective shot often includes a tracking camera movement and characters' turning to the camera—both techniques suggesting Diego's optical point of view—but these are not always present. And no single sound cue will unequivocally assure us that a subjective sequence is coming up or in progress. Given the silence within Diego's mental image, the sound track may let dialogue in the present continue (e.g., Jude's chatter in the first scene) or supply diegetic noise from the present (e.g., the two men's footsteps in scene 5), nondiegetic music, the voice-over, silence in the present, or any combination of these. For example, Diego's anticipations of Nadine in scene 5 are accompanied by piano music for nine of the ten shots and dialogue in the present during eight of them. This means that the subjective sequences may be accompanied by a rich variety of sounds. In scene 1, Jude's complaining about the vacation he had hoped for while Diego is occupied with his own anticipations exemplifies how the range of sonic options can indirectly reinforce the image.

The narration can also withhold some cues. We have already seen that the first anticipatory sequence can be construed as Diego's subjective "insert" even though it ends not with a shot of Diego but with a shot of Jude. Such slight deviations from extrinsic norms can suffice to destabilize our expectations. A subjective insert can thus come along in a wide range of circumstances. There is no need for a lead-in shot of Diego, or a musical cue, or explicit discussion of the subject of the anticipation. This is comparable to the variation of cues for order and duration at work in *The Spider's Stratagem*. The narration can also mislead us by foregoing a subjective passage when we might expect one. On several occasions, Diego will pause reflectively—on a train, in his study—and the next shot will prove *not* to be an index of his thoughts. When Diego burns his false passport photo, we hear his voice, as if in voice-over; yet it is not the internal voice that addresses him, and we must conclude that he is murmuring offscreen. Such a play with our expectations remains within the boundaries codified by the film. It is the trigger and the timing of the mental imagery that the spectator can never exactly predict. To the end, the eruption of a subjective sequence remains only more or less probable, never certain.

The narration maintains its game with the viewer in still more ways. Consider, for instance, the difficulty that crops up if we cut from a shot of Diego to a close-up of some act, say a valise being slid into a locker. If there is no "present-tense" sound on the track, there are two possible assumptions: that it is a subjective flashforward or that it is the first shot of a new, objective scene. One effect of some flashforwards can thus be an uncertainty as to whether we are yet "into" the next present-tense scene. There are several other, equally slight, dislodgings of expectation that the anticipatory sequences create, but I want here to focus on two of great importance, both revolving around time.

By scene 5, I have argued, redundant cues have established the reigning hypothesis for grasping narrational disjunctions: when in doubt, look for cues for Diego's subjective anticipations. This hypothesis is strengthened in scene 6, when at Hendaye station Diego reflects on how Juan might be captured and how Diego might prevent it. In scene 7, aboard the train to Paris, the narration provides a summary of most of the subjective motifs we have seen: Diego getting out of a cab, Diego arriving at Juan's apartment,

Diego meeting his leftist cronies, Juan being captured, Diego spotting young women who might be Nadine. Both scenes 6 and 7 are accompanied by present-tense sound: dialogue in the first, the train rumble and whistle in the second. The film is now in danger of becoming predictable. In the next scene, some ground rules get modified, albeit in equivocal fashion.

We are first given to wonder whether Diego is now not occasionally conjuring up *past* events. In scene 8, a quick shot of Madame Lopez and a longer take of the apartment complex are accompanied by voice-over remarks that suggest flashbacks: "You visited Juan a year ago—building G, tenth floor, number 107—care of Madame Lopez, you thought." The case for a flashback is not clear-cut, though, since one could also consider the shots of Madame Lopez and the apartment complex as anticipatory; only the commentary would then pertain to the past. There follows a shot of Juan driving off which can be taken as Diego's imagining of a past event ("Juan has probably already left") but could also be taken as another anticipation ("If Juan has yet to leave . . ."). In scene 11, the promise is fulfilled. When Diego leaves Ramon's, the narration gives us another ambiguous image—a track back from the corridor of Juan's apartment—and then a definite flashback: a shot of Madame Jude, as she had been seen earlier that day when Diego talked with her. Here we have a case of foregrounding, the violation of an established intrinsic norm. It is not, however, a strong case, for it varies along only one dimension, temporal order. (Recall that foregrounding gets stronger according to how many dimensions of syuzhet or style are involved and how predictable the deviation is with respect to intrinsic and extrinsic norms.) Indeed, this deviation quickly gets absorbed into the intrinsic norm. From this point on, the film will have occasional recourse to flashbacks. Thus the narration teasingly asks the spectator to modify the initial hypothesis: assign any deviation from objective continuity to Diego's mind, either *most probably* as an anticipation or *secondarily* as a flashback. The strategy suits the art-cinema mode. Instead of opening the film with the more conventional device of the flashback and moving on to include flashforwards, the narration starts with the more unpredictable device and introduces the conventional one in a way which yields uncertainty.

Along with the flashback there is another foregrounded temporal device, used only once. We have seen that as a rule Diego's subjective flashforwards are presented as silent images, although they may be accompanied by dialogue or noise in the present. The temporal disjunction occurs only on the image track. But in one scene we are disoriented by an apparent violation of this rule. Diego and Nadine have agreed to meet at the Bullier Building at 6:00. There follows a pursuit: Nadine and her boyfriend, Miguel, are followed by a policeman, who is in turn followed by Diego. Over the third shot of the pursuit, nondiegetic xylophone music gives way to the disembodied voices of Nadine and Diego. He is telling her that she has been followed; she denies it. After several moments of conversation, cut to Nadine, turning in medium shot and saying: "Miguel?" Now she and Diego are in the Bullier Building, their rendezvous point. Like the images in earlier scenes, the sound track here is equivocal. It could represent Diego's anticipation of what their conversation will be, in which case it would be the only auditory anticipation in the film. Or the passage can be taken as a more "objective" aural flashforward: the sound of their conversation at Bullier at one point of fabula time is laid over images of action at an earlier point. Either way, the narration is only stretching the rules. Allowing one instance of auditory anticipation still adheres to the basic principles of Diego's subjectivity, while the "authorial" trick of letting the sound of scene *B* lie over the end of scene *A* would be quite conventional in the art cinema generally. In either event, the image/sound interaction here, like the occasional flashbacks, works to keep the film from falling into easily predictable patterns.

One more way that the narration maintains its game with viewer expectation deserves notice because it is quite particular to *La guerre est finie*. We have already seen that the film spectator's interest is essentially future oriented; under the pressure of time created by the viewing situation, we are more geared to suspense than curiosity. To some extent, the art cinema works against this by stressing curiosity and delaying expositional material. But the narration of *La guerre* trades upon future-oriented interest to a great degree. Obviously, at the level of causality, there is the what-will-happen-next sort of interest. At the level of narration, the handlings of the intrinsic norms also solicit spectator surprise. (Will the device of sequence 1 be explained? Once it is explained in sequence 5, will it vary?) The peculiarity of this film is that the particular narrational tactics it exploits create diffused gaps with respect to past events but unusually focused expectations about future ones. Because Diego is constantly anticipating his actions, our awareness of them is sharpened. Will the events he envisions take place? If so, will they occur in the way that he expects? The most obvious and pervasive instance is Juan's trip. Since the film enacts (and not merely recounts) many possible fates which could befall Juan, we take a keen interest in finding which will be actualized. On a more local level, Diego's anticipations of what Nadine will look like, where she will live, how he will encounter Juan's wife, and how he and his colleagues will conduct their meeting are all precise enough to let us look forward to measuring the fit between subjective image and objective event. To some degree, the film makes up for the widely distributed and delayed exposition of prior fabula events by an unusually high degree of control over the spectator's hypotheses about upcoming ones. Our hypotheses are highly exclusive (Diego constructs clearly defined alternatives) and often simultaneous. Which is to say that because of the narration's enactment of Diego's mental activity, the film invites us to make his expectations our own.

Yet this tactic too is modified so as not to become predictable. At two points, Diego doubts the efficacy of his (and our) hypothesis forming. His chief charges him with subjectivism, with misjudging the danger to Juan, and though he puts up resistance he ends by accepting the criticism. More vividly, in scene 30, Nadine's Leninist group confronts him with the possibility that he led the police to them. Surprised, he imagines an *agent* filming from a car (another "speculative flashback"). One effect of any highly restricted and deeply subjective narration is to make us forget the extent to which we and the character may be led astray. In the course

of the narration, Diego is forced to consider that his hypotheses are often not as probable or as exclusive as he had assumed. Once we learn the narration's devices, we are inclined to trust Diego's judgment; when that fails, we suffer what Sternberg calls the "rise and fall of first impressions."[11]

The anticipatory image and its varied manifestations, functions, and effects maintain the intermittent overtness of narration characteristic of the art cinema. That stress is also apparent in the way that the film employs ambiguity. The complexity of certain images and sounds is not a reflection of their ambiguity *for Diego*. (He knows who Juan is, when he must have left, what was actually said to Nadine at the Bullier Building.) The ambiguity is largely the result of an omniscient narration's overt play with audience expectation. Sometimes it is a matter of communicativeness—holding back the identification of Juan in the first scene, for instance. Sometimes it is a question of self-consciousness, as when the narration supplies images and sounds that are most comprehensible as coming from an overriding consciousness (the narrator).

A simple example is the love scene with Nadine. After Diego has met her, they make love. But the scene is staged and cut in a stylized fashion uncharacteristic of the rest of the film. A montage of body parts is accompanied by high-key lighting, overexposed images, and abstract white backgrounds. The effect is to code the scene as both "reality" (the couple did make love) and "fantasy" (connotations of impossibly pure pleasure). In retrospect, the treatment appears even more stylized by comparison with Diego and Marianne's lovemaking later, handled in longer takes and without the abstract visual effects. The question is: to "whom" do we attribute the fantasy connotations in the scene with Nadine? We can take it as a piece of character psychology (Diego "seeing" Nadine as a fantasy of desire) or as commentary (the narration informs us of this fantasy as Nadine's role, although Diego is unaware of it). The ambiguity plays between a relatively unselfconscious presentation of character subjectivity and a highly self-conscious intervention of the "author."

While the love scene is fairly ordinary in its ambiguity, the narration is somewhat more inventive in its use of the voice-over commentary. We have already noticed that this internal speaker, using a voice which is not Diego's and addressing him as "you," is inherently equivocal. It could be the "subjectively objective" voice of his own mind, a kind of internalized Other that ponders his actions in an impersonal way. This alternative is reinforced by the commentary's habit of coldly summing up what has happened and of projecting future possibilities that accord with what we see. "Antoine's right," the voice says. "Go to Paris"—this over a shot of Diego jumping on a train. The commentary often chimes with the anticipatory images, giving us a greater confidence that it is in some mediated way Diego talking to himself. Yet one could also construe the voice as that of a highly knowledgeable and unusually intimate narrator, one deliberately letting us "overhear" its address to Diego. This would justify the use of "you," the disparity in vocal qualities, and Resnais's own comment that the narration aims to admit to the spectator, "We are in the cinema."[12] The difficulty of choosing one source over another is revealed in two later scenes.

When Diego is meeting with his leftist colleagues, a voice-over commentary is heard. At first, we might be inclined to take the voice as Diego's inner Other ("Again the feeling you've lived through this experience before . . ."), but when Diego and the chief start to debate in Spanish, the voice comes to function as a translator's. It renders the speeches into French, while in an undercurrent we still hear the characters speaking Spanish—a technique transtextually coded as "documentary" from its use in television reportage. When Diego speaks, the commentary continues to render his Spanish with a shift in person: "You never said that, that we ought to give ourselves up to spontaneity . . ." We are forced to posit either that Diego is thinking in French while speaking in Spanish or that a self-conscious narrator is translating this speech for the benefit of the viewer while still retaining access to Diego's attitudes. Moreover, in this scene the commentary utilizes a *new* voice, not the one we have heard over earlier scenes. This of course exacerbates the problem of the source. There is no way to resolve these disparities; we can only note them as ambivalent effects,

working to jar our expectations and to make the film an object of interpretation.

The most striking ambiguity surrounding the voice-over commentary occurs when we last hear it. In scene 31, Diego returns to his compatriots' apartment. Manolo is standing morosely by the window. As Diego walks in, the commentary delivers a remarkable passage.

> You didn't know that Ramon was dead, they're going to announce the news to you in a second. Dead Sunday night, a few hours after you saw him. His heart gave out, as the saying goes. And now you're going to leave in his place, because the work has to go on, no single death can interrupt it.[13]

This is most plausibly grasped as the voice of an omniscient narrator who has decided to intervene overtly. Only such an entity could confidently assert, "They're going to announce the news to you . . ." Yet some degree of ambiguity remains. Leaps into the future are compatible with Diego's habits of mind, however unlikely it is that he could anticipate Ramon's death in such detail. Moreover, the trip planning is soon interspersed with Diego's anticipation of Ramon's funeral, at which he is sometimes seen as present, sometimes treated as absent. To make Diego the source of the voice-over is tantamount to granting him second sight, but it could well be the climax of the film's use of subjective anticipation. Self-conscious narrator, or unselfconscious character? The uncertainty is never dispelled.

It is at the film's close that the play between clear, even redundant narration and the expansion of ambiguity becomes strongest. Diego meets his new driver, Salart, and they set off for Spain. In extreme long shot, the car drives off (fig. 10.22). This is the first time we have been so spatially distant from Diego. And now there is a dissolve to Juan, walking toward us as the camera tracks back (fig. 10.23). The image hangs suspended between character and narrator. Until now, we have seen Juan only through Diego's imaginings, so this shot may constitute his last anticipation. But many of the previously affirmed cues for subjectivity are absent: no cut (rather, a dissolve); no subjective camera; no

10.22
10.23   *10.24*

interrogation of Nadine with shots of Diego and Salart speeding to the border. Nadine learns that the police have set out to trap Diego and she calls her father, telling him to warn his Spanish friends. As soon as she hangs up, there is a curt shot of Diego's passport being stamped at the border. Side by side stand a highly ambiguous shot and a passage that employs unrestricted narration for the sake of suspense.

The same juxtaposition occurs in the very last scene. Manolo and Marianne are at Orly airport. She will depart for Barcelona to warn Diego. The spatial and temporal construction of the scene is unequivocal, with shot/reverse shot predominating. Then there is a cut from Manolo at Orly to Diego riding in a car (fig. 10.24), much as we have seen him in the first sequence (fig. 10.7). A very slow dissolve takes us back to Orly, where Marianne hurries down a corridor toward the camera. Diego's face is held superimposed over her, as guitar and choral music rises on the sound track (the same music used in their lovemaking scene). Diego's face finally fades out, leaving only Marianne hurrying toward us as Juan had at the closing of the earlier sequence (fig. 10.25).

The scene reveals that the narration has moved us to

contextual cues that could trigger a flashforward (Diego has departed, we hear no dialogue).

Immediately after this equivocal, foregrounded image, however, the narration supplies a highly normalized sequence. The long shot turns out to be our farewell to Diego as a bearer of information. Now the film crosscuts a cop's

10.25

A full analysis would have to study the film's political themes—its debates about commitment and its stress on individual responsibility. But all I have aimed to show is how the political material has been appropriated and transformed by formal conventions. The film has in fact blatantly announced its conjunction of political substance and narrational protocols. On his way to Ramon's, Diego reflects that Roberto gets upset when "the reality of the world resists us, because he saw what we did as being a dream of infinite progress. He hates it when reality fails to coincide with his dream." Here the political struggle is made analogous to the film's own principal narrational operation—Diego's dreams coinciding more or less with actual events—and, more generally, to the familiar dream/reality theme of the art cinema. By focusing on the individual psyche and maintaining a shifting narrational game with the spectator, *La guerre est finie* transmutes political material into a unique treatment of the conventions of a particular narrational mode.

The Art Cinema in History

As a mode of narration, the art cinema forms a paradigm. But as we saw when considering classical Hollywood narration, putting the paradigm into a historical context reveals some narrational options as more likely at certain points than at others. *La guerre est finie*'s use of time and ambiguity would be improbable in a 1950s film, or a 1984 one. The drama of a family's emigration to the city is rendered with "objective" verisimilitude in Visconti's *Rocco and His Brothers* (1960), while a comparable story is refracted through flashbacks, fantasy scenes, hallucinations, and overt authorial address in Francesco Rosi's *Three Brothers* (1980). In sum, we have now to sketch out how the weight assigned to narrational options, the shifting of "dominants," has varied across history.

Art-cinema narration has become a coherent mode partly by defining itself as a deviation from classical narrative. This may seem most obvious in the postwar decades, when the dismantling of the studio system enabled highly individual-

closure. The characters have become predictable, their actions thoroughly motivated, the alternative outcomes simplified. Just before this scene, Diego's psychological crisis has been resolved: he has broken with Nadine, has offered to take Marianne to Spain, and has renewed his political commitment by envisioning Ramon's funeral as an occasion for solidarity: "You're caught up again by the fraternity of long combats, by the stubborn joy of the action." Now Marianne has found the place in Diego's life that she has sought. Yet the last scene also generates considerable ambiguity. Two flaunted gaps in the syuzhet become permanent ones: we will never learn what became of either Juan or Diego. The dissolved image of Diego, like that of Juan earlier, can be understood as the narration's self-conscious juxtaposition (Marianne runs to Diego, or Marianne will become Diego, or Marianne will become Juan) or as her anticipation of Diego's drive (making her the sort of restricted, deeply subjective narrational vehicle that Diego has been during the bulk of the film). It would be wrong to settle on one interpretation, since the film works to create a limited but still "open" ending; in this it fulfills yet another convention of the art cinema.

10.26
10.27

ized international auteurs to emerge. Historically, however, the art cinema has its roots in an opposition to Hollywood nurtured within various national film industries of the silent era and sustained by concepts borrowed from modernism in theater and literature.

During the 1920s, when modern art was strongly influencing avant-garde cinema, the grounds for conventions of expressive realism and overt narrational address were laid. The influential *Cabinet of Dr. Caligari* (1920) took up theatrical techniques (distorted settings, *Schrei* acting) for representing subjective states, and its equivocal frame story can be seen as a very early case of applying ambiguity to an entire narrative structure, since we must wonder whether the stylized settings proceed from the "narrator" or (as the film tries to suggest at the end) from the character's mind. The film also appears to leave a permanent gap: the distorted settings remain constant to some degree when they reappear in the frame story, and the Doctor's final "I think I know how to cure him now," addressed to the camera, strikes modern viewers as unsettling.[14] It was in Germany as well that the *Kammerspielfilm* was initially developed. Films like *Scherben* (1921), *Hintertreppe* (1921), and *Sylvester* (1923), with their confinement of the action to a single locale and a brief time span, showed that cinema could represent existential boundary situations with the same concentration as that achieved in Strindberg's dramas.

In France, the Impressionist school was cultivating a set of devices for the representations of characters' inner states. Abel Gance's *La roue* (1923) sought to dramatize its characters' fleeting thoughts and moods through superimpositions and other optical effects, point-of-view shots, and rapid editing. In Epstein's *Coeur fidèle* (1923), the heroine's mental distress as she rides a whirling carnival ride is conveyed by frantic cutting. Theorists of the period advocated subjective camera movements to enhance the audience's identification with characters' feelings.[15] The French filmmakers also explored ways to convey narrational comment. Irises and vignettes could soften the image for lyricism. At the start of *Coeur fidèle*, Epstein uses mismatched close-ups—the barmaid's unmoving face alternating with her arms tiredly per-

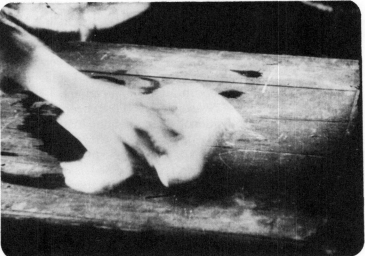

forming her chores—to imply a dissociation between her sensitive temperament and her sordid life (figs. 10 26– 10.27). The impressionists were much influenced by post-Symbolist art, so it is not surprising to find Germaine Dulac comparing a film to a Debussy piece, or to see in the complex multiple-narrator structure of Epstein's *La glace à trois faces* (1927) the influence of Proust, Gide, or Romains. At the same period, Surrealist films like *Un chien andalou*, in their savage play with the conventions of mainstream storytelling, opened up new paths for the achievement of narrational ambiguity.[16]

Not until after World War II, however, did the art cinema emerge as a fully achieved narrational alternative. Hollywood's dominance of exhibition, both at home and abroad, began to wane. In the United States, judicial decisions (the Paramount decrees) created a shortage of films. Production firms needed overseas markets; exhibitors needed to compete with television. In Europe, the end of the war reestablished international commerce and facilitated film exports. Thomas Guback has shown how, by 1954, many films were being made for international audiences.[17] It would be wrong to see this as a case of "Hollywood versus Europe." American firms underwrote much foreign production, and foreign films helped American exhibitors fill screen time. The postwar "art house," a film theater in a city or campus town, was a symptom of the new audience: college-educated, middle-class cinéphiles looking for films consonant with contemporary ideas of modernism in art and literature. Parallel audiences emerged in European intellectual centers.

In the light of these developments, Italian neorealism may be considered a transitional phenomenon. Institutionally, films like *Shoeshine* (1946), *Rome Open City* (1945), *Paisà* (1946), *Bicycle Thieves* (1948), and *Umberto D* (1952) functioned as international reportage, addressed as much to the outside world as to Italians. Along with certain French efforts (notably *Les enfants du paradis*, 1945) and Scandinavian films (e.g., *Day of Wrath*, 1943), the Neorealist films broke into worldwide markets. Formally, the films contributed to founding conventions of objective verisimilitude. Bazin pointed out the importance of chance (*Bicycle Thieves* "unfolds on the level of pure accident") and of narrational omission, which he justified as the construction of the film out of "component blocks of reality."[18] By the early 1950s, then, filmmakers had at their disposal a tradition embracing both character subjectivity and authorial intervention. And some filmmakers had begun to explore the objective realism of open-ended narratives, a dramaturgy of chance encounters, and above all the essential ambiguity of the fabula world. At this point, however, objective verisimilitude on the Italian model was the dominant narrational convention. It was chiefly the flashback films, such as *Rashomon* (1950), *Miss Julie* (1950), *Ikiru* (1952), *Waiting Women* (1952), and *Lola Montes* (1955) that chose to explore subjectivity.

If, in retrospect, art-cinema narration seems so distinctly a creature of the late 1950s and the 1960s, it is partly because the richest play among its three defining schemata took place then. During this period, the ambiguous interaction of objective and subjective realism reached its apogee. Consider just some of the output of those years:

1957: *Nights of Cabiria, Wild Strawberries, Aparajito, The Cranes Are Flying*

1958: *Eroica, Ashes and Diamonds, Brink of Life, The Face, Nazarin, Black Orpheus*

1959: *L'Avventura, La Dolce Vita, Hiroshima mon amour, The 400 Blows, The Virgin Spring, The World of Apu, Kagi*

1960: *Les bonnes femmes, Shoot the Piano Player, Zazie dans le métro, Une aussi longue absence*

1961: *Through a Glass Darkly, Cleo from 5 to 7, Jules and Jim*

1962: *The Exterminating Angel, 8½, Knife in the Water, The Loneliness of the Long-Distance Runner, Winter Light, The Soft Skin*

1963: *The Silence, Muriel, The Leopard, The Passenger, The Servant, This Sporting Life*

1964: *Red Desert, Before the Revolution, The Gospel according to St. Matthew, Identification Marks: None, King and Country*

1965: *Juliet of the Spirits, Le Bonheur, Walkover, Darling*

1966: *La guerre est finie, A Man and a Woman, The Hawks and the Sparrows, Barrier, Daisies, Night Games, Young Törless, Persona, Man Is Not a Bird*

1967: *Belle de Jour, La collectionneuse, China Is Near, Love Affair, Accident, How I Won the War*

1968: *Everything for Sale, Artists at the Top of the Big Top: Disoriented*
1969: *My Night at Maud's, The Damned, If . . ., The Girls*

In retrospect, *L'année dernière à Marienbad* (1961) must be seen as a film of great influence, pushing the art cinema toward extreme exploration of character subjectivity. (It was a double-edged influence, however, as I shall show later.) It was still possible, of course, for a film to exploit the objective verisimilitude of Neorealism, either for drama (*The Fiancés*, 1963) or Chekhovian comic pathos (*Closely Watched Trains*, 1966). Generally, though, in this period, formal process and economic demands merge: the tendency to play a cognitive game with the spectator, to modify and foreground the text's operations, matches the institution's need for the salable differentiated product. The fullest flower of the art-cinema paradigm occurred at the moment that the combination of novelty and nationalism became the marketing device it has been ever since: the French New Wave, New Polish Cinema, New Hungarian Cinema, New German Cinema, New Australian Cinema . . .

A cinema of ambiguity required machinery to interpret it. During the 1960s, film criticism took up a task it has for the most part clung to ever since. Now a critic was expected to explain what a film meant—to fill in the gaps, explicate the symbols, paraphrase the filmmaker's statement. The *Cahiers du cinéma* critics unashamedly interpreted works, sometimes in pseudophilosophical or pseudoreligious terms. In Britain, *Movie* subjected films to a detailed explication in the tradition of Oxbridge "practical criticism." Journals like *Sight and Sound, Film Culture, New York Film Bulletin, Moviegoer, Brighton Film Review, Artsept, Positif, Image et son, Jeune cinema, Film Quarterly*, and their counterparts all over Europe ran analytical and interpretive essays as well as interviews from an auteurist standpoint. Publishers began to bring out monographs on art-cinema directors and surveys of the art cinema as a whole, such as Parker Tyler's *Classics of the Foreign Film* (1962), Penelope Houston's *The Contemporary Cinema* (1963), John Russell Taylor's *Cinema Eye, Cinema Ear* (1964), and Gilles Jacobs' *Le cinéma moderne* (1964). The onus of interpretation fell even upon journalist-reviewers. Some (e.g., John Simon) took it up gladly, while others—Pauline Kael and Dwight MacDonald are notable instances—somewhat nervously mocked their duty by welcoming films that did not require hyperintellectual exegesis. The role of critical discourse in comprehending the art film was confessed by Bergman in *Not to Speak about all These Women* (1964), wherein a shot of a man running down a corridor waving fireworks is interrupted by a title warning critics not to interpret the fireworks symbolically.

So strong an intellectual presence was the 1960s art cinema that it shaped conceptions of what a good film was. Because the film was to be understood as a "personal statement" by the filmmaker, the art cinema effectively reinforced the old opposition between Hollywood (industry, collective creation, entertainment) and Europe (freedom from commerce, the creative genius, art). In 1965, Arthur Knight compared the Hollywood product with the European approach:

> Art is not manufactured by committees. Art comes from an individual who has something that he must express, and who works out what is for him the most forceful or affecting manner of expressing it. And this, specifically, is the quality that people respond to in European pictures—the reason why we hear so often that foreign films are "more artistic" than our own. There is in them the urgency of individual expression, an independence of vision, the coherence of a single-minded statement.[19]

To this personalization of creation, the director as artist, there corresponded certain narrational aspects which critics could highlight. Through an emphasis on "character," the cinema could now achieve the seriousness of contemporary literature and drama, insofar as the latter were thought to portray modern man's confrontation with a mysterious cosmos. The individualization of political action in *La guerre est finie* is only one instance of how the art film's concentration on the boundary situation reinforced widely held notions of the existential problems of the solitary character.

It is in this context that the *auteur* approach to criticism can be understood historically. The art cinema accustomed critics to looking for personal expression in films, and no one doubted that it could be found in the works of Antonioni, Bergman, et al. Auteur critics went further and applied art-cinema schemata to classical Hollywood films. The critic did not usually bother to explain how individual expression seeped into the Hollywood commodity.[20] More commonly, the critic concentrated on describing and interpreting selected films; as Jim Hillier put it in 1975: "The strategy was to talk about Hawks, Preminger, etc. as artists like Buñuel and Resnais."[21] Scenes in Ray, Minnelli, or Hitchcock could be taken as informed by subjective realism or authorial commentary. (The house in *Bigger Than Life* imprisons the protagonist; a camera angle in *The Birds* expresses the narrator's judgment.) V. F. Perkins could interpret a shot in *Carmen Jones* as if it were by Antonioni: "A metal strut at the center of the widescreen divides the image so as to isolate and confine each character within a separate visual cage. . . . [This shot] begins as a graphic expression of Joe's personality. It shows us his world as he wishes to see it—a world of order and stability."[22] Sirk's objects and decor could be justified as symbols of characters' mental states or as the narrator's ironic asides to the audience. The style of a Hawks or Walsh, on the other hand, was conceived of as avoiding authorial address or expressive realism; these were the "objective" directors. And there was always the possibility of complexity and ambiguity, as in the work of Hitchcock, Preminger, and the American Lang. Ironically, the "rereading" of Hollywood, which has been so central to film theory in recent years, has its roots in the schemata of European "artistic" filmmaking.

Nor were the lessons of art-cinema narration lost on filmmakers. The wheel turned almost full circle: classical Hollywood influenced the art film (often negatively); the art film influenced the "New Hollywood" of the late 1960s and the 1970s. Everything from freeze frames and slow motion to conventions of gapping and ambiguity has been exploited by filmmakers like Donen (*Two for the Road*, 1967), Lester

(*Petulia*, 1968), Hopper (*Easy Rider*, 1968), Coppola (*The Rain People*, 1969), Nichols (*Catch-22*, 1973), and Altman (*Images*, 1972; *Three Women*, 1977). Like its European "New Wave" forebears, the New Hollywood took up an explicit intertextuality, often alluding to the Old Hollywood in parody (*Play It Again, Sam*, 1972) or pastiche (De Palma's work). More broadly, art-cinema devices have been selectively applied to films which remain firmly grounded in classical genres—the Western (*Little Big Man*, 1970; *McCabe and Mrs. Miller*, 1971), the domestic melodrama (*The Last Picture Show*, 1971), science fiction (*2001*, 1968), the thriller (*Sisters*, 1973), and the detective film (*Klute*, 1971; *The Conversation*, 1974; *The Long Goodbye*, 1973; *Night Moves*, 1975). The force of the European art film lay in large measure in making not genre but the author's oeuvre the pertinent set of transtextual relations, but the Hollywood cinema absorbed those aspects of art-cinema narration which fitted generic functions.[23] The process was assisted by those filmmakers like Antonioni and Truffaut who occasionally made Hollywood genre pictures (e.g., *Zabriskie Point* and *Fahrenheit 451*).

I write this in 1983, when the intense subjectivity of the 1960s art film is less in evidence. Most current works emphasize an ambiguous play between objective realism and authorial address. Antonioni, Resnais, Fellini, Bergman, Truffaut, Buñuel, and others of the 1950s and 1960s have been content to repeat themselves, sometimes skillfully. The possibility of authorial differentiation can still be exploited for novelty, as the Tavianis, Bertolucci, Ruiz, Herzog, Fassbinder, and Wenders have shown.

From another angle, the art cinema brought out more radical possibilities. For the postwar decades, the key work is—again—*L'année dernière à Marienbad*. Constructed like a *nouveau roman*, the film solicits comprehension within an art-film frame of reference but goes beyond the limits of that paradigm. The syuzhet is so wrought as to make it impossible to construct a fabula. Cues are either too few or contradictory. One order of scenes is as good as any other; cause and effect are impossible to distinguish; even the spatial reference points change. This might seem the very incarnation of the dream of significant ambiguity, but it is not. Once there is no longer a fabula to interpret, once we have no stable point of departure for constructing character or causality, ambiguity becomes so pervasive as to be of no consequence. Art-cinema narration self-consciously points to its own interventions, but the aim is still to tell a discernible story in a certain way. These schemata are of no help when everything in the film may represent both subjective vision and authorial address. By teasing us to construct a fabula but always thwarting us, *Marienbad*'s narration radically separates the potential "story" from the syuzhet and stylistic patterning that are presented to us. *Marienbad* invokes conventions of subjectivity only to surpass them, and constitutes an example of yet another mode of film practice, one I shall discuss in Chapter 12 as "parametric" narration. The "realism" of art-cinema narration, as have so many "realisms" before, opened the way for a new stylization.

11. Historical-Materialist Narration
The Soviet Example

In its widest scope, leftist political cinema has no pertinence as a mode of narration. Political fiction films can appeal to classical narrational norms (e.g., the work of Costa-Gavras) or to conventions of the art-cinema mode (e.g., *Man of Marble*, 1976). But within left-wing filmmaking we can discern one clear-cut narrational tradition. Although this tradition has influenced both classical and art-cinema norms, it possesses a distinct set of narrational strategies and tactics. These originate in the Soviet "historical-materialist" cinema of the period 1925–1933. I will take twenty-two films as prime instances of this mode: *Strike* (1925), *Potemkin* (1925), *The Devil's Wheel* (1926), *Mother* (1926), *Moscow in October* (1927), *The End of St. Petersburg* (1927), *October* (1928), *Zvenigora* (1928), *Lace* (1928), *Storm over Asia* (1928), *Arsenal* (1929), *The Ghost That Never Returns* (1929), *The New Babylon* (1929), *Fragments of an Empire* (1929), *Old and New* (1929), *Goluboi Express* (1929), *Earth* (1930), *Mountains of Gold* (1931), *Ivan* (1932), *A Simple Case* (1932), *Twenty-six Commissars* (1933), and *Deserter* (1933). (Certainly *By the Law* (1926), *Bed and Sofa* (1927), *Alone* (1931), and others might be added to the list, but the above seem to me the least disputable cases.) After considering the Soviet variant, I will sketch out how the mode changed in later years.

Narration as Rhetoric

Like much Soviet art of the 1920s, the historical-materialist film has a strong rhetorical cast. It uses narrational principles and devices opposed to Hollywood norms for purposes that are frankly didactic and persuasive. Within Soviet culture generally, artists and political workers debated how aesthetic practices could be translated into utilitarian ones. One position, exemplified by the extreme left wing of Constructivism, called for an end to "art," a hopelessly bourgeois category. But on the whole, both artists and politicians wanted to maintain "the aesthetic" as a distinct (if subordinate) space. Some, like Kuleshov, saw their work as part of a long-range process of basic research; pursued in the scientific spirit, their experiments could eventually reveal the laws of socialist art. Other creators made art obedient to "social command." Here the artwork was endowed with immediate utility as "agitprop." Patriotic music, the mass spectacles celebrating the October Revolution, and much of Mayakovsky's poetry are examples. No matter how practical the end, the social-command view clung to a conception of the distinctly aesthetic. "Art," wrote Lunacharsky and Slavinsky in 1920, "is a powerful means of infecting those around us with ideas, feelings, and moods. Agitation and propaganda acquire particular acuity and effectiveness when they are clothed in the attractive and mighty forms of art."[1] Thus, the instrumental aim provided—at least for a time—an acceptable framework for experiment.

In Soviet cinema, the double demand of poetic and rhetoric shapes basic narrational strategies. There is the tendency to treat the syuzhet as both a narrative and an argument. Soviet cinema is explicitly tendentious, like the *roman à thèse*; the fabula world stands for a set of abstract propositions whose validity the film at once presupposes and reasserts. *Strike* offers a very clear instance. Not only is this the story of a single strike, it is a discourse on all the Russian strikes that occurred before 1917. The exact locale and time are unspecified; instead, the film is broken into six parts explicitly labeled as typical stages: seething in the factory; "Immediate Cause of the Strike"; "The Factory Stands Idle";

"The Strike Is Prolonged"; "Engineering a Massacre"; "Liquidation." The film concludes:

Extreme close-up: Eyes stare out at us.
Expository title: "And the strikes in Lena, Talka, Zlatovst, Yaroslavl, Tsaritsyn, and Kostroma left bleeding, unforgettable scars on the body of the proletariat."
Extreme close-up: Eyes stare out at us.
Expository title: "Proletarians, remember!"

The film's argument works by appeal to example; the narrative cause and effect demonstrate the necessity for the working class to struggle against capital. While later films did not utilize the nakedly argumentative structure of *Strike*, they did rely on the presupposition that the narrative should constitute an exemplary case for Marxist-Leninist doctrine.[2] Furthermore, *Strike*'s example is a historical one; the fabula is based on fact. Other Soviet films take up this referential impulse, creating a "realistic" motivation for the fabula events.

The most obvious result of "rhetoricizing" the fabula world is the changed conception of character. Narrative causality is construed as supraindividual, deriving from social forces described by Bolshevik doctrine. Characters thus get defined chiefly through their class position, job, social actions, and political views. Characters also lose the uniqueness sought to some degree by classical narration and to a great degree by art-cinema narration; they become prototypes of whole classes, milieux, or historical epochs. Diego's existential crisis in *La guerre est finie* would be unthinkable in Soviet historical-materialist cinema. As M. N. Pokrovsky put it, "We Marxists do not see personality as the maker of history, for to us personality is only the instrument with which history works."[3] The single character may count for little, as seen in some films' attempt to make a group of peasants or workers into a "mass hero." Such an approach to character had already been evident in Soviet revolutionary literature and theater of the 1918–1929 era.[4]

True, the Soviet cinema recognized degrees of individuation: the anonymous agents of *Moscow in October*, Eisenstein's physically vivid but generally apsychological characters like the sailor Vakulinchuk, the more detailed delineation of individual behavior in Pudovkin, and the intensely subjective characterization in Room's films. Nonetheless, psychological singularity remains quite rare. Sometimes, as in *October*, the more psychologically motivated the character (e.g., Kerensky, with his Napoleonic lust for power), the surer the character is to be denigrated as a bourgeois.

Character types find their roles within specific generic motivations. There is the genre of "studies of revolution," either in historical or contemporary settings. Here the film tells a story of successful struggles (*Potemkin, October, The End of St. Petersburg, Moscow in October, Zvenigora*) or currently emergent ones (*Storm over Asia, Mountains of Gold, The Ghost That Never Returns, Goluboi Express, Twenty-six Commissars*). The revolution film may also pay tribute to heroic failures (*Strike, Mother, Arsenal, The New Babylon*). A second genre portrays contemporary problems in Soviet life, usually involving remnants of capitalist or feudal behavior (*Fragments of an Empire, Lace, The Devil's Wheel*). There is also a genre that matches the literary formula of the "production" novel: a dam must be built (*Ivan*), or the countryside must be collectivized (*Old and New, Earth*). Some films combine genres: *A Simple Case* (historical revolution and problems of contemporary life) or *Deserter* (emergent revolution plus production goals). All these genres evidently give the film an opportunity to create a fabula that will make each character emblematic of forces within a politically defined situation.

One task of tendentious narrative art is to create conflicts that both prove the thesis and furnish narrative interest. In these films, the viewer is likely to know, or quickly guess, the underlying argument to be presented and the referential basis of the fabula world. (There can be no doubt that the October Revolution will succeed.) Most of our interest thus falls upon the question of how history takes the course it does.

In a general sense, the Soviet historical-materialist film answers this by adhering to the two schematic patterns which Susan R. Suleiman identifies in the *roman à thèse*. There is what she calls the "structure of confrontation," in which a psychologically unchanging hero represents a group in his struggle against adversaries.[5] Such is Marfa in *Old and New*, or the Chinese coolie in *Goluboi Express*. This structure provides a fairly traditional curve of dramatic conflict. There is also the "structure of apprenticeship" in which the typical individual moves from ignorance to knowledge and from passivity to action.[6] The specific shape which this dramatic development takes in Soviet literature of the period has been summarized by Katerina Clark. She points out that the Socialist Realist narrative often centers on a character who moves from a spontaneous, instinctive form of activity to a disciplined, correct awareness of political ends and means.[7] *Mother*, as both novel and film, is the canonic instance. The mother acts spontaneously but incorrectly, and her positive qualities are offset by the danger she poses to the revolution. By accepting the tutelage of her son and the Party, she is able to become a martyr to conscious revolutionary activity. The result of this pattern is that potentially affirmative characters are shown initially in a rather bad light: they may be naive (Mother, the sailor in *The Devil's Wheel*, Filiminov in *Fragments of an Empire*) or worse— cowardly (Renn in *Deserter*), lascivious (Pavel in *A Simple Case*), rowdy (the delinquents in *Lace*), treacherous (the peasant in *The End of St. Petersburg*) or greedy (the peasant in *Mountains of Gold*). The cause-and-effect chain then works to convert the character(s) to disciplined socialist activity. The drama—and the spectator's hypotheses—come to be based on how and when the apprentice's conversion will take place.

To some extent, the didactic aim of the Soviet cinema created a storehouse of *topoi*, or argumentative commonplaces, which the filmmaker could use to structure the syuzhet. But these were not so narrow that they stifled experimentation. The narrative-plus-argument pattern was open to poetic exploitation in many ways. The use of character prototypes—the sturdy worker, the activist woman, the bureaucrat, the bourgeois "man out of time"—allowed stylistic embroidering. "The figure of a cinematic character," declared Pudovkin, "is the sum of all the shots in which he appears."[8] It was up to the director not to give the character individuality but to use film form to make the type vivid.

Pudovkin could draw on the techniques of poster art and contemporary fiction, Eisenstein on theater and caricature, Dovzhenko upon cartoon art and Ukrainian folklore. Commonplace rhetorical points could be sharpened by stylistic devices. The opening sequence of *Arsenal* powerfully demonstrates how, given the topos "The czar's war destroys the Russian peasantry," a film's shot-to-shot relations could still be made highly unpredictable. Similarly, in *Old and New*, Marfa's decision to organize a collective is presented so that her misery in the fields ("Enough!") is alternated with her oratory before her friends; impossible to say where one scene leaves off and the other begins. Rhetorical demands provided generic and realistic motivation for an experimentation with the medium akin to that in Soviet avant-garde art generally. Thus *Old and New*'s localized breakdown of classical order and duration is motivated by the whole film's juxtaposition of past and present. In Russian Formalist terms, the rhetorical aim enabled the films to "defamiliarize" classical norms of space and time.

Once the film uses poetic procedures for rhetorical ends, the narrational process becomes quite overt. The narration comes forward as a didactic guide to proper construction of the fabula.

There is an especially clear index of this. In the classical Hollywood cinema of the silent era, the narration almost invariably employed many more dialogue titles than expository ones—usually four to twelve times as many. In some films of the late 1920s, there are no expository titles at all. The reason is obvious: an expository title creates a self-conscious narration that is only occasionally desirable in the classical film. But the Soviet films I am considering here have a much higher proportion of expository titles. In most of these films, dialogue titles outweigh expository ones by a ratio of only four to one, and some of the films actually contain more expository than dialogue titles. In later years, the Soviets' use of nondiegetic or "contrapuntal" sound montage had a comparably overt effect.

Overt narration is also signaled through nonlinguistic means. Some cinematographic techniques—the dynamic camera angle that creates many diagonals; the abnormally high or low horizon line; slow and fast motion; the extreme close-up that picks out a detail; the 28-mm lens that distorts space; vignetting and soft focus—were quickly identified with the Soviet cinema, but despite their often clichéd employment, we must see them as striving to suggest a narrational presence behind the framing or filming of an event. It is here that Pudovkin's concept of an "ideal observer" has some relevance. Critics were quick to spot and personify this camera eye; one wrote of *Potemkin*: "It is like some grotesque record of a gargantuan news photographer with a genius for timing and composition."[9]

"Realistic" though such films as *Potemkin* and *The End of St. Petersburg* were often felt to be, the staging of the action tends to create highly self-conscious narration. The set may present a perspectively inconsistent space, as in the warden's office in *The Ghost That Never Returns* or in the cafe in *The New Babylon*. Lighting may also be manipulated, as when in *Storm over Asia* the cut-in close-ups of the fox fur are lit in ways completely unfaithful to the overall illumination of the Mongol home. Figures are often placed against neutral background, either realistically motivated ones (a peasant or worker fiercely silhouetted against a cloudless sky) or more stylized ones, as in the initial attack on the woman on the Odessa Steps (fig. 11.1) or the abstract cut-ins from *The End of St. Petersburg* which we examined earlier (fig. 7.50–7.55). The figures will often be placed in unnaturally static poses as well. While Dovzhenko made the most systematic use of this, we find the device in other films as well: in *The Ghost that Never Returns*, characters freeze in place during an attempted suicide; in *Twenty-six Commissars*, a crowd listens to a speech while standing in abnormally fixed postures. In contrast, the figure behavior may be what was called at the time "grotesque" or "eccentric"—stylized figure movement that makes the scene difficult to construe as a real event. *Strike*'s dwarfs and clownish bums are usually cited here, but we could add the petty thieves in *The Devil's Wheel*, Kerensky and company in *October*, the priest in *Earth*, and the prison warden in *The Ghost That Never Returns*.

What gives the narrational presence away completely is

11.1. Potemkin

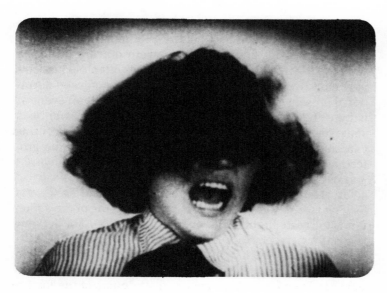

the propensity for frontality of body, face, and eye in these films. We have seen how the classical film favors a modified frontality of figure placement; our sight lines are marked out, but the characters seldom face or look directly toward us. The Soviet cinema tends to stage the action much more frontally. Furthermore, the characters frequently look out at the camera. Sometimes this is motivated as another character's point of view, but not nearly as often as it would be in Hollywood. And at some point, frontality becomes an unabashedly direct address to the camera. Again and again characters turn "to us" without the slightest realistic motivation. The end of *Strike*, with its staring eyes, is probably not the best example, since such concluding confrontations form a minor convention of classical epilogues too.[10] But when, in the middle of a scene, a soldier gazes out and asks us, "What am I fighting for?" (*End of St. Petersburg*), or when a character confides in us (*Zvenigora*), or mugs and winks at us (*Lace*), or asks whether it is all right to kill the enemy (*Arsenal*), or turns to us for help during a fistfight (*Twenty-six Commissars*), we must acknowledge that narration is not simply relaying some autonomously existent

profilmic event. Now the narration overtly *includes* the profilmic event, has already constituted it for the sake of specific effects. Ideas of montage within the shot, montage "before filming," and montage "within the actor's performance," so current in the late 1920s, testify to filmmakers' notion that narration should include self-conscious manipulation of the profilmic event, the material that normally pretends to go unmanipulated. This narration is not only omniscient; it announces itself as omnipotent.

What brings together film techniques like intertitles, cinematography, and mise-en-scène is the key concept of Soviet film theory and practice: editing, usually called montage. As conceived in Soviet artistic practice during the 1920s, montage in any art implies the presence of a creative subject actively choosing how effects are to be produced. Summarizing the views of many practitioners, Félicie Pastorello writes aptly: "Montage is an act (and not a look), an act of interpreting reality. Like the engineer and the scholar, the artist constructs his object, he does not reproduce reality."[11] In objecting that Soviet montage "did not give us the event; it alluded to it," Bazin was putting his finger on exactly this refusal to treat film technique as a neutral transmitter.[12] The didactic and poetic aspects of Soviet cinema meet in a technique which insists, both quantitatively and qualitatively, upon the constant and overt presence of narration.

It comes as no news that Soviet montage films rely upon editing, but some comparative figures may spruce up the obvious. The Soviet films I am considering contain between 600 and 2,000 shots, whereas their Hollywood counterparts of the years 1917–1928 typically contain between 500 and 1,000. (I am counting intertitles as shots.) Hollywood canonized the average shot length as five to six seconds, yielding a common figure of 500–800 shots per hour. The Soviet films, however, average two to four seconds per shot and contain between 900 and 1,500 shots per hour. This means that only the very fastest cut Hollywood films of the teens (such as *Wild and Woolly*) approach the Soviet standard, while the fastest-cut Hollywood films of the 1920s fall at the slower end of the Soviet scale. And nowhere in Hollywood filmmaking of any period can one find editing as quickly paced as in the most rapid montage films: an average shot length of under two seconds in *Potemkin, Deserter, Goluboi Express,* and *A Simple Case.*

The reliance on cutting has qualitative consequences. In the Hollywood film, especially after the coming of sound, a few sequences will be fairly heavily edited while others will contain longer takes. By rejecting such a "crossbred" decoupage, the Soviet films provide a ubiquitous and constant level of rhetorical intervention. This cinema goes beyond those narrational asides which we found in the art cinema; these films do not offer a reality (objective, subjective) inflected by occasional interpolated "commentary"; these films are signed and addressed through and through, the diegetic world built from the ground up according to rhetorical demands.

Thus there are always more cuts than needed for lucid cueing of fabula construction. Even the simplest gesture may be broken into several shots. Crosscutting endlessly juxtaposes actions in different locales. By virtue of what the Soviets called "concentration" cuts, a simple transition from long shot to medium shot gets splintered into several shots. Jump cuts break up a single camera position. Montage also operates on intertitles: in *October,* the narration chops speeches into brief phrases. The relentless presence of montage in these films aims to keep the spectator from construing any action as simply an unmediated piece of the fabula world. Whereas Bazin worried that cutting changed the profilmic event from something real into something imaginary, the Soviet filmmakers believed that *not* cutting would change the syuzhet from a rhetorical construct into something (falsely) descriptive.

Montage makes the narration self-conscious in yet another way: through rhetorical tropes. The Soviet films furnish an anthology of both "tropes of thought" and "tropes of speech." The former are buried or ellided formal arguments, such as the schematic argument-from-example that undergirds the Soviet film and the tendency of the narration to argue by analogy (as when crosscutting links two social agents and makes us infer a shared motive or political view: bourgeoisie/police, proletarian/peasant). Tropes of speech,

or figures of adornment, can be mimicked by editing too. These films teem with rhetorical questions, metaphors or similes (the bull and the strikers in *Strike*), synecdoches (a general's medals substituting for the general in *The End of St. Petersburg*), personifications (the squirming concertina in *Arsenal*), understatements, hyperbole, antitheses, and many other classical figures. *October* uses paranomasia, or punning, when the narration presents Kerensky's political rise as a climb up an apparently endless flight of stairs; the play is based on the Russian word *lestnitsa* (stairs), as used in the phrase *ierarkhicheskaia lestnitsa,* or "table of military ranks." In the same film, the intercutting of Kerensky with a Napoleon statue cites the simile Lenin used in a 1917 *Pravda* article, "In Search of a Napoleon," while the montage of statues and artillery probably is meant to revive Lenin's synecdoche "With icons against cannons."[13] The prominence of stylistic organization in these films cannot be read as sheer artistic motivation; the didactic ends often make film style operate as compositionally justified ornamentation.

All these techniques invest the narration with a high and consistent degree of overtness in all the respects we have been considering since Chapter 4.

Degree and depth of knowledge. The narration of these Soviet films is omniscient. The conventional knowledgeability afforded by crosscutting is particularly visible in these works because the crosscutting is not only that of a last-minute rescue: crosscutting is constantly drawing marked comparisons. Firing cannons are likened to popping champagne corks (*Goluboi Express*). While a boy is borne to his grave, his lover is at home, in an ecstasy of despair (*Earth*). More unusually, the syuzhet will "flash back" without the motivation of character memory, as when at the close of *Old and New* the narration gives us glimpses of earlier scenes of Marfa's struggle. The narration may also overtly anticipate what will happen later in the film. The most striking example comes from the opening of *Storm over Asia,* where shots of landscapes are interrupted by near-subliminal flashes of the saber that the protagonist will wield in the *last* scene. The narration likewise has no need to justify spatial manipulations by character knowledge: we can cut to any locale. In *Potemkin*, as the marines prepare to fire, the narration cuts away to the bugle, the imperial crest, and other objects which yield ironic juxtapositions. In *The End of St. Petersburg*, the narrator can situate the political activity in relation to lyrical landscapes. In *The Ghost That Never Returns*, when the police agent fires his pistol, the narration prolongs suspense by holding on such details as drifts of sand and a hat rolling in the wind. In *Lace*, a quarrel is interrupted by cutaway shots of a poster on the wall.

Communicativeness. The narration's authority rests in part on its refusal to withhold what the mode defines as crucial fabula information. Such information includes the story's historical context, political arguments, and character background. The film's fabula action consists either of the struggle of a protagonist to achieve a goal or of the growth of a spontaneous protagonist to socialist discipline and awareness. It is this linearity that the narration respects. The syuzhet does not equivocate about characters' motives or behavior. The exposition is concentrated and preliminary, furnishing relevant and valid information about the characters' pasts; there will never be what Sternberg calls "anticipatory caution," let alone a "rise and fall of first impressions." The narration, in fact, takes the opportunity to be "overcommunicative" by using many devices that ensure redundancy: conformity of character to type, of type to situation, or of situation to historical-political presuppositions. In *Ivan*, a street loudspeaker will often reiterate the narrational information already supplied by other means. The celebrated overlapping editing of Soviet practice displays not only the narration's authority (ability to restage the profilmic event, to "remount" it in editing) but also the narration's urge to insist on certain gestures. Scenes like that of the woman running through the doors in *Ivan* and the cream separator test in *Old and New* resemble traditional oratorical amplifications of set topics (grief, success).

Self-consciousness. We have already seen the extent to which camera position and lens length, frontality of figures, static poses, to-camera address, and the constant use of montage all create the sense of a self-conscious address to the audience. The expository title can focus this effect. The narration can interject maxims (a quotation from Lenin in *Potemkin*), slogans ("All power to the Soviets!" in *October*), and rebuttals (in *Goluboi Express*, a reactionary cries, "Stop the train!" and an expository title shoots back: "But can you stop a revolution?"). The narration will also usurp the characters' own voices. In many Soviet films, information that could easily be given in dialogue titles will be supplied by expository titles, as in the beginning of *The End of St. Petersburg*, when the peasant family must send some members to work in the city. In one episode of *Twenty-six Commissars*, the narration becomes a witness's testimony to the action. And some titles could plausibly come from the fabula world but, because they are not signaled as quotations, instead suggest that the words are routed through the narration. *Moscow in October* intercalates an orator and expository titles, while in *Arsenal*, we cannot locate a speaker for such lines as "Where is father?" Nothing could be stronger evidence for this tendency than the insistence on retaining exhortatory expository titles after the arrival of lip-synchronized sound. In the remarkable *Mountains of Gold*, expository titles repeat what we have already heard a character say, and they even argue with a speaking character! Unlike their contemporaries in Europe, who envisioned the titleless film as the goal of a "pure" experimental cinema, the Soviet filmmakers saw the linguistic resources of the expository title as an instrument for rhetorical narration.

Attitudinal properties. The very constitution of genres and the didacticism of the narration in this mode make the narration openly and unequivocally judgmental, often satirically and ironically so. Judgments can be carried by intertitles, especially in the exposition: how many Soviet films begin by rendering an oppressive state of affairs in the images and then interjecting ironic titles ("All is calm . . ." etc.)? The narration throws its voice to cheer for the opposition or quotes characters to mocking effect (the figure known to classical rhetoric as "transplacement"). In *Goluboi Express*, decadent bourgeois proclaim, "Ah, Europe, culture, civilization"; later the narration intercuts the same phrases with statues, policemen, and troops. In *October*, the

11.2. Mountains of Gold

Bolsheviks arrested during the July Days are called traitors and spies; later, when Kerensky releases them to defend Petrograd, the narration sarcastically recalls the epithets. The ne plus ultra of this process may be seen in the intercutting of battlefield and stock exchange in *The End of St. Petersburg,* in which the same phrases ("Forward!" "The deal is over!" "Both parties are satisfied!") apply with brutal irony to both milieux. Once this "tone of voice" has been established, the images can reinforce it by typage (grotesque costumes and demeanor of the bourgeois types, valorization of protagonists), camera work (the low angle as connoting power or solitude), lens length (the wide-angle lens for distortion and caricature; see fig. 11.2), and music (e.g., comic music to parody the opposition). The specific rhetorical tropes already mentioned will often, of course, work to judgmental effect as well.

Predictable Fabula, Unpredictable Narration

By treating the syuzhet as an argument by example, and by gathering a powerful rhetorical thrust, the Soviet historical-materialist cinema created a distinct organization of narration, with effects on cinematic style already discussed. Another result was an idiosyncratic approach to the spectator, one that is neither as "totalitarian" as liberal-humanist critics often assume nor as radical as some recent theorists of textuality have claimed. The films' mixture of didactic and poetic structures calls for viewing procedures which deviate from classical norms yet remain unified by protocols specific to this mode.

Broadly speaking, the viewer brings to these films a few highly probable schemata. Already-known stories, drawn from history, myth, and contemporary life, furnish a fairly limited range of options for the overall cause-effect chain. Knowledge of the different genres, especially when the film treats a historical subject, further limits what can plausibly happen. The viewer also possesses a sense of how the mode creates character and signals salient conflicts. And the ending is likely to be known, at least in general outline. In syuzhet terms, the narration further strives to eliminate any ambiguity at the level of causality (motives, goals, preconditions) or at the level of the rhetorical point made. Most narrational difficulties presented by these films cannot be explained under the rubrics of realism or subjectivity; the problems are clearly marked as proceeding from the self-conscious narration. On the whole there is little room for the gamelike equivocations and the interpretive subtlety valorized by art-cinema norms.

These films therefore sacrifice many resources of other narrational modes. There is relatively little curiosity about how events came to be as they are; macrosocial historical causes are often taken for granted. Suspense is limited to questions of how the inevitable will occur or, in the case of characters who are not "public" personages, whether the character will survive, move to correct consciousness, and so forth. The syuzhet may assume that because the historical event or rhetorical point is already known, not all of the links need to be shown. In *Deserter,* the process of converting the German worker Renn from a traitor to a good proletarian is completely skipped over; the narration simply assumes that a stay in the Soviet Union suffices to bring him around. The end of *Potemkin* neglects to mention that the rebelling sailors were eventually captured, but the viewer is supposed to understand that whatever the outcome of this episode, the entire 1905 revolution was a harbinger of 1917. Moreover, if there are political disputes within Soviet communism about the case considered, it is often wiser for the filmmaker to omit explanation than to risk being criticized. Vance Kepley has shown that many elliptical moments in Dovzhenko's films result from skirting sensitive issues.[14] We shall later see how *The New Babylon* tries to avoid disputes about why the Paris Commune failed. Again, the omnipotent narration works as a reliable guide: any "permanent" breaks in the causal chain signal not a lack of communicativeness but a tacit appeal to the audience's referential schemata.

The historical-materialist film compensates for its limited narrative schemata by unusually innovative spatial and temporal construction. If the story outline is often predictable, stylistic processes often are not. At the barest perceptual level, narration will jolt the spectator. Consider the opening of *Twenty-six Commissars*:

1. Long shot: Oil field
2. Title: "Baku"
3. Explosion
4. Title: "1918"
5. Explosion
6. Explosion

This is our introduction to the revolutionary brigade. *Strike* begins with abstract shots of the factory, including silhouettes and an upside-down, reverse-motion reflection of the factory in a puddle. The narration of *Deserter* establishes the river docks in a lyrical tranquillity before startling us with shots of chains dropped from ships—shots that intersperse black frames with bursts of imagery and thus create an almost annoying flicker. The conventionality of the large-scale narrative articulations promotes a moment-by-moment "microattention" to the unfolding syuzhet. Like the orator embroidering a commonplace, the narration takes for granted that we understand that part of World War I was fought around Baku, that *Strike* will be about a workers' walkout, that *Deserter* is set in a dockyard. The task is to

make these givens vivid, or as the Soviet directors were fond of saying, *perceptible*.

What renders these stylistic processes more unpredictable than the procedures of classical narration? Most obviously, the Soviet films I am considering define themselves against many spatial and temporal norms of classical Hollywood narrative. All the procedures of titling, cinematography, editing, and mise-en-scène I have already mentioned constitute an alternative stylistic paradigm. Eyelines will not necessarily cut neatly together; characters will not necessarily ignore the audience; framing will not necessarily be symmetrical or centered. Similarly, principles of spatial and temporal continuity, of tight linkage of cause and effect, and so forth do not hold in this mode. As in the art cinema, style becomes more prominent here because of its deviation from the classical norm.

To the extent, however, that the Soviet devices function within a paradigm, the viewer can apply schemata based on *this* extrinsic norm to make sense of the films. But this process is more difficult than in the classical mode because of the great emphasis the Soviets placed upon deviating from extrinsic norms. Again as in the art cinema, variations often proceed from authorial differences: Dovzhenko is more likely to use slow motion than Eisenstein is, Room is more apt to match shots "classically" than are his contemporaries. Still, nothing in *Strike* prepares us for the alternating of two successive scenes in *Old and New*; nothing in *Mother* anticipates the montage of black frames in *Deserter*. It is not just that the filmmakers developed; the search for ever more "perceptible" effects pushed them to try new devices in every film. In general, narration became more elliptical, images became briefer, gaps became greater, fabula events underwent more expansion and amplification. Virtually any device—soft focus, slow or fast motion, upside-down camera positions, single-source lighting, handheld camera movement—could create a film's distinctive intrinsic norm. It would be up to the viewer to make sense of the unpredictable procedure by slotting it into accustomed syuzhet functions and patterns. We have already seen this at work in our examples of spatial discontinuity in *Earth* and *The End of St.*

11.3. Earth

Petersburg in Chapter 7. Because each film strives to attain great stylistic prominence—the intrinsic norms marking significant differences within the "Soviet style" itself—the viewer must use the extrinsically normalized principles as guidelines. The task, as in art-cinema narration, is to grasp each film's unique reworking of the paradigm. This is done by calling on procedural schemata that urge: when in doubt, construct a fabula event as perceptually forceful and politically significant.

Faced with the shocks of this jarring style, the spectator can, at least up to a point, deal with it cognitively. The important strategies are those of "filling in" and "linking and distinguishing." Such activities form a part of the viewer's task in any narrational mode, but, with Soviet montage cinema, they play a major role at the level of temporal and spatial construction.

The very idea of montage demands that we fill in gaps. As Shklovsky put it in describing intellectual montage, the editing works "through its non-coincident components—its aureoles."[15] Every shot change offers the filmmaker a chance to create a break in time and space. Classical editing usually avoids perceptible gaps at this level; at most they are suppressed or temporary. Soviet montage flaunts its spatiotemporal gaps and will not always plug them. The Soviet tendency to minimize or omit establishing shots asks the spectator to fill in the overall milieu. For similar reasons, the Soviet directors never canonized the over-the-shoulder reverse shot; instead of this extra cue that the classical style provides we are often presented with no clear information about characters' distances or angles of interaction. Thus when the cutting pattern violates the 180-degree rule of Hollywood practice, the viewer must construct a set of hypotheses about character position. Entire sequences (e.g., Pavel's trial in *Mother*) or whole films (*Earth*) can make sense on the basis of comparatively few cues for characters' placement.

From the elimination of the establishing shot the Soviet directors drew two conclusions, one quite radical. First, you need not find or create an entire profilmic event: partial views can create a locale that need never have existed in front of the lens. The spectator will infer a unified space based on assumptions about real spaces and about the sort of space that films usually present. The more radical discovery was that viewers could be asked to unify spaces in physically impossible ways. Supplied with strong spatial cues, such as character eyelines or earlines, the spectator will infer an "abstract" space that could not exist empirically. In *Twenty-six Commissars*, the Bolshevik prisoners are massacred in the desert. A wounded man staggers to the top of a hill and shouts: "Be calm, comrades!" There is a cut to the oil fields of Baku, many miles away. Suddenly workers in the fields freeze in place, as if hearing his cry. There follows a series of shots in which a striker at Baku "watches" the execution of the commissars. And after the massacre, the workers stand in silent homage before a spectacle they could not possibly see or hear. Comparably "abstract" spaces can be found in many Soviet films; as we shall see, *The New Babylon* relies on them to a considerable degree.

The spectator must fill in temporal gaps too. Here is a passage from *Earth*:

1. Medium shot: In his house the father bellows (fig. 11.3).

2. "Ivan!"
3. Long shot: Against sky, he calls, rightward (fig. 11.4).
4. "Stephen!"
5. Medium shot: He calls, rightward (fig. 11.5).
6. "Grigori!"
7. Medium close-up: He calls, leftward (fig. 11.6).
8. "Have—"
9. "you killed—"
10. "my—"
11. "Vassily?"
12. Long shot, as (3): The father looks straight out (fig. 11.7).
13. Extreme long shot: Empty landscape (fig. 11.8).
14. Medium shot: Over father's shoulders, two men together (fig. 11.9). Track back with father as he strides to the camera, revealing a third man in the background (fig. 11.10).
15. Medium shot: The father walks up to Khoma (fig. 11.11).

The narration has created a spatial gap—the abrupt transition from the house to the outdoors in shots 1–3—and some temporal ones. If the father shouted "Ivan!" in the house, we must assume that he consumed time in getting out to the hillside. Yet the rhythmic alternation of title and image suggests that perhaps "Ivan!" was shouted outside too. This yields an ambiguity about the frequency of the fabula event. Later, after the father has hollered and apparently gotten no response (shots 12–13), another cut takes us immediately to a group of three men (shot 14)—presumably those he summoned by name. Without warning, the cut has skipped over the fabula duration required for the group to assemble. But when the father turns and walks away, shot 15 reveals that a fourth man is present—Khoma, the youth who did kill Vassily. His arrival has been withheld for the sake of surprise. Dovzhenko's style is unusually oblique, but his reliance on ellipses is only an extension of a general Soviet tendency to ask the spectator to see any cut as embodying a possible break in fabula time.

Because these Soviet films suggest that we fill in missing pieces of space and time, the spectator must tolerate a degree

11.12. Potemkin
11.13. Potemkin

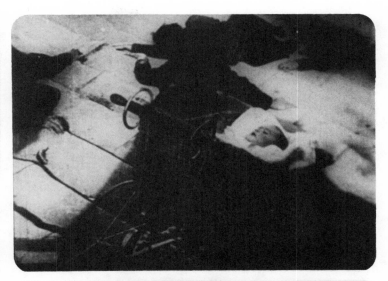

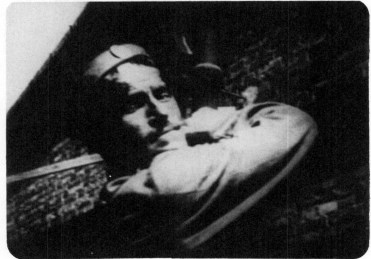

of cognitive strain. At the start of a sequence, we may be uncertain about exactly what is happening; the narration has plunged us abruptly into a stream of details. We must patiently trust that the narration will eventually clarify or justify what seems unsettled. Early in *Old and New* we see men sawing timbers while families look on; only gradually do we grasp (thanks chiefly to an intertitle) that brothers are dividing their property by sawing the family house in two. In *Arsenal*, the fight for possession of the locomotive is interrupted by a series of very close shots of a woman turning to the camera and leaping up; cut back to the locomotive; only after this do we get a shot that establishes the woman at the telegraph key in a railroad office. It is as if the narration, rushing to give us the emotional core of the situation, later takes the opportunity to flesh out time, place, and causality. In Chapter 7, we have already seen how sequences in *Earth* and *End of St. Petersburg* create "open" spatial relations that only eventually get closed: father and son quarreling (back to back or not?), troops firing (on the Bolsheviks or on the general?). In sum, the stability of broad causal schemata in these films allows the narration to create a process of hypothesis testing in a film's moment-by-moment unfolding. Film style works to retard the likeliest meaning, and the spectator adopts a wait-and-see strategy.

Occasionally we wait and never see. Some spatiotemporal gaps we can never close at any denotative level. At the end of the Odessa Steps sequence in *Potemkin*, the baby carriage jitters down the steps, intercut with shots of the staring woman with the pince-nez. Then:

1. Medium shot: The carriage begins to flip over (fig. 11.12).
2. Medium shot: A swordsman starts to swing his saber (fig. 11.13).
3. Close-up: He slashes downward (fig. 11.14).
4. Close-up jump cut: He slashes (fig. 11.15).
5. Close-up jump cut: He draws back and starts to slash again, shouting (fig. 11.16).
6. Close-up: Blood runs from a woman's eye, and her pince-nez is shattered (fig. 11.17).

We can, I think, construct the fabula action in several ways. (A) The soldier has slashed at the woman with the pince-nez. Reasons: shots 2–6 can be construed as a group, making shot 6 a reaction shot; the frontality of the soldier's attack (perhaps a subjective point of view) is congruent with that of the woman's orientation. (B) The soldier has slashed

11.14. Potemkin   *11.16.* Potemkin
11.15. Potemkin   *11.17.* Potemkin

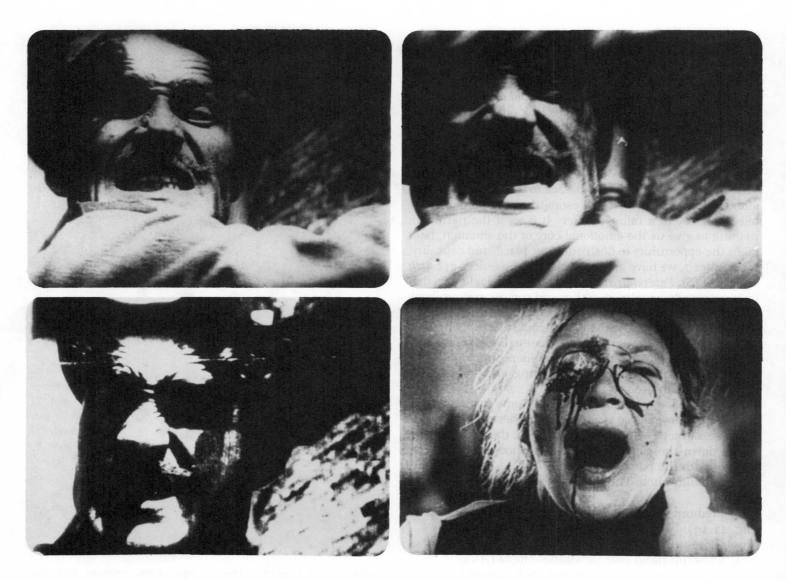

at the baby in the carriage. Reasons: shots 1–5 hang together; the cossack is observed from a low angle, befitting his assault on the carriage; the woman has earlier been seen some way up the steps; the woman's wound is not plausible as coming from a saber. (C) The baby carriage overturning, the cossack slashing, and the wounding of the woman are unconnected events, crosscut. Reason: all the inadequate and incompatible cues present in (A) and (B). (D) The cossack slashes at both the carriage and the woman: an "impossible" profilmic event. Rather than decide on a single

11.18. Potemkin

11.19. Potemkin

construction, we should recognize that exactly this mixing of cues, this shaking of scenic components loose from a univocal fabula world, enables the narration to create an "open" space from which can be selected maximally forceful images of brutality—with five of the six addressed directly to the viewer. The spatial gaps become permanent ones, creating vivid rhetorical effects.

The act of filling in must then include our willingness to accept, in the name of perceptibility, very great violations of conventional or internally consistent space and time. What else can explain the spectator's assimilation of shots in which the film strip is flipped side-to-side or upside down? The fabula event may be presented not as ambiguous but as contradictory: an officer sits in inconsistent positions from shot to shot (*Storm over Asia*); a coolie is slapped once, but in a different way from shot to shot (*Goluboi Express*); a worker assaults his boss in two locales at once (*The End of St. Petersburg*); a priest raps his cross in one palm, then—or rather also—in the other (*Potemkin*; see figs. 11.18–11.19). The Soviet directors assumed that if syuzhet material cannot be unified at the denotative level, the spectator will look for ways to unify it connotatively. Thus ideologically defined

argumentative schemata and the explicit and constant presence of a narrator allow the viewer to place incompatible presentations within a larger affective dynamic.

Besides filling in gaps, the spectator must link and distinguish elements. One consequence of Soviet film's stress upon "perceptibility" is that we are expected to fine tune our sensitivity to the representation of space and time. Similarities and dissimilarities among images weigh more in this mode than in the classical narrative. Soviet directors are fond of calling on short-term memory in order to permute images in palpable ways, as Dovzhenko does in the *Earth* segment (figs. 11.3–11.11) or as Boris Barnet does in *Moscow in October* by varying the same shot (figs. 11.20–11.22). In *Potemkin*, the narration frequently cuts from one character to another as each executes a similar gesture (making a fist, running a machine); denotatively we must pick different individuals out of a smooth passage of movement (even while connotatively we must see them as linked in the performance of similar actions). By using editing to achieve temporal dilation, these films rely on the viewer's ability to construct one movement out of several overlapping representations onscreen. And some films, in particular Pudov-

11.20. Moscow in October
11.21. Moscow in October

11.22. Moscow in October

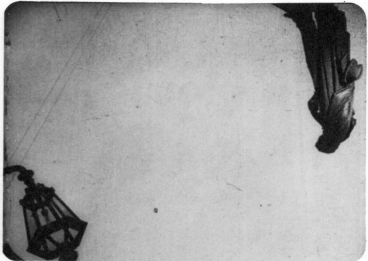

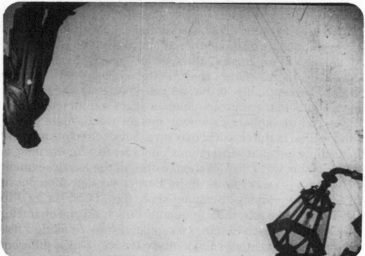

kin's, utilize devices which lie on the very threshold of perceptual discrimination, such as sporadic black frames, single-frame montage, and barely discernible jump cuts.

The spectator's ability to draw likenesses and contrasts can work closely with the rhetorical aims of the mode. *Storm*

over Asia features a celebrated sequence in which the British commander and his wife prepare to visit the Buddhist temple. The narration crosscuts the couple's preparation—shaving, washing, dressing—with functionaries scurrying around cleaning the temple. More than temporal simultaneity is evoked here. The narration draws analogies between objects in each line of action: the temple feather duster is likened to the wife's powder puff, the priest's collar to her necklace. Expository titles remark ironically, "There are ceremonies / and rites / among all races." Since the immediate causal function of the scene is minimal, the fact that it is given extensive treatment invites the viewer to dwell on its rhetorical implications. The spectator must take the visual similarities between the British and the Buddhists as cues to a conceptual likeness; the intertitles reinforce the link. The rhetorical effect is double: to satirize fastidious upper-class hygiene, as solemn and self-righteous as a religious ritual; and to mock the church as a thing of this world, as vain as the decadent imperialists. Like many crosscutting episodes in Soviet film, this sequence asks the viewer to liken "unlike" things. Conceptual parallelism replaces causal logic as the basis of the syuzhet. Ultimately, however, these argumentative connotations "feed back" into the causal nexus, since the similarity between imperial and Buddhist authorities anticipates the complicity of rulers to be exhibited during the colonialists' visit to the temple.

The locus classicus of this abstract tendency is the notorious "intellectual montage" of Soviet cinema, of which the *Storm over Asia* sequence could count as a fair example. But note that the narration can achieve high-level "intellectual"—that is, rhetorical—judgments in two ways. The possibility that entranced Eisenstein was what Metz has called the nondiegetic insert—one or more images that possess no denotative reality in the fabula world. The slaughter of the bull intercut with the massacre of the workers (*Strike*) is a pure case, as are the Kerensky/peacock comparisons and the "God and Country" sequence in *October*. More common Soviet practice, however, was the rhetorical combination of images taken from the diegetic world. The sequence from *Storm over Asia* is an instance: both the commander's household and the temple exist on the same level of fabula "reality." In fact, this second possibility proves to be the richer one, since it allows the narration to present images initially designed to denote fabula information and then to recall them for more connotative purposes. Eisenstein had a penchant for repeating identical shots in very different situations across the film. In *October*, images hailing the February revolution—for instance, troops with upraised rifles—are repeated during the October Revolution. After the *Potemkin*'s crew has pitched Smirnov overboard, the narration inserts an image of the maggoty meat that had precipitated the mutiny. Such a shot becomes what one theorist of the time calls a "refrain."[16] At the start of *Arsenal*, a worker is shown in a very disjointed series of images; much later in the film, as urgings to strike sweep through the arsenal, the same worker suddenly looks up. The use of the refrain multiplies the potential functions of each montage fragment, making the film a collection of intrareferential bits frozen in a mosaic, a total "spatial" order.

It may seem odd that I have said so little about what is for most viewers the salient quality of Soviet montage: the speed of the cutting. All of the films I have picked out contain passages of rapid editing, and some present shots only one frame long. Often this technique is motivated by violent action or by tense emotional confrontations; the rapidly cut battle scene or police attack is a convention of these works. Just as often, though, accelerated rhythmic editing functions as the narration's instrument. Fast cutting not only embodies causal climaxes but creates rhetorical ones. Any rapidly cut sequence becomes ipso facto significant (not least because fast cutting tends, paradoxically, to stretch out the syuzhet duration devoted to an episode). For the spectator, rapid editing is the most self-conscious effort of the rhetorical narration to control the *pace* of hypothesis formation. We have repeatedly seen that any rapid flow of fabula information, via editing or other means, compels the spectator to make simple, all-or-nothing choices about story construction. Under the pressure of time—certainly long before half a second—we must give up trying to predict the next image and simply accept what we are given. Soviet fast cutting takes care to combine and repeat shots or actions that we have already seen, so that we can gather a total impression from repeated bursts. Far from being passive subjects inundated by the film's spray of imagery, we continue to apply rhetorical and narrative schemata; we continue to fill in, to liken, to discriminate; but we do so at a suprashot level, unifying the sequence from the top down by using prototypes like "battle," "strike rally," "police attack," or whatever—all the while registering the sheer perceptual force of the style.[17]

The New Babylon

The film work of Grigori Kozintsev and Leonid Trauberg grew out of their experimental theater group, Factory of the Eccentric Actor ("Feks" for short). These young men were initially interested in achieving grotesque effects by manipulating the profilmic event. Feks's *The Cloak* (1926) transposes verbal grotesquerie (Gogol's *skaz* style) into visual terms through setting, costume, and acting. The stylization of the profilmic event serves to emphasize narrational intervention and thus links Feks to more montage-oriented directors. *The Devil's Wheel* (1926) was an attempt to integrate such staging with Soviet editing techniques. By the time of *The New Babylon* (1929), Kozintsev and Trauberg were able to achieve original effects within the norms of the Soviet historical-materialist mode.

That one of the two books which Lenin carried into hiding in Finland was Marx's *Civil War in France* suggests the importance he attached to the lessons of the 1871 Paris Commune. After 1917, the Commune passed into official mythology as a principal antecedent of the Bolshevik Revolution. The subject was thus eminently suited for a Soviet film. *The New Babylon* portrays highlights of the Franco-Prussian war of 1870 and the Commune which sprang up the following year. The film's opening presents the war hysteria manifesting itself in emotional farewells to the troops, buying sprees in a department store, and frenzied celebration in a cabaret. In the first two sequences the narration introduces Louise, a salesgirl at the New Babylon store; her boss; various workers; a cabaret singer; a member of the Chamber of Deputies; and a journalist who bursts into the restaurant with news of French defeat. Eventually the French capitulate to the Prussians, but proletarian women prevent the French soldiers from taking the cannons to Versailles. Later, after the Commune occupies Paris, the boss, the deputy, and the singer encourage the Versailles troops to fire on the city. Soon the Commune takes to the barricades, and after a fierce battle the French forces capture Paris. Communard prisoners are assaulted by the bourgeoisie, with the boss leading the charge. At the film's close, Louise and her comrades are executed.

The film shares with others in its mode a use of historical referentiality and stock types. Louise the salesclerk resembles Louise Michel, the "Red Virgin" of the Commune. The emphasis on women as active fighters is faithful to most accounts of the civil war. The film's very title plays on a historical reference: there apparently was a New Babylon department store, but at the time Paris itself was known as the "Modern Babylon," celebrated for decadence and frivolity. More generally, the film expects the viewer to supply historical background and to identify emblematic moments. When the boss catches the deputy wooing the singer backstage, his pledge of silence in exchange for a state subsidy can be taken to symbolize what Marx denounced as the Second Empire's "joint-stock government . . . the undisguised subservience of government to the propertied classes."[18] Nonetheless, the conventional roles of bourgeois, politician, and worker are given more vividness by the film's referential exactitude. Kozintsev and Trauberg drew ideas for costume and typage from caricatures of the period. The tableau of Victorious France in the cabaret is especially evocative of the spirit of Commune and anti-Commune broadsides of 1870–1871.[19]

The New Babylon is notable for the episodic quality of its organization. The syuzhet's eight parts correspond to the film's projection reels (common enough in a country whose theaters often had only one projector), but most Soviet films which divide themselves into distinct acts remain somewhat tighter-knit than this. Sequences skip from the autumn of 1870 to January of 1871 (the moment of surrender) to 18 March, when crowds swarm over the Montmartre troops, and the film concludes in late May, with the battle for Paris and the execution of the Communards. The first two parts concentrate on depicting the decadence of the Second Empire, while the later portions show the Commune as doing little more than meeting, fighting, and suffering. These gaps in referential time can be explained by the fact that Soviet thinkers were not agreed upon the Commune's political significance. By 1929, historians had begun to quarrel about whether the Commune overrated purely democratic reforms, whether it paid too little attention to military strategy, and whether it failed for want of a central state machinery (this last being a favorite Stalinist view). On these points of controversy the film remains silent, choosing simply to condemn the bourgeoisie and eulogize the revolutionaries according to generic convention. (The film is more direct in drawing on already-canonized interpretations. In one very brief scene, a worker suggests to the leaders that the Commune seize the factories and banks, but the proposal is rejected in favor of a peaceful solution. This interchange puts into the mouth of the proletariat exactly the criticism made by Engels in 1891 and Lenin in 1917.)

There is, however, one occasion where realistic motivation makes the narrative swerve from conventional lines. Another contemporary debate centered on the Commune's failure to forge links with the peasants in the French army; as a result, the peasants took the side of the bourgeoisie. *The New Babylon* makes reference to this issue by including as a major character Jean, a country lad who comes to know Louise and her family. Jean is characterized as tense and fearful in his soldier's role. When he meets the workers, Louise gives him bread and her father mends his boots. Louise and other Communards extend offers of solidarity throughout the film; she even follows him in a drenching rain to beg him to desert the army. Nonetheless, Jean is always wavering. Again and again he halts, as if on the brink of understanding his class allegiance, but then—motivated by a desire to end the war and go home—he sides with the oppressor. Once the Communards have seized the cannons, Jean refuses to join them. Encamped at Versailles, he is haunted by memories of Louise, but once the battle for Paris begins he participates frenziedly. Jean searches for Louise among the prisoners and is thrown out of the cafe of the class for whom he has fought. In a cemetery, Jean stares frozen as Louise defies the officer; then he joins other soldiers in digging graves for the victims. The usual pattern would be for Jean to shift from spontaneous feeling to political consciousness, as Louise does; but instead Jean remains impotent and terrified, more romantically interested in Louise than politically aware of the situation. Jean's progress conforms to the "negative" apprenticeship Suleiman finds in the *roman à thèse* generally, the pattern whereby a character moves from naive ignorance and passivity to an obstinate blindness and a refusal of action.[20] More specifically, Jean poses an ideological difficulty for the film. To portray him as utterly villainous would be risky at a moment when Stalin was at pains to celebrate the peasantry; to portray him as joining the Commune would gainsay a historical interpretation going back to Marx. The solution is to make Jean an unstable element whose presence conforms to ideological

necessity but whose exact function lacks some narrative and rhetorical clarity.

In *The New Babylon*, the narration foregoes many devices—overlapping editing, static poses—that are common in other Soviet historical-materialist films. Instead, the film amplifies the sort of abstract, empirically false scenographic space I have mentioned in connection with *Twenty-six Commissars* and the Odessa Steps. *The New Babylon* raises one tendency of the extrinsic norm to the level of an intrinsic one. The film uses crosscutting, "Kuleshov effect" editing (that is, the omission of the establishing shot), the eyeline match, double-voiced intertitles, and figure frontality to produce a loose, "open" space that can forge rhetorical connections. Some fairly static fabula situations are thus dynamized by the narration's constant manipulation, and the spectator's task is not only to fill in the missing spatial connections but to liken and distinguish the fabula elements shown.

The expository norm gets locked into place during the first segment, which depicts war fever gripping Paris. The film's first block of shots ranges over four locales, all of which will be intercut throughout the scene: the railroad station, as the troops depart; a cabaret; the New Babylon department store; and an unspecified group of settings I shall call the workers' spaces. The chart shows the film's first thirty-one shots, grouped by locale. The shifts from place to place proceed overtly and unambiguously from the narration. (Contrast the way that the opening of *La guerre est finie* motivates its imagery by the play of Diego's consciousness.) Crosscutting conventionally signifies simultaneity, but the sequence makes the viewer downplay temporal considerations and connect fabula events by purely connotative similarities and differences. The cabaret repeats the railroad scene by use of what will become a central motif: spectacle. As crowds cheer the troop train, so the couples in the cabaret applaud the skit enacting France's crushing of Prussia (figs. 11.23–11.24) and one slogan—"Death to the Prussians!"—appears in both. The train and the cabaret are linked to the department store by the stress on buying (titles 10, 20); later, chants of "Bargain!" and "Buy!" will echo through the New Babylon's aisles. At the same time, the store's display of parasols and

The New Babylon: Opening

1. "War!"
2. "Death to the Prussians!"

Railroad Station	Cabaret	Department Store	Workers' quarters
3. Locomotive	11. Couple applaud	20. "War! Prices have risen!"	
4. Four women applaud	12. Stage: France victorious	21. Displays of umbrellas	
5. One woman cheers	13. Stage: Prussia crushed	22. Fans on display	
6. "Scatter their blood to Berlin!"	14. "Death to the Prussians!"	23. "The Department Store 'New Babylon'"	
7. Cheering women	15. Stage: Three singers	24. Stairs and goods for sale	
8. "Scatter their blood!"	16. Stage: France		
9. Long shot: Train and crowd	17. Long shot: Stage and crowd		
10. "War! All the places are sold!"	18. Stage: Woman and crown		
	19. Couple applauds		
	25. "The boss"		28. Young women at sewing machines
	26. Drumroll		29. Cobbler
	27. Medium close-up: The boss, seated		30. Washerwomen
			31. Woman at suds

fans (fig. 11.25) and the frantic women customers (fig. 11.26) recall the cheering women at the station.

From the New Babylon we cut back to the cabaret; the shift is motivated by the fact that the store's owner is there, finishing his meal. Finally, the shots of workers—seamstresses, cobbler, and washerwomen—are justified not only as an expected antithesis in this mode but also by the fact that these workers make and maintain the clothes sold at such stores and worn at the cabaret and the station: they form the infrastructure of the fashion-conscious Second Empire. Although the workers we see will become causally significant (the cobbler is Louise's father, one washer-woman her mother), they are introduced as prototypes of exploited labor; their class identity overshadows their personal individuality, as is suggested by lining up the figures in ranks into the depths of the shot (figs. 11.27–11.28). In general, the effect of the crosscutting is to create an omniscient survey of a society that treats war as spectacle and commodity consumption. The tone of the exposé is of course accusatory: shots 21 and 22 (figs. 11.29–11.30) compare the objects on display with those wielded by the customers, a drumroll announces the entry of the boss (fig. 11.31), and the first two expository titles make the narration participate, by ironic ventriloquism, in the war whoops.

The rest of the first reel builds upon the intercutting of elements defined in the initial portion. Two locales become principal stockpiles of imagery—the department store and the cabaret. We shift between Louise hawking lace ("It's a good buy") and her boss idly studying the menu, between Louise furtively gnawing a piece of bread and the boss ordering dessert. Louise works before an immense mannequin, who in stance and drapery recalls the cabaret tableau of Victorious France (fig. 11.32). (The shallow focus makes the dummy in fact a backdrop for Louise.) Then the manager

invites Louise to join the boss at the ball later; significantly, the omniscient and self-conscious narration has explicitly linked the saleswoman and her boss long before the two will meet.

Louise, the manager, and a salesman take up a frantic spiel, which becomes the occasion for the most rapid shifts so far. From one salesman's "Buy!" we cut to the railroad station, repeating the analogy between commerce and war. Then back to another salesman shouting, "For sale!"; back to the cabaret skit personifying France—now also an object

11.31
11.32

of commerce. Customers at the New Babylon fight for the goods on sale; cut from the daemonic salesman to men in the cabaret; "Buy!" Cut to the laundress, exhausted over her steaming tub; her image reiterates the contrast between rich and poor, and the following shot of the boss reinforces it.

Then a couple in the cabaret applaud. Cut to the crowd at the station applauding the soldiers with the old cry, "Scatter their blood!" The sequence closes with a shot of the train identical to the opening image (shot 3).

My description makes crosscutting the most obvious device here, but the abstraction of the fabula space is accomplished by other means as well. Within locales, characters are never defined in an establishing shot, so that even the long shots of the cabaret or the station do not unequivocally "place" the characters. Louise and the sales staff are never situated with respect to the customers, and the workers are never shown in any single locale. What links characters within most settings is one component of the Kuleshov effect: the eyeline match. On the basis of glances, we assume that the train (shot 3) is the object of the women's applause (shot 4), that Crowned France (shot 18) is the object of the couple's delight (shot 19), and that Louise is addressing the customers in her harangue. This cue is somewhat helped by a frontality of figure position even more self-conscious than in most Soviet shots. Characters' bodies and faces are turned almost completely to us; only their eyes "just miss" addressing the camera. Consequently, when we see Lady France very frontally and then see a shot of a couple, also frontal, we will construct an eyeline running "between" them, on which we sit. But since the space within locales is defined only by eyelines and figure position, it becomes possible for crosscutting to exploit these cues to create *an abstract space of spectacle.* Hinted at in shot 11, the effect emerges most clearly near the close of the sequence. The narration cuts from the department store salesman to cabaret customers, looking off slightly left and laughing and rocking as if watching the sale that occurs in a wholly different place. The narration cuts from an applauding couple at the cabaret to applauding women at the station, creating a metaphoric sign of equality—as if the couple were cheering the train, as if the women were egging on the performance (figs. 11.33–11.34).

In this respect, Feks was carrying on approved precedent. *The Civil War in France* portrays the Second Empire bourgeoisie as entranced by spectacle. Marx describes polite

11.33
11.34

The Paris of M. Thiers was not the real Paris of the "vile multitude," but a phantom Paris, the Paris of the *francs-fileurs*, the Paris of the Boulevards, male and female—the rich, the capitalist, the gilded, the idle Paris, now thronging with its lackeys, its blacklegs, its literary *bohème*, and its *cocottes* at Versailles, St.-Denis, Rueil, and Saint-Germain; considering the civil war but an agreeable diversion, eyeing the battle going on through telescopes, counting the rounds of cannon, and swearing by their own honor and that of their prostitutes, that the performance was far better got up than it used to be at the Porte St. Martin. The men who fell were really dead; the cries of the wounded were cries in good earnest; and besides, the whole thing was so intensely historical.[21]

By creating "eyeline matches" across impossible spaces, the opening sequence of *The New Babylon* depicts the bourgeoisie as Marx did: as feckless spectators.

The film's second segment reinforces the intrinsic norm while presenting some amplifications. The setting remains, almost to the end, the cabaret. The viewer must now construct a more concrete sense of place out of the fragments supplied by montage: men and women toasting "Gay Paris," dancers on and offstage, the singer's act, the boss's table, couples sitting at various tables, and the boss and the deputy striking their bargain backstage. Thus when the chanteuse sings, "We all need love," and the narration cuts to a series of couples—old rake and young woman, young man and old woman, a girl ravenously eating while an old man slobbers over her neck (fig. 11.35)—we are to understand these commentaries on the cash nexus of romance as arising from the depiction of a fairly stable narrative space. These couples are all in the cabaret. Moreover, Louise's presence helps anchor the scene: the shots of her and the boss approach conventional long shots and over-the-shoulder reverse angles (figs. 11.36–11.37). Against the quite conceptual space of the opening sequence, the relative contiguity of these elements becomes apparent. But the narration still opens up this space to a considerable extent by exploiting devices which were subordinate during the first episode.

ladies watching mob atrocities from a balcony. He cites an English reporter on the bourgeoisie's addiction to cabaret, even under shellfire. And Kozintsev has quoted one scathing passage as the source of Feks's approach:

For one thing, the sharp disparity of foreground and background is given new emphasis. No matter what character we see, she or he is in the foreground and the rest of the cabaret forms a vague flat. (There is never anything *between* the camera and the figure.) So absolute is the split between the plane of action and the rearward space that we cannot get any sense of where couples sit or stand in the set. (In this respect, the uniformly blurred backgrounds constitute the functional equivalent of the neutral sky in other Soviet films or the bleached walls of Dreyer's *La Passion de Jeanne d'Arc*.) The narration strives to keep all action played to us; so that when the journalist is informed of the French defeat (fig. 11.38), he rises from his table to address the crowd in the background, turning from the camera (fig. 11.39). But then we cut to a frontal shot, with as great an extent behind him now as there was in the previous shot (fig. 11.40). In the absence of an establishing shot, the cabaret becomes indefinitely large, elastic, always stretching out to infinity behind whatever we see; and yet a paucity of depth cues makes the cabaret hang as flatly behind the characters as does the sunbeam backdrop setting off Crowned France.

The cabaret sequence goes beyond frontality of body and face by making characters look more or less directly to the camera. The very first shot (fig. 11.41) announces the saliency of the device, which recurs almost every time a customer toasts Paris (fig. 11.42). By combining relatively flat backgrounds with self-conscious eye contact, the se-

quence makes the cabaret a very "open" locale. This is most evident when Louise is watching the frenzied dancing:

133. Women dance the cancan to the camera.
134. Top-hatted men dance to the camera.
135. Louise turns to look behind her.

136. As (133): Women dance to the camera.
137. Louise turns to look off right.
138. Men and women dance the cancan diagonally left.
139. An old man and some women dance diagonally left.
140. Medium close-up: Louise turns to look left.

11.42 *11.43*

141. Medium shot: A diner raises his glass to the camera.

142. "To well-fed Paris!"

143. Medium shot: An old man nibbles a woman's neck while she eats.

144. Medium shot: An old man raises his glass.

145. "To carefree Paris!"

146. A man dances with a bottle in his arms.

147. Medium shot: Louise, still looking left, shrinks back.

148. As (134): Men dance to the camera.

149. As (133): Women dance to the camera.

By classical principles of point of view, the to-camera movements in this passage cannot be justified. Louise cannot be watching behind her (shot 136) what she will see in front of her and to the left in shot 149. Rather than take this as a transcription of her subjective experience interrupted by overt narrational commentary (e.g., from "Well-fed Paris" to a man's lecherous appetites in shot 143), the best hypothesis is that Louise is simply the approximate center of a fluid, circular space. Her eyelines do not furnish cues for the precise location of each element but rather heighten the vividness of the swirling dance: the revelry is taking place "all around her."

As the second sequence develops, its space is further opened up by a return to crosscutting. The journalist's announcement that the French army has been beaten is interspersed with shots of the crowds at the train (with whip pans linking this locale to the cabaret), and then shots of the Prussian horsemen charging. The narration now asks us to distinguish among several lines of action: the smiling dancers juxtaposed with the shocked bourgeois customers, the ironic refrain "To Paris!" no longer a toast but a battle cry. After treating the cabaret as the bourgeoisie's dream of Paris, Marx's phantom Babylon ("the misery of the masses was set off by a shameless display of gorgeous, meretricious, and debased luxury"), the narration opens that phantasmagoric space onto a wider political context: a class dancing on the edge of a precipice. The cabaret empties out, and our one establishing shot comes too late to reveal anything but a solitary drunkard (fig. 11.43). Cut to the tableau of victorious France, woefully clinging to the set as the curtain falls (fig. 11.44). Since we have seen other acts occupy the stage since this one, we are entitled to doubt that this image has an unequivocal story "reality" here. It functions as a spatially and temporally abstract reprise of the jingoist spectacle of

11.44
11.45

the first reel and as a self-conscious narrational aside. (The comedy is over.) The device of plucking an image from an earlier moment in the film, creating a flashback without benefit of character memory, will become emphasized in later segments.

"Paris is under siege." The film's third sequence displays a clear obedience to Soviet montage norms. The fabula action consists of an account of life under the siege and a lengthy scene in which the peasant Jean, as a member of the National Guard, meets Louise and her family. The narration is constantly overt, employing many extrinsically conventionalized processes. Crosscutting juxtaposes the battlefield, life in the streets, the sufferings of a washerwoman and her daughter, and a meeting of the journalists and Louise's family. The narration ironically recalls phrases from the previous scene: "Gay Paris" / A woman washing clothes / "Carefree Paris" / A sick girl lies in bed. The narration also permutes the cutaway image of the battlefield landscape, adjusting the composition each time (e.g., fig. 11.45). And the narration routes its own commentary through character speech. When the French surrender is announced, warnings issue first from the journalist. Then subsequent dialogue titles link characters in different spaces, so that we have to assume a collective reaction manifested by the narration. In general, however, the space of proletarian life is more unified than that of the bourgeoisie in earlier scenes. Now, contrary to the most probable expectations in this mode and this film, a medium shot is placed within a total space (figs. 11.46–11.47). Later, Jean's troubled acceptance of the workers' comradeship is rendered in a coherent 180-degree space with homogeneous eyeline matches (figs. 11.48–11.49), even though, à la Kuleshov, there is no establishing shot.

Segment 4, "18 March," initiates a return to the more conceptual space and time of segment 1. On a hillside, proletarian women confront the army and strive to keep the Montmartre artillery in Paris. Meanwhile, in the cabaret the boss and the deputy watch the chanteuse rehearse a new operetta. The narration is able to exploit all the double meanings latent in the parallel situations, asking us to draw out rhetorical analogies and differences. Moment-by-moment uncertainties in the syuzhet issue from our realization that any piece of information may reinforce or undercut what went before, or may operate in different rhetorical senses. For instance, after three shots of the rehearsal, the title "Preparations" refers back to the show and forward to the

11.46   *11.48*
11.47   *11.49*

next image, the beginning of the army's attack on the can-non guards. Again, exploits in the political sphere are likened to spectacle and associated with bourgeois manipu-lation. As the singer croons, "We all need love," the cannon sentry falls dead. The spectacle motif will come to a climax when, as the workers' militia succeeds in seizing the can-nons, the boss will shout that the show is done for.

This sequence also prolongs the "false vision" we glimpsed in the first sequence when cafe clients seemed to be applauding the troop train. Now a sustained "dialogue"

arises between disparate spaces. When the officer says, "More horses and we're ready," the narration cuts to the boss and the deputy applauding, as if congratulating him on the capture. Soon Louise's mother asks the officer, "Whom do you serve?" He turns abruptly, and the narration again cuts

to the boss and the politician. When an old soldier flings down his rifle to join the workers' militia, there is a cut to the boss, furiously rising from his seat. Later the journalist looks right and shouts, "To the Hôtel de Ville!" (fig. 11.50), and the deputy answers (in a perfect if impossible eyeline match) by shouting, "To Versailles! We have to start over!" (fig. 11.51). Denotatively, the deputy means that they must retire to Versailles for more rehearsal, but the narration asks us to construe this as an emblem of the bourgeoisie's emigration from Paris. Overall, we must be prepared to accept physical impossibilities—such as the causal interplay of independent locales—for the sake of intensified narrational comment.

In the art cinema, overt narration emerges intermittently to play a game of ambiguity with the spectator. In the Soviet historical-materialist cinema, thanks to the pervasiveness and the discontinuity of the montage, the narration tends to be constantly overt; but it seldom creates connotative ambiguity. In general, the Soviet films choose simply to vary their narrational tactics within well-defined bounds, recombining them in different portions of the film. *The New Babylon* is a good example. We have already seen how sequence 1 relies upon crosscutting to establish the possibility of an abstract conceptual space, while sequence 2 uses frontality and foreground/background interactions to create an "open" space within the cabaret. The third sequence develops a more intimate and less disjunctive space, associated with the workers and the future Communards. And we have seen how sequence 4 goes further than any earlier episode by building character interactions across impossibly great distances. Because each narrational option was latent in the first scene, we cannot say that later foregroundings startle or puzzle the viewer (in the way that, say, Diego's ambivalent conversation with Nadine in *La guerre est finie* is foregrounded as a deviation from the film's norm). In the same way, the last half of the film develops and recombines devices that we have already encountered.

The fifth segment, that of the Commune's occupation of Paris, is structurally and substantially similar to the first episode. Seven distinct locales are crosscut: Paris exteriors, the workers' space, the Communards' meeting room, a bar at

11.52
11.53

Versailles, the army's hillside camp, the cabaret, and the department store. The characteristic narrational tone of Soviet historical-materialist cinema is present from the start. After a title, "Paris survived for centuries," we get several tourist views of the city, ending with close-ups of gargoyles on Notre Dame. Immediately another expository title challenges the earlier one. "Paris is no more!" In extreme close-up a hammer strikes. The Vendôme column topples. After a series of shots of the washerwomen and seamstresses (as in the first segment), we discover that the hammer that "felled" the column is that of the cobbler (Louise's father). The narration's rhetoric has shown the Paris of boulevards and monuments transformed by the proletariat's seizure of power. Workers raise their heads in praise: "Why do we work with such gaiety? . . . We work for ourselves, not for a boss! The Commune has decided so!" As in the first segment, the characters' direct address is presented very frontally. Finally, by quickly crosscutting the workers' labor with debates in the Commune, the narration makes the Commune the official leadership of the struggle. This portion of the sequence concludes with more shots of the gargoyles that had initiated the crosscutting.

The scene shifts to Versailles, where the boss, the deputy, and the cabaret singer join some French soldiers in a bar. The boss and the deputy address the men in tones of patriotic fervor, while the singer approaches the moping Jean and revives his memories of Louise. Now the narration juxtaposes the boss and deputy with the gargoyles before cutting back to a rapid montage of the men's harangues. While the journalist advocates peaceful methods, the deputy and the boss lash the soldiers into a violent mood. And once more the bourgeoisie represents war hysteria as spectacle. The singer leads the men in the "Marseillaise" while a dazed Jean becomes dimly aware of the band's frenzy. The boss is intercut with the band's side drum, a refrain of the drumroll that had introduced him in the cabaret. The narration now reverts to two devices: the spatialized, mosaic form and the "dialogue" between disparate spaces. As the sequence develops, the cutting begins to integrate material from earlier episodes, treating the first portion of the film as a repository

of images. The narration crosscuts the trumpets with the stage tableau of Victorious France in the cabaret (scenes 1 and 2); it intercuts the singer in this bar with the bourgeois women fighting for lace at the New Babylon; it then juxtaposes her with the flashing cancan legs of scene 2. Thus this

chauvinist spectacle is firmly classified with the earlier ones. The singer then kisses the bayonet and calls for blood (fig. 11.52). The officer on the hillside, as if hearing her call (fig. 11.53), turns abruptly from the camera and orders his troops "on to Paris" (fig. 11.54), an echo of the Prussians' cry in

scene 2. The narration gives us three shots of the target—the women workers—before a quick montage of firing cannons, blaring trumpets, roaring drums, and the boss's expression concludes the sequence.

The sixth principal episode brings to a climax the specta-

tional analogy. Louise is ransacking the New Babylon for material for the barricades.

798. Long shot: Louise looks for goods (fig. 11.55).

799. Medium close-up: The mannequin is lifted out of the store (fig. 11.56).

800. Louise grabs lace and begins to unwind it (fig. 11.57).

801. *Plan américain*, low angle: A young woman wearing lace and twirling a parasol looks left (fig. 11.58).

802. "On the hill of Versailles, the bourgeoisie watched."

803. Medium shot: The boss looks down to the left, holding a parasol (fig. 11.59).

804. Medium shot: The singer, seated, watches through binoculars (fig. 11.60).

Shots 798–801 build toward an equation of the dummy in white and the bourgeois woman (shot 801), with lace as a connecting factor. But the intertitle and subsequent shots emphasize that the bourgeoisie are literally watching—if not Louise's pillaging of the store, then at least the Commune's activities. (Again, the citation is to Marx, who described the bourgeoisie as "considering the civil war but an agreeable

cle motif that has run through the film. The Communards, realizing that all is lost, take to the streets. The Battle of Paris is rendered through another recombining of intrinsically normalized devices—crosscutting and the "impossible" eyeline match. The result at first seems only another narra-

diversion, eyeing the battle going on through telescopes . . .") No small-scale spectacles now; the civil war
becomes the ultimate cabaret show, to be enjoyed from a
distance. Correspondingly, the narration produces the most
grandiose conceptual space in the film—at once concrete

(the locales are for once proximate) and abstract (the
bourgeoisie could not, on empirical grounds, see all the
incidents that we see).

And the battle indeed becomes both spectacle and dialogue. The bourgeoisie call across the chasm for blood, and

the soldiers obey, attacking the barricades. Motifs from the first two parts recur, in parodic form: the lace wraps wounds, Louise rolling it out as if for sale (fig. 11.61) before taking up a rifle; a pianist entertains the Communards during a break in the fighting. As the Commune dies, it creates its own participatory spectacle: the pianist plays, the women sing. An old man shouts: "You want Paris? . . . The old Paris? . . . For the bosses?" and we cut to the boss raging, as if he heard the dying Communard. Once the ramparts are overrun, Jean is on the scene and the sequence concludes with him in the foreground, turning slowly to look out at the camera (fig. 11.62) and to "see" and "hear" the boss and his friends applauding his performance (fig. 11.63).

The last two segments develop the film's narrational norm in more modest and conventional ways, probably because these scenes aim to evoke the most sympathy and the smallest amount of conceptual "distance." The Communard prisoners are marched past a cafe, where the boss recognizes Louise and begins to beat her. This precipitates a riot in which the bourgeoisie attack the prisoners. There are echoes of earlier narrational procedures: the ironic title ("Peace and order rule Paris"), the interjected shots of "Vive la Commune" scrawled on a wall, intercutting within a locale, and a frontality with foreground/background stylization (even during a massacre; see fig. 11.64). On the whole, however, this is the most concrete space yet depicted in the film, defined by an establishing shot (fig. 11.65) and plausible eyeline matching (fig. 11.66). The geographical exactitude is appropriate, for this is the first time that the narration has shown workers and bourgeoisie concretely inhabiting the same locale.

The last segment, "The Judgment," again swerves from its immediate predecessor in creating a fluid and "open" space within a circumscribed setting, as sequence 2 had done with the cabaret. In Père-Lachaise cemetery, as Communards are questioned and executed in the savage rain, the narration return to almost total frontality and foreground/background planification (fig. 11.67), while connecting portions of the space by Kuleshovian eyeline matching. As Jean watches tensely, Louise refuses to betray the Commune. Sentenced to death, she cries out in agony, but then turns and looks off, laughing. "We will return, Jean!" As the group is executed, a man cries, "Vive la Commune!" and the film ends with three quick shots, one per word, of the same phrase scrawled on a wall. The narration has fused character voice and narrational commentary into a simple rhetorical flourish.

The New Babylon asks the viewer to undertake activities I have argued to be characteristic of its mode: filling in spatial constructs of various degrees of abstraction, likening and differentiating juxtaposed elements, submitting to a texture of abrupt disjunctions, and wrestling with cognitive incompatibilities (e.g., characters watching what they cannot see) for the sake of perceptual and didactic vividness. The film's syuzhet and style create a constantly overt narration, knowledgeable to the point of omniscience, highly communicative, self-conscious in its address to the viewer, and unambiguous in its attitudes and conclusions. At the same time, *The New Babylon* innovates within its mode not only by introducing new subjects (the Paris Commune) and motifs (the spectacle-centered bourgeois life) but also by varying its exploitations of narrational conventions. In particular, the film's intrinsic norm—the abstract, empirically impossible space—gets developed in unique ways to fulfill rhetorical ends.

Toward an Interrogative Cinema

It would take a volume to explore the various aspects of Soviet culture and politics that shaped the development of the historical-materialist mode. We would have to survey two decades of debate about the role of agitprop art; a range of experiments in painting, literature, sculpture, theater, and architecture; the growing Party control of the Soviet film industry; the experience of studying and recutting American films of the teens and early twenties; developments in literary theory, such as Formalism (Kozintsev has claimed that the critic Yuri Tynianov was the major influence on Feks at the time of *The New Babylon*);[22] and the influx of European experimental films of the 1920s, especially from France. We would also need to consider the seminal importance of Lev Kuleshov's writings and teachings, especially in their "Sovietization" of principles of Hollywood découpage. We would have to spread our net to include those films in other genres—comedy, adventure, and literary adaptation—that exploited some aspects of historical-materialist narration (chiefly, of course, montage). A chapter alone could be devoted to the emergence of models and prototypes of the mode. (*Pravda* called *Strike* "the first revolutionary creation of our cinema.")[23] It would also be necessary to stress both authorial differences and the uniqueness of each of these extraordinary films. Finally, a complete survey should consider the extent to which many films, while aiming at ideological clarity, became subject to debate; the didactic schemata for construing the films were never as neat or unqualified as an overview tends to make them.

Here I want only to suggest the extent to which the historical-materialist mode of narration has gained some purchase beyond its use in the USSR between 1925 and 1933. These Soviet filmmakers permanently affected film history—not only by making influential films but by forging an approach to storytelling that has remained a strong, if minority, alternative to classical narration.

Hollywood's fast cutting and analytical approach to the scene had prompted Soviet filmmakers to explore montage; soon, however, classical Hollywood filmmaking drew upon some stylistic resources of the Soviet mode. American films had already borrowed superimpositions and prismatic optical effects from the German cinema in order to create special transitional sequences, and it was through these devices that montage was assimilated. One could present a violent spectacle, such as the earthquake in *San Francisco* (1936), with a Soviet-style montage technique. More usually, one could present a significant lapse of time by means of a rapid series of symbolic images linked by dissolves, wipes, or superimpositions. We have seen that *Say It with Songs* (1929) offers many instances. (Hollywood's use of canted setups, low angles, and rapid rhythm seems clearly influenced by such films as *The End of St. Petersburg*.) By the mid-1930s, "montage" had passed into Hollywood jargon, but the force and deeper implications of the Soviet conception were lost. Shots were never very short, the perceptual impact of cutting was softened by the ever-present dissolves, and the whole procedure was relegated to a transitional role, becoming an isolated and stereotyped gesture.[24]

If the Hollywood cinema drew the argumentative and perceptual sting from montage, Soviet socialist realism after 1933 abandoned the technical basis. In general, the historical-materialist films paved the way for Socialist Realism in their use of referentiality, exemplary heroes, and the apprenticeship pattern. What was lost was the constant narrational presence and overt rhetorical address of the historical-materialist style. At the level of fabula structure, Socialist Realism is significantly different from the classical Hollywood cinema; but its narrational principles and procedures do not vary drastically. *Chapayev* (1934) is the conventional example here, but a more technically proficient work like Vera Stroyeva's *Generation of Conquerors* (1936) shows just as clearly how the rhetorical impulses of the narration pass wholly over to the characters (here, a band of student revolutionaries from czarist days) and how classical technique is at the center of the style. (Only one scene, in which a police chief addresses his staff but is presented as addressing the spectator, faintly echoes the self-consciousness of earlier works.) What remains is a story of typical individuals, each given one humanizing idiosyncrasy and each exemplifying some aspect of the prerevolutionary situation in Russia.

Outside the Soviet Union, the historical-materialist mode had an influence on political filmmaking. Charles Dekeukeleire's *La flamme blanche* (1930) owes a good deal to Pudovkin (and Vertov). It intercuts documentary footage of demonstrations by the Flemish People's Party with staged footage of battles between demonstrators and police, framed against white backgrounds and edited in rapid montage. The most famous example of Soviet influence is, of course, *Kuhle Wampe* (1932), a film which shows a fascinating mingling of conventions drawn from the more radical silent films and from the emerging canons of Socialist Realism. The German left had strong ties with the Soviet Union between 1929 and 1933, and Brecht visited Moscow for the world premiere of *Kuhle Wampe*. In many respects the film is quite "classical," but its first part, "One Unemployed Less," displays a remarkable synthesis of Soviet devices. Unable to find a job, the young Bonicke son has come home for lunch, and his mother remarks: "If you don't try at all, you're bound to fail." Cut to a shot of men on bikes pedaling down the street looking for work. Later, after the boy has committed suicide and the neighbors are gathered around, there is a shot of a woman speaking to the camera: "One unemployed less." And at the end of the chapter, an old woman remarks: "He had his loveliest years before him"; cut to the next portion, entitled "The Loveliest Years," which portrays the family's eviction. Such uses of intellectual montage, direct address, and ironic interplay of character dialogue and overt narrational intervention all demonstrate that the lessons of Soviet historical-materialist narration were not lost on Brecht and Slatan Dudow.

Just as influenced by this mode was *La vie est à nous* (1936), supervised by Jean Renoir for distribution by the French Communist Party. Like *Kuhle Wampe* and *La flamme blanche*, this is a mélange of newsreel footage and staged scenes, but the constant direct address intertitles, the asynchronous sound, and the abstract and figurative editing reveal a direct borrowing from the Soviets. Rich idlers fire pistols at cardboard cutouts with workers' caps; cut to ranks of French fascists on the firing range. When Hitler rants, we hear a dog bark; Mussolini looks around him and "sees" his bombing of Ethiopia. One of the film's three episodes sketches the familiar movement from spontaneity to consciousness: with the backing of a PCF cell, exploited factory workers confront the boss and win concessions. The film concludes with a series of speeches by party leaders, addressed both to us and to a fictional audience composed, impossibly, of characters from the various episodes we have seen. At the close, several groups of workers march toward us singing, while "refrain" shots from the film's start create a Kuleshovian space that is nothing less than the entire landscape of France.

At the level of theory, the Soviet historical-materialist films had strong appeal to a European intelligentsia already interested in montage in a broad sense. Novels like Johannes R. Becher's *Levisite* (1926) and Alexander Döblin's *Berlin Alexanderplatz* (1930) and dramatic productions like Piscator's *In Spite of Everything* (1925) and Brecht's *Mahagonny* (1930) also laid claim to montage as a modernist and socially critical practice.[25] By 1935, Ernst Bloch was identifying montage as the formal means for attacking petit bourgeois normality.[26] As is now well known, Georg Lukács objected to such elevations of montage, criticizing the technique as a principle of subjectivist self-expression and calling for a holistic art that manifests true essences "as immediacy, as life as it actually appears."[27] Lukács charged naturalistic techniques of description with fragmenting point of view and thus whittling reality down to atomic data and isolated episodes.[28] From this angle, montage becomes the culmination of naturalistic description, assembling scraps of fact and judgment and exposing disparities. Lukács rejects the overt narrational presence implied by the artist as *monteur*: "The slice of life shaped and depicted by the artist and re-experienced by the reader should reveal the relations between appearances and essence without the need for any external commentary."[29] Lukács advocates a return to the technique of classical realism, in which an omniscient author establishes the correct proportions of an event and integrates all aspects into a larger whole.

On the particular issue of montage, it is of course Brecht who stands most clearly opposed to Lukács. He cites Döb-lin's definition of the "epic" *Berlin Alexanderplatz*: a work which "lets itself be cut up, as if with scissors, into parts capable of continuing to lead their own life."[30] *Kuhle Wampe*, he claimed, constitutes "a montage of quite autonomous little plays."[31] As if in retort to Lukács, Brecht writes in 1939 that didactic elements must be introduced into a play by means of montage. "They would have no organic link with the totality but would find themselves in contradiction with it; they would break the course of performance and actions; cold showers for sensitive souls, they would block all identification."[32] More generally, we can see Brecht's early theory of drama as quite congruent with the narrational model established by Soviet historical-materialist film.

By 1930, Brecht had clearly formulated a conception of "dialectical" theater. One source was Piscator's "epic" theater; another was Döblin's conception of the "epic" novel, which was indebted to Joyce and Dos Passos. Yet another source was the Soviet cinema. Brecht's epic theater was to be overtly pedagogic and didactic. As in Soviet cinema, the epic theater's syuzhet was to exhibit a "non-Aristotelian" causality by breaking with the depiction of isolated individuals. "The spectator must perceive the masses behind the individual, consider the individuals as particles which manifest themselves as a reaction, a way of behaving, a development of the mass."[33] Most significantly, the Aristotelian "mimetic" theater was to be, in our terms, "diegeticized." In epic theater, "the stage begins to narrate. The fourth wall no longer makes the narrator disappear."[34] Projections, films, titles, and captions create abstract discussions confirming or contradicting what the characters say and do. The "literarization" of the theater consists in a narration that is constantly "punctuating 'representation' with 'formulation'"—a good description of what happens with many Soviet intertitles.[35] In a move recalling the Soviet film's use of "refrain images," Brecht proposes that "footnotes, and the habit of turning back in order to check a point, need to be introduced into play-writing too."[36] Performance can be "diegeticized" by processes that make the actor appear to be quoting the words and deeds of an absent character. Just as Soviet films had created an all-powerful narration governing the very constitution of the filmed event, Brecht seeks to install an overt narration at the center of the theatrical experience, mediating between the imaginary fabula world and its presentation on stage. And as the film required constant montage to keep the spectator from taking the image as a simple record of a preexistent event, so epic theater requires montage to interrupt the performance, to break up scenes, to proceed "by fits and starts."[37] In 1947 Brecht followed Lukács in contrasting naturalism to realism, but the terms were almost exactly reversed: the naturalist lets events "speak for themselves," but in true realism, the author interrupts to make them intelligible.[38]

It was chiefly through the theory, practice, and example of Brecht that norms of the historical-materialist mode were perpetuated. Brecht's Berliner Ensemble productions remained influential models of modernist political theater: one French critic wrote in 1955 that "for Brecht, the stage narrates, the audience judges."[39] Brecht indeed constitutes the link to the historical-materialist cinema of the late 1960s. In Germany, around 1960, the "documentary theater" movement emerged under the auspices of Piscator (especially his Berlin production of *The Deputy* in 1962) and of Peter Weiss, both influenced by Brecht.[40] This movement was greatly to affect the work of Jean-Marie Straub and Danièle Huillet. In 1962, Godard made *Vivre sa vie* in conscious imitation of Brechtian methods. Not until somewhat later, however, did filmmakers and theorists turn to a scrutiny of the Soviet cinema of the 1920s. In France, Althusser's reinterpretation of Leninism, the impact of structuralism and Russian Formalism on intellectual circles, the new availability of films by Vertov and Feks, the efforts of journals like *Tel Quel* and *Change* to link Marxism to a literary avant-garde, and crucially the revolutionary activities of May 1968 all intensified interest in Soviet silent cinema. Writing of the Etats généraux du cinéma, René Micha predicted in the summer of 1968 that the Soviet directors would become the model for a revolutionary cinema.[41] In January of 1969, Eisenstein's essays and memoirs began to appear in *Cahiers du cinéma*; the series would run for over two years. In a special 1970 number on Soviet cinema of the 1920s, Jean Narboni wrote: "This is the only cinema capable of comprehending itself as a signifying practice, aware of its materiality, detaching itself

at last from the ideology of 'lived experience.' . . . A cinema which belongs not to the prestigious silence of the archives but is active *today*, before us and with us."[42]

One theoretical consequence of the rediscovery of Soviet historical-materialist cinema was a broadening of the concept of montage. Thanks partly to Bazin, "modernity" in cinema had come to imply long takes and intrashot effects, but New Wave films forced theorists to reconsider editing as a significant technique. Moreover, films like *Not Reconciled* (1965) and *Méditerranée* (1963), not to mention Godard's work, made the question of montage quite pressing. A 1969 *Cahiers* panel defined montage as "all notions of liaison, juxtaposition, combination (and their corollaries: difference, rupture, analysis)."[43] The political efficacy of montage emerged in its ability to shatter the homogeneity of the spectacle. J.-L. Comolli put it emphatically, if circuitously:

> All montage, even formalist montage, produces at least some *effects of work*: it multiplies traces, cuts, gaps, fractures, in short the signs of writing [*écriture*] which affirm it as being an operation by which, again at the very least, it shows that there is a work of signifying production: it *watches* itself. . . . Reworking the status of the images in the signifying network, redistributing their positions, reorganizing their relations according to systems of opposition or recurrence, dividing and denaturalizing their mechanical linkup, montage *superimposes* upon that flowing emergence of an impression of reality, which every series of images (edited or not) necessarily produces, another movement, that of meaning, of reading.[44]

Montage thus became absorbed into the general issue of what I have been calling self-conscious narration.

Such theoretical developments were preceded and paralleled by filmmaking practice. The Soviet directors had forged a tendentious "Socialist Formalism." The 1960s and 1970s saw a movement, within the conventions of the historical-materialist mode, toward an interrogative cinema. Films such as those of Straub and Huillet, Jancsó, the Dziga-Vertov Group, and more recent British independent filmmakers preserve basic tenets of the Soviet model: the refusal of a psychologically defined, individual-centered syuzhet; the emphasis upon typicality and historical referentiality; the insistence upon continuous transformation of the fabula by an overt and politically conscious narration. But these films also refuse the fixed doctrine and clearly didactic purpose that had informed the Soviet approach. Here the narration stages an inquiry into political issues. The characters and/or the narration pose questions about political theory and practice—including the practice of cinematic representation. In these works, the need for revolutionary change is often posited, but a film's own capacity for social analysis and change is subjected to a scrutiny that was never undertaken in the Soviet films we have considered.

That political issues tend to be questioned, and not solved by fiat, is explicable by the fact that no fixed doctrine serves as a point of departure. After 1956, with the Soviet Communist Party's denunciation of Stalin and the USSR's suppression of the Hungarian uprising, the European left was in disarray. In no country was there an official "line" that these filmmakers could promote without falling into some version of realism. "The cinema," remarked Godard in 1970, "is a party instrument and we find ourselves in countries where the revolutionary party is far from existing."[45] The Dziga-Vertov Group, sometimes believed to be the most tendentious element of "left-wing modernism," had no fixed ties to a Maoist organization (Althusser comes in for criticism in Vent d'est),[46] while Jancsó's work constitutes a steady critique of centralized power within actually existing socialism. Thus the films raise political problems: the return of fascism (Not Reconciled), Soviet revisionism (Pravda), spontaneous revolutionary outbursts (The Confrontation, Vent d'est), the relations of ideology to the economic infrastructure (British Sounds). This is not to say that these films can be seen as utterly open-ended; as one critic remarks of The Confrontation: "It certainly does not accept any alternative to socialism."[47]

Given an interrogative political stance, some films use a "collage" principle to create forms incorporating debate and dialogue. Entire films will be staged as debates or discussions. The Confrontation lays out various positions—anarchist, humanist, sectarian, democratic centrist, and party centered.[48] Similarly, Godard's Un film comme les autres frames its footage of May 1968 within a conversation among unseen students and workers who argue about the failures of May. Besides such moot forms there are more pedagogical attempts to analyze a problem or period. Straub and Huillet treat History Lessons (1972) as an assemblage of representations of Caesar's reign; Le gai savoir (1969) proposes a three-year curriculum concentrating on decomposing images and sounds from a Marxist perspective. At a local level, the narration can juxtapose texts or voices to map out arguments surrounding an issue, as when, in Jonathan Curling and Susan Clayton's Song of the Shirt (1979), a Parliamentary debate is recreated on two video monitors. Or the sound track can interrogate the image, as in Godard's Dziga-Vertov Group films. Rethinking Soviet montage as a collage of documents created a looser, still more conceptual texture, seen perhaps at the limit in Godard's work, as Serge Daney describes it:

> It consists of taking note of what is said (to which one can add nothing) and then looking immediately for the *other* statement, the *other* sound, the *other* image which would counterbalance *this* statement, this sound, this image. . . . More than "Who is right? Who is wrong?" the real question is, "What can we oppose to this?"[49]

This cinema also interrogates cinematic representations. Here is its "Brechtian" heritage. The work of Straub and Huillet constitutes a running violation of dominant figures of style: shot/reverse shot, eyeline matching, the framing of figures, the use of landscape, sound/image relations.[50] Similarly, what Ferenc Feher has called Jancsó's synthesis of parable and pantomime (which owes something to Brecht's theatrical parables) also serves to question socialist-realist demands for a plausible and homogeneous diegetic world.[51] The Dziga-Vertov Group emphasizes crude, obviously constructed images and overloaded sound tracks, thus challenging the supremacy of the visual in cinema. Noël Burch's In the Year of the Bodyguard (1982) juxtaposes primitive cinema's staging and shooting practices with more modern alternatives (e.g., to-camera interviews, volumetric space, *cinéma-vérité*) in order to suggest comparisons between suffragist struggles and contemporary feminist acitivity.

Central to the interrogation of cinematic representation is another link to Soviet cinema: the overtness of the narrational operations. The marked angles and empty frames in Straub and Huillet's films and our pervasive awareness of manipulation in Jancsó's camera movements encourage the viewer to construct a constantly present narration. The film's own operations will not necessarily escape observation, as in the recording sessions in *Introduction to Arnold Schoenberg's Accompaniment for a Film Scene* (1972), the black frames which create spaces for reflecting on the pre-ceding shots in *Luttes en Italie* (1970), and the critique of one part of the film by another in *Pravda* (1969).

It seems likely that the interrogative tendency has an ambivalent relation to another set of extrinsic norms—that of art-cinema narration. Certainly the psychologically complex protagonist and the crisis of individual values have been effectively countered by such films as *Chronicle of Anna Magdalena Bach* (1967), *Not Reconciled* (1965), *Tout va bien* (1972), and Jancsó's *Allegro Barbaro* (1978). Nonetheless, the ability of art-cinema narration to maximize ambiguity for symbolic effect has suggested avenues for an open-ended political cinema. Thus the recent interrogative strain in the historical-materialist mode of narration has selectively absorbed some norms of its rival.

12. Parametric Narration

This is the least "public," most rarely discussed sort of narration I shall consider, and it will be the most controversial. The very name poses a problem. I could call it "style centered," or "dialectical," or "permutational," or even "poetic" narration. "Parametric" was chosen in reference to Noël Burch's *Theory of Film Practice*, in which he uses the term "parameters" to describe what I call film techniques. But nomenclature is only the start of the difficulties. This type of narration is not linked to a single national school, period, or genre of filmmaking. Its norms seem to lack the historical concreteness of the three modes I have considered so far. In many ways, the pertinent historical context is less that of filmmaking than that of film theory and criticism. To some extent, then, this mode of narration applies to isolated filmmakers and fugitive films. I shall also be pointing to formal processes that film criticism typically ignores, even when studying the films I will mention. Making these processes my central focus will inevitably strike some readers as implausible. Here I can ask only patience and a willingness to consider that, at least in some films, apparently trivial aspects may turn out to be essential.

A New Role for Style

As previous chapters have shown, stylistic patterns tend to be vehicles for the syuzhet's process of cueing us to construct the fabula. This is most apparent in classical narration, in which film technique, though highly organized, is used principally to reinforce the causal, temporal, and spatial arrangement of events in the syuzhet. The "invisibility" of the style is a function both of its role in supporting the syuzhet and of its conformity with extrinsically normalized principles and procedures. In art-cinema narration and historical-materialist narration, style is more prominent by virtue of its deviation from classical norms and its tendency to deviate, however slightly, from extrinsic norms of the mode. But the film's unique deployment of stylistic features nonetheless remains subordinate to syuzhet-defined functions: to create realism, expressive subjectivity, authorial commentary, or a play among such factors (art-cinema narration); or to create vivid perceptual heightening of a narrative/rhetorical construct (historical-materialist narration).

Yet there exists another sort of narration, one in which the film's stylistic system creates patterns *distinct from the demands of the syuzhet system*. Film style may be organized and emphasized to a degree that makes it at least equal in importance to syuzhet patterns.

Most critics and theorists are inclined to recognize the dominance of style only in abstract or nonnarrative films, when there is no syuzhet present at all. Yet there is also the possibility of what Tynianov called as early as 1927 "style-centered" narative cinema.[1] We can imagine a narrative cinema in which there is still a syuzhet, but "the rise and fall of the stylistic masses" come to the fore.[2] This split, however, is too simple. We must also allow the possibility that syuzhet and style may become equal in importance. Moreover, since a film operates through time, we must consider that syuzhet processes and stylistic processes may alternate in emphasis.

Analogies with other arts may be helpful here. Most films resemble novels or short stories in that the stylistic surface functions chiefly to expose syuzhet patterns. But parametric narration is more like what goes on in "mixed" arts. In a narrative poem, the construction of a story is often subordinated to the demands of verse. Poe's Raven croaks "Nevermore," and the narrator loves someone named Lenore, partly because of the requisites of rhyme. In opera or the art song, the music's unfolding may not simply accompany the text but impose its own patterns on it. Cinematic style, the repetition and development of instantiations of film technique, may likewise become what Tynianov calls the "dominant," the factor that is pushed forward at the expense of others, "deforming" them.[3]

Another way to clarify the parametric idea is to trace its historical development. Certainly the notion that stylistic organization could achieve formal saliency has been around for some time. As my citations from Tynianov imply, the Russian Formalists granted stylistic factors considerable importance. In poetic language, writes one Formalist, "linguistic patterns acquire independent value."[4] The Czech structuralist Jan Mukařovský distinguished between linguistic distortion that was motivated by the poem's subject matter and linguistic distortion operating for its own sake.[5] This tendency was not confined to the criticism of verse. As early as 1919, Viktor Shklovsky argued that narrative involved parallels between syuzhet composition and linguistic patterning—a distinction which presumed the possibility of noncoincidence between the two systems.[6] In the domain of cinema, Eisenstein suggested that in shot conflict and "overtonal" montage, purely stylistic features can create patterns independent of immediate narrative needs.[7] Still, it was not for some decades that such ideas were systematically applied.

One of the most important trends in European music of the 1950s was "total serialism." The model is usually held to be Messiaen's 1948 piece, *Mode de valeurs et d'intensités*, which extended the idea of the scale from pitch to the spheres of duration, loudness, and attack. Young composers such as Pierre Boulez, Karlheinz Stockhausen, Luigi Nono, and Jean Barraqué began to use Schoenberg's principles of the twelve-tone row to generate music of unprecedented formal complexity. By assigning codified values to the intervals in the pitch row, or series, the composer could systematically vary meter, rhythm, timbre, dynamics, and attack. Schoenberg had chiefly used the row for harmonic and melodic purposes, but according to the young composers, Webern had glimpsed the generative possibilities of serial functions. Now, wrote Boulez, "the architecture of the work derives directly from the ordering of the series."[8] The composer could select certain "parameters" (pitch, rhythm, etc.) to be serialized and then lay out a table of all possible permutations based on intervals in the row, or rhythmic "cells," or whatever.[9] The goal of integral serialism was a new unity, in which a single structure dictates the entire piece, from local texture to overall form.[10] For our purposes, the crucial aspect of serialist doctrine is the possibility that large-scale structure may be determined by fundamental stylistic choices.

Although exact causal links are hard to find, many experimental trends in French literature of the period resemble serial thinking. The *nouveau roman*, which rose to prominence in the mid-1950s, was also concerned with the generation of large-scale forms out of limited verbal material. Michel Butor's *L'emploi du temps* (1956), Alain Robbe-Grillet's *La jalousie* (1957), and Claude Mauriac's *Toutes les femmes sont fatales* (1957) mixed together fragmentary blocks of time in a way that suggested a hidden formula controlling surface variants. The so-called *nouveau nouveau roman*, associated with the journal *Tel Quel*, went still further in exposing the novel's structural armature. At the same time, Raymond Queneau and other writers formed OuLiPo, a group devoted to building new poetic texts out of existing ones by use of rule-governed procedures.

Structure, wrote Boulez in 1963, was a key word in his theory, and he went on to cite Lévi-Strauss as showing that this concept transcended the dichotomy of form and content.[11] That heterogeneous intellectual movement known as structuralism significantly changed the way linguists, literary critics, and philosophers conceived of textual form. In the late 1950s and early 1960s, several influential structuralist thinkers introduced concepts that encouraged "parametric" thinking. Although we must take care not to conflate serialism and structuralism, there are several important points of similarity. All involve the relation of local structure, or stylistic events, to large-scale structure.

Both serialism and structuralism held that textual components form an order that coheres according to intrinsic principles. In more technical terms, the structuralist looks first at the organization of signifiers; only then does the analyst correlate that to a system of references or signifieds. Roman Jakobson's theory holds poetry to be autotelic, relying upon the play of linguistic categories to block referential meaning. Similarly, Boulez emphasizes that the series creates its meaning immanently, by virtue of its unique ordering of parameters. Many literary experiments in the wake of the *nouveau roman* rely solely upon the generative powers of the signifier—anagrams, puns, or other verbal ploys that get stretched out to form large-scale patterns.[12] This line of thought suggests that style (often called *écriture*) may form an independent structure in the text. Style need be governed only by internal coherence, not by representational function.

Serial and structuralist theory also treat textual form as a "spatial" phenomenon. This notion can be defined in two ways. First, the "visible," phenomenal text gets treated as a configuration whose parts exist simultaneously. In analyzing a myth, Lévi-Strauss lays out the actions in a horizontal line.[13] Boulez speaks of a piece as a "concrete sound object" occupying "musical space."[14] Jakobson tends to treat the poem as a simultaneous order, a design in language stretched across the page. Claude Simon's novel *La route de Flandres* (1960) possesses an overt shape: there are three passes through the same point, and successive events are presented as if simultaneous. In a 1964 essay, "Le langage de l'éspace," Michel Foucault discusses several other *nouveaux romans* which undertake a similar project.[15] The outstanding spokesman for the spatiality of the literary text has been Michel Butor, who suggests taking the three-dimensional connotations of *volumen* literally. He treats the book as possessing "a mobility which most nearly approximates a simultaneous presence of all parts of work."[16] He itemizes many features—horizontals and verticals, oblique patterns, margins, typography, layout—through which the text creates a spatial order.

There is another sense in which the aesthetic text may be considered as having spatial form, and this bears on "invisible" properties. The ordering of parts can be treated as a *distribution* of elements drawn from a fixed storehouse "behind the scenes." In serial music, the series is not a simple succession of pitches but what Boulez calls an underlying hierarchy of functions.[17] Strings of notes, rhythm, attack, and other temporal features of the piece spring from an unchanging generative formula. In other media, this process was theorized by Jakobson and Roland Barthes according to the Saussurean principles of syntagm and paradigm. The syntagm is the combined string of items visibly present in the text. The paradigmatic axis is that set from which each item is selected. The presence of one item thus inevitably signals the absence of others that could substitute for it.

That the paradigmatic dimension creates a "virtual space" in the text is especially emphasized in the work of Lévi-Strauss and Jakobson. In 1955, Lévi-Strauss argued that myth is a particular kind of story composed of "gross constituent units." These are defined not only by their position in a horizontal chain of actions but by their relation to purely conceptual ("vertical") categories. The mythologist could analyze the text by spatializing it: write each action on a card, then lay out the cards in a two-dimensional array in order to discover both the syntagmatic and the paradigmatic axes.[18] At a 1958 conference, Roman Jakobson proposed a comparable theory of stylistic construction in poetry by claiming that the poetic function of language was characterized by the projection of "the principle of equivalence from the axis of selection into the axis of combination."[19] That is, in poetry, a string of signs tends to embody in linear form the paradigmatic groups basic to its constitution. "The cat sat on the mat" projects the paradigmatic category of phonological similarity (rhyme) onto the syntagmatic level of the line. Any sequence of units—phonological, syntactic, semantic—strives to build an equality with others, creating designs within the poem, "similarity superimposed upon contiguity."[20]

One consequence of these ideas is that the phenomenal form of the text tends to be seen as a permutational distribution of the invisible set. According to Boulez, the piece is only "a sort of probable fragment" drawn from hundreds of possible variants of chosen parameters.[21] Lévi-Strauss treats different versions of myths in the same way; any one mythical text is only one manifestation of a larger permutation group. The *nouveau roman* and its successors made much of this principle. Robbe-Grillet's novels characteristically make each scene a slightly incompatible variant upon a central event, which may never be presented in an authoritative fashion. Jean-Louis Baudry's *Personnes* (1967) contains eighty-one sections, each one playing out a different combination of personal pronouns; the last page obligingly maps out all the possibilities on a nine-by-nine square. Perhaps the limit case is Marc Saporta's *Composition no. 1* (1962), an unbound sheaf of leaves without pagination, to be read in any order. "The number of possible combinations," the author announces, "is infinite."[22]

Where, one might now ask, does all this leave the perceiver? Perceiving a poem, novel, or a piece of music is a time-bound activity; yet the concept of a frozen textual design deliberately ignores that process. The perceiver may not grasp the signifiers as forming a total order, and the paradigmatic dimension and permutational play may go unnoticed. At one point, Boulez admits that serial music's structures are not necessarily audible.[23] I shall consider this point in more detail later, but it is worth mentioning that both serialism and structuralism are often hard pressed to show that the work's formal principles are registered by the perceiver.

In sum, serialism and structuralism both reveal new conceptions of form that give style great significance. In integral serialism, local textural choices could be seen as generating the entire work's form. The self-referring aspects of stylistic patterning could create an independent level of the text, as in Jakobson's account of poetry. At the macroscopic level, structuralism and serialism provide a conception of spatial form which treats any discrete configuration as one paradigmatic possibility, and thus only a variant of a hidden order. There are, however, important differences between the two schools. Serialism is a means of composition, structuralism a method of analysis. For Lévi-Strauss, structuralism is to serialism as religion is to free thought.[24] Umberto Eco develops this point by suggesting that, as a musical practice, serial composition challenges the intertextual codes which are the chief objects of structural analysis.[25] Both schools emphasize the organization of signifiers, the spatialization of form, permutation, and nonperceptible structures, but serialism values transgression and the need for each artwork to construct a unique system. In other words, structuralist thought tends to emphasize the extrinsic norms that constrain syntagm and paradigm, while serialist thought emphasizes the creation of prominent intrinsic norms. It is significant that when self-consciously parametric films and a theory of parametric cinema emerged, both owed more to serialism and the *nouveau roman* than to structuralism.

Two films are landmarks in the cinema of parametric narration. *L'année dernière à Marienbad* (1961), the product of a collaboration between Robbe-Grillet and Alain Resnais, is virtually a *nouveau roman* on film. Each scene, while teasing the spectator with the possibility of causal and temporal relations with other scenes, remains finally significant as a variant of abstract narrative topoi (e.g., a man tries to persuade a woman to leave with him). In this respect, the film relies on what Stephen Heath calls Robbe-Grillet's characteristic *bricolage* of "syntagmatic elements of traditional narrative."[26] At the same time, *L'année dernière à Marienbad* elevates various stylistic features to the level of intermittently dominant structures: the splitting of image from sound, the use of false eyeline matches and matches on action, the refusal of camera movement to adhere to the action or to reveal a coherent offscreen space.[27] The film thus treats syuzhet and style as organizations of fixed elements, varied and circulated across the text, suggesting a coherent fabula world while again and again denying that any such entity can be constructed.

What *L'année dernière à Marienbad* was to the *nouveau roman*, *Méditerranée* (1963) was to the *Tel Quel* group. Few films can have been so seldom seen and so often cited. Like *Marienbad*, *Méditerranée* resulted from a collaboration,

here between poet and novelist Philippe Sollers and filmmaker Jean-Daniel Pollet. The film consists of 261 brief shots, musical passages, and a poetic commentary by Sollers. The visual track is based on a small set of elements: the sea, statuary, pyramids, ruins, an ingot forged in a factory, a garden, a bullfight, a woman on an operating table, and so forth. Most of the shots are clichés of "the Mediterranean," and it is part of the film's aim to recombine images in ways that drain them of their stereotyped associations. *Tel Quel* adherents praised the film as an "open" text, organized wholly as a play of signifiers, and Pollet has suggested that the film was composed by permuting a series.[28] *Méditerranée* thus operates with a thoroughly spatialized form, putting itself, according to Sollers, within a cinema of "*differed* presence": "literal but also partial presence, a presence which presents an absence and, here, a film which manifests *another*, invisible film of which the voice injected into the film records the fluctuations."[29]

Both *L'année dernière à Marienbad* and *Méditerranée* were made in full consciousness of the serialist aesthetic. It remained to show that this esthetic could be applied to films that had no direct influence from experimental literature or music. In 1967, Noël Burch published several articles in *Cahiers du cinéma* that were later collected in the volume *Praxis du cinéma* (1969; in English, *Theory of Film Practice*, first published in 1973). These writings constitute a powerful argument for a serialist theory of film.

Burch arranges film techniques into parameters, or stylistic procedures: the spatial-temporal manipulation of editing, the possiblities of framing and focus, and so forth. He constructs each parameter as a set of alternatives: sometimes as oppositions (soft focus/sharp focus, direct sound/mixed sound), sometimes as sets (the fifteen types of spatiotemporal matches, the six zones of offscreen space). He goes on to extend the concept of parameter to include narrative factors (subject matter, plot line, etc.). Burch then takes a crucial step. He posits that technical parameters are as functionally important to the film's overall form as are narrative ones. "Film is made first of all out of images and sounds; ideas intervene (perhaps) later."[30] Instead of simply manifesting the plot, the film's decoupage can become a system in its own right.

This is accomplished, Burch suggests, by a process of dialectical structure. Here "dialectics" refers to "the conflictual organization to which these elementary parameters have been subjected."[31] The poles of selected parameters are in effect paradigmatic alternatives. Burch thus expects both poles of the dialectic to be manifested in the film, just as Jakobson treats poetry as projecting paradigmatic equivalences onto the text's syntagmatic succession. The film's dialectic must also be justified by some systematic quality, by an overall structure possessing its own logic. Burch evidently has permutational principles in mind. The fifteen different ways of combining shots, for instance, are capable of "rigorous development through such devices as rhythmic alternation, recapitulation, retrogression, gradual elimination, cyclical repetition, and serial variation, thus creating structures similar to those of twelve-tone music."[32] Thus stylistic structure can become as thoroughly organized as narrative structure. "It is only through a systematic and thorough exploration of the *structural* possibilities inherent in the cinematic parameters I have been describing that film will be liberated from the old narrative forms and develop new 'open' forms that will have more in common with the formal strategies of post-Debussyan music than with those of the pre-Joycean novel."[33]

Burch's debt to serial thought is already evident in these quotations. In 1961, he had translated into English André Hodeir's *Since Debussy*, a book deeply infused with serial assumptions and a model, in its use of terms like "dialectics" and the "spatial organization of sound," for Burch's nomenclature. Boulez's *Penser la musique d'aujourd'hui* (1963) is another source for the exhaustive taxonomies and the polemical fervor of *Praxis du cinéma*. Both Hodeir and Boulez emphasize the way in which serial practice challenges established procedures, a point echoed constantly by Burch in his assault on "zero-degree filming." And Burch often uses serial music as a formal model, as when he suggests that the film's narrative can be generated out of technical parameters, just as the tone row generates large-scale

forms.[34] But he is careful not to push the analogy too far. A film cannot be organized as rigorously as a musical piece, for the former is not susceptible to mathematical schematization and is usually committed to concrete representation.[35] Musical practice offers a suggestive analogy, not a recipe.

The years immediately after the publication of Burch's volume reveal that he had some influence on the *Cahiers* group.[36] Oudart's theory of the "suture" and Bonitzer's 1972 essay on offscreen space can be interpreted as complex replies to Burch's work.[37] On the whole, though, the idea of a parametric cinema became of secondary importance in a film culture drawn to semiology, Lacanian psychoanalysis, and Althusserian Marxism. After May 1968, not only did these theoretical systems seem more politically pertinent; they also allowed critics to turn their attention to films which Burch frankly despised—the products of Hollywood classicism. Not until somewhat later did his work start to appear more significant. In America and Britain, the serial implications of Burch's theory had some impact.[38] Participants in a 1977 colloquium, "Cinemas of Modernity," used Burchian concepts to analyze films by Eisenstein and Robbe-Grillet.[39] And Burch's next major book, *To the Distant Observer: Form and Meaning in Japanese Film* (1979), aroused considerable interest—partly for its contribution to a stylistic history of the cinema, but also perhaps because its limitation to the conventional category of a national cinema and its eclectic Marxism made its argument seem less intransigently "formalist" than the ultimately more fruitful reflections of *Praxis du cinéma*. That very few film scholars have followed up Burch's insights (and those of Eisenstein and the Formalists, for that matter) is no reason to ignore them, especially if they can help us explain the specific workings of particular films.

This history of the concept of "parametric" narration sketches the outline of an aesthetic theory, but it cannot provide a rationale. In logical terms, it is difficult to deny that style could be promoted to the level of a shaping force in the film, but many critics will suggest that in practice this never happens. It remains to show that such objections fail and to suggest how style may achieve this role.

12.1. Lady Windermere's Fan
12.2. Lady Windermere's Fan

Shapes and Strategies

In general, a film's stylistic patterning splits away from the syuzhet when only "artistic" motivation can account for it. That is, if the viewer cannot adequately justify the stylistic work as necessary for some conception of realism, for transtextual ends such as genre, or for compositional requirements, then he or she must take style as present for its own sake, aiming to become palpable as such.

Let us take a set of comparisons involving one stylistic procedure, the "graphic match." This is inherently a nonnarrative device: lines, shapes, colors, movement, or other graphic qualities in one shot are closely "matched" by a similar configuration in the next shot, regardless of the space or time depicted. Consider first of all two contiguous shots from *Lady Windermere's Fan* (figs. 12.1–12.2). The overall similarity of composition is apparent—each figure is in the same spot, head and body are roughly comparable, light and dark values are somewhat consistent. In the classical narrative cinema, this "approximate" graphic match screens out irrelevant data and guides our attention to narratively salient differences from shot to shot, such as expressions and angle of character orientation. Next, consider the graphic matches during one of Diego's reveries in *La guerre est finie* (figs. 10.19–10.21). Here the graphic continuity is much stronger, and it is motivated for compositional ends typical of art-cinema narration. The matches convey the subjective alternatives that Diego posits: Nadine may look like this, or this, or that. . . . In comparison, there is the vivid graphic match of father and son arguing in *Earth* (figs. 7.26–7.27). Here again, the stylistic device is subordinate to syuzhet ends—thwarting the construction of a denotative space and cueing a connotative construction (the expression of fierce opposition). Finally, consider the graphic match of two schoolboys playing with a globe in Ozu's *What Did the Lady Forget?* (figs. 12.3–12.4). The similarities of composition across the cut create a much more precise graphic match than in *Lady Windermere's Fan*. And these cuts are not explicable on art-cinema or historical-materialist grounds, unless one contends that the cuts present a narra-

tional commentary that the boys are somehow "alike." But this justification would be unspecific (it could apply to any of the graphic matches we have considered) and banal (I shall suggest shortly why parametric narration drives critics to banality): in a word, desperate. The most adequate motiva-

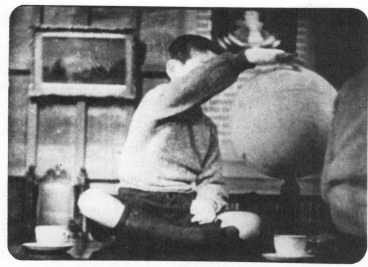

flourish—a gratuitous camera movement, an unexpected and unjustified color shift or sound bridge. In the visual arts, the flourish is an embellishment, expressing what E. H. Gombrich describes as "the joyful exuberance of a craftsman who displayed both his control and his inventiveness."[40] The flourish exhibits aesthetic motivation because it makes the artwork's materials and forms perceptually salient. Ozu's graphic match, however, is not a flourish; the device recurs frequently and systematically. (Here is another reason for resisting the banal interpretation that these boys are "alike," for to apply this principle to all of Ozu's graphic matches would lead merely to vacuity.) In parametric narration, style is organized *across the film* according to distinct principles, just as a narrative poem exhibits prosodic patterning or an operatic scene fulfills a musical logic. Godard's *Vivre sa vie* will illustrate this process.

Vivre sa vie announces itself as "a film in twelve episodes." Each episode includes one or more scenes and is bracketed off by fades and numbered intertitles. At the level of visual style, each segment is characterized by one or more variants on possible camera/subject relations. In the credits sequence, Nana is presented in three close-up views: one of her left profile, one frontal shot, and one of her right profile. This announces the "theme" of varying camera/figure orientations. In the first episode, the camera presents Nana talking with her husband; both are framed from the rear. This completes the circuit around her begun during the credits and emphasizes that in the film's narrative, Nana's spatial relations with her surroundings will function as material for the stylistic variants. Later sequences explore a range of alternatives. Two characters in dialogue will be filmed by a camera right on the 180-degree line between them (Episodes 4 and 5). There are various options with respect to camera movement as well: a laterally tracking camera (Episode 2), a forward tracking camera (6), a simple pan shot (12). There are variants upon an arcing camera movement, one in which the conversing figures are arranged perpendicular to the lens axis (Episode 3), another in which they sit parallel to it (Episode 7). Episode 8 is a montage sequence highly fragmented by editing, while Epi-

tion for Ozu's cut is a purely aesthetic one. Incongruity and humor arise from the palpable manipulation of the stylistic parameters of composition and cutting. Syuzhet needs are subordinated to the play of graphic space.

Now, any film might contain an aesthetically motivated

sode 9 consists of very long takes. The only moments in which a conversation is handled in classical shot/reverse shot come within a "quoted" passage—the excerpt from Dreyer's *La Passion de Jeanne d'Arc* in Episode 3—and within the penultimate episode, during the conversation with Brice Parain. "Quoting" and postponing the most orthodox stylistic option throw the other alternatives into higher relief. Stylistically, the film moves through a paradigm of alternatives to orthodox shot/reverse shot, forming a clear instance of what Jakobson calls the projection of the axis of selection into the axis of combination.[41]

A skeptic cannot, I think, deny that the stylistic organization of the film exhibits these features. The problem is what to do with them. Someone might claim that they are just ornamentation. But this would be like saying that rhythm and rhyme merely embellish a poem. The exhaustive way in which these stylistic alternatives are presented in the film would militate against their being simply filler material. V. F. Perkins writes of the film as "a series of dialogues on which Godard's camera plays a suite of variations, offering both an actual *mise en scène* and a string of suggestions as to how one *might* film a conversation."[42] Against the background of classical narration, *Vivre sa vie*'s stylistic devices achieve a structural prominence that is more than simply ornamental.

Granted that these stylistic patterns are present and important, the critic is tempted to "read" them, to assign them thematic meanings. My skeptic might posit that *Vivre sa vie* is about the problem of communication, and therefore the stylistic devices can be taken as symbolizing the distance between people. Or—to take a currently fashionable interpretive line—perhaps *Vivre sa vie* is actually "about cinema." On this account, the filmmaker's ambivalent relation to his medium is represented through a varied camera handling. Such interpretive moves seek to insert parametric narration into the art-cinema mode. Yet although films like *Vivre sa vie* are made and seen within the art-cinema *institution*, it does not follow that they answer to the sort of symbolic *readings* we have seen art-cinema narration solicit.

The urge to read stylistic effects in this way must also be traced to a broader tendency, that of assuming that everything in any film (or any good film) must be interpretable

thematically. Thematization of this sort typically loses the specificity of a film's narrational work. Every stylistic element gets read the same way: long shots unite characters, cuts divide them; vertical lines isolate or split a character, horizontal lines evoke freedom; point-of-view shots create power relations by making one character the "object" of another's look. In this game, though, every card is wild. Whenever Nana is in the same shot with the pimp Raoul, the interpreter can posit a "unity" between them. If you point out that Raoul will exploit her and eventually let her be killed, then the critic claims that Godard is being ironic in positing such a unity. If Nana and her lover look at each other, and if this is rendered in alternating optical point-of-view shots, then the critic can say that Nana remains feminized (object of the male look) or not (appropriation of the power to look). If we are prepared to equate camera and director, every film can be interpreted as "making a statement" about cinema.

Interpretation of this sort is wholly appropriate to such narrative forms as allegory, in which abstract, often doctrinal meanings constitute the dominant structuring force of the text. In other forms, however, thematic meaning is only one component in the system, and not necessarily a very important one. The critic who thematizes technique in every film risks banalizing works which take as their "dominant" the perceptual force of style. For the problem is not just that thematization tends to rely on the clichés of sophomore literary criticism. Even at its best, thematization aims to assimilate the particular to the most general, the concrete to the woolly. It is perhaps for this reason that parametric filmmakers have tended to employ strikingly obvious themes. Not much acumen is needed to identify *Play Time* as treating the impersonality of modern life, *Tokyo Story* as examining the decline of the "inherently" Japanese family, or *Vivre sa vie* as dealing with contemporary urban alienation and female desire. It is as if stylistic organization becomes prominent only if the themes are so banal as to leave criticism little to interpret.

Possessed of a *horror vacui*, the interpretive critic clings to theme in order to avoid falling into the abyss of "arbitrary" style and structure. The critic assumes that everything in the film should contribute to meaning. If style is not decoration, it must be motivated compositionally or realistically or, best of all, as narrational commentary. Yet the error lies in assuming that style and syuzhet have a fixed relation to one another. It is important to recall that in any film, syuzhet structure—the selection and organization of story events—does not unequivocally determine a single stylistic presentation. (See p. 50.) There is always a degree of arbitrariness, which parametric cinema exploits. In the first episode of *Vivre sa vie*, Nana's conversation with Paul could be staged, shot, and cut in many ways and still convey the fabula information about their separation. As Perkins puts it: "Scenes whose action is static are filmed with a mobile camera, but the precise nature of the camera's movements is so far irrelevant to the recorded settings, faces, movements, and gestures that the various treatments could be interchanged from scene to scene without affecting our knowledge or understanding of the action in any substantial way."[43] If a film's stylistic devices achieve prominence, and if they are organized according to more or less rigorous principles, independent of syuzhet needs, then we need not motivate style by appealing to thematic considerations.

Is such narration a widespread filmmaking strategy? No, but significant filmmakers have employed it, especially those not aligned with national schools or movements. Some, such as Ozu and Bresson, seem to have done so intuitively; others have been more theoretically self-conscious, as we have seen in French cinema of the 1960s. Godard, for example, could not have been unaware of combinatory theories of serial music and the *nouveau roman* when he made *Vivre sa vie*. And what of the spectator? Do parametric principles constitute a widespread viewing norm? Certainly not as such. I shall suggest later, however, that parametric narration does tend to produce effects that many spectators register. Furthermore, as Perkins's remarks on *Vivre sa vie* suggest, viewers who are sensitive to style can notice such patterns. Of course, many viewers do not have such a sensitivity. Just as serial music may require training, practice, and some theoretical knowledge to become intelligible, so too may parametric narration. Burch puts it corrosively: "And why shouldn't the eye exercise itself? Why should filmmakers not address themselves to an elite, just as composers have always done at different periods? We define 'elite' as those people willing to take the trouble to see and resee films (many films), as one must listen and relisten to a lot of music in order to appreciate the last quartets of Beethoven or the work of Webern."[44]

I can imagine one more objection to the concept of parametric narration. Can the play of style in such narration possess the perceptual and cognitive coherence that the syuzhet patterning does? The spectator unifies the syuzhet system causally, temporally, and spatially. Its units are events. We can identify intersubjective assumptions, hypotheses, and inferences with respect to it. If the syuzhet system omits a story event, we can make more or less sound guesses about it. But what does stylistic patterning offer us? It cannot have causal unity, and it must achieve an "immanent" organization of cinematic space and time. It seems to have no clearly designated units, perhaps only the notion of the "stylistic figure." And how could a spectator create a purely stylistic hypothesis or inference, or know that a stylistic element has been omitted, or that a stylistic development is taking place? If a stylistic pattern is not dependent on the syuzhet, it would seem at best highly unpredictable and at worst simply random, never salient. Could the spectator ever perceive the stylistic structures of parametric narration?

This is a very strong objection. A counterargument could start with Gombrich's suggestion that there is a difference between the perception of *meaning*, which he links to representational art, and the perception of *order*, which he associates with decorative and abstract art.[45] Normally, the activities are not easily distinguished, since our perception of order is shot through with assumptions and expectations about meaning. But in art, representational meaning may be played down or withheld, and sheer perceptual order may become strongly profiled. This happens in abstract painting, which either expels denotative meaning or overwhelms it by pure design. One can see a table and a guitar in a Cubist still life, but their identifiable meaning is secondary to the spatial organization of the whole. Much the same thing occurs through the organization of cinematic space and time in parametric cinema.

Can this order be empirically perceived? We know that

this problem has haunted discussions of integral serialism in music. Many composers and theorists, anxious to permute every sonic parameter, recognized that the new music was so complex that the generating series and its transformations might never be grasped in performance.[46] The "spatial" structuring was evident on paper but not necessarily in performance. The result, as Nicolas Ruwet suggested in 1959, is often a perceived *simplicity*, as if the intricate manipulation of pitch, duration, timbre, dynamics, and touch yielded only a music of brute instants.[47] A sharp theoretical challenge has been laid down by Leonard Meyer, who has sought to show that the form of serial music tends to be imperceptible on four grounds.[48]

1. All communication requires redundancy, but serial music is insufficiently redundant. The total ordering of all parameters makes the basic formal pattern difficult to perceive. Serial music also relies upon subtle shades of difference among various parameters, but when no parameters are held constant, such differences cannot be spotted.

2. Because serial music rejects traditional forms, we have no schemata as aids to memory or guides for anticipation. When every piece is unique, no one can grasp any of them.

3. Some tonal combinations are more easily perceived and recalled than others; specifically, pitch and duration seem more "basic" than timbre and attack. But serial music ignores natural patterns of comprehension.

4. Attention is a matter of allocating perceptual-cognitive resources. The perceiver thus has a limited "channel capacity." By packing so much novelty into a piece, the serial composer creates an overload that prevents more and less relevant events from being distinguished. Meyer is not saying that ordinary listeners typically cannot follow serial music. He is proposing that total serialist works may be formally imperceptible to all listeners. "Even if . . . a coterie of aficionados devoted their full perceptual capacities to this music, it is doubtful that they would ultimately succeed in really learning to *understand* it aurally."[49]

It is possible to agree with Meyer and hold that a wholly parametric use of film style is not perceivable in viewing. Noël Burch writes: "A structure exists when a parameter evolves according to some principle of progression that is apparent to the viewer in the theater, or perhaps only to the film-maker at his editing table, for, even though there may be structures that are 'perceptible only to those who have created them,' they nonetheless play an important role in the final aesthetic result."[50] This sounds much like Boulez's claim that even if the ear does not perceive serial structures, it "registers" them.[51] The locus classicus of this sort of defense has been Berg's opera *Wozzeck*, which unifies its score by an intrinsically musical logic: each act consists of pieces in different forms; each piece's tempo evolves from that of the preceding passage; each act ends with a cadence to the same chord; and so on.[52] Yet Berg insisted that his particular achievement was the music's "invisibility":

> No one in the audience, no matter how aware he may be of the musical forms contained in the framework of the opera, of the precision and logic with which it has been worked out, no one, from the moment the curtain parts until it closes for the last time, pays any attention to the various fugues, inventions, suites, sonata movements, variations, and passacaglias about which so much has been written.[53]

Later I shall suggest that "unseen" structures can play some broader role in our response to a film. In general, however, an appeal to objectively present but imperceptible structures does not offer a strong explanation of parametric practices. After all, many structures in an artwork go unnoticed but also remain irrelevant to the work's aesthetic effect. Michael Riffaterre, in a devastating critique of Roman Jakobson's poetic analyses, has shown that not every pattern in a work is aesthetically functional or perceptually salient.[54] A better line of defense is to argue that the most clear-cut cases of parametric narration can definitely be perceived in viewing.

In a parametric film, stylistic events can be noticed, their relation to the syuzhet can be hypothesized, aspects of their patterning can be noted and recalled. Parametric narration meets all four of Meyer's criteria:

1. *Sufficient redundancy.* Parametric cinema is not totally serial, since typically only a few parameters are highlighted and varied across the film. *Vivre sa vie*, for instance,

operates with distinct camera positions and editing options. Moreover, the syuzhet often provides a constant basis for stylistic change.

2. *Prior schemata.* Parametric narration does not as a whole reject schemata as sources of order and expectation. The syuzhet will often be comprehensible according to the norms of classical narration or art-cinema narration. (There is in fact a predilection for quite predictable plot patterns.) Stylistically, the film will have a strong inner unity: a prominent intrinsic norm and patterned reiterations of that. Moreover, the style can be seen as "preformed" to a great degree, especially across a body of work. Ozu, Bresson, and other directors possess virtually preexistent stylistic systems which can reduce almost any subject to their own terms.

3. *Recognition of "natural" predispositions.* Burch has pointed out that certain parameters seem more basic than others: image/sound relations, onscreen/offscreen space, editing alternatives. Whether these are more "natural" or not, it is likely that these are the most obvious targets of attention.

4. *Recognition of limited "channel capacity."* Since cinema normally programs the order and duration of viewing, questions of redundancy and allocation of cognitive resources become pertinent. Parametric cinema is not totally serial, so the viewer's capacities are not necessarily taxed by an overwhelming range of stylistic elements. There is also, as we shall see, a tendency for this mode to work with simply additive forms. But there is no hiding that some parametric film do create "overload"; Tati's *Play Time* is a famous case.[55] And even with more ascetic films, such as those of Bresson and Dreyer, the overall organization of parameters may well exceed detailed comprehension. At the close of this section I shall try to show that particular connotative effects may follow from the spectator's limited ability to construct intelligible patterns of style. Parametric cinema is thus, theoretically at least, perceptible in Meyer's terms. As we consider this mode's principles of organization, we must concentrate upon those that yield precise and intersubjective aesthetic effects.

In order for style to come forward across the whole film, it must possess internal coherence. This coherence depends on establishing a distinctive, often unique intrinsic stylistic norm. We can distinguish two broad strategies. One is the "ascetic" or "sparse" option, in which the film limits its norm to a narrower range of procedures than are codified in other extrinsic norms. The Mizoguchi of the mid- and later 1930s selects the long take in long shot or medium long shot; Bresson confines himself to the straight-on medium shot, often of body parts; Tati utilizes long shots with decentered framing in deep space; and so on. Announced at the film's outset, such a limitation of devices constitutes a powerful intrinsic norm which "processes" each syuzhet event according to a recognizably "preformed" style.

By contrast, a more "replete" intrinsic norm creates an inventory or a range of paradigmatic options. We have already seen that *Vivre sa vie* brings many disparate stylistic procedures to bear on the problem of representing character encounters. Burch has found the same to hold true in Lang's *M*, in which each sequence plays a variant upon spatial and temporal discontinuity.[56] Typically, the ascetic option presents a material similarity of procedures across differentiated syuzhet passages; the replete option creates parallels among distinct portions of the syuzhet and varies the material procedures used to present them. The strongly articulated sequences in *Vivre sa vie* and *M* permit a clear comparison of different paradigmatic options at the level of style. Redundancy is achieved either by limiting the range of stylistic procedures or by strictly paralleling segments of the syuzhet.

Establishing a distinctive intrinsic norm, either sparse or replete, may create deviations within the film. The replete approach is constantly foregrounding stylistic events in that each discrete stylistic event will tend to instantiate a deviant procedure. More complex cases are Dreyer's *Ordet* and *Gertrud*. Each film takes a "sparse" approach by restricting itself to slow lateral camera and figure movements and long takes; but each also sparingly cites isolated devices more characteristic of classical style (shot/reverse shot, eyeline matches, analytical cutting). Thus Dreyer's foregrounded moments achieve a kind of "repleteness," sampling—but only in passing—a wider paradigmatic range than the film draws on generally.[57] More often, the ascetic tendency in paradigmatic narration tends to conform closely to its intrinsic stylistic norm. This is achieved by creating a narrow and strongly individual bunch of parametric qualities and then repeating them regularly across the film. In particular, the ascetic mode plays upon what psychologists call "just-noticeable differences." Given a stringently limited range of procedures, the sparse approach can create a barely perceptible threshold between identical repetition and slight variation. In the films of Ozu, for instance, a return to a familiar locale will be treated in a slightly rearranged sequence of views or with small changes of objects. How noticeable the differences are will vary. I shall suggest shortly that they cannot be minute, since spectators cannot spot or recall very slight changes; but it is one aim of the sparse approach to explore the boundary between what is and is not recognizable.

Once the intrinsic stylistic norm is in place, it must be developed. Style must create its own temporal logic. But because the viewer's schemata for film style are limited, it is unrealistic to expect parametric form to exhibit detailed intricacies. As in serial music, the more convoluted and the less redundant such form is, the more imperceptible it is likely to be. Consequently, parameters cannot all be varied simultaneously. Several must be held constant if repetition and variation are to be apparent. Moreover, the spectator is less likely to observe an isolated parameter than the stylistic "event," a recurrent local texture created by a cluster of devices. In *Vivre sa vie*, it is the combination of several factors—characters in spatial proximity, varied camera positions, and the editing patterns (or lack of them)—that creates the stylistic event that the narration permutes. Ozu's style achieves prominence through a similar effect of the interaction among figure position, frame composition, camera placement, use of offscreen space, and so on; the typical Ozu "moment" is a node of such parameters. This is not to say that each event will repeat every parameter, or that parameters cannot move off and recombine elsewhere in the film—only that if parametric play is to be perceived as ordered, it will be grasped in relation to some recurrent factors.

Despite Burch's call for "rhythmic alternation, recapitulation, retrogression, gradual elimination, cyclical repetition, and serial variation," parametric form must develop simply. The most adequate musical models are additive forms such as strophic patterns, the rondo, and theme and variations. Here parts are related not by a hierarchical process but by structural parallelism and/or similarity of device. In parametric narration the syuzhet may well possess a cumulative overall shape, often of great structural symmetry, but the stylistic patterning tends to be additive and open-ended, with no predictable point of termination. *Vivre sa vie*'s survey of paradigmatic options betrays no evolving logic, while the succession of slightly varied procedures in Dreyer or Ozu is completely "reversible." As in the musical rondo or the theme and variations, the number of stylistic events can be indefinitely large, and there is room for many unexpected repetitions and differences.

In the replete approach, additive development displays a tendency toward permutational exhaustion of options within a paradigm. This we saw in *Vivre sa vie*'s variants on "how to shoot and cut character interaction." Burch has been astute in finding films possessing paradigmatic principles; among his examples are *Une simple histoire, Cronaca di un Amore*, and Renoir's *Nana* ("a model of the exhaustive use of offscreen space").[58] The sparse approach, as I have mentioned, uses additive form to create "just-noticeable differences." Kristin Thompson has revealed this process at work in *Play Time* and in Bresson's *Lancelot du Lac*.[59] To take another instance: One does not think of Fassbinder as an ascetic filmmaker, yet his *Katzelmacher* (1969) exemplifies how the sparse approach can produce slight variations. By reducing the number and types of setting, the angle of view (perpendicular, with few depth cues), the number of shots (one per scene), character movements (typically a tableau), shot transitions (the cut only), and camera movements (none, except as noted below), *Katzelmacher* creates a sparse intrinsic norm. An ambiguous durational scheme also encourages us to arrange the scenes in "columnar" rather than linear fashion. The narration develops as a combinatory scheme: same locale, different characters; different locale, same characters; same locale, with or without figure movement. One shot, which includes nondiegetic music and camera movement, at first works as a deviation from the film's intrinsic norm, exemplifying Burch's suggestion that a dialectical structure can operate by "emphasizing one of the two poles of a parameter by using it rarely or perhaps only once."[60] As the film goes on, however, this stylistic event is also repeated, each time with different characters, thus entering into the overall variation structure. As in the films of Dreyer, Ozu, Bresson, and Mizoguchi, *Katzelmacher*'s additive form invites us to notice nuance.

In this mode, the spectator's task becomes one of recognizing stylistic repetition and staying alert for more or less distinct variations. We may speak of suspense hypotheses (how will this scene be handled?) and a "scanning" strategy that compares one stylistic event with preceding ones, giving the earlier one the status of "statement." For instance, in *Ordet* and *Gertrud*, the lateral tracking shots following characters build up purely spatiotemporal expectations. When and where will the character pause? Will another character enter the shot? Mizoguchi uses long takes to generate hypotheses about whether a character will fill a vacant portion of the frame. Ozu achieves a more playful rotation of hypotheses by juggling shot combinations in unpredictable ways. In *An Autumn Afternoon*, the first transition to Tory's Bar employs three shots: medium shot of a row of bar signs, none of which is Tory's (so will we now move inside one?); then a long shot of the street (so will a scene take place on the street?); then a medium shot of Tory's sign (so will the action take place inside?). The next transition to this locale begins in more orthodox fashion, with a shot of Tory's sign. This should suffice to signal any future scenes in Tory's. Yet the next scene at the bar begins with a long shot of the bar signs across the street; there follows a cut to a long shot (comparable to shot 2 in the first series) as our protagonist, Hirayama, staggers down the street and into the bar; cut inside as he arrives. The narration spreads the three shots of the first set out in different order, across two other transitions. This cues the spectator to notice the variants. Moreover, of the two earlier scenes in Tory's Bar, one had ended with a cut back to

the sign, and one had not. A cut to the sign in this last variant is thus not clearly likely. And yet when Ozu does cut to the sign at the end of the third scene, this shot is revealed to complete the theme-and-variations pattern, since this shot is the one "missing" from the most recent variant! Such playful, constantly self-correcting shot combinations are among the most salient aspects of Ozu's parametric narration.

Additive stylistic structures do not have a strong directional quality, but the syuzhet does. Even if style becomes the "dominant," in Tynianov's sense, the syuzhet system operates partly to throw repeated and varied stylistic shapes into relief. Like the guitar in a Cubist still life, the syuzhet episode—a character conversation in *Vivre sa vie*, a visit to a bar in *An Autumn Afternoon*—becomes a reference point for stylistic departures, a stable support for a freer pattern making.

Parametric narration can make syuzhet and style interact in three ways. Style may completely and constantly dominate the syuzhet. This occurs rarely, but *Wavelength* (1967) affords a clear example. A plot (the events of a routine day and a mysterious murder) is wholly subordinated to the internal progression of cinematographic parameters (lens length, light, color). Or style may be seen as equal in importance to the syuzhet. Burch has suggested the possibility of "cellular" form analogous to that in serial music, whereby a single structure dictates both local texture and large-scale form. This might seem to resemble the "generative" poetics of narration associated with the later films of Robbe-Grillet. As Robbe-Grillet explains: "*L'Eden et après* (1970) is doubtless the only fiction film—or in any case the first one—where the story itself is produced by the organization of themes into successive series according to a system that is somewhat comparable to that of Schoenberg in music."[61] But in Robbe-Grillet's films these themes are only motifs, such as objects or colors, or abstractions, such as "opposition." The themes give rise to syuzhet patterning, but as Roy Armes points out, they determine nothing about *stylistic* configurations.[62] A more truly generative account of parametric narration is Burch's description of *Play Time* as possessing a "cell"—a dialectic between gags centered in the shot and gags in a "bad" position—which generates the overall structure of the film's sequences as well.[63] Kristin Thompson's analysis of *Ivan the Terrible* shows how a basic opposition controls both the syuzhet structure and the stylistic patterning.[64] In her work on *Les vacances de M. Hulot*, Thompson demonstrates that a very Robbe-Grilletian variation among sequences (the various routines of a vacation week) proceeds from the same "cell" as do the manipulations of film technique.[65]

Even if syuzhet and style do not issue from a single donnée, they can function as equals. In Dreyer's *Ordet*, repeated camera movements across a parlor create a systematic scanning independent of local narrative needs; the camera will track only with characters "going its way," able to assist its achievement of a global, nonnarrative pattern. Late in the film, when a group of mourners has assembled in the parlor, the camera punctiliously surveys the space, tracking right and then back left with a striking lack of economy. Stylistically, this is another variant on the to-and-fro movements of earlier scenes. Yet in its summative quality the shot signals the exhaustion of this locale (we will not see it again) and prepares not only for a shift in style but for narrative closure.[66] Style indubitably comes forward, but it functions to mark both its own functioning and syuzhet patterns. In what Burch calls "a fully composite work," stylistic structures "retain their autonomous, 'abstract' function, but in symbiosis with the plot which they both support and challenge."[67]

In most parametrically narrated films, syuzhet and fabula shift in importance. This is not surprising. An analogous situation occurs in opera: The story action needs to continue, but the music needs to repeat. Hence the levels alternate in significance. In parametric narration, style will sometimes accompany the syuzhet, reinforcing it. For example, Nana's conversation with Brice Parain in *Vivre sa vie* is handled in conventional shot/reverse-shot fashion, which makes syuzhet construction dominant. At other times, parametric narration will subordinate the syuzhet to stylistic structures, as in the back-to-the-camera sequence of *Vivre sa vie*. When this occurs, the constant potential tension between style and syuzhet can manifest itself—as it does often in *Vivre sa vie*,

whose "gratuitous" survey of paradigmatic options frustrates our fabula-constructing activity. Burch describes this alternating process as "a dialectical rhythm that sometimes joins and sometimes separates what used to be called form and content."[68]

Note, however, that even when the syuzhet comes forward, it tends to do so on the style's own terms. Once the intrinsic stylistic norm has established itself, the syuzhet is grasped and the fabula constructed within the constraints of that norm. For instance, after *Katzelmacher*'s combinatory patterning becomes apparent as a stylistic principle, we can take it for granted, and the syuzhet becomes easier to assimilate. And even the relative downplaying of style in *Vivre sa vie*'s scene with Brice Parain is achieved within the framework of a string of codified alternatives.

The parametric syuzhet will thus tend to be recognizable by its deformities. One symptom is an abnormal ellipticality. Causes and effects may be disjoined, major scenes may be omitted, duration may be skipped over. *M* is one example, but *Katzelmacher* and *Vivre sa vie* are better ones. Each has an episodic construction that yields only glimpses of character psychology and presents unmarked excerpts from an indeterminate fabula duration. A contrary symptom is an abnormal repetiveness, such as that in Dreyer's *Ordet* and *Gertrud*. Here the syuzhet is telling us too little too often, flattening big scenes and trivial gestures to the same level. Some filmmakers are notable for using both tactics. The films of Ozu and Bresson manage to be both elliptical (omitting big scenes, halting a scene before its climax, suddenly switching locale, not marking duration) and repetitious (reiterating trivial linking actions in Bresson, locales in Ozu). Both severe ellipticality and repetition indicate that the constraints of stylistic patterning are imposing their will on the syuzhet, or at least that the narration limits itself to presenting events that display the style to best advantage.

To sum up: Parametric narration establishes a distinctive intrinsic norm, often involving an unusually limited range of stylistic options. It develops this norm in additive fashion. Style thus enters into shifting relations, dominant or subordinate, with the syuzhet. The spectator is cued to construct a prominent stylistic norm, recognizing style as motivated neither realistically nor compositionally nor transtextually. The viewer must also form assumptions and hypotheses about the stylistic development of the film.

The strategy of treating the stylistic pattern as a rigorous but additive set of differences laid over the syuzhet does challenge our normal processes of perceiving a film narrative. In particular, it thwarts the chief method of managing viewing time—constructing a linear fabula. (The parametric film battles against time, carrying to an extreme the tendency toward "spatialization" which we observed in historical-materialist narration. This is very evident in *Katzelmacher* and in Ozu's films, in which stylistic repetition encourages the viewer to "stack" scenes by technique, in opposition to the horizontal unrolling of the action. This mode strains so vigorously against habitual capacities that it risks boring or baffling the spectator. *Vivre sa vie* or *Katzelmacher* can be treated as art films by critics who neglect the workings of style. Because of the complex and inherently open nature of stylistic construction in such films, a viewer may move quickly to connotative interpretation and miss the parametric play.

Here we can locate the more general effects of a mode whose structures may be invisible but still "registered" in the sense remarked by Burch and Boulez. It is significant that the most celebrated exponents of the sparse parametric strategy—Dreyer, Ozu, Mizoguchi, and Bresson—are often seen as creating mysterious and mystical films. It is as if a self-sustaining style evokes, on its edges, elusive phantoms of connotation, as the viewer tries out one signification after another on the impassive structure. The recognition of order triggers a search for meaning. Noncinematic schemata, often religious ones, may thus be brought in to motivate the workings of style. It is possible to recuperate these films in art-cinema terms, invoking subjectivity or authorial commentary to explain isolated stylistic events. But one reason to hold onto the possibility of parametric narration is that it points up the limits upon the art film's extrinsic norms—limits, we have seen, of insipidity and banality—and lets us acknowledge a richness of texture that resists interpretation.

The Parameters of *Pickpocket*

Michel takes up a life of theft, while his friends Jacques and Jeanne and a police inspector try to dissuade him. Close to being captured, he flees Paris and returns two years later. Jeanne now has a child and has been abandoned by Jacques, the father. Michel offers to take care of them. He gets a job and gives Jeanne money. Tempted to return to picking pockets, he succumbs and is arrested. Jeanne visits him in prison, where they declare their love for one another.

Such an emaciated outline of *Pickpocket's* story cannot suggest the rich play of syuzhet and style in the narrational activity of the film. This process gets set in motion from the film's first frame. There is initially a prologue, a crawl title on a black ground while a Lully piece swells up on the sound track.

> The style of this film is not that of a thriller.
> The author attempts to explain, in pictures and sounds, the nightmare of a young man, forced by his weakness into an adventure in theft for which he was not made.
> Yet this adventure, by strange paths, brings together two souls who otherwise might never have known one another.

And within this extradiegetic frame there is a recounting in the story world. After the credits, a hand writes in a notebook while a voice (later to be identified as Michel's) recites the text. The first entry follows the prologue.

> I know that normally those who have done these things keep quiet, while those who talk have not done them.
> And yet I have done them.

We could not ask for a more blatant signal of the difference between syuzhet and style: Michel's hand and voice telling the things he has done, an omniscient authorial voice announcing that these events will be "explained" in images and sounds. There is much to be said about this double-barreled opening, but let us first consider the syuzhet's relation to the fabula in the film as a whole.

There are two lines of story action: the relation of Michel to his mother and to his friends Jacques and Jeanne; and Michel's pickpocket career. In syuzhet presentation, these two lines are initially linked by the actions of various characters. Jacques tries to find Michel a job so that he won't steal, while the inspector steps into Michel's life, apparently to warn him off. But not until the inspector visits Michel does the fundamental causal connection emerge. The inspector announces that a year previously Michel's mother had reported a robbery and then sent Jeanne to withdraw the complaint. Thus the police have suspected Michel of being a thief all along, and his personal life has been bound up with the investigation from the start. The Russian Formalists would here point out that the protagonist, far from being a creature with great psychological depth, is constructed as the point of intersection of two lines of material, becoming the splice between domesticity and petty crime.[69] This conclusion gains some weight when, in the next scene, Michel comes as close as he ever does to naming the cause of his actions. "I couldn't achieve anything," he says. "It drove me mad." If this is the weakness mentioned in the film's prologue, it is explained in fairly perfunctory fashion. What did he try to achieve? And why theft rather than other acts? The film does not posit psychological ambiguity, as in art-cinema narration, but opacity.

The syuzhet also brings out certain temporal patterns. Here is an outline of the fabula.

A. Michel's mother reports the robbery to police.

B. A month later: Michel robs the woman at the racetrack.

C. Over the next eleven months: Michel meets Jeanne, his mother dies, and he becomes a professional thief. He flees to England.

D. Over the next two years, Michel stays in England.

E. He returns to Paris.

F. Over one or two weeks: He works to support Jeanne and her child. He is arrested at the racetrack.

G. Over several weeks: He is in prison.

The syuzhet manipulates our construction of this fabula by starting (like Michel's written account) in medias res,

with (B), the racetrack robbery. The first three-fifths of the film are concerned with the eleven-month series of events in (C). Near the end of this section, Michel learns of event A, his mother's report to the police, and it is only then recounted to us. The syuzhet goes on to render the sojourn in England (D) by a single laconic journal entry, thus letting two years elude dramatization. The rest of the film dramatizes events in (E), (F), and (G). There are, however, equivocations. Within the fabula world, it is hard to tell how much time elapses, chiefly because the seasons seem constant and Michel wears an unvarying costume. In *La guerre est finie*, Diego wears the same suit throughout the film, but there costuming functions as a cue for a short syuzhet duration. Here the same device renders fabula and syuzhet duration vague.

The syuzhet goes further in marking its manipulation of the fabula. Story events are buckled into loops. The first scene shows Michel stealing at Longchamps racetrack; three years later he is caught in the same locale. After his capture, a series of scenes in prison, itself symmetrically constructed, forms a pendant to the main syuzhet action. Retardation is also flagrantly present. As Roy Armes has pointed out, "The whole film is ultimately a vast *temps mort*, a detour that takes in exile and imprisonment for [Michel] and abandonment and an illegitimate pregnancy for Jeanne, only to bring the two of them back to a love they could have enjoyed to begin with."[70] From this standpoint, Jacques, the inspector, and the entire adventure in crime constitute an extensive series of realistically motivated delays in the consummation of the couple's relations. When the inspector objects to Michel's belief in superior thieves on the grounds that these men would not stop stealing, his remark prophesies Michel's persistence in folly and at the same time justifies the inclusion of more robbery scenes. Indeed, the acts of theft are remarkably "dysfunctional," concentrating upon Michel's progress toward self-sufficient virtuosity, with no concomitant effects on his attitudes. Similarly, the encounters which Michel has with Jacques and Jeanne are highly repetitious and contribute little to any linear development. The retardation is laid bare in the prologue, with its warning that "strange paths" will eventually unite two souls. This is quite analogous to Shklovsky's example of *Tristram Shandy*, in which the narrator graphs the book's digressive syuzhet as a knot of squiggles and whorls.[71]

In most respects, the syuzhet reflects the constraints of Michel's written text. We are confined almost completely to his range of knowledge at the moment when the story events occurred. Indeed, the diegetic recounting in the notebook does not as rule fill in prior information or anticipate events. And the device of the written record enables Michel to explain his feelings and thoughts. In thirty-six of the forty-nine sequences, his voice will interject a report of his mental state. There is thus some "subjective" depth on the sound track to compensate for the notable impassivity of face and demeanor. Ellipses are also subjectively motivated by the recounting. When Michel goes abroad, his notebook summarizes the hiatus with two sentences, and we never see him in England. On either side of this gap there is also a revealing asymmetry. He rides to the station in a cab, tensely expecting pursuit and arrest. Upon his return, however, we dissolve from the railroad station to him climbing a flight of stairs. Why no shot of him driving from the station to the apartment? "I was there again," the commentary explains, "without knowing how."

In a classical film, technique would faithfully reflect the syuzhet's degree of communicativeness and its limited range and depth of knowledge. But this film's prologue announces the overt presence of an omniscient narration which will operate through style. The crawl title ("The style of this film is not that of a thriller . . ." and so on) is highly self-conscious, emphasizing the spectator as someone in a theater to whom pictures and sounds can be explicitly addressed by an "author." Here is a case where the narrational process mimics a communication from sender to receiver. (See p. 62.) It is significant that the credit sequence follows the prologue, as if identifying Bresson the filmmaker with the self-nominated source of images and sounds. Furthermore, the prologue claims absolute knowledge of distant origins (Michel "was not made" for theft), immediate causes (he has a "weakness"), psychological reactions, vari-

ous events along the way, and the eventual outcome. The narration also proposes particular schemata to try on the film. We are to watch for theft, for the motivation for actions, and for digressive developments that will eventually unite two characters. This prologue is also more communicative than its Hollywood counterpart, but it remains tantalizingly obscure on certain points. What are the "strange paths"? Is Michel one of the two souls? Who is the other? Certain explanations will be kept vague, such as the exact weakness that led Michel into thievery. By such gaps and equivocations, the narration maintains an overt uncommunicativeness that provokes our curiosity about how the predicted events will occur.

From the start, Michel's diegetic writing and voice-over commentary are at the mercy of the extradiegetic voice. The master of "pictures and sounds" chooses to start at a point well along in Michel's text. A bit of the preceding paragraph (*dans la rue . . .*) can be seen. Did it recount his theft from his mother a month before? We will never know. Nor will we learn the context of Michel's act of recounting. Is this a diary, addressed to himself? Is it a confession to the police? Is it a letter to Jeanne? (Compare the relatively explicit definition of the narrating circumstances in *Murder My Sweet*, discussed on pp. 66–67.) By not revealing Michel's recounting, in its entirety, the overarching narration cuts it free of immediate fabula causality and makes it a self-conscious address to the audience. (This will lead to a crucial equivocation at the very end.) Furthermore, Michel's writing is not clearly located with respect to the events it recounts. How long afterward does it take place? The narrating situation is never defined as it is in, say, *Kind Hearts and Coronets*. Indeed, at the film's close we do not return to Michel's written record at all—another indication of the power of extradiegetic narration to curtail syuzhet information.

Narration in *Pickpocket* would be highly self-conscious by virtue of the striking syuzhet handling alone, but the syuzhet is in turn subjected to an internally organized parametric system, preformed and defined wholly in terms of cinematic space and time. Using a "sparse" approach, the film selects only a few technical procedures from the classi-

12.5
12.6

cal paradigm. These devices become organized into an additive, spatialized form that coheres as a unique stylistic world. *Pickpocket*'s intrinsic norm thus achieves prominence by virtue of its narrow range of technical choices, its quantitative repetition of those, and its qualitative subordination of Michel's recounting to stylistic patterning. The crawl title defines the work's prominence immediately: "The style of this film is not that of a thriller." Thereafter the narration literally *stylizes* the represented events; images and sounds stand like translucent filters between the syuzhet organization and the spectator.

The work on film style begins with the organization of the profilmic event itself. Although shot on location, *Pickpocket* is hardly "realistic." The manipulation of the sound track owes nothing to classical verisimilitude. No métro platfroms ever sounded so quiet; in these bank lobbies and train stations you can hear every rustle of banknotes, each footfall. The figures' behavior is equally stylized. After Jeanne and Jacques return to a cafe table where Michel had been sitting, they sit down, pause, and only then does Jacques lift his eyes and remark that Michel is gone. In the bank, Michel blocks the exit of a businessman by simply stepping up to him; the two hold their postures for a long moment before they separate. Such abstraction of figure movement is at its height during the pickpocket scenes. These passages are not the plausible representations of efficient thievery which classical cinema would present. Victims stand unnaturally still and let strangers grasp their wrists or lapels with impunity. When Kassagi steals from a man about to take a cab, the gull must halt motionless and silent before climbing in. At the racetrack, there is an unnatural divorce between the rigid position of Michel's body (in frontal shots) and the flexible mobility of an arm creeping toward a purse or pocket. (See figs. 12.5–12.6.) The stylization of the profilmic event includes costumes as well. Black suits mask off chunks of space and allow diving hands to stand out against a neutral ground. Perhaps the most outrageous example is Michel's outfit, his rumpled dark suit and his loosened tie that is usually skewed a constant angle. One function of the unvarying costumes, as I have mentioned, is to create uncertainty about duration. But Michel's suit also acts as a uni-

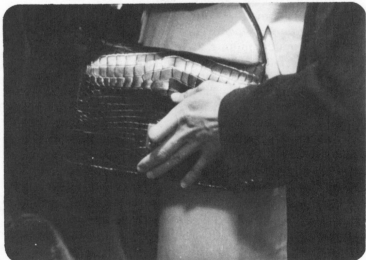

form, so that we can always pick him out of a crowd or identify him in a frontal midriff shot. Michel's suit and tie could stand as emblems of the extent to which rigorous and restricted regularities of mise-en-scène bear the trace of an all-powerful parametric system.

12.7

A comparable restraint operates in the choice of framing and cutting patterns. Bresson restricts his camera to a straight-on or a slightly high angle, most typically in medium-shot or medium-close-up range, and he uses only a 50-mm lens. He relies upon eyeline matches and shot/reverse-shot combinations. The recurrent devices derive from the paradigm characteristic of classical Hollywood narration. Yet in Bresson's films devices gain great prominence with respect to the classical norm, for several reasons. First, Bresson typically does not employ other classical devices, such as the establishing long shot, the low-angle framing, match-on-action cuts, or analytical editing. Certain devices thus get pried loose from their codified role and move forward as pure parameters. Second, there is the matter of timing. In a classical film, the completion of the glance determines the moment of an eyeline-match cut, as we saw in *Rear Window*. Jeff looks, we see what he sees, then we see Jeff reacting. In *Pickpocket*, though, the cut will be delayed. In a favorite variant, a figure will look, lower the eyes, look again, lower the eyes again, then finally raise them; only then will we see the object of the glance. A slower timing is also created by having characters leave a shot and then

holding the empty framing for a noticeable interval before cutting away. With Bresson, the urge to "cover" offscreen movement by the slight lag in cutting away that we saw in William deMille and Lubitsch (pp. 171, 182) becomes a palpable emphasis on vacant space. The same prolongation of what Hollywood would accelerate occurs in conversation scenes. In a Hollywood dialogue, the pace is often governed by cutting to the listener before the speaker has finished the line. Bresson instead makes his speaker pause after every line, so that the cut to a reverse angle never interrupts dialogue. This simple device (also used by Ozu) makes the cut slightly more apparent than when continuous dialogue smoothes it over. Bresson thus "defamiliarizes" classical découpage by prolonging what leads into and out from cuts.

All these parameters of sound, mise-en-scène, framing, and cutting break sharply from the realistic and compositional motivation codified by classical norms. As a result, the relation of syuzhet and style becomes more dynamic. Syuzhet patterning comes forward at various points when the style is most impalpable, such as the opening racetrack scene, in which Michel's first theft is represented through point-of-view shots and close-ups of details. At other points, the syuzhet and style become more or less equivalent in interest. The best examples of the latter are the film's several shot/reverse-shot scenes.

As a classical figure of style, the shot/reverse shot is readily graspable and thus well suited for the neutral transmission of story information. The device is easy to motivate compositionally; each cut shows each character as she or he speaks. But in Bresson's hands the device gains a new emphasis. We have already seen how the general tendency to omit establishing shots gives more prominence to other découpage devices. A Bresson scene will typically start in one of two ways. The camera may frame a detail which will then be situated in a wider locale (by camera movement or figure movement).[72] Or the scene will start with a character's entering a space which is defined as contiguous to that occupied by another character; the relation of the characters is defined through glances and/or portions of a body intruding into the shot. Once the scene has begun, it tends to be

12.8
12.9

12.10
12.11

analyzed—or, rather, processed—by a ruthless shot/reverse-shot technique. For example, when Michel first goes to the cafe, a panning long shot follows his scanning of the crowd for Jacques (fig. 12.7). Michel enters the cafe. Dissolve to the two of them at the bar, seen from the outset in a shot/ reverse-shot configuration (figs. 12.8–12.9). After several exact repetitions of these setups, Michel notices the inspector offscreen and walks to him; the inspector comes into the frame and creates a new over-the-shoulder composition (fig. 12.10). Dissolve again as the three men go to a table and sit,

creating another over-the-shoulder setup (fig. 12.11). They talk, and there follows a shot/reverse-shot passage of only four setups, two of which (figs. 12.12–12.13) are presented eight times apiece. After another dissolve, Michel and Jacques come to the cafe door and talk. This initiates a brief shot/reverse-shot sequence (figs. 12.14–12.15) before Michel drifts off into the night (fig. 12.16; cf. fig. 12.7). The three brief scenes are unusual by virtue of their refusal of variety: no variation of camera angle or distance within each shot/reverse-shot stretch and nearly none between the two

exchanges between Michel and Jacques (figs. 12.8–12.9, 12.14–12.15); no figure movement that would change the relative positions of the interlocutors. Striking also is the "preformed" nature of the découpage, whereby characters *move into position* for the shot/reverse-shot combination, as if figure behavior and camera position secretly collaborated to fulfill an abstract stylistic formula. With the establishing shot virtually abolished, the very first shot in a character encounter must become the first phase of a shot/reverse-shot exchange.

But you can see I have no job...

The sense of characters moving to fulfill a preordained découpage is even stronger in the remarkable scene in which Michel visits Jeanne to ask about the police investigation. Their talk is presented in twenty-eight reverse shots. Here the repetition is nuanced in that a shot will start to develop in a way that varies slightly from the norm. At one point, Michel begins to pace, turning from Jeanne (fig. 12.17), and the camera follows him by tracking in (fig. 12.18). He turns to her and walks back (fig. 12.19), and the camera tracks back to its initial position over Jeanne's shoul-

12.24   *12.25*

der (fig. 12.20). She replies to him in a reverse shot. Cut to a repetition of the earlier setup, and track in again as Michel once more moves to the window (figs. 12.21–12.22). He turns and comes forward again, but now her shoulder is not in the frame (fig. 12.23). The shifting distance between the characters is measured by a precise decoupage: one step makes a "just noticeable" compositional difference. Later in the scene, when Michel asks her if she thinks he is a thief, she retreats out of the frame, he takes one step forward, and the camera tracks back far enough to reposition her shoulder exactly as at the outset (fig. 12.24). Thus, repetitions and minute variations reveal powerful but simple rules of framing and cutting which figure movement must obey, beyond the dictates of the syuzhet. Unlike Soviet historical-materialist narration, which often withholds spatial cues entirely, *Pickpocket's* narration reorients us hyper-redundantly through a very narrow range of cues.

In the shot/reverse-shot scenes, stylistic rigor and syuzhet development operate as equals. In other passages, stylistic devices and patterns subordinate, even deform, syuzhet operations. At the very start, the extradiegetic narration declared itself to be an explanation "in pictures and sounds":

cinematic style may take charge of the syuzhet. The tendency is apparent at a very local level. The first shot of the first scene of story action is a close-up: a woman's gloved hands take bills out of a purse and pass them to the hands of a man. One aspect of the stylistic norm, the close-up of hands, is thus supplied at the outset. Later, a scene may begin in an apparently comparable way but then go on to disorient us. Michel watches a theft on the subway. The scene ends with a close-up of the thief's hand as it grasps a newspaper in which a wallet has been nestled. Dissolve to a close-up of a hand sliding a notebook out from a creased newspaper. But this hand belongs to a different thief: a track back reveals Michel at home practicing the feat. Similarly, when Kassagi instructs Michel in picking pockets, we get a dissolved "montage sequence" of hands executing moves. We cannot tell if these all take place in a single evening's session or if they are excerpted from many days or weeks. A shot of Michel flexing his fingers on a table's edge retrospectively becomes at once the last shot of the montage and the first shot of a new scene. Unlike the narrative "hooks" between scenes in classical films, here Bresson creates purely visual and sonic linkages that make syuzhet relations equivocal.

At a broader level, the sparse techniques become palpable through development of a richly spatialized form. A simple example is offered by the portrayal of "insignificant," often routine story actions. In shot 22, Michel enters his apartment building and leaves the frame (fig. 12.25). Cut to a shot of the top of the stairs; Michel passes through, walking up (fig. 12.26). In shot 24, we see the door of his room standing ajar, and he enters (fig. 12.27). The spatial gaps here invite us to imagine Michel starting at the foot of the staircase (an absent shot between shots 22 and 23), arriving at his land-

12.30
12.31

ing, and walking down the hall to his room (two shots to be inserted between shots 23 and 24). Later in the film we get to see the first flight of stairs, when Michel stands looking out at Kassagi (fig. 12.28). Still later do we see him walk down the hallway outside his door (fig. 12.29). The trivial process

of Michel's coming and going has been broken up into several bits, and all of them are never present in any one sequence. The narration plays a remarkable series of variants on these simple elements and even extends the handling to other locales. The first time Michel visits his mother, we start with a shot of him leaving the front doorway (fig. 12.30) and cut to a shot of him climbing the stair (fig. 12.31), very much as we have seen in the earlier scene. Behind all these "surface" manifestations there lurks an absent structure, a "shot row" which, like the series in music, can only be inferred.

These examples also suggest how the "spatialized" tendency of the narration emerges through unusual regularities of stylistic handling. However classical the sources of *Pickpocket*'s parametric operations, through rigorous repetition those procedures form a closed system unique to this film. Now, every narration requires repetitions in order to reinforce spectatorial assumptions and to signal the intrinsic norms that will govern the work. Normally, however, stylistic repetitions operate to emphasize syuzhet informational processes without calling attention to style as such. Consider, for instance, the reiterated camera setups in the sequence from *Miss Lulu Bett* analyzed back in Chapter 9. The repetition of orientation and framing sinks below awareness because our perception is geared to noticing significant changes in the characters' behavior—expression, gesture, or dialogue. But by Bresson's famous tactic of expressionless performance, *Pickpocket* deprives the shot of much informational content. When each character wears a blank face and stands motionless or walks without idiosyncrasy, the repetitions of camera setup come forward to a greater degree. It is not just that 36 per cent of the shots in *Pickpocket* repeat earlier setups in the scene, for a classical film might have an even higher degree of spatial redundancy. (In *Heaven Knows, Mr. Allison*, one out of every two shots repeats a setup.) In a classical film, repeated camera setups serve as a neutral ground for changes in the human agents. In *Pickpocket*, the neutrality of performance makes the repetition of camera position part of the film's intrinsic norm.

The "preformed" quality of framing, cutting, and figure movement becomes most prominent across scenes, when

repetitions and variations of prior camera setups create a strong sense of a style that reduces every event to the same coordinates. Sometimes the symmetries are in neighboring shots, as when we see Michel descend to the métro platform to board a train, and then, after a quick dissolve, get off a train and walk up the opposite stairs. A similar effect proceeds from the graphically matched dissolves to newspapers, hands, door frames, and so forth. More powerful are the far-reaching parallels. Each time Michel visits his mother's apartment, the same camera movement follows his route.

On the second and third occasions that Michel meets Jacques at their cafe, shot/reverse-shot series are played out in terms very close to the first one (figs. 12.32–12.33; cf. figs. 12.14–12.15). On his third visit to the cafe, he talks with the inspector, in a series that recalls the first occasion (figs. 12.34–12.35; cf. figs. 12.12–12.13). Michel's two visits to the inspector's office are rendered in strikingly similar reverse shots, and Michel's visit to Jeanne, discussed above, is an echo of their first meeting on the landing outside his mother's room. The repetition becomes dizzying in those

12.40
12.41

teases Jacques into leaving (fig. 12.40), and when Michel goes to interrogate Jeanne (fig. 12.41). Another director would vary our views of this locale far more. The fact that this narration usually lingers on the hallway after the characters have gone only augments the tendency of these events to register as nearly identical variants of a single stylistic unit.

The hand that writes in the notebook implies, I have suggested, that we will be restricted to Michel's range and depth of knowledge in spelling out the syuzhet. But the narration of images and sounds creates a further set of restrictions on our knowledge, somewhat analogous to the sheerly stylistic constraints on knowledge which we saw in Jancsó's long takes in *The Confrontation.* The style confines itself to those syuzhet acts it can "process" within its own limits and with regard to its own patterns. To get to the formulaically edited exchanges, the narration excludes certain other activities, such as striding across a room. In the cafe scenes, for instance, Michel is never shown walking to the bar; the film regularly omits this slight action. At one remarkable point, a dissolve skips over only a few seconds—just enough to move the inspector, Jacques, and Michel from one shot/reverse-shot passage at the bar to another one at a table. The syuzhet might have rendered Michel's theft of the man's watch at the carnival in intensely subjective terms, but the style diverges from the terms of the written recounting: Michel leaves the frame, and the camera holds on the empty table. Later we will learn that he had run and fallen, scraping his hand. It is as if such a melodramatic action cannot be sufficiently transformed by the style, so it is omitted. The most flagrant example of the style's exclusivity is Michel's trip abroad. The elision is partially justified by a syuzhet tactic: Michel's passage in his notebook summarizes the hiatus in two sentences. But the style processes the ellipsis in a thoroughly characteristic manner. In scene 38 Michel leaves his apartment house. In scene 39, after he has boarded the train, the camera pans left with the train as it pulls away. Dissolve to his hand writing in his notebook. Dissolve to the train platform two years later, and pan right with Michel walking through the crowd. Dissolve to a shot of him climbing a staircase (fig. 12.42), in a framing that calls

oblique shots of the hall outside Michel's apartment: when Jeanne and Jacques visit (fig. 12.36), when Michel and Jeanne arrive after his mother's death (fig. 12.37), when Michel enters to meet Jacques (fig. 12.38), when Jacques and Michel go to meet Jeanne (fig. 12.39), when Michel

12.42

up the whole set of such shots earlier in the film (e.g., figs. 12.25–12.29). The syuzhet has not followed him to England, and the style has treated his departure and return just as symmetrically and repetitively as it had treated his life in Paris.

We come at last, and again, to the problem of perceptibility. How does *Pickpocket*'s narration engage the spectator by means of processes characteristic of parametric cinema? As usual, the initial portions of the film establish the intrinsic norm. The prologue, the credits, and the hand writing emphasize narrational authority and the calculated play between extradiegetic and diegetic factors. The first ordinary scene, in which Michel steals from a woman's purse and then is quickly captured by the police, sets out several stylistic features: the close-up of hands, the repetition of setups, the use of Michel's optical point of view, the sparse sound track, the impassive figure behavior, and so on. I would argue, though, that the style does not dominate syuzhet patterning in this or in other early scenes. The style is neither as obtrusive nor as equivocal as it will later become. Rather, it is somewhat suited for the scene, and the fabula action is presented with sufficient suspense to make syuzhet

construction the primary interest. Gradually the stylistic rules begin to assert themselves. Michel returns home in the spatially "gapped" fashion we have already considered (figs. 12.25–12.27). He visits Jacques in the cafe, and the scene's symmetries, both of shot/reverse shot (figs. 12.8–12.15) and of scenic construction, begin to emerge. The parametric system becomes apparent, however, only after the syuzhet starts to recycle itself.

After the prologue and the shot of the hand writing, the first five segments constitute a condensed phase within Michel's life. He commits the theft at Longchamps, is taken to the police station, is interrogated and freed, returns to his room, visits his mother and speaks with Jeanne, and meets Jacques at the cafe. These sequences introduce all the major characters and locales and establish a rhythm of theft/interrogation/encounter that will be repeated throughout the film. After Michel leaves the cafe, he goes to the métro, where he spies a pickpocket at work. We are back to the theft phase. As Leonard Meyer notes, "Immediate repetition tends to emphasize the differences between like events, while remote repetition—that is, return—tends to call attention to their similarities."[73] Soon the viewer is able to assume that a narrow set of parallel syuzhet units is at work. There are scenes of Michel alone, practicing in his room or on the street. There are scenes of Michel's encounters with Jacques and Jeanne, at a cafe or in Michel's room. There are the discussions with the inspector, again at the cafe or in his room. There are also scenes of tutelage, either by the anonymous pickpocket on the métro or by Kassagi later. We can also predict the outcome of most of these scenes: Michel will try to increase his virtuosity; he will bait the inspector and remain unrepentant; in any encounter with Jacques or Jeanne he will probably rebuff them and leave abruptly. And in general the stylistic handling comes to be taken for granted: shot/reverse shot for character confrontation, sudden transitions on details, interjections of the voice-over, and so on. The overall repetition of syuzhet modules, the combinations of relatively fixed character relations, and the narrow range of stylistic variation create very firm assumptions and hypotheses.

In this context the pickpocket scenes stand out vividly. They are much less predictable, involving the greatest variety of locales, characters, objects, and methods. Michel goes solo in the métro; then he is, unexpectedly, nabbed by a victim; he acts in partnership with Kassagi outside the bank; solo, he lifts men's watches in the street; he works as part of a trio at the train station; solo again, he is caught at the racetrack. Stylistically too the pickpocket scenes are more varied, though always within the sparse norm established at the outset. We get almost abstract close-ups of hands roaming against black suits, complex camera movements trailing victims' torsos, cutting that severs arms from bodies, and almost complete silence. In context, the pickpocket scenes gather their excitement from such nuances of handling as the fact that now the shots no longer hold on empty frames—a "minimal" means of picking up pace. If the film did not break its cyclical repetition of set units with the more unpredictable and comparatively spectacular pickpocket scenes, it would be closer to the monodic construction of Bresson's later *Procès de Jeanne d'Arc* (1961).

It is necessary for the narration to geometricize syuzhet patterning in predictable ways to establish the unity of style and to prompt the viewer to perceive repetitions, disjunctions, and differences in parametric handling. By virtue of all the stylistic regularities considered above, various cafes and rooms become extensions of the same rudimentary locales. Uncertainty about when a scene ends is created by such stylistic play as dissolving in the middle of a dialogue or action or holding on an empty space once a character has exited. The narration can create unwarranted stylistic hypotheses by using such tactics as misleading transitions from one close-up to another. The spectator must also notice how far the style will go in its ruthless processing of the syuzhet. To create the intermittent dominance of style over syuzhet, the narration must generate firm expectations that in this film certain actions will be rendered only according to specific parameters organized as stylistic events, and that there will be some additive variation of them in the course of the film.

Among other advantages, an analysis of parametric form helps reveal the formal causes of that aura of mystery and transcendence which viewers and critics commonly attribute to Bresson's work. One source of this effect is that stylistic patterning is somewhat distinct from syuzhet patterning. In the 1960s art cinema, stylistic organization makes sense within schemata of objectivity, subjectivity, and authorial commentary. In *La guerre est finie*, the rhythmically edited shots of Diego boarding trains create psychological ambiguity. But in parametric narration, the style cannot be accounted for by such schemata. The shots of Michel's departure from and return to Paris possess no subjective cues, the author makes no comment. In parametric cinema, the syuzhet is subordinated to an immanent, impersonal stylistic pattern. Because no evident denotative meaning is forthcoming from such obvious patterning, the viewer itches to move to the connotative level. Yet nothing very certain is evident here either. When a powerful and internally consistent style refuses conventional schemata for producing narrative meaning, we are tantalized into projecting other schemata onto it, and the flickering oscillation of such alternatives contributes to the sense of uncertainty. Order without meaning tantalizes.

Without leisure to linger, the viewer may also attribute ineffability to the ungraspable differences generated by the style. The spectator cannot spot all the variants of every parameter and cannot keep them in mind all at once. The minute variations of lighting or framing in recurrent shots (for instance, figs. 12.36–12.41) put too great a strain on attention and memory. Instead, the viewer sacrifices variations in individual parameters for a synoptic recognition of stylistic events: "This again!" To quote Meyer once more: "What we perceive and respond to is not the order or regularity of individual parameters, but the pattern—or lack of pattern—which their combination creates. To put it simply, a perceptual pattern is more than, and different from, the sum of the parameters that create it."[74] Slight differences among instances are not easily recognized. The viewer forgets, say, how many times a shot recurs, and sacrifices the ability to compare aspects of each occurrence. Thus the narration strains against its materials and against the per-

12.43
12.44

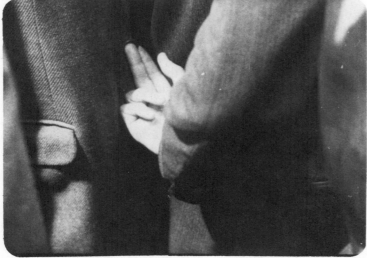

ceptual norms of the cinema as we know it. More is put in than we can assimilate, even on repeated viewings. Like decorative art, parametric cinema exploits the very limits of the viewer's capacity.[75] The sense of an order whose finest grain we can glimpse but not grasp helps produce the con-

notative effects of which thematic criticism records the trace. These effects arise from a formal manipulation that is, in a strong sense, *nonsignifying*—closer to music than to the novel.

Pickpocket's stubborn resistance to interpretation, its preference for order over meaning, reappears in the final four segments. After a great many repetitions of the theft/interrogation/encounter cycle, the film's major portion completes itself with a second visit to the racetrack. Enticed by a plainclothes policeman, Michel attempts to pick his pocket. Predictably, his effort is rendered as a variant upon the first scene (compare figs. 12.43–12.44 and figs. 12.5–12.6). The last four scenes take place in prison and constitute a new cycle with its own symmetrical syuzhet structure. In scene 47, Michel leaves his cell and goes to the visitors' room to talk with Jeanne. In scene 48, he waits in his cell, but Jeanne does not return. In scene 49, he gets a letter from her announcing that she will come see him. In scene 50, Michel leaves his cell and goes to the visitors' room. Jeanne is there, and they embrace. As an obsessive itinerary of Michel's comings and goings, the scenes recapitulate in tiny compass his movement in earlier parts of the film. The same camera movement tracks Michel back from his bed and through the cell doorway in scene 47 and scene 50. The style also creates a negative symmetry in the two scenes of Jeanne's visit. In (47), he leaves his cell and we dissolve to him in the visitors' room; we never see him arrive, but we do see him leave. In (49), we see him leave his cell and arrive to stand before Jeanne, but we never see him leave the visitors' room. Bresson's "preformed" style goes still further, making the prison scenes exact extensions of earlier ones. The beginnings of the shots in his cell echo shots of Michel on his bed in his apartment. The encounters with Jeanne are handled in scrupulous shot/reverse shot like those earlier in the film (figs. 12.45–12.46; cf. figs. 12.17–12.24). Most remarkably, the prison corridor is filmed to resemble the hallway outside Michel's apartment (figs. 12.47–12.48; cf. figs. 12.36–12.41). The prison scenes thus summarize both syuzhet patterns and stylistic protocols.

The final scene continues the trend toward symmetries.

Michel and Jeanne face each other in a pair of reverse shots (figs. 12.49–12.50) barely different from prior ones. He presses the bars and she rises and comes to him (fig. 12.51). A shot/reverse-shot series (figs. 12.52–53) recalls their brief embrace in her apartment (figs. 12.54–12.55). As the Lully music starts, and while he kisses her forehead and she kisses his hand, the camera tracks slowly forward to them (fig. 12.56). In but one other scene has the camera tracked in during a shot/reverse-shot exchange, and that was the scene in Jeanne's apartment (figs. 12.17–12.23). Only in the con-

text of such a sparse style can such a simple device and such a minute variation of an intrinsic norm take on such perceptual power.

The stylistic symmetries become even more significant in relation to the asymmetrical presentation of the framing narration. The shot of the couple (fig. 12.56) is the film's last image. Since we never return to Michel's journal, our initial "frame" of his recounting is left incomplete. The shot we get forms a stronger *stylistic* coda than would a neutral shot of the hand writing. We do, however, hear Michel's voice: "O

12.53
12.54

12.55
12.56

Jeanne, what a strange way I had to take in order to reach you." Since Jeanne's face blocks Michel's mouth as this line is heard, we cannot tell if it is a line of dialogue he murmurs to her, or the final voice-over commentary. Thus the narration creates a partial frame and a diegetic effect simul-taneously. Similarly, there is no return to the extradiegetic voice of the prologue. But again an implicit, partial symmetry emerges. As the image fades out, the Lully music continues over the black frame for almost a full minute. *Pickpocket* ends as if the images and sounds with which the tale was to be told have abolished the need for written commentary altogether. Which is to say that authorial presence was no more than a label for the shots, noises, voices, and music that gain their final effect as an impersonal stylistic system.

The Problem of Modernism

Throughout this book I have refrained from using the term "modernism." By spelling out the differences among various modes and norms, we can see that several different sorts of narration could qualify as "modernist." If we look to the traditions of twentieth-century fiction and drama, running roughly from James, Proust, Joyce, and Kafka through Faulkner, Camus, and the Theater of the Absurd to Cortázar and Stoppard, we find that art-cinema narration could be called modernist; for these are among its important sources.[76] If we take modernism to be more closely allied with the experimental work of political artists like Grosz, Lissitzky, Heartfield, Brecht, and Tretyakov, then historical-materialist narration will be a better candidate for the label.[77]

And if we consider parametric narration as a distinct mode, its modernist pedigree can be traced back to the work of the Russian Formalists—a movement deeply involved with contemporary avant-garde poetry and fiction—and to the continental serialism and structuralism of the 1950s and 1960s. Thus parametric films might be considered modernist.[78] The important difference is that we cannot posit any influence of such movements upon all parametric films. For reasons that have to be explained in each particular context, filmmakers in widely differing periods and cultures have utilized parametric principles. Some have done so consistently (Ozu, Bresson), others sporadically (Lang, Dreyer, Fassbinder, Godard). Whether we call this "modernism" is not as important as recognizing that only after an aesthetic was formulated explicitly was it possible for critics and spectators to construct an extrinsic norm that helps us grasp certain problematic films. Comprehension of films changes through time as we construct new schemata. In their ability to change our perspective on films both old and new, the norms of parametric narration epitomize the historicity of all viewing conventions.

13. Godard and Narration

Like any artistic tradition, however antitraditional it may be, the avant-garde also has its conventions. In the broad sense of the word, it is itself no more than a new system of conventions, despite the contrary opinion of its followers. . . . Disorder becomes a rule when it is opposed in a deliberate and symmetrical manner to a pre-established order.

Renato Poggioli[1]

The films made by Jean-Luc Godard between 1959 and 1967 raise so many issues that I hesitate to broach them when this book is drawing to a close. But Godard's work of this period offers a valuable occasion to test many of the narrational concepts I have proposed. The peculiar problems posed by Godard's work become more intelligible in the light of the theory set forth in earlier chapters.

Our point of departure is a recognition of just how firmly these films resist narrative comprehension. This is not simply a problem of interpretation, as if Godard were creating thematically ambiguous or profound works. He usually is not. In fact, Godard's films readily succumb to high-level "readings." The real problem is that they remain elusive on a simple denotative level. It is fairly easy to say what *Pierrot le fou* or *Made in USA* is "about" (especially if one has mastered a set of clichés about Godard the social critic, the romantic, the Brechtian, etc.), but it is quite hard to say what literally happens in each film's fabula. It is as if the very indeterminacy of narrative denotation encourages a random itemization of themes. But what if the simplicity of isolated connotations permits a complexity at the levels of syuzhet and style? Godard's films invite interpretations but discourage, even defy, analysis. To grasp how the films work we must start with the flagrant and peculiar obstacles they create at the most fundamental levels of storytelling and spectator activity.

Take a typical instance. Psychology has long known the difficulty of attending to two simultaneous spoken discourses (the "cocktail-party effect"). Typically the listener can follow only one. The task is even harder if either discourse is grammatically incoherent.[2] Yet Godard's sound track habitually overlaps one discourse with another, and often at least one is ungrammatical. Moreover, the audience must assimilate them under the pressure of time. (The film moves on.) No viewer can grasp the important plot information spewed out in the concurrent to-camera speeches of Widmark and Paula in *Made in USA*. A comparable strain occurs when disparate information is presented in image and in sound, as when Godard scatters writing and photos within the frame, often running letters sidewise or backward while a commentary intones unrelated phrases. (The best examples come from *Deux ou trois choses que je sais d'elle* and *La chinoise*.) Much of Godard's film practice leads to perceptual and cognitive overload.

"Transtextuality" exacerbates this. In Godard's films we find intertextuality aplenty—citations, allusions, borrowings—as well as what Gérard Genette calls "hypertextuality," the derivation of one text from another by transformation (satire, parody) or imitation (pastiche, remake).[3] The difficulties here are many. We may not recognize the allusion or the satirized target. (Who would have known that the soldiers' letters home in *Les carabiniers* are excerpted from actual war correspondence if Godard had not told us? How many such citations has he not yet revealed?) Or the citations may come so quickly that we have no time to assimilate them. Or the attribution may be false, as Godard claims of one in *Le petit soldat* ("That's a quote from Gorky, but in the film I have him say it's Lenin, because I like Lenin better").[4] Most drastically, the suspicion dawns that every shot or line can be treated transtextually. Godard remarked in 1967: "Everything is a quotation. If I shoot a scene of the Arc de Triomphe it's a quotation. If I'm in the street I thumb through a book. In a film I continue to do it—it carries more weight but it's quite the same thing."[5] Although many films have exploited transtextuality, none but Godard's create what Rivette has aptly called intertextual terrorism.[6]

Most nagging of all, perhaps, is the problem of function.

Why does the camera careen out of kilter in *Une femme mariée*? What purpose is served by the elimination of sound in the penultimate scene of *Vivre sa vie*? What justifies the switches to negative in *Alphaville* or the repetition of the car wash scene in *Deux ou trois choses*? This sort of problem runs all the way back to *A bout de souffle*, in which the timing and context of the jump cuts remain inexplicable by any consistent principle of narrative relevance. Godard, in other words, raises as does no other director the possibility of a sheerly capricious or arbitrary use of technique.

On the whole, critics have ignored such problems. They have been content to rely on two comforting but empty explanations. One account sees Godard's 1959–1967 work as belletristic. These films, we are told, are not narratives but essays. Now, this claim is suspect, since all the films do tell stories about fictional characters, and essays typically do not. Perhaps, though, Godard uses narrative elements in order to suggest or demonstrate a point, as an essayist might refer to historical events or fictional characters. But what essayistic point is made in *Alphaville* or *Deux ou trois choses* that cannot be reduced to the clichés which a critic might ascribe to any critical fiction set in the contemporary world (e.g., "the technology of the future already exists," or "modern life commodifies human relations")? Moreover, the essay is not just a genre but a form, however loose. An essay organizes reflections around a body of evidence or examples and proceeds in logical or emotional order to a conclusion. But Godard's films of this period are organized around narrative cause and effect; the films' digressions (often flagrant ones) do not make them essays any more than the interpolated material in *Tristram Shandy* and *Ulysses* turns them into something other than novels. The notion of "essay" is, I believe, relevant to Godard's work only as a filmmaker's historically conditioned alibi for unusual narrational strategies.

A second cliché treats Godard's work as being in some sense scientific. Specifically, his films are said to be concerned with analysis—of Hollywood conventions, of contemporary life, of sign systems. Depending on the critic's perspective, Godard is said to conduct investigations into his historical moment, political problems, or the history of cinema. It is especially tempting to see him as a semiologist without portfolio, demonstrating the arbitrariness of the signifier or exposing the commodity basis of late capitalism. We might, however, distinguish between the subject matter of his films—which undeniably includes what semiologists call sign systems—and the films' approach to it. The approach follows no coherent research program: no statement of assumptions, no chains of inference, no conclusion. One need only recall the systematic investigative procedures of semiological inquiry launched by Barthes or Umberto Eco to see that Godard does not analyze anything. His films mobilize a variety of perspectives, and these are sometimes drawn from scientific discourse, as when in *Deux ou trois choses* the narrator declares himself to resemble a biologist relating an individual to its species. But no biologist would collect specimens in the scattered fashion Godard handles his *elle*; and what scientist would equivocate about whether his object of study is Paris or Juliette? Godard's work was undoubtedly influenced by semiology, and influential upon it; but Godard uses concepts like "analysis" and "science" poetically, as counters in a formal game. These films suggest much but prove nothing.

I assume, then, that conventional labels like "film-essay" and "investigation" do not help us to come to grips with the orneriness of these films' styles and forms. Such problems cannot be solved completely; part of the films' aim is to make us wrestle with them. The critic's task is not to find the correct meaning, to domesticate the extraordinary, but rather to explain the conditions within which the difficulties emerge and have consequences. What creates these problems? What effects do they generate? While I do not believe that any single approach to Godard's work is entirely adequate, we can situate the pre-1967 output, in its peculiar difficultness, within the history of filmic narration. His work embodies ways of mixing established narrational modes in disorienting ways; it creates a syuzhet whose paradigmatic tendencies war with syntagmatic ones; and it suggests unique ways of unifying a film by constructing a strongly characterized narrator.

Schemata in Conflict

Why is a concept of narration relevant to Godard's work? Simply because from *A bout de souffle* to *La Chinoise*, the films are always fundamentally narratives. The viewer still struggles to create a fabula of one sort or another, still treats intertextual material as digression, commentary, amplification, or retardation measurable in reference to a (more or less determinable) story.

If the films are, however eccentrically, narratives, one objection to privileging particular elements—citations, fragments of themes, isolated moments of reflexivity or social critique—emerges. Such an approach says nothing about what narrational schemata we employ to comprehend an element *as* a citation or a theme or a critique. For instance, before we decide to puzzle out the meaning of a book jacket inserted into a scene in *Deux ou trois choses*, we have already employed particular viewing conventions. If the book is not determinably present in the scene, the cut violates classical continuity and thus is not subsumable under Hollywood narrative norms. The conventions of the art cinema allow us to take the shot as either character subjectivity or authorial commentary. If the former is improbable (Juliette is unlikely to have flashbacks to book jackets), then we opt for the latter. But then we would ask why the narration chooses to comment by means of a book jacket rather than by an intertitle. Probable hypothesis: because the jacket really exists in the Parisian bookstalls of late summer 1966, and this adds to the referential verisimilitude of the film. Only some such grid of narrational comprehension could engender the feeling that a passage is "essayistic" or "analytical"; only narration can essay or investigate. I belabor this simply to stress that Godard's films, like other directors', cohere and make sense only within particular narrational modes. And lest my instance seem trivial or obvious, I suggest that just the sorts of choices I have adumbrated constantly confront us in the process of watching a Godard film. Whereas in comprehending a Borzage or a Resnais film, we need not switch between conventions of different narrational modes, Godard constantly interrelates these modes, to the point of refusing to let us unify a film around any single one. Jan Mukařovský's description of the artwork that tangles norms is worth recalling. "Being full of internal harmonies and disharmonies, it represents a dynamic equilibrium of heterogeneous norms applied in part positively, in part negatively."[7]

Critics quickly recognized Godard's deployment of Hollywood genre conventions, but what is more important is the extent to which he accepts many basic norms of classical narrative. Goal-oriented heroes entering into conflicts and achieving some resolution are at the center of *A bout de souffle, Le petit soldat, Une femme est une femme, Les carabiniers, Bande à part, Alphaville,* and *Made in USA.* Furthermore, these films make sense to some degree by virtue of classical norms of narration: the privileging of the investigator-protagonist as the vessel of knowledge; crosscut alternation of scenes; the use of "montage sequences" to compress time or convey lengthy or habitual processes. At many moments in a Godard film, one is invited to apply schemata that will unify the action in terms congruent with classical Hollywood cinema.

Yet Godard will also solicit us to apply norms more appropriate to the art cinema. Uncertain, psychologically ambiguous characters (e.g., Patricia in *A bout de souffle,* Nana in *Vivre sa vie,* Juliette in *Deux ou trois choses,* Paul in *Masculin féminin*) are akin to the protagonists of Fellini and Bergman. Character subjectivity is signaled by monologues and voice-overs (*Une femme mariée, Pierrot, Masculin féminin, Deux ou trois choses*). Characters recount experiences (Corinne and her lover in *Weekend*) and tell each other their dreams (Juliette and her son in *Deux ou trois choses*). There are meditations on lack of communication (the first ending of *Bande à part,* the opening of *Masculin féminin:* "Never do two glances meet . . ."). There are also clear authorial marks, so many that I need not itemize them. (Let one instance suffice: *Alphaville*'s credits announce it as "le neuvième film de Jean-Luc Godard.") The tendency to valorize the ideas presented by chatty sages—Melville, Parain, Lang, Leenhardt, and so on—is also grounded in the art-cinema convention of finding some character who formulates the "correct" authorial attitude. Perhaps we can take *Le mépris*

as the fullest flower of art-film conventions in Godard's early work. Paul and Camille are psychologically complex and ambivalent; the narration creates a permanent gap (Paul's half-hour delay in arriving at Prokosch's); the characters debate character motivation in the *Odyssey*; there are inserts that we can grasp as either character subjectivity or authorial commentary; and the last shot brings us back to a reflexive stance announced in the opening credits, when a camera dollies toward us.

We have already seen that one convention of the art cinema is an appeal to the realism of concrete behavior and locales. Godard employs this as well, often by drawing on documentary techniques. A conversation will be shot in direct-cinema style, as in *A bout de souffle* or *Bande à part.* This is most explicit in *Masculin féminin,* in which ordinary dialogue exchanges take on an interview quality. We are also asked to apply criteria of documentary realism in order to appreciate the shooting in real locations (e.g., a cafe, an apartment) and to make allowance for ambient noise and limited camera positions. Even the gag of letting one minute of silence pass (*Bande à part*) or the reference to *La Chinoise* as "a film in the act of being made" invites the viewer to situate the film with respect to a norm of documentary recording.

Other norms are brought into Godard's work. Chapter 12 has already considered *Vivre sa vie* as an instance of parametric narration; shortly I will suggest some broader affinities with the concept of "spatialized" form. *La Chinoise* and perhaps some other works call upon norms of rhetorical montage present in Soviet historical-materialist narration, though this mode does not become salient in Godard's career until 1968. We can also see films like *Une femme mariée* and *Deux ou trois choses* as appealing to norms drawn from advertising, especially the television commercial and the theatrical publicity film.

But an inventory of the norms mobilized by the films is only a first step. For it might be thought that Godard simply shapes each film around a given mode: *A bout de souffle* and *Bande à part* would then become *policiers, Le mépris* and *Une femme mariée* become art films, and so on. What creates problems of comprehension is principally the fact that any one Godard film also undercuts its appeal to a single set of norms. Parody is the most obvious instance, since Godard seldom uses classical conventions straight. (*Alphaville* and *Made in USA* satirize the hardboiled detective tale, *Une femme est une femme* parodies the musical.) Similarly, Godard will mock the art cinema as well, with Bergman forming a frequent target (the film-within-a-film of *Masculin féminin*, Corinne's erotic monologue in *Weekend*). Still, a parody is not necessarily of another order than its target. There are more radical ways of undermining a film's adherence to one narrational mode.

Two quantitative strategies might be considered first. Sometimes Godard will oversaturate a passage with cues. In *Une femme mariée*, for instance, Madame Céline's name suffices to make her scene a citation; but then Godard redundantly inserts a cover of *Mort à credit*. During the English lesson in *Bande à part*, when Odile receives the mash note from Arthur, her shy smile is exaggeratedly underscored by the sound of a beating heart. When Lemmy Caution replies to Alpha 60 that he is interested only in gold and women, he is laying bare what goes without saying in a *film noir*. Godard's recourse to intertitles and voice-over commentary has alienated many aficionados of the art cinema, since such obviousness challenges the subtlety sought by art-film narration. (Symbols and commentary ought not to be so blatant.) Alternatively, Godard will refuse to supply *enough* conventional cues. In particular, his shot composition is almost never organized along conventional lines: no interplay of high and low angles, few carefully balanced compositions, seldom any significant foreground/background interplay, little virtuosity of lighting. The shots usually do not inscribe the trajectory of the action into the visual design, as did the shots we considered in Chapters 6 and 7 (figs. 6.1–6.4, figs. 7.28–7.32). The "documentary" looseness of framing and figure placement works against the economical denotative significance of classical narration and the carefully symbolic connotations cultivated by the art film. One cannot "read off" character relations or thematic significance from a Godard frame the way one can with

Welles, Antonioni, or Fassbinder, yet the shot will also not have the compact balance of one by Hawks or the subtle effects of volume achieved by Ford. A paucity of cues does not let the viewer wholeheartedly apply the codified schemata appropriate to either mode.

Most important in Godard's undercutting of various narrational modes is his tendency to mix incompatible cues. As Jean-André Fieschi pointed out as early as 1962, Godard's originality lies in "the manner in which he plays with different possibilities without submitting from one film to the next or within the same film to the necessities of tone and style."[8] In the terms proposed in this book, the Godard film emits cues that one schema is most appropriate but these conflict with other cues signaling us to apply other schemata. Godard has been explicit about this, calling *Le mépris*, for instance, "an Antonioni film shot by Hawks or Hitchcock."[9]

How does this clash of schemata occur? A passage soliciting comprehension within one frame of reference may be followed by a passage that requires a different one. In *Le mépris*, after a half-hour quarrel between Paul and Camille, she announces that she no longer loves him. Just before they leave, Paul takes a pistol down from the bookshelf. Suddenly we are asked to construct Paul's character along new lines: no longer the Antonioniesque intellectual, he becomes more like a character in *Some Came Running*. Yet in turn this melodramatic gesture is canceled; Paul does not use his gun on Camille, Prokosch, or anyone else. Something along opposite lines happens in *Made in USA*, when the detective plot is retarded by a lengthy art-cinema discussion in a bar; we must shift gears from Paula Nelson's investigation to a pseudophilosophical consideration of some problems of language. The clash is quite apparent in the last portion of *Bande à part*. First there is the art-cinema ending (the death of Arthur, Franz and Odile musing together alone), then comes classical closure (the couple united on shipboard, the narrator's voice assuring us of a happy end). Or a single scene will contain cues for disparate narrational modes, as when in *Le mépris* the portrayal of Camille adheres to art-film conventions of verisimilitude, but Jack Palance's performance as the maniacal Prokosch seems to have been lifted intact from an Aldrich film. In many scenes of *Masculin féminin*, there is a continual tension between the classical conventions of the romance plot and the relation of image to sound characteristic of direct cinema. And *La Chinoise* contains scenes in which episodes of teenaged romance mingle with elements characteristic of historical-materialist narration; this may be what leads some viewers to think that Godard's film satirizes the Maoists, as if a love scene irredeemably tainted a political fiction.

A skeptical reader might object that here Godard is not so different from Truffaut, who merges classical narrative form with art-cinema narration. But Truffaut exemplifies the degree to which the norms of classical and art-cinema narration can peacefully coexist. He takes an intrigue plot (*policier* as in *La mariée était en noir*, romance in *Le dernier métro*) and then "enriches" it by injecting the psychological depth and ambiguity associated with the art cinema. *Sirène du Mississipi* (1969) tells the story of Louis Mahé, owner of an isolated tobacco factory who falls in love with a mail-order bride only to find that she is a cheat and a murderer. When she abandons him, he vows to kill her. He trails her to a nightclub in Lyon and confronts her. An iris shot of his pistol clinches the canonic, melodramatic tone of the scene. But then Marion tells Louis of her unhappy life before they met, and he weakens: "There's nothing magic about a revolver; I can't pull the trigger." What is usually discussed as Truffaut's tempering of Hitchcockian plotting with Renoirian characterization comes down to the synthesizing of certain Hollywood norms with art-cinema notions of psychological realism.

Godard does not synthesize norms; he makes them collide. In one scene in *Une femme mariée*, Charlotte meets her lover, Robert, in the Orly cinema. Not only is her arrival played satirically (she looks around furtively, peering over dark glasses), but abrupt narrational asides keep appearing: a pan across a sign (PAS . . . SAGE), close-ups of her legs on the escalator, an insert of the emergency stop button (ARRET D'URGENCE), intercut close-ups of her glance and the cinema sign, and, once she has entered, an exaggerated close-up of a Hitchcock cardboard cutout accompanied by a sting in the music. In its characteristic overkill, the sequence manages to parody both the suspense conventions of the thriller and the commentative interjections of the art-film narrator. The character and her decision are treated in no psychological depth. Once Charlotte is in the theater, the tone shifts; of all films at which to meet, they have chosen *Nuit et brouillard*. Now we must apply an art-cinema frame of reference in all seriousness: we can connect their impassive viewing of the film with Charlotte's obtuseness about the concentration camps earlier (revealed in the airport encounter with Roger Leenhardt). But once the couple leave, we are back to satire, with an elaborately furtive walk to the hotel interrupted by another insert of a sign: PRENEZ PARTI! The characters have a different psychological status from moment to moment: at one point, shallow caricature (the Errant Wife); then more "solid" individuals; then caricature again. (Unlike Truffaut's characters, these behave abnormally in normal situations.) In Godard films, a character becomes an uneasy construct out of cues appropriate to various narrational modes. Rather than assimilate one narrational strategy to another in the humanizing manner of Truffaut, Godard simply juxtaposes one set of conventions with another, dehumanizing each mode and revealing its relative arbitrariness.

On the whole, then, a Godard film solicits comprehension according to several narrational schemata, but then it denies the ability of any single schema to unify syuzhet/fabula relations. Moreover, we must shift schemata abruptly, and they will often conflict with one another. This is to say that Godard's films exhibit a continual foregrounding, constant deviations from any intrinsic narrational norm presented earlier in the film. Undoubtedly Godard influenced practitioners of parametric narration, but the net effect of his films is not a systematic exhaustion of a few parameters but a sense of sheer multiplicity and difference, a tendency toward the "absolute unpredictability" envisaged by Boulez and other advocates of total serialism.[10] This constitutes one major source of problems for the viewer. The interaction of disparate narrative schemata will not, however, account completely for all the perceptual and cognitive dislocations of Godard's work. We need other tools.

Spatializing Narration

The chief critical concept for discussing Godard's style has been "collage." As early as 1962, Jean-André Fieschi was comparing *Vivre sa vie*'s inclusion of a scene from *La Passion de Jeanne d'Arc* to Braque's insertion of a tobacco packet into a painting.[11] In 1964, Andrew Sarris spoke of Godard as employing a "collage of styles" in the manner of Eliot in *The Waste Land*.[12] By 1966, critics commonly applied the term to *Une femme mariée*, *Masculin féminin*, and *Deux ou trois choses*. The concept, never defined with care, has some historical justification, reaching back to Parisian Cubism and identifying Godard's disruption of cinematic unity with Braque's and Picasso's experiments in fragmenting the depicted scene. During the 1950s, Paris had seen a rebirth of collage art in such movements as *tachisme* (an art of assemblage deriving from Surrealist automatic writing), *art brut*, and the mechanical assemblage typified by Jean Tinguely's machines.[13] The work of the American Robert Rauschenberg and of the Britisher Richard Hamilton (usually considered the "founder" of Pop Art) was also important in revitalizing collage construction, as was Butor's book *Mobile* (1962).

Whatever its historical appropriateness, though, "collage" offers only general help in specifying Godard's formal work. The urge to call these films collages reflects critics' underlying awareness of formal principles which we have seen at work in other modes of narration. Like Robbe-Grillet, Bresson, Ozu, and the Soviet filmmakers, Godard works toward a "spatialization" of narration. The temporal thrust of the process of fabula construction is checked to some extent by the accumulation of "paradigmatic" materials.

One way this occurs is familiar from previous chapters. Throughout the narration will be scattered images and sounds which, by their similarity and their relative independence of immediate context, belong to the same paradigmatic set. In *Alphaville*, we have the set of "city landscape at night" shots, the set of "traffic sign" shots, the set of "neon formulas" shots, and so forth. Members of each set are distributed across the film, sometimes in conventional ways (e.g., a landscape shot signifying a change of locale) but sometimes purely as disruptions (e.g., the flashing formula cut into Lemmy's interview with Harry Dickson). Shots from Fritz Lang's tests for the *Odyssey* film circulate throughout *Le mépris*, often acting as punctuation for a sequence. In *La Chinoise*, we have the group of images bearing on the cause-effect chain of the fabula, the shots belonging to the "interview" set, the shots belonging to the stockpile of mass culture and political images, and the set of intertitles. The film's découpage consists of one particular combination of all these, often scarcely related to the narrative action. The same spatialization is frequently present in the use of sound, as when a brief musical motif (e.g., Beethoven in *Deux ou trois choses*) or sound effect (e.g., a pistol ricochet in *Masculin féminin*) is replayed at various points in the film. At the limit, the same image or sound will reappear immediately: Paula's repeated entry into the garden (*Made in USA*) or Corinne's duplicated march to the woods (*Weekend*) or the repetition of a line of dialogue from the end of shot *A* at the beginning of shot *B* (especially common in *Masculin féminin*). This image-and-sound recycling goes beyond the "refrains" of Soviet film, moving toward the serial variation of *Méditerranée* or *Katzelmacher*. As Godard puts it, "For me, to make a film is to seize in one gesture a whole through fragments. Each shot is not organized with respect to the dramatic function. A film is not a series of shots but an ensemble of shots."[14] Or, more cryptically: "Two shots which follow each other do not necessarily follow each other."[15]

In other cases—though the borderline is not easy to mark—the syuzhet gets "spatialized" by an unorthodox succession of items that implies alternative temporal arrangements. The order of war episodes in *Les carabiniers* is almost completely arbitrary. In *Weekend*, a unified sequence of Roland and Corinne's drive is broken by the miraculous episode of Joseph Balsamo ("The Exterminating Angel"): the scene could more logically have come before or after its appearance here. At a more local level, there is the famous rearranged scene in *Pierrot le fou*, which I shall consider shortly. Michel Butor writes of the contemporary novel:

When we pay so much attention to the order in which materials are presented, we inevitably wonder whether this order is the only possible one, whether the problem does not admit of several solutions, whether we may not, indeed must not, anticipate within the novel's structure, different trajectories of reading, as in a cathedral or town. The writer must then control the work in all its different versions, take responsibility for them, much like the sculptor, who is responsible for all the angles from which his statue would be photographed and for the moments which connect all these views.[16]

One result of the process of spatialization is that an image or sound becomes evoked by its stressed absence. In *A bout de souffle*, our two necking lovers in the movie theater are shown and we infer a picture offscreen; we hear a citation from Aragon (fed through a theater's sound system) and are expected to supply the film's "real" dialogue that has been suppressed. In *Pierrot le fou* and *Masculin féminin*, characters hold voice-over conversations; these must be occurring before, after, or during the action we are watching, but we will never find out. The existence of one image or sound creates Butor's textual "volume" by conjuring up ghostly counterparts.

In a broader perspective, Godard's syuzhet evokes a sense of textual space in ways quite different from other approaches. Because Godard typically mixes cues for various narrational modes, the film as a whole tends to present itself as a survey of those modes. When elements of classical causality on the image track jostle against the meditative intervention of the author in the sound track (as in *Bande à part*), we are expected to measure the gap between the modes. When characters in a murder plot are named after Hollywood directors and actors (*Made in USA*), we must recognize the incompatibility between classical "transparency" and the citational inclinations of the art film. More specifically, Godard's eclecticism allows him to slam stylistic alternatives endlessly against one another. Richard Roud points to the way a Godard film alternates "block-like

tableaux"[17] with passages of brief shots; we could also mention the more or less arbitrary juxtaposition of lighting options, color schemes, camera angles, découpage options, musical styles, and so forth. The "organic dialectics" of parametric cinema expand to the point where no system becomes visible: in the absence of a sparse range of techniques or an exhaustive inventory of one set of parameters, all that issues from Godard's eclecticism is a sense of the entire range of paradigmatic choice available at any point. Godard's spatialization, we shall see, tends to be not systematically oppositional but purely "differential." He makes a whole film out of discrete narrational flourishes.

A compact specimen of Godard's strategy is the famous scrambled escape scene in *Pierrot le fou*. (See the following pages for a shot breakdown.) The first four shots lead us out of the previous scene; while the talk could conceivably be a continuation of Marianne and Ferdinand's breakfast conversation, the images may be postcards on the wall (thus diegetically adjacent to the characters) or nondiegetic inserts. In tandem with the voice-overs, the shots of paintings create a timeless shot/reverse-shot dialogue between images. Near the end of the fourth shot, Marianne's voice intrudes in the past tense ("Marianne told . . . a story"). The rest of the voice-over passage has no defined temporal site; there is no present from which to measure the pastness of what we see. Moreover, the voice-overs are laid out in chunks, alternating with blocks of nondiegetic music and containing a great deal of repetition, all of which enhances their qualities as paradigmatic units. On the visual plane, a series of fragmented close-ups (shots 1–6) is followed by a virtuosic long take (shot 7) that plays games with characters' locations in offscreen space. The abstract contrast between the options of montage and *plan-séquence* is thus immediately realized in the visual texture.

At the very end of shot 7, as Marianne walks leftward along the balcony, there is another quickly cut series (shots 8–19) that depicts the couple's flight. This is rendered with several ellipses and out of fabula order. The sequence invites us to rearrange the shots into "correct" chronology (that is, 9, 11–14, 17, 15, 8, 10, 16, 18, 19). As an extra fillip, one

Pierrot le fou: Escape Sequence

1. Medium shot: Picasso painting, *Pierrot au masqué*.

MARIANNE, voice-over: "Your wife was here this morning."

2. Medium shot: Modigliani woman.

FERDINAND, voice-over: "Know what? I don't give a damn."

3. As (1)

M: "That's not all."

4. Medium shot: Woman in Renoir painting.

F: "I don't give a damn, I said."

5. Medium close-up: Lamp and gun on table.

M: "Marianne tells . . ."
F: "Ferdinand . . ."
M: "A story . . ."
F: "All mixed up . . ."
M: "I knew some people . . ."
F: "Like in the Algerian war . . ."
M: "I can explain it all . . ."

6. Close-up: Gun on table, different place.

7. *Plan américain*: Pan up from body on bed as Ferdinand enters. They speak, but no voices on track. As man enters, they hide.
They emerge from hiding.

F: "Frank had the key?"
M: "I can explain it all . . ."

Sombre music up, cut voice.

As man peers into other rooms, Ferdinand darts through the frame. Man comes back out onto balcony with Marianne. Pan and track with them going back in. They kiss. She sits him down with a comic book. Ferdinand comes in and circles them.

Marianne sneaks behind man and whacks him. Ferdinand drags man out; track back.

Pan left to balcony and Marianne.

Marianne on balcony; she looks down and runs back inside.

M: "A story . . ."
F: "All mixed up . . ."
M: "Leave in a hurry . . ."
F: "Escape from a bad dream . . ."
M: "I knew some people . . ."
F: "Politics . . ."
M: "An organization . . ."
F: "Getaway . . ."
M: "Gun running . . ."
F: "In silence—in silence . . ."

Pan and track in as Ferdinand drags body off.
Marianne goes to get rifle from table and walks left onto balcony, looking down. Track left with her as she walks on balcony.

F: "In silence . . ."
Noble music up, under voice.
M: "It's me, Marianne . . ."
F: "He kissed you . . ."
M: "A story . . ."
F: "All mixed up . . ."
M: "I knew some people . . ."
F: "You were in love . . ."
M: "Use—

8. Long shot: High angle, pan right as Ferdinand jumps into moving car.

9. *Plan américain*: In apartment; Marianne and Ferdinand come down corridor.

                   my apartment . . ."
F: "The Algerian war . . ."

10. Extreme long shot: Car driving down street, tracked behind.

M: "My brother . . ."

11. Long shot: Rooftop; Ferdinand and Marianne step onto it. Pan left.

F: "Escape from a bad dream . . ."

12. Long shot: High angle; two men get out of car in lot below.

　　M: "Leave in a hurry . . ."

13. Long shot: Couple at edge of roof, looking down.

　　M: "Leave in a hurry . . ."

14. Long shot: Drainpipe and street. Ferdinand stumbles, then helps Marianne down. They run left.

　　M: "Leave in a hurry . . ."
　　F: "Answer . . ."
　　M: "Clobber him . . ."
　　F: "Argument . . ."
　　M: "Garage . . ."
　　F: "Who is it?"
　　M: "Down south . . ."
　　F: "Getaway . . ."
　　M: "No money . . ."

15. Long shot: Almost as (8). Ferdinand climbs into car moving right.

16. Extreme long shot: Car drives down street, tracked by camera; similar to (10).

17. Extreme long shot: Marianne climbs into red car and drives it to the right.

　　F: "It was time to leave that rotten world anyway . . ."
　　M: "We left Paris by a one-way street."

18. Extreme long shot: Car drives, similar to (16).

　　F: "Recognizing two of her children . . ."

19. Long shot: From speeding car; point of view of Statue of Liberty replica

　　F: "The Statue of Liberty gave us a friendly wave."

action—Ferdinand's leaping into the car—is represented twice (in 8 and 15), but he performs the action differently each time. By the end of the sequence, the voice-over has recycled itself and added a new significance: Marianne's "mixed-up story" was initially an exposition of her past (shot 4 to start of 7), but its recurrence (end of shot 7) points ahead to the scrambled editing of shots 8–18. With shot 19, image and voice pull abreast; the preceding shots and sounds create a whimsically spatialized narration.

I need not add that such spatialization fluctuates in degree throughout Godard's oeuvre (it is perhaps strongest in the films from 1963 to 1967) and that it is never total. There is always, as I have said, a chronological chain of cause and effect that forces the film forward. In parametric cinema, the stylistic system develops "to one side" of syuzhet representation; both are retrievable as systems. In Godard's work (with the exception of *Vivre sa vie*, apparently his only excursion into purely paradigmatic regions), there is no coherent stylistic system. It is as if Godard has extended the principle of "replete" parametric cinema to so many parameters that we

grasp each stylistic event only as a discrete burst of technique, immediately arresting our attention and disrupting the construction of a unified fabula. The narration shifts violently and without warning between many principles of organization.

This exacerbates the demands which the film places on attention and memory. The cocktail-party effect gets extended to relations among images and between images and sounds. Can any viewer piece together the *Pierrot* escape sequence on one viewing? (Compare the redundancy of Diego's mental flashes in *La guerre est finie*.) The overload effect increases the aggressiveness of the paradigmatic strategy. The eventual result is to tease the spectator with a spectral totality, triggering a search for an elusive pattern— the film behind the film—that will never be confirmed.

Spatializing the narration cooperates with the impossibility of ordering the film according to one narrational mode. The chief effect is to fragment the process of viewing into a series of moments. When we cannot confidently project a schema to explain all that syuzhet and style display, we are forced to choose strategies on a very atomic level. We can decide to follow one strand, perhaps that of the characters' interaction, discarding all else as secondary; but then the narration chops that strand up into many short lengths, so separated by stretches of tangential material that our attention alternates between briefly focused bits and annoyingly empty passages. Moreover, the simultaneous presentation of different pieces of fabula information creates an overload that forces us simply to let certain material pass without scrutiny. Or we can simply take the syuzhet as it comes, refusing to privilege one strand and treat others as digressions; but then we accede to the film as an ensemble of instants.

This fragmentation of the syuzhet, its refusal to answer to demands of any higher order, may explain why early critics saw Godard as a cineaste of the isolated moment. Like *nouveaux romans*, André Labarthe noted in 1961, Godard's films exist wholly in the present; he is not interested in Valéry's problem of when the Marquise went out: "What interests him is to watch her leave."[18] Marie-Claire Ropars claimed that Godard discovered how to express "what existence offers to perception in an instant."[19] Those who dislike Godard's films may well find the works' resistance to large-scale coherence intolerably frustrating; those who admire the films have probably learned to savor a movie as a string of vivid, somewhat isolated effects.

It may seem, in all this spatial opening out of the film, that Godard becomes the cineaste of late structuralism, the one most attuned to theoretical fashion. It is certainly true, for instance, that Godard's tendency to spatialize the narration has strong roots in his cultural circumstances: the *nouveau roman* came to renown when he was making his short films, and the writings of Barthes, Lévi-Strauss, and Jakobson made a theoretical explanation of paradigmatic form highly visible in his intellectual milieu. Similarly, his use of montage to create highly "plural" films accords not only with the avant-garde literary theories circulating in Paris in the 1960s but also with protocols of Vertov's theories. For Vertov, montage was not dialectical (*pace* Eisenstein) but *differential*, grounded in the notion of the "interval"—any measurable

difference (graphic, ideational) between shots. Godard similarly treats montage as a way of controlling intervallic distances between images or sounds or both. Here is his gloss on a sequence from *La Chinoise*:

> One of the texts in the presentation is a speech by Bukharin. Right after it's read there comes a title: "Bukharin made this speech." Next you see a photo of Bukharin's accuser. Of course, I could have used a photo of Bukharin himself. But I didn't need to: you'd just "seen" him in the person who reads the speech. So, I had to show his adversary: Vichynski—and, eventually, Stalin. Okay: Photo of Stalin. And because it's a young man who speaks in the name of Bukharin, the Stalin in the photo is young. That takes us then to the time when the young Stalin was already at odds with Lenin. But by that time Lenin was married. And one of Stalin's greatest enemies was Lenin's wife. So, right after the photo of the young Stalin: photo of Ulianova. That's quite logical. What has to come next? Well, it's revisionism that toppled Stalin. So next you see Juliette reading an ad in France-Soir: Soviet Russia is busy publicizing Tsarist monuments. Right after you see the men who in their youth killed the Tsar.[20]

To many viewers this explanation will seem about as comprehensible as ballet over the radio, but it could be adduced as evidence that Godard has followed Vertov's declaration that "to edit means to organize pieces of film (shots) into a film, to 'write' a film with shots, and not to select pieces for 'scenes.'"[21] At the same time, however, the passage suggests that the open, "plural" qualities of a Godard film are in fact governed by one overriding principle of unity, one that does allow us to grasp and "close" the film to some degree. The same principle is expressed more concisely in *Charlotte et Véronique*: "From the mere fact that I say a sentence, there is necessarily a connection with what came before."

Narrator and Palimpsest

"I need to talk and show me talking, to show and to show me showing."[22]

At the end of *Numéro deux* (1975), Godard is seen at the console of his video equipment. He adjusts the controls and, as the voice of the female protagonist comments on her role, he slumps forward onto his arms. However one interprets this image, it seems to me emblematic of Godard's approach to filmmaking throughout his career. Despite the manifold problems posed by his films, the process of narration is organized, with a thoroughness seldom attained elsewhere in the cinema, around an overt narrator. This narrator is characterized, assigned specific traits that color the representation of the fabula. Most important, this narrator is given a concrete role that leads us to understand the syuzhet in unique ways.

In the art cinema, self-conscious narration may stress a point or introduce ambiguity, but there remains a continuous, independent diegetic world into which narration occasionally intrudes. In *La guerre est finie* or *8½*, the "author" steps into objectively or subjectively "realistic" passages. But in Godard's films, the narrator is present to a much greater degree, pervading the film to the extent that the work must be seen as his total construct. To this extent, Godard's narrational mode resembles that of "parametric" cinema, which finds ways of continually making style palpable. But parametric cinema tends not to offer any strong characterization of a narrator; syuzhet and style constitute relatively impersonal systems. Godard's films do not do this: by avoiding any consistent system, the narrational manipulations get justified as the work of a distinct persona.

The central aspect of Godard's narrational processes is self-conscious address to the audience. In a Godard film, from the credit sequence on, we recognize a narration signaling its presence. To-camera address is of course a clear cue here, but, even if repeated and prolonged, it remains sporadic. Godard has amassed a battery of other devices—titles, voice-overs, nondiegetic inserts, frontal staging, color design, camera movements, editing patterns—calculated to designate the narration's direct address to the audience. And this presence is *continuous*: far from the occasional interventions of the art-film narration, Godard's self-consciousness is pervasive. It is not too much to say that in every scene, sometimes at every moment, the narration becomes overt in one fashion or another. (Recall our *Pierrot* scene.)

The self-consciousness of Godard's narration colors the range and depth of knowledge the narration claims. These questions are of course bound up with the fact that a Godard character is, to various degrees, presented as a sketchy construct, a precipitate out of the mixture of narrational modes. This means that instead of the narration's asserting its ability to swell or contract its range of fabula information to "match" that of a character, the character's range of knowledge at any moment works as a function of the goals of the narration. Instead of claiming the ability to plunge into the mental life of the character, the narration creates those portions of that mental life which can play a part in the tissue of self-conscious address to the viewer. When character subjectivity operates through vision—e.g., point-of-view shots—the objects seen are seized and labeled by the narrator. Such is the case with the magazines and books at which characters may glance; such is also the case in this brief passage from *Le petit soldat*:

1. Medium shot: Sitting on the train, Bruno looks right.
2. Medium shot: Pan down from a woman to her child.
3. Medium shot: Bruno turns back to look left.
4. Long shot: POV; Gland station approaching.
5. Long shot: POV; Gland station retreating.
6. Medium shot: Bruno looks right.

By inserting a marked temporal ellipsis within the character's optical viewpoint, the narration reveals its own controlling presence. Similarly, the use of the sound track to render a character's subjective interior monologue is skewed in *Le mépris*, *Une femme mariée*, and *Masculin féminin*: we cannot be sure whether the voice-over phrases directly express the characters or are simply the narrator's mimicry. There is also the overt intervention of the narrator via voice-over, claiming to describe (or not to describe) characters' feelings in *Bande à part* and *Deux ou trois choses*. In sum, range and depth of knowledge are but occasions to reveal the self-consciousness of the narration in constantly changing ways.

Thus, the Godard film requires us to build the fabula on the basis of knowledge that comes to us with fingerprints all over it. The narration can be completely uncommunicative, leaving many permanent gaps. What happens to Nana between episodes in *Vivre sa vie*? What triggers Paul's death in *Masculin féminin*? What is Marianne's connection with the gang of *Pierrot le fou*? And, as we have seen, the narration can be overcommunicative, loading the syuzhet with too much information and distracting us from crucial fabula events. The narration can also communicate its awareness that it need not communicate, thus distracting us from what should have been plain in the first place: "We might now open a parenthesis on Odile's, Franz's, and Arthur's feelings, but it's all pretty clear. So we close our parenthesis and let the images speak." This line from *Bande à part* is extreme but not untypical in its flaunting of the narration's sovereignty over what we know. As a result, any lack of communicativeness seems arbitrary; if the narration does not tell us something, it is not because of any self-imposed restrictions of range or depth. Furthermore, the fact that the self-conscious narrator can shift from channel to channel at any moment to reveal or conceal fabula information raises the hypothetical possibility of total disclosure, the unmasking of the whole film as a construct, nothing less than the "spatialized" absent-present totality we have considered already.

In any film, expositional passages are privileged. In the classical and the art-cinema modes, the opening reveals a marked degree of overt narration that will recur at codified moments later. Godard openings tend to announce not only the fabula information (often in elliptical ways) but also the sort of self-conscious narration that will pervade the film. The opening of *La Chinoise* affords a good instance.

Under the first title ("A film in the making") we hear a voice reading about a crisis in French capitalism. Cut to a young man on the balcony continuing to read aloud. When he finishes, he goes inside. Cut to a title: "THE." Cut to a white wall, against which one hand joins and clasps with another while voices (off or over?) describe themselves as "the discourse of others." Fade out, and fade in to a long shot of the apartment, empty of characters, while voices over (Guillaume and Yvonne) discuss how long the owners will be gone and how liberalism is a threat to the workers. Cut to a living room in which a young woman sits writing while a figure comes in and out of frame unexpectedly. Cut to a title: "THE IMPERIALISTS." Then a shot of hands filling a shelf with Mao's writings while voices talk offscreen (or over). Cut to a close-up of a dark young man smoking. Cut to a photo of Castro; voices over, or off, consider what to call their cell. Cut, finally, to a long shot of the doorway: the young woman opens the door and another fellow helps the first young man in, wounded in a street fight.

What is remarkable is how little redundancy is assigned to the fabula. Characters are introduced in dissociative ways: isolated from the group; split between sound and image (we have no way of knowing whose voices speak offscreen or over, since Véronique, Guillaume, and Yvonne do not speak when they are on screen); and abstracted to a diagrammatic degree (the clasping hands, the red books). The intertitle "THE" cannot be interpreted in the light of adjacent material, so we must suspend making sense of it until the next title, "IMPERIALISTS"; but this too cannot designate what we see, so we must wait still longer until the phrase is completed. (No hurry: the last word is put into place in shot 297.) Characteristically, Godard delays and distributes his exposition more than any other director. The most solid first impressions we can form pertain to the subject of the film and the narration's strategies of address. The initial thirteen shots of *La Chinoise* indicate the principal paradigmatic sets from which the film will be generated: the filmmaking set, titles, found images, and narrative actions. Only gradually will a coherent fabula crystallize out of these self-conscious images and sounds. The characters are indeed created by the "discourse of others"—not only in social interaction but in the film's formal procedures.

In discussing basic principles of narration (chapter 4), I argued that we ought not to attribute narration to a narrator unless invited by textual cues and historical context. Godard's work offers perhaps the best instance of how a film's narration asks us to unify it around a distinct organizing personality. The narration is playful, fragmenting its materials (from PISCINE to CINE . . . PIS), pulling jokes in its credit sequences and intertitles ("Nothing left but a woman and a man and a sea of spilled blood"), misleading us about a film's overall structure (the "Fifteen Precise Actions" of *Masculin féminin*) or a scene's antecedent. It is virtuosic, able to mimic and parody other styles and narrational modes, and to cite many texts from many sources. It can be casual, insisting on its incompleteness and spontaneity ("Fragments of a Film Made in 1964," "An Action-Film"). And it is digressive, treating the skeletal cause-effect chain of the fabula as a basis for more or less free association. Indeed, by inviting us to construct a constantly present narrator within the syuzhet, the films have encouraged us to collapse the theoretically distinct categories of narrator and filmmaker.

In 1960, Luc Moullet asserted that the only thing that held a Godard film together was his personality.[23] Moreover, Godard explained the breakdown of narrative unity in his films by claiming to think of himself as an essayist.[24] Once this became a critical commonplace, it had the effect of identifying the film's narration with the voice of an essayist, a voice traditionally conceived of as being closer to that of the real author than is the voice of the narrator in fiction. Like Edouard in Gide's *Counterfeiters*, who wanted his novels to be all-inclusive, Godard embraces multitudes: "Everything can be put into a film. Everything should be put into a film."[25] Or: "I can put together a certain number of things which have struck me and which I find interesting, some of which I can explain, some of which I can't."[26] As these remarks indicate, Godard has been willing to "explain" his films (usually to no avail) in interviews, lectures, and essays. As a result, in no contemporary filmmaking is the distance between textual persona and historical individual so small. The self-conscious, playful narrator comes to be identified with the self-conscious, playful, flesh-and-blood Godard.

It is therefore significant that the narrator and the filmmaker are only characterized in certain respects. It is rare, for instance, to find anything straightforwardly autobiographical in Godard's work; the narrator does not incarnate Godard as husband or friend. The films' drive to collapse narrator and person assigns the narrator only one role: that of cineaste. The real filmmaker becomes a narrator who is characterized as (ideal) filmmaker.

In this egocentric cinema, the narrator comes forward as the manipulator of film material, the master of production, creator of all that appears in the narration. That there is no discernible pattern to the jump cuts in *A bout de souffle* creates the impression of a whimsical narrator-filmmaker, but it also defines that being's authority principally by the power to sit down at an editing table armed with splicer and cement. The unity of the narration in a Godard film proceeds from our constructing a narrator and personifying him as "the total filmmaker," sovereign over images and sounds—the very figure embodied in the Wizard of Video dozing at the end of *Numéro deux*.

Some critics will argue that to portray the narrator as I have done provides too much of a center for what are essentially dispersed and "open" films. Peter Wollen stresses Godard's intertextuality: "What seemed at first to be a kind of jackdaw mentality, a personal trait of Godard himself, begins to harden into a genuine polyphony, in which Godard's own voice is drowned out and obliterated behind that of the authors quoted. The film can no longer be seen as a discourse with a single subject, the filmmaker/auteur."[27] But a narrator can be identified not as a speaker but as a builder and combiner, the source of the "open" stylistic texture and syuzhet composition. And equating the narrator with the publicly available image of the filmmaker is, as we have seen, encouraged by the formal working of the film and by extratextual activities (e.g., interviews). Even a polyphony is composed, and here it is designed in a way that stresses the whimsicality, resourcefulness, and virtuosity of the composer.

To some extent my argument seems to coincide with Serge Daney's and J. P. Oudart's discussion of how the modern cinema has equated narrator and filmmaker under the rubric of the "Name-of-the-Author." The characteristically serpentine passage has to be quoted in full:

In the film practice immediately springing from the tendency toward cinephilia (*A bout de souffle, Le beau Serge*), the marking-out done by the camera and the insistent effects of shooting have the result of designating the film's *scripteur* (that is, the camera eye) no longer as the author of a fiction including all the effects of production of its *écriture* (in the sutured cinema, the author is identified with the fictive other of the mise-en-scène, the absent one), but as the author of a fiction which consists of the exteriorized relation of a cineaste (lens plus consciousness) with the objects filmed: in other words, the operation of filming becomes, in this cinema, the fiction itself. Filming is understood as a fiction of filmic inscription, an inscription which *fetishizes* what sutured cinema *forecloses*: the "edge" of the iconic film image (the frame), the materiality of the displacement of the camera.[28]

To some extent, this remark applies to Godard: the shooting of the film becomes part of the film's narrational process. But the account does not go far enough. The narrator-as-cineaste emerges not solely from effects of filming, but from every stage of production, each layered over the others. What Godard's narration offers is neither a coherent style nor simply an inscription of the shooting phase but what we might call *superscription*—littering the narration with traces of different stages of the filmmaking process and then "writing over" them at a later phase. In our *Pierrot* sequence, the character dialogue in the scene is eradicated, replaced by "subsequent" voice-over exchanges between Marianne and Ferdinand. Then the "original" order of the couple's escape is scrambled, again accompanied by dialogue taking place elsewhere, possibly later. Over all this is added, more or less arbitrarily, chunks of music fading in and out. In the opening of *La Chinoise*, commentary seems to be at once simultaneous with the image (voice off) and laid over it afterward, and the fragmentation of the "imperial-

ists" sentence forms a structure evidently added at the editing phase. The film's texture becomes that of a palimpsest, a document which has been written upon several times, leaving earlier, partly erased writing still visible. Such a process appeals even more to the cinephilia Oudart and Daney mention, since it fetishizes the film as the palpable residue of the entire production process.

In the mainstream film, Jean-Louis Comolli reminds us, each production stage strives to reproduce the preceding one.

Thus the project of the film is repeated for the first time in the scenario, which is repeated by the cutting continuity which is in turn itself repeated by rehearsals [*répétitions*] (appropriately so named). The latter are then reproduced for the filming, the editing of which is simply its reconstruction with post-synchronization, finally closing the cycle of re-presentations. This process of reduplication, far from allowing (as one might wrongly suppose) for new and decisive interventions at each new stage, on the contrary imposes auto-fidelity of the most extreme kind (on pain of seeing the whole edifice crumble, as for example in cases of re-editing by producers). It permits only the most minor retouches or variations. Thus each new operation must really be a false operation, a quasi-mechanical recommencement of the preceding one, and therefore imitative and non-productive. Though a hundred times reworked, the film is not thereby changed a hundred times, but simply repeated a hundred times, each time a copy of itself.[29]

With Godard, however, the stages of production are represented in the stylistic texture as acts of transformation, signs of "new and decisive interventions at each stage." For one thing, there are outcroppings of apparently raw or partially processed material. On the other hand, the polished working of some moments points to the presence of the diligent craftsman standing between us and the work. This in turn implies that the traces of incompatible elements are left there deliberately by a cunning narrator-cineaste: not actual "rawness" but *signs* of it. The rawness is no less a fictional—

and narrational—strategy than the polishing is. From staging and shooting to editing and sound mixing, all phases of
production are intermittently visible in this palimpsest.

In classical cinema, to stage the profilmic event—to put
actors into a setting, to light the action—is usually to create
by implication the diegetic world. Like Soviet filmmakers,
however, Godard refuses to identify the profilmic with the
diegetic. The clearest example is the use of to-camera
address. This is not simple "reflexivity" (reminding us we're
watching a film) but a self-conscious demonstration of the
filmmaker's power over the profilmic event, a virtuosic display of the ability to govern what we see. Citations affect the
status of the profilmic event too. It is one thing for characters
to allude to films, as when in *A bout de souffle* Michel
imitates Bogart. It is something else when characters *become*
citations, such as Veronika Dreyer (*Le petit soldat*), Nana
(*Vivre sa vie*), Alfred Lubitsch (*Une femme est une femme*),
Kirilov and Shokolov (*La Chinoise*), and virtually all characters in *Les carabiniers*, *Alphaville*, and *Made in USA*. By
peopling the fiction with clichés, Godard cuts it away from
the profilmic event: the actor is tangible enough, but
"Donald Siegel" or "Leonard Nosferatu" constitutes a character scarcely the thickness of cardboard. And sometimes
the profilmic event cannot be understood as equivalent to a
diegetic event. In *Alphaville*, we construct a piece of fabula
action: "Lemmy Caution thrashes a guard in a car lot." Yet
the profilmic event we see is a series of shots in which the
actors assume postures evocative of stages of an altogether
implausible fight. Similarly, in the opening of *La Chinoise*,
the two hands meeting against the wall can be construed as
representing the political and romantic union of Véronique
and Guillaume, but we do not assume that the fictional
characters ever choreographed their fists in this way within
the diegetic world: it is the self-conscious narrator's address
to the viewer through the medium of the actor.

Godard even lets the profilmic event be invaded by tactics
characteristic of techniques operating at "later" stages of
production. Fragmentation? In *La Chinoise*, Véronique and
Guillaume hurl phrases at each other, creating an aleatory
poem. Arbitrary sound/image connections? In the same film,

Véronique puts a Mozart record on the phonograph as background to her (faked) breakup with Guillaume. Detached
sonic commentary on the image? In *Une femme mariée*,
Charlotte switches on a record of a woman's laughter which
continues (though often interrupted) through the scene.
Rapid editing of still images? It is common for a Godard
character to flip through pages of a book or magazine, with
the fluttering pages creating a montage of words and pictures. Harsh sound cuts? In *Masculin féminin*, the recording studio is rendered as two spaces: output (blasting sound
of the song with full accompaniment) and input (a vacuum
with only Madeleine's thin voice audible). By allowing us to
construct a fabula only after passing through the "relay" of
recognizing the narrator as *meneur de jeu*, Godard's films
acknowledge the extent to which the profilmic event in any
film is always manipulated for the purpose of narration.

The narrative action we infer will thus oscillate between
being a "direct" derivation of the profilmic event and a manipulated "superscription" imposed upon that event. Godard
leaves traces of the act of staging through several production
practices. He does not improvise but writes the dialogue at
the last minute. For nonactors, he uses ear microphones
through which he transmits the lines he wants them to
repeat.[30] In either case, he preserves signs of "documentary"
spontaneity while still controlling the performance. The
syuzhet announces that the narrator can shape the profilmic
event in any fashion, from the apparently natural dialogues
in the bedroom in *A bout de souffle* or in the kitchen in
Masculin féminin to the impossibly stylized cocktail party of
Pierrot le fou (the characters talk advertisements) or the
implausible capture of Lemmy Caution in *Alphaville*. The
to-camera addresses of characters become principal instances of shifting between "natural" staging and acknowl-
edgement of authorial intervention.

The shooting phase also peers through the palimpsest. On
one hand, the shots are seldom designed to be dense with
significance. Countering this relative rawness of the composition is an identification of the camera with the narrator.
This is a convention of the art cinema as well, but Godard
exploits it in order to characterize the narrator as master

13.1. Pierrot le fou
13.2. Pierrot le fou

cineaste reworking an empirical space. The choice of actual locations is often mitigated by the use of long lenses (especially in the widescreen films) and flat lighting, both of which tend to minimize depth and abstract the space of the scene. The camera is also endowed with a presence that can react to the action, as when the hero of *Charlotte et son Jules* asserts, "Cinema is an illusory art" and the camera responds by canting left and right. The camera can comment on the action by tilting from a character to a picture on the wall (*A bout de souffle* and *Le petit soldat*). The unexpected canted shots in *Une femme mariée, Made in USA,* and *Deux ou trois choses* function in part to signal the presence of a narrator intervening between character and viewer.

More generally, Godard employs camera movements to assert the cineaste's presence. There are the virtuoso tracking shots that weave around the action (*Vivre sa vie*) or pursue a rectilinear course independent of character movement (*Le mépris, Weekend*). Here the narrator comes forward in a traditional way as the master of our vision. Alternatively, Godard will employ the hand-held camera, which by panning or tracking to follow characters generates slight tremblings and gratuitous reframings that make us continually aware of the filming subject. In *A bout de souffle*, for instance, even before Michel turns to talk to us, we know that the cameraman is riding in the front seat of the car. In a sense, direct sound recording, with its ambient noise and "unnatural" volume and timbres, is the sonic equivalent to the use of real locations and the hand-held camera: the sign of not the reality of an event but the real presence of the recording of that event.

The editing phase makes itself known in complex ways. Mainstream French filmmaking of the 1950s of course presupposed classical editing as a norm, but Godard's films violate nearly every tenet of correct continuity. As early as *Charlotte et son Jules*, we find him crossing the axis of action, using false eyeline matches and jump cuts, and mismatching on action. Thereafter he will cut together opposed camera or figure movements, overlap shots, and reshuffle temporal order. From this standpoint *A bout de souffle* constitutes a virtual anthology of incorrect matches.

In the sequence we have already examined from *Pierrot*, at the end of shot 7 Marianne walks out from behind a balcony pillar (fig. 13.1); cut to the high angle of Ferdinand getting into the car (fig. 13.2). The force of the cut arises not only from the dismemberment of time we have already noted. There is also a strong graphic tension, whereby shapes (balcony pillar and Marianne's face / tower and Pierrot's head) are compositionally continuous but the directions of movement clash from shot to shot (Marianne to the left, Ferdinand and the car to the right).

What is striking about Godard's approach to editing, however, is its unsystematic character. Throughout no film does the editing consistently block our creating a coherent space and time for the fabula action—as, say, Dreyer does in *La Passion de Jeanne d'Arc*. In every Godard film, there are some passages which are edited in conventional fashion. The disjunctions that do arise can be attributed to the fact that Godard often treats the cut less as a way to combine shots than as a way to halt one shot and commence another.

1956: "Knowing just how long one can make a scene last is already montage."[31]

1965: "As if by chance, the only great problem with cinema seems to me more and more with each film when and why to start a shot and when and why to end it."[32]

1978: "[Normal shot length] let me avoid this essential question: Why stop a shot? When must it be cut off?"[33] Significantly, during filming Godard typically shoots each action from only one setup; he seldom retakes the same action from different camera positions. The duality of master shot and insert (upon which much of classical cutting is predicated) is absent from Godard's work; there is virtually no orthodox analytical cutting. Since Godard's shots are often staged with no idea about how they will be joined in the editing, each shot retains a degree of independence, forming a block (big or small) that will necessarily strike some friction against whatever gets spliced to it.

This friction may be minimal, eased by an eyeline match, the most common cut within a Godard scene. The friction increases when, as is often the case, there is no establishing shot, so that like the Soviet filmmakers of the 1920s Godard can exploit our drive to synthesize a whole out of parts. At the limit, we have Godard's most original approach to disjunction: using the cut simply to interrupt the shot. Resnais's or Bresson's editing, however rapid, presents shots complete in themselves; the brief images of *La guerre est finie* or *Pickpocket* each make a distinctly rounded-off point. In the same way, the Soviet directors' tendency to plan each shot in advance assured that each shot, however it would fragment the scenographic space, retained its own curve of development. Godard, however, gives us shots that seem to run too long or to be curtailed before they have finished. In accordance with the palimpsest principle, he reminds us of the distinction between the shot as it comes from the camera and the shot after it has been whittled down (or not) for insertion into the final edited film.

Godard's propensity for long takes emphasizes the interruptive function of the cut. Brian Henderson describes the spectacular tracking shots of the rural traffic jam in *Weekend* as basic to the film: "The cuts are mainly connective; once outside the Paris apartment, the film might as well be a single fixed-distance traveling shot along the highway and across the provincial landscape."[34] But this claim ignores how the survey of the traffic jam is disrupted by intertitles.

26. Long shot: Track rightward down traffic jam. Music abruptly up at end. (2 min 34 sec)

27. Title: 13H40. (1.5 sec)

28. Long shot: Track past bus and a couple saying farewell. (1.5 sec)

29. Title: WEEKEND. (1.5 sec)

30. Long shot: Track past bus, as (28). Music cuts out. (2.5 sec)

31. Title: 14H10. (1.5 sec)

32. Long shot: Track down traffic jam. (5 min 11 sec)

The odd-numbered shots contaminate the "Bazinian" purity of the tracking shots by virtue of their annoying brevity and their nature as intertitles. As if by contagion, two of the tracking shots (28 and 30) also become fragments. Moreover, each inserted title creates a different temporal disjunction: a slight ellipsis (appropriate to the length of the interposed title) between 26 and 28, no ellipsis between 28 and 30, a greater ellipsis (not appropriate to the length of the interposed title) between 30 and 32. The titles lead us to expect a greater duration than we can find on the basis of the next shot. Finally, the unmodulated entry and exit of the musical score intensifies the interruptive quality of some cuts. The spectator cannot predict how long a shot will continue because the cut may break in at any moment. If the Soviet montage school often uses the cut to rupture the *action*, Godard often uses it to interrupt the *shot*, as if the narrator at the editing table needed long takes to give him plenty of choice about when to make a splice.

The interruptive function of the cut is exemplified by another device. The jump cut has been associated with Godard's work since *A bout de souffle*, and it crops up in other early films. The jump cut is one which yields the impression that footage has been excised from within the shot. In Godard's films, the device signals one thing unequivocally: the intervention of the filmmaker at the editing stage. As such, the jump cut is a perfect index of the superscription I have mentioned. The film is finished, but the narrator fiddles with it, chopping out a frame here and there, leaving traces of the act of editing. This yields the characteristic effect of Godardian montage, noted by Jacques Rivette:

> What distinguishes his films from those of Chytilova, Eisenstein, or Pollet is that with him one feels there was (or used to be) an earlier state of the film, an inference the others do not permit. In *Made in USA*, Godard leaves the impression of an earlier film, rejected, contested, defaced, torn to shreds; destroyed as such, but still "subjacent."[35]

Although Godard's cuts are often registered as interruptions, important positive effects arise from the combinations of shots. The central devices of Godard's editing all point to the "superscriptural" form I am analyzing: they suggest the presence of a narrator running a conventionally finished film through the moviola, skipping over some passages and recomposing others at will, in caprice, or by chance. Let us take one sequence as an example.

In *Alphaville*, Natasha and Lemmy are talking in his suite in daylight. He tells her he is in love with her. After a very precise shot/reverse-shot exchange, these shots ensue:

226. Extreme close-up: Natasha turns rightward.

227. High angle: Police car driving though streets.

228. Medium Shot: Lemmy comes to Natasha and circles her. She walks to the window, asking, "So what is love, then?"

229. High angle: Police car stopped. Doors swing open.

230–236. Abstract shots of Natasha and Lemmy embracing, kissing, dancing as light flashes on them.

237. Long shot: City landscape at night. Pan right to the silhouettes of Natasha and Lemmy. She circles to the table to the lamp.

238. Medium long shot: Outside window, day. Natasha looks out and up, the book pressed to her chest.

239. *Plan américain*: Lemmy in bathroom washing up. Pan to Natasha coming to him. They discuss how he may be duped. Lemmy grips her throat.

240. Close-up: Natasha.

241. Long shot: The two of them in bedroom, talking.

Lemmy tries to use the telecommunication system, but it is shut down. They try to flee, but they back into the shot, followed by four cops.

This brief passage exemplifies several of Godard's pet editing devices. There is the "free montage sequence," obviously derived from Hollywood norms but revised almost out of recognition. Shots 230 through 236 are linked by music and Natasha's disjointed offscreen commentary and are somewhat abstractly shot (flashing lights, to-camera looks); they might pass for an elliptical version of a night spent together, except that because of the inconsistent daylight-nighttime cues, we cannot be sure that a night has in fact passed. (Compare the lovemaking scenes in *La guerre est finie*.) The sequence is, in a sense, the answer to her question, "So what is love?" but it is hardly a straightforward one. Such a loosening of the traditional montage sequence can be found as early as *A bout de souffle* (e.g., when Michel searches for a car to steal); it reappears in almost every Godard feature. The meditative narrator inserts footage in a way that gives the segment an arbitrary autonomy with respect to the diegetic action that surrounds it: a poetic digression composed at the editing table.

The *Alphaville* sequence instantiates another editing device, that of the equivocal transition. We do not know if the day/night/day montage (shots 230–238) counts as a separate sequence, or the end of the prior sequence (and day), or the start of a new sequence (and day). The boundaries of the episode are thrown into question by an interruption of the normal cues for continuity of time. (Shot 228, of Natasha going to the window, would cut fairly smoothly with shot 238—her standing there.) Like the editing in Soviet montage cinema, Godardian cutting challenges our expectations about where a scene will end or begin. Sometimes, as here, he simply avoids the conventional punctuation of fades and dissolves. At other times, he will use such punctuation in ambivalent ways. In *Weekend* and *La Chinoise*, a scene fades in, then quickly fades out with no action having transpired; then it fades in again, and the action starts. By 1965, it becomes almost impossible to break a Godard film into incontrovertible sequences.

Conventionally treated, the cutaway is a classical device: to cover a gap in fabula duration, we cut away from the principal action, either to something else within the scene or, more likely, to another action elsewhere. A simple case occurs in *Charlotte et son Jules*, when Jules's frenetic display is interrupted by cutaways to Charlotte's lover waiting in the car outside. Similarly, in *Charlotte et Véronique*, there is a cut from the two women by the bed to a Picasso print on the wall. Across Godard's career, however, the cutaway becomes a more abrupt and disorienting device. Sometimes the shot simply "glances" at an item: the poster for *Ten Seconds to Hell* in *A bout de souffle*, or the cover of Elsa Triolet's *L'âge du nylon: L'âme* in *Une femme mariée*. Although these objects are within the diegetic space, the abrupt insertion of such exaggerated close-ups makes the cut a self-conscious narrational gesture. In our *Alphaville* example, a shot of a speeding police car (shot 227) interrupts the dialogue in Lemmy's suite. Natasha walks to the window (shot 228). Cut to an overhead shot of a stopped police car, the doors opening (shot 229). Our first assumption is that the police have arrived, perhaps seen from Natasha's point of view. But there follows the lengthy "free montage" of the couple. At the end (shot 238), she is back at the window looking *upward*. Lemmy and Natasha continue their conversation. Only then do the police burst into Lemmy's suite (shot 241). The cutaways to the cops have misled us; instead of covering a gap in fabula time, they have confused us about the duration of the action in the suite. The shot of the car's arrival "belongs" after the montage sequence (say, between 238 and 239), just before the cops burst in.

When the cutaways have even less causal import than in this case, they become "nondiegetic inserts." The flashing neon formulas that interrupt scenes in *Alphaville* can be grasped only as the interjections of a omniscient narrator. The inserted ads and comic strips in *Made in USA* and *Deux ou troix choses*, the paintings and comics of *Pierrot*, the proliferations of such material in *La Chinoise*—all these must be attributed to a self-conscious intelligence. It is here that the "collage" metaphor seems most apt, since the term traditionally implies the cutting up of a preexistent body of material. What remains raw here is the actually existing detritus of mass culture; the juxtaposition of such material, however, points to a *collagiste* at the editing bench assembling, from the bits and pieces of modern life, disruptions of the fabula.

In 1978, Godard remarked that when making *A bout de souffle* he wished that he could avoid the problem of editing (when to start or stop a shot) by inserting intertitles between shots.[36] As in Soviet montage cinema, Godard's intertitles addressed to the viewer mark the intrusion of a self-conscious narrator. But with Godard the intertitle also tags another component of the film as "added at the editing stage." In the early works, titles tend to break the film into segments: the twelve parts of *Vivre sa vie*, the interpolated letters home in *Les carabiniers*. With *Masculin féminin*, the intertitles proliferate, creating a running commentary and, at one point, identifying their source as the storymaker/filmmaker: "The philosopher and the filmmaker share a certain attitude, a certain view of the world which is that of a generation." In subsequent works like *La Chinoise* and *Weekend*, titles pervade the film, breaking into the action and supplying epigrammatic asides. As a final touch, Godard will occasionally handwrite credits (*Charlotte et son Jules, Charlotte et Véronique, Les carabiniers*) or write over inserted imagery (*La Chinoise*), as if to stress the ex post facto intervention of the narrator (and his equation with Godard the man). It is with the post-1968 work that literal superscription takes over, creating a dry calligraphy that etches every stray advertisement, news photo, or pinup with the graffiti of the cineaste, refusing to allow us to take any vision as unmediated.

Just as chopping down an image grants the individual shot some autonomy as a piece in the narrator's game, so sonic montage frees each sound track to become a discrete component at the editing stage. Godard again begins from basic elements, such as characters' conversation, portions of which can be erased (the after-dinner monologue and the girls' exchange in *Une femme mariée*) or repeated (the replaying of a line of dialogue after a cut in *Masculin féminin*). Another component is voice-over commentary. In *Bande à part*, Godard intones a voice-over text, exhibiting unlikely knowledge of the poetic side of these characters. During the "Madison" dance sequence, the narrator arbitrarily fades down the jukebox tune to which the trio dances and overlays his remarks—while all the while retaining the shuffle and stamp of their feet on the cafe floor. The narrator has here foregrounded his power to become the sound mixer, creating *une bande à part*. The same thing occurs in the opening of *Les carabiniers*: we hear a voice ordering the construction of the sound track ("Hello, hello! Military march!"). *Le mépris* has the credits recited by Godard over the opening shot. In *Deux ou trois choses*, the narrator's voice whispers to us, as if just out of camera range, stressing the choices made at the moment of filming. The voice-over parallels the injected intertitles: both gloss the fabula action as we construct it.

There is also a great deal of character voice-over in Godard's films. The most coherent instance is *Le petit soldat*, which strictly separates the image track (Bruno's past action) from the voice-over reflections (taking place in the narrating present). Thereafter, however, Godard begins to violate the temporal uniformity associated with character voice-over. In *Le mépris*, he inserts characters' voice-over during a sequence whose reality status is uncertain; the voices of Paul and Camille mingle and alternate without any evidence that either character speaks of what we see. The same problem comes up in *Alphaville, Pierrot le fou, Masculin féminin*, and *Made in USA*: we cannot assign any narrating present to the inserted character voice-overs that we hear. The effect is to cut the voice-overs free of any strict relation to the fabula action and to make them fragments running parallel to the image. By minimizing any realistic motivation for their presence, the syuzhet makes them attributable to the will of an omniscient sound engineer. This is especially evident in *Pierrot le fou*, when the characters' interspersed voice-overs take on tasks normally assigned to the author (Ferdinand will announce, "Chapter Two"). In another case, *Vivre sa vie*, a character's voice-over (the pimp Raoul's exposition of prostitution) bleeds indistinguishably into the narrator's commentary.

Music and sound effects operate in the same fashion.

Their disjunctiveness makes them stand out as material elements "applied" or "rubbed out" at a late production phase. In place of smoothly modulated sound bridges (what Hollywood calls "sneaking in" and "sneaking out"), the narration usually offers only shards of sound. Often a cut on the image track is accompanied by an abrupt sound cut, as in *Charlotte et son Jules*: first shot—music; second shot—silence; third shot—music; fourth shot—silence. The abrasiveness of *Deux ou trois choses* arises partly from its alternation of silent landscape shots with ear-splitting ones. More complex are the cases when the sound constitutes a montage level distinct from the image track. Typically Godard chooses fragments of noise and music and welds them momentarily into the verbal chain. *Made in USA* is the most striking instance, wherein chunks of Beethoven and the roar of jet planes are looped, again and again, in multiple combination with the images. In many films the same musical passage will be faded up and out so arbitrarily that its original evocative power becomes replaced by our awareness of a hand twiddling a dial. A scene may begin in silence, with sound entering abruptly and coinciding with the opening of a door. Alan Williams points out that in the theater audition in *Le mépris*, a single shot is accompanied by chunks of the song in playback and chunks of synced dialogue, "two alternate and incompatible renderings of the acoustic environment."[37] Like other paradigmatic uses of sound, this displays the filmmaker's act of selection at the sound-mixing stage. And Godard's use of already-existing sound—bits of classical music or pop tunes—further reinforces our sense of montage as a final arrangement of materials in different degrees of rawness. "Music is a living element," he noted in 1965, "just like a street, or cars. It is something I describe, something pre-existent to the film."[38]

Still other effects can be traced to the creation of the cineaste-narrator. The switches into negative footage (in *Une femme mariée* and *Alphaville*) or into tinted color (in *Le mépris* and *Anticipation*) create a narrator who can doctor the tonality of the film strip. The more or less arbitrary partitioning of the film comes almost to seem an afterthought. The abrupt or altogether absent credit sequences can be attributed to the image manipulator. Even the insistence of Godard (the man) upon giving each film a distinct source—novel, Balzac short story (*Masculin féminin*), press clipping (*Deux ou trois choses*), other films (*Alphaville, Made in USA*)—only emphasizes the transformation that his work has wrought. The palimpsest has many layers, but each inscription bears witness to one identifiable hand. We can now repeat the line from *Charlotte et Véronique*, but with a new stress: "From the mere fact that *I* say a sentence, there is necessarily a connection with what came before." The unity of the subject—the narrator-cineaste-cinephile—lends unity to the syuzhet.

Not a complete unity, of course; most of my examples show the gulf between the films' narrational disjunctions and their motivation as the work of the cineaste-auteur. Yet the disunity is, as we have seen, an effect over which our narrator labors. The spontaneous and rushed qualities of the scribbles on Godard's palimpsest constitute as carefully created an illusion as the effect of speed arising from the heavily worked-over Cubist collages. The story has gaps not because there are any constraints on the narrator's range or depth of knowledge but because the narrator has skipped decisions, or just hasn't worked it all out yet. Godard is like a painter who leaves a pencil grid or a patch of underpainting visible in the finished picture, not only as a compositional element but also as a fastidiously preserved sign of process.

It should now be evident that Godard's narration is not fully reducible to the current critical notion of "reflexivity." His films do declare their own artificiality, but so do all films. Rather, and more specifically, Godard's work could have been created only in the era of the art cinema, with its valorization of an authorial presence hovering over the text, its drift toward confusing narrator and creator, and the concomitant sense that we know vaguely how a film is produced. Other collage films—say, *Song of the Shirt* (1979)—might be considered reflexive, but there is no personification of the narrator, and no palimpsest as a "record" of the stages of production. Godard gives us *cinéma d'auteur* with a vengeance; the narrator becomes "superauteur," flaunting his command of the entire production process. It is not simply reflexivity that is at stake, but the constitution of a narrator who engages the viewer as a virtuoso "playing" cinema. ("You have the impression that Buñuel plays cinema the way Bach at the end of his life could play the organ.")[39]

The "cinephilia" of this narrator is perhaps clearest in "Camera Eye," Godard's contribution to *Loin du Viêt-Nam* (1969). Shots of Godard in Paris manipulating a camera alternate with inserts of documentary footage, stills, posters, and takes from *La Chinoise*. The episode's structure looks forward to the 1968 work and the films of the Dziga-Vertov Group. It is a good example of interrogative cinema, though in a nonnarrative form. Yet we are back again to the image of the filmmaker as sorcerer: peering through his viewfinder, snapping on a floodlight (and illuminating, via the Kuleshov effect, a fleeing Vietnamese), winding up soundtape, and editing together found footage and staged action. As in *Numéro deux*, the narrator assumes center stage, acknowledging his role as creator and encouraging us to unify the narration around the (divided) consciousness of the cineaste. How typical then that while proposing that we let Vietnam invade us, Godard's voice also insists: "The only thing we can do is make films."

1968 and After

Critics commonly break Godard's work into the "nonpolitical" films (chiefly those before 1968) and the "political" efforts afterward. Even Marxist critics have forgotten, however, that most of the pre-1968 films are political in a sense that Godard and his contemporaries would have acknowledged: they take as subject matter the politics of everyday life, a notion that owes a good deal to Henri Lefebvre and other existential Marxists.[40] (Mark Poster has convincingly argued that it is this strain, not Party or Althusserian versions of Marxism, that had the most influence upon the uprising of May 1968, in which Godard became deeply involved.)[41] From the standpoint of this book, the periodization by "politics" thus does not reflect the change in narra-

13.3. Ici et ailleurs

tional procedures that Godard's work undergoes. The crucial dividing line is "Camera Eye," which marks the emergence of truly essayistic forms in his work. (Later examples would be *Pravda* and *Letter to Jane.*) Broadly speaking, three narrational tendencies emerge in the post-1967 films, all related to principles of the early period.

First, we find films (the *Cinétracts, Le gai savoir, Un film comme les autres, One Plus One, British Sounds, Pravda, Ici et ailleurs*) which expand the principles behind the digressions that swarmed into the earlier films. Now there is no narrative, at best a framing situation of conversation (*Le gai savoir, Un film comme les autres*). The film becomes an assemblage out of documentary footage, photographs, television images, recorded sound. The films draw upon genres of documentary cinema (publicity film, reportage, interview) and utilize techniques of Soviet historical-materialist film (the "intellectual montage" of *Le gai savoir*, the contrapuntal sound/image relations and the rhetorical intertitles in all the Dziga-Vertov Group films). The occasional mixing of modes has the overtly political aim of searching for a "grammar" for revolutionary cinema. And the principle of the palimpsest is still in force, as the film displays the transformations of the profilmic event by all manner of superscriptions: writing over printed images ("Les rois de l'imperialisme"), blotting out one sound track by another, or layering images atop one another (*Letter to Jane*). In these works, the spatialization of the text (no longer a narration, since there is no fabula to be constructed) reaches its apogee. A shot will appear, be commented on, then reappear in a new context and with new commentary. More than ever is there a sense of a stockpile of images picked over by a *grand imagier*. *Ici et ailleurs* constitutes a summary case. Here a debate (between Godard and Anne-Marie Miéville in voiceover) about Palestinian footage is accompanied by titles sprayed out as video characters; black frames; a recasting and reframing of earlier images with a new sound; and insistent effects of montage (people successively showing pictures to the camera, slides popping up in a tiny viewer, four television monitors filling a frame). When Henry Kissinger's name is wiped away leaving only SS (fig. 13.3), we

recognize how an entire film has been built out of what were interpolations in *La Chinoise*.

A second tendency lies in a more direct line from the 1960–1967 output. Here we have a narrative punctuated by insertions and paralleled by sonic manipulations. At one extreme are the minimal, allegorical narratives contained in some Dziga-Vertov Group films: *Vent d'est, Luttes en Italie, Vladimir and Rosa.* Far more conventional is *Tout va bien.* And somewhere in between stand the more fragmented but still coherent *Numéro deux* and *Comment ça va?* All these films require us to construct a more or less conventional fabula on the model of classical cinema (*Vent d'est*, with its parody of the Western) or on that of art-cinema narration. Again, however, the modes mix: an interrogative historical-materialist narration challenges and corrects other cues. The art-cinema conventions of subjectivity and character reflection in *Luttes en Italie* and *Tout va bien* run up against devices that demand political formulation: voice-overs, black frames (in *Luttes en Italie*, to allow time for viewer reflection), and self-conscious Brechtian devices (especially in *Tout va bien*). In *Numéro deux*, scenes of family life as an updated Neorealism become highly mediated by Godard's use of video monitors to carry the imagery, thus surrounding every shot with a black void, wiping one image out by another, and creating a montage effect among several screens. *Comment ça va?* intermingles footage from the framing narrative (a couple making a militant videotape) with material that may or may not be on the tape, thus yielding a complex interplay of documentary, art-cinema, and historical-materialist schemata. Again, like the pre-1968 films, the narration gets spatialized, as sounds and images recombine and segments evoke what we do not see. The identification of narrator and filmmaker is again very strong, although the voice-overs often split narrational functions to create a dialogue. And of course superscription is constant, to the point of marking up the film strip itself (*Vent d'est*).

The most recent tendency in Godard's work is difficult to assess because it appears to be a regression. *Sauve qui peut (La vie)* and *Passion* seem to be almost completely assimilable to the art cinema's narrational mode. Serious protagonists revealing more or less consistent character traits, loose narratives hinging on chance encounters and psychological crises, a degree of causal resolution accompanied by many permanent gaps—in such respects, the films recall middle-period Antonioni. Many technical effects come close to being readable as authorial commentary (however ambiguous) upon a fundamentally coherent and uniform diegetic world. (I am thinking of the mistimed sound synchronization in *Passion* or the slowed frames in *Sauve qui peut*.) Superscrip-

tion is thus much less overt, often only a matter of volume or uncertain diegetic status. In the opening of *Sauve qui peut*, for instance, only Paul's annoyed pounding on the wall tells us that the soprano's voice, which cuts abruptly off, is diegetic. There also remains a paradigmatic impulse, especially in the exploration of various image-sound relations, but it manifests itself in subtle ways. Overall, these films operate on two levels: the fairly straightforward usage of art-film schemata, and a quiet process of disjunction which never poses the glaring problems of the early films but which can, once opened up to critical scrutiny, reveal a stylistic work no less experimental than that in the years immediately after 1968.

For some viewers and critics, this will seem too much of a step backward. But an artist's work need not move in a straight line, as Godard cryptically reminds us in a two-page insert he designed for a 1981 number of *Cahiers*.[42] On the left page there is a photomontage of Freud looking on as Eisenstein works at his editing bench. Beside Freud there is the sentence, "Where id was ego shall be" (*Là où c'était, je serai*); beside Eisenstein we find, "Where ego shall be, ego has already been" (*Là où je serai, j'ai déjà été*). On the facing page is a photo of Godard at his editing machine, with the caption: "Where id will be, one will be better" (*Là où ça ira, on sera mieux*). What has not changed is the image of the narrator as total filmmaker, one capable of presenting an apparently conservative career turn as only the willed fluctuation of a mercurial self-consciousness.

Conclusion

The main purpose of this book has been to build a theory of how films, in their formal and stylistic operations, solicit story-constructing and story-comprehending activities from spectators. Part 2 laid out the theoretical concepts necessary to explain this process. There is the goal-directed spectator, equipped with schemata and ready to make assumptions, form expectations, motivate material, recall information, and project hypotheses. There are the formal features of the film itself: first, syuzhet tactics that cue the spectator to execute inferential moves; second, qualities of knowledge-ability, communicativeness, self-consciousness, and tone that shape the spectator's evolving story construct. There are also the temporal and spatial properties of the film medium itself, any of which can contribute to a film's narrational process.

The third part of the book argued that narrational devices and principles tend to cluster historically, to form extrinsic norms within which a great many films are produced and consumed. While the narrational activity is logically open to any textual innovation, a few modes have proven to have great historical weight. I have concentrated upon four of these: classical narration, art-cinema narration, historical-materialist narration, and parametric narration. Each has its own relatively stable compositional "dominants" and its fundamental choices about how the viewing activity will occur. This is not to say that there are not also problematic works that call on norms in conflicting ways; Godard was our (glaring) example. Nor is this to say that a film produced within the protocols of one mode cannot be construed according to protocols of another; we saw this occuring with Hollywood films at the hands of auteur critics, or with *L'an-née dernière à Marienbad* in relation to the art-cinema and the parametric modes.

What advantages accrue to this theoretical, historical, and critical account of narration in fictional filmmaking? Most obviously, it should be judged by the criteria used in gauging all theories. Is it sufficiently comprehensive? Does it discriminate in interesting and handy ways? Does it cohere logically? Does it correspond to what we take to be the domain of data? If I am right in thinking that it passes these tests reasonably well, we have something useful: a partial theory of narrative in fictional cinema.

I stress the qualifier "partial." This theory will not answer every interesting question we might ask about cinematic storytelling. Being an account of narration, it will not necessarily help define matters of narrative representation or narrative structure. Dependent upon a perceptual-cognitive account of the spectator's activity, it will not address issues such as sexuality and fantasy, for which psychoanalytic theories are better suited. Taking the history of the cinema as its most proximate context, it will of course not answer broader cultural, economic, or ideological questions about the filmmaking institution. Such limitations seem to me symptoms of strength. A theory that explained everything would be uninteresting; it might also verge upon religion. Knowledge often benefits from a circumscribed domain of inquiry.

Nonetheless perhaps some concepts and distinctions made in previous pages can help clarify accepted or emergent critical categories. Notions of authorship in cinema could be recast in narrational terms, especially with respect to norms. Genre study might benefit, as I propose in Chapter 5, from an attention to variations in narrational strategies. Critics interested in "reception theory" might consider how the sorts of norms I have sketched here could be specified in particular historical conjunctures. Studies of ideology in cinema can usefully recognize that through schemata a society's ideological constructs are taken up by its members; and that narrational modes are central mediations between ideology and its manifestations in artworks, so that, for instance, kindred political positions may get represented very differently in classical narration, art-cinema narration, and historical-materialist narration. If ideological analysis is to avoid vacuous overgeneralization, it must reckon in the concrete ways that narrational processes function in filmic representation.

It may be, then, that the theory proposed here can define, describe, and analyze processes that other approaches should take into account. This possibility would be in the spirit of the Russian Formalist critics, who, in Eichenbaum's term, considered themselves "specifiers." I do not, however, offer this work as one ingredient in the eclectic mixing of doctrines that often passes for film theory. This book was written in the conviction that film study needs not blanket programs but a discrimination among questions that can be answered according to more or less powerful conceptual frames of reference.

One more test of a good theory is its fecundity. Does it generate interesting new questions? Some of the claims set out here will, I hope, lead readers to study the process of narration and to disclose fresh areas of investigation. Certainly the relations of syuzhet and style, the possibility of other narrational modes, the interaction of intrinsic and extrinsic norms, and the full range of perceptual-cognitive operations performed by the spectator are all matters for more detailed inquiry. None of what I have said is definitive, but this account of narration may encourage the growth of a valuable realm of knowledge: the historical poetics of cinema.

Notes
Photo Credits
Selected Bibliography
Index

Notes

INTRODUCTION

1. V. Propp, *Morphology of the Folktale*, trans. Laurence Scott, 2d ed. (Austin: University of Texas Press, 1968); Tzvetan Todorov, *The Poetics of Prose*, trans. Richard Howard (Ithaca: Cornell University Press, 1977), 218–233.

2. Claude Lévi-Strauss, "The Structural Study of Myth," *Structural Anthropology*, trans. Claire Jacobson and Brooke Grundfest Schoepf (Garden City, N.Y.: Anchor, 1967), 202–228.

3. John Holloway, *Narrative and Structure* (Cambridge: Cambridge University Press, 1979).

4. Boris Eichenbaum, "The Theory of the 'Formal Method,'" in Lee T. Lemon and Marion J. Reis, eds., *Russian Formalist Criticism: Four Essays* (Lincoln: University of Nebraska Press, 1965), 104.

5. See, for example, Jim Kitses, *Horizons West* (Bloomington: Indiana University Press, 1970); Colin MacArthur, *Underworld USA* (New York: Viking, 1972); John G. Cawelti, *The Six-Gun Mystique* (Bowling Green, Ohio: Bowling Green Popular Press, 1975); and most of the essays in Rick Altman, ed., *Genre: The Musical* (London: Routledge and Kegan Paul, 1981).

6. Christian Metz, "Problems of Denotation in the Fiction Film," *Film Language*, trans. Michael Taylor (New York: Oxford University Press, 1974), 108–146.

7. See Stephen Heath, "Film and System: Terms of Analysis," *Screen* 16, 1 (Spring 1975): 7–77, and *Screen* 16, 2 (Summer 1975): 91–113; Raymond Bellour, *L'analyse du film* (Paris: Albatros, 1979); and Thierry Kuntzel, "The Film-Work," *Enclitic* 2, 1 (Spring 1978): 39–62, and "The Film-Work, 2," *Camera Obscura* no. 5 (1980): 6–69.

8. This conception of a "poetics" is discussed in Benjamin Hrushovski, "Poetics, Criticism, Science: Remarks on the Fields and Responsibilities of the Study of Literature," *PTL: Poetics and Theory of Literature* 1 (1976): iii–xxxv, esp. xv–xvii.

CHAPTER 1

1. Aristotle, *Poetics*, trans. Gerald F. Else (Ann Arbor: University of Michigan Press, 1967), 13.

2. Gerald F. Else, " 'Imitation' in the Fifth Century," *Classical Philology* 53, 2 (April 1958): 78.

3. Samuel Y. Edgerton, Jr., *The Renaissance Rediscovery of Linear Perspective* (New York: Harper and Row, 1975), 173n.

4. Quoted in John White, *The Birth and Rebirth of Pictorial Space* (New York: Harper and Row, 1972), 251.

5. For an account of the development of perspective, see Lawrence Wright, *Perspective in Perspective* (London: Routledge and Kegan Paul, 1983), 33–180.

6. Quoted in Michael Baxandall, *Painting and Experience in Fifteenth-Century Italy* (New York: Oxford University Press, 1972), 127.

7. Leon Battista Alberti, *On Painting*, trans. John R. Spencer (New Haven: Yale University Press, 1966), 56.

8. Nikolai Taraboukine, *Le dernier tableau*, trans. A. B. Nakov and Michel Petris (Paris: Champ Libre, 1972), 117.

9. White, *Birth and Rebirth of Pictorial Space*, 190–191.

10. George R. Kernodle, *From Art to Theatre: Form and Convention in the Renaissance* (Chicago: University of Chicago Press, 1943), 188.

11. See Dene Barnett, "The Performance Practice of Acting: The Eighteenth Century. Part I: Ensemble Acting," *Theatre Research International* 2, 3 (May 1977): 157–186.

12. E. H. Gombrich, *Art and Illusion: A Study in the Psychology of Pictorial Representation* (Princeton: Princeton University Press, 1961), 129–138.

13. Quoted in Walter Allen, ed., *Writers on Writing* (New York: Dutton, 1949), 123.

14. Ibid., 168.

15. Quoted in Joseph A. Kestner, *The Spatiality of the Novel* (Detroit: Wayne State University Press, 1978), 58.

16. Quoted in Allen, *Writers on Writing*, 123.

17. Quoted in Richard Stang, *The Theory of the Novel in En-*

gland, *1850–1870* (New York: Columbia University Press, 1959), 101.

18. Ibid., 92–99.

19. Henry James, "The Future of the Novel," *The Future of the Novel*, ed. Leon Edel (New York: Vintage, 1956), 33.

20. Henry James, *The Art of the Novel*, ed. R. P. Blackmur (New York: Scribner's, 1934), 46.

21. Henry James, "The Art of Fiction," in Gay Wilson Allen and Harry Hayden Clark, eds., *Literary Criticism: Pope to Croce* (Detroit: Wayne State University Press, 1962), 558.

22. James, *Art of the Novel*, 306.

23. Percy Lubbock, *The Craft of Fiction* (New York: Viking, 1962), 9.

24. Ibid., 10.

25. Ibid., 65.

26. Ibid., 71.

27. Ibid., 74.

28. Ibid., 65.

29. Ibid., 73.

30. Ibid., 113.

31. Quoted in Allen, *Writers on Writing*, 186.

32. Roger Fowler, *Linguistics and the Novel* (New York: Methuen, 1977), 74.

33. Frances Marion, "Scenario Writing," in Stephen Watts, ed., *Behind the Screen: How Films Are Made* (New York: Dodge, 1938), 33.

34. V. I. Pudovkin, *Film Technique and Film Acting*, trans. and ed. Ivor Montagu (New York: Grove, 1970), 70–71.

35. Ibid., 254.

36. Karel Reisz and Gavin Millar, *The Technique of Film Editing*, 2d ed. (New York: Hastings House, 1968).

37. Ivor Montagu, *Film World: A Guide to Cinema* (Baltimore: Penguin, 1964), 102.

38. Frederick Y. Smith, "The Cutting and Editing of Motion Pictures," *The Technique of Motion Picture Production* (New York: Interscience, 1944), 130–139.

39. Montagu, *Film World*, 141.

40. André Bazin, "The Evolution of the Language of Cinema," *What Is Cinema?* trans. Hugh Gray (Berkeley: University of California Press, 1967), 24.

41. Quoted in S. Y. Kuroda, "Réflexions sur les fondements de la théorie de la narration," in Julia Kristeva, Jean-Claude Milner, Nicolas Ruwet, eds., *Langue, discours, société*. (Paris: Seuil, 1975), 281.

42. "The Rehearsal Method," *Kuleshov on Film: Writings by Lev Kuleshov*, trans. and ed. Ronald Levaco (Berkeley: University of California Press, 1974), 147–158.

43. S. M. Eisenstein, *Izbranniie proizvedeniia v chesti tomakh* (Selected works in six volumes), Vol. 4: *Regissura* (Direction) (Moscow: Iskusstvo, 1966), 605–630. Hereafter cited as *Direction*.

44. Sergei Eisenstein and Sergei Tretyakov, "Expressive Movement," *Millennium Film Journal* no. 3 (Winter/Spring 1979): 37.

45. Ibid., 38.

46. Sergej Eisenstein and Sergej Jutkevič, "L'Ottava Arte," *Bianco e Nero* 32, 7–8 (July–August 1971):111.

47. Eisenstein and Tretyakov, "Expressive Movement," 36–37.

48. S. M. Eisenstein, "Montage of Attractions," *The Drama Review* 18, 1 (March 1974): 78.

49. S. M. Eisenstein, "Les deux crânes d'Alexandre de Macédoine," *Au-delà des étoiles*, trans. Jacques Aumont et al. (Paris: Union Générale d'Editions, 1974), 169–170; Sergei Eisenstein, "The Unexpected," *Film Form*, ed. and trans. Jay Leyda (Cleveland: World, 1957), 20n.

50. Eisenstein, *Film Form*, 103.

51. Ibid., 53.

52. Ibid., 80.

53. See David Bordwell, "Narration and Scenography in the Later Eisenstein," *Millennium Film Journal* no. 13 (Fall-Winter 1983–1984): 62–80.

54. Eisenstein, *Direction*, 711–712.

55. S. M. Eisenstein, *Mémoires*, Vol. 1, trans. Jacques Aumont (Paris: Union Générale d'Editions, 1978), 62–63.

CHAPTER 2

1. Plato, *The Republic*, *The Collected Dialogues of Plato*, ed. Edith Hamilton and Huntington Cairns (New York: Pantheon, 1963), 638.

2. Ibid.

3. Etienne Souriau, Préface, in Etienne Souriau, ed., *L'univers filmique* (Paris: Flammarion, 1953), 7. See also Gérard Genette, *Narrative Discourse: An Essay in Method*, trans. Jane E. Lewin (Ithaca: Cornell University Press, 1980), 27n.

4. Roland Barthes, *Writing Degree Zero* and *Elements of Semiology*, trans. Annette Lavers and Colin Smith (Boston: Beacon, 1970), 9.

5. Roland Barthes, "Introduction to the Structural Analysis of Narratives," *Image Music Text*, ed. and trans. Stephen Heath (New York: Hill and Wang, 1977), 112.

6. Ibid., 113.

7. Yuri Tynianov, "On the Foundations of Cinema," in Herbert Eagle, ed., *Russian Formalist Film Theory* (Ann Arbor: University of Michigan Slavic Publications, 1981), 90–91.

8. Boris Eichenbaum, "Problems of Cinema Stylistics," in Eagle, *Russian Formalist Film Theory*, 56–62.

9. Colin MacCabe, *James Joyce and the Revolution of the Word* (London: Macmillan, 1978), 13–14.

10. Colin MacCabe, "Realism and the Cinema: Notes on Some Brechtian Theses," *Screen* 15, 2 (Summer 1974): 10.

11. Ibid.: 11.

12. Colin MacCabe, "Theory and Film: Principles of Realism and Pleasure," *Screen* 17, 3 (Autumn 1976): 11.

13. Tarski, however, is concerned to show the possibility of a semantic definition of truth by defining the referential dimensions of formalized languages; he takes no notice of literary or fictional discourse. See not only Tarski's "The Semantic Conception of Truth and the Foundations of Semantics," *Journal of Philosophy and Phenomenological Research* 4 (1944): 341–375 but also the discussion in George D. Romanos, *Quine and Analytic Philosophy: The Language of Language* (Cambridge: MIT Press, 1983), 135–172.

14. MacCabe, "Realism and the Cinema": 15.

15. Roland Barthes, "Reponses," *Tel Quel* 47 (Autumn 1971): 97.

16. See Geoffrey N. Leech and Michael H. Short, *Style in Fiction: A Linguistic Introduction to Fictional Prose* (London: Longman, 1981), 323.

17. See David Lodge, "*Middlemarch* and the Idea of the Classic Realist Text," in Arnold Kettle, ed., *The Nineteenth-Century Novel: Critical Essays and Documents*, 2d ed. (London: Heinemann, 1981), 218–231. Many of MacCabe's generalizations are also challenged by the extent to which even "realistic" nineteenth-century novelists like Scott, Austen, and Trollope indulge in parody, reflexivity, and narrative devices which confess their own artificiality. For a discussion, see George Levine, *The Realistic Imagination: English Fiction from Frankenstein to Lady Chatterley* (Chicago: University of Chicago Press, 1981).

18. MacCabe, "Realism and the Cinema": 8.

19. For a discussion of these registers, see Shlomith Rimmon-Kenan, *Narrative Fiction: Contemporary Poetics* (London·

Methuen, 1983), 106–116, and Leech and Short, *Style in Fiction*, 318–334.

20. Catherine Belsey, who follows MacCabe's definition of the classic realist text, at least realizes this problem, but her solution is draconian. According to her, *Bleak House* presents two discourses, that of a third-person narrator and that of a first-person narrator; they alternate and never become framed in a metalanguage. Belsey suggests that there must then be a third discourse containing the other two: a "privileged but literally unwritten discourse . . . the single and non-contradictory invisible discourse of the reader" (*Critical Practice* [London: Methuen, 1980], 80–81). If discourse can be literally unwritten, MacCabe's conception of discourse as a textual entity collapses. And if the reader produces a discourse or metalanguage, nothing stops us from positing many such entities, each corresponding to a different critical interpretation of the work. A discourse is, at least, a piece of text, and a reader's comprehension, however it may "unite" discourses, is not a piece of text.

21. For a thorough analysis of the poetics of quotation and "direct speech" in narrative texts, see Meir Sternberg, "Point of View and the Indirections of Direct Speech," *Language and Style* 15, 2 (Spring 1982): 67–117. The passages most pertinent to MacCabe's argument are pp. 108–114.

22. M. M. Bakhtin, "Discourse in the Novel," in *The Dialogic Imagination: Four Essays*, ed. Michael Holmquist, trans. Caryl Emerson and Michael Holquist (Austin: University of Texas Press, 1981), 366.

23. Ibid., 415–416.

24. For a comparable critique of MacCabe on this point, see Mary Ann Doane, "The Dialogical Text: Filmic Irony and the Spectator" (Ph.D. diss., University of Iowa, 1979), 73–77.

25. MacCabe, "Realism and the Cinema": 11.

26. Catherine Kerbrat-Orecchioni, *L'énonciation: De la subjectivité dans le langage* (Paris: Colin, 1980), 7.

27. Emile Benveniste, "L'appareil formel de l'énonciation," *Problèmes de linguistique générale*, Vol. 2 (Paris: Gallimard, 1974), 80–85.

28. Kerbrat-Orecchioni, *L'énonciation*, 32.

29. Emile Benveniste, "Structure des relations de personne dans le verbe," *Problèmes de linguistique générale* (Paris: Gallimard, 1966), 242.

30. Ibid., 239.

31. Ibid., 241.

32. For a discussion of the structuralists' reworking of Benveniste, see Jonathan Culler, *Structuralist Poetics: Structuralism,*

Linguistics, and the Study of Literature (Ithaca: Cornell University Press, 1975), 197–200.

33. Roland Barthes, "To Write: An Intransitive Verb?" in Richard Macksey and Eugenio Donato, eds., *The Structuralist Controversy: The Languages of Criticism and the Sciences of Man.* (Baltimore: Johns Hopkins University Press, 1972), 136–145.

34. Gérard Genette, "Frontières du récit," *Figures II* (Paris: Seuil, 1969), 67.

35. Jenny Simonin-Grumbach, "Pour une typologie des discours," in Julia Kristeva, Jean-Claude Milner, and Nicolas Ruwet, eds., *Langue, discours, société* (Paris: Seuil, 1975), 103.

36. Christian Metz, "Story/Discourse (A Note on Two Kinds of Voyeurism)," *The Imaginary Signifier*, trans. Celia Britton et al. (Bloomington: Indiana University Press, 1981), 91.

37. Ibid., 96.

38. Ibid., 94.

39. Ibid., 96.

40. Mark Nash, "*Vampyr* and the Fantastic," *Screen* 17, 3 (Autumn 1976): 29–67.

41. Janet Bergstrom, "Alternation, Segmentation, Hypnosis: Interview with Raymond Bellour," *Camera Obscura* 3–4 (Summer 1979): 98.

42. Claude Bailblé, Michel Marie, and Marie-Claire Ropars, *Muriel: Histoire d'une recherche* (Paris: Galilée, 1974), 244–245.

43. Nash, "*Vampyr* and the Fantastic": 39.

44. François Jost, "Discours cinématographique, narration: Deux façons d'envisager le problème de l'énonciation," in J. Aumont and J. L. Leutrat, eds., *Théorie du film* (Paris: Albatros, 1980), 127; Nick Browne, "The Rhetoric of the Specular Text with Reference to *Stagecoach*," in John Caughie, ed., *Ideas of Authorship* (London: Routledge and Kegan Paul, 1981), 253.

45. Jacqueline Suter, "Feminine Discourse in *Christopher Strong*," *Camera Obscura* 3–4 (1979): 135.

46. Alain Bergala, "L'homme qui se lève," *Cahiers du cinéma* no. 311 (May 1980): 25–26.

47. Marie-Claire Ropars-Wuilleumier, "Fonction du montage dans la constitution du récit au cinéma," *Revue des sciences humaines* no. 141 (January–March 1971): 33.

48. Nash, "*Vampyr* and the Fantastic": 41.

49. Christian Metz, "Montage et discours dans le film," *Essais sur la signification au cinéma*, Vol. 2 (Paris: Klincksieck, 1972), 96.

50. Raymond Bellour, "Hitchcock the Enunciator," *Camera Obscura* 2 (Fall 1977), 68.

51. Browne, "Rhetoric of the Specular Text with Reference to *Stagecoach*," 254.

52. Marie-Claire Ropars-Wuilleumier, "Narration et signification: Un exemple filmique," *Poétique* 12 (1972): 526; Bellour "Hitchcock the Enunciator": 68.

53. Bellour, "Hitchcock the Enunciator": 68.

54. Stephen Heath, "Narrative Space," *Questions of Cinema* (London: Macmillan, 1981), 26.

55. Ibid., 65.

CHAPTER 3

1. Reviews may be found in John R. Anderson, *Cognitive Psychology and Its Implications* (San Francisco: Freeman, 1980), 367–399, and in Dan I. Slobin, *Psycholinguistics* (Glenview, Ill.: Scott, Foresman, 1974), 97–133.

2. Cited in E. H. Gombrich, *The Sense of Order: A Study in the Psychology of Decorative Art* (Ithaca: Cornell University Press, 1979), 1.

3. Irwin Rock has suggested that any perceptual activity might be explicable in light of such cognitive processes as description, problem solving, and so on. See *The Logic of Perception* (Cambridge: MIT Press, 1983), especially 17–20.

It is in relation to this point that I should draw attention to two differences between my account of filmic perception and cognition and a version of Constructivism offered by Bill Nichols in *Ideology and the Image* (Bloomington: Indiana University Press, 1981). First, Nichols describes the brain as "organizing sensory impressions into patterns and then conferring meaning upon various kinds of patterns" (12). This, like Nichols's account generally, seems to me to overemphasize bottom-up processing, in the world and in cinema. More seriously, Nichols conflates *non*-conscious perceptual processes with *un*conscious mental activity in the Freudian sense (27–28). The move is crucial to Nichols's overall project—to link "the image" to "ideology" via Jacques Lacan—but it relies upon an equivocal notion of the unconscious. Perceptual processes are often inaccessible in that we have no phenomenological awareness of them. But this is not to identify, as Nichols does, the "site" of these activities with what Freud called the "primary process" (29). Freud himself seems to have considered perception a matter of consciousness, not the unconscious; see also his tendency in his late work to treat perception as a function of the ego. A summary of these views may be found in Richard Wollheim, *Sigmund Freud* (New York: Viking, 1971), 40–45, 213–215.

4. Gombrich, *Sense of Order*, 5.

5. See Jerome S. Bruner, "On Perceptual Readiness," *Psychological Review* 64 (1957): 123–152.

6. Jerry Fodor calls them "aboriginal prototypes" of voluntary processes. See *The Modularity of Mind* (Cambridge: MIT Press, 1983), 43.

7. A review of the concept of "schema" may be found in Deborah Tannen, "What's in a Frame? Surface Evidence for Underlying Expectations," in Ray O. Freedle, ed., *New Directions in Discourse Processing* (Norwood, N.J.: Ablex, 1979), 137–144.

Incidentally, readers of David Bordwell, Janet Staiger, and Kristin Thompson, *The Classical Hollywood Cinema: Film Style and Mode of Production to 1960* (New York: Columbia University Press, 1985) will have noticed that in Chapter 2 of that book I adopted E. H. Gombrich's term "schema" to describe the inherited stylistic pattern from which an artist starts the process of "making and matching." (See *Art and Illusion: A Study in the Psychology of Pictorial Representation* [Princeton: Princeton University Press, 1961], 73–77.) In the present work, I have confined myself to including such traditional patterns within the broader concept of norms. What Gombrich calls a "mental set" corresponds to what I call a schema here.

8. Reid Hastie, "Schematic Principles in Human Memory," in E. Tony Higgins, C. Peter Herman, and Mark P. Zanna, eds., *Social Cognition: The Ontario Symposium*, Vol. 1 (Hilldale, N.J.: Lawrence Erlbaum, 1981), 40–41.

9. Julian Hochberg, "Visual Art and the Structures of the Mind," in Stanley S. Madeja, ed., *The Arts, Cognition, and Basic Skills* (St. Louis: CEMREL, 1978), 162–164; Ulric Neisser, *Cognition and Reality: Principles and Implications of Cognitive Psychology* (San Francisco: Freeman, 1976), 124.

10. Keith Oatley, *Perceptions and Representations: The Theoretical Basis of Brain Research and Psychology* (New York: Free Press, 1978), 167–207.

11. Strictly speaking, this process includes both the *phi* phenomenon (seeing pure, disembodied movement) and *beta* movement (seeing moving light). For a good discussion, see Susan J. Lederman and Bill Nichols, "Flicker and Motion in Film," in Nichols, *Ideology and the Image*, 297–298.

12. R. L. Gregory, *Eye and Brain: The Psychology of Seeing*, 3d ed. (New York: McGraw-Hill, 1978), 111–113; R. L. Gregory, "The Confounded Eye," in Gregory and E. H. Gombrich, eds., *Illusion in Nature and Art* (London: Duckworth, 1973), 73. See also Shimon Ullman, *The Interpretation of Visual Motion* (Cambridge: MIT Press, 1979), and Rock, *Logic of Perception* 165–176.

13. Ralph Norman Haber and Maurice Hershenson, *The Psychology of Visual Perception*, 2d ed. (New York: Holt, Rinehart, and Winston, 1980), 122.

14. For this reason, there is no reason to take talk of "schemata" as immediately tainted by neo-Kantian idealism. A Constructivist account can be reconciled with a functionalist developmental psychology, such as that advanced by L. Vygotsky and his followers. See James V. Wertsch's introduction to his anthology *The Concept of Activity in Soviet Psychology* (Armonk, N.Y.: M. E. Sharpe, 1981), 9–33, and, for more anecdotal speculation, Jerome Bruner, *In Search of Mind: Essays in Autobiography* (New York: Harper and Row, 1983), 138–146.

15. Gillian Cohen, "The Psychology of Reading," *New Literary History* 4 (Autumn 1972): 89.

16. Gombrich, *Art and Illusion*, 50–68, 98ff, 200ff, 279ff.

17. For examples, see David E. Rumelhart, "Notes on a Schema for Stories," in D. G. Bobrow and A. Collins, eds., *Representation and Understanding: Studies in Cognitive Science* (New York: Academic Press, 1975), 211–236; Jean Mandler and Nancy Johnson, "Remembrance of Things Parsed: Story Structure and Recall," *Cognitive Psychology* 9 (1977): 111–151; Perry W. Thorndyke, "Cognitive Structures in Comprehension and Memory of Narrative Discourse," *Cognitive Psychology* 9 (1977): 77–110; Walter Kintsch, "On Comprehending Stories," in Marcel A. Just and Patricia A. Carpenter, eds., *Cognitive Processes in Comprehension* (Hilldale, N.J.: Erlbaum, 1977), 33–62; Nancy L. Stein, "The Comprehension and Appreciation of Stories," in Madeja, *Arts, Cognition, and Basic Skills*, 231–249.

18. More particularly, preliterate cultures require very different skills of their storytellers and audiences, and their narratives are characterized by distinctive organizational principles. For a general review, see Walter J. Ong, *Orality and Literacy: The Technologizing of the Word* (London: Methuen, 1982), 57–71, 139–155. Literate narrative traditions other than those of the post-Renaissance West may also inflect story form in unique ways, as Robert Alter shows in *The Art of Biblical Narrative* (New York: Basic Books, 1981), 49–154. Walter Kintsch and Edith Greene discuss the general point in "The Role of Culture-Specific Schemata in the Comprehension and Recall of Stories," *Discourse Processes* 1 (1978): 1–3.

19. Hastie, "Schematic Principles in Human Memory": 40–43.

20. Mandler and Johnson, "Remembrance of Things Parsed": 130–131; Thorndyke, "Cognitive Structures in Comprehension and Memory of Narrative Discourse": 79.

21. Thorndyke, "Cognitive Structures in Comprehension and Memory of Narrative Discourse": 84–96.

22. Roland Barthes, "Action Sequences," in Joseph Strelka, ed., *Patterns of Literary Style* (University Park: Pennsylvania State University Press, 1971), 9. Whether these "concepts or labels" necessarily involve natural language we do not know. For an interesting discussion, see Lawrence Crawford, "Actional Nameability and Filmic Narrativity: From Inner Speech to Identification," *Quarterly Review of Film Studies* 6, 3 (Summer 1981): 265–277.

23. Boris Tomashevsky, "Thematics," in Lee T. Lemon and Marion J. Reis, eds., *Russian Formalist Criticism: Four Essays* (Lincoln: University of Nebraska Press, 1965), 78–87.

24. Teun A. van Dijk, "Cognitive Processing of Literary Discourse," *Poetics Today* 1, 1–2 (1979): 153.

25. Fodor, *Modularity of Mind*, 56–57.

26. Frederic C. Bartlett, *Remembering: A Study in Experimental and Social Psychology* (Cambridge: Cambridge University Press, 1950), 205.

27. Meir Sternberg, *Expositional Modes and Temporal Ordering in Fiction* (Baltimore: Johns Hopkins University Press, 1978), 245–246. See also Edward Branigan, *Point of View in the Cinema: A Theory of Narration in Classical Film* (New York: Mouton, 1984), 50–56.

28. Roland Barthes, "Introduction to the Structural Analysis of Narratives," *Image Music Text*, ed. and trans. Stephen Heath (New York: Hill and Wang, 1977), 91–97.

29. Gombrich, *Sense of Order*, 108.

30. Van Dijk, "Cognitive Processing of Literary Discourse": 155.

31. Sternberg, *Expositional Modes and Temporal Ordering in Fiction*, 94.

32. Viktor Shklovsky, "On the Connection between Devices of Syuzhet Construction and General Stylistic Devices," *Twentieth Century Studies* nos. 7/8 (December 1972): 54–61.

33. Sternberg, *Expositional Modes and Temporal Ordering in Fiction*, 177.

34. Neisser, *Cognition and Reality*, 28.

35. See Leonard B. Meyer, *Emotion and Meaning in Music* (Chicago: University of Chicago Press, 1956), 13–42, and George Mandler, *Mind and Emotion* (New York: John Wiley, 1975), 65–172.

36. Alfred Hitchcock, "*Rear Window*," in Albert J. Lavalley, ed., *Focus on Hitchcock* (Englewood Cliffs, N.J.: Prentice-Hall, 1972), 45.

37. Noël Carroll, "Toward a Theory of Film Suspense" *Persistence of Vision* no. 1 (Summer 1984): 65–89.

38. Hitchcock, "*Rear Window*," 42.

CHAPTER 4

1. Sigmund Freud, "The Unconscious" (1915), in *Collected Papers*, Vol. 4, ed. James Strachey (London: Hogarth Press, 1956), 106. On this point, see also Noël Carroll, "Address to the Heathen," *October* no. 23 (Winter 1982): 130–134.

2. Vladimir Nizhny, *Lessons with Eisenstein*, trans. and ed. Ivor Montagu and Jay Leyda (New York: Hill and Wang, 1962), 110.

3. See Aristotle, *Poetics*, commentary by D. W. Lucas (Oxford: Clarendon Press, 1968), 53–54, 100.

4. Yuri Tynianov, "Plot and Story-Line in the Cinema," *Russian Poetics in Translation* 5 (1978): 20.

5. Since writing Chapters 1–7 of David Bordwell, Janet Staiger, and Kristin Thompson, *The Classical Hollywood Cinema: Film Style and Mode of Production to 1960* (New York: Columbia University Press, 1985), I have reconsidered the plot/story distinction. There Chapter 2 asserted that plot (syuzhet) consists of "the totality of formal and stylistic materials in the film," and Chapter 3 called narration that aspect of plot which transmits story information. This formulation now seems to me inadequate, both as a reading of the Formalists and as an account of film form. For the reasons presented in the present chapter, I take narration to be the all-inclusive process which uses both *syuzhet* and style to cue spectators to construct a *fabula*, or story. This revision of theoretical terms does not seem to me to affect the analytical and descriptive claims I make in *The Classical Hollywood Cinema*, but it does offer greater theoretical precision.

6. Boris Tomashevsky, "Thematics," in Lee T. Lemon and Marion J. Reis, eds., *Russian Formalist Criticism: Four Essays*, (Lincoln: University of Nebraska Press, 1965), 66–67.

7. My emphasis upon the fabula as an emergent spectatorial construct is characteristic of "late" Russian Formalist poetics; the early writings of Shklovsky in particular tend to treat the fabula as a preexistent raw material for artistic elaboration. Nonetheless, at times we must use the language of carpentry or sculpture in describing the syuzhet's operations. For the narrative artist does in

some sense work "on" the fabula *as he may assume that the perceiver will construct it*. In the previous chapter, I claimed that the narrative film is so made as to encourage the spectator to execute story-constructing activities. These activities can in turn be presupposed by the filmmaker. For the artist, presenting a story "out of" chronological order is just that: a transformation of that arrangement which a spectator would presumably make when presented with more "linear" cues. (Here a theoretical approach emphasizing narrative as a *structure* overlaps with that treating narration as a temporal *activity*.) The perceiver, given a narrative text, is invited to recognize a syuzhet and infer a fabula from it, whereas the artist constructs a syuzhet according to assumptions about how the spectator could infer a fabula from it. And these assumptions will form part of the artist's material.

8. Most Russian Formalist narrative theory assumes a distinction between syuzhet and style, as witnessed in the title of Viktor Shklovsky's 1919 essay, "On the Connection Between Devices of Syuzhet Construction and General Stylistic Devices" (*Twentieth-Century Studies* nos. 7/8 [December 1972]: 48–72). Although Shklovsky believed that syuzhet construction and stylistic elements often parallel each other, he presupposed them to occupy distinct domains. Boris Tomashevsky and Boris Eichenbaum also held this view. More recently, both Meir Sternberg and Seymour Chatman exclude style from the realm of the syuzhet. See Sternberg, *Expositional Modes and Temporal Ordering in Fiction* (Baltimore: Johns Hopkins University Press, 1978), 34; and Chatman, *Story and Discourse: Narrative Structure in Fiction and Film* (Ithaca: Cornell University Press, 1978), 10–11, 24. Yuri Tynianov speaks of the syuzhet as "the story's dynamics, composed of the interactions of all the linkages of material (including the story as a linkage of actions)—stylistic linkage, story linkage, etc." ("On the Foundations of Cinema," in Herbert Eagle, ed., *Russian Formalist Film Theory* [Ann Arbor: University of Michigan Slavic Publications, 1981], 96). The passage is cryptic, but it suggests that the syuzhet includes both "story linkage" and style, in which case Tynianov's conception would be structurally congruent with mine: what I and others call "syuzhet," he calls "story linkage," and what he calls "syuzhet" I call narration.

9. See p. 31, above.

10. Sternberg, *Expositional Modes and Temporal Ordering in Fiction*, 34.

11. Cf. Chatman, *Story and Discourse*, 19–20; Gérard Genette, *Figures II* (Paris: Seuil, 1969), 66.

12. Tynianov, "Plot and Story-Line in the Cinema": 20.

13. Roland Barthes, "The Third Meaning," *Image Music Text*, trans. and ed. Stephen Heath (New York: Hill and Wang, 1977), 64.

14. Kristin Thompson, *Ivan the Terrible: A Neoformalist Analysis* (Princeton: Princeton University Press, 1981), 287–295.

15. Ibid., 302.

16. Sternberg's term "gap" does not coincide with the usage of phenomenological theorists of narrative like Wolfgang Iser. For Iser, a gap is any "indeterminate" portion of a text which calls forth "a free play of interpretation" ("Indeterminacy and the Reader's Response," in J. Hillis Miller, ed., *Aspects of Narrative* [New York: Columbia University Press, 1971], 11). He finds gaps between action segments, between character thought and deed, between different points of view. For Sternberg, however, gaps arise only from the relation of syuzhet to fabula. I shall suggest that they are usually quite determinate, especially given the canonic schemata of story construction.

17. Sternberg, *Expositional Modes and Temporal Ordering in Fiction*, 161–162.

18. Ibid., 129.

19. Ibid., 98–99.

20. Tzvetan Todorov, "La lecture comme construction," *Les genres du discours* (Paris: Seuil, 1978), 89.

21. Edward Branigan, *Point of View in the Cinema: A Theory of Narration and Subjectivity in Classical Film* (New York: Mouton, 1984), 40–49.

22. Wayne Booth, *The Rhetoric of Fiction* (Chicago: University of Chicago Press, 1961), 71–75.

23. Albert Laffay, *Logique du cinéma: Création et spectacle* (Paris: Masson, 1964), 81.

24. But not necessarily. The works of S. Y. Kuroda, Ann Banfield, and others suggest that literary narration may be defined by its inability to be taken as proceeding from a speaker. See Ann Banfield, *Unspeakable Sentences: Narration and Representation in the Language of Fiction* (London: Routledge and Kegan Paul, 1982).

25. Chatman, *Story and Discourse*, 147–151.

CHAPTER 5

1. Quoted in Peter Bogdanovich, *The Cinema of Howard Hawks* (New York: Museum of Modern Art Film Library, 1962), 25.

2. We see Carroll Lundgren kill Joe Brody and the thug Canino

kill Harry Jones. By the end of the film Marlowe learns that Owen Taylor killed Arthur Geiger and Carmen Sternwood killed Sean Regan. But who killed Taylor, the Sternwood chauffeur found floating in the family Packard? Under Marlowe's questioning, Joe Brody admits that he followed Taylor, knocked him out, and stole the incriminating film. As he recounts this, Joe is notably evasive, stammering and avoiding Marlowe's eyes. Marlowe accuses Joe of killing Taylor. Joe: "You can't prove I did it." Marlowe: "I don't particularly want to." In the absence of competing candidates, and given the laconic nature of this film, we must assume that Joe is the culprit. He will be sleeping the big sleep in a moment anyhow.

3. Dorothy L. Sayers, Introduction, *The Omnibus of Crime* (Garden City, N.Y.: Garden City Publishing Company, 1929), 33.

4. Ibid., 34–36.

5. Raymond Chandler, *The Big Sleep* (New York: Ballantine, 1972), 20–21.

6. Daniel Gerould, "Russian Formalist Theories of Melodrama," *Journal of American Culture* 1, 1 (Spring 1978): 16.

CHAPTER 6

1. Julian Hochberg and Virginia Brooks, "The Perception of Motion Pictures," in *Handbook of Perception*, Vol. 10: *Perceptual Ecology,* ed. Edward C. Carterette and Morton P. Friedman (New York: Academic Press, 1978), 286–288. For a general orientation to this approach see J. S. Bruner, "On Perceptual Readiness," *Psychological Review* 64 (1957): 130–131.

2. R. L. Gregory, "A Speculative Account of Brain Function in Terms of Probability and Induction," *Concepts and Mechanisms of Perception* (New York: Scribner's, 1974), 526.

3. Jerome S. Bruner, Jacqueline J. Goodnow, and George A. Austin, *A Study of Thinking* (New York: Wiley, 1956), 61.

4. Meir Sternberg, *Expositional Modes and Temporal Ordering in Fiction* (Baltimore: Johns Hopkins University Press, 1978), 17.

5. J. P. Simon, "Remarques sur la temporalité cinématographique dans les films diégétiques," in Dominique Chateau, André Gardiès, and François Jost, eds., *Cinémas de la modernité: Films, théories* (Paris: Klincksieck, 1981), 63.

6. My categories are drawn from Gérard Genette, *Narrative Discourse: An Essay in Method*, trans. Jane E. Lewin (Ithaca: Cornell University Press, 1980), 33–160.

My debt to Genette ought not, however, to blur the theoretical differences between our approaches. Genette's temporal categories

pertain to the difference between *histoire* and *récit*, and these terms are not quite congruent with the fabula/syuzhet pair. To take the most significant difference, Genette's *récit* designates "the discourse, oral or written, which tells [the story events]"—that is, it constitutes the phenomenal text before us. (See Genette, *Nouveau discours du récit* [Paris: Seuil, 1983], 10.) The syuzhet is a system already at one remove from the phenomenal text. (See Chapter 4, pp. 51–52.) Nonetheless, Genette's categories of temporal relations hold good for the relations between narration (syuzhet plus style) and the story narrated (fabula)—fortunately for me, since Genette's discussion of time is one of the triumphs of contemporary poetics.

7. Chatman, *Story and Discourse*, 32.

8. The recounting/enactment distinction is not reducible to the immemorial showing/telling split criticized by Edward Branigan. He attacks the latter on the grounds that any narration's telling can be regarded as a showing, and vice versa. (In effect, he is playing off the mimetic and diegetic theories we have already considered.) But I am not saying that the narration directly "tells": characters tell, or recount, even if they "show" a videotape of prior events. See Branigan, *Point of View in the Cinema: A Theory of Narration and Subjectivity in Classical Film* (New York: Mouton, 1984), 190–196.

9. Noël Burch, *Theory of Film Practice*, trans. Helen R. Lane (New York: Praeger, 1973), 5–7.

10. A "frame cut" (the term is Edward Branigan's) is a variant of the match on action. It occurs when the match is made as the moving object crosses a frame line and enters a new shot. For example, in classical Hollywood continuity, a man will walk out frame right. Cut as the body crosses the frame line. The man walks into the next shot, his body now crossing the left frame line. For a discussion of this editing device, see David Bordwell, Janet Staiger, and Kristin Thompson, *The Classical Hollywood Cinema: Film Style and Mode of Production to 1960* (New York: Columbia University Press, 1985), Chap. 5.

CHAPTER 7

1. For reviews of these theories, see Margaret A. Hagen, "A New Theory of the Psychology of Representational Art," in C. F. Nodine and D. F. Fisher, eds., *Perception and Pictorial Representation* (New York: Holt, Rinehart, and Winston, 1979), 196–212; and Julian Hochberg, "Art and Perception," in *Handbook of Perception,*

Vol. 10: *Perceptual Ecology,* ed. Edward C. Carterette and Morton P. Friedman (New York: Academic Press, 1978), 225–258.

2. James J. Gibson, *The Ecological Approach to Visual Perception* (Boston: Houghton Mifflin, 1979), 302.

3. Rudolf Arnheim, *Art and Visual Perception: A Psychology of the Creative Eye,* 2d ed. (Berkeley: University of California Press, 1974), 263.

4. Rudolf Arnheim, *Film as Art* (Berkeley: University of California Press, 1957), 57.

5. See Richard L. Gregory, "The Space of Pictures," in Nodine and Fisher, *Perception and Pictorial Representation,* 230; J. Fodor and Z. Pylyshyn, "How Direct Is Visual Perception?" *Cognition* 9 (1981): 171–172.

6. See Jerry A. Fodor, *The Modularity of Mind* (Cambridge: MIT Press, 1983), 45.

7. William H. Ittelson, *The Ames Demonstrations in Perception: A Guide to Their Construction and Use* (Princeton: Princeton University Press, 1952), 26.

8. R. L. Gregory, *The Intelligent Eye* (New York: McGraw-Hill, 1970), 29–30.

9. E. H. Gombrich, *Art and Illusion: A Study in the Psychology of Pictorial Representation* (Princeton: Princeton University Press, 1961), 249.

10. E. H. Gombrich, "The Evidence of Images," in Charles S. Singleton, ed., *Interpretation: Theory and Practice* (Baltimore: Johns Hopkins University Press, 1969), 51–56.

11. Hochberg, "Art and Perception," 240–241.

12. For a summary of this argument, see Ralph Norman Haber and Maurice Hershenson, *The Psychology of Visual Perception,* 2d ed. (New York: Holt, Rinehart, and Winston, 1980), 313–314; and Julian Hochberg, "Pictorial Functions and Perceptual Structures," in Margaret A. Hagen, ed., *The Perception of Pictures,* Vol. 2 (New York: Academic Press, 1980), 67–80.

13. Julian Hochberg, "Some of the Things that Paintings Are," in Nodine and Fisher, *Perception and Pictorial Representation,* 18.

14. Julian Hochberg, "The Representation of Things and People," in E. H. Gombrich, Max Black, and Julian Hochberg, *Art, Perception, and Reality* (Baltimore: Johns Hopkins University Press, 1972), 68–69.

15. Gombrich, "Evidence of Images," 57–59.

16. Rudolf Arnheim, *The Power of the Center: A Study of Composition in the Visual Arts* (Berkeley: University of California Press, 1982), 155–169.

17. B. A. R. Carter, "Perspective," in H. Osborne, ed., *The Oxford Companion to Art* (Oxford: Clarendon Press, 1970), 847.

18. John White, *The Birth and Rebirth of Pictorial Space* (New York: Harper and Row, 1972), 194–196.

19. Antonio di Tuccio Manetti, quoted in Isabelle Hyman, ed., *Brunelleschi in Perspective* (Englewood Cliffs, N.J.: Prentice-Hall, 1974), 67. See also Michael Baxandall, *Painting and Experience in Fifteenth-Century Italy* (New York: Oxford University Press, 1972), 119–150.

20. Stephen Heath, "Narrative Space," *Questions of Cinema* (Bloomington: Indiana University Press, 1981), 30–32.

21. Ibid., 31.

22. See Erwin Panofsky, *The Life and Art of Albrecht Dürer* (Princeton: Princeton University Press, 1945), 261; and Panofsky, *The "Codex Huygens" and Leonardo da Vinci's Art Theory* (London: Warburg Institute, 1940), 106.

23. Samuel Y. Edgerton, Jr., *The Renaissance Rediscovery of Linear Perspective* (New York: Harper and Row, 1975), 162.

24. E. H. Gombrich, "Image and Code: Scope and Limits of Conventionalism in Pictorial Representation," in Wendy Steiner, ed., *Image and Code* (Ann Arbor: Michigan Studies in the Humanities, 1981), 17–21; Hochberg, "Art and Perception," 236.

25. Ernest A. Lumsden, "Problems of Magnification and Minification: An Exploration of the Distortions of Distance, Slant, Shape, and Velocity," in Margaret A. Hagen, ed., *The Perception of Pictures,* Vol. 1 (New York: Academic Press, 1980), 92–93.

26. Jean-Pierre Oudart, "Cinema and Suture," *Screen* 18, 4 (Winter 1977/1978): 35, 39.

27. See Daniel Dayan, "The Tutor-Code of Classical Cinema," *Film Quarterly* 28, 1 (Fall 1974): 22–31. For a critique, see William Rothman, "Against the System of the Suture," *Film Quarterly* 29, 1 (Fall 1975): 45–50.

28. Nick Browne, "The Rhetoric of the Specular Text with Reference to *Stagecoach,*" in John Caughie, ed., *Ideas of Authorship* (London: Routledge and Kegan Paul, 1981), 254. Browne's own example from *Stagecoach* disconfirms his general claim. He confuses frontality of character position with optical point of view, and he overlooks the fact that the characters' eyelines are not directed at the camera.

29. Oudart, "Cinema and Suture," 46.

30. Ibid., 43.

31. Serge Daney and Jean-Pierre Oudart, "Le Nom-de-l'Auteur," *Cahiers du cinéma* nos. 234–235 (December 1971, January–February 1972): 90.

32. Oudart, "Cinema and Suture," 37; italics mine.

33. Ibid., 41–42.

34. Julian E. Hochberg, *Perception*, 2d ed. (Englewood Cliffs, N.J.: Prentice-Hall, 1978), 208.

35. For a detailed discussion of a film's graphic space, see Eric Rohmer, *L'organisation de l'espace dans le 'Faust' de Murnau* (Paris: Union Générale d'Editions, 1977), 113–172.

36. Albert Yonas, "Attached and Cast Shadows," in Nodine and Fisher, *Perception and Pictorial Representation*, 101–103.

37. For a general discussion, see Shimon Ullman, *The Interpretation of Visual Motion* (Cambridge: MIT Press, 1979).

38. James J. Gibson, *The Perception of the Visual World* (Westport, Conn.: Greenwood Press, 1974), 118–144; James J. Gibson, *The Senses Considered as Perceptual Systems* (Boston: Houghton Mifflin, 1966), 161–162, 195–201.

39. Donald L. Weismann, *The Visual Arts as Human Experience* (Englewood Cliffs, N.J.: Prentice-Hall, 1974), 170–173.

40. Ibid., 186–215.

41. Brian Henderson writes: "Godard avoids depth: he arranges his characters in a single plane only—none is ever closer to the camera than another. . . . His moving camera . . . eliminates the succession of aspects. . . . Godard's planes, even where multiple, are strictly parallel—they do not intersect or interrelate. . . . The fixed, 90° camera angle . . . arranges all planes in parallel to the borders of the frame itself" (*A Critique of Film Theory* [New York: Dutton, 1980], 64n, 75–78). All these claims, purporting to apply to shots like the traffic jam sequence in *Weekend*, are inaccurate. Henderson also suggests that the shots eliminate the very close foreground of Wellesian deep focus: Godard arranges his elements "all within the long-shot range" (77). This is true (at least of this shot, not of other shots in Godard), but it does not make the image "flat"; it simply defines significant depth within a narrower zone of the scenographic space. Were Wellesian depth the norm, most films in world cinema would present a flat space. If Godard had sought the extreme flatness Henderson claims, he could have shot the scene from a lower and less angular position, arranged the jam against a neutral background of sky, moved it steadily in tempo with the camera, and employed color in a more subdued fashion.

42. Noël Carroll, "Toward a Theory of Film Editing," *Millennium Film Journal* no. 3 (1978): 94–95.

43. Arthur C. Handy and R. W. Conant, "Perspective Considerations in Taking and Projecting Motion Pictures," *Transactions of the Society of Motion Picture Engineers* 12, 33 (1928): 117–118.

44. Laurence E. Marks, "Multimodal Perception," in *Handbook of Perception*, Vol. 8: *Perceptual Coding*, ed. Edward C. Carterette and Morton P. Friedman (New York: Academic Press, 1978), 330–333.

45. See Alan Williams, "Is Sound Recording like a Language?" *Yale French Studies* no. 60 (1980): 58–64; Alan Williams, "Godard's Use of Sound," *Camera Obscura* nos. 8/9/10 (1982): 193–208.

46. For related discussions, see Edward Branigan, "What Is a Camera?" in Patricia Mellencamp and Philip Rosen, eds., *Cinema Histories, Cinema Practices* (Frederick, Md.: University Publications of America, 1984), 86–107, and David Bordwell, "Camera Movement and Cinematic Space," *Cine-Tracts* no. 2 (Summer 1977): 19.

47. Noël Burch, *Theory of Film Practice*, trans. Helen R. Lane (New York: Praeger, 1973), 17.

48. Ibid., 21.

49. See André Gardiès, "L'espace du récit filmique: Propositions," in Dominique Chateau, André Gardiès, and François Jost, eds., *Cinémas de la modernité: Films, théories* (Paris: Klincksieck, 1981), 75–92.

50. The term "omnipresence" comes from Seymour Chatman, *Story and Discourse: Narrative Structure in Fiction and Film* (Ithaca: Cornell University Press, 1978), 212.

51. Edward Branigan, *Point of View in the Cinema: A Theory of Narration and Subjectivity in Classical Film* (New York: Mouton, 1984), 103–121.

52. William Simon, "An Approach to Point of View," *Film Reader* 4 (1979): 147–148.

53. Graham Petrie, *History Must Answer to Man: Hungarian Cinema Today* (Gyoma, Hungary: Corvina, 1978), 95.

54. Quoted in Giovanni Buttafava, *Miklós Jancsó* (Florence: Castoro, 1974), 10.

55. A similar effect, in Dreyer's *Vampyr* and *Ordet*, is discussed in David Bordwell, *The Films of Carl-Theodor Dreyer* (Berkeley: University of California Press, 1981), 103–107, 155–157.

56. Quoted in Robert Ban, "La quête de la vérité," *Etudes cinématographiques* nos. 73–77 (1969): 134.

57. Yvette Biró, *Jancsó* (Paris: Albatros, 1977), 117.

58. Miklós Jancsó, "Entretiens avec Jean-Louis Comolli et Michel Delahaye," *Cahiers du cinéma* no. 212 (May 1969): 30.

59. André Bazin, *Jean Renoir*, ed. François Truffaut, trans. W. W. Halsey II and William H. Simon (New York: Simon and Schuster, 1973), 87.

60. Gyula Hernádi and Miklós Jancsó, "Sur 'Silence et cri,'" *Positif* no. 105 (May 1969): 33.

61. Petrie, *History Must Answer to Man*, 67–68.
62. Bordwell, *Films of Carl-Theodor Dreyer*, 158–164.
63. Hernádi and Jancsó, "Sur 'Silence et cri,'" 33.

CHAPTER 8

1. Jan Mukařovský, *Aesthetic Function, Norm and Value as Social Facts*, trans. Mark E. Suino (Ann Arbor: Michigan Slavic Contributions, 1979), 33.
2. Felix Vodička, "The Concretization of the Literary Work," in Peter Steiner, ed., *The Prague School: Selected Writings, 1929–1946* (Austin: University of Texas Press, 1982), 118.
3. Lest this seem farfetched, I refer the reader to an essay which maintains that sequences from *The Scarlet Empress* exhibit "a regular alternation between mainly light and mainly dark tones in the center of the frame" at a "fixed interval" of 160 frames. (See Barry Salt, "Sternberg's Heart Beats in Black and White," in Peter Baxter, ed., *Sternberg* [London: British Film Institute, 1980], 103.) Put aside the fact that the author's excerpted frames prove nothing of the sort. (See figs. I.13–18 for six frames that violate the rule.) Overlook the indeterminacy of many frames, in which light and dark are mixed in equal measure. Waive the author's own admission that there are several exceptions and that "the period of pulsation is not quite completely steady at 160 frames" (106). Ignore the fact that in a black-and-white film, the center of every 160th frame can be *only* light *or* dark, so the likelihood of change is strong. We are still left with the problem of pertinence. Such a purely quantitative pattern may lack not only any narrative function (the author happily grants this); it need not have any stylistic saliency either. Measuring the alternations through arbitrarily selected points says nothing about the tempo of movement, lighting, or cutting that produces the putative changes: what happens in frames 1 through 159 could be a rapid flickering which the 160-frame cross section simply catches at various points, or a more gradual shift of tonality that takes 160 frames to complete. It is, of course, such phenomena as these that the viewer actually sees; the viewer has no access to the 160th, 320th, 480th, etc., frames as distinct entities. Taken in isolation, these frames are as irrelevant to style as dirt specks and cinch marks, which can also come at quantifiable intervals.
4. Jan Mukařovský, "Standard Language and Poetic Language," in Paul L. Garvin, ed., *A Prague School Reader on Esthetics, Literary Structure, and Style* (Washington, D.C.: Georgetown University Press, 1964), 20.

5. V. F. Perkins, "The Cinema of Nicholas Ray," in Ian Cameron, ed., *The Movie Reader* (New York: Praeger, 1972), 66.
6. Felix Vodička, "The History of the Echo of Literary Works," in Garvin, *Prague School Reader on Esthetics, Literary Structure, and Style*, 74.
7. See David Bordwell, Janet Staiger, and Kristin Thompson, *The Classical Hollywood Cinema: Film Style and Mode of Production to 1960* (New York: Columbia University Press, 1985).
8. Jan Mukařovský, "The Aesthetic Norm," *Structure, Sign, and Function*, ed. and trans. John Burbank and Peter Steiner (New Haven: Yale University Press, 1977), 52.

CHAPTER 9

1. Much of what follows is discussed in greater detail in Chapters 1–7 of David Bordwell, Janet Staiger, and Kristin Thompson, *The Classical Hollywood Cinema: Film Style and Mode of Production to 1960* (New York: Columbia University Press, 1985).
2. Perry W. Thorndyke, "Cognitive Structures in Comprehension and Memory of Narrative Discourse," *Cognitive Psychology* 9 (1977): 84–96.
3. Eugene Vale, *The Technique of Screenplay Writing* (New York: Grosset and Dunlap, 1972), 135–160; Stephen Heath, "Film and System: Terms of Analysis," *Screen* 16, 1 (Spring 1975): 48–50.
4. See Bordwell, Staiger, and Thompson, *Classical Hollywood Cinema*, Chapters 14–18.
5. Rick Altman stresses the need to consider the importance of character parallels as "paradigmatic" relations in the classical text. It is true that analogies and contrasts of situation or character occur in classical films, but these relations are typically dependent upon logically prior causal relations. See "The American Film Musical: Paradigmatic Structure and Mediatory Function," in Rick Altman, ed., *Genre: The Musical* (London: Routledge and Kegan Paul, 1981), 197–207.
6. Christian Metz, *Film Language*, trans. Michael Taylor (New York: Oxford University Press, 1974), 108–146.
7. Raymond Bellour, "The Obvious and the Code," *Screen* 15, 4 (Winter 1974/1975): 7–8. See also Alan Williams, "Narrative Patterns in 'Only Angels Have Wings,'" *Quarterly Review of Film Studies* 1, 4 (November 1976): 357–372.
8. Raymond Bellour, "To Analyze, to Segment," in Altman, *Genre: The Musical*, 107–116.

9. Thierry Kuntzel, "The Film-Work, 2," *Camera Obscura* no. 5 (1980): 25.

10. Parker Tyler, *The Hollywood Hallucination* (New York: Simon and Schuster, 1970), 177.

11. Meir Sternberg, *Expositional Modes and Temporal Ordering in Fiction* (Baltimore: Johns Hopkins University Press, 1978), 178.

12. See Richard Dyer, *Stars* (London: British Film Institute, 1979), 65, and David Bordwell, "Happily Ever After, Part II," in *The Velvet Light Trap* no. 19 (1982): 2–7.

13. Bertolt Brecht, *Collected Plays*, Vol. 2, ed. Ralph Manheim and John Willett (New York: Vintage, 1977), 331.

14. Vale, *Technique of Screenplay Writing*, 81.

15. Jean-Paul Sartre, "Quand Hollywood veut faire penser," *L'écran français* no. 5 (3 August 1945): 3.

16. I borrow the term from Seymour Chatman, *Story and Discourse: Narrative Structure in Fiction and Film* (Ithaca: Cornell University Press, 1978), 103.

17. A. Lindsley Lane, "The Camera's Omniscient Eye," *American Cinematographer* 16, 3 (March 1935): 95.

18. The clearest statement of the "invisible observer" notion is to be found in V. I. Pudovkin, *Film Technique* (New York: Grove, 1960), 67–71.

19. André Bazin, *What Is Cinema?* trans. Hugh Gray (Berkeley: University of California Press, 1967): 32.

20. See Hal Herman, "Motion Picture Art Director," *American Cinematographer* 28, 11 (November 1947): 396–397, 416–417; Herman Blumenthal, "Cardboard Counterpart of the Motion Picture Setting," *Production Design* 2, 1 (January 1952): 16–21.

21. Susan Rubin Suleiman, *Authoritarian Fictions: The Ideological Novel as a Literary Genre* (New York: Columbia University Press, 1983), 159–171.

22. Herb Lightman, "The Subjective Camera," *American Cinematographer* 27, 2 (February 1946): 46, 66–67.

23. Yuri Tynianov, "Fundamentals of the Cinema," in Christopher Williams, ed., *Realism in the Cinema* (London: Routledge and Kegan Paul, 1980), 149. I have modified this translation by substituting "syuzhet" for "plot."

24. Peter Bogdanovich, *Alan Dwan* (Berkeley: University of California Press, 1970), 86.

25. Quoted in Thomas Elsaesser, "Why Hollywood," *Monogram* no. 1 (April 1971): 8.

26. Because norms are guidelines that rank options probabilistically, we ought not to be too quick to disclose "transgressions" of classical style. For instance, Peter Lehman claims that subjective framings of a character's to-camera stare in *Dr. Jekyll and Mr. Hyde* (1932) are "quite at odds with the usual Hollywood paradigm." Yet optical point-of-view shots are not forbidden by classical protocols; they are just less likely than other alternatives. Similarly, Lehman points out a discontinuity when Jekyll leaves an establishing shot and supposedly turns his back; cut to Ivy looking at the camera and tossing a garter at it. I would suggest three things here. First, the cues seem ambiguous as to whether Jekyll in fact turns his back; he could still be watching offscreen. A later shot, of his feet turned toward Ivy as the garter lands before him, reinforces some such spatial hypothesis. Second, the playfulness of the point-of-view pattern is not unlike the whimsical jugglings of space in Lubitsch and other innovative classical directors. Finally, we should recall that *Dr. Jekyll and Mr. Hyde* begins with a lengthy traveling shot from Jekyll's optical point of view, before we have been introduced to the character. Optical subjectivity thus constitutes an important part of the film's intrinsic norm. One could argue that Ivy's glance into an ambivalent offscreen eye simply plays with this norm. See Peter Lehman, "Looking at Ivy Looking at Us Looking at Her: The Camera and the Garter," *Wide Angle* 5, 3 (1983): 59–63.

27. "There are, of course, periods tending toward maximally attainable harmony and stability; they are usually called periods of classicism." Jan Mukařovský, "The Aesthetic Norm," *Structure, Sign, and Function*, trans. and ed. John Burbank and Peter Steiner (New Haven: Yale University Press, 1978), 54.

28. Frances Marion, *How to Write and Sell Film Stories* (New York: Covici-Friede, 1937) 144.

29. Richard Mealand, "Hollywoodunit," in Howard Haycraft, ed., *The Art of the Mystery Story* (New York: Grosset and Dunlap, 1946), 300.

30. It is thus somewhat misleading for Vance Kepley to assert that the restaurant scene in *His Girl Friday* creates "a shifting cinematic space not unlike what Burch finds in *Ivan the Terrible* and what other theorists find in such non-classical directors as Ozu." Eisenstein and Ozu make mismatches more prominent than does Hawks. The point is not that Hawks's scene has no spatial incompatibilities, but that the classical spectator is simply cued to overlook them. See Vance Kepley, Jr., "Spatial Articulation in the Classical Cinema: A Scene From *His Girl Friday*," *Wide Angle* 5, 3 (1983): 50–58.

31. Sternberg, *Expositional Modes and Temporal Ordering in Fiction,* 71.

32. Michèle Lagny, Marie-Claire Ropars, and Pierre Sorlin,

"Analyse d'un ensemble filmique extensible: Les films français des années 30," in J. Aumont and J. L. Leutrat, eds., *Théorie du film* (Paris: Albatros, 1980), 132–164.

33. Noël Burch, "Fritz Lang: German Period," in *Cinema: A Critical Dictionary*, Vol. 2, ed. Richard Roud (New York: Viking, 1980), 583–588.

34. Sternberg, *Expositional Modes and Temporal Ordering in Fiction*, 20–26.

35. Frederick Palmer, *Photoplay Writing* (Los Angeles: Palmer Photoplay Corporation, 1921), 29.

36. Ibid., 9.

37. François Truffaut, *The Films in My Life*, trans. Leonard Mayhew (New York: Simon and Schuster, 1978), 53.

38. For another example, see the discussion of *Vampyr* in David Bordwell, *The Films of Carl-Theodor Dreyer* (Berkeley: University of California Press, 1981), 97–109.

39. Tyler, *Hollywood Hallucination,* 55. It is important to note the extent to which such a sequence represents a vulgarization of the Soviet concept of montage, resulting from complicated historical causes. A crucial stylistic effect was Hollywood's use of the dissolve and superimposition to soften the pictorial conflicts that Soviet montage sought to maximize. The rise of montage sequences thus encouraged the development of sophisticated optical printing equipment.

40. Herb A. Lightman, "The Magic of Montage," *American Cinematographer* 30, 10 (October 1949): 361.

41. On this distinction, see Chatman, *Story and Discourse,* 68–72.

42. Louis Marcorelles, "*His Girl Friday,*" *Cahiers du cinéma* no. 139 (January 1963): 29.

43. See David Bordwell and Kristin Thompson, *Film Art: An Introduction* (Reading, Mass.: Addison-Wesley, 1979), 234–239.

44. Fred J. Balshofer and Arthur C. Miller, *One Reel a Week* (Berkeley: University of California Press, 1967), 192.

45. Quoted in Donald Chase, *Filmmaking: The Collaborative Art* (Boston: Little, Brown, 1975), 44.

46. Michel Butor, *Passing Time*, trans. Jean Stewart (New York: Simon and Schuster, 1960), 179.

47. See Charles G. Clarke, "Practical Filming Techniques for Three-Dimension and Wide-Screen Motion Pictures," *American Cinematographer* 34, 3 (March 1953): 138; Clarke, "CinemaScope Techniques," *International Photographer* 27 (1955): 11–12; Gayne Rescher, "Wide Angle Problems in Wide Screen Cinematography," *American Cinematographer* 37, 4 (May 1956): 301–302, 322–323.

48. François Truffaut, "En avoir plein la vue," *Cahiers du cinéma* no. 25 (August 1953): 22–23.

49. Clarke, "CinemaScope Techniques": 362.

50. Leon Shamroy, "Filming the Big Dimension," *American Cinematographer* 34, 5 (May 1953): 232.

51. Clarke, "CinemaScope Techniques": 362.

52. Michel Mardore, "Vingt ans après," *Cahiers du cinéma* no. 172 (November 1965): 30.

53. Quoted in Robert Carringer and Barry Sabath, *Ernst Lubitsch: A Guide to References and Resources* (Boston: G. K. Hall, 1978), 23.

54. See Leonard B. Meyer, "Toward A Theory of Style," in Berel Lang, ed., *The Concept of Style* (State College, Pa.: University of Pennsylvania Press, 1979), 27.

CHAPTER 10

1. Marcel Martin, "Les voies de l'authenticité," *Cinéma 66* no. 104 (March 1966): 52–79.

2. André Bazin, *What Is Cinema?*, Vol. 2, trans. Hugh Gray (Berkeley: University of California Press, 1971), 35.

3. André Bazin, *What Is Cinema?* trans. Hugh Gray (Berkeley: University of California Press, 1967), 134.

4. Horst Ruthrof, *The Reader's Construction of Narrative* (London: Routledge and Kegan Paul, 1981), 102.

5. Edward Branigan, *Point of View in the Cinema: A Theory of Narration and Subjectivity in Classical Film* (New York: Mouton, 1984), 73–142.

6. V. V. Ivanov, "Functions and Categories of Film Language," *Russian Poetics in Translation* 8 (1981): 33–35.

7. V. F. Perkins, *Film as Film* (New York: Penguin, 1972), 149.

8. Marie-Claire Ropars-Wuilleumier, "Fonction du montage dans la constitution du récit au cinéma," *Revue des sciences humaines* no. 141 (January–March 1971): 51

9. Veronica Forrest-Thomson, *Poetic Artifice* (Manchester: Manchester University Press, 1978), 53.

10. Quoted in Robert Benayoun, *Alain Resnais: Arpenteur de l'imaginaire* (Paris: Stock, 1980), 224.

11. Meir Sternberg, *Expositional Modes and Temporal Ordering in Fiction* (Baltimore: Johns Hopkins University Press, 1978), 99–109.

12. See Benayoun, *Alain Resnais*, 219.

13. As translated by Richard Weaver in Jorge Semprun, *La guerre est finie* (New York: Grove, 1967), 176–177.

14. See Michael Budd, "Retrospective Narration in Film: Re-reading *The Cabinet of Dr. Caligari,*" *Film Criticism* 4, 1 (Fall 1979): 35–43.

15. A typical discussion is Pierre Porte, "Une loi du cinéma," *Cinéa-Ciné pour tous* no. 8 (1 March 1924): 8–9; no. 9 (15 March 1924): 11–12.

16. For a close analysis, see Philip Drummond, "Textual Space in *Un chien andalou,*" *Screen* 18, 3 (Autumn 1977): 86–90.

17. Thomas H. Guback, *The International Film Industry* (Bloomington: Indiana University Press, 1969), 7–15, 68–83.

18. Bazin, *What Is Cinema?* Vol. 2, 59, 43.

19. In Michael F. Mayer, *Foreign Films on American Screens* (New York: Arco, 1965), vii.

20. V. F. Perkins eventually provided a plausible account in *Film as Film,* 158–186.

21. "The Return of *Movie,*" *Movie* 20 (Spring 1975): 17.

22. Perkins, *Film as Film,* 80.

23. An example is analyzed in David Bordwell, Janet Staiger, and Kristin Thompson, *The Classical Hollywood Cinema: Film Style and Mode of Production to 1960* (New York: Columbia University Press, 1985), Chap. 30.

CHAPTER 11

1. Anatolii Lunacharsky and Yuvenal Slavinsky, "Theses of the Art Section of Narkompros and the Central Committee of the Union of Art Workers concerning Basic Policy in the Field of Art," in John E. Bowlt, ed., *Russian Art of the Avant-Garde: Theory and Criticism, 1902–1934* (New York: Viking, 1976), 185.

2. For historical background on the didactic premises of Soviet film, see Richard Taylor, *Film Propaganda: Soviet Russia and Nazi Germany* (London: Croon Helm, 1979), 44–68.

3. Quoted in John Willett, *The New Sobriety: Art and Politics in the Weimar Period, 1917–1933* (London: Thames and Hudson, 1978), 106.

4. See Richard Freeborn, *The Russian Revolutionary Novel: Turgenev to Pasternak* (Cambridge: Cambridge University Press, 1982), 87–91; Harold B. Segel, *Twentieth-Century Russian Drama: From Gorky to the Present* (New York: Columbia University Press, 1979), 147–181; A. M. Van Der Eng-Liedmeier, *Soviet Literary Characters: An Investigation into the Portrayal of Soviet Men in Russian Prose, 1917–1953* (The Hague: Mouton, 1959), 11–74.

5. Susan Rubin Suleiman, *Authoritarian Fictions: The Ideological Novel as a Literary Genre* (New York: Columbia University Press, 1983), 101–109.

6. Ibid., 64–78.

7. Katerina Clark, *The Soviet Novel: History as Ritual* (Chicago: University of Chicago Press, 1981), 15–20.

8. Quoted in Barthélémy Amengual, *Vsevelod Pudovkin* (Paris: Premier Plan, 1968), 28.

9. Evelyn Gerstein, "*Potemkin,*" *New Republic* 48 (20 October 1926), 243.

10. See David Bordwell, Janet Staiger, and Kristin Thompson, *The Classical Hollywood Cinema: Film Style and Mode of Production to 1960* (New York: Columbia University Press, 1985), chap. 3.

11. Félicie Pastorello, "La catégorie de montage chez Arvatov, Tretiakov, Brecht," in D. Bablet, ed., *Collage et montage au théâtre et dans les autres arts durant les années vingt* (Lausanne: L'Age d'homme, 1978), 125.

12. André Bazin, *What is Cinema?* trans. Hugh Gray (Berkeley: University of California Press, 1967), 25.

13. See V. I. Lenin, *Collected Works,* Vol. 20: *The Revolution of 1917* (New York: International Publishers, 1929), Book 1, 241; Book 2, 69.

14. See Vance Kepley, "The Fiction Films of Alexander Dovzhenko: A Historical Reading" (Ph. D. diss., University of Wisconsin, 1978), 9–20, 186–190.

15. Viktor Shklovsky, "Eisenstein's 'October,'" *Screen* 12, 4 (Winter 1971/1972): 89.

16. S. Timoshenko, *Iskusstvo kino i montazh fil'ma* (The art of the cinema and the montage of films) (Leningrad: Academia, 1926), 50–51.

17. For a more detailed study of the Soviet montage style, see Kristin Thompson, *The Promised Land of the Cinema* (forthcoming).

18. Karl Marx, "The Civil War in France," in K. Marx and F. Engels, *Selected Works,* Vol. 2 (Moscow: Progress Publishers, 1977), 218–219.

19. See James A. Leith, ed., *Images of the Commune* (Montreal: McGill-Queen's University Press, 1978).

20. Suleiman, *Authoritarian Fictions,* 84–100.

21. Marx, "Civil War in France," 230.

22. Grigori Kozintsev, "Propos," *Positif* no. 194 (June 1977): 43.

23. Quoted in Jay Leyda, *Kino: A History of the Russian and Soviet Film* (London: Allen and Unwin, 1960), 181.

24. See Bordwell et al., *Classical Hollywood Cinema.*

25. See Willett, *New Sobriety,* 51, 108–110.

26. Quoted in Philippe Ivernal, "Gestaltung et montage dans la gauche littéraire allemand: Lukács et les trois B," in Bablet, *Collage et montage au théâtre et dans les autres arts,* 107.

27. Georg Lukács, "Realism in the Balance," in Ernst Bloch et al., *Aesthetics and Politics* (London: New Left Books, 1977), 39.

28. Georg Lukács, "Narrate or Describe?" *Writer and Critic and Other Essays* (New York: Grosset and Dunlap, 1970), 116–138.

29. Lukács, "Realism in the Balance," 33–34.

30. Bertolt Brecht, "Théâtre récréatif ou théâtre didactique?" *Ecrits sur le théâtre,* Vol. 1 (Paris: L'Arche, 1972), 258.

31. Quoted in Johnny Ebstein, "Le montage politique dans le film de Brecht/Dudow *Kuhle Wampe,*" in Bablet, *Collage et montage au théâtre et dans les autres arts,* 88.

32. Bertolt Brecht, "Sur le théâtre expérimental," *Ecrits,* Vol. 1, 287.

33. Bertolt Brecht, "La causalité dans la dramaturgie non aris-totélicienne," *Ecrits,* Vol. 1, 275.

34. Brecht, "Théâtre récréatif ou théâtre didactique?" 259.

35. Bertolt Brecht, "The Literarization of the Theatre (Notes to the *Threepenny Opera*)," *Brecht on Theatre,* ed. John Willett (New York: Hill and Wang, 1964), 43.

36. Ibid., 44.

37. The phrase is Walter Benjamin's. See *Understanding Brecht,* trans. Anna Bostock (London: New Left Books, 1973), 99.

38. Bertolt Brecht, *Journal de travail, 1938–1955,* trans. Philippe Ivernel (Paris: L'Arche, 1976), 446–447.

39. Roland Barthes, "Mother Courage Blind," *Critical Essays,* trans. Richard Howard (Evanston: Northwestern University Press, 1972), 34.

40. Jack Zipes, "Piscator and the Legacy of Political Theater," *Theater* 10, 2 (Spring 1979): 85–93.

41. René Micha, "'The Cinema Rises in Rebellion,' 'The Cinema Is Liberty,'" *Art and Confrontation: The Arts in an Age of Change,* trans. Nigel Foxell (Greenwich, Conn. New York Graphic Society, 1970), 173.

42. Jean Narboni, "Introduction to *Poetika Kino,*" in Ian Christie and John Gillett, eds., *Futurism/Formalism/Feks: "Eccentrism" and Soviet Cinema, 1918–1936* (London: British Film Institute, 1978), 59.

43. Jacques Rivette et al., "Montage," *Rivette: Texts and Interviews,* ed. Jonathan Rosenbaum (London: British Film Institute, 1977), 70.

44. Jean-Louis Comolli, "Technique et idéologie: Caméra, perspective, profondeur de champ," *Cahiers du cinéma* nos. 234–235 (December 1971, January–February 1972): 100.

45. Quoted in Sylvia Harvey, *May '68 and Film Culture* (London: British Film Institute, 1978), 31.

46. Gérard Leblanc, "Sur trois films du groupe Dziga-Vertov," *VH 101* no. 6 (1972): 26; see also "Le 'Groupe Dziga-Vertov,'" *Cahiers du cinéma* nos. 238–239 (May–June 1972): 34.

47. Ferenc Feher, "A Parable and Pantomime of Revolutionary Power," *Hungarofilm Bulletin* 1 (1969): 31.

48. For a comparison of Jancsó's work and Soviet montage films, see Yvette Biró, *Jancsó* (Paris: Albatros, 1977), 103–106.

49. Serge Daney, "The T(h)errorized," *Thousand Eyes* no. 2 (1977): 34–35 (translation of "Le t(h)érrorisme [pédagogie godardienne]," *Cahiers du cinéma* nos. 262–263 [January 1976]: 32–39).

50. An account of such violations may be found in Martin Walsh, *The Brechtian Aspect of Radical Cinema* (London: British Film Institute, 1981), 37–107.

51. Feher, "Parable and Pantomime of Revolutionary Power": 32.

CHAPTER 12

1. Yuri Tynianov, "On the Foundations of Cinema," in Herbert Eagle, ed. *Russian Formalist Film Theory* (Ann Arbor: University of Michigan Slavic Publications, 1981), 97.

2. Yuri Tynianov, "Plot and Story-Line in the Cinema," *Russian Poetics in Translation* 5 (1978): 20.

3. Yuri Tynianov, *The Problem of Verse Language,* ed. and trans. Michael Sosa and Brent Harvey (Ann Arbor: Ardis, 1981), 33.

4. Leo Jakubinsky, quoted in Boris Eichenbaum, "The Theory of the Formal Method," in Lee T. Lemon and Marion J. Reis, eds., *Russian Formalist Criticism: Four Essays,* (Lincoln: University of Nebraska Press, 1965), 108.

5. Jan Mukařovský, "Standard Language and Poetic Language," in Paul L. Garvin, ed. and trans., *A Prague School Reader on Esthetics, Literary Structure, and Style* (Washington, D.C.: Georgetown University Press, 1964), 28.

6. Viktor Shklovsky, "On the Connection between Devices of

Syuzhet Construction and General Stylistic Devices," *Twentieth Century Studies* nos. 7/8 (December 1972): 48–72.

7. Sergei M. Eisenstein, "A Dialectic Approach to Film Form," *Film Form: Essays in Film Theory*, ed. and trans. Jay Leyda (Cleveland: World, 1957), 53–57.

8. Pierre Boulez, *Notes of an Apprenticeship*, trans. Herbert Weinstock (New York: Knopf, 1968), 12. Reginald Smith-Brindle and Paul Griffiths point out that Webern probably did not want the series to govern all parameters. See Smith-Brindle, *The New Music* (London: Oxford University Press, 1975), 13, and Griffiths, *A Concise History of Avant-Garde Music from Debussy to Boulez* (New York: Oxford University Press, 1978), 144.

9. For a discussion of the permutational principle in Boulez's *Structures*, see Smith-Brindle, *New Music*, 25–33.

10. Boulez, *Notes of an Apprenticeship*, 53–57.

11. Pierre Boulez, *Boulez on Music Today*, trans. Susan Bradshaw and Richard Rodney Bennett (London: Faber and Faber, 1975), 32.

12. Bruce Morissette, "Post-Modern Generative Fiction: Novel and Film," *Critical Inquiry* 2, 2 (Winter 1975): 254–262.

13. Claude Lévi-Strauss, "The Structural Study of Myth," *Structural Anthropology*, trans. Claire Jacobson and Brooke Grundfest Schoepf (Garden City, N.Y.: Anchor, 1967), 209–212.

14. Boulez, *Notes of an Apprenticeship* 41, 83–98. See also Pierre Schaeffer, *Traité des objets musicaux* (Paris: Seuil, 1966).

15. Michel Foucault, "Le langage de l'éspace," *Critique* no. 203 (1964): 378–382.

16. Michel Butor, *Inventory*, trans. Richard Howard (New York: Simon and Schuster, 1968), 42.

17. Boulez, *Notes of an Apprenticeship*, 194.

18. Lévi-Strauss, "Structural Study of Myth," 206–209.

19. Roman Jakobson, "Closing Statement: Linguistics and Poetics," *Style in Language*, ed. Thomas A. Sebeok (Cambridge: MIT Press, 1960), 358.

20. Ibid., 350.

21. Boulez, *Notes of an Apprenticeship*, 204.

22. Quoted in Reinhold Grimm, "Marc Saporta: The Novel as Card Game," *Contemporary Literature* 19, 3 (Summer 1978): 281n. Saporta's novel is also discussed in Sharon Spencer, *Space, Time and Structure in the Modern Novel* (Chicago: Swallow Press, 1976), 85–87, 209–212.

23. Boulez, *Notes of an Apprenticeship*, 88.

24. Claude Lévi-Strauss, *The Raw and the Cooked: Introduction to a Science of Mythology I*, trans. John and Doreen Weightman (New York: Harper, 1969), 27.

25. Umberto Eco, *La structure absente* (Paris: Mercure de France, 1972), 352.

26. Stephen Heath, *The Nouveau Roman: A Study in the Practice of Writing* (Philadelphia: Temple University Press, 1972), 135.

27. See David Bordwell and Kristin Thompson, *Film Art: An Introduction* (Reading, Mass.: Addison-Wesley, 1979), 252–257.

28. "La terre intérieure: Entretien avec Jean-Daniel Pollet et Jean Thibaudeau," *Cahiers du cinéma* no. 204 (September 1968): 36. Cf. Jean-Paul Fargier, "Vers le récit rouge," *Cinéthique* nos. 7–8 (1970): 13–14.

29. Philippe Sollers, "Une autre logique," *Cahiers du cinéma* no. 187 (February 1967): 38.

30. Noël Burch, *Theory of Film Practice*, trans. Helen R. Lane (New York: Praeger, 1973), 144.

31. Ibid., xx.

32. Ibid., 14.

33. Ibid., 15.

34. Ibid., 143.

35. Ibid., 67, 107–108.

36. See, for example, Jean-André Fieschi, "Le Carrefour Tati," *Cahiers du cinéma* no. 199 (March 1968): 25–26, and Pascal Bonitzer, "Les vases communicants: The Party," *Cahiers du cinéma* no. 216 (October 1969): 52.

37. Jean-Pierre Oudart, "Cinema and Suture," *Screen* 18, 4 (Winter 1977/1978), 35–47; Pascal Bonitzer, "Hors-champ," *Cahiers du cinéma* nos. 234–235 (December 1971, January–February 1972): 18–20.

38. See Edward Branigan, *Point of View in the Cinema: A Theory of Narration and Subjectivity in Classical Film* (New York: Mouton, 1984), 103–121; Kristin Thompson and David Bordwell, "Space and Narrative in the Films of Ozu," *Screen* 17, 2 (Summer 1976): 41–73; Edward Branigan, "The Space of *Equinox Flower*," *Screen* 17, 1 (Summer 1976): 74–105.

39. See Dominique Chateau, "Méthodologies possibles pour des films improbables," and François Jost, "Vers de nouvelles approches méthodologiques," in Dominique Chateau et al., eds. *Cinémas de la modernité: Films, théories* (Paris: Klincksieck, 1981), 7–39.

40. E. H. Gombrich, *The Sense of Order: A Study in the Psychology of Decorative Art* (Ithaca: Cornell University Press, 1979), 239.

41. For a discussion of permutational musical patterning in

Vivre sa vie, see Royal S. Brown, "Music and *Vivre sa vie,*" *Quarterly Review of Film Studies* 5, 3 (Summer 1980): 319–333.

42. V. F. Perkins, "*Vivre sa vie,*" in Ian Cameron, ed., *The Films of Jean-Luc Godard* (New York: Praeger, 1969), 33.

43. Ibid., 35.

44. Noël Burch, *Praxis du cinéma* (Paris: Gallimard, 1969). This passage was omitted from the English translation.

45. Gombrich, *Sense of Order,* 116–117.

46. Boulez, *Notes of an Apprenticeship,* 180; Henry Pousseur, "The Question of Order in New Music," in Benjamin Boretz and Edward T. Cone, eds., *Perspectives on Contemporary Music Theory* (New York: Norton, 1972), 106.

47. Nicolas Ruwet, "Contradictions du langage sériel," *Langage, musique, poésie* (Paris: Seuil, 1972), 23–24.

48. Leonard B. Meyer, *Music, the Arts, and Ideas: Patterns and Predictions in Twentieth-Century Culture* (Chicago: University of Chicago Press, 1967), 284–293.

49. Ibid., 291.

50. Burch, *Theory of Film Practice,* 67.

51. Boulez, *Notes of an Apprenticeship,* 213.

52. René Leibowitz, *Schoenberg and His School,* trans. Dika Newlin (New York: Da Capo, 1975), 162–170; Willi Reich, "A Guide to *Wozzeck,*" *Musical Quarterly* 38 (January 1952): 3–5.

53. Alban Berg, "Postscript," *Musical Quarterly* 38 (January 1952): 21.

54. Michael Riffaterre, "Describing Poetic Structures: Two Approaches to Baudelaire's *Les chats,*" in Jacques Ehrmann, ed., *Structuralism* (New York: Anchor, 1970), 195–202.

55. See Kristin Thompson, "*Play Time:* Comedy on the Edge of Perception," *Wide Angle* 3, 2 (1979): 18–25.

56. Noël Burch, "Fritz Lang: German Period," in *Cinema: A Critical Dictionary* Vol. 2 (New York: Viking, 1980), 593.

57. David Bordwell, *The Films of Carl-Theodor Dreyer* (Berkeley: University of California Press, 1981), 63–65, 164–186.

58. Burch, *Theory of Film Practice,* 18.

59. Thompson, "*Play Time,*" 18–25; Thompson, essay on *Lancelot du Lac* (forthcoming).

60. Burch, *Theory of Film Practice,* 56.

61. Quoted in Roy Armes, *The Films of Alain Robbe-Grillet* (Amsterdam: Johns Benjamins, 1981), 134.

62. Ibid., 162.

63. Noël Burch, "Notes sur la notion de forme chez Tati," *Cahiers du cinéma* no. 199 (March 1968): 26–27.

64. Kristin Thompson, *Eisenstein's "Ivan the Terrible": A Neoformalist Analysis* (Princeton: Princeton University Press, 1981), 63–67.

65. Kristin Thompson, "Parameters of the Open Film: *Les vacances de M. Hulot,*" *Wide Angle* 2, 1 (1977): 23, 30.

66. Bordwell, *Films of Carl-Theodor Dreyer,* 153–168.

67. Burch, "Fritz Lang," 594.

68. Burch, *Theory of Film Practice,* 79.

69. Boris Tomashevsky, "Thematics," in Lemon and Reis, *Russian Formalist Criticism,* 90.

70. Roy Armes, *The Ambiguous Image: Narrative Style in Modern European Cinema* (London: Secker and Warburg, 1976), 86.

71. Viktor Shklovsky, "Sterne's *Tristram Shandy:* Stylistic Commentary," in Lemon and Reis, *Russian Formalist Criticism,* 56.

72. P. Adams Sitney describes this two-framings-in-one-shot technique in "The Rhetoric of Robert Bresson," in P. Adams Sitney, ed., *The Essential Cinema* (New York: New York University Press, 1975), 188.

73. Leonard B. Meyer, *Explaining Music: Essays and Explorations* (Chicago: University of Chicago Press, 1973), 51.

74. Ibid., 285.

75. Gombrich, *Sense of Order,* 95–101.

76. See William C. Siska, *Modernism in the Narrative Cinema* (New York: Arno Press, 1980).

77. This would constitute one of the two trends discussed by Peter Wollen in "The Two Avant-Gardes," *Reading and Writings: Semiotic Counter-Strategies* (London: New Left Books, 1982), 93–96.

78. See Bordwell and Thompson, "Space and Narrative in the Films of Ozu": 42, 70–73.

CHAPTER 13

1. Renato Poggioli, *The Theory of the Avant-Garde,* trans. Gerald Fitzgerald (New York: Harper and Row, 1971), 56.

2. Donald A. Norman, *Memory and Attention: An Introduction to Human Information Processing* (New York: John Wiley, 1976), 16–18, 48.

3. Gérard Genette, *Palimpsestes* (Paris: Seuil, 1982), 8–16.

4. Michèle Manceaux, "Learning Not to Be Bitter," in Royal S.

Brown, ed., *Focus on Godard* (Englewood Cliffs, N.J.: Prentice-Hall, 1972), 27.

5. Quoted in Herbert R. Lottman, "Cinéma-Vérité: Jean-Luc Godard," *Columbia University Forum* 11, 1 (Spring 1968): 28.

6. Jacques Rivette et al., "Montage," *Rivette: Texts and Interviews*, ed. Jonathan Rosenbaum (London: British Film Institute, 1977), 74–75.

7. Jan Mukařovský, "The Aesthetic Norm," in *Structure, Sign, and Function: Selected Essays by Jan Mukařovský*, trans. and ed. John Burbank and Peter Steiner (New Haven: Yale University Press, 1978), 52.

8. Jean-André Fieschi, "The Difficulty of Being Jean-Luc Godard," in Toby Mussman, ed., *Jean-Luc Godard: A Critical Anthology* (New York: Dutton, 1968), 65.

9. Jean-Luc Godard, "L'Odyssée selon Jean-Luc," *Cinema 63* no. 77 (June 1963): 21.

10. On the pursuit of unpredictable order, see Pierre Boulez, *Notes of an Apprenticeship*, trans. Herbert Weinstock (New York: Knopf, 1968), 14ff., and Henri Pousseur, "The Question of Order in New Music," in Benjamin Boretz and Edward T. Cone, eds., *Perspectives on Contempoary Music Theory* (New York: Norton, 1972), 99–107. Alan Williams makes a point similar to mine in his essay, "Godard's Use of Sound," *Camera Obscura* nos. 8/9/10 (1982): 206.

11. Fieschi, "Difficulty of Being Jean-Luc Godard," 73.

12. Andrew Sarris, "Waiting for Godard," in Mussman, *Jean-Luc Godard*, 136.

13. Eddie Wolfram, *History of Collage* (New York: Macmillan, 1975), 143–147.

14. Quoted in Philippe Maillat, "*Une femme mariée*," *Télé-ciné* no. 123 (June 1965): 23.

15. *Godard on Godard*, trans. Tom Milne (New York: Viking, 1972), 215.

16. Michel Butor, *Inventory*, trans. Richard Howard (New York: Simon and Schuster, 1968), 24.

17. Richard Roud, *Jean-Luc Godard*, 2d ed. (Bloomington: Indiana University Press, 1970), 66.

18. André S. Labarthe, "La chance d'être femme," *Cahiers du cinéma* no. 125 (November 1961): 54.

19. Marie-Claire Ropars-Wuilleumier, "Form and Substance, or the Avatars of the Narrative," in Brown, *Focus on Godard*, 95.

20. "Struggle on Two Fronts: A Conversation with Jean-Luc Godard," *Film Quarterly* 21, 2 (Winter 1968–1969): 25. Godard's description does not accord with the finished film, which has the following series of shots after Henri's speech: Title: "These words were spoken by N. Bukharin on the last day of the Moscow trials"; shot of young Stalin; shot of Yvonne reading *France-Soir*; shot of revolutionary baring his chest (from *Arsenal*). Evidently Godard condensed the associations into the more dense chain: Bukharin/Stalin/revisionism/authentic revolution.

21. Dziga Vertov, "The Vertov Papers," *Film Comment* 8, 1 (Spring 1972): 48.

22. Quoted in Colin MacCabe, *Godard: Images, Sounds, Politics* (London: Macmillan, 1980), 160.

23. Luc Moullet, "Jean-Luc Godard," in Mussman, *Jean-Luc Godard*, 35.

24. *Godard on Godard*, 171.

25. Ibid., 239.

26. Maillat, "*Une femme mariée*": 23.

27. Peter Wollen, "Godard and Counter Cinema: *Vent d'est*," *Readings and Writings: Semiotic Counter-Strategies* (London: New Left Books, 1982), 86.

28. Serge Daney and Jean-Pierre Oudart, "Le Nom-de-l'Auteur," *Cahiers du cinéma* nos. 234–235 (December 1971/January–February 1972): 90.

29. Jean-Louis Comolli, "Detour by the Direct" in Christopher Williams, ed., *Realism and the Cinema* (London: Routledge and Kegan Paul, 1980), 239–240.

30. See James Blue, "Excerpt from an Interview with Richard Grenier and Jean-Luc Godard," in Mussman, *Jean-Luc Godard*, 252; see also *Godard on Godard*, 172–173.

31. *Godard on Godard*, 40.

32. Ibid., 214.

33. Quoted in Alain Remond, "La 'réalisation' me dégoûtait, la 'mise en scène' me paraissait noble," *Télérama* (22–28 July 1978): 60.

34. Brian Henderson, *A Critique of Film Theory* (New York: Dutton, 1980), 68.

35. Rivette, "Montage," 74.

36. Quoted in Alain Remond, "'A bout de souffle' c'était le petit chaperon rouge," *Télérama* (29 July–4 August 1978): 60.

37. Alan Williams, "Godard's Use of Sound," 201.

38. *Godard on Godard*, 234.

39. "Lutter sur deux fronts: Entretien avec Jean-Luc Godard," *Cahiers du cinéma* no. 194. (October 1967): 69.

40. For an account, see Arthur Hirsh, *The French New Left: An*

Intellectual History from Sartre to Gorz (Boston: South End Press, 1981); for an example, see Henri Lefebvre, *Everyday Life in the Modern World,* trans. Sacha Rabinovitch (New York: Harper and Row, 1971).

41. Mark Poster, *Existential Marxism in Postwar France: From Sartre to Althusser* (Princeton: Princeton University Press, 1975), 361–398.

42. See *Cahiers du cinéma* nos. 323/324 (May 1981): 58–59.

Photo Credits

Any illustrations not credited are from the author's private collection. The printing of all frame enlargements was done by Kristin Thompson.

Audio-Brandon Films: 7.56–7.127 (© 1969).

Elvehjem Museum of Art, University of Wisconsin–Madison: 7.4 (Gift of Samuel H. Kress); 7.5 (Bequest of John Hasbrouck Van Vleck): 7.6 (Lent by Mrs. Earnest C. Watson).

Goldwyn Pictures Corporation: 7.9 (© 1938).

New Line Cinema: 10.1–10.25 (© 1968).

New Yorker Films: 6.23–6.51, 7.8 (© 1969); 7.20–7.22 (© 1968).

RKO General: 5.1 (© 1944).

Twentieth-Century Fox Films: 7.28–7.43 (© 1927); 9.69–9.77 (© 1957).

United Artists: 7.16–7.17 (© 1942).

Universal Pictures: 9.67–9.68 (© 1946).

Warner Bros. Pictures: 1.1–1.3 (© 1925); 5.2 (© 1942); 7.24–7.25 (© 1938); 7.44–7.49 (© 1946); 9.52–9.53 (© 1929); 12.1–12.2 (© 1925).

Cover photo from the motion picture *Rear Window*, courtesy of Universal Pictures.

Selected Bibliography

Alberti, Leon Battista. *On Painting.* Translated by John R. Spencer. New Haven: Yale University Press, 1966.

Aristotle. *Poetics.* Translated by Gerald F. Else. Ann Arbor: University of Michigan Press, 1967.

Armes, Roy. *The Ambiguous Image: Narrative Style in Modern European Cinema.* London: Secker and Warburg, 1976.

Arnheim, Rudolf. *Art and Visual Perception: A Psychology of the Creative Eye.* 2d ed. Berkeley and Los Angeles: University of California Press, 1974.

Arnheim, Rudolf. "Inverted Perspective in Art: Display and Expression." *Leonardo* 5 (1972): 125–135.

Arnheim, Rudolf. *The Power of the Center: A Study of Composition in the Visual Arts.* Berkeley and Los Angeles: University of California Press, 1982.

Aumont, Jacques, and J. L. Leutrat, eds. *Théorie du film.* Paris: Albatros, 1980.

Bailblé, Claude; Michel Marie; and Marie-Claire Ropars. *Muriel: Histoire d'une recherche.* Paris: Galilée, 1974.

Bartlett, Frederic C. *Remembering: A Study in Experimental and Social Psychology.* Cambridge: Cambridge University Press, 1950.

Bazin, André. *What Is Cinema?* Translated by Hugh Gray. Berkeley and Los Angeles: University of California Press, 1967.

Bellour, Raymond. *L'analyse du film.* Paris: Albatros, 1979.

Benveniste, Emile. *Problèmes de linguistique générale.* Paris: Gallimard, 1966.

Benveniste, Emile. *Problèmes de linguistique générale.* Vol. 2. Paris: Gallimard, 1974.

Booth, Wayne C. *The Rhetoric of Fiction.* Chicago: University of Chicago Press, 1961.

Bordwell, David; Janet Staiger; and Kristin Thompson. *The Classical Hollywood Cinema: Film Style and Mode of Production to 1960.* New York: Columbia University Press, 1985.

Bordwell, David, and Kristin Thompson. *Film Art: An Introduction.* Reading, Mass.: Addison-Wesley, 1979.

Branigan, Edward. *Point of View in the Cinema: A Theory of Narration and Subjectivity in Classical Film.* New York: Mouton, 1984.

Browne, Nick. *The Rhetoric of Filmic Narration.* Ann Arbor: UMI Research Press, 1982.

Bruner, Jerome S. "On Perceptual Readiness." *Psychological Review* 64 (1957): 123–152.

Burch, Noël. "Fritz Lang: German Period." In *Cinema: A Critical Dictionary,* Vol. 2, edited by Richard Roud. New York: Viking, 1980.

Burch, Noël. *Theory of Film Practice.* Translated by Helen R. Lane. New York: Praeger, 1973. Originally published as *Praxis du cinéma* (Paris: Gallimard, 1969).

Carroll, Noël. "Address to the Heathen." *October* no. 23 (Winter 1982): 89–163.

Carroll, Noël. "Toward a Theory of Film Editing." *Millennium Film Journal* no. 3 (1978): 79–99.

Chambers, Ross. *Story and Situation: Narrative Seduction and the Power of Fiction.* Minneapolis: University of Minnesota Press, 1984.

Chateau, Dominique; André Gardiès; and François Jost, eds. *Cinémas de la modernité: Films, théories.* Paris: Klincksieck, 1981.

Chatman, Seymour. *Story and Discourse: Narrative Structure in Fiction and Film.* Ithaca: Cornell University Press, 1978.

"Cinema et récit." Special number of *Cahiers du XXe siècle,* no. 9 (1978).

Daney, Serge, and Jean-Pierre Oudart. "Le Nom-de-l'Auteur." *Cahiers du cinéma* nos. 234–235 (December 1971, January–February 1972): 79–92.

Doane, Mary Ann. "The Dialogical Text: Filmic Irony and the Spectator." Ph.D. diss., University of Iowa, 1979.

Dubery, Fred, and John Willats. *Perspective and Other Drawing Systems.* New York: Van Nostrand Reinhold, 1983.

Dubois, Jean. "Enoncé et énonciation." *Langages* no. 13 (March 1969): 100–110.

Eagle, Herbert, ed. and trans. *Russian Formalist Film Theory.*

Ann Arbor: University of Michigan Slavic Publications, 1981.

"Enonciation et cinéma." Special number of *Communications* no. 38 (1983).

Erlich, Victor. *Russian Formalism: History-Doctrine.* The Hague: Mouton, 1969.

Friedman, Norman. "Point of View in Fiction: The Development of a Critical Concept." In *The Theory of the Novel,* edited by Philip Stevick. New York: Free Press, 1967.

Garvin, Paul L., ed. and trans. *A Prague School Reader on Esthetics, Literary Structure, and Style.* Washington, D.C.: Georgetown University Press, 1964.

Gaudreault, André. "Récit scriptural, récit théâtral, récit filmique: Prolégomènes à une théorie narratologique du cinéma." *Thèse de doctorat de 3e cycle,* Université de Paris-III, 1983.

Genette, Gérard. *Narrative Discourse: An Essay in Method.* Translated by Jane E. Lewin. Ithaca: Cornell University Press, 1980.

Genette, Gérard. *Nouveau discours du récit.* Paris: Seuil, 1983.

Glass, Arnold Lewis; Keith James Holyoak; and John Lester Santa. *Cognition.* Reading, Mass.: Addison-Wesley, 1979.

Gombrich, E. H. *Art and Illusion: A Study in the Psychology of Pictorial Representation.* Princeton, N.J.: Princeton University Press, 1961.

Gombrich, E. H. *The Image and the Eye: Further Studies in the Psychology of Pictorial Representation.* Oxford: Phaidon, 1982.

Gombrich, E. H. *The Sense of Order: A Study in the Psychology of Decorative Art.* Ithaca: Cornell University Press, 1979.

Gombrich, E. H.; Julian Hochberg; and Max Black. *Art, Perception, and Reality.* Baltimore: Johns Hopkins University Press, 1972.

Gregory, R. L. *Eye and Brain: The Psychology of Seeing.* 3d ed. New York: McGraw-Hill, 1978.

Gregory, R. L. *The Intelligent Eye.* New York: McGraw-Hill, 1970.

Gregory, R. L., and E. H. Gombrich, eds. *Illusion in Nature and Art.* London: Duckworth, 1973.

Haber, Ralph Norman, and Maurice Hershenson. *The Psychology of Visual Perception.* 2d ed. New York: Holt, Rinehart, and Winston, 1980.

Hagen, Margaret. A., ed. *The Perception of Pictures.* 2 vols. New York: Academic Press, 1980.

Heath, Stephen. "Le Père Noël." *October* no. 26 (Fall 1983): 63–116.

Heath, Stephen. *Questions of Cinema.* London: Macmillan, 1981.

Hochberg, Julian. *Perception.* 2d ed. Englewood Cliffs, N.J.: Prentice-Hall, 1978.

Hochberg, Julian, and Virginia Brooks. "The Perception of Motion Pictures." In *Handbook of Perception.* Vol. 10: *Perceptual Ecology,* edited by Edward C. Carterette and Morton P. Friedman. New York: Academic Press, 1978.

Ittelson, William H. *The Ames Demonstrations in Perception: A Guide to Their Construction and Use.* Princeton, N.J.: Princeton University Press, 1952.

Jakobson, Roman. *Selected Writings.* Vol. 3: *Poetry of Grammar and Grammar of Poetry.* Edited by Stephen Rudy. The Hague: Mouton, 1981.

James, Henry. *The Art of the Novel.* Edited by R. P. Blackmur. New York: Scribner's, 1934.

Kawin, Bruce. *Mindscreen: Bergman, Godard, and First-Person Film.* Princeton, N.J.: Princeton University Press, 1977.

Kerbrat-Orecchioni, Catherine. *L'énonciation: De la subjectivité dans le langage.* Paris: Colin, 1980.

Kernodle, George R. *From Art to Theatre; Form and Convention in the Renaissance.* Chicago: University of Chicago Press, 1943.

Laffay, Albert. *Logique du cinéma: Création et spectacle.* Paris: Masson, 1964.

Lanser, Susan Sniader. *The Narrative Act: Point of View in Prose Fiction.* Princeton, N.J.: Princeton University Press, 1981.

Lemon, Lee T., and Marion J. Reis, eds. *Russian Formalist Criticism: Four Essays.* Linclon: University of Nebraska Press, 1965.

Lintvelt, Jaap. *Essai de typologie narrative: Le "point de vue."* Paris: Corti, 1981.

Lubbock, Percy. *The Craft of Fiction.* New York: Viking, 1962.

MacCabe, Colin. "Realism and the Cinema: Notes on Some Brechtian Theses." *Screen* 15, 2 (Summer 1974): 7–27.

MacCabe, Colin. "Theory and Film: Principles of Realism and Pleasure." *Screen* 17, 3 (Autumn 1976): 7–27.

Mandler, Jean, and Nancy Johnson. "Remembrance of Things Parsed: Story Structure and Recall." *Cognitive Psychology* 9 (1977): 111–151.

Matejka, Ladislav, and Krystyna Pomorska, eds. *Readings in*

Russian Poetics: Formalist and Structuralist Views. Cambridge: MIT Press, 1971.

Mendilow, A. A. *Time and the Novel.* London: Peter Nevill, 1952.

Metz, Christian. *Film Language.* Translated by Michael Taylor. New York: Oxford University Press, 1974.

Mukařovský, Jan. *Structure, Sign, and Function.* Translated and edited by John Burbank and Peter Steiner. New Haven: Yale University Press, 1977.

Neisser, Ulric. *Cognitive Psychology.* New York: Appleton-Century-Crofts, 1967.

Nichols, Bill. *Ideology and the Image.* Bloomington: Indiana University Press, 1981.

Ornstein, Robert E. *On the Experience of Time.* New York: Penguin, 1969.

Oudart, Jean-Pierre. "Cinema and Suture." *Screen* 18, 4 (Winter 1977–1978): 35–47.

Panofsky, Erwin. *La perspective comme forme symbolique.* Translated by Guy Ballange. Paris: Minuit, 1975.

Perry, Menakhem. "Literary Dynamics: How the Order of a Text Creates Its Meanings." *Poetics Today* 1, 1 (Autumn 1979): 35–64, 311–361.

Pirenne, M. H. *Optics, Painting, and Photography.* Cambridge: Cambridge University Press, 1970.

Prince, Gerald. *Narratology: The Form and Function of Narrative.* Berlin: Mouton, 1982.

Riffaterre, Michael. "Describing Poetic Structures: Two Approaches to Baudelaire's *Les chats." Yale French Studies* 36–37 (October 1966): 300–342.

Rimmon-Kenan, Shlomith. *Narrative Fiction: Contemporary Poetics.* London: Methuen, 1983.

Rock, Irwin. *The Logic of Perception.* Cambridge: MIT Press, 1983.

Ropars-Wuilleumier, Marie-Claire. *De la littérature au cinéma.* Paris: Colin, 1970.

Rumelhart, D. E. "Notes on a Schema for Stories." In *Representation and Understanding: Studies in Cognitive Science,* edited by D. G. Bobrow and A. Collins. New York: Academic Press, 1975.

"Russian Formalism." Special number of *Twentieth Century Studies* nos. 7/8 (December 1972).

Ruthrof, Horst. *The Reader's Construction of Narrative.* London: Routledge and Kegan Paul, 1981.

Scholes, Robert and Robert Kellogg. *The Nature of Narrative.* New York: Oxford University Press, 1966.

Sternberg, Meir. *Expositional Modes and Temporal Ordering in Fiction.* Baltimore: Johns Hopkins University Press, 1978.

"Story Comprehension." Special number of *Poetics* 9, 1–3 (June 1980).

Suleiman, Susan Rubin. *Authoritarian Fictions: The Ideological Novel as a Literary Genre.* New York: Columbia University Press, 1983.

Thorndyke, Perry W. "Cognitive Structures in Comprehension and Memory of Narrative Discourse." *Cognitive Psychology* 9 (1977): 77–110.

Todorov, Tzvetan. *Introduction to Poetics.* Translated by Richard Howard. Minneapolis: University of Minnesota Press, 1981.

Todorov, Tzvetan. *The Poetics of Prose.* Translated by Richard Howard. Ithaca: Cornell University Press, 1977.

Torney, Alan. "Seeing Things: Pictures, Paradox, and Perspective." In *Perceiving Artworks,* edited by John Fisher. Philadelphia: Temple University Press, 1980.

Uspensky, Boris. *A Poetics of Composition: The Structure of the Artistic Text and Typology of a Compositional Form.* Translated by Valentina Zavarin and Susan Wittig. Berkeley: University of California Press, 1973.

Warren, William H.; David W. Nicholas; and Tom Trabasso. "Event Chains and Inferences in Understanding Narratives." In *New Directions in Discourse Processing,* edited by Roy O. Freedle. Norwood, N.J.: Ablex, 1979.

White, Allon. *The Uses of Obscurity: The Fiction of Early Modernism.* London: Routledge and Kegan Paul, 1981.

White, John. *The Birth and Rebirth of Pictorial Space.* New York: Harper and Row, 1972.

Wollen, Peter. *Readings and Writings: Semiotic Counter-Strategies.* London: New Left Books, 1982.

Wright, Lawrence. *Perspective in Perspective.* London: Routledge and Kegan Paul, 1983.

Index